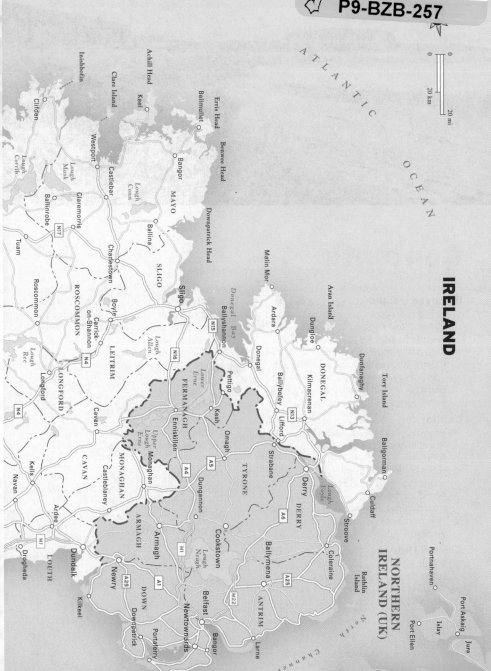

IRELAND

ATLANTIC

OCEAN

0
0
20 km
20 mi

Inishbofin

Achill Head

Clare Island

Keel

Bellmullet

Erris Head

Benwee Head

Downpatrick Head

Clifden

Westport

Lough Corrib

Lough Mask

Castlebar

Bangor

MAYO

Lough Conn

Ballinrobe

Claremorris

Charlestown

Ballina

N17

Tuam

Roscommon

Boyle

Carrick-on-Shannon

ROSCOMMON

SLIGO

Sligo

N4

N16

LEITRIM

Lough Allen

Lough Ree

Longford

LONGFORD

N4

Cavan

Kells

Navan

Ardee

CAVAN

M1

Drogheda

LOUTH

Dundalk

Kilkeel

Newry

A25

A1

ARMAGH

Castleblaney

MONAGHAN

Armagh

M1

DOWN

Newtownards

Portaferry

Downpatrick

Bangor

Belfast

M22

Lough Neagh

Cookstown

Dungannon

A4

A5

Enniskillen

FERMANAGH

Lower Lough Erne

Upper Lough Erne

Lough Monaghan

Kesh

Omagh

TYRONE

Ballymena

ANTRIM

Larne

A25

Coleraine

Stroove

DERRY

A6

Derry

Strabane

Lifford

N13

Ballybofey

Pettigo

Ballyshannon

N15

Donegal Bay

Donegal

DONEGAL

Kilmacrenan

Dungloe

Ardara

Malin Mor

Aran Island

Duntanaghy

Culdaff

Ballygorman

Portnahaven

Tory Island

Rathlin Island

Islay

Port Askaig

Port Ellen

Jura

NORTHERN IRELAND (UK)

North Channel

Lough Foyle

Contents

Discover Ireland **6**
   10 Top Experiences 8
   Planning Your Trip 14
   Ireland's Best Trips 20
   Sacred Sites and Pilgrimages 25
   • Can't-Miss Castles 26
   • Sporting Ireland 28
   Ghosts of Ancient Ireland 29
   Family Fun 31

Dublin **32**
   Sights 39
   Activities and Recreation 55
   Food 57
   Entertainment and Events 63
   Shopping 68
   Accommodations 69
   Information and Services 72
   Transportation 73
   Vicinity of Dublin City 76

Around Dublin **80**
   Meath 85
   Louth 97
   Wicklow 106
   Kildare 117

The Southeast **120**
   Wexford 125
   Kilkenny 138
   Tipperary 148
   Waterford 153

Cork **162**
   Cork City 167
   Around Cork City 176
   West Cork 182
   The Mizen Head Peninsula 188
   The Sheep's Head Peninsula 190
   The Beara Peninsula (Cork Side) 193

Kerry **199**
   The Dingle Peninsula 204
   The Iveragh Peninsula 217
   The Beara Peninsula (Kerry Side) 240
   North Kerry 241

Clare and Limerick **243**
   Eastern Clare 248
   The Clare Coast 257
   The Burren 268
   Limerick City 276

Galway **284**
  Galway City 288
  The Aran Islands 300
  Connemara 311
  Southern and Eastern Galway 323
  Detour to Clonmacnoise 327

The Northwest **332**
  Mayo 337
  Sligo 357
  Donegal 369

Northern Ireland **389**
  Belfast 394
  Antrim 404
  Derry 417
  Down 426
  Armagh 435
  Fermanagh 437

Background **444**
  The Landscape 445
  History 447
  Government and Economy 456
  People and Culture 458

Essentials **466**
  Transportation 467
  Food and Accommodations 471
  Travel Tips 474
  Information and Services 477

Resources **480**
  Glossary 480
  Suggested Reading 484
  Internet Resources 486

Index **488**

List of Maps **502**

DISCOVER

Ireland

Ireland is the sort of place you long to visit one day—and then, once you've been, you forever dream of returning. Boom times or bust, whether her children are emigrating or coming home again for good, this country is as proud of its rebels, saints, and bards as it ever was.

It isn't only the remote abbey ruins, fairy-tale castles, and prehistoric stone monuments that give Ireland its haunting flavor. Evidence of ordinary lives is everywhere, too: the rural farmsteads rendered bleak by the lashing rain, statues of the Madonna in roadside niches, the Irish language stubbornly reasserting itself on every road sign. These glimpses of a vanishing Ireland can only add to the texture of your visit.

For all its smartphones, wind turbines, and modern enterprise, it's safe to say this country's most beloved attributes will never change: Potatoes are still the fifth food group, stout is still a meal in a glass, a traditional music session is the perfect end to the day, and the Irish are as hospitable as ever. In its people, legends, and landscapes, Ireland ignites the imagination in a way few other earthly places can.

Clockwise from top left: West Cork; Clonmacnoise, the most important monastery in medieval Ireland; the graveyard at St. Declan's Monastery in Ardmore; the Mussenden Temple at Downhill; 9th-century high cross at Kilree; the Cliffs of Moher.

10 TOP
EXPERIENCES

1 **The Cliffs of Moher:** No postcard can convey the misty magnificence of this natural wonder standing sentinel over the waves (page 262).

2 **Ruins:** History haunts the landscape at sites such as **Brú na Bóinne** (page 85), with passage tombs older than Stonehenge; **Glendalough** (pictured, page 110), Ireland's best-known monastic site; and the **Rock of Cashel** (page 148), a dramatically perched castle-fortress.

3 **Killarney National Park:** This glorious park's glens, mountains, lakes, and waterfalls are among Ireland's most fantastic scenery (page 231).

4 **Scenic Drives:** The Emerald Isle abounds with breathtaking drives. Two of the most dramatic are the **Ring of Kerry** (page 217) and **Slea Head Drive** on the **Dingle Peninsula** (pictured, page 212).

<<<

5 **The Book of Kells:** Pages of Ireland's most famous illuminated manuscript are on display at Trinity College's **Old Library** in Dublin (page 41).

>>>

6 **Galway City:** This sparkling medieval city on the west coast has a friendly, laid-back vibe and bohemian vitality (page 288).

<<<

7 Aran Islands: Off the Galway coast these three enchanting islands are romantic and remote, echoing with an old way of life (page 300).

8 Traditional Music: Head to a pub to experience Ireland's folk music, by turns rollicking and otherworldly (page 294).

<<<

9 Belfast's Black Taxi Tour: This eye-opening excursion explores working-class, sectarian Belfast and its **murals,** with a running commentary on the city's political history (page 398).

>>>

AND HISTORY IS MADE BY THE PEOPLE

10 Derry City Walls: Derry's 17th-century walls offer views of both the old city and the **Bogside peace murals** (page 417).

<<<

Planning Your Trip

Where to Go

Dublin

Unless you're flying into Shannon, the fast-paced, cosmopolitan capital of the Irish Republic will be your first stop. Many visitors tour the Guinness Brewery and go for afternoon pub crawls in the Temple Bar neighborhood—but be sure to seek out culture *outside* the pubs, too. Art, architecture, archaeology, and book lovers can occupy themselves for days at **Trinity College,** where the **Book of Kells** is on display; the **National Gallery;** the neo-Gothic **Christ Church Cathedral;** and the **National Museum of Archaeology and History.** It's worth passing an hour or two on **St. Stephen's Green** just watching all of Dublin go by.

Around Dublin

The first Neolithic farmers settled in the fertile Boyne River valley. The best-known prehistoric site at **Brú na Bóinne** is **Newgrange,** but for a glimpse of unexcavated tombs, visit the more remote **Loughcrew Cairns.** "Wee" County Louth offers distinguished monastic sites at **Mellifont Abbey** and **Monasterboice.** County Wicklow is called the "Garden of Ireland" for its green vales and Italianate terraces, most notably at **Powerscourt House and Gardens.** Drive less than half an hour south from Dublin for the gorse-dotted **Wicklow Mountains National Park** and the early Christian monastery at **Glendalough.**

The Southeast

County Wexford is the sunniest in the country; it also boasts Europe's oldest **lighthouse** at **Hook Head.** Kilkenny City offers medieval atmosphere

Christ Church Cathedral in Dublin

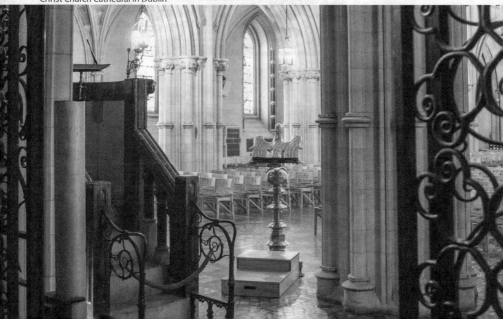

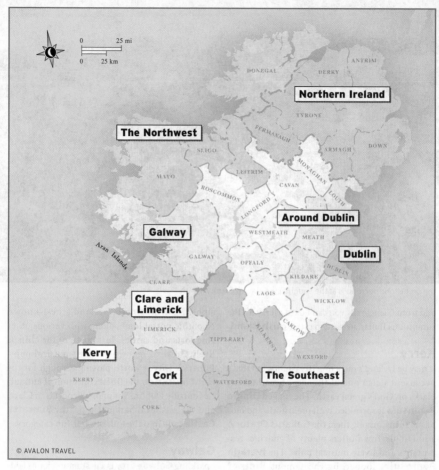

© AVALON TRAVEL

in its narrow winding streets, **Kilkenny Castle,** and **St. Canice's Cathedral** with its climbable round tower. The county features quiet, picturesque villages along the River Nore and **Jerpoint Abbey,** one of the country's finest monastic ruins. The fields of Tipperary and Waterford are some of the island's most fertile; here you'll find the awe-inspiring **Rock of Cashel,** where Patrick baptized the king of Munster. The highlights of the sunny Waterford coast are the breathtaking ruins of **St. Declan's Monastery,** at the start of a bracing cliff walk, and the pretty village of **Dunmore East.**

Cork

Cork is Ireland's largest county, and its capital city has enjoyed a cultural renaissance in recent years. Climb the tower and play a tune on the bells of **St. Anne's Church.** Admire the Harry Clarke windows and whimsical floor mosaics at the **Honan Chapel. Kinsale** is one of Cork's most touristy towns for its reputation as "Ireland's Gourmet Capital"; if serenity is what you're after, head out to West Cork with its three lovely peninsulas—the **Beara, Sheep's Head,** and **Mizen Head.** The enchanted forests at **Gougane Barra** and **Glengarriff** are lovely, too,

the prehistoric necropolis at the Loughcrew Cairns in County Meath

and from Glengarriff you can board a ferry for the sumptuous Italianate garden on **Garnish Island.**

Kerry

It may be Ireland's most touristy county, but that's because it's also one of the most breathtaking places on God's green earth. The rugged **Dingle Peninsula** is sprinkled with prehistoric and monastic ruins, among them the **Gallarus Oratory,** and Dingle Town offers plenty of gourmet restaurants and lively musical pubs. The **Iveragh Peninsula,** looped by the famous **Ring of Kerry,** has a few hidden places you'll want to seek out, from the Skellig Ring to the quiet highlands. A visit to the 6th-century monastery perched atop jagged **Skellig Michael** is well worth the nausea of a rough ferry ride. Kerry is a slice of heaven; you just have to plan ahead to escape the crowds.

Clare and Limerick

County Clare is best known for the **Cliffs of Moher:** breathtaking, but try to visit in low season if you can. West of here stretches a deceptively barren-looking limestone plateau, the **Burren,** where you'll find another famous sight, **Poulnabrone,** Ireland's best-known Neolithic portal tomb, along with various other ring forts and castles. Just north of the cliffs is lively **Doolin,** renowned for its musical pubs. Limerick City is worth passing through for the **Hunt Museum,** the finest collection of antiquities outside Dublin. Shannon Airport is in Clare, and the medieval banquet at nearby **Bunratty Castle** falls into the touristy-but-fun category.

Galway

Sparkling **Galway City** is a destination for its laid-back atmosphere and excellent pubs and restaurants. Head west to the brooding heather-covered mountains and glittering black lakes of **Connemara.** Highlights include the early Victorian manor house **Kylemore Abbey** and **Killary Harbour,** Ireland's only fjord. The three **Aran Islands** in Galway Bay are just as enchanting. Southern Galway offers its own delights: **Dunguaire Castle** in the seaside village of **Kinvara;** the poet Yeats's restored summer home, **Thoor Ballylee;** and the monastic site at **Kilmacduagh** with its leaning tower. Make a detour into the midlands to **Clonmacnoise,** Ireland's most important monastic site.

Counties Cork and Kerry share the pretty Beara Peninsula.

The Northwest

In Mayo it feels like you have the county to yourself. Climb **Croagh Patrick,** one of Ireland's most popular pilgrimages. County Sligo is touted as "Yeats country"; it's also known for its megalithic burial sites, including **Carrowmore, Knocknarea,** and **Creevykeel,** not to mention some relaxing **seaweed baths.** Donegal's **rugged landscapes** are well worth the longer travel time; make the five-hour trek across the **Slieve League** sea cliffs in the Gaeltacht parish of **Glencolmcille.** You'll hear plenty more Irish spoken farther north in **Gweedore,** where crimson sunsets stain the so-called **Bloody Foreland.**

Northern Ireland

Northern Ireland's **Causeway Coast** is a feast of green cliffs and glittering sea vistas, from **Giant's Causeway** and the **Carrick-a-Rede rope bridge** to precarious **Dunluce Castle** and the **Mussenden Temple** at Downhill. For an unvarnished history lesson, take a **Black Taxi tour** through the working-class neighborhoods of **Belfast.** In **Derry,** check out the **Bogside peace murals** after you've made the nine-furlong circuit around the intact **city walls.** In County Down, wander through spooky **Grey Abbey** or the formal gardens at **Mount Stewart House.** The lonely **Mourne Mountains** are perfect for walking or cycling.

Know Before You Go

When to Go

Ireland can be beautiful at any time of year. **July** and **August** are **peak months,** when the sheer volume of tourists in Kerry, Clare, and other popular destinations can be downright irritating.

Planning to do any **water sports** or **camping?** Crowds or no, **June through August** is your window (though **May** and **September** may also suit, depending on the activity).

Do those tour buses really get on your nerves? Visit during the **spring** or **autumn**—the **"shoulder seasons"**—or in winter, better yet. Want to get **off the beaten track? Late spring** or **early autumn** is best, but transportation can be limited to more remote locales (especially the various islands off the west coast) between November and April. Note that late autumn can be the rainiest time of year.

There is much to be said for a **winter** visit. New Year's is a good choice; listening to a live traditional music session with a pint in hand sure beats watching the ball drop. Irish winters are milder than those of New England—the low/high temperatures run 0-11°C (32-52°F)—and the rare snowfall wreaks both magic and chaos (the former in the landscape; the latter in the national bus system). Aer Lingus and other airline carriers post their lowest fares in January and February, and many hotels, B&Bs, and hostels offer better off-season rates, though many others close altogether.

You may also wish to time your visit to coincide with a particular event. For instance, there's the **Dublin Theatre Festival** in early October, the **Cork Jazz Festival** in late October, and the **Cúirt International Festival of Literature** in Galway in late April.

Planning Your Time

If you take only one piece of advice, let it be this: Relax! Don't try to see seven counties in as many days. If you do that, you'll spend half of each day behind the wheel of a rental car. It's worth noting that when the Irish go on vacation, they tend to pick one place and stay put. So choose two or three places you really want to see and see them properly. Savor them. Factor in a couple more days for poor weather (particularly if you want to take a ferry to any offshore islands) or a case of love at first sight: "If we can't buy a cottage here, can we at least spend one more night?" It's not as easy to keep your itinerary flexible in high season when you've got to book accommodations well in advance, but in the off or shoulder seasons, to a great extent, you can plan as you go.

Passports and Visas

Upon arrival, an immigration official will stamp your passport for a **three-month tourist visa**—easy as pie—although officials are much friendlier and more relaxed at Shannon. When you land in Dublin, come prepared with proof of departure within the 90-day window.

What to Pack

Bring lots of comfortable clothing to wear in **layers,** as well as a **waterproof jacket.** Pack a couple of **sweaters** even in summertime—but don't let the threat of rain keep you from applying **sunblock.** On lucky days when the temperature's in the high 20s C (80s F), you'll find the beaches (or "strands") crowded with pasty-skinned locals of all ages reveling in the sun.

Dress is quite **informal,** even in the fancier pubs and restaurants. Though **raingear** is sensible, you will find that the Irish don't wear galoshes unless farming is their business. Getting soaked, followed by drinking tea while warming by the fire, is an Irish ritual. Throw a few **tissue travel-packs** in with your skivvies.

If you plan to do a lot of hill-walking or other **outdoor activities,** you might want to bring a pair of **Wellingtons** along with your **hiking boots.** If you don't mind the occasional case of damp feet, however, keep your load light. Umbrellas are nearly useless, as the wind makes the rain seem like it's falling sideways. Be optimistic and pack your **sunglasses.**

Hill-walkers and **cyclists** should also bring the usual compass, flashlight, medical minikit, pocketknife (in your checked luggage), and so forth.

Purchase a **plug adapter** for electronic devices before you leave. (The Irish plug has two horizontal prongs and one vertical.)

Transportation

GETTING THERE

International flights arrive in either **Dublin Airport** or **Shannon Airport** (on the border of Counties Clare and Limerick); the most commonly used carriers from the United States and Canada are Aer Lingus and United Airlines. If you are planning to travel in summertime, book as far in advance as possible for the best fares. Flights from Europe (London, Paris, Amsterdam, et al.) on **budget airlines** like Ryanair can be extremely economical. It's also possible to arrive by **ferry** from England or France.

GETTING AROUND

If you're planning to stick to classic destinations like the Cliffs of Moher, the Ring of Kerry, Newgrange, and Glendalough, you'll do just fine with **public transportation** (Bus Éireann and Irish Rail) and perhaps a **coach tour** or two out of Dublin or Galway. To explore less-traveled areas, or if you are covering a lot of territory in a week, rent a **car.** Gas is quite expensive compared to American prices, but competition keeps rental fees surprisingly affordable.

If you have the time and energy, a long-distance **walking** or **cycling** trip—be it a long weekend or a month or more—is the ideal way to experience Ireland's landscape, history, and culture. The **Wicklow Way, Kerry Way,** and **Táin Trail** (for cyclists) are just three of many options, and you can do any portion of the route.

Ireland's Best Trips

On these three trips you will explore the famous sights of southern Ireland, traditional culture in Galway and the northwest, and the coastal treasures of Northern Ireland and Donegal. All of them begin and/or end in **Dublin;** for suggestions on how to spend time in the capital city, see page 38.

The South

This nine-day route takes in Ireland's best-known destinations—the Cliffs of Moher, the Ring of Kerry, Killarney National Park—as well as equally beautiful places you may not have heard of yet, like Ardmore in County Waterford. While it's possible to reach most of these places by bus (and bicycle), allow yourself more time to complete the itinerary if you're not driving.

DAY 1

Fly into Shannon and head for the **Cliffs of Moher,** a 75-minute drive from the airport. Take the car ferry from Killimer in south Clare

to Tarbert in north Kerry, and proceed south through Tralee to the **Dingle Peninsula.** Drive **Slea Head,** visit **Gallarus Oratory** and the **Riasc Monastic Settlement,** and spend the night in **Dingle Town** after a fine meal and some live trad.

DAY 2

Drive from Dingle to **Killarney National Park** and go for a walk or bicycle ride—this is one of Ireland's most popular tourist destinations, and you'll see why as soon as you arrive. Spend the night in **Killarney Town.**

DAY 3

From Killarney, do the **Ring of Kerry** counterclockwise; the earlier your start, the fewer tour buses you'll get stuck behind. Have another lovely dinner in **Kenmare.**

DAY 4

Do the **Beara Peninsula** today, driving the

cliffs of the Dingle Peninsula

dazzling **Healy Pass** from Lauragh in Kerry to Adrigole in Cork, all relatively quiet little places even in summertime. End up in **Glengarriff,** rambling through the forest park and up the steep steps to **Lady Bantry's Lookout.** Or take the ferry to **Garnish Island** with its formal Italianate garden.

DAY 5

Drive from Glengarriff to **Kinsale** for lunch at one of its famed gourmet restaurants. Finish the day in **Cork City,** climbing the tower at **St. Anne's Church** to ring the bells. Also make a point of visiting the lovely **Honan Chapel** at University College Cork. Take in a play or concert at one of Cork's many fine theaters.

DAY 6

Head east to **Ardmore** in County Waterford, and take a short walk uphill from the village's main street to the spectacular ruins of **St. Declan's Monastery.** Then go for the gorgeous five-kilometer cliff walk all around the headland, ending up back on the main street.

DAY 7

Drive north to **Cashel** in County Tipperary, and visit the **Rock of Cashel** (also called "St. Patrick's Rock"); don't miss the spooky Romanesque **Cormac's Chapel.** Have dinner at the atmospheric **Chez Hans,** a worthwhile splurge if there ever was one.

DAY 8

Drive east from Cashel to **Kilkenny City** and visit **Kilkenny Castle.** Have lunch in Kilkenny, then head south to Thomastown to see **Jerpoint Abbey.** Then drive through Carlow and Wexford north to **Wicklow Mountains National Park;** stay near **Glendalough.**

DAY 9

Spend the early morning on one of Glendalough's shorter walking trails, take one last stroll through the monastic city, and then head north for **Powerscourt House and Gardens.** Spend your last night in **Dublin** (there is express bus service back to Shannon, though, if you need it).

the majestic Rock of Cashel

Connemara National Park

Galway and the Northwest

This travel plan, covering the western province of Connaught plus Donegal in Ulster, highlights some of the very best aspects of traditional Irish culture, from live music sessions to woolen textiles and cottage museums offering glimpses into the old fishing and farming lifestyles.

DAY 1

Fly into **Donegal Airport** (via Dublin), pick up your rental car (using Enterprise), and spend a leisurely day soaking up the wild beauty and lilting Irish Gaelic of **Gweedore.** Catch a traditional music session at **Teach Hudí Beag.**

DAY 2

Drive south to **Ardara** to visit John Molloy's tweed shop and Eddie Doherty's handweaving studio, pausing for lunch before continuing south to **Kilcar** for Studio Donegal. Spend the night in Donegal Town.

DAY 3

Visit **Donegal Castle** and the **Donegal Craft Village** before heading south to **Sligo.** Check out works by Jack B. Yeats and Sean Keating at the **Model Gallery.**

DAY 4

Make an early start for **Westport** in County Mayo, stopping for an early lunch before continuing on to Murrisk to climb **Croagh Patrick** in the afternoon. This is Ireland's most famous (not to mention breathtaking) Catholic pilgrimage. Stay the night in Westport, catching a session at **Matt Molloy's.**

DAY 5

Take the N59 south to **Letterfrack** and go for an easy but visually rewarding ramble in **Connemara National Park.** When you arrive in **Galway,** you can return your rental car to any of the Enterprise locations in the city, and then you have another night of excellent traditional music to look forward to. Try **Tigh Coili, The Crane,** or **Monroe's.**

DAY 6

Take the Aran Islands ferry from Rossaveal to **Inis Meáin** and visit **Teach Synge** and **Cniotáil Inis Meáin.**

DAY 7

Catch the morning ferry to **Inis Mór** and learn about traditional island culture at **Ionad Árann,** the Aran Heritage Centre. Hail a taxi to take you out to **Dún Dúbhchathair,** the Black Fort (or walk, if it's still early enough in the day).

DAY 8

Cycle out to **Dún Aengus** first thing in the morning, pausing at the **Kilmurvey Craft Village** to shop for hand-knit Aran jumpers for yourself and your family. Catch a trad session at **Tigh Fitz, Joe Watty's,** or **Tí Joe Mac's.**

DAY 9

Take the ferry back to Galway and spend a laid-back afternoon popping into the shops and classic pubs of the charming old city center. **Neachtain's** is a must for excellent pints and people-watching.

DAY 10

Take the express bus back to Dublin for your flight home.

Northern Ireland and Donegal

This one-week driving itinerary in Ulster takes in the coastal highlights of Northern Ireland plus a few wonderful places in Donegal not covered by the *Galway and the Northwest* itinerary. At the finish you'll be traveling from Donegal back to Dublin by air, so you'll need to use Enterprise (www.enterprise.ie), the only car rental company at tiny Donegal Airport. (Otherwise, you'll be driving back to the capital.)

DAY 1

Heading north from Dublin, take a scenic drive through the **Mourne Mountains** in County Down, have lunch in **Strangford,** a lovely village on an eponymous lake, and spend the night at **Anna's House** in **Lisbane,** unofficially the best B&B on the island.

DAY 2

Arrive in Belfast and take a **Black Taxi tour** for an exceedingly vivid history lesson. Spend the afternoon at the **Botanic Gardens** or **Cave Hill Country Park** if the weather's fine, but if not, take the **Belfast City Hall** tour. After a terrific

numinous vistas at Glenveagh National Park

meal at one of the city's many outstanding eateries, see what's on at the **Grand Opera House** or **Ulster Orchestra.**

DAY 3
Traveling northeast from Belfast on the A2, head for **The Gobbins** Edwardian-era cliff walk (be sure to book your tickets ahead of time). Continue on through the **Glens of Antrim,** spending the night in quiet **Ballintoy** or cheerful, family-friendly **Ballycastle.**

DAY 4
Clamber across the **Carrick-a-Rede rope bridge,** once traversed daily by local salmon fishermen but now a worthwhile tourist draw, before continuing on the **Causeway Coast** route. Have lunch at **The Nook** before ambling down to **Giant's Causeway** with its 40,000 hexagonal basalt columns. Stay the night in the Bushmills area rather than rushing through all this gorgeous scenery.

DAY 5
Return to the coastal route for the precariously situated **Dunluce Castle.** Drive on to **Downhill**

to check out the ruins of Bishop Hervey's estate and the charming **Mussenden Temple.** Arrive in **Derry City.**

DAY 6
Walk the **Derry City walls** and view the **Bogside peace murals.** Continue west into Donegal, pausing at the hilltop ring fort of **Grianán of Aileách** before driving north to the **Inishowen Peninsula.** Spend the evening at the fabulous McGrory's pub in **Culdaff,** where you can catch a well-known musical act any night of the week.

DAY 7
Another long but rewarding day's drive: Get an early start from Inishowen down to **Glenveagh National Park,** where you can walk through a numinous landscape of lakes, mountains, and moor grass to 19th-century **Glenveagh Castle.** Continue west to **Gweedore,** with its dramatic **Bloody Foreland** viewing point and friendly Irish-speaking locals.

DAY 8
Drive to Donegal Airport just south of Gweedore for your flight back to Dublin.

Giant's Causeway

the Iron Age ring fort of Grianán of Aileách

Sacred Sites and Pilgrimages

Whether your interest is religious or archaeological, this itinerary covering some of the most important cathedrals and monastic ruins in Ireland is for you. The Skellig Islands—which offer the remains of an early Christian monastery atop a jagged peak jutting out of the ocean—will be the highlight, but factor in an extra day (or two) in case the weather's bad on the morning you wish to visit. A rental car is essential for this one.

Day 1

Fly into **Dublin** and visit **Christ Church Cathedral, St. Patrick's Cathedral,** and **St. Michan's Church,** three Anglican churches (all but the last have pre-Reformation histories, and thus may be of interest to Catholics as well). True pilgrims will want to visit the shrine of St. Valentine at **Our Lady of Mount Carmel.**

Day 2

Make a day trip to County Louth to visit **Mellifont Abbey,** once one of the most prosperous Cistercian abbeys on the island (guided tours available in high season), and **Monasterboice,** which offers scant ecclesiastical ruins and Ireland's two most important high crosses.

Day 3

Quit Dublin for **Glendalough** in the **Wicklow Mountains National Park.** Spend the night here so you can experience the site first thing in the morning, before the arrival of the tour buses. St. Kevin's monastic city is even more memorable when few others are around to share the experience.

Day 4

Rise early and take a walk along Glendalough's **Upper and Lower Lakes.** Then make the drive to **Kilkenny City,** where you'll base yourself while visiting the area's monastic remains.

Day 5

South of the city, tour **Jerpoint Abbey** and examine its intricate carvings. Also visit **Kells Priory** and other smaller, more secluded ruins like the **Kilfane and Kilree Churches.**

Day 6

A couple days from now, weather permitting, you'll visit Skellig Michael off the coast of the Iveragh Peninsula in County Kerry. To break up the journey from Kilkenny, spend the night in **Killarney.** Pop inside the austere, cavernous, Catholic **St. Mary's Cathedral.**

Day 7

Rise early and visit **Muckross Abbey** in **Killarney National Park.** Before skipping town, check out the Harry Clarke studio window and ornate Flemish-style altar at the **Franciscan Friary.** Spend the night in **Portmagee.**

Day 8

Take the ferry from Portmagee to **Skellig Michael.** Bring a picnic lunch to enjoy on a grassy peak outside the monastery, with its beehive huts and tiny whitewashed chapel, and take the excellent tour. Spend another night in Portmagee.

Day 9

Head through northern Kerry and take the Tarbert-Killimer ferry to County Clare. Visit **Quin Abbey,** the Franciscan **Ennis Friary,** and the church at **Dysert O'Dea,** and spend the night in **Ennis** or **Corofin.** Guided tours of Quin Abbey and the Ennis Friary are available in the summer months.

Day 10

Keep driving north to **Galway City,** stopping at the **Kilmacduagh** monastic site en route, with

Can't-Miss Castles

Many Irish castles are still inhabited, some by descendants of the original owners (who were members of the Protestant Ascendancy). Some of these families open a wing of their homes to tour groups on weekends in the summer, and others have beautiful gardens that are open to the public even if the manor itself isn't. Some castles are now hotels; others are made available for weddings, conferences, films, and other private events (a few even offer aristocratic holiday accommodations to the tune of €20,000-75,000 a week!). Still others are ruins on private property—whether ivy-clad and picturesque, or literally a pile of rubble. Organized by region, here are Ireland's must-see castles.

DUBLIN AND AROUND

If you visit only one castle in the Dublin area, let it be **Malahide**: It retains much of its original furnishings, and the ghost stories are deliciously spooky. **Dublin Castle** houses several government offices, but you can tour the excavations of the 13th-century foundation. **Trim Castle,** in County Meath, is the country's largest Anglo-Norman fortress. And if you can, spend the night at wonderful **Ross Castle** on Lough Sheelin (it's relatively affordable!).

THE SOUTH

Kilkenny Castle is a must-see for its sumptuous 1830s period furnishings and atmospheric Long Gallery lined with portraits of the Butler family, who lived here from the 1390s to the 1930s. The Butlers acquired **Cahir Castle** in County Tipperary, with its distinctive portcullis and feudal-style courtyard, around the same period. (And while you're in the area, visit the **Rock of Cashel**, originally the seat of the kings of Munster.) At **King John's Castle** in Limerick City you can tour archaeological excavations dating to the 9th and 10th centuries. Take a tour with **Bunratty Castle**'s wonderfully informative guides, visit the folk park, and return to the castle in the evening for the kitschy-but-fun medieval banquet. There are evening entertain-

Cahir Castle

ments available at **Knappogue Castle** and **Dunguaire Castle** as well.

NORTHERN IRELAND

A short drive or train ride from Belfast, **Carrickfergus Castle** is the island's most complete medieval stronghold. On the Causeway Coast, **Dunluce Castle** is the most precariously situated—on a cliff that has, on at least one tragic occasion, crumbled into the sea. It's technically the ruin of an 18th-century manor house, not a castle, but **Downhill Estate** is even more haunting than ruins five times its age.

inside St. Patrick's Cathedral in Dublin

Jerpoint Abbey has a wealth of curious effigies.

its tall, complete, but precariously tilted round tower. Take time to enjoy the Galway nightlife.

Day 11

Drive through northern Connemara into County Mayo. Spend the night in **Murrisk** and enjoy a wonderful meal at **The Tavern,** just across the road from the ruins of 15th-century Murrisk Abbey.

Day 12

Climb **Croagh Patrick.** It's two hours up and an hour and a half down—it's a challenging climb if you aren't in great shape. Stay another night in Murrisk, but spend the evening listening to a trad session at one of Westport's many musical pubs.

Day 13

Return to Galway and visit its **cathedrals,** both named for St. Nicholas: the Catholic cathedral just over the Salmon Weir Bridge and the Anglican church on Lombard Street.

Day 14

Your last day brings another highlight: **Clonmacnoise.** Head east from Galway, and if you have time, stop at Clonfert to admire the medieval cathedral's stunning Romanesque doorway. Then proceed to Clonmacnoise. Founded by St. Ciarán, this was once Ireland's greatest monastic city, and its ruins alongside the Shannon are truly fascinating. Administered by Dúchas, Clonmacnoise always has guided tours available. Be sure to take a walk down to the **Nuns' Church,** which has another remarkable Hiberno-Romanesque doorway. Drive back to Dublin.

Whatever your favorite activity, you'll be able to build your whole Irish vacation around it. Here are suggested destinations organized by sport, chosen for both scenery and tourist infrastructure.

CLIMBING

Get up to County Donegal to hike **Mount Errigal** and the sea cliffs at **Slieve League. Macgillicuddy's Reeks,** west of Killarney National Park, constitute the country's highest mountain range. Joining in on a guided hike couldn't be easier.

LONG-DISTANCE WALKS

The 127-kilometer **Wicklow Way** and 214-kilometer **Kerry Way** are the most established routes, making accommodations and luggage transfer a snap, but if you'd prefer to go the path less traveled, see the **Irish Trails** website (www.irishtrails.ie) for many more choices.

CYCLING

Ireland's relatively quiet regional and local roads are great for cycling. For a day excursion, try cycling in the **Burren** in County Clare, **Connemara** or **Inis Mór** in County Galway, or on the **Great Western Greenway** in County Mayo. Long-distance options are popular, too. The **Ring of Kerry** cycling route covers 216 kilometers (round-trip from Killarney) and is best traveled in a clockwise direction over a one-week period; for more details, visit **Discover Ireland** (www.discoverireland.ie). Another choice is the 138-kilometer **Beara Way,** which has County Cork's loveliest scenery to offer. For many more options and a very handy route-planning app, check out **Cycle Ireland** (www.cycleireland.ie).

SURFING

Get yourself to "The Hollow" at **Enniscrone** in County Sligo for some of the best waves on this side of the Atlantic.

KAYAKING AND CANOEING

For ocean kayaking, try **Atlantic Sea Kayaking** (www.atlanticseakayaking.com) in Union Hall, West

scenery along the Wicklow Way

Cork. For kayaking on Ireland's only fjord, contact **Killary Adventure Company** (www.killaryadventure.com) outside Leenane in Connemara, County Galway.

DIVING

Contact **Scuba Dive West** (www.scubadivewest.com) in Renvyle, Connemara, which offers excursions in a private sheltered cove, or **Valentia Island Sea Sports** (www.valentiaislandseasports.com) in County Kerry, with trips that include the Skellig Islands and the clear waters around Valentia Island. For more scuba diving and snorkeling opportunities, visit the **Irish Underwater Council** online (www.diving.ie).

HANG-GLIDING

You can sightsee from above in the **Blackstairs Mountains** (along the Carlow-Wexford border) in summer. For details, visit the **Irish Hang Gliding and Paragliding Association** online (www.ihpa.ie).

The Neolithic burial mound at Newgrange is Ireland's most famous prehistoric monument.

Ghosts of Ancient Ireland

Amateur archaeologists can have a field day on the Emerald Isle—pun intended! If you don't have a rental car, you can still do much of this itinerary (Loughcrew and Carrowkeel being the only places you'll have to skip, as public transportation is nonexistent and taxis unfeasible). You'll be flying into Dublin and out of Shannon for this one (which typically isn't any more expensive).

Day 1

Spend your first day in **Dublin** at the **National Museum of Archaeology and History,** which houses the vast majority of the country's treasures from prehistory to the present.

Day 2

Base yourself in County Meath for the next two nights. Visit **Brú na Bóinne** today, Ireland's most important Neolithic site. **Newgrange** is the most famous passage tomb here, though **Knowth** is also accessible by guided tour, and you can take a walk around unexcavated **Dowth.**

Day 3

Visit the **Loughcrew Cairns** for a sense of what Newgrange might have been like before it was excavated and turned into the country's most popular attraction.

Day 4

From Meath, drive northwest to County Sligo, stopping first at **Carrowkeel** just over the Roscommon border. This one vies with Loughcrew for Ireland's creepiest megalithic cemetery. Spend the night in **Sligo Town.**

Day 5

Visit the **Carrowmore** and **Creevykeel** sites outside Sligo Town; these prehistoric tombs aren't as dramatically situated as Carrowkeel or Loughcrew, but they are interesting in their own right. Spend a second night here.

Day 6

Drive west from Sligo to northern Mayo to visit

the prehistoric Poulnabrone portal tomb in County Clare

the excellent interpretive center at **Céide Fields.** Heck, why not stop in **Enniscrone** first for a seaweed bath? Then you can spend the night in **Ballycastle,** a very quiet one-street town (and the closest to Céide Fields).

Day 7

Drive south from Ballycastle to **Galway City.** This is going to be the least interesting day of your trip, but no matter—tomorrow, Inis Mór is going to be the number one highlight. This, the largest of the Aran Islands, is rich in prehistoric and early Christian ruins (the clifftop fort of **Dún Aengus** is the most popular, though there's plenty more to see besides) and still surprisingly traditional in attitude.

Day 8

Take the ferry from Rossaveal to **Inis Mór** and spend the afternoon at **Dún Dúbhchathair** ("Black Fort"). This ruin is much less popular than Dún Aengus, but just as picturesque.

Day 9

Rise early and get to **Dún Aengus** before the morning ferries arrive full of day-trippers. Spend the afternoon exploring the less popular destinations, like **Dún Eochla.**

Day 10

Take morning ferry back to Galway. Drive south into the **Burren,** checking out dramatically situated **Poulnabrone,** which marks a prehistoric burial site, in the early dusk when the site is spookiest. Stay in the **Doolin** area (you can rise early and hightail it to Shannon for your early afternoon flight; if this isn't feasible, stay in Ennis).

Family Fun

Focused on Kerry and West Cork, this itinerary balances fun family outings with chilled-out beach days and other kid-friendly recreational activities. After the first two nights in Killarney and Kenmare, choose a B&B or self-catering accommodation in Glengarriff, using your rental car for relatively short excursions.

Day 1

Fly into Shannon Airport, pick up your rental car, and head south on the N21 for **Killarney.** After lunch in town, head for **Muckross House and Gardens** and **Muckross Traditional Farms.** If you have time, you can visit **Ross Castle** or go for a jaunt in the **Gap of Dunloe.**

Day 2

Drive the **Ring of Kerry,** stopping in **Cahersiveen** for lunch and a quick side trip to the **Cahergall ring fort.** Spend the night in **Kenmare.**

Day 3

Head out to the end of the **Beara Peninsula** for a ride on the **Dursey Island cable car.** After a happy hour or two on the beautiful **Ballydonegan Strand** at **Allihies,** drive back east on the R572 for Glengarriff.

Day 4

Spend the day in **Glengarriff:** Visit the **Glengarriff Bamboo Park,** or take the ferry to **Garnish Island** for a wander through the gardens at **Ilnacullen.**

Day 5

Explore the **Mizen Head** peninsula: check out the **Mizen Vision** visitors center and signal tower, and relax on the beach at **Barley Cove.**

Day 6

Another day in Glengarriff: Explore the tranquil forest trails of the **nature reserve,** making the short-but-steep climb up to **Lady Bantry's Lookout.**

Day 7

Save the best for last, and go **kayaking** in **Schull** or **Baltimore.** And if you aren't completely zonked, check out the **Schull Planetarium.**

Day 8

Return to Shannon for your flight home.

Dublin

Sights 39

Activities and Recreation 55

Food 57

Entertainment and Events 63

Shopping...................... 68

Accommodations.............. 69

Information and Services 72

Transportation................. 73

Vicinity of Dublin City.......... 76

I t's not just the world's best (and fresh-est!) Guinness that brings people to Ireland's capital city. They come to observe the ubiquitous reminders of the city's fascinating, checkered history.

It's a history that traces from Viking origins, through the long centuries of British domination, becoming a nationalist tinderbox during the second decade of the 20th century, and eventually emerging as the capital of a free and independent state in December 1922. The Easter Rising centennial celebrations in 2016 reinvigorated the city's already steady sense of historic pride.

Today Dublin is as fast, modern, and style-conscious as any European capital—and it feels more fast-paced and cosmopolitan every time you visit. Any of the 12 genuine Dublin accents are increasingly rare to hear; the city has become like New York in that most of its 527,000 residents (within the city limits) were born and raised elsewhere. It's also a remarkably youthful place, with more than half its population under the age of 30.

Like other European metropolises, the city has an abundance of neoclassical architecture mixed with fast food places, clothing chains, and souvenir shops—and sometimes exorbitant admission and accommodation prices (though the economic downturn has kept those fees more or less stable ever since). It was perhaps inevitable that the "Celtic Tiger" economic boom of the 1990s and the economic prosperity of the early 2000s would turn the capital city into a mixed bag of excellent gourmet restaurants and Mickey D's, chic nightclubs and tacky tourist traps. But the city is truly what you make of it. Load up on life-altering cultural experiences, spend your afternoon drinking Guinness and talking "sport"—or better yet, do a little bit of both.

Most of the greater county is made up of sprawling commuter suburbs, though there are a few seaside towns worth an afternoon excursion in fine weather. The fertile plains of Meath to the northwest and the verdant hills and valleys of Wicklow Mountains National Park to the south provide opportunities for unforgettable day trips as well.

Previous: *The Eve of St. Agnes* by Harry Clarke at the Hugh Lane Gallery; the Ha'penny Bridge across the River Liffey. **Above:** mural on a wall in Temple Bar.

Look for ★ to find recommended sights, activities, dining, and lodging.

Highlights

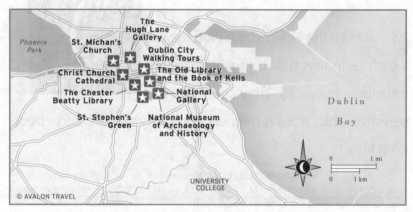

★ **The Old Library and the Book of Kells:** Two pages at a time of Ireland's most famous illuminated manuscript are on display under glass (page 41).

★ **National Gallery:** Check out great paintings by Irish and international artists from the 16th century to the present; Caravaggio's *The Taking of Christ* is the highlight of the European collection (page 41).

★ **National Museum of Archaeology and History:** Once discovered, every Irish treasure from every period in history—including the Tara Brooch, Ardagh Chalice, and Cross of Cong—has found its way into the country's most important museum (page 42).

★ **St. Stephen's Green:** Europe's largest city square features colorful parterres, interesting sculptures and memorials, and many opportunities for people-watching and bird-feeding (page 42).

★ **The Chester Beatty Library:** This

well-presented collection of priceless manuscripts is housed on the grounds of Dublin Castle (page 43).

★ **Christ Church Cathedral:** Wander down the central aisle of the city's grandest Gothic edifice, with its precariously tilting columns and strange artifacts (page 44).

★ **The Hugh Lane Gallery:** Revel in a close-up view of Harry Clarke's stained-glass masterpiece, *The Eve of St. Agnes,* and take a peek inside Francis Bacon's infamously chaotic studio (page 47).

★ **St. Michan's Church:** The medieval limestone crypt of this Anglican church offers the city's most macabre sights. Handel used the organ upstairs to practice his *Messiah* for its first performance in 1742 (page 48).

★ **Dublin City Walking Tours:** Whether you're interested in history, ghost stories, or whiskey, the city's various walking tours offer something for you (page 55).

Though Dublin originates from the Irish "Dubh Linn" ("Dark Pool"), today its official name in Irish Gaelic is Baile Átha Cliath ("Town of the Hurdles"), the name of an adjoining settlement north of the Liffey.

HISTORY

Actually, the Vikings didn't found Dubh Linn. Ptolemy recorded the existence of a settlement here on his famous map of AD 140; he called it Eblana Civitas. It's said that St. Patrick arrived in 448 and got busy making converts. Then the Vikings came in 841 with the intent of setting up a trading post (trading human cargo, that is) using the existing native Irish settlement. They were driven out by Brian Boru at the Battle of Clontarf in 1014.

But that wasn't the end of the foreign invaders—far from it. The Normans arrived in the 12th century at the plea of the deposed king of Leinster, Diarmuid Mac Murrough. Mac Murrough was only hoping to reclaim his throne, but one imagines he lived to regret his actions when the Normans cast their eyes over the entire island. Henry II, who had sent his troops under the ambitious and opportunistic Strongbow to "aid" the Leinster king, established a court in Dublin to keep an eye on his power-hungry knights—and thus was British domination established. Greater Dublin became known as "the Pale" for its complete subjugation to English government control.

The Norman adventurers settled into their confiscated lands and after a few generations considered themselves Irish—though they still swore loyalty to the British Crown, and those who rebelled swiftly lost their holdings through bloodshed. Still more Plantationers arrived to claim territories allotted by Elizabeth I (the native Irish farmers were forced to work as tenants on what had been their own land). Dublin City was the stronghold of this British Ascendancy, where the Anglo-Irish landowners usually kept townhomes. For them, city artisans—furniture-makers, silversmiths, and architects—kept up a busy practice. Dublin in Georgian times would have been quite an exciting place for all its wealth and prestige.

As a consequence of the failed island-wide rebellion in 1798, the 1801 **Act of Union** stripped Dublin of its independent parliament. A Kerry lawyer, Daniel O'Connell, was sent to London to represent County Clare, and he succeeded in rolling back the Catholic-oppressive Penal Laws in 1829. He was elected the first Catholic Lord Mayor of Dublin in 1841 but died six years later feeling like a failure for having left so much unaccomplished. History would judge him otherwise, but the struggle for civil rights and political independence for Irish Catholics continued.

The city bore the fruits of the **Irish Literary Revival** with the establishment of the **Abbey Theatre,** the world's first English-speaking repertory theater, in 1904. Auspiciously enough, the venue on Lower Abbey Street (purchased for the company by Annie Horniman) was on the site of a morgue. Not all Dubliners were open-minded enough to appreciate the efforts of Lady Augusta Gregory and William Butler Yeats; the use of the word "shift" (as in a ladies' undergarment) during a performance of John Millington Synge's *The Playboy of the Western World* led to a riot in the theater in January 1907. The original theater burned down in July 1951 and was rebuilt and reopened in 1966. (Despite its ugly new premises, the Abbey is still showcasing the finest in classic and contemporary Irish drama.)

One of the most crucial events in Irish history took place in Dublin on a single day, Easter Sunday 1916, when a nationalist guerrilla group, the Irish Republican Army, took over the General Post Office and declared Ireland a free and independent republic. The British attacked, and citywide chaos and bloodshed ensued. The rebellion was eventually suppressed, and 90 participants (including future Taoiseach and president Eamon de Valera) were sentenced to death. (Only de Valera's American citizenship saved his neck.) Ultimately, 14 of those 90 were executed at

Dublin

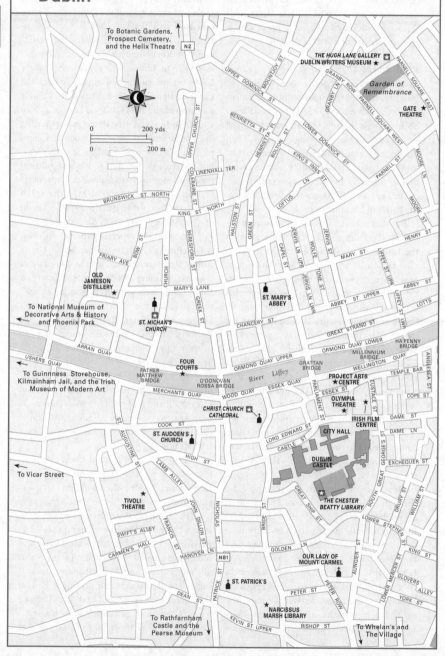

To Botanic Gardens,
Prospect Cemetery,
and the Helix Theatre

N2

THE HUGH LANE GALLERY
DUBLIN WRITERS MUSEUM ★

*Garden of
Remembrance*

GATE ★
THEATRE

UPPER DOMINICK ST

MOUNTJOY ST

GRANBY ROW

GRANBY LN

PARNELL SQUARE EAST

PARNELL SQUARE WEST

PARNELL SQUARE WEST

HENRIETTA ST

HENRIETTA PL

BOLTON ST

KING'S INNS ST

LOWER DOMINICK ST

PARNELL ST

MOORE ST

MOORE LN

0   200 yds
0   200 m

UPPER CHURCH ST

LINENHALL TER

BRUNSWICK ST NORTH

COLERAINE ST

KING ST NORTH

HALSTON ST

GREEN ST

LOFTUS LN

JERVIS LN UPR

WOLFE TONE ST

JERVIS ST

MARY ST

HENRY ST

HENRY ST

FRIARY AVE

BOW ST

CHURCH ST

BERESFORD ST

GREEK ST

CAPEL ST

JERVIS LN LWR

ABBEY ST UPPER

LIFFEY ST UPR

ABBEY ST

LIFFEY ST LWR

LOTTS

OLD
JAMESON
DISTILLERY ★

MARY'S LANE

ST. MARY'S
ABBEY

To National Museum of
Decorative Arts & History
and Phoenix Park

ST. MICHAN'S
CHURCH

CHANCERY ST

GREAT STRAND ST

ARRAN QUAY

ORMOND QUAY LOWER

MILLENNIUM
BRIDGE

HA'PENNY
BRIDGE

ANGLESEA ST

USHERS QUAY

FATHER
MATTHEW
BRIDGE

FOUR
COURTS ★

ORMOND QUAY UPPER

River Liffey

GRATTAN
BRIDGE

WELLINGTON QUAY

ORMOND QUAY

TEMPLE BAR

To Guinnness Storehouse,
Kilmainham Jail, and the Irish
Museum of Modern Art

O'DONOVAN
ROSSA BRIDGE

ESSEX QUAY

PARLIAMENT ST

EUSTACE ST

ESSEX ST

PROJECT ARTS
★ CENTRE

COPE ST

MERCHANTS QUAY

WOOD QUAY

OLYMPIA
THEATRE ★

DAME ST

DAME LN

CHRIST CHURCH
CATHEDRAL

IRISH FILM
CENTRE

COOK ST

ST. AUDOEN'S
CHURCH

HIGH ST

LORD EDWARD ST

CASTLE ST

CITY HALL

GEORGE'S ST

EXCHEQUER ST

AUGUSTINE ST

LAMB ALLEY

DUBLIN
CASTLE

GREAT SHIP ST

SOUTH GREAT

DRURY ST

WILLIAM ST

To Vicar Street

TIVOLI
THEATRE

JOHN DILLON ST

FRANCIS ST

NICHOLAS ST

BRIDE ST

THE CHESTER
BEATTY LIBRARY

LOWER STEPHEN ST

KING ST

SWIFT'S ALLEY

CARMEN'S HALL

HANOVER LN

N81

GOLDEN LN

OUR LADY OF
MOUNT CARMEL

AUNGIER ST

LOWER MERCER ST

GLOVERS
ALLEY

ST. PATRICK'S

PETER ROW

PETER ST

YORK ST

DEAN ST

NARCISSUS
MARSH LIBRARY

To Rathfarnham
Castle and the
Pearse Museum

KEVIN ST UPPER

BISHOP ST

To Whelan's and
The Village

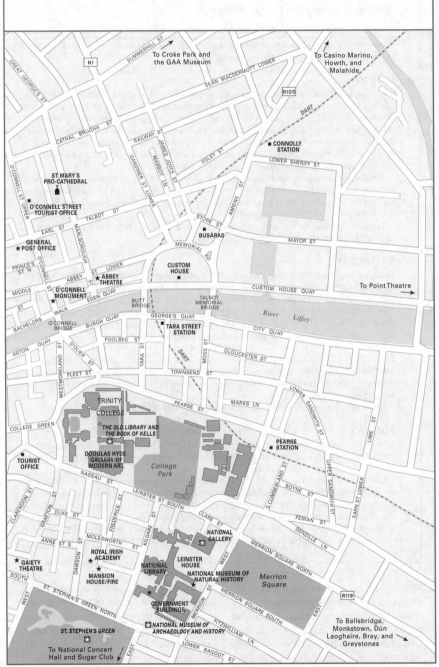

Three Days in Dublin

Three days in Dublin is just enough time to hit the highlights (and take an excursion to get a little breather from all the urban hustle and bustle).

FRIDAY

When you arrive Friday morning, refresh yourself with a stroll through **St. Stephen's Green,** pausing for coffee at **Kaph** or at one of the **Powerscourt Townhouse** cafés a block off **Grafton Street** before making your way to **Trinity College Dublin** and the **Book of Kells** exhibition. For lunch, you have your pick of fantastic eateries along Dame and South Great Georges Streets; **The Bank** is perhaps the most atmospheric (and the food is aces), though it may be a little early in the day yet for a cocktail. Pop into the **Market Arcade** on South Great George's Street for a browse through the quirky shop stalls.

In the afternoon, sign up for the guided tour at **Christ Church Cathedral** so you'll be able to climb up to the belfry and ring one of the bells. If you haven't run out of steam yet, head to the **Chester Beatty Library** to view a dazzling collection of manuscripts, engravings, and decorative art pieces from all over the world.

Tonight, buy yourself a pint and settle in for a traditional music session at **O'Donoghue's, Hughes',** or the **Stag's Head.**

SATURDAY

Today, explore Dublin's Northside. After breakfast, stroll up O'Connell Street to the **Garden of Remembrance** and learn everything you ever wanted to know about Joyce, Yeats, Wilde, and Synge across the street at the **Dublin Writers Museum.** Then pass a happy hour a few doors down at the **Hugh Lane Gallery,** viewing Harry Clarke's stained-glass scenes from John Keats's poem *The Eve of St. Agnes* up close and personal; then check out Francis Bacon's insanely messy studio to console yourself about the state of your own house!

After lunch at the courtyard café downstairs at the Hugh Lane, take a 15-minute stroll west to **St. Michan's Church** to tour the over-the-top spooky crypts—because who wouldn't want a hardcore spell of *memento mori* while they're on holiday? Now you'll be needing a drink, of course; fortunately the **Old Jameson Distillery** is right around the corner, and the price of admission includes a shot of whiskey.

Take it easy this evening with dinner at **Gallagher's Boxty House** in Temple Bar.

SUNDAY

It's time for an excursion north of the city! Take the DART to Malahide to stroll the grounds of **Malahide Castle,** popping into the **Avoca food hall** for gourmet souvenirs and an early lunch before joining the hourlong castle tour.

Back in Dublin proper, spend the rest of your afternoon at either the **National Gallery** or the **National Museum of Archaeology and History** (both are centrally located, south of Trinity College between St. Stephen's Green and Merrion Square, and are open on Sunday afternoon). For dinner, treat yourself to a meal you'll remember for decades to come at nearby **Restaurant Patrick Guilbaud** (but be sure to book well ahead!). Then stop for one last pint at an atmospheric **Victorian pub,** like **John Kehoe's, William Ryan's,** or the **Long Hall.**

Kilmainham Jail, and the nationalist papers declared them martyrs for the cause.

Since the country asserted its freedom from constitutional monarchy in the Republic of Ireland Act of 1949, Dublin's history has been marked by economic stagnation. Membership in the European Economic Community (later European Union) starting in 1973 slowly began to turn things around, and from the mid-1990s to the end of 2008 the city enjoyed an economic boom. The global economic downturn killed the Celtic Tiger for good, however, and Dublin will be handling the consequences of its €85 billion bailout from the E.U. and I.M.F. for years to come.

PLANNING YOUR TIME

As in all European capitals, no amount of time in Dublin will allow you to see everything worth seeing—not even if you stay a month. Rather than exhaust yourself on a one- or two-day visit, be selective in what you choose to see, and spend a bit of time just watching the world go by in a pub, café, or on a park bench in St. Stephen's Green. You'll soak up as much "culture" in those places as you would in the National Museum of Archaeology and History.

Some attractions (especially churches and small museums) close for lunch, so be sure to arrive early enough in the morning to get the most out of your visit. For maximum efficiency, the more ambitious visitor should divide the city into sections and explore one area per day. For instance, plan to visit Kilmainham Jail, the Irish Museum of Modern Art at the Royal Hospital Kilmainham, and the Guinness Storehouse on the same day, since they're all on the western end of the city. Hop-on, hop-off bus tours are a popular means of seeing a lot of places in just a few hours.

As for day trips out of Dublin, there are several possibilities, whether you join in on a bus tour or rent a car. Nestled in the Wicklow Mountains in County Wicklow is Glendalough, one of Ireland's most important monastic sites; Newgrange, part of the Brú na Bóinne funerary complex in County Meath, is one of the most significant Neolithic sites on the whole continent. Other worthwhile excursions include Trim Castle, the largest Anglo-Norman fortress in the country, also in County Meath, and Castletown, Ireland's grandest Palladian manse, in County Kildare, accessible by Dublin Bus. All these places are within an hour and a half of the capital. Or you could just take the DART to one of the county's seaside towns for the afternoon; Killiney south of the city has a great beach, and Howth and Malahide to the north each have several attractions as well.

Sights

Though Dublin sprawls for miles, almost everything you'll want to see is concentrated within an easily walkable area on either side of the River Liffey, wedged between the city's two major train stations (Heuston on the west side and Connolly on the east). North of the Liffey, or "Northside," is a grittier neighborhood, traditionally blue collar and of less interest to tourists; this characterization is becoming somewhat less apt, however, as widespread commercial redevelopment progresses. The Northside's main thoroughfare is O'Connell Street.

South of the river are Temple Bar, Trinity College, St. Stephen's Green, Dublin Castle, Christ Church and St. Patrick's Cathedrals, and many other attractions. Dame Street runs parallel to the river, linking Christ Church with Trinity, and hungry visitors should turn south onto South Great Georges Street for its array of great eateries. Grafton Street, the famous pedestrian shopping strip, links the Trinity College campus to the north with St. Stephen's Green to the south. Wedged between St. Stephen's Green and Merrion Square, a couple of blocks east of Grafton Street, are lots of important buildings within one square block—the National Library, Museum, and Gallery, along with Leinster House (the Irish equivalent of the U.S. Capitol).

SIGHTSEEING PASSES

The Dúchas **Heritage Card** (tel. 01/647-6587, www.heritageireland.ie, €25), available for purchase at all Dúchas sites, will get you into Kilmainham Jail, Phoenix Park Visitor Centre

(Ashtown Castle), and the Casino Marino. If you're up for a really ambitious round of sightseeing, though, it's wise to have more than the Heritage Card on hand. The **Dublin Pass** (contact the tourist office for details, tel. 01/605-7700, www.dublinpass.ie, 1/2/3/5-day pass €49/69/79/99, discounts available online) gets you into Dublin Castle, the Dublin Writers Museum, Kilmainham Jail, the Old Jameson Distillery, the Guinness Storehouse, and several other places. (Though it advertises free admission to the Irish Museum of Modern Art, the National Museums, and the Chester Beatty Library, note that there is no charge to these places anyway!) One free Aircoach ride is also included in the pass, though this isn't of much use unless yours is a fly-by-night visit, and there are "special offers" available at many shops and restaurants. Compare a list of the places you want to see with the list of covered attractions on the website, and if the admission charges exceed the price of a pass, pick one up at the tourist office.

TRINITY COLLEGE

Chartered in 1592 by the Virgin Queen for "the planting of learning, the increasing of civility, and the establishment of the true religion"—that's Protestantism—"within the realm," **Trinity College Dublin** (TCD, College Green, at the eastern end of Dame St.) remains the island's most prestigious university. The college was opened in 1594 on the grounds of the Augustinian Priory of All Hallows, which was dissolved under Henry VIII's decree in 1537; the oldest extant buildings date to the early 18th century. Though the college had permitted the admission of Catholics since the late 18th century (provided they converted to Protestantism), it was not until 1970 that the Catholic Church officially permitted it. Now, of course, a majority (roughly 70 percent) of TCD's 12,500 students are Catholic.

The **guided campus tour** (tel. 01/608-1724, departs the main gate every 40 minutes 10:15am-3pm daily mid-May-Sept., ticket €13) is pricey but worthwhile: The tour itself is informative but entertaining, and your ticket includes admission to see the Book of Kells, in the Old Library. Even if you don't have time for the Book of Kells exhibition or a guided campus tour, take 10 or 15 minutes to wander around the perimeter of the immaculate campus green (known as Parliament Square) lined with dignified Georgians (you might even want to duck into the campus chapel, on your left after you pass through the main gate).

prestigious Trinity College

★ The Old Library and the Book of Kells

The **Old Library,** which dates to the 1720s, houses the **Book of Kells** (tel. 01/608-2308, www.tcd.ie, 9:30am-5pm Mon.-Sat. all year, 9:30am-4:30pm Sun. June-Sept., noon-4:30pm Sun. Oct.-May, admission without campus tour €11), the best known of all Ireland's illuminated monastic manuscripts. A different two-page spread is on display each day, under thick glass of course; with so much company, you'll be lucky to get a close extended look. Before you get to the viewing room, there's an engaging exhibition, "Turning Darkness into Light," that puts the book into historical and religious context.

The Old Library also houses the Book of Armagh, the Book of Dimma, the Book of Durrow, and the Yellow Book of Lecan, which contains a partial version of the *Táin Bó Cúailnge* ("The Cattle Raid of Cooley"), one of Ireland's greatest medieval epics. Either get here early in the day so you don't waste your afternoon in the queue to get in, or spring for the "fast track" option available for purchase online (€14).

Douglas Hyde Gallery of Modern Art

Named for the first president of Ireland, the **Douglas Hyde Gallery of Modern Art** (entrance on Nassau St., tel. 01/608-1116, www.douglashydegallery.com, 11am-6pm Mon.-Fri., until 7pm Thurs., 11am-4:45pm Sat., free) is in the Arts and Social Science Building, south of the Old Library. Two temporary exhibitions are on at a time in separate galleries, and feature paintings, sculpture, and textile arts from an international roster of artists.

SOUTH OF TRINITY

Dublin's political hub, as well as the National Gallery, Library, and Museum, is contained within a single block northeast of St. Stephen's Green, between Kildare and Merrion Streets. One block west, on Dawson Street, is the early Georgian Mansion House, the official home of the Lord Mayor of Dublin since 1715. Dawson Street is lined with other grand old buildings with interesting architectural details; several ground floors have been converted into chic bars and eateries.

Leinster House

Leinster House (entrance on Kildare St., tel. 01/618-3271, www.irlgov.ie/oireachtas, free), once home of the 20th Earl of Kildare (and later Duke of Leinster), now houses the Irish Parliament, the Oireachtas na hÉireann. The Parliament comprises a lower house, the Dáil (pronounced "doll"), and an upper house, the Seanad ("SHAN-add"); meetings (only 90 days out of the year Nov.-May) are open to the public. Tickets are available at the entrance on Kildare Street. Guided tours are also available occasionally; ring for more information.

For a free tour of the Irish **Government Buildings** (Upper Merrion St., tel. 01/645-8813, 10:30am-1:30pm Sat., free), head to the National Gallery lobby first for a ticket. Built between 1904 and 1911 and renovated to the nines in the late 1980s, the Government Buildings house the Taoiseach's offices as well as the Council Chamber (where the cabinet meets) and the Department of Finance. It's a worthwhile stop if you're interested in the Irish government or Edwardian architecture. Another item of interest is the huge stained glass window with nationalist motifs by Evie Hone in the entrance hall, which was commissioned for the New York World Trade Fair in 1939.

★ National Gallery

The **National Gallery of Ireland** (Merrion Sq. W., tel. 01/661-5133, www.nationalgallery.ie, 9:30am-5:30pm Mon.-Sat., until 8:30pm Thurs., noon-5:30pm Sun., free) is well worth a visit for its comprehensive collection of Irish art (plan to linger in the Yeats hall—bet you had no idea the whole family was so talented!) as well as works by Caravaggio, El Greco, Goya, Rembrandt, Vermeer, and Picasso. Other highlights include *The Marriage of*

Strongbow and Aoife, a humonguous tableau scene painted by Daniel Maclise in the 1850s, and the Millennium Wing, which houses a permanent collection of contemporary works as well as visiting exhibitions. There's also a quality bookshop and an airy, modern café with pretty good food.

National Library

Check out the main reading room with its coffered dome at the **National Library of Ireland** (Kildare St., tel. 01/603-0200, www.nli.ie, 10am-9pm Mon.-Wed., 10am-5pm Thurs.-Fri., 10am-1pm Sat., free), which usually has a downstairs exhibition featuring scribbled pages from first drafts of beloved works and other interesting tidbits.

National Museum of Natural History

A better official name for the **National Museum of Natural History** (Merrion St., tel. 01/677-7444, www.museum.ie, 10am-5pm Tues.-Sat., 2pm-5pm Sun., free) might just be the Victorian Taxidermy Museum—it's already commonly known as the "Dead Zoo." Most visitors will probably end up skipping this one, but for those with antiquarian taste this quirky museum will provide an hour's diversion.

★ National Museum of Archaeology and History

There's more than one **National Museum,** but this one (Kildare St., tel. 01/677-7444, www.museum.ie, 10am-5pm Tues.-Sat., 2pm-5pm Sun., free) is the one you hear most about, for its phenomenal collection of artifacts from every period in Irish history: prehistoric tools and pottery; stunning gold torcs and other jewelry from the Bronze Age; ornate chalices, crosses, crosiers, bells, and brooches from the early Christian and medieval eras; Viking jewelry and weaponry; 18th- and 19th-century lace, silver, and musical instruments; and clothing and wooden sculptures—even a body!—found preserved in the bogs. The museum's three most important medieval

artifacts are the Tara Brooch, an exquisite example of Celtic gold and silver metalwork dating to the beginning of the 8th century; the early 9th-century Ardagh Chalice, made of silver, gold, and bronze, found with other smaller treasures in a Limerick potato field in 1868; and the 12th-century Cross of Cong, an ornate silver reliquary that supposedly houses a splinter of the True Cross. Basically everything of archaeological importance found anywhere in the country is brought here and put under glass (even the bog man, and the effect is disconcerting to say the least). Visiting exhibitions complement a permanent collection of ancient Egyptian, Cypriot, Roman, and Byzantine artifacts.

Dawson Street

The first meeting of the Dáil took place on January 22, 1919, in the early-18th-century **Mansion House,** around the block from Leinster House on Dawson Street, as did the adoption of the Declaration of Independence and signing of the Anglo-Irish Treaty in 1921. The Mansion House is the official residence of the Lord Mayor of Dublin, elected by the city council for a one-year term, and is not open to the public.

Bibliophiles, take note: The **Royal Irish Academy** (19 Dawson St., tel. 01/676-2570, www.ria.ie, 10am-5:30pm Mon.-Thurs., 10am-5pm Fri., free) has a trove of priceless medieval illuminated manuscripts, including *The Cathach,* the oldest Irish psalter (dating to the 6th century, and associated with St. Columba). Generally only one manuscript is on display at a time, though.

★ ST. STEPHEN'S GREEN

Possibly Europe's largest city square, **St. Stephen's Green** is tranquil and immaculately kept. All these verdant walkways, duck ponds, and tidy flowerbeds (nine hectares in all) belie a dark history, however: Before the mid-17th century the area was commonly used for rowdy public executions (including burnings). The space was closed off from "rabble" in 1663 and gradually spiffed up for use by Dublin's elite. In 1877 Arthur Guinness introduced an Act of Parliament to open the green to the public, and this finally happened in 1880. The main entrance is through the **Fusiliers' Arch** at the bottom of Grafton Street; modeled after the Arch of Titus in Rome, it memorializes the 200-plus Royal Dublin Fusiliers killed in the Boer War. The park is dotted with smaller memorials to 1798 rebels Theobald Wolfe Tone and Robert Emmet, William Butler Yeats, Constance Markievicz, nationalist poet and translator James Clarence Mangan, and several other luminaries. The park is perfect for a leisurely stroll at any time of day, or just pick a bench and watch half of Dublin go by on their lunch breaks.

DUBLIN CASTLE AND AROUND

Dublin Castle (Dame St., Cork Hill, tel. 01/677-7129, www.dublincastle.ie, tours 10am-4:45pm Mon.-Fri., 2pm-4:45pm Sat.-Sun. and holidays, €8.50), built by order of King John in 1204, served as the seat of British power in Ireland for more than 700 years. Little of the original castle survives due to many half-hearted refurbishments and a widespread fire in 1689; today you can tour the excavations of the 13th-century foundations (called the "Undercroft," where the old castle joined the city walls), but otherwise it's just the Record Tower, finished in 1258, that remains. Most of the current structure dates from the mid-1700s. Despite its dank and crumbling walls, the castle continued to be used for official balls and banquets into the 20th century. During the Victorian era as many as 15,000 people were entertained there in the five-week period culminating in the annual St. Patrick's Ball (a festivity that, it is safe to say, the holy man would have scarcely approved of). In 1907 the Irish Crown Jewels were purloined from Bedford Tower and never seen again.

Today Dublin Castle is home to many government offices and a neo-Gothic chapel,

which was converted to Catholicism in 1943. Guided tours usually include the state apartments, Undercroft, and chapel, but if the state rooms are unavailable due to official business the abridged tour will cost you a euro less.

City Hall

Opposite the castle entrance is **Dublin City Hall** (Dame St., tel. 01/222-2222, www.dublincity.ie, exhibition 10am-5pm Mon.-Sat., 2pm-5pm Sun., free). Built for the Royal Exchange in the 1770s, this neoclassical edifice boasts a gold-leaf dome supported by a dozen fluted columns, as well as plasterwork crafted by one of Dublin's mayors, Charles Thorp. While admission was free at time of writing to celebrate the Easter Rising centennial, there will likely be an admission charge again in 2017. Unless you're in the mood for a history lesson at the exhibition in the downstairs vaults, just pop inside to admire the rotunda with its statue of Daniel O'Connell.

★ The Chester Beatty Library

Bibliophiles and art lovers should put **The Chester Beatty Library** (on the grounds of Dublin Castle, signposted from the car park through the front gates, tel. 01/407-0750, www.cbl.ie, 10am-5pm Mon.-Fri., 11am-5pm Sat., 1pm-5pm Sun., closed Mon. Oct.-Apr., free) at the top of their sightseeing list. Arthur Chester Beatty (1875-1968), a prosperous American businessman living in London, moved his exquisite collection of illuminated manuscripts (and plenty of other treasures) to Dublin in 1950. The shrewd but soft-spoken Beatty spent the remainder of his life here, and he was the first person to be made an honorary Irish citizen. After a 10-minute audiovisual on Beatty's life and times, you make your way up to the galleries to peruse the collections of Chinese snuff bottles and embroidered garments, Japanese inro (lacquered wood containers suspended from a kimono sash), and a wealth of Islamic, Indian, and Asian manuscripts, working your way to the rooms of medieval and Renaissance books and engravings (including several by the late-15th/early-16th-century German master Albrecht Dürer). It's worth lingering in several rooms to watch the demonstration videos on illumination, book-binding, engraving, and other arts. The top-floor exhibits analyze three world religions (Christianity, Islam, and Buddhism) through manuscripts and other sacred objects. Behind glass are fragments of letters written as early as the second century AD, epistles that would eventually be included in the New Testament. There's also a rooftop garden and a classy café on the ground floor. The Beatty collection would be a must-see even if admission weren't free; it's just all the more worthwhile because it is!

TEMPLE BAR

Probably named for a local family in the late 17th century, this area stretches between Dame Street (which turns into Lord Edward Street) and the river, the western and eastern boundaries being Fishamble Street, where Handel first conducted his *Messiah* in 1742, and Trinity College, respectively. **Temple Bar**—what *The New York Times* called "that dilapidated medieval neighborhood"—underwent an ambitious government-sponsored facelift in the 1990s using the designs of several local cutting-edge architectural firms. Today it's a hyper-commercialized hive of pubs, clubs, restaurants, and atmospheric alleyways.

Tucked between Sycamore and Eustace Streets just a couple of blocks south of the river, **Meetinghouse Square** is the hub of the neighborhood, buzzing at all hours with locals and tourists alike. The **Temple Bar Food Market** (tel. 01/671-5717, 10am-4:30pm) transpires here on Saturdays.

You can traverse Temple Bar's alleyways after nightfall without a backward glance, though the proliferation of (albeit harmless) drunken rowdies late at night can sure get on one's nerves. Unless you believe this . . . shall we say, *festive* atmosphere is an integral part of the Dublin experience, you might want to avoid the area after 10pm.

CHRISTCHURCH AND AROUND
★ Christ Church Cathedral

Though the marvelous **Christ Church Cathedral** (Christchurch Place, west end of Lord Edward St., tel. 01/677-8099, www.cccdub.ie, €6, guided tour €4) has its origins in the late 12th and early 13th centuries, much of the building was structurally unsound, and it was almost entirely rebuilt through the generosity of Henry Roe in the 1870s. Roe's chosen architect, George Edmund Street, preserved as much of the original edifice as possible and faithfully replicated the rest in the Romanesque and Early English Gothic styles.

In the yard are the foundations of a 13th-century chapter house, and in the southern aisle you'll spot the tomb of a knight whose nose is worn off; though it is identified as Strongbow's, we know for a fact that his tomb was destroyed when the south wall collapsed in 1562. Cathedral literature states this tomb is a replica of the original, but it's more likely someone else's tomb entirely. A reliquary in the Peace Chapel contains the heart of 12th-century archbishop Laurence O'Toole, patron saint of Dublin. The cathedral offers a few more weird surprises, like the mummified cat-and-rat pair found in a pipe of the church organ and the massive arches on the north side of the aisle leaning at an unnerving angle. Creepy statues of Charles I and II greet you as you enter the crypt, where you can watch a 12-minute audiovisual on the cathedral's history and check out the ornate silver plate presented to the cathedral by William of Orange in celebration of his victory at the Battle of the Boyne.

The cathedral is open daily (9am-6pm weekdays June-Aug., 9:45am-5pm or 6pm weekdays Sept.-May, 10am-4:30pm Sat. and 12:45pm-2:45pm Sun. all year). Evensong, which features music dating to the Reformation period, is performed in the cathedral at 3:30pm Sunday, 6pm Wednesday and Thursday, and 5pm Saturday. Admission to the belfry (where you can ring one of the bells!) is by guided tour only.

Patrick Street and Around

Dublin's second Anglican cathedral is **St. Patrick's** (Patrick St., tel. 01/475-4817, www.stpatrickscathedral.ie, €6), built in the Early English Gothic style at the turn of the 13th century near a well where Ireland's patron saint was said to have performed baptisms. St. Patrick's is the largest of Ireland's medieval cathedrals, though it has no crypt because it was built above the trickly River Poddle. Jonathan Swift, who served as Dean from 1713 to 1745, is entombed here beside his mistress, Esther Johnson. Come at the end of the day (weekdays excepting Wednesday) to hear the choir perform evensong; their 18th-century predecessors were the first to sing Handel's *Messiah*. St. Patrick's is open daily (9am-6pm Mon.-Sat. and 9am-11am, 12:45pm-3pm, and 4:15pm-6pm Sun. Mar.-Oct.; 9am-6pm weekdays, 9am-5pm Sat., 10am-11am and 12:45pm-3pm Sun. Nov.-Feb.).

Down the street is the **Narcissus Marsh Library** (St. Patrick's Close, tel. 01/454-3511, www.marshlibrary.ie, 9:30am-5pm Mon. and Wed.-Fri., 10am-5pm Sat., €3). Ireland's first public library was established in 1701 by Narcissus Marsh, who was the Anglican Archbishop of Cashel, Dublin, and Armagh (though not all at once). The archbishop opened the library with 10,000 volumes from his personal collection, and today there are more than 25,000 ancient (and somewhat moldy-looking) tomes arranged carefully on the original shelves in two cathedral-ceilinged galleries. Rotating exhibits under glass feature centuries-old books with hand-painted illustrations, and another case houses Jonathan Swift's death mask. The library staff are very friendly and informative, the volunteers delightfully quirky and garrulous; bibliophiles will find the Marsh library well worth a visit.

Catholics and lovebirds might want to step inside **Our Lady of Mount Carmel** (entrance at 56 Aungier St., tel. 01/475-8821), which houses "some of" the remains of St. Valentine in a niche on your right as you walk up the aisle.

St. Audoen's Church

The Anglican **St. Audoen's Church** (Cornmarket, High St., tel. 01/677-0088, 9:30am-5:30pm daily June-Sept., free) is the only remaining medieval parish church in Dublin, flanked by a chunk of the old city wall. St. Audoen's Arch here is the last extant city gate. The Catholic **St. Audoen's** around the corner on High Street is an imposing neoclassical edifice with a huge and hideous

a view of Christ Church Cathedral from the walkway to the belfry, accessible by guided tour

Corinthian portico. The two churches form a somewhat amusing study in architectural contrasts. Here too is **St. Mary's Abbey** (Mary's Abbey St., Meetinghouse Ln., off Capel St., tel. 01/833-1618 or 01/647-6587 in winter, 10am-5pm Mon.-Sat. mid-June-mid-Sept., free), once the richest Cistercian monastery in the country. Here "Silken Thomas," Lord of Offaly, had the chutzpah to renounce his allegiance to Henry VIII in 1534, thus sparking a yearlong, nationwide insurrection.

NORTHSIDE

Head north of the Liffey for a glimpse of everyday life in the capital city. The "Northside" neighborhood consists of everything north of the river and south of the M50 motorway skirting the city, and the word is used to refer to a blue-collar attitude as often as it is indicative of urban geography. The "post-code snobbery" of the Dublin elite has eased as developers have erected sparkling new shopping centers, and every just-opened eatery is hipper than the one before it. There is plenty in the way of sightseeing north of the Liffey as well: the Dublin Writers Museum, Old Jameson Distillery, and St. Michan's Church are just a few of the highlights.

O'Connell Street

The Northside's primary thoroughfare, O'Connell Street is a transportation hub where you'll find the General Post Office (headquarters of the ill-fated Easter Rising in 1916) as well as a few decorations of hilariously questionable taste: the "Floozy in the Jacuzzi" (you'll see!), a statue of James Joyce to which locals chain their bicycles, and the "Dublin Spire," a 120-meter light-up metal spoke Dubs know better as the "stiffy by the Liffey."

Erected in 1854 in memory of the "Great Liberator," the **O'Connell Monument** is flanked by four winged figures representing patriotism, fidelity, eloquence, and courage. Farther up O'Connell Street (formerly Sackville), the **General Post Office,** or GPO

(tel. 01/705-7000, 8am-8pm Mon.-Sat., free), an imposing neoclassical edifice built between 1815 and 1817, served as rebel stronghold during the Easter Rising of 1916. Here Patrick Pearse (also spelled Pádraic or Pádraig) read the Proclamation of the Irish Republic from the front steps, and the shell marks are still visible on the facade.

Just off O'Connell Street is **St. Mary's Pro-Cathedral** (83 Marlborough St., tel. 01/874-5441, www.procathedral.ie, 7:30am-6:45pm Mon.-Fri., 7:30am-7:15pm Sat., 9am-1:45pm and 5:30pm-7:45pm Sun., 10am-1:30pm public holidays, free), the seat of the Catholic Archbishop of Dublin ("pro" indicating the church is an "acting cathedral"; Dublin has two Anglican cathedrals, St. Patrick's and Christ Church, but the Catholic Church still recognizes the latter as its official cathedral because it was designated as such in the 12th century). "The Pro," as locals call it, was designed by amateur architect John Sweetman in 1816 with a Greek revival facade and a richly decorated interior evocative of the great basilicas of Rome.

At the top of O'Connell Street is the **Parnell Monument,** an obelisk pillar topped with a bronze statue by Augustus St. Gaudens.

Parnell Square

At the **Dublin Writers Museum** (18 Parnell Sq., tel. 01/872-2077, www.writersmuseum.com, 10am-5pm Mon.-Sat., 11am-5pm Sun. year-round, closing at 6pm Mon.-Sat. June-Aug., €7.50), you can peruse exhibition boards (presenting Ireland's literary heritage in chronological order, with plenty of biographical details) and glass cases containing typewriters, first editions, original correspondence, and other stuff; an audio guide is included in the admission price. The foyer and upstairs rooms feature portraits and bronze busts of luminaries from Yeats and Beckett to Elizabeth Bowen and Mary Lavin, and there is generally a rotating exhibit upstairs as well.

Across the street is the **Garden of Remembrance** (Parnell Sq. E., tel.

01/874-3074). Opened in 1966 to commemorate the 50th anniversary of the Easter Rising, it features a sculpture by Oisin Kelly depicting the legend of the Children of Lir (who were turned into swans by their sorceress stepmother).

★ The Hugh Lane Gallery

A couple doors down from the Dublin Writers Museum is the **Hugh Lane Municipal Gallery of Modern Art** (22 N. Parnell Sq., tel. 01/874-1903, www.hughlane.ie, 10am-6pm Tues.-Thurs., 10am-5pm Fri.-Sat., 11am-5pm Sun., free), in the erstwhile townhome of the first Earl of Charlemont and designed by William Chambers in the 1760s. The fantastic permanent collection includes works by Monet, Renoir, Degas, Corot, Millais, and Burne-Jones, and native works by Sean Keating, Paul Henry, and Jack B. Yeats, most of which were collected by Sir Hugh Lane before his demise on the *Lusitania* in 1915. The gallery also includes an authentically chaotic re-creation of **Francis Bacon's studio** in London, and Harry Clarke's stained-glass masterpiece, *The Eve of St. Agnes,* is another highlight. The downstairs courtyard café is a very good choice for lunch, with good coffee and friendly service.

Croke Park

Croke Park is Ireland's largest stadium, with 84,000 seats. Those interested in **Gaelic football** and **hurling** should check out the **GAA Museum** (Gaelic Athletic Association, New Stand, Croke Park, Clonliffe Rd., north of the Royal Canal, tel. 01/855-8176, http://museum.gaa.ie) for a high-tech history of the games, including a 15-minute audiovisual. In addition to visiting the museum (9:30am-5pm Mon.-Sat. and noon-5pm Sun. Apr.-Oct., 10am-5pm Tues.-Sat. and noon-4pm Sun. Nov.-Mar., €6.50), you can take a one-hour stadium tour (€13). The All-Ireland finals take place here every September. To get here, take **Dublin Bus** (#3, #11/A, #16/A, or #123) from O'Connell Street.

Four Courts

Notice that striking (not to mention humongous) green-domed neoclassical structure on the quay? It's the **Four Courts** (Inns Quay, tel. 01/872-5555, 11am-1pm and 2pm-4pm weekdays, free), home of the Irish law courts since 1796; the name comes from the four traditional divisions of the judicial system (Chancery, King's Bench, Exchequer, and Common Pleas). Designed by James Gandon in the 1780s, the building was bombarded by

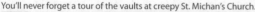

You'll never forget a tour of the vaults at creepy St. Michan's Church.

provisional forces and gutted by republican "irregulars" during the Civil War; the restoration work dates to 1932. The public is admitted only when court is in session.

★ St. Michan's Church

Named for a Danish bishop who built the original church on the site of an ancient oak grove, the Anglican **St. Michan's Church** (Church St., tel. 01/872-4154, www.stmichans.com, €6) houses the organ on which Handel practiced the *Messiah* before its first performance at the old Dublin Music Hall on Fishamble Street on April 13, 1742. That's not why teenagers come here in droves, though—it's to see the uncannily preserved remains in the medieval crypt, a phenomenon caused by a combo of methane gas and the limestone foundations, which absorb the moisture in the air. This is, bar none, the most macabre sight in the city, and not for the faint-hearted. Hours vary seasonally (10am-12:45pm and 2pm-4:30pm Mon.-Fri. and 10am-12:45pm Sat. mid-Mar.-Oct., 12:30pm-3:30pm Mon.-Fri. and 10am-12:45pm Sat. Nov.-mid-Mar.).

Access to the crypt is by guided tour, which takes place whenever there are enough visitors. Stringy cobwebs dangle from the rough stone ceiling in these dimly lit subterranean vaults, each one belonging to a different aristocratic Dublin family. In the second section, the first cell on your right displays the death mask of Theobald Wolfe Tone as well as the gruesome execution order of John and Henry Sheares, all of whom were patriots in the 1798 rebellion. (The brothers' remains are here too.) You'll pass family vaults on either side, a couple of which have been illuminated to show you how the coffins have been stacked upon those of the previous generation—many of which have collapsed, with undecomposed limbs poking through the splintered wood. You can see the fingernails and everything.

The vault at the end of the first section contains the remains that St. Michan's is known for. You used to be able to touch the hand of the so-called "Crusader," who has been dead for at least 600 years—he was almost two

meters tall, and his feet were actually sawn off to fit him in the coffin!—but these days the church caretakers are being more responsible about preserving these formerly human curiosities. The tour guide is still amusingly theatrical, even if he can no longer give you the run of the place.

Old Jameson Distillery

If you have time for only one tipple tour, go for the **Old Jameson Distillery** (Bow St., Smithfield, 1 block north of Arran Quay, tel. 01/807-2355, www.whiskeytours.ie, 9:30am-5:30pm daily, €16, 10% discount online) rather than the Guinness Storehouse; it's a bit less expensive and more engaging, and unlike at Guinness you get a real guided tour (departing every half hour). And of course, a whiskey-tasting is included in the price of admission.

Collins Barracks

The **National Museum of Decorative Arts and History** at the Collins Barracks (Benburb St., one block north of Wolfe Tone Quay, tel. 01/677-7444, 10am-5pm Tues.-Sat., until 8:30pm Thurs., 2pm-5pm Sun., free), opened in 1999, may not be as exciting as the National Museum of Archaeology and History, but it's still worth a visit. Here you'll find collections of silver, coins, period clothing and furniture, ceramics, glassware, and weaponry. There's a special gallery devoted to long-stored items just recently dusted off. On a darker note, the 14 executed Easter rebels were buried on **Arbour Hill** directly behind the barracks.

WEST OF THE CITY CENTER
Guinness Storehouse

Perhaps the biggest tourist trap in Dublin is the **Guinness Storehouse** (St. James' Gate, tel. 01/408-4800, www.guinness-storehouse.com, 9:30am-5pm daily, €16, 20% discount with online booking). It's one thing if you're a devoted stout drinker, but don't feel like you ought to go just because everyone else is. Note that the tour is self-guided—and even

Greater Dublin

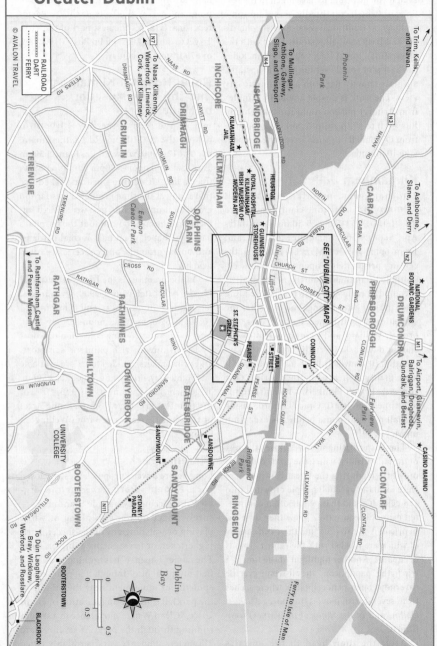

© AVALON TRAVEL

RAILROAD
DART
FERRY

Phoenix Park

To Trim, Kells, and Navan

To Mullingar, Athlone, Galway, Sligo, and Westport

N4

N3

To Ashbourne, Slane, and Derry

N2

To Airport, Glasnevin, Balriggan, Drogheda, Dundalk, and Belfast

M1

CASINO MARINO

NATIONAL BOTANIC GARDENS

CLONTARF

CLONTARF RD

FAIRVIEW

Fairview Park

DRUMCONDRA

PHIBSBOROUGH

CABRA

CABRA RD
OLD CIRCULAR RD
NAVAN RD
NORTH CIRCULAR RD
CLONLIFFE RD
RING ST
DORSET ST
CHURCH ST

INCHICORE
ISLANDBRIDGE

NAAS RD
PETERS RD
DRIMNAGH RD
DAVITT RD
CHAPELIZOD RD

KILMAINHAM JAIL
KILMAINHAM
ROYAL HOSPITAL KILMAINHAM/ IRISH MUSEUM OF MODERN ART
HEUSTON
GUINNESS STOREHOUSE

River Liffey

SEE 'DUBLIN CITY MAPS'

CONNOLLY
TARA STREET
PEARSE
PEARSE ST
GRAND CANAL ST
HOUSE QUAY
EAST WALL
ALEXANDRA RD

CRUMLIN
DRIMNAGH
CRUMLIN RD
SOUTH CIRCULAR RD
DOLPHINS BARN
CROSS RD

TERENURE
TERENURE RD
RATHGAR
RATHGAR RD
RATHMINES
RING

Eamon Ceaont Park

ST. STEPHEN'S GREEN

BALLSBRIDGE
SANDFORD RD
DONNYBROOK
DUNDRUM RD
MILLTOWN

To Naas, Kilkenny, Waterford, Limerick, Cork, and Killarney

N7

To Rathfarnham Castle and Pearse Museum

UNIVERSITY COLLEGE
STILLORGAN RD
BOOTERSTOWN
ROCK RD
N11

SANDYMOUNT
LANSDOWNE
SANDYMOUNT
SYDNEY PARADE
BEACH RD

Ringsend Park
RINGSEND

Ferry to Isle of Man

To Dún Laoghaire, Bray, Wicklow, Wexford, and Rosslare

BOOTERSTOWN
BLACKROCK

Dublin Bay

0   0.5
0   0.5

N

cheekier, you have to pay the admission fee even if you just want to have lunch in the restaurant (which, admittedly, serves up some really good traditional meals like shepherd's pie and Irish stew, all liberally laced with the black stuff). But at least your ticket includes the best pint you'll ever taste in the upstairs, all-glass Gravity Bar with a panoramic city view. The walk is doable (about 15 minutes from Trinity), but you could also take Dublin Bus #51B or #78A from Aston Quay or #123 from O'Connell or Dame Street; the trip will take 10 minutes.

Kilmainham Jail

Another very popular attraction, **Kilmainham Jail** (or "Gaol," Inchicore Rd., tel. 01/453-5984, 9:30am-6pm daily Apr.-Sept., 9:30am-5:30pm Mon.-Sat. and 10am-6pm Sun. Oct.-Mar., €7) is a late-18th-century prison that is open to the public essentially to commemorate the 14 nationalists executed in early May 1916 for their leading roles in the Easter Rising. You can enter the stonebreakers' yard where Patrick Pearse, his brother William, and 12 other patriots were shot at daybreak. Over the course of a fascinating (if crowded) hour-long tour, you'll hear plenty of heart-tugging stories. One concerns Joseph Plunkett, who married his longtime sweetheart, Grace Gifford, inside the jail just four hours before his execution on May 4, 1916.

The Easter Rising nearly eclipses the rest of the jail's history, which the guide discusses only briefly; during the Great Famine there were as many as 9,000 people crowded into 188 cells. It's said that people often committed crimes because they knew they'd be fed in prison. You can peep into these cells, many of which are labeled with their most famous occupants. Another highlight of the tour is a trip to the "panopticon," the all-seeing eye, the cavernous open-plan cell block where scenes from several Irish movies (including *Michael Collins* and *In the Name of the Father*) were filmed.

After the tour, head to the upstairs exhibition and look out for a red-lighted side hallway, which is lined with display cases of poignant personal effects of the 14 Easter rebel-martyrs. It's the best part of the visit. To get to the jail, take Dublin Bus #51/B, #78A, or #79 from Aston Quay.

Royal Hospital Kilmainham and the Irish Museum of Modern Art

Just up the road is the **Royal Hospital Kilmainham** (Military Rd., Kilmainham, tel. 01/612-9900, www.rhk.ie, 10am-5:30pm Tues.-Sat. and noon-5:30pm Sun. June-Sept., free), a late 17th-century neoclassical edifice that many at the time grumbled was far too grand for its inhabitants, who were retired soldiers. In summer you can tour the hospital's baroque chapel, great hall, formal gardens, and burial grounds, and concerts are often held here.

On the premises is the **Irish Museum of Modern Art** (tel. 01/612-9900, www.imma. ie, 10am-5:30pm Tues. and Thurs.-Sat., 10:30am-5:30pm Wed., noon-5:30pm Sun., free), with an intriguing collection of works by lesser-known Irish painters, sculptors, and printmakers. Guided tours are available on Wednesday, Friday, and Sunday at 2:30pm. To get here, take Dublin Bus #51/A/B, #78A, or #79 from Aston Quay, #123 from Dame Street or O'Connell Street, or #26 from Wellington Quay.

Phoenix Park

Long before it was Europe's largest enclosed park, **Phoenix Park** served as the largest Viking cemetery outside Scandinavia—surely a fact no one's thinking of while playing or watching any of the soccer, hurling, cricket, or horse racing going on here! The name "Phoenix" has nothing to do with that mythical bird (though it appears on an eponymous monument near the middle of the park); it's just the anglicization of Fionn Uisce, "Clean Water," a reference to a stream running through the park. At seven square kilometers, Phoenix Park is roughly twice

The Wraiths of Kilmainham

The long, dark history of Kilmainham Jail—Ireland's largest uninhabited prison—and its tragic association with the Easter rebellion, make ghost stories nearly inevitable. Along with the doomed patriots, the jail housed everyone from common criminals to ordinary citizens who'd fallen on especially hard times. In fact, many victims committed crimes simply because they knew they'd be fed in prison. Even children were incarcerated here. Records indicate that Kilmainham saw approximately 150 executions in its 128-year history, and many of those prisoners were buried in the stonebreakers' yard (where 14 Easter rebels met their deaths). Furthermore, the jail was built on the site of a gallows.

So it comes as no surprise that many folks, visitors and employees alike, will testify that Kilmainham has quite an accumulation of restless spirits. Those volunteers who set about restoring the jail during the 1960s had plenty of chilling stories to share: lights turning on by themselves in remote sections of the building late at night, inexplicable gusts of wind, and heavy phantom footsteps. According to the Paranormal Research Association of Ireland, most of the supernatural activity occurs in the west wing, where you'll find the political prisoners' dark, dank cells.

During the tour your guide will draw your attention to an excerpt of a poem by Patrick Pearse, "The Rebel," scrawled on the wall above a doorway:

Beware of the thing that is coming, beware of the risen people,
Who shall take what ye would not give.
Did ye think to conquer the people,
Or that law is stronger than life and than men's desire to be free?
We will try it out with you, ye that have harried and held,
Ye that have bullied and bribed, tyrants, hypocrites, liars!

Pearse, one of the leaders of the Easter rebellion, was among those executed in May 1916, and his words are as much a contribution to the spooky atmosphere as they are a reminder of Ireland's centuries-old political struggle.

the size of Central Park in Manhattan; like Central Park, it has several busy through-roads. Every day as many as 20,000 cars travel through the park, and the Office of Public Works hopes eventually to eliminate all through traffic.

The park's two main entrances are at Parkgate Street (at the southeast corner) and at Castleknock Gate (at the northwest corner), with Chesterfield Avenue being the thoroughfare that bisects the park. Phoenix Park is bordered by North Road to the north and Chapelizod Road to the south.

Once inside, it's quite easy to orient yourself by a 63-meter obelisk, the **Wellington Monument,** at the southeastern corner. Across Chesterfield Avenue is the **People's Garden,** laid out in 1864, and **The Hollow,** where a bandstand in a natural amphitheater hosts brass and swing bands in the summertime.

On the far side of the park, the **Phoenix Park Visitor Centre** (tel. 01/677-0095, www.phoenixpark.ie, 10am-5pm Wed.-Sun. Nov.-Mar., 10am-5:30pm daily late Mar. and Oct., 10am-6pm daily Apr.-Sept., free) offers a 20-minute audiovisual on the park's history, certainly worthwhile if you've purchased the Dúchas Heritage Card. It's also your point of entry for nearby 17th-century **Ashtown Castle.** This restored tower house is rather small and unfurnished, though, so the half-hour tour is of only moderate interest.

The park holds several official buildings, including the residence of the U.S. ambassador and Garda Síochána headquarters. There's also the home of the Irish president, **Áras an Uachtaráin** (tel. 01/670-9155, hour-long

Phoenix Park

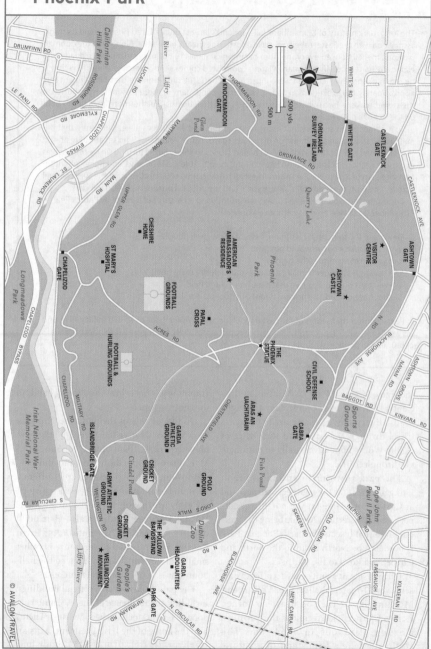

tours 10:30am-4:15pm Sat. summer, 9:30am-3:30pm Sat. winter, free). The "Irish White House" is in the northeastern section of the park, and you can sign up for a visit on a Saturday morning at the visitors center. After an introductory audiovisual presentation, you'll be whisked off to the president's house in a minibus for an hour-long tour of the main state reception rooms and gardens. There are no reservations and spots are limited, so it's wise to arrive when the Phoenix Park Visitor Centre opens at 9:30am to obtain tickets for the first tour at 10:30am. State business can sometimes lead to cancellation of all tours, and note that backpacks and cameras aren't permitted. To get to the visitors center by Dublin Bus, the route that drops you the closest (Ashtown Gate) is #37, which you can board from Lower Abbey Street (Northside).

In the southeast corner is **Dublin Zoo** (tel. 01/677-1425, www.dublinzoo.ie, €17), established in 1830—making it the second-oldest zoo in Europe. Dublin Bus #10 from O'Connell Street will get you here. Hours vary seasonally (9:30am-6pm Mon.-Sat. and 10:30am-6pm Sun. May-Sept., 9:30am-4pm Mon.-Fri., 9:30am-5pm Sat., and 10:30am-5pm Sun. Oct.-Apr.).

GLASNEVIN

An erstwhile suburb three kilometers north of the Liffey, Glasnevin is home to Dublin City University (DCU) as well as two of the city's most important attractions.

National Botanic Gardens

The 19-hectare **National Botanic Gardens** (Botanic Rd., 3.5 km north of Trinity College, tel. 01/837-7596 or 01/837-4388, www.botanicgardens.ie, 9am-6pm Mon.-Sat. and 10am-6pm Sun. in summer, 10am-4:30pm daily in winter, free, guided tour €5) are home to more than 20,000 plant species, 300 of which are endangered and 6 of which are already extinct in the wild. Established in 1795, the gardens feature superb Victorian glasshouses by Richard Turner. It was here in August 1845 that the then-curator, David Moore, first noted the

potato blight and correctly predicted its devastating consequences.

To get to the gardens, catch Dublin Bus #13/A from Merrion Square or O'Connell Street, or #19 from O'Connell Street (4/hour daily, 15-minute trip, fare €0.95).

Glasnevin Cemetery

Just west of the botanic gardens is Glasnevin Cemetery, also known as **Prospect Cemetery** (Finglas Rd., 3.5 km north of Trinity College, tel. 01/830-1133, www.glasnevin-cemetery.ie, 9:30am-6pm Mon.-Sat., 9:30am-5pm Sun., closes earlier in winter, free), the largest in the country at 124 acres. Here is the final resting place of many of Ireland's most beloved patriots: Daniel O'Connell (just look for the faux round tower), Charles Stewart Parnell, Michael Collins, Eamon de Valera, Maud Gonne MacBride, Constance Markievicz, Patrick Pearse, and Arthur Griffith. Much of the statuary here bears overt republican and patriotic motifs, apt considering it was established as a Catholic burial ground in 1832, after the Act of Emancipation. Note the watchtowers in the graveyard's southeastern section, which were used to keep an eye out for bodysnatchers. A free 90-minute guided tour departs the main gate at 2:30pm every Wednesday and Friday. Alternatively, there's a map and guide available from the flower shop at the front gate for €3.50.

The cemetery is on Dublin Bus #40 from Parnell Street (5/hour daily, 35-minute trip).

EAST OF THE CITY CENTER

The Dúchas-run **Casino Marino** (Cherrymount Crescent, off the Malahide Rd., 4 km east of the city center, tel. 01/833-1618, 10am-5pm daily May and Oct., 10am-6pm daily June-Sept., noon-4pm weekends Nov.-Mar., noon-5pm weekends Apr., €4) is, in the words of *Irish Times* writer Frank McDonald, "surely our most peculiar national monument. It was designed by an English architect who never set foot in this country for an Irish aristocrat and aesthete who almost went bankrupt trying to recreate

Italy in Ireland." These men were William Chambers and James Caulfield (the first Earl of Charlemont), respectively. As a young man, the earl had dragged his Grand Tour of Europe into a nine-year odyssey, and he became good friends with Chambers while both were staying in Rome. He later had Chambers design his "summer home," what is still widely considered one of the best examples of small-scale neoclassical architecture; difficult as it is to picture now, this section of Dublin was still part of the boonies back in the 18th century, and the casino (as in "small house") had a great view of Dublin Bay and the surrounding countryside. Now it's something of an oasis amid the urban sprawl.

Ironically, Chambers never laid eyes on one of his very finest achievements, which is larger and grander than it appears from the exterior. Ingenious touches abound, like chimneys disguised as decorative urns on the roof and rainwater pipes hidden in columns, and the nearly hour-long guided tour offers plenty more interesting historical and architectural tidbits.

The building was taken into state care in 1932, but the 10-year restoration effort commenced only in 1974. To preserve the original flooring, visitors are asked to wear disposable booties over their shoes. To get here, take Dublin Bus #123 from O'Connell Street (4+/hour daily), or ride the DART from Connolly to Clontarf Road (4/hour daily), which is much faster.

SOUTH OF THE CITY CENTER

In the "village" of Rathfarnham is **Rathfarnham Castle** (Rathfarnham bypass, between Rathfarnam Rd. and Grange Rd., Dublin 14, tel. 01/493-9462, 9:30am-5:30pm daily May-Oct., €4), an impressive 16th-century structure with 18th-century interiors by two of England's most prominent architects, William Chambers and James "Athenian" Stuart (he got that moniker after publishing *Antiquities of Athens,* which greatly influenced the neoclassical movement in late-18th-century British architecture). Conservation work is ongoing in the castle itself, where access is by a guided tour of 45 minutes to an hour. Take Dublin Bus #16/A from South Great Georges Street.

Patrick Pearse, one of the Easter rebels executed in May 1916, was a devoted learner and teacher of the Irish language. The nearby **Pearse Museum and St. Enda's National Historic Park** (Grange Rd., Rathfarnham, Dublin 16, tel. 01/493-4208, 10am-1pm and 2pm-5:30pm daily May-Aug., until 5pm Feb.-Apr. and Sept.-Oct., until 4pm Nov.-Jan., free) is housed on the premises of the school he founded in 1909; it features an exhibition on Pearse's life and work with a collection of letters and photographs and a 20-minute audiovisual. The adjacent St. Enda's Park includes a waterfall, walled garden, and self-guiding nature trail. Take bus #16/A to get here.

Activities and Recreation

TOURS

All tours are bookable through Dublin's central **tourist office** (25 Suffolk St., tel. 01/884-7871, www.visitdublin.com, 9am-5:30pm Mon.-Sat., 10:30am-3pm Sun.).

★ Walking Tours

Get some exercise, learn a lot, and maybe even have yourself a tipple on one of Dublin's many excellent guided walking tours. The best known, running since 1988, is the **Dublin Literary Pub Crawl** (tel. 01/670-5602, www.dublinpubcrawl.com, tours at 7:30pm daily and noon Sun. late Mar.-late Nov., Thurs.-Sun. only in low season, 2.25 hours, €12), hosted by local actors who'll perform the work of Ireland's most beloved poets and playwrights at each of the four pubs on the itinerary. The tour starts at The Duke pub on Duke Street off Grafton Street. The performances come between frequent 20-minute beer breaks.

If you love a good old-fashioned ghost story, sign up for a **Haunted History Dublin** walking tour (tel. 085/102-3646, www.hidden-dublinwalks.com, runs Mon., Thurs., and Sat. at 8pm, 1.5-2 hours, €13). This company offers both bus and walking tours to several creeptastic destinations, including the infamous Hellfire Club in the Wicklow Mountains. The rendezvous point is opposite Eddie Rocket's on Dame Street.

Want something a little more serious? Then you'll admire your hardworking guides on the **Historical Walking Tour** (tel. 01/878-0227 or 087/688-9412, www.historicalinsights.ie, 11am and 3pm daily Apr.-Sept., noon Fri.-Sat. Oct.-Mar., €12), all postgraduate history students. The two-hour walk departs from the Trinity College entrance. Themed tours, available between May and September, include "Architecture and Society," the "Sexual History of Ireland," and another focusing on the Easter Rising.

Another reputable company does an **Easter Rising Walk** (tel. 01/707-2493 or 087/830-3523, www.1916rising.com, 11:30am Mon.-Sat. and 1pm Sun. Apr.-Sept., €13), which departs the International Bar on Wicklow Street and also lasts two hours.

City Bus Tours

Dublin Bus (59 O'Connell St., tel. 01/873-4222, www.dublinsightseeing.ie) offers tours in and around the city. The **Hop-On Hop-Off Tour** (buses every 15 minutes 9:30am-4:30pm daily, €22) is a 90-minute circuit that includes pretty much all the city center attractions, plus Phoenix Park and the Guinness Storehouse, and your ticket entitles you to discounts at several places. The **Ghost Tour** (7pm and 9pm Sat.-Sun., 8pm Tues.-Fri., 2-hour tour €25) offers, among other grisly tidbits, a "crash course in body-snatching." The **Coast and Castles Tour** (10am-2pm daily, 3-hour tour €25) covers the National Botanic Gardens, Casino Marino, Malahide Castle, and Howth Harbour. You can book any of these tours at the Dublin Bus office at 14 Upper O'Connell Street or at the Suffolk Street tourist office, though you can usually get at least a 10 percent discount online; all tours depart the O'Connell Street office.

Boat Tours

One of the most fun and original (if touristy) ways to see more of the city is on a **Viking Splash Tour** (tel. 01/707-6000, www.viking-splash.com, tours generally every half hour 10am-5pm daily Mar.-Oct., Wed.-Sun. in Feb. and Tues.-Sun. in Nov., €22, €25 June-Aug.). Tours depart 64-65 Patrick Street (near St. Patrick's Cathedral) and St. Stephen's Green North (at Dawson Street). You'll spend the first 50 minutes on this 75-minute tour walking around the city wearing "Viking" hats and behaving outrageously in public at the behest of your guide. In between, of course, you'll learn a lot of historical tidbits. The tour culminates in a 20-minute boat trip on the Grand Canal Basin in a "Duck"—a reconditioned WWII amphibious military vehicle. There is not much "splashing" involved, however.

Day Trips from Dublin

Brú na Bóinne (Newgrange and two other passage tombs), **Powerscourt,** and **Glendalough** in Wicklow Mountains National Park are commonly experienced on a day tour out of the city.

Over the Top Tours (tel. 01/838-6128 or 087/259-3467, freephone tel. for reservations 1800/424-252, www.overthetoptours.com, departs O'Connell St. outside Gresham Hotel at 9:20am and Suffolk St. tourist office at 9:45am daily, returning 5:30pm, ticket €28) offers smallish (max. 14 people) tours of Glendalough and Wicklow Mountains National Park as well as Newgrange and Knowth (€17, same departure points at 8:45am and 9am, admission to site not included).

Game of Thrones fans will definitely want to sign up for a daylong tour (tel. 01/513-3033, www.gameofthronestours.com, €55) of the Winterfell filming locations, which includes two three-kilometer walks in Tollymore forest and Castle Ward Estate in County Down. The tour bus departs Jurys Inn, Custom House Quay at 8am daily.

OTHER ACTIVITIES AND RECREATION
In the City

Be a temporary Dubliner and stretch your legs on the nine-hectare **St. Stephen's Green** (at the bottom of Grafton St., tel. 01/475-7816), or go for a run or longer walk at the seven-square-kilometer **Phoenix Park** (main entrance on Parkgate St., at the southeast corner, tel. 01/677-0095) on the western perimeter of the city center.

Built for the 2003 Special Olympics summer games, the **National Aquatic Centre** (Snugborough Rd., Blanchardstown, Dublin 15, tel. 01/646-4364 or 01/646-4367, www.nac.ie, 9am-8:45pm weekdays, 9am-7:45pm weekends, €7.50-15) features plenty of kiddie delights (slides, wave and surf machines, the works) as well as the official Olympic-size pool. Dublin Bus #38A from Hawkins Street (or Berkeley St., outside St. Joseph's Church) will get you here.

Outside the City

Don't stay in the city center if the weather's fine! There are several sandy beaches in the Dublin burbs; some of them, like **Killiney** (kill-EYE-nee, 16 km south of the city), **Portrane** (24 km north), and **Donabate** (21 km north), have even been awarded the coveted Blue Flag. Killiney is particularly attractive; some say it even has a vaguely Mediterranean vibe on fine summer days. Many Irish celebs (Bono, Enya, and director Neil Jordan, among others) have homes here. Fortunately, you can reach all these beaches via the **DART** (tel. 01/805-4288, www.dart.ie, 2-3/hour daily from Connolly Station, 20-minute trip, get off at Donabate for Portrane as well, single/day return fares €3.80/6.85). **Dollymount,** another Blue Flag beach (and UNESCO Biosphere Reserve, for its web-footed population), is immediately north of Dublin Harbour. The strand is linked to the Dollymount neighborhood by an old wooden bridge. Get here via Dublin Bus #130 from Lower Abbey Street (4-6/hour daily).

If you are using a fair bit of public transportation in the Dublin area, it might be worth purchasing a **Leap travel card** (www.leapcard.ie, €19.50), a three-day transit pass valid on the Luas light rail, the DART (within County Dublin), and all Dublin Bus and Airlink buses (excluding day tours). Purchase a Leap ticket at the Dublin airport, either at the information desk or at the Spar grocery shop in the arrivals hall. The card expires 72 hours after the first time you use it.

For a day tour including Glendalough and Powerscourt in Enniskerry, look into **Walkabout Wicklow** (tel. 087/784-9599, www.walkaboutwickow.com). The base price is €25, €35 if you'd like to add a guided walk, and €75 if you'd like to add a horseback riding excursion. Tours depart the Gresham Hotel on O'Connell Street at 9:20am and the central tourist office on Suffolk Street at 9:35am, returning to Dublin around 5:30pm. Walkabout Wicklow also offers longer guided treks of 3-15 days.

Not many folks can say they've sailed over Ireland in a hot air balloon. Want bragging rights? Contact **Irish Balloon Flights** (80 Cypress Grove Rd., Templeogue, Dublin, tel. 01/408-4777 or 087/933-2622, flight-check line 087/743-7575, www.balloons.ie, 1/2/3 or more passengers €195/190/185 pp). Most flights depart Rathsallagh House in Wicklow (60 km south of Dublin) or Trim Castle in Meath (55 km northwest), though there are other launch locations around the country. The hefty ticket price includes a glass of champagne after a one-hour flight.

Spectator Sports

Catch a **hurling** or **Gaelic football** match at the country's largest stadium, **Croke Park** (Clonliffe Rd., north of the Royal Canal in Drumcondra, tel. 01/836-3222, €25-55), on Sunday afternoons May-September. Except for playoff games (when tickets can be mighty hard to come by), you can purchase admission at the door. For more background on these native sports, check out the **Gaelic Athletic Association** website (www.gaa.ie).

Dublin Bus routes #3, #11/A, #16/A, and #123 frequently link O'Connell Street with Croke Park.

Football (i.e., soccer) and rugby matches are played at **Lansdowne Stadium** (Ballsbridge, tel. 01/668-9300, www.lrsdc.ie) on the south side of the city; capacity is 50,000. Take the DART to the Lansdowne Road Station, a short walk from the park, or ride Dublin Bus #7, #8, #45, or #84.

Food

Whether you want a (relatively) cheap, no-frills meal or a lavish three-course affair, Dublin's eateries run the gamut. So long as you know where to go, you might just end up eating better here than you did in Paris. Plus, finding good-value eats in this city isn't as difficult as you might think.

Some restaurants have started tacking a 10-15 percent "service charge" onto your bill (regardless of the number in your party). If you weren't satisfied with your meal in any way, don't hesitate to ask your server to deduct it.

AROUND GRAFTON STREET

It may be the historic jewel of Grafton Street—Harry Clarke windows, mahogany banisters and all—but unfortunately **Bewley's Oriental Café** (78-79 Grafton St., tel. 01/672-7720, www.bewleys.com) was closed at time of writing. The famous tearooms are supposedly undergoing refurbishments, though the Dublin press has speculated that the exorbitant annual rent of €1.5 million led to the closure. Hopefully it'll be open again by the time you're reading this.

You'll find the best pub grub in the area at **O'Neill's** (2 Suffolk St., tel. 01/679-3656, www.oneillspubdublin.com, food served 3:30pm-9:30pm Mon.-Thurs. and noon-9:30pm Fri.-Sun., €11-14), a commodious, old-fashioned watering hole—open more than three centuries—with excellent carvery lunches that call to mind a Thanksgiving feast (though there's a vegetarian quiche on the menu as well).

You can choose either cafeteria-style or table service at ★ **Cornucopia** (Wicklow St., noon-8pm Mon.-Sat., noon-7pm Sun., €10-14), the city's most beloved vegetarian eatery. The hearty-yet-gourmet fare is so darn good it's a fave lunch spot for omnivores, too—not to mention delicious desserts, many of which are dairy free.

Dublin Food and Accommodations

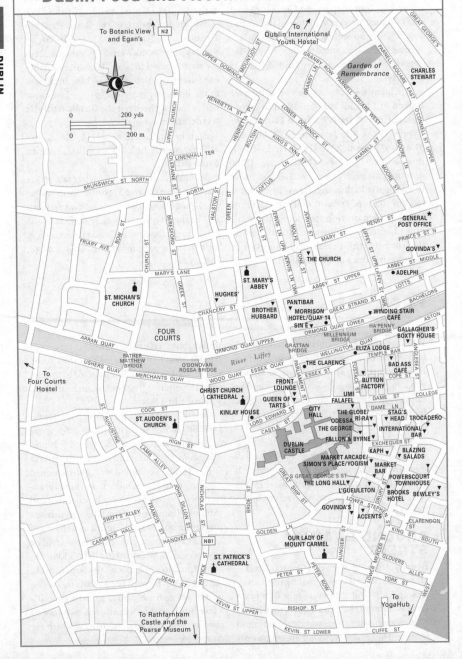

To Botanic View
and Egan's | N2

To
Dublin International
Youth Hostel

Garden of
Remembrance

CHARLES
STEWART

0   200 yds
0   200 m

UPPER DOMINICK ST
MOUNT JOY
GRANBY ROW
PARNELL SQ EAST
PARNELL SQ WEST
PARNELL SQUARE EAST
PARNELL SQUARE WEST
HENRIETTA ST PL
HENRIETTA ST
UPPER CHURCH ST
LOWER DOMINICK ST
PARNELL ST
MOORE ST
MOORE LN
O'CONNELL ST UPPER
GREAT GEORGE'S
LINENHALL TER
BOLTON ST
KING'S INNS ST
LOFTUS LN

BRUNSWICK ST NORTH
KING ST NORTH
HALSTON ST
GREEN ST
CAPEL ST
WOLFE TONE ST
JERVIS LN UPR
JERVIS ST
MARY ST
HENRY ST
GENERAL
POST OFFICE
PRINCE'S ST N
GOVINDA'S
ABBEY ST MIDDLE
ADELPHI
LIFFEY ST UPR

FRIARY AVE
BOW ST
CHURCH ST
BERESFORD ST
GREEK ST
MARY'S LANE
THE CHURCH
ABBEY ST UPPER
LOTTS
BACHELORS

ST. MICHAN'S
CHURCH
HUGHES'
ST. MARY'S
ABBEY
CHANCERY ST
PANTIBAR
MORRISON
HOTEL/QUAY 14
SIN É
GREAT STRAND ST
WINDING STAIR
CAFÉ
ASTON

FOUR
COURTS
BROTHER
HUBBARD
ORMOND QUAY LOWER
HA'PENNY
BRIDGE
GALLAGHER'S
BOXTY HOUSE
ANGLESEA ST

ARRAN QUAY
FATHER
MATTHEW
BRIDGE
ORMOND QUAY UPPER
MILLENNIUM
BRIDGE
River Liffey
GRATTAN
BRIDGE
WELLINGTON
ELIZA LODGE
TEMPLE BAR

To
Four Courts
Hostel
USHERS QUAY
O'DONOVAN
ROSSA BRIDGE
MERCHANTS QUAY
WOOD QUAY
ESSEX QUAY
ESSEX ST
THE CLARENCE
EUSTACE ST
BAD ASS
CAFÉ
COPE ST

COOK ST
CHRIST CHURCH
CATHEDRAL
FRONT
LOUNGE
PARLIAMENT ST
BUTTON
FACTORY
COLLEGE

ST. AUGUSTINE ST
ST. AUDOEN'S
CHURCH
HIGH ST
KINLAY HOUSE
LORD EDWARD ST
QUEEN OF
TARTS
CITY
HALL
UMI
FALAFEL
DAME LN
DAME ST
THE GLOBE/
RI-RA
STAG'S
HEAD
TROCADERO

LAMB ALLEY
CASTLE ST
ODESSA
THE GEORGE
FALLON & BYRNE
INTERNATIONAL
BAR

JOHN DILLON ST
NICHOLAS ST
DUBLIN
CASTLE
EXCHEQUER ST
KAPH
BLAZING
SALADS

SWIFT'S ALLEY
FRANCIS ST
MARKET ARCADE/
SIMON'S PLACE/YOGISM
MARKET
BAR
POWERSCOURT
TOWNHOUSE

CARMEN'S HALL
HANOVER ST
S GREAT GEORGE'S ST
THE LONG HALL
L'GUEULETON
LOWER STEPHEN ST
DRURY ST
BROOKS
HOTEL
BEWLEY'S

GOLDEN LN
GOVINDA'S
ACCENTS
CLARENDON
ST
KING ST SOUTH

BRIDE ST
OUR LADY OF
MOUNT CARMEL
AUNGIER ST
PETER ROW
GLOVERS
ALLEY

PATRICK ST
N81
ST. PATRICK'S
CATHEDRAL
PETER ST
LOWER MERCER ST
YORK ST

DEAN ST
KEVIN ST UPPER
BISHOP ST
To
YogaHub

To Rathfarnham
Castle and the
Pearse Museum
KEVIN ST LOWER
CUFFE ST

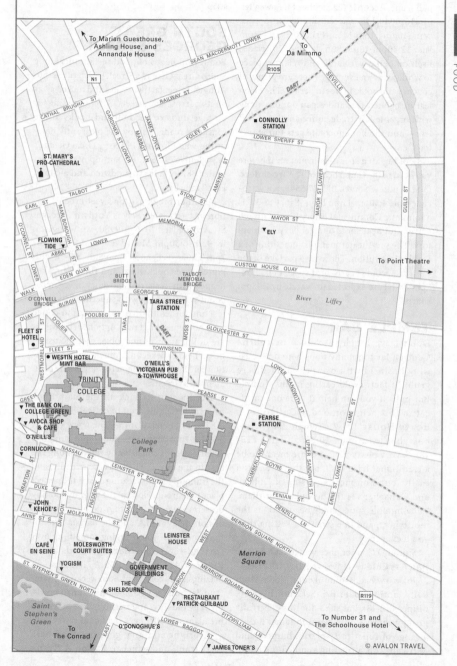

To Marian Guesthouse, Ashling House, and Annandale House
To Da Mimmo
R105
N1
DART
SEVILLE PL
SEAN MACDERMOTT LOWER
RAILWAY ST
GARDINER ST LOWER
JAMES JOYCE ST
MABBOT LN
FOLEY ST
CONNOLLY STATION
LOWER SHERIFF ST
ST. MARY'S PRO-CATHEDRAL
CATHAL BRUGHA ST
TALBOT ST
STORE ST
AMIENS ST
MAYOR ST LOWER
GUILD ST
EARL ST
MARLBOROUGH ST
MEMORIAL RD
MAYOR ST
ELY
O'CONNELL ST LOWER
FLOWING TIDE
ABBEY ST LOWER
EDEN QUAY
BUTT BRIDGE
TALBOT MEMORIAL BRIDGE
CUSTOM HOUSE QUAY
To Point Theatre
WALK
O'CONNELL BRIDGE
BURGH QUAY
GEORGE'S QUAY
River Liffey
TARA STREET STATION
CITY QUAY
FLEET ST HOTEL
D'OLIER ST
POOLBEG ST
TARA ST
DART
MOSS ST
GLOUCESTER ST
WESTMORELAND
FLEET ST
TOWNSEND ST
WESTIN HOTEL/ MINT BAR
O'NEILL'S VICTORIAN PUB & TOWNHOUSE
MARKS LN
LOWER SANDWITH ST
LIME ST
TRINITY COLLEGE
PEARSE ST
THE BANK ON COLLEGE GREEN
GREEN
PEARSE STATION
AVOCA SHOP & CAFE
O'NEILL'S
College Park
UPPER SANDWITH ST
ERNE ST LOWER
CORNUCOPIA
NASSAU ST
LEINSTER ST SOUTH
S. CUMBERLAND ST
BOYNE ST
GRAFTON ST
DUKE ST
FREDERICK ST
KILDARE ST
CLARE ST
FENIAN ST
DENZILLE LN
JOHN KEHOE'S
DAWSON ST
MOLESWORTH ST
WEST
MERRION SQUARE NORTH
ANNE ST S
LEINSTER HOUSE
CAFÉ EN SEINE
MOLESWORTH COURT SUITES
Merrion Square
YOGISM
ST. STEPHEN'S GREEN NORTH
GOVERNMENT BUILDINGS
MERRION ST
MERRION SQUARE SOUTH
EAST
Saint Stephen's Green
THE SHELBOURNE
RESTAURANT PATRICK GUILBAUD
R119
To Number 31 and The Schoolhouse Hotel
To The Conrad
EAST
O'DONOGHUE'S
LOWER BAGGOT ST
FITZWILLIAM LN
JAMES TONER'S

© AVALON TRAVEL

Established as a late-night alternative to the pub scene, **Accents** (23 Stephen St. Lower, tel. 01/416-0040, http://accentslounge.wordpress.com, 10am-11pm Mon.-Fri., 10:30am-11pm Sat., 12:30pm-10pm Sun., under €10) prides itself on being a friendly and relaxing place to while away an evening. There are plenty of couches and bookshelves to peruse. The menu features gluten-free and vegan options along with organic fair-trade coffee and loose-leaf teas—and the hot chocolate gets top marks too.

Looking for a special gourmet meal before you head to the Gate Theatre? The **Trocadero** (3 St. Andrew St., tel. 01/677-5545, www.trocadero.ie, 4:30pm-11pm Mon.-Sat., €16-30) is a romantic Continental eatery lined with red velvet and headshots of legendary Irish actors. The pre-theater menu is something of a Dublin institution. Those who partake of the €27 three-course early-bird special (4:30pm-7pm daily) are expected to "vacate by 7:45pm sharp."

TEMPLE BAR

Don't leave lunch to chance in Tourist Central; far too many pubs here do a bustling business with overpriced, mediocre grub. In fact, avoid eating in any Temple Bar pubs if you can help it. The one must-eat in this neighborhood is **Gallagher's Boxty House** (20-21 Temple Bar, www.boxtyhouse.ie, noon-10:30pm daily, €15-18). Savory boxty pancakes are meant to be a traditional Irish dish, but they aren't too easily found on menus outside of Dublin, and Gallagher's is the best place for them. "The humble spud, made beautiful" is the motto here, and in a swankier setting than you'd expect.

Sinead O'Connor once waited tables at the **Bad Ass Café** (9-11 Crown Alley, tel. 01/671-2596, www.badassdublin.com, noon-11pm daily, until 1:30am Fri.-Sat., lunch €8-10, dinner €12-18), but she's not this cheerfully grungy eatery's only claim to fame: It does a range of super-tasty pizzas, burgers, and Mexican grub, attracting a chilled-out crowd who'd otherwise steer clear of this touristy strip.

SOUTH GREAT GEORGES STREET

You'll find heaps of good restaurants along South Great George's Street, which turns into Aungier Street farther south, and tucked away on its narrow side streets. After browsing for vintage duds or secondhand books at the Market Arcade, pop by the pleasantly hole-in-the-wall **Simon's Place** (S. Great George's St., tel. 01/679-7821, 8:30am-6pm Mon.-Sat., under €8) for a hefty sandwich and a cup of Fair Trade brew.

Another breakfast (or sweet lunch?) option just across the way is **Yogism** (Georges St. Arcade, tel. 01/679-9980, www.yogism.ie, 9am-6:30pm Mon.-Wed. and Sat., 9am-7pm Thurs.-Fri., noon-6pm Sun., €5-9), with gluten-free (buckwheat and flax) pancakes heaped with fresh fruit and dairy or vegan coconut yogurt along with superfood smoothies, not-so-healthy fro-yo cones, and coffee with homemade nut milk options. These guys are doing an awesome job at diet-inclusiveness. There's a second, much smaller location on Dawson Street on the north side of St. Stephen's Green.

Need a spot to duck off the main tourist strip for a quiet cup of coffee? Try **Kaph** (31 Drury St., tel. 01/613-9030, www.kaph.ie, 8:30am-7pm Mon.-Sat., noon-6pm Sun., €5). Their coffee is consistently rated among the best in the city, the baristas are friendly, and the tranquil upstairs seating area is the perfect place to regroup. None of the yummy-looking desserts are vegan, but they do offer a choice of non-dairy milks, and the baristas are totally cool with you bringing something over from all-vegetarian **Blazing Salads** across the street (42 Drury St., tel. 01/671-9552, www.blazingsalads.com, 9am-6pm weekdays, 9am-5pm Sat., under €8). Smoothies, salad bowls, pizza by the slice, and freshly baked cakes and breads are on offer here, but for takeaway only.

A bright and airy gourmet food hall, restaurant, and winebar, **Fallon & Byrne**

Brunch at **Odessa** (13 Dame Ct., off Exchequer St., tel. 01/670-7634, 6pm-late daily, 11:30am-4:30pm Sat.-Sun., €14-22) is a modern legend. It's been so popular for so long that calling Odessa "trendy" doesn't quite fit, but it's still true this loungy eatery attracts a come-to-be-seen crowd (that there's an adjacent "supper club" says something, doesn't it?).

There isn't actually a sign out front at ★ **L'Gueuleton** (1 Fade St., tel. 01/675-3708, www.lgueuleton.com, 12:30pm-4pm and 5:30pm-10pm Mon.-Sat., noon-4pm and 5:30pm-9pm Sun., lunch €11-17, dinner €18-26). This place serves up divine French fare that doesn't take itself too seriously, and in a wonderfully relaxed dining room with exposed brick walls and tasteful yet funky modern art. Lunch is a much better value (the portions are generous), and you don't have to worry about getting a table if you show up around two. Oh, and the token vegetarian dish is excellent as well.

You'd never know it from the entrance off a dingy alleyway, but ★ **Yogahub** (27 Camden Pl., tel. 01/478-9043, www.theyogahub.ie, 7am-9:30pm Mon.-Thurs., 7am-7pm Fri., 9:30am-5pm Sat.-Sun., €6-11) is an urban oasis, with the serene atmosphere you'd expect from a café adjoining a yoga studio. Here you can order the most satisfying full vegan breakfast on the whole island, with chickpea hash, lentil sausages, and sliced avocado and tomato on fresh sourdough. It'll keep you going till dinnertime. The raw gluten-free desserts are scrummy too.

DAME STREET

A sure bet for a pub lunch is **The Stag's Head** (1 Dame Ct., tel. 01/679-3687, food served noon-6pm daily, €8-14), an atmospheric Victorian bar perfect for a leisurely meal (or a meal in a glass).

You'll find some of Dublin's best Middle Eastern grub (plus fresh juices) at the all-vegetarian **Umi Falafel** (13 Dame St., tel. 01/670-6866, noon-10pm daily, €5-8), which offers

The Stag's Head pub, an ideal spot for an afternoon pint

(11-17 Exchequer St., tel. 01/472-1010, www.fallonandbyrne.com, 8am-9pm Mon.-Fri., 9am-9pm Sat., 11am-7pm Sun., lunch €8-17, dinner €18-34) sells mostly organic prepared foods and delectables from all over the world along with fresh coffee and baked goods. While you won't find vegan sweets behind the bakery counter, the restaurant does offer dairy-free dessert options on a separate vegan menu. Best values are the set lunch (2/3 courses €20/25) and the pretheater dinner menu (2/3 courses €26/30, available 5:30pm-7pm Wed.-Sat., all night Sun.-Tues.), though you might want to book a table online for an evening meal.

For a hefty helping of vegetarian heaven, try cafeteria-style ★ **Govinda's** (4 Aungier St., tel. 01/475-0309, www.govindas.ie, noon-9pm Mon.-Sat., €7-10). Linger at a table by the window watching all of Dublin go by while you dig into your *mattar paneer* curry (or one of many vegan options). Unless the hunger of the world's on you, the "small" lunch portions will keep you going until dinnertime.

sit-down service or lightning-fast takeaway with a smile.

It's a shame the **Queen of Tarts** (Dame St. at Parliament St., tel. 01/670-7499, 7:30am-6pm weekdays, 9am-6pm Sat., 9:30am-6pm Sun., €6-9) is in such a tiny space; you can keep passing by, squinting through the window, and noting with disappointment there *still* isn't a table free. This bakery-café is utterly charming and deservedly popular; along with a dazzling array of gourmet desserts, you can order from an extensive breakfast menu, or try a sandwich or savory tart at lunchtime.

MERRION SQUARE

Widely praised as Dublin's best, ★ **Restaurant Patrick Guilbaud** (21 Upper Merion St., tel. 01/676-4192, www.restaurantpatrickguilbaud.ie, 12:30pm-2:15pm and 7:30pm-10:15pm Tues.-Sat., 2/3-course lunch €45/55, 2/3/4-course dinner €90/105/130) has been doing exquisite French fare using local meats and produce for more than 35 years. There's an eight-course "degustation menu" (€185) featuring French twists on traditional Irish dishes like colcannon and braised crubbeens (that's pig's feet, for the uninitiated). And if 25 quid for a chocolate fondant induces a gasp, be assured you'd give your first- *and* secondborn children for it. Reservations are recommended.

NORTHSIDE

There are fewer notable restaurants north of the Liffey, though this is slowly beginning to change. Locals adore **Brother Hubbard** (153 Capel St., tel. 01/441-1112, www.brotherhubbard.ie, 7:30am-9:30pm Mon.-Fri., 9:30am-5pm Sat.-Sun., lunch €7-12, 2/3-course dinner €25/30) for its homebaked brownies and epic weekend brunches as well as some of the best coffee in the city.

You'll find the other all-vegetarian ★ **Govinda's** (83 Middle Abbey St., tel. 01/872-9861, www.govindas.ie, noon-9pm Mon.-Sat., €8-15) beside Eason Books just off O'Connell Street. Hot tip for shoestring travelers: If you show up just before closing time, say 8:45, they'll be giving full portions away for a euro a pop!

If you want really good Italian food, you have to go to the Italians. The owners of **Da Mimmo** (148 N. Strand Rd., tel. 01/856-1714, 10am-3pm and 5:30pm-10pm Mon.-Fri., 12:30pm-10pm Sat.-Sun., €8-18) hail from Lazio, and as soon as you step in the door you can tell how seriously they take their cuisine, though the atmosphere and prices are super casual. It's well worth the longish walk or taxi ride out here for top-notch pizzas and pastas, and worth waiting a few minutes for a table to open up in this tiny place. It's close to Croke Park, so you might want to eat here before or after a match.

Named after a Yeats poem, the **Winding Stair Café** (40 Lower Ormond Quay, tel. 01/872-7320, www.winding-stair.com, 12:30pm-3:30pm and 6pm-10:30pm daily, €14-24) used to be a cheap-and-cheerful café, a favorite student haunt; now it's an upscale modern Irish restaurant. Gone are the murals and checkered tablecloths, but the food is delicious (if fancy), the wine list is exhaustive, and the waiters are nice. Reservations are a good idea. It's not quite as cool as the original Winding Stair, but better a new, posh version than none at all.

★ **The Church** (Mary St. at Jervis St., tel. 01/828-0102, www.thechurch.ie, bar food served noon-9:30pm Mon.-Wed., noon-10pm Thurs.-Sat., and 12:30pm-8pm Sun., gallery restaurant noon-10pm Mon.-Wed., noon-11pm Thurs.-Sat., and 12:30pm-10pm Sun., bar meals €12, restaurant €12-24) is a fabulously unique bar-cum-restaurant in a converted Methodist church. The fare is relatively traditional—steak, salmon, beef-and-Guinness pie, the usual vegetarian pasta dish—though the cocktails will prove almost as memorable as the setting.

Entertainment and Events

TRADITIONAL PUBS

There're always traditional music sessions on at the chintzy tourist traps of Temple Bar, but you're better off seeking out more low-key venues. Nothing's quite "authentic" in this town—you'll have to go out to the boonies for a session that doesn't have a heavy element of tourist-driven theatricality to it—but some spots are certainly more "authentic" than others. Avoid any place that charges a cover for entry.

Tucked away behind the Four Courts, **Hughes'** (19-20 Chancery St., tel. 01/872-6540) offers live trad nightly into the wee hours and is far less touristy than the musical pubs of Temple Bar. Similarly atmospheric is the upstairs bar at **Cobblestones** (N. King St., tel. 01/872-1799, www.cobblestonepub.ie), where you'll also find trad or folk on a nightly basis. It's a bit more touristy, but that's because **O'Donoghue's** (15 Merrion Row, tel. 01/661-4303, www.odonoghues.ie) offers (arguably) the city's best trad. The walls are covered with pictures of The Dubliners, the '60s folk group that got its start here, and the courtyard/alleyway leading to the entrance is always packed with a youngish crowd more interested in chat than music.

It claims to be Ireland's oldest pub, a hotbed of seditious activity in rebellions gone by, but the **Brazen Head** (Bridge St., tel. 01/677-9549, www.brazenhead.com) is pushing the limits on tourist-kitsch with its silly castellated facade and extremely overpriced drinks (even for Dublin). The nightly session is meant to be traditional, but the guys play a lot of Van Morrison or Thin Lizzy, with only the occasional jig or reel thrown in. Having said all this, there's still a fair bit of *craic* to be found, especially in the spacious courtyard beer garden.

A delightfully "crusty old man's pub" (it used to sell groceries as well), **James Toner's** (Lower Baggot St., tel. 01/676-3090, www.

tonerspub.ie) hums with an after-work crowd of all ages. This is believed to be the only pub in Dublin William Butler Yeats ever visited.

A classy yet understated Victorian pub with all the period details, **William Ryan's** (28 Parkgate St., tel. 01/677-6097) is in a residential neighborhood off the tourist circuit, which means the ambience is refreshingly workaday. The same goes for **The Long Hall** (51 S. Great Georges St., tel. 01/475-1590), though weirdly enough, it's smack-dab in the middle of touristville. After a satisfying meal at one of the great restaurants on or near South Great Georges, you can chill out to the strains of Annie Lennox—another nice surprise, in a place like this. Another great Victorian snug-lined pub is **John Kehoe's** (9 S. Anne St., tel. 01/677-8312), where you can have a drink upstairs in the late proprietor's old living room. **The Stag's Head** (1 Dame Ct., tel. 01/679-3687) is another delightful Victorian relic, complete with the requisite hunting trophy above the bar. There's live trad on Fridays and Saturdays starting at 10pm.

BARS AND CLUBS

Dublin has amassed a reputation for one of the hottest club scenes in Europe, though it's difficult to party properly when even the hippest places close their doors at 3am! Cover charges vary from €5-10 during the week to €15-20 at weekends. Check *inDublin* (www.indublin.ie), a free weekly, for a listing of what's on when that's as comprehensive as it gets. Not into grinding? The city center offers plenty of trendy bars—some you might call "novelty"—where you can kick back with a fancy cocktail and let the night slip by in a whirl of funky lighting and stimulating conversation.

It's within spitting distance of the Trinity College gates, but **The Bank** (20-22 College Green, tel. 01/677-0677, www.bankoncollegegreen.com) is more popular with 20- and 30-something professionals. The stunning

What's the *Craic?*

You may be wondering why the Irish are always talking about crack—*craic,* that is, an Irish word meaning fun times, news, or enjoyable conversation, though it's one of those special terms that means so much more than its translation. *Craic* can be "mighty," "savage," or "deadly," and it's often (but not always) experienced at the nearest pub. Someone somewhere along the way defined *craic's* essential components by acronym: *ceol* ("kyole," music), *rince* ("RIN-keh," dance), *amhrain* ("OW-rin," songs), *inis scealta* ("IN-ish SHKEEL-tuh," storytelling), and *cainte* ("CAHN-chuh," gossip). At any rate, you'll know great *craic* when you're having it!

Victorian details—polished mahogany, plasterwork, mosaic flooring, open fireplaces, a wrought-iron mezzanine above the horseshoe bar—belie a relaxed atmosphere and down-to-earth staff. Somewhat trendier is the **Market Bar** (14A Fade St., off S. Great Georges St., tel. 01/677-4835, www.marketbar.ie, tapas €4-15), in an old sausage factory. It's an atmospheric space, with tall walls of exposed brick, a ceiling made all of skylights, comfortable seating, and another wall of shelves lined with wooden shoe-trees thrown in for quirky good measure. There are plenty of meaty, cheesy tapas choices along with several tasty vegan plates.

With a breathtaking, impeccably assembled interior, the commodious belle-epoque **Café en Seine** (40 Dawson St., tel. 01/667-4567) draws a youngish, well-heeled crowd of those who don't mind the high drink prices. Get here early, order your cocktails, score a couple of plush armchairs by an ornate period fireplace, and people-watch to your heart's content.

Here's one to write home about: an 18th-century Methodist church converted into a swanky new bar and restaurant, complete with original pipe organ, stained glass windows, and marble wall memorials. Ask the bartender at **The Church** (Mary St. at Jervis St., tel. 01/828-0102, www.thechurch.ie) how the owner achieved this entrepreneurial feat—isn't it sacrilegious, or something?—and the bartender will sagely point out to you that this church was fast plummeting into ruin when John M. Keating purchased the property in the late '90s (and wouldn't the people buried beneath you prefer a swanky

bar over a crumbling edifice littered with empty crisp bags?). Millions of euros later, here we are in the coolest, most unusual nightspot on either side of the Liffey. The old crypt has also been converted into a second bar down a long set of stairs, but the main bar is far more atmospheric. You might want to have your dinner up in the organ gallery, a highly unusual feature in ecclesiastical architecture regardless of the denomination.

The swanky **Mint Bar** (Westmoreland St., tel. 01/645-1322, www.westin.com) at the Westin Hotel offers salsa Fridays and "Velvet Lounge" Saturdays, with a mix of lounge, jazz, and swing; the music starts at 10pm both nights, and bar nibbles are available until 10:30. The Morrison Hotel also has a chic bar, **Quay 14** (Lower Ormond Quay, tel. 01/887-2400, www.morrisonhotel.ie); with a stylish (if at times pretentious) crowd, hip ambience, and titillating cocktail menu, it's perfect for "pre-clubbing."

A hip place to pass the day away with coffee and nibbles, after dark **The Globe** (11 S. Great George's St., tel. 01/671-1220, www.globe.ie) is a perennial pre-club favorite with Dublin's fashion-conscious trend-setters. There's an evening tapas menu, trip hop and acid jazz on the stereo, and a collection of faux-classical marble statues. There's also live jazz on Sunday afternoon. After closing, the Globe becomes part of **Rí-Rá** (Dame Ct., tel. 01/677-4835, www.rira.ie, open at 11:30pm Mon.-Sat., free before midnight during the week, cover €10), possibly the best nightclub in the city for its eclectic crowd, great funk

LGBTQ in Dublin

DUBLIN
ENTERTAINMENT AND EVENTS

Ireland has come a long, long way since homosexuality was legalized in 1993. The positive outcome of the republic's same-sex marriage referendum in November 2015 means that it's easier than ever to be yourself, and not just in the capital city. Dublin is embracing LGBTQ culture like never before. You're spoiled for choice entertainment-wise; May is a great time to be here, for the **Dublin Gay Theatre Festival** (tel. 01/677-8511, www.gaytheatre.ie), when you'll spot Oscar Wilde's mug hanging on banners all over town (though the plays put on are mostly contemporary). Another event worth planning a trip for is the **Gay Pride Parade**, established in 1992; the parade is the culmination of the **Dublin LGBTQ Pride Festival** (www.dublinpride.org), a two-week event toward the end of June. There's also the city's Lesbian and Gay Film Festival, **Gaze** (6 Eustace St., tel. 01/679-3477, www.gaze.ie), for four days in early August, where international flicks are screened at the Irish Film Institute (www.ifi.ie).

There are a couple all-gay clubs in Dublin: **The George** is the oldest (89 S. Great Georges St., tel. 01/478-2983), with something fun on every night of the week. Sunday-night bingo (free admission before 10pm) is still a local favorite. Or catch a drag show at **PantiBar** (7-8 Capel St., tel. 01/874-0710), which is open until 2:30am on Saturdays. Mainstream venues sometimes offer LGBTQ nights, though they don't tend to last for more than a year or two at a stretch. One hopefully safe bet is **Glitz** at Dandelion (130-133 St. Stephen's Green W., tel. 01/476-0870, www.welovedandelion.com, €5 cover) on Tuesday nights.

As for LGBT-friendly hangouts, try **The Front Lounge** (33 Parliament St., tel. 01/670-4112, www.thefrontlounge.ie) for a quiet drink (unless it's karaoke night!), or **Accents** (23 Stephen St. Lower, tel. 01/416-0040, http://accentslounge.wordpress.com) if you're not in the mood to drink. Either way, you'll probably want to plan on an afternoon or evening at **The Boiler House** (12 Crane Ln., tel. 01/677-3130, www.the-boilerhouse.com, noon-5am Mon.-Thurs., noon Fri. to 5am Sun., €22), which has jacuzzi, sauna, and steam rooms along with massage treatments, a coffee bar (sans alcohol), and a "play room." There's a nightclub here one Saturday a month; check the website for details.

Now on to the practical stuff. Stop by the **Outhouse** (105 Capel St., Northside, tel. 01/873-4999, www.outhouse.ie), the city's most established resource center, and peruse the notice boards before having lunch at the café (1pm-9:30pm Mon.-Fri., 1pm-5:30pm Sat.). The **Gay Switchboard Dublin** (tel. 01/872-1055, www.gayswitchboard.ie) also provides advice and information. **Gay Dublin** (www.gaydublin.com) is a decent source of entertainment info, and better yet is the nationwide **Gay Ireland** (www.gay-ireland.com).

and lounge tunes, and astonishingly friendly bouncers.

Friday nights bring "Salsa Palace" and Saturdays "The Soul Stage" (jazz, soul, hip-hop, and Motown) at the **Gaiety Theatre** (King St. S., tel. 01/677-1717, www.gaietytheatre.com, open at midnight, Fri./Sat. cover €15/20). Both nights feature live bands, four different bars, and old films playing on the main stage until 4am. The motto is "sweets for the sweet" at the classy **Sugar Club** (8 Lower Leeson St., tel. 01/678-7188, www.thesugarclub.com, cover €10/15 before/after 10pm), where a live show prefaces a night of dancing. The lineup is eclectic, from indie rock

bands to ska, blues, or Latin. The acoustics are fab, the seats slouchy velour, and the cocktails killer.

LIVE ROCK VENUES

There's something on every night of the week—rock, jazz, blues, trad, you name it—at **Whelan's** (25 Wexford St., tel. 01/478-0766, www.whelanslive.com, €10-23) and at its "sister" venue, the **Village** (26 Wexford St., tel. 01/475-8555, www.thevillagevenue.com). Featuring some high-profile performers (Damien Rice, Rodrigo y Gabriela, and the Flaming Lips just for starters), **Vicar Street** (58-59 Thomas St., tel. 01/454-5533, www.

vicarstreet.com, €20-35) is a cozy enough place to catch a show—with its main level dotted with round tables and theater-style balcony, it holds only 1,000.

The city's largest pop/rock venue is the **3Arena** (East Link Bridge, North Wall Quay, tel. 01/819-8888, www.3arena.ie, €40-70), which has hosted Prince, Pearl Jam, Diana Ross, Paul Simon, and many other greats over the years in this converted railway depot that seats up to 8,500.

The **Olympia Theatre** (72 Dame St., tel. 01/677-7744, www.olympia.ie) sometimes offers experimental or unusual drama (like, say, Shakespeare's *Twelfth Night* by a Russian company, in Russian), but it's better known for its eclectic range of concerts at the weekend. The Goo Goo Dolls, Lyle Lovett, Pentatonix, and Sufjan Stevens have all played here.

Another popular space for indie gigs is the **Button Factory** (Curved St., Temple Bar, tel. 01/670-9105, www.buttonfactory.ie), which turns into a nightclub with visiting DJs on Saturday evenings.

If you're not looking for a concert as such, another option is a dimly lit Northside pub, **Sin É** (which means "That's it"; 14-15 Ormond Quay, tel. 01/555-4036), which has live pop/indie/rock music nightly. There's no cover and the bartenders are nice as can be.

OTHER MUSIC VENUES

Venues abound for the listener with more "refined" tastes as well. The National Symphony Orchestra performs nearly every Friday night at the **National Concert Hall** (Earlsfort Terrace, just south of St. Stephen's Green, tel. 01/475-1666, www.nch.ie, 8pm, €10-25), and on other nights there are international bands and orchestras, jazz ensembles, and traditional music performances. Northside, the **Hugh Lane Municipal Gallery of Modern Art** (22 N. Parnell Sq., tel. 01/874-1903, www.hughlane.ie) also hosts classical concerts.

Serious jazz fans should check out **Jazz on the Terrace** (www.jazzontheterrace.com), which "represents Irish jazz artists abroad and international jazz artists in Ireland." There's

a listing of upcoming concerts, gigs, and festivals as well as links to local band websites.

Founded in 1951 in an attempt to preserve the country's musical traditions, **Comhaltas Ceoltóiri Éireann** (32 Belgrave Sq., Monkstown, tel. 01/280-0295, www.comhaltas.com, 9pm Mon.-Thurs. July-Aug., €10) offers a *seisiún* of top-notch singing and dancing along with the jigs, reels, and airs you'd hear in a pub session. Friday nights all year there's a "country set dance" starting at 9pm, where the €8 admission fee basically gets you an informal lesson (and a lot of *craic*). To get here, take the DART from Tara Street in the city center southbound to Seapoint Road.

THEATER AND CINEMA

Ireland's national theater, the **Abbey** (Lower Abbey St., tel. 01/878-7222, www.abbeytheatre.ie, €15-30) commissions new works from Irish playwrights and occasionally revives classic plays by O'Casey, Beckett, Behan, and many lesser-known dramatists. In addition to the rather out-of-date main theater, there's a smaller venue downstairs, **The Peacock**. Afterward, if you feel like chatting about the play with random strangers, the pub to head to is the **Flowing Tide** (9 Lower Abbey St., tel. 01/874-0842).

Other Dublin mainstays include the **Gaiety Theatre** (King St. S., tel. 01/677-1717, www.gaietytheatre.com, €17-55), opened in 1871, which puts on everything from Riverdance to Mother Goose to the more mainstream productions of the annual Dublin Theatre Festival; and the **Gate Theatre** (1 Cavendish Row, tel. 01/874-4045, www.gate-theatre.ie, €15-30), founded by the flamboyant duo of Hilton Edwards and Micheál MacLiammóir in 1928, which offers a range of Irish classics—from Oscar Wilde to Brian Friel—as well as quirkier works along the lines of Harold Pinter.

Dublin has **Bewley's** (www.bewleyscafetheatre.com) to thank for its venerable **lunchtime theater** tradition, and while the original café is closed for refurbishment the café-theater continues at the **Powerscourt Townhouse** (S. William St., tel. 01/671-7000, www.powerscourttheatre.com). The top-floor townhouse venue will likely continue its own program after Bewley's has reopened. Performances of one-act plays begin at 1pm Monday-Saturday. Tickets are €8-12, with a light lunch of vegetarian soup and brown bread an additional €4.

Opened by President Mary McAleese in 2002, **The Helix** (Collins Ave., Glasnevin, DCU campus, tel. 01/700-7000, www.thehe-lix.ie, €15-25) sports an art gallery and three separate venues for an eclectic (but fairly mainstream) calendar of plays and concerts. Take Dublin Bus #4, #11/A/B, #13/A, or #19 to Ballymun Road.

If you're more into the experimental side of things, see what's on at the **Tivoli Theatre** (135-136 Francis St., tel. 01/454-4472). The **Project Arts Centre** (39 E. Essex St., tel. 1850/260-027, www.projectartscentre.ie, €12-20) is another solid venue.

For arthouse and classic film screenings, the place to go is the **Irish Film Centre** (6 Eustace St., tel. 01/679-3477, www.ifi.ie, €9).

COMEDY

One of the best comedy venues in the city is the **Comedy Cellar** at the **International Bar** (23 Wicklow St., tel. 01/677-9250, www. dublincomedycellar.com, cover €8), which has shows on Tuesday and Wednesday nights starting at 9pm. As many as 10 jokemeisters will pass the evening, which lasts until clos-ing time.

FESTIVALS AND EVENTS

Naturally, Dublin's **St. Patrick's Festival** (tel. 01/676-3205, www.stpatricksfestival.ie) is Ireland's largest: The parade attracts as many as 1.5 million spectators, and there's everything from concerts to street theater to fireworks over the four days leading up to St. Paddy's Day. If you've come too early in the year for these festivities, there's always **Tradfest** (tel. 01/703-0700, www.temple-bartrad.com) at the end of January, show-casing the island's best traditional and folk musicians.

The **International Literature Festival Dublin** (tel. 01/222-5455, www.ilfdublin.com) brings an international roster of authors to town toward the end of May. The **Dublin City Soul Festival** (www.dublincitysoulfestival. ie) takes place in Merrion Square around the same time. Admission is by donation, which benefits the Musical Youth Foundation char-ity for at-risk children. Another fun option this month is the **Dublin Dance Festival** (tel. 01/679-8658, www.dublindancefestival. ie), which features modern and international styles rather than traditional Irish.

One of the biggest and most exciting events on the city's calendar, the **Dublin Theatre Festival** (tel. 01/677-8899, www.dublinthe-atrefestival.com, €10-35) takes place over the first two weeks in October. Productions are Irish and international, classic and avant-garde, and plays are put on at theaters all over the city. The well-established **Fringe Festival** (tel. 01/872-9016, www.fringefestival.com) offers comedy as well as more experimental work.

And the last weekend in October brings the **Dublin City Marathon** (tel. 01/623-2250, www.dublincitymarathon.ie), established in 1979 and sponsored by Adidas. This race is widely known as the "friendly marathon" for the especially supportive crowds it attracts.

For an exhaustive list of festivals in Dublin and elsewhere, check out **Entertainment.ie** (www.entertainment.ie/festivals).

Shopping

GRAFTON STREET

Though everyone thinks Grafton Street is the best place to shop in Dublin, if you take a walk down the crowded pedestrian street you'll notice that most of the shops are midscale women's clothing boutiques (and the same goes for the huge, glass-domed **St. Stephen's Green Shopping Centre** where Grafton meets the park). You can skip Grafton altogether if you're looking for souvenirs; head for **Powerscourt Townhouse** (59 S. William St., one block west of Grafton St. and signposted, tel. 01/679-4144), which includes several smallish but ultra-classy clothing and jewelry shops along with three quality cafés.

Just around the corner from Grafton Street is a spacious **Avoca Handweavers** shop (11-13 Suffolk St., tel. 01/677-4215, www.avoca.ie), full of delightful gifts—blankets, sweaters (colorful and modern, not the old-fashioned Aran kind), and jewelry, along with household items (aerodynamic spatulas, spice racks, hardcover cookbooks, and so forth) downstairs and a top-floor café, a nice spot for lunch or tea.

Another gem just off Grafton Street is **Ulysses Books** (10 Duke St., tel. 01/671-8676, www.rarebooks.ie), which rightly bills itself as "Ireland's leading antiquarian bookshop." Serious bibliophiles should note that its catalog is available online.

SOUTH GREAT GEORGES STREET

Full of delights is the **Market Arcade** on South Great Georges Street (at Exchequer), with shops and stalls of secondhand books and vintage clothing. Food stalls sell fudge, juices and smoothies, and olives-and-cheese type munchies perfect for picnicking in St. Stephen's Green.

SOUTH OF TRINITY COLLEGE

There is a wealth of sweater and knickknacky shops along Nassau Street, just east of Grafton Street and south of Trinity, but most of them aren't worth browsing. If it's an Aran sweater you're after, try **Cleo** (18 Kildare St., tel. 01/676-1421, www.cleo-ltd.com), which has

The Grafton Street flower vendors offer a bright note on even the rainiest days.

an exquisite selection (and, as at those shops selling machine-knit ganseys, you do get what you pay for). Then spend an hour or two at **Kilkenny Design** (5-6 Nassau St., tel. 01/677-7066, www.kilkennydesign.com), an upscale chain store renowned for its stock of cutting-edge Irish fashion, housewares, pottery, silverware, jewelry, sculpture, and framed art. There's also a fantastic upstairs café.

TEMPLE BAR

This area's better known for its tourist-trap pubs, but there are several shops worth

an extended browse. The Wilde-inspired **Gutter Bookshop** (Cow's Lane, tel. 01/679-9206, www.gutterbookshop.com) often launches books by local authors (check the website for an events calendar) and stocks a range of classic kids' toys. **Claddagh Records** (2 Cecelia St., tel. 01/677-0262, www.claddaghrecords.com) sells recordings of traditional music.

For funky clothing (new and secondhand), try **Fresh** (1 Crown Alley, tel. 01/671-8423, www.freshtemplebar.com) or **Lucy's Lounge** (11 Fownes St. Upper, tel. 01/677-4779).

Accommodations

Securing clean, relatively good-value accommodations in Dublin can sometimes be a challenge, particularly when there's a festival or other major event going on. Aside from the Irish Tourist Board seal of approval, your best bet is word of mouth (from someone who's stayed at the place in question within the last year). At any rate, be smart and book well in advance.

TEMPLE BAR

It's central, but accommodations in Temple Bar can be noisy. You probably don't want to stay in this neighborhood unless you're planning to be out pubbing and clubbing every night.

Despite an inefficient reception area and a rather inexperienced staff, ★ **Four Courts Hostel** (15-17 Merchants Quay, tel. 01/672-5839, www.fourcourtshostel.com, dorms €16-25, private rooms €28-36 pp) is still one of the best hostels in the city. The location is superb, security is adequate, the rooms are clean and the mattresses comfortable, and there are separate rooms for socializing and quiet pastimes. This place isn't quite as bohemian as it likes to think it is (there are cartoon murals along the staircase spouting random statistics—did you know that lefties live an average of nine years less than right-handers?—and

the impossibly buxom blonde carrying a U.S.A. tote bag annoys you more every time you pass her), but the Four Courts still attracts a fun crowd. Basic continental breakfast (i.e., vending-machine coffee is extra) is included in the price.

The top guesthouse/hotel in this neighborhood is the **Eliza Lodge** (23-24 Wellington Quay at Eustace St., tel. 01/671-8044, www.elizalodge.com, rooms €190-228, s €120), You can expect friendly and accommodating staff, mod but comfortable rooms (with in-room safes), and an outstanding breakfast in Elizablues, the downstairs restaurant. Some of the rooms have Jacuzzis and/or balconies overlooking the Liffey and Millennium Bridge.

If you want the convenience of a temporary Temple Bar address without any stress or fuss, the **Fleet Street Hotel** (19-20 Fleet St., tel. 01/670-8124, www.fleethoteltemple-bar.com, rooms €120-190, s €70-130) is a safe bet. Rooms are smallish but well appointed, and surprisingly quiet.

Owned by Bono and The Edge, **The Clarence** (6-8 Wellington Quay, tel. 01/407-0800, www.theclarence.ie, rooms €220-370, suites €700-900, penthouse suite €2,500) is unsurprisingly a favorite with celebrities. The individually designed rooms are luxuriously furnished with king-size beds with Egyptian cotton sheets, Shaker-style furniture, a CD and DVD collection, and laptop-sized safes. Check out the website for last-minute deals as low as €179. This hotel is definitely worth maxing out the credit card for.

CHRISTCHURCH

You can see the cathedral out your dorm room window at another of Dublin's most reliable hostels, **Kinlay House** (2/12 Lord Edward St., tel. 01/679-6644, www.kinlaydublin.ie, dorms €17-25, private rooms €30-40 pp). It's big, sure, but not overwhelmingly so. Atmospheric yet well-maintained, Kinlay House has ample kitchen and dining facilities, comfy beds, and professional staff. You can't go wrong booking a bed here.

AROUND TRINITY COLLEGE

Owned and run by the O'Neill family for more than 100 years, **O'Neill's Victorian Pub and Townhouse** (36-37 Pearse St., tel. 01/671-4074, www.oneillsdublin.com, rooms €125-200) offers comfortable new mattresses, hearty breakfasts, and fine period details in both the rooms and the delightful downstairs pub. Street noise from the DART passing nearby can be a problem, so this one is not recommended for light sleepers, and though the location is pretty central, just north of Trinity College, the immediate neighborhood is not especially nice.

Built in 1865 to house the Allied Irish Bank, the five-star **Westin Hotel** (Westmoreland St., tel. 01/645-1000, www.westin.com, rooms €320-600, package deals from €180 pp) retains its Victorian elegance in the reception areas, though the bedrooms are thoroughly modern: in-room massage treatments, laptop safes, minibars, private balconies, and so forth. The Westin is especially known for its trademarked "Heavenly Bed," featuring the most sumptuous bedclothes in all Dublin. Breakfast is extra (€25) unless you've booked a package deal.

AROUND ST. STEPHEN'S GREEN

You'll pay handsomely for the central location, but the range of top-quality accommodations near and around the green is well worth a splurge. Popular with families, ★ **Molesworth Court Suites** (35 Schoolhouse Ln., off Kildare St., tel. 01/676-4799, www.molesworthcourt.ie, 1/2-bedroom suite €180/200, 2/3-bedroom penthouse suite €260/320) offers swanky, spacious self-catering apartments in a stellar location with the attentive service of a five-star hotel. Each apartment comes equipped with CD and DVD players and a kitchenette.

If you appreciate finding mints on your pillow when you return to your hotel room, try the small, plush, and friendly ★ **Brooks Hotel** (Drury St., tel. 01/670-4000, www.brookshotel.ie, rooms €175-360), where you'll also find plasma TVs in the bedroom—*and* bathroom! The in-room foot spa and pillow menu (from which to select your pillow of choice) are other nice touches. Delicious full breakfasts are cooked to order and included in the room price.

One of Dublin's best guesthouses is **Number 31** (31 Leeson Close, Lower Leeson St., tel. 01/676-5011, www.number31.ie, rooms €200-280), with individually designed bedrooms in two wings: the retro-'50s coach house (with its sunken sitting room and mirrored bar) and the more staid Georgian townhouse. A top-notch breakfast menu, served in the conservatory, features homemade breads and salmon and kippers cooked to order. Top this off with a friendly staff, big comfy beds, and relaxing vibe, and you have a hotel with significant repeat business.

A five-star Hilton hotel, **The Conrad** (Earlsfort Terrace, tel. 01/602-8900, www.conradhotels.com, rooms €360-570) is conveniently located across the street from the National Concert Hall. Rooms are comfortable and well appointed, if a bit on the sterile business-class side, and feature bathrobes and slippers, minibar, HiFi with CD player, ergonomic desk chairs, and converter plugs in case you've forgotten yours.

The Shelbourne (27 St. Stephen's Green, tel. 01/663-4500, www.marriott.co.uk, rooms €330-470) offers incomparably elegant Georgian reception rooms, and the modern bedrooms (featuring down comforters, bathrobes and slippers, minibar, and suchlike) have historically inspired touches. The complimentary on-site parking is a major plus; you won't find this at other city five-star hotels. The full-size swimming pool's kinda nice to have, too.

NORTHSIDE

Accommodations north of the Liffey are generally less expensive. The An Óige **Dublin International Youth Hostel** (61 Mountjoy St., tel. 01/830-1766, www.anoige.ie, dorms €14-21, twins/triples €25-30 pp) is huge and therefore utterly chaotic with so many school groups coming and going, so obviously it isn't your number one choice. That said, the security is tight, the dorms and bathrooms are so clean they're sterile (not a bad thing, considering all the horror stories you hear about the hostels in this city), and continental breakfast in the lovely chapel-turned-dining hall is included in the price. You can also "upgrade" to a reasonably priced fry (€4.50 full Irish or vegetarian, porridge €1 extra).

Good-value budget B&Bs abound along Gardiner Street and Parnell Square, though you may want to choose the room-only option and go for breakfast downtown (especially if you're a vegetarian). These guesthouses are usually well-maintained Georgian townhouses, or a row of them renovated into one property. One option is the **Charles Stewart** (5-6 Parnell Sq., tel. 01/878-0350, www.charlesstewart.ie, €55 pp), which offers clean but slightly nondescript en suite rooms with television and hostess tray. The 24-hour reception is handy. Check the website for even better specials, usually at midweek. The rooms are homier at the **Marian Guesthouse** (21 Upper Gardiner St., tel. 01/874-4129, www.

marianguesthouse.ie, €25-40 pp, s €35-45), though not all are en suite. The full Irish fry will keep you going till dinnertime.

Another good option is **Adelphi** (67-68 Lower Gardiner St., tel. 01/836-3859, www. adelphidublin.com, €55-80 pp, s €60-230), with friendly staff and super-clean, freshly decorated rooms with large flatscreen TVs. Rates vary considerably based on what's going on in town, so it's a good idea to book well in advance; bedrooms with shared bath are quite a bit less expensive.

The **Morrison Hotel** (Lower Ormond Quay, tel. 01/887-2400, www.morrisonhotel. ie, rooms €325-590, penthouse €1,500) has a great riverside location. Rooms are high-tech, featuring CD players or iPod docking stations, and there's a safe and minibar in every room. Six "studio" rooms have flatscreen Apple computers and sunken bathtubs with leather head- and footrests. The hotel also has one of the most sophisticated bars in the city. The in-house spa offers Turkish baths, seaweed wraps, and aromatherapy.

BALLSBRIDGE

A wonderfully atmospheric hotel with an ever-present sense of history, the oldest section of ★ **The Schoolhouse Hotel** (2-8 Northumberland Rd., tel. 01/667-5014, www. schoolhousehotel.com, rooms €160-230) served as St. Stephen's Parochial School beginning in 1861, and you can see stray bullet holes in the wall of the hotel pub that date to the Easter Rising. The school closed its doors in 1969 and lay empty until 1997, when hotel renovations commenced. The food's fairly good for hotel fare, and the bedrooms are decorated with William Morris reproduction wallpaper to maintain the Victorian flavor. Even if you can't afford to stay here, it's well worth finding your way here for a pint in the gorgeously old-fashioned and very cozy bar, with its soaring pitched wooden ceiling, loft seating area, and cheerful open fire. The hotel is right by the Grand Canal, a 20-minute walk east of Merrion Square.

OUTSIDE THE CITY CENTER

You'll often find better value for your money outside the city center. Here are a few top guesthouses in Drumcondra and Glasnevin, both a couple kilometers north of town.

A very good budget guesthouse is tidy red-brick **Ashling House** (168 Drumcondra Rd. Upper, tel. 01/837-5432, www.ashlinghouse. ie, €24-45 pp, s €40-74), with clean, modern, no-frills rooms and an add-on continental breakfast option. Ask for a room at the back of the house for a quieter night's sleep. The more upscale **Annandale House** (84 Grace Park Rd., Drumcondra, tel. 01/804-0822, www.annandalebnb.com, €40-60 pp) is recommended for its bright, homey rooms. In fine weather you can take your breakfast (with homemade jam and very good coffee) in the lovely garden out back. These two Drumcondra guesthouses are good options if you're planning on a match at Croke Park, which is only 2.5 kilometers away.

Convenient for a morning stroll through the National Botanic Gardens, **Botanic View** (25 Botanic Ave. at Iona Rd., Glasnevin, tel. 01/860-0195, www.botanicview.com, €40-60 pp, s €50-60) offers immaculate (if a bit pink and frilly) rooms with cable television, a friendly and helpful proprietor, and the full fry at the breakfast table. Take Dublin Bus #13, #19/A, or #83; otherwise it's a brisk 35-minute walk to/from the city center. Nearby **Egan's** (7 Iona Park, Glasnevin, tel. 01/830-3611, www.eganshouse.ie, €50-60 pp, s €75-100) is a bit more upscale, with quaint and tranquil rooms, though the buffet breakfast is an additional €10.

Information and Services

INFORMATION

As you would expect, Dublin's central **tourist office** (25 Suffolk St., tel. 01/884-7871, www.visitdublin.com, 9am-5:30pm Mon.-Sat., 10:30am-3pm Sun.)—which does not accept inquiries by phone—is so busy you could spend all afternoon in line. There is a **secondary office** at 14 Upper O'Connell Street (tel. 01/605-7700, 9am-5pm Mon.-Sat.). You're best off just stopping by to pick up flyers and free listings of upcoming events; *inDublin* (www.indublin.ie) is a great free weekly magazine you can find here or in many hostels and cafés.

Other sources for entertainment info are the twice-monthly *Dublin Event Guide* (www.dublineventguide.com) and the *Evening Herald* (along with its freebie sister paper, the *Herald AM,* www.herald.ie), which is published every day but Sunday.

Dublin's city-center **public library** (Ilac Shopping Centre, Henry St., tel. 01/873-4333, www.dublincitypubliclibraries.ie, 10am-8pm Mon.-Thurs., 10am-5pm Fri.-Sat.) is on the Northside, two blocks west of O'Connell Street.

SERVICES

Banks

Bureaux de change abound in the city center, but the commission charges are lowest at the banks: **Bank of Ireland** (2 College Green or 6 Lower O'Connell St.), **AIB** (40-41 Westmoreland St. or 1-3 Lower Baggot St.), or **Ulster Bank** (33 College Green or George's Quay).

Embassies

The **U.S. Embassy** (42 Elgin Rd., Ballsbridge, tel. 01/668-8777, http://dublin.usembassy.gov) is on Dublin Bus routes #4, #5, #7, #7A, #8, #45, #63, and #84 to Lansdowne Road. The **Canadian Embassy** (65/68 St. Stephen's Green, 4th fl., tel. 01/417-4100, www.dfait-maeci.gc.ca) is more conveniently located. For a complete embassy listing, visit the Irish **Department of Foreign Affairs** online (http://foreignaffairs.gov.ie/embassies).

Emergency and Medical Services

Dial 999 for an emergency. Crime against tourists is relatively rare, though pickpocketing is a problem. Ring the 24-hour **Tourist Victim Support Service** (tel. 01/478-5295 or freephone tel. 1800/661-771) if you need any assistance. The fastest way to reach the Garda (the Irish police) is by dialing 999, which will connect you with the Command and Control center at Harcourt Square (tel. 01/475-5555).

Hospitals in the city center include **St. James'** (James St., tel. 01/453-7941, just south of Heuston Station and the Guinness Storehouse) and **Mater Miserichordiae** (Eccles St., between Berkeley Rd. and Dorset St., north of Parnell Sq., tel. 01/830-1122).

Both branches of **O'Connell's Pharmacy** (21 Grafton St., tel. 01/679-0467, and 55-56 O'Connell St., tel. 01/873-0427) stay open until 10pm daily.

Left Luggage

You can leave that ungainly suitcase in a coin-operated locker at **Busáras** (Store St., 7am-10:30pm daily, €4-10 for 24 hours). Better yet, for around €6, **Connolly** (east side, north of the Liffey at Amiens St., tel. 01/836-6222, 7am-10pm Mon.-Sat., 8am-10pm Sun.) and **Heuston** (west side, Victoria Quay, same phone and hours) train stations also offer locker rooms; a (usually helpful and very chipper) attendant will squeeze your bag into the smallest locker possible to save you a couple bob.

Transportation

GETTING THERE

Dublin is 217 kilometers east of Galway on the M6, 166 kilometers south of Belfast on the M1, and 256 kilometers northeast of Cork City on the M8.

Air

Flights depart **Dublin International Airport** (tel. 01/814-1111, www.dublinairport.com) for more than 140 destinations in Europe, Asia, and North America. The most commonly traveled airlines from the United States and Canada are **United Airlines** (tel. 1890/925-252, www.united.com), **Aer Lingus** (tel. 1800/474-7424 from the U.S. and Canada, tel. 01/886-8888 for reservations, tel. 01/886-6705 for departures/arrivals, www.aerlingus.com), **Air Canada** (tel. 1800/709-900, www.aircanada.ca), and **American Airlines** (tel. 01/602-0550, www.aa.com).

An alternative to **British Airways** (tel. 1800/626-747, www.britishairways.com) is the most popular budget airline to Britain and mainland Europe, **Ryanair** (tel. 0818/303-030, www.ryanair.ie), which offers daily service from Berlin (Schonefeld), Birmingham, London (Gatwick, Luton, and Stansted), Edinburgh, Glasgow (Prestwick), Paris (Beauvais), Venice (Treviso), Milan (Orio al Serio), Rome (Ciampino), and other destinations.

Car-rental agencies on the arrivals hall lower level include **Europcar** (tel. 01/812-0410, www.europcar.ie), **Avis** (tel. 01/605-7500, www.avis.ie), and **Budget** (tel. 01/844-5150, www.budget.ie).

A **left luggage service** (tel. 01/814-4633, www.greencaps.ie, 5am-11pm daily) will run you €8-12 per day per item.

Train

Iarnrod Éireann, also known as **Irish Rail** (tel. 01/836-6222, www.irishrail.ie) operates from **Connolly** (east side, north of the Liffey at Amiens St., points north) and **Heuston** (west side, Victoria Quay, points west and south); the stations are linked by the Luas light rail line. Traveling by train is much more expensive than by bus, but the trip is also far more comfortable. Round-trip (or "return") tickets are always a much better value, especially if purchased online.

If you're traveling a lot by train, pick up either a **Trekker Pass** (€110 for four consecutive days) or an **Explorer Pass** (€160 for five days' travel in a 15-day period); these passes are available for purchase only at the ticket desks at Connolly and Heuston Stations.

Bus

Busáras (Store St., tel. 01/836-6111, www. buseireann.ie), the central bus depot, can take you anywhere you need to go via **Bus Éireann.** Buses depart regularly for Drogheda and Belfast (#1), Kilkenny, Cahir, and Cork (#7, or #8 for Cork via Cashel), Limerick and Ennis (#12), Tralee (via Limerick, #13), Killarney (#14), Athlone and Galway (#20), Westport (via Athlone, #21), Sligo (#23), Donegal (#30), and Derry (#33).

This none-too-pleasant station is made even more chaotic by frequent construction work; it's also swarming with pickpockets, so summon all your street smarts. If you plan to do three or more days of bus travel during your holiday, pick up an **Open Road** pass at the central ticket office (3 days' travel over a 6-day period €60, each additional day €16.50).

Citylink (tel. 01/626-6888, www.citylink. ie, at least 14/day daily, single/return €14/18) offers frequent Galway-Dublin service, continuing to the airport. The Dublin city stop is at Burgh Quay, south of the Liffey, one block north of Trinity College. Citylink prices are comparable to Bus Éireann's, but the buses are newer and more comfortable (and the drivers are friendlier). Another option is Galway-based **GoBus** (tel. 091/564-600, www.gobus. ie), which will get you from Dublin to Galway (single/return €13/23 from the city center, €18/28 from the airport) or Cork (€17/27 from the city center, €20/30 from the airport), with at least five departures daily in each direction. The bus picks up at Burgh Quay for Galway and Busáras for Cork. Save a euro by booking online.

Boat

Reach Dublin by ferry from Liverpool or Holyhead. For Liverpool, take **P&O Irish Sea Ferries** (tel. 01/407-3434, www.poirishsea.com, 2/day Tues.-Sun., 1/day Mon., crossing 7.5-8 hours, car and driver €150-185, additional passengers €22-37), which does not carry pedestrians. Two meals are included in the fare. The Holyhead-Dublin route is served by **Irish Ferries** (tel. 01/638-3333, www.irishferries.com, 2/day daily, crossing 1.75 hours, car and driver €89, additional adult €25, pedestrians €27). It is also possible to travel between Dublin and the Isle of Man via **Steam Packet** (tel. 1800/805-055, www. steam-packet.com, usually 2/day daily, crossing 2.75 hours, fare €80-260 for car and two passengers, pedestrians €25).

Ferries pull into the **Ferryport Terminal** (Alexandra Rd., tel. 01/855-2222) at North Wall, and there are Bus Éireann shuttles to meet every incoming boat (fare €3). Buses leave Busáras for the ferry terminal 75 minutes before scheduled departures.

GETTING AROUND

The city center is easily walkable, but if you're planning to spend a good bit of time traipsing around the city outskirts, you will probably want to pick up a **Leap visitor card** (www. leapcard.ie, €19.50), a three-day transit pass valid on the Luas light rail, the DART (within County Dublin), and all Dublin Bus and Airlink buses (excluding day tours). Purchase a Leap ticket at the Dublin airport, either at the information desk or at the Spar grocery shop in the arrivals hall. The card expires 72 hours after the first time you use it.

To and from the Airport

The airport is off the M1 12 kilometers north of Dublin, and parking in the short-term lot costs €3/hour.

Dublin Bus (tel. 01/873-4222) operates a frequent **Airlink** service (#748) from the street directly outside the arrivals hall; buy a ticket (single/return €6/10) at the kiosk or on board (with exact change) and look out for the bright green-and-blue double-decker. The bus will take you to O'Connell Street, Busáras, and Connolly and Heuston Stations. The ride is more comfortable on **Aircoach** (tel. 01/844-7118, www.aircoach.ie, departures from O'Connell St. every 15 minutes, every 30 minutes midnight-5am, single/return fare €7/12), which offers 24-hour service. **Citylink** (tel. 01/626-6888, www.citylink.ie, at least 14/day daily, single/monthly return ticket €19/29) offers a frequent Dublin Airport-Galway coach service.

A taxi to or from the airport will run you €36-40.

Train

Dublin's spiffy light rail system, **Luas** (free-phone tel. 1800/300-604, www.luas.ie, departures every 5-10 minutes 7am-10pm, runs until 12:30am Sat. and 11:30pm Sun., fare within city-center zone €1.90), whisks commuters in from the burbs, but it's also useful for tourists looking to get from Heuston to Connolly Station or any point in between (including the National Museum at Collins Barracks, the Four Courts, Abbey Street, and Busáras). Buy a ticket at the bus stop kiosk before boarding.

For travel outside the city, you'll want to take the **DART,** or Dublin Area Rapid Transit (tel. 01/805-4288, www.dart.ie, fares usually under €10), which is much faster than the bus. There is frequent service (2-3 trains hourly) to Drogheda in County Louth (from Connolly, with other routes to Malahide and Howth), Kildare (from Heuston), or Dun Laoghaire, Killiney, Bray, and Greystones (from Pearse or Connolly).

Bus

For Kilmainham Jail, Phoenix Park, the National Botanic Gardens, and other attractions on the city fringe, take **Dublin Bus** (tel. 01/873-4222, www.dublinbus.ie, single ticket to most destinations under €3). Maps and departure times (generally three or more per hour during the day) are posted at each stop.

Exact change is not necessary, though notes are not accepted and if you overpay you won't get change from the driver. You can redeem your passenger change receipt (bring the original ticket as well) at the Dublin Bus office at 59 Upper O'Connell Street.

The Dublin Bus **Airlink** service is the second-least expensive way to get to the airport (#748, fare €6, frequent departures from Ormond Quay, O'Connell St., Busáras, and Connolly and Heuston Stations, 30-minute trip). The least expensive way is to take the local bus (#16A from O'Connell St. or #41 from Lower Abbey St., 3/hour, fare €2.70, 40-minute trip).

Car

It's possible to rent a car without returning to the airport. Rental agencies with city center branches include **Europcar** (Baggot St. Bridge, tel. 01/614-2800, www.europcar.ie), **Dan Dooley** (42 Westland Row, tel. 01/677-2733, www.dan-dooley.ie), and **Hertz** (149 Upper Leeson St., tel. 01/660-2255, www.hertz.ie).

That said, pick up the rental only when you're ready to leave the city, as driving in Dublin can be confusing and stressful even for natives. Pay-and-display parking in the city center will run you €2.90/hour.

Bicycle

With so much traffic and construction work going on, getting around by bike can be pretty risky; don't forget to wear your helmet. It's also pricier to rent a bike (around €20/120 per day/week, plus a €100-200 deposit) than elsewhere in the country. Try **Irish Cycling Safaris** at the Belfield Bike Shop (near the running track on the University College Dublin campus, on Dublin Bus routes #3, #10, and #11B from O'Connell St., tel. 01/716-1697, www.cyclingsafaris.com, until 6pm weekdays and 10am-2pm Sat.), which also offers weeklong themed cycling trips, or **Cycleways** (185-186 Parnell St., tel. 01/873-4748, www.cycleways.com, until 6pm Mon.-Sat., 8pm Thurs.).

Taxi

There are 79 **taxi ranks** (www.taxi.ie) all over the city, most of which operate 24 hours a day. Between the hours of 8pm and 6am, bus lanes at the following locations also serve as taxi ranks: Dame Street, outside the Bank of Ireland, near Trinity but facing Christchurch; Merrion Row, near St. Stephen's Green; Dawson Street, opposite the Mansion House; and, Northside, on Talbot Street, on the O'Connell Street side of the railway bridge.

Alternatively, ring **National Radio Cabs** (tel. 01/677-2222) or **City Cabs** (tel. 01/872-2688). There are surcharges galore across the board: late-night pickups, phone bookings, luggage handling per bag (even if you load it yourself), and extra passengers.

Vicinity of Dublin City

NORTH OF DUBLIN CITY
Howth

A charming fishing village on a small peninsula north of the city, Howth (rhymes with "both," from the Norse for "headland"; Bínn Eádáir, "Hill of Eadair," after a chieftain of the mythical Tuatha de Danann) makes a fine afternoon excursion, what with its rhododendron gardens and spooky, poorly tended 14th-century abbey ruins overlooking the harbor. There's also a bracing six-kilometer **cliff walk** clearly signposted from the train station, which will take you 1.5-2.5 hours depending on the length of the route you choose.

Howth Castle has remained in the same family, the St. Lawrences and their descendants, for more than 800 years. The current structure dates from 1564 and has been restored and rebuilt many times since then. The most interesting story about this castle regards the pirate queen Grace O'Malley, who dropped by for dinner once in 1575 only to be snubbed by Christopher St. Lawrence. O'Malley promptly kidnapped his son and heir and sailed him back to Mayo. (He was eventually returned to his family, but not before the St. Lawrences had much humbled themselves.) Though the castle is not open to the public (they do make exceptions for educational groups), their **cookery school** (www.

the rhododendron gardens at Howth Castle, north of Dublin City

Vicinity of Dublin City

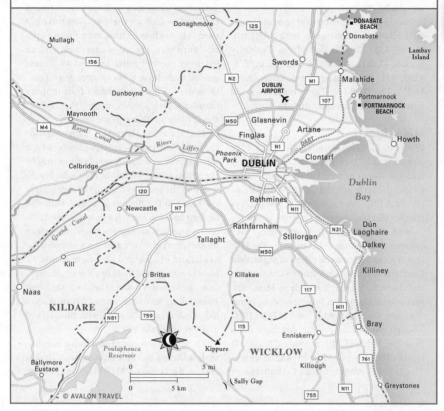

howthcastlecookeryschool.ie) offers classes. The Howth Castle **gardens** are open in summer (try to go in May or June when the rhododendrons are in bloom), and on the grounds is a prehistoric dolmen known as **Aideen's Grave** (Aideen being the wife of a dead warrior, a little legend attached to the formation much later on). Access to the rhododendron gardens is via the Deer Park Hotel and Golf Course.

To get here, make a right out of the DART station and cross the street, following the main road for about five minutes. Make a left for the Deer Park Hotel entrance (passing the Anglican St. Mary's Church with its small memorial garden), and after another five minutes you'll see the castle on the right (the turnoff is here for a rather ramshackle "transport museum" as well). It's another 10-minute walk straight on for the hotel. Once there, walk along the right side of the building, past the bar, and you'll see a clearly trodden path leading you into the woods (where the rhododendrons are). A short climb up this secret-gardenesque path will afford you a phenomenal view over Dublin Bay. The dolmen is on the wooded path to the fourth tee.

Feeling peckish? Instead of risking the hotel food, try the grub at the dimly lighted, atmospheric **Abbey Tavern** (Abbey St., tel. 01/839-0307, www.abbeytavern.ie, food served 12:30pm-10pm daily, lunch €12-28).

Dinner in the upstairs restaurant is over-priced, but the simple, reasonably priced pub lunches hit the spot.

Howth is 16 kilometers northeast of Dublin on the R105, and is served by both **DART** (tel. 01/805-4288, 2/hour daily from Connolly Station, €1.60) and **Dublin Bus** (tel. 01/873-4222, #31, 3/hour daily from Eden Quay, €1.55). The DART will get you there in 20 minutes, but the bus takes nigh an hour.

Malahide

With its pleasant promenade, Blue Flag strand, shady tree-lined avenue, and hip boutiques—not to mention the second-most haunted castle on the island—Malahide (Mullach Íde, "Promontory of St. Ita") makes another pleasant day trip.

With the exception of one lord's temporary eviction at the hands of Cromwell in the 17th century, the Talbot family lived at **Malahide Castle & Gardens** (tel. 01/846-2184, www.malahidecastle.com, 10am-5pm Mon.-Sat. year-round, 10am-6pm Sun. Apr.-Sept., 11am-5pm Sun. Oct.-Mar., €12) from 1174 to 1976. Though most of the present structure dates from the 17th and 18th centuries, Malahide retains the title of oldest inhabited castle. The Talbots converted from Catholicism in 1779, and the exquisitely carved Flemish panels in the Oak Room—depicting various Old Testament tales along with the Coronation of the Virgin—indicate that the room was once used as their chapel. Other rooms feature period furniture, rococo plasterwork, and an extensive portrait collection, and 35-minute guided tours leave every quarter of an hour. Outside, the botanic gardens feature more than 4,500 plant species, many of them exotic; this is a fine spot for a picnic lunch.

The Malahide Historical Society claims the castle houses at least five ghosts (whose sightings are well documented). Some may be the spirits of the 14 Talbot men who breakfasted in the banquet hall on the morning of the Battle of the Boyne—a meal destined to be their last. Another wraith is that of a 15th-century sentry named Puck who fell asleep on duty, thus allowing an enemy to storm the castle, and who hanged himself in shame; he hasn't been spotted in 30 or so years, though. (An alternate version of the story says that Puck fell in love with one of his mistress's lady visitors, and did away with himself out of unrequited love.)

There's a new **Avoca food hall** and mini-mall adjacent to the castle, or you have a choice of eateries on Malahide's main drag.

Malahide Castle

For excellent Greek and Cypriot victuals, try **Cape Greko** (Unit 1, 1st floor, New St., tel. 01/845-6288, www.capegreko.ie, 5pm-11pm Mon., noon-11pm Tues.-Thurs., noon-midnight Fri.-Sat., noon-10pm Sun., lunch €9-15, dinner €15-25). The service is as quick and polite as the food is delish, and veggie-lovers are well-catered for.

Malahide is 15 kilometers north of Dublin on the R107. Get there via **DART** (tel. 01/805-4288, 2/hour daily from Connolly Station, single/return fare €3.25/6.15). **Dublin Bus** service (tel. 01/873-4222, #32A, 9-11/day daily from Eden Quay, or 3/hour daily on #42 from Lower Abbey St., €3.30) is much slower (the DART journey is 22 minutes, but the bus takes nearly an hour).

SOUTH OF DUBLIN CITY
Dún Laoghaire

Thirteen kilometers south of the city, Dún Laoghaire ("dun LEER-y") is an uneasy mix of seaside resort and industrial harbor. The town has been hyped as a lower-cost alternative regarding food and accommodations, but this seems a little like going to Paris to dine on PB&J. Most folks take the DART down here to visit the **James Joyce Tower & Museum** (1 km east of town in Sandycove, signposted on the R119, tel. 01/280-9265,

10am-5pm Mon.-Sat. and 2pm-6pm Sun. Feb.-Oct., free), housed in a martello tower that features in the opening scene of Joyce's best-known work, *Ulysses*. The 22-year-old Joyce spent just a week here in August 1904 before leaving for Italy to live the life of a literary expat (teaching English, naturally) with future bride Nora Barnacle. On the seaside of the tower is a swimming hole, known as the **Forty Foot Pool** (named not for height, but for the 40th Regiment of the British Army stationed at the tower above). In years gone by the pool was forbidden to women, as men liked to bathe there in the nude. Today, alas, there are few exhibitionists carrying on the tradition.

Another reason to come to Dún Laoghaire is if you're leaving the country by ferry. The **Stena Line** (tel. 01/204-7777 or 01/204-7799 for timetable, www.stenaline.ie, 4/day daily, 2-hour trip, advance reservations recommended, single fare €164-210) links Dún Laoghaire with Holyhead in North Wales. Book online for the best rates.

Dún Laoghaire is 13 kilometers south of Dublin on the R118 coastal road. The **DART** (tel. 01/805-4288, 3-4/hour daily, get off at Sandycove for the Joyce museum, single/daily return €3.25/6.15) can get you down here in 20 minutes or less from Pearse Station.

Around Dublin

Meath 85   Wicklow 106
Louth 97   Kildare 117

Dublin's surrounding counties may be sampled by coach tour easily enough, but these areas are so rich in history—and offer such a lovely respite from the capital's hectic pace—that you'll be glad you decided on an extended exploration.

Wedged between Dublin and Northern Ireland on the east coast, Meath (An Mhí, "The Middle") and Louth (An Lú, "The Least") boast some of the island's most important megalithic and early Christian remains. Newgrange, a Neolithic passage tomb that predates the pyramids at Giza, is arguably the country's most popular tourist attraction, but there are also lesser-known sites (equally worthwhile) in Meath and Louth.

Counties Wicklow (Cill Mhantáin, "Church of Mantáin," a disciple of Patrick) and Kildare (Cill Dara, "Church of the Oak Wood"), on the other hand, are something of a study in contrasts. Half an hour due south of Dublin and you're in another world entirely, verdant hills and winding backroads: That's Wicklow, aptly nicknamed the "Garden of Ireland." Half an hour west and you're in Kildare, marked by a chain of commuter suburbs and flat green pastures—racetrack country.

These counties do, of course, have more than their share of humdrum commuter suburbs. Navan and Dundalk in particular are bulging with anonymous cookie-cutter estates to meet the overwhelming demand for affordable housing within an hour or so of Dublin. Keep on driving, as the few sights in these towns aren't all that worthwhile.

HISTORY

Though Ireland has more than 1,200 megalithic tombs (in varying states of preservation, of course), archaeologists have learned the most about everyday life in the Stone Age from the sites of County Meath. From remains at Brú na Bóinne—the megalithic funerary complex of which Newgrange is the centerpiece of sorts—we know plenty more than what they ate (livestock, nuts, wheat, and barley). They "cleaned" their teeth with soot, cleared tracts of forest for growing grain and raising animals brought over from England,

Look for ★ to find recommended
sights, activities, dining, and lodging.

Highlights

★ **Brú na Bóinne:** At this funerary complex, Newgrange, one of Europe's most famous Stone Age monuments, and two other tombs, Knowth and Dowth, attract as many as 200,000 yearly visitors, who admire their astonishing architecture and striking Neolithic art (page 85).

★ **The Hill of Tara:** Go for an outdoor guided tour of the legendary seat of the High Kings of Ireland (page 89).

★ **Loughcrew Cairns:** Set in a stunning hilltop location, these spooky Stone Age cairns are nicknamed the "Hills of the Witch" (page 90).

★ **Trim Castle:** The huge cruciform keep of this mighty Anglo-Norman fortress has been restored with vertiginous catwalks and detailed historical models, but what really makes Trim worth your while is the excellent guided tour (page 94).

★ **Monasterboice:** Along with the remains of a round tower and two small churches, this 6th-century monastic site features the two most magnificent high crosses in all Ireland (page 102).

★ **Powerscourt House and Gardens:** Exquisitely manicured Italianate gardens and statuary, leisurely walking trails, gourmet eats, retail therapy—it's all here (page 106).

★ **The Wicklow Way:** Hike all or part of this 132-kilometer trail from southern Dublin through the Wicklow Mountains and placid green farmlands north of Carlow (page 109).

★ **Glendalough:** Nestled in the gorse-dotted

hills of the Wicklow Mountains National Park around two placid lakes, this fantastic 6th-century monastic site was once one of Ireland's most important centers of learning (page 110).

★ **Glenmalure:** The country's longest glacial valley is far removed from the manicured gardens Wicklow is renowned for, but this quiet, utterly remote locale has an appeal all its own (page 113).

Around Dublin

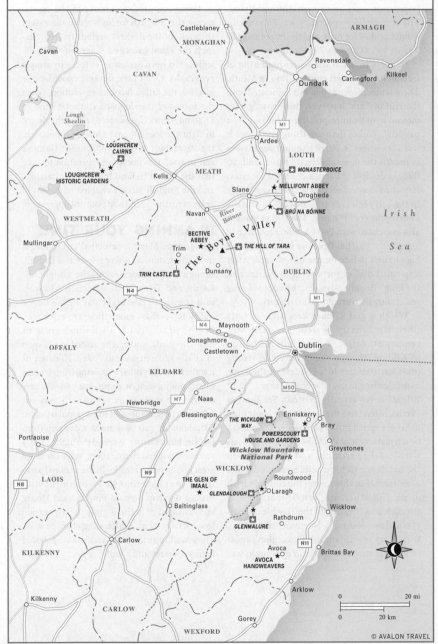

ARMAGH

MONAGHAN

Castleblaney

Cavan

CAVAN

Ravensdale

Kilkeel

Carlingford

Dundalk

Lough
Sheelin

LOUGHCREW
CAIRNS

M1

Ardee

LOUTH

LOUGHCREW
HISTORIC GARDENS

Kells

MEATH

MONASTERBOICE

Slane

MELLIFONT ABBEY

Drogheda

WESTMEATH

Navan

River
Bóinne

BRÚ NA BÓINNE

Irish

Mullingar

BECTIVE
ABBEY

The Boyne Valley

THE HILL OF TARA

Sea

Trim

DUBLIN

N4

TRIM CASTLE

Dunsany

OFFALY

M4

Maynooth

Donaghmore

Castletown

Dublin

KILDARE

M50

Newbridge

M7

Naas

Blessington

THE WICKLOW
WAY

Enniskerry

Bray

POWERSCOURT
HOUSE AND GARDENS

Portlaoise

Wicklow Mountains
National Park

Greystones

LAOIS

N9

WICKLOW

THE GLEN OF
IMAAL

Roundwood

GLENDALOUGH

Laragh

Baltinglass

Wicklow

N8

Rathdrum

GLENMALURE

KILKENNY

Carlow

Avoca

N11

Brittas Bay

AVOCA
HANDWEAVERS

Kilkenny

Arklow

0   20 mi

CARLOW

0   20 km

Gorey

WEXFORD

© AVALON TRAVEL

and decorated their pottery and tomb walls with elegant tri-spiraling motifs. And the population stats are downright horrifying: The average life expectancy was 26 years for women and 29 for men, and the infant mortality rate was as high as 75 percent.

In pre-Christian times the high king of Ireland had his royal court at Tara in Meath. There is more legend than fact associated with the Hill of Tara, however; this broad grassy mound with its unimpressive ruins is more a national symbol than anything else, since it was Tara where St. Patrick sought permission to preach the new religion on this island. St. Buite, a disciple of Patrick, founded a monastery at Monasterboice near the River Boyne in the early 6th century. "Boyne" is actually a corruption of his name. The Hill of Slane is also associated with Patrick, who according to legend lit a paschal fire here in view of King Laoghaire's palace on the hill of Tara. After a spiritual duel of sorts between Patrick and the king's druidic advisors, the enraged king reluctantly converted to Christianity.

Wicklow and Kildare were hives of early Christian activity as well. The early 6th-century St. Brigid is the unofficial patron of Kildare, though the county had strong pre-Christian ties to a goddess of the same name (leading many to speculate that a "Saint Brigid" never actually existed). Yet another Patrick legend has the saint, at the beginning of his evangelist mission, desiring to land on a beach just south of Wicklow Town. The locals were less than friendly, and in a scuffle on the beach one of his disciples, Mantáin, lost a few teeth. For this reason the county's Irish name, Cill Mhantáin, can be more loosely translated as "Church of the Toothless One." ("Wicklow" is Anglo-Norman, and has no such story to explain it.) The region's most important monastic site, Glendalough, was founded in the 6th century as well, by the hermit St. Kevin.

These counties' proximity to the capital meant that English forces were omnipresent throughout the darkest periods in Irish history; the Penal Laws and other anti-Catholic legislation were easiest to enforce by simple geography. One of the darkest epochs came in 1690, the failed Jacobite revolution, when the forces of the deposed Catholic king of England, James II, assembled along the Boyne to fight the Parliament's choice of monarch, the Protestant William of Orange (James's son-in-law). It is not an exaggeration to state that the fate of Ireland hung in the balance, and the English victory enabled hundreds of years of further social and political oppression.

PLANNING YOUR TIME

Newgrange, Meath's principal attraction, is most often done as a day trip out of Dublin, though there's more here—the Loughcrew Cairns and Trim Castle especially—to warrant at least an overnight stay in the Boyne Valley. It is perhaps most efficient to experience Louth's sights—nearly all of which are in or near Drogheda, and can be visited in the span of a day—while en route to Belfast. Kildare's attractions can be visited in passing from Dublin to any points west or south, but you will certainly want to linger in Wicklow. The county's most important (and most popular) sight, Glendalough, can be done in a day trip from Dublin, but it's better to spend the night; ideally you should spend two or three, since there are great hiking opportunities in the national park. If you don't have time for an overnight visit, make a day trip here, to Powerscourt House and Gardens, or to the slightly shabby seaside town of Bray for an exhilarating cliffside walk. Those walking the whole Wicklow Way should bank on a week and a half.

Meath

Meath is often referred to as "The Royal County," since the pre-Christian seat of the high kings was here, on the Hill of Tara. Originally there were five Irish provinces—Leinster, Munster, Connaught, Ulster, and Meath—but the fifth and smallest was subsumed into Leinster by an Act of Parliament under Henry VIII in 1543, which formed two new counties, Meath and Westmeath.

Newgrange and the other Boyne Valley sights can be done in a day tour out of Dublin, but it's far better to base yourself in Trim or Slane and take your time. And if you're interested in the archaeology but can't stand crowds (you'll find 'em at Newgrange even in winter), consider visiting the spooky, yet-to-be-excavated Loughcrew Cairns instead of Brú na Bóinne. The views from those "hills of the witch" will literally take your breath away.

THE BOYNE VALLEY

From superstitious Stone Age farming communities to the seat of royal power, home of saints and scholars and a bloody battle for the English throne: The history of the Boyne River valley is even richer than the soil. A day tour out of Dublin, such as the one offered by **Mary Gibbons Tours** (tel. 01/283-9973, www.newgrangetours.com, departs the Dublin tourist office on Suffolk St. at 10:15am Mon.-Sat., returning at 4:30pm, €35, includes admission fees), will take you to Brú na Bóinne, the Hill of Tara, and the Battle of the Boyne site. **Bus Éireann** also offers a **Newgrange and Boyne Valley tour,** though it doesn't run daily (Busáras, Store St., tel. 01/836-6111, www.buseireann. ie, departs bus station 10am on Thurs. and Sat. and returns at 5:45pm, €29, includes admission fees).

Locally, the village of Slane makes a very pleasant base for visiting the Boyne Valley sights, though Trim and Drogheda are good options as well.

★ Brú na Bóinne

Opened in 1997, the very informative **Brú na Bóinne Visitor Centre** (2 km west of Donore on Staleen Rd., clearly signposted from Drogheda/M1 and Slane/N2, tel. 041/988-0300, www.worldheritageireland.ie or www. newgrange.com, €3 exhibition only, €6 with Newgrange, €5 with Knowth, €11 combo ticket) is your access point (via quick shuttle bus ride) for three of Europe's most important prehistoric burial chambers: Newgrange, the best-known and most-visited, as well as Knowth and Dowth, the latter of which has yet to be excavated. (It's also the only monument you can check out without going through the visitors center.) Newgrange and the interpretive center are open year-round (9:30am-5:30pm daily Mar.-Apr. and Oct., 9am-6:30pm daily in May, 9am-7pm daily June-Sept., 9:30am-5pm Nov.-Feb.); Knowth is open the same hours but only late March through October. On this UNESCO World Heritage Site there are more than 90 monuments and earthworks in all.

You need only to look at the lush river valley around you to understand why the first Neolithic farmers chose to settle here between 3800 and 3400 BC. The Boyne provided rich soil, fish, drinking water, and a means of transport, and the surrounding forests provided plenty of timber. The river attained spiritual significance as well, a symbol in their pagan religion of the sometimes-hazy boundary between the "real" and "other" worlds.

These elaborately constructed megalithic passage tombs were the product of that belief, and the 40 burial mounds at Brú na Bóinne are the first signs of human activity in this region. **Newgrange** (Sí an Bhrú) was built between 3300 and 2900 BC, making it 500 years older than the Giza pyramids and a thousand years older than Stonehenge. This type of

Meath and Louth

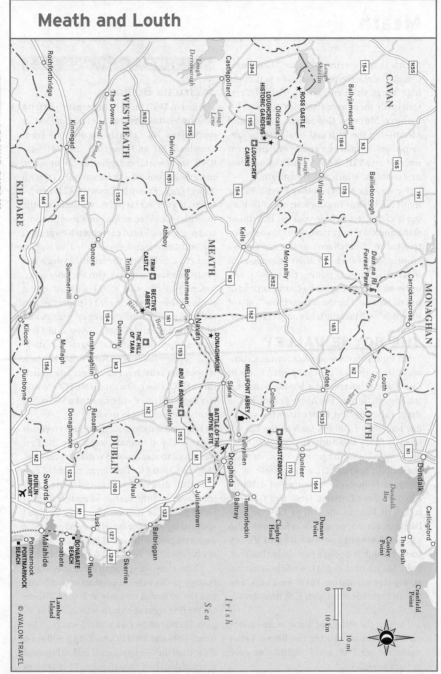

© AVALON TRAVEL

megalithic tomb was built all over western and northern Europe during the fourth millennium BC, however, and it's somewhat ironic that the architects and laborers who spent at least 15 years erecting Newgrange would never be entombed there themselves. Yes, even in Neolithic times a rigid social hierarchy was firmly in place.

You may be startled at first by the tomb's spiffy white quartz facade, a reconstruction based on the findings of University College Cork (UCC) archaeologist Michael J. O'Kelly. The entry stone is carved with exquisite triple spirals, the most common interpretation being that this motif symbolizes the cycles of nature. The mound alone weighs 200,000 tons and covers a full acre; grooved channels in the upper surfaces of the roof stones siphon off the rainwater, keeping the chamber dry. Clearly, this monument, a marvel of Stone Age technology, was built to last.

Dr. O'Kelly's discoveries between 1962 and 1975 included the cremated remains of five bodies in the niches around the cruciform central chamber, though they were not cremated inside the tomb (no soot was found on the walls). Dearly departed members of the Neolithic upper crust were probably deposited here until the next winter solstice, when the dawning light streaming through the roof box would have, so they believed, transported their spirits to the afterlife. After the solstice these remains would have been transferred to other graves nearby, though probably not beneath the myriad "satellite tombs" around each of the three primary monuments; these would have been reserved for families lower on the social ladder.

Dr. O'Kelly also alighted—pun intended—on the roof box above the doorway and was the first person in modern times to witness the solstice illuminate the burial chamber. Today you can view a simulated version toward the end of the tour, and once back in the visitors center you can enter your name into a drawing to see it for real come December 20. Before you go, though, spend a few minutes

deciphering the eerie early-19th-century graffiti.

The guided tour of Newgrange is not for claustrophobics, as the passageway is very low and narrow and the central chamber is too small for the number of visitors per group.

Knowth (Cnóbha), roughly the same size as Newgrange, is accessible by a second shuttle bus. Excavated by George Eogan from Trinity College Dublin in 1967 and 1968, this passage tomb is encircled by 127 large curbstones, and the two chambers within see the light of the spring equinox. Knowth alone contains 45 percent of Irish tomb art, and more than 25 percent of the tomb art in all Europe, so it's a real disappointment that you can't actually enter either of its two passages (you can only take a peek inside). According to UCC archaeologist Elizabeth Shee Twohig, many motifs in megalithic art were probably "derived from altered states of consciousness." A replica of a carefully carved phallic stone found at Knowth is on display in the exhibition; whatever their intention in building such monuments, clearly these Stone Agers were having their fun.

Though **Dowth** (Dubhadh)—with its 115 curbstones and two westward-facing tombs—is comparable in size to Newgrange and Knowth, it has never been properly excavated. Archaeologists believe that, like Knowth, this site was still a hive of activity in early Christian times. The crater at the center of the mound is the result of excavations in the 1840s; like Newgrange, Dowth's west face was quarried by local builders. You can walk around the site, though entrance to the mound is not possible.

The **Brú na Bóinne interpretive center** is kid-friendly without being dumbed down, featuring replicas of Neolithic clothing, tools, and tchotchkes. Birdcalls play on a speaker above a full-scale model of a circular thatched hut, a speculative reconstruction based on the post holes and foundation trenches uncovered during the excavation. There's also a seven-minute audiovisual inside an ersatz planetarium, and a low stone doorway on the far side leads into a full-scale model of the inner chamber at Newgrange. Along with the usual tearoom and gift shop, the center also houses a full-fledged tourist office.

Brú na Bóinne is one of Ireland's top tourist attractions, which means you need to be strategic in planning your visit. In high season it's wise to arrive at opening to beat most of the coach tours and school groups. Come in the afternoon and you may not be able to visit the sites at all—spaces on the tours fill up extremely quickly. Purchase a combo ticket for the interpretive center and both monuments, and consider buying the Dúchas Heritage Card if you'll be visiting other OPW (Office of Public Works) sites on your trip.

Brú na Bóinne is 55 kilometers northwest of Dublin off the N2, and the site is also clearly signposted from Slane and Drogheda on the N51. Those not driving can do Brú na Bóinne as a day tour out of Dublin.

But if you'd like to spend the night, there is accommodation just across the road at **Newgrange Lodge** (Staleen Rd., tel. 041/988-2478, www.newgrangelodge.com, dorm beds €21, private rooms €25-30). This hostel-slash-guesthouse is large, clean, and well-appointed (with kitchens for self catering), but its size makes it very popular with

groups, who can be a bit overwhelming if you are hoping for a quiet evening. That said, you may be interested in kayaking, archery, paintball, or guided hikes at the adjoining activity center (www.activitynation.ie).

Bective Abbey

The substantial ruins of **Bective Abbey** (on the L4010 7 km north of Trim, signposted off the Navan road/R161, always accessible, free) are well worth seeking out. This is Ireland's second Cistercian monastery, founded in 1147 as a "daughter house" of Mellifont Abbey in County Louth and converted into a mansion after minions of Henry VIII forcibly dissolved it. Romantically labyrinthine, the abbey's highlight is a lovely arcaded cloister—and if it seems familiar, it may be because one of the scenes in *Braveheart* (with Sophie Marceau and Jeanne Marine) was filmed here. What a perfect spot for a picnic!

If you'd like to spend the night in these lovely pastoral surroundings, eco-conscious **Bective Mill** (signposted on the L4010 opposite Bective Abbey, 100m down a local road, tel. 087/396-2399, www.bectivemill.com, €40 pp, s €50) is a cozy, well-kept B&B with its own duck eggs on the breakfast menu. This waterside guesthouse is a particularly good

the romantic ruins of Bective Abbey

choice for anglers, who have access to three kilometers along the River Boyne. For dinner, try **The Station House** (Kilmessan, 3.5 km southeast of Bective Abbey on the L4010, tel. 046/902-5239, www.stationhousehotel.ie, food served 12:30pm-10pm daily, €17-28, B&B rooms €80-180), a converted railway station that has happily retained much of its 19th-century charm.

★ The Hill of Tara

As with Rome, all roads once led to the **Hill of Tara** (12 km south of Navan off the M3, tel. 046/902-6222, visitors center 10am-6pm daily late May-mid-Sept., exhibition €4), legendary seat of the high kings of Ireland from the 3rd through the 10th century AD—and fortunately, the M3 motorway hasn't destroyed the site's tranquility, as many locals feared it would. Here St. Patrick obtained permission from King Laoghaire to preach Christianity on the island after explaining the concept of the Holy Trinity using a shamrock plucked from the grass. For this reason the site is often called the **Ráth of the Synods** (a synod being, essentially, a religious assembly). The 20-minute guided tour takes you by the **Mound of the Hostages,** a Bronze Age passage tomb built between 2500 and 2000 BC; remains of several ring forts and earthenworks, including a "banquet hall" (more likely used as another burial site) and the **Fort of King Laoghaire,** supposedly entombed standing up and in full armor; and the **Lia Fáil,** the overtly phallic "Stone of Destiny," where the kings were crowned—suspiciously Arthurian, eh? The tour, coupled with a 20-minute audiovisual at the visitors center (housed in a deconsecrated church), will give you a sense of the historic importance around this sheep-dotted hill. The site is fairly popular with locals (some walking their dogs) any time of year, and you don't have to pay a fee just to walk around.

In more recent history, Tara was the site of an Irish defeat in the rebellion of 1798, and in 1843 the "Great Liberator," Daniel O'Connell, held a mass rally on this hill. It's said as many as a million people turned up to hear his call for the repeal of the Act of Union. Even if that figure is exaggerated, most agree at least half a million people were there that day—still a stunning statistic, considering the pre-famine population was somewhere in the neighborhood of eight million.

Once you've taken a wander around the site, pop into **Maguire's** (tel. 046/902-5534, 9:30am-6pm daily) for coffee and a sandwich. Bibliophiles should budget at least half an hour at **The Old Book Shop,** a veritable trove of wonders. This tourist complex, such as it is, is refreshingly untouristy!

To get to Tara from Dublin (40 km), head north for Cavan on the M3. The **Bus Éireann** (tel. 01/836-6111) Dublin-Navan route (#109, at least one departure per hour daily) can leave you off at Tara Cross within easy walking distance of the site, if requested.

The Battle of the Boyne

The largest battle in Irish history was fought on July 1, 1690, between supporters of William of Orange and the Jacobites, who sought to restore the Catholic king he had deposed. There were more than 61,000 troops amassed on the **Battle of the Boyne site** (Oldbridge Estate, 6 km west of Drogheda via the L16014, tel. 041/980-9950, www.battleoftheboyne.ie, 9:30am-4:30pm daily Mar.-Apr., 10am-5pm daily May-Sept., 9am-4pm daily Oct.-Feb., €4) on that fateful morning. The date of the battle is still seared on the Irish national psyche, especially in the north, where Protestant schoolboys continue to celebrate the "marching season" with truly frightening zeal.

As at the Hill of Tara, you really need some context (provided by a 13-minute audiovisual and weaponry displays in the exhibition center) to get anything out of a visit to the battle site; otherwise it's just an ironically peaceful riverside stroll. To get here, take the N51 west from Drogheda (5 km) or east from Slane (13 km), or take the N2 or M1 motorway out of Dublin; the site is clearly signposted from the N51. If you're relying on public transport, the **Bus Éireann** route out of Drogheda (#163, 6/day Mon.-Sat., 5/day Sun.) stops in the nearby village of Donore. From Dublin, take the #110 bus (6/day Mon.-Sat., 5/day Sun.) and transfer in Drogheda. It's much more efficient to take one of the Boyne Valley day tours, however.

Loughcrew Historic Gardens

The complex at **Loughcrew Historic Gardens** (Loughcrew House, 5 km south of the village of Oldcastle, signposted off the R195/Mullingar road, tel. 049/854-1060, www.loughcrew.com, 9:30pm-5:30pm Mon.-Fri. and 11am-5:30pm Sat.-Sun. mid-Mar.-Oct., 11am-4pm Sat.-Sun. and upon request Nov.-Mar., €6) is yet another example of 21st-century big-house enterprise: You can wander through the restored 17th- and 19th-century gardens (which include the ruin of St. Oliver Plunkett's family church), go ziplining or tree-climbing at the **adventure center** (tel. 049/854-1356, half/full day of activities €32/52), and have lunch in the adjoining café. The neoclassical **Loughcrew House** used to offer B&B, but caters primarily to wedding and stag/hen parties now. The estate mounts a music and opera festival on a circular stage in the garden (€35), and a weekend **jazz festival** (€60) attracts some pretty high-profile performers. Visit the website for more details on both events, which take place in the month of June.

If you're visiting in low season, you'll need to pick up the key here if you wish to venture inside one of the Neolithic passage tombs at the Loughcrew Cairns.

Loughcrew House is 106 kilometers northwest of Dublin. To get to the house, garden, and cairns, take the M3 from Dublin to Kells and pick up the westbound Oldcastle road, the R154, and follow the signs for Loughcrew Gardens from the village.

Unfortunately, Bus Éireann's Drogheda-Oldcastle service is too infrequent and convoluted to be of any use to the tourist. Consider renting a car if Loughcrew is at the top of your destination list.

★ Loughcrew Cairns

If the prospect of elbowing through the crowds at Newgrange in summer gets you seriously queasy, consider a visit to the relatively quiet (and "undeveloped") necropolis of the **Loughcrew Cairns** (Corstown, 3 km east of Oldcastle off the R154, tel. 049/854-2009 or 041/988-0300 for off-season inquiries, 10am-6pm mid-June-mid-Sept., free), constructed around 3000 BC. These 30 megalithic tombs (scattered on three neighboring hills) are known as the Hills of the Witch, for legend claims a beldam jumped from one hill to the next, dropping stones from her pocket to form them. Sliabh na Caillighe (meaning "Hill of the Witch") is the highest at 280 meters, and supposedly provides a view of 17 counties. The other two hills are known as Carnbane East (195 meters) and Carnbane West (205 meters). (You don't need to be a mountaineer to scale these hills, but for heaven's sake, put on sensible footwear!) The Neolithics decorated the largest tomb, Cairn T (on Carnbane East), with their trademark stone carvings; as at Newgrange (which was erected around the same time), New Agers flock here on the equinoxes to watch the morning light stream inside. If you'll be visiting around the spring or fall equinox (March 19-21 or September 19-21), you may want to take part in the **Loughcrew Equinox Festival** (www.facebook.com/carnbane), organized by the Oldcastle Tourism Group.

There are guides on-site during official opening hours, from whom you can obtain the key to Cairn L (on Carnbane West). Otherwise, to borrow the key to Cairn T from the Loughcrew Gardens visitors center, you are required to leave your passport or driver's license, a laundry list of contact details, and/or a €50 deposit. Contact **Loughcrew House** directly (tel. 049/854-1356, info@loughcrew.com) should you wish to borrow the key outside visitors center opening hours (key available 10am-4pm only). Bring a flashlight!

To get to the cairns, take the M3 from

Dublin to Kells and pick up the westbound Oldcastle road, the R154; follow the signs for Loughcrew Gardens from the village. You'll have to double back on that road once you've picked up the Cairn T key (though you can still wander around the site without it, of course).

Backpackers will definitely want to crash at **Loughcrew Megalithic Centre** (tel. 086/736-1948 or 087/397-4295, www.lough-crewmegalithiccentre.com, dorm beds €23), which includes a 16-bed hostel and campsites, a pleasant tearoom, and **Maggie Heaney's Cottage,** restored to its humble 18th-century roots. If you're busing it from Dublin (#109), the hostel offers pickup service from Kells. If you're driving, take the R163 west from Kells; the center is liberally signposted because the way there is very twisty-turny on potholed local roads.

Note that the café at Loughcrew Megalithic Centre is not to be confused with the Loughcrew House tearoom, where you can obtain the key to the Loughcrew cairns (although the owners are hoping to obtain their own key at some point). There is a route from here up to the top of the hill, and if you're here in the summer there'll be an OPW employee on site who can let you in.

LOUGH SHEELIN

Tucked away in the quiet western corner of County Meath, Lough Sheelin makes for a relaxing stopover once you've explored Newgrange, Tara, and Loughcrew by car. If you're charmed by the idea of staying in a castle without signing away your firstborn child, ★ **Ross Castle** (5.5 km southwest of the village of Mount Nugent on the L7081, turnoff is signposted on the right, tel. 087/125-0911, www.ross-castle.com, rooms €120-200) is the place for you. This 16th-century tower house overlooking Lough Sheelin comes with its very own Romeo-and-Juliet-style ghost story—it's said the maiden of the castle still wanders the grounds at night searching for her lost love. On a more practical note, this B&B is absolutely first rate, from the warm welcome and tranquil lake views to the beautiful (but not too stuffy) antique furniture, including four-poster beds and the full-sized suit of armor greeting you in the entryway. Nothing's too much trouble for caretaker Jackie Moran—breakfasts are bountiful and the coffee is delish. The original tower rooms are positively oozing with medieval atmosphere, so much so that some folks will be more comfortable staying in one of the more modern rooms in the ground-floor annex.

Climb up to the Loughcrew Cairns for gorgeous green views over County Meath.

You'll definitely want to eat dinner at the castle (three-course meal €30), but in low season your best option is the lakeside **Crover House Hotel** (signposted off the R154 west of Mount Nugent, tel. 049/854-0206, www.croverhousehotel.ie, food served 12:30pm-9pm daily, €12-24), which is just over the border in County Cavan. The atmosphere is reminiscent of an American golf club, but the fare is above average and the staff are friendly. To get here, drive back to Mount Nugent and turn left onto the R154; the hotel is signposted on the left about two kilometers down the road, and it's another two kilometers or so from there.

DONAGHMORE

The small graveyard and 11th- or 12th-century round tower at **Donaghmore** (Domhnach Mór, "Big Church," 3km northeast of Navan on the N51 en route to Slane, always accessible, free) are worth a stop for the eerie 16th-century church ruin: There's only one wall left, and the doorway and two bell arches above look disconcertingly like a screaming face. There's also a collection of finely carved 18th- and early-19th-century headstones. It's nice to see an old Irish burial ground so exceptionally well cared for. The monastic community was founded in the 5th century by St. Cassán, a disciple of St. Patrick.

SLANE

If you're planning to do the Newgrange-Tara-Battle of the Boyne circuit, **Slane** (Baile Shláine) is far and away the most pleasant base—it's only 9 kilometers northwest, 24 kilometers northeast, and 12 kilometers west of those respective sites. Despite the occasional high-profile concert at Slane Castle, the village is delightfully quiet, friendly, and down-to-earth, priding itself on its illustrious sons: the early 20th-century poet Francis Ledwidge and John Boyle O'Reilly, a Fenian who became editor of a Boston newspaper, the *Pilot*, after escaping an Australian penal colony in the late 1880s.

Sights

Slane Castle (on the N51 just west of the village, tel. 041/988-4400, www.slanecastle.ie, noon-5pm Sun.-Thurs. May-July, €7), on whose grounds a natural amphitheater is now the country's coolest concert venue, was built in the 1780s using several prominent British and Anglo-Irish architects. Today you can tour several of the drawing rooms and bedrooms, among them the chamber in which King George IV enjoyed the occasional rendezvous with the lady of the house. The current Lord Conyngham, an enterprising chap, seems to be squeezing a profit out of his ancestral home in every manner feasible.

The **Hill of Slane,** where St. Patrick lit his paschal fire in a sort of religious competition with the druids at Tara in 433, is crowned with the atmospheric ruins of the 15th-century **Slane Abbey.** Above a gorgeous mullioned window rises a dramatic belfry—look up and you'll find you can see up all the way to the roof. To get here, take Chapel Street away from the river (past George's Patisserie) to the signpost on your left, just beyond the modern Celtic cross that serves as a 1798 monument. The road winds gently uphill for another kilometer, and at the crest you'll find lovely panoramic views of the Boyne River valley.

Francis Ledwidge, a tremendously promising poet who grew up just outside Slane, was killed in the first World War. He was just shy of 30. **The Ledwidge Museum** (Janeville, Slane, tel. 041/982-4544, www.francisledwidge.com, 10am-5pm daily mid-Mar.-Oct., 10am-3:30pm Nov.-Mar., €3) commemorates Ledwidge's life and poetry in a small exhibition and garden.

A two-hour **Slane historical walking tour,** led by Mick Kelly (tel. 087/937-7040), departs the Conyngham Arms every evening at 7pm.

Activities and Recreation

Slane is on the **Táin Trail** cycling route. Since there's no bike shop in the village proper, pedaling to Newgrange isn't really an option

The Táin Trail and the Cattle Raid of Cooley

The Táin Trail cycling route is 504 kilometers long, a loop that extends from Roscommon to Carlingford on the Cooley Peninsula—hitting Longford, Athlone, Trim, Slane, and Kells, and plenty of sleepy midland villages along the way. County Louth includes 150 kilometers of this route, which hits the various settings of the medieval epic *Táin Bó Cúailnge* (literally "The Driving-Off of Cows of Cooley," but the anglicized title is *The Cattle Raid of Cooley*).

The epic follows the exploits of the teenage Ulster warrior Cuchulainn and his nemesis, Maeve (queen of Connaught). In an attempt to best her husband's wealth, Maeve (also spelled "Medb") plots to steal the finest bull in Ulster, and because the rest of the Ulster army is incapacitated by a mysterious curse, Cuchulainn is the only one who can stop her. Drawn-out battles ensue, some pitting Cuchulainn against his own loved ones.

If you're planning to cycle the Táin Trail, contact **Táin Tours** (Carlingford, tel. 087/239-7467, kmckeybushire@gmail.com) for bike rental (€15/80 per day/week). Bicycles are delivered to your accommodation and they'll give you all the maps and resources you need. More information is available through the **East Coast & Midlands Tourism** office (tel. 044/934-8761, www.discoverireland.ie).

unless you've brought one with you. Climbing the **Hill of Slane** (it's a leisurely kilometer) is a nice way to pass an afternoon, as both the monastic ruins and the view at the top are eminently picture-worthy; alternatively, head over the bridge (just south of the square) and pick up the path along the Boyne. Otherwise, there's always the **Stackallen Tennis and Pitch and Putt Club** (Stackallen, Pig Hill, 2 km from Slane on the Navan-bound N51, tel. 041/982-4279 or 087/977-3213, info@stackallen.com).

Food and Entertainment

Savor a *pain au chocolat* and a *café au lait* at **George's Patisserie** (Chapel St., tel. 041/982-4493, www.georgespatisserie.com, 9am-6pm daily, €6). The ornate three-tier cakes on display conjure daydreams of a grand old-fashioned wedding. Though the café offers only sweet things, there's a delicatessen on the premises featuring local meats and cheeses, and the freshly baked breads (including gluten-free options) make for good picnic fixings.

The old-style tearoom is no more, but the dark, spacious, comfortable **Boyle's** (Main St., tel. 041/982-4195, www.boylesofslane.ie) is still the best spot in town for an afternoon drink. The friendly bartenders show plenty of traditional Irish hospitality, too. **The Village Inn** (Main St., tel. 041/982-4230) has a fun collection of pictures and posters from castle concerts gone by. There's also good *craic* to be found at the old-school pub at the Conyngham Arms.

The **Conyngham Arms** (Main St., tel. 041/988-4444, food served noon-8pm daily, €15-25) does pub grub as well as more formal meals in the restaurant; your other option in the village is **The Poet's Rest** (Chapel St., tel. 041/982-0738, 12:30pm-9:30pm Mon., 5pm-9:30pm Thurs.-Fri., 12:30pm-9:30pm Sat., 12:30pm-8:30pm Sun., €12-20), which will get the job done with smiling service. But if your budget allows, try the **Brabazon** (Rathkenny, 7 km north of Slane on the N51, tel. 041/982-4621, www.tankardstown.ie, 6pm-8:30pm Wed.-Thurs., 6pm-9:30pm Fri.-Sun., also 12:30pm-3:30pm Sun., vegetarian/omnivore's fixed-price dinner €55/70), part of the swanky 18th-century Tankardstown House.

Accommodations

Whether you're looking for budget beds or charming self-catering digs, head on over to the IHH **Slane Farm Hostel and Cottages** (Harlinstown, 2 km from the village on the

Kells road, the R163, tel. 041/988-4985, www. slanefarmhostel.ie, Mar.-Nov., dorms €18, doubles €25 pp, singles €30, cottages €80/350 per night/week), a converted 18th-century stablehouse all done up in cheerful green trim. The kitchen, sitting room, and dormitories are amazingly clean and homey, stocked and decorated with far more care than most people give their own living spaces. Breakfast is €5 and includes eggs from the resident hens and produce from the vegetable garden.

B&Bs in and around Slane are strangely sparse. As far as hotels go, the **Conyngham Arms Hotel** (Main St., tel. 041/988-4444, www.conynghamarms.com, rooms €115-150) is about as old-fashioned as it gets, with cathedral ceilings, four-poster beds (not in every room, though), and that certain air of faded gentility. The restaurant fare is far better than average, too—but don't plan on an early night, as the noise from the pub can be heard even on the top floor. The finest accommodation in the area is a restored Georgian manor, **Tankardstown House** (Rathkenny, 7 km north of Slane on the N51, tel. 041/ 982-4621, www.tankardstown.ie, B&B €100-200 pp). Book online for a package including dinner, spa treatments, high tea, and/or sightseeing excursions.

Information and Services

You'll find the local **tourist office** (Main St., tel. 041/982-4010, www.meathtourism.ie, 9:30am-5pm Mon., Thurs., and Sat.) across the street from the Conyngham Arms Hotel.

There's an ATM in the Londis supermarket on the Collon road (the N2). Pick up cough drops at **Breen's Pharmacy** (Main St., tel. 041/982-4222).

Getting There

Slane is 15 kilometers west of Drogheda on the N51 and 48 kilometers northwest of Dublin on the N2. **Bus Éireann** passes through Slane on the following routes out of Dublin: Letterkenny (#32, 5/day daily), Derry (#33, 3-4/day daily), Portrush (#36, 3-4/day daily), and Clones in County Monaghan

(#177, 6/day daily). There is also direct service from Drogheda (#183 or #188, at least 6/ day Mon.-Sat.).

Getting Around

Newgrange Bike Hire (Drumree, tel. 086/069-5771, kevinohand@eircom.net, ring for rates) is 300 meters from the Brú na Bóinne visitors center.

For a taxi in the Slane area, ring **M&L Cabs** (tel. 087/214-3088 for a cab, tel. 086/360-1338 for a minibus).

TRIM

Dominated by the fascinating ruins of an Anglo-Norman castle, **Trim** (Baile Átha Troim) is a tidy little town on the River Boyne 40 minutes northwest of Dublin. It's a quiet place—some may find it a bit too quiet, especially after dark—but its medieval attractions and a couple of delightfully scruffy pubs make Trim a pleasant spot to spend the night.

Between the humongous castle and the town's smallish size, orienting yourself is fairly easy. The street that hugs the castle ruins changes names from the New Dublin Road to Castle Street to Bridge Street—here crossing the Boyne—to High Street to Navan Gate Street as it curves northward. Most of the town's amenities are on Market Street, which shoots westward off the main drag where Castle meets Bridge Street. Turn off the west end of Market Street onto Emmet Street, home to several pubs offering live trad.

★ Trim Castle

Granted the land by Henry II, Hugh de Lacy and his son Walter built a motte-and-timber tower in 1172 on the site of the Boyne-side **Trim Castle** (tel. 046/943-8619, 10am-6pm daily Apr.-Oct., 10am-5pm weekends Nov.-Mar., admission with/excluding the keep €4/2), only to burn it down the following year to prevent the Irish from taking it by force. They rebuilt the castle over the following three decades, and it was—and remains—the largest Anglo-Norman castle in the country. Before its restoration in the late 1990s, Trim was partially rebuilt (and filled with various livestock and ragamuffin extras) for the filming of *Braveheart,* and you can flip through a photo album available from the admission desk.

Only the service tower is missing from the imposing, three-story, cruciform keep, accessible by guided tour only; it's an informative-but-interesting 45 minutes. On the ground level, three large and wonderfully detailed models of the castle at three different periods in its history highlight many notable architectural features, like the "roof scars" that are all that remain of a double A-framed, red-tiled roof, or the squinches that still lend structural support. Metal catwalks allow visitors to peruse the upper levels, and the view from the parapet is worth the vertigo on the spiral stairs.

Elsewhere on the castle grounds, the Barbican Gate has five parallel murder holes (there are also two in the town gate, from which you enter the grounds), and the jail features an oubliette.

Other Sights

Just across the Boyne are the **yellow steeple,** once the bell tower of the Augustinian Abbey of St. Mary (its present ruined state thanks, yet again, to Cromwell), and the **Sheep's Gate,** the only extant gate from the old town walls. The early-15th-century **Talbot Castle** (High St.) incorporates a portion of the old abbey and was once owned by Jonathan Swift (he lived there for only one year, though his mistress spent much more time there). The Millennium Bridge at the end of Castle Street connects the medieval ruins on either side of the river.

Newtown Abbey (Lackanash Rd., 1.5 km east of town, always accessible, free) contains the ruins of the **Cathedral of Saints Peter and Paul,** remarkable for its well-worn double tomb effigy of a knight and his wife. The sword that separates them has inspired locals to refer to them as "the jealous man and woman." The rainwater that collects in the carvings is said to have curative

properties—for warts, that is—and the space between the effigies is littered with rusted safety pins. To get here, take the New Road/Navan exit at the roundabout at the end of New Dublin Road (just east of the castle), cross the Boyne, and make the first right onto Lackanash Road, a residential street. It's a 20-minute walk or a 3-minute drive from town.

Trim is also a viable base for the Boyne Valley's prime attractions (Tara is 23 km, Newgrange 34 km). Need a break from driving, or don't have wheels? Contact Anne Leavy at **Tours na Mí** (tel. 046/943-2523, abirdyleavy@iol.ie).

Activities and Recreation

Tee off at the **County Meath Golf Club** (Newtonmoynagh, 1.5 km outside town, tel. 046/943-1463, www.trimgolf.net), which has an 18-hole parkland course.

You have a choice among equestrian centers in the area (no more than a 10-minute drive): There's the **Kilcarty Horse Riding Centre** (Kilcarty, Dunsany, tel. 046/902-5877 or 086/088-7841), the **Pelletstown Riding Centre** (Pelletstown, Drumree, tel. 01/825-9435, www.pelletstownridingcentre.com), or the **Moy Riding Centre** (Summerhill, Enfield, tel. 04/055-8115, www.moyriding-centre.com).

Food

You don't have a ton of choice here, but there are a few decent eateries. For breakfast (a bagel sandwich or the full fry) or lunch (lasagna and such), try **Java Juice** (1 Haggard Court, Haggard St., across the river from the castle, tel. 046/943-8771, 9am-5pm Mon.-Sat., 10am-5pm Sun., under €10), which boasts the best coffee in town.

For dinner, Trim's top eatery is the family-run **Stock House** (Emmet House, Finnegan's Way, tel. 046/943-7388, www.stockhouserestaurant.ie, 5pm-9pm Tues.-Thurs., 5pm-10pm Fri.-Sat., 1pm-8:30pm Sun., €16-23). Though steak is (unsurprisingly) the specialty here, there are several veg and seafood options, and the service is first rate. If you can't get a table at the Stock House, try **Franzini's** (5 French's Lane, tel. 046/943-1002, www.franzinis.com, 6:30pm-10pm Mon.-Sat., 5pm-9pm Sun., €12-26). The menu is strangely eclectic: You can order a burger, pasta . . . or duck glazed in peach sauce! You have a choice of fun cocktails too. This place is overpriced, however—the food is good, but by no means exceptional.

Entertainment and Events

You can't leave Trim without taking a pint at **Marcie Regan's,** a.k.a. **David's Lad** (Lackanash Rd., Newtown, tel. 046/943-6103, open at 9pm Thurs.-Tues.), which claims to be Ireland's second-oldest pub. Granted, with the rough stone walls, grungy chairs, and cement floors it feels like drinking in your uncle's basement, but the fact that everybody knows everyone here makes for an authentically Irish night out. The half dozen snow-haired gents who play traditional music here on Friday nights (starting a bit after 10:30) have been jamming together longer than you've been alive. To get here, take the New Road/Navan exit at the roundabout at the end of New Dublin Road (just east of the castle), cross the Boyne, and make the first right onto Lackanash Road, a residential street. The pub is directly across the road from Newtown Abbey.

Another delightfully old-fashioned pub is **James Griffin's** (21 High St., tel. 046/943-1295, www.jamesgriffinpub.ie), but if it's more trad you want, check out **The Emmet Tavern** (Emmet St., tel. 046/943-1378), with sessions Thursday-Saturday; **The Olde Stand** (Emmet St., tel. 046/943-1286) Friday-Sunday; or **The Steps** (Emmet St., tel. 046/943-7575) on Thursday. The **Castle Arch Hotel** (Summerhill Rd., tel. 046/943-1516, www.castlearchhotel.com) offers trad every Saturday night.

Accommodations

Built in 1810, the marvelous **Highfield House** (Maudlins Rd., tel. 046/943-6386, www.highfieldguesthouse.com, €45 pp) was once a maternity hospital. The house is situated on a hill a couple minutes' walk from the castle, and its imposing stone facade, with bright flowers tumbling from the window boxes, matches the amazingly authentic decor. Gilded mirrors, cathedral ceilings and ornate plasterwork, high windows and sumptuous curtains, original oil paintings of young ladies in powdered wigs—it might sound on the stuffy side, but the rooms are actually quite comfortable (with new showers). Just keep in mind you're staying here for the atmosphere, not the breakfast. For the full fry done up right, try **Tigh Cathain** (Longwood Rd., 1 km from town on the R160, tel. 046/943-1996, www.tighcathain-bnb.com, €35-38 pp, s €50), a Tudor-style bungalow surrounded by carefully tended gardens, or **Crannmór Country House** (Dunderry Rd., 1.5 km northeast of the town center, tel. 046/943-1635, www.crannmor.com, €35-40 pp), a spacious, ivy-clad farmhouse in equally tranquil surroundings.

Trim's swankiest beds are found at the **Castle Arch Hotel** (Summerhill Rd., on the southern end of town, tel. 046/943-1516, www.castlearchhotel.com, €75-100 pp). Formerly known as Wellington Court (there's a monument to the duke of Waterloo fame nearby, on the corner of Emmet St. and Patrick St.), the town's only hotel often has terrific weekend packages up for grabs, so check the website before you go. Alternatively, you might be able to book a last-minute B&B for as little as €43 per person sharing.

Information and Services

The **tourist office and heritage center** (Mill St., tel. 046/943-7111 or 046/943-7227, www.meathtourism.ie, 9:30am-5:30pm Mon.-Sat., noon-5:30pm Sun. May-Sept., 9am-5pm Mon.-Sat. Oct.-Apr., exhibit €3.20) offers a 20-minute audiovisual show on Trim's medieval history (unfortunately, not included in the castle admission price).

The **AIB** (Market St., tel. 046/943-6444), **Bank of Ireland** (Market St., tel. 046/943-1230), and **Ulster Bank** (High St., tel. 046/943-1233) all have ATMs. There are two pharmacies on Market Street, **Kelly's** (tel. 046/943-1279) and **Farrell's** (tel. 046/943-6600).

Getting There and Around

Trim is 56 kilometers northwest of Dublin off the M3, picking up the R154 in the hamlet of Black Bull 26 kilometers outside the city. **Bus** **Éireann** (tel. 01/836-6111) operates a local service from Dublin (#111, 9/day Mon.-Fri., 8/day Sat., 4/day Sun.), though to get here from anywhere else by bus, you'll have to head back to Dublin first.

If you need a taxi, ring **Donal Quinn** (tel. 046/943-6009 or 087/222-7333), who offers 24-hour service.

Louth

Considering it's the smallest county on either side of the border, Louth has quite a fair bit to offer the visitor, including the truly magnificent high crosses of Monasterboice and the remains of once-powerful Mellifont Abbey with its unusual octagonal lavabo. Pass through the county's principal town, Dundalk, to reach the Cooley Peninsula, with its thoroughly lovely medieval heritage town of Carlingford. This is the setting for the 8th-century epic *The Cattle Raid of Cooley,* an oral tradition finally set to paper by the monks of Clonmacnoise and Noughaval (in Wexford) in the 12th and 14th centuries. Thomas Kinsella's 1969 translation is the definitive one.

Base yourself in Carlingford or in far less touristy Drogheda, a pleasantly workaday place in the throes of citywide redevelopment.

DROGHEDA

A gritty-but-lively industrial town about an hour's drive north of Dublin, Drogheda ("DROH-heh-duh," Droichead Átha, "Bridge of the Ford") is slowly shedding its dormitory town image. Ongoing construction may be unsightly, but it definitely adds to the sense that this is a city on the upswing. It's delightfully untouristy, and your best choice for a base if you want to sample the local nightlife after a day at Newgrange and all the other Boyne Valley attractions. There are plenty of sights in Drogheda proper as well, including a folk and archaeology museum and craft complex, and a liberal sprinkling of vivid historical reminders—after all, Drogheda was one of Ireland's most important medieval walled towns 600 years back. The city was devastated more than any other by the advent of Oliver Cromwell in 1649; his forces slaughtered more than 2,700 members of the town's garrison on September 11 of that year. Sir Arthur Aston, commander of the resistance, was beaten to death with his own wooden leg by Cromwell's henchmen.

Sights

Drogheda's medieval heritage allows for a full day of sightseeing. Seven hundred years ago the town wall was a mile and a half long, and the area enclosed was twice that of medieval Dublin. There were eight defense gates, of which the 13th-century **Butter Gate** (Barrack St., just north of Millmount) and **St. Laurence's Gate** (between Laurence St. and Cord Rd. at Francis St.) remain (though the Butter Gate is nearly a century older). An even more dramatic sight is the **Magdalene Tower** (on the northern end of town, at the end of Magdalene St.), which is said to be haunted by the spirit of a nun—though there is very little left to haunt! The belfry is all that remains of a 13th-century Dominican friary, though the tower itself probably dates from the following century: downright precarious, and downright eerie. But wait, there's more—excavations unearthed a skeleton of a woman who must have stood seven feet tall!

The town's primary tourist attraction is the **Millmount Museum** (Millmount, on the southern end of town, clearly signposted

Drogheda

© AVALON TRAVEL

from town center, tel. 041/983-3097, www.
millmount.net, 10am-6pm Mon.-Sat.,
2:30pm-5:30pm Sun., admission to museum/
tower/combo €3.50/3/5.50), housed within
an early-18th-century military complex
that also includes a martello tower (offering
a nice panoramic view of the river valley).
The museum itself is a motley assortment
of religious artifacts, rare rocks, and cottage
industry antiques, and the pre-1800 guild
banners are supposedly the only ones left in
the country.

On the site of a Franciscan monastery
and center of learning founded in the early
15th century, the **Highlanes Gallery** (56-57
West St., tel. 041/983-7869, www.highlanes.
ie, 10:30am-5pm Mon.-Sat., suggested donation €2) now houses Drogheda's civic art collection as well as traveling exhibitions from

Ireland and abroad. The building itself dates
from 1829.

Before the construction of the **Boyne
Viaduct** in the 1850s, northbound passengers had to disembark at Drogheda and secure
alternative transportation to the next station
10 kilometers away. No wonder the architect,
a Louth man named John Mac Neill, was
considered a genius in his day. At 427 meters
long, with 18 arches each 18 meters wide, this
bridge spanning the river on the eastern side
of town is still a formidable sight.

St. Peter's Roman Catholic Church
(West St.) is the final resting place of St. Oliver
Plunkett's head. Tried for "treason" (having
allegedly taken part in the "Irish Popish plot")
and martyred in 1681, Plunkett's noggin was
"rescued" and brought to Drogheda by a
group of French nuns. What remains is now

on display—a truly frightening sight—in a tall, ornate brass-and-glass case. Another glass reliquary nearby holds three of the saint's ribs, a scapula, and other carefully labeled bones. This is the most morbid attraction in Louth, if not the entire eastern seaboard.

Still more morbid attractions are to be found at the mid-18th-century **St. Peter's Church of Ireland** (William St.). In the churchyard you will find a relatively rare cadaver tomb (depicting the departed in a decayed state, something of a fad in the century or so after the bubonic plague). Furthermore, the previous edifice had a wooden steeple, where as many as 100 people took refuge during Cromwell's rampage in 1649. Cromwell set fire to the tower, and no one survived.

Take in Plunkett's head along with a load of other historical sights—the old town walls, St. Mary's Catholic and Protestant churches, Millmount, and more—on the **Medieval Drogheda** walking tour (tel. 041/983-7070, departs the tourist office on Mayoralty St. at 11am and 2pm Tues.-Fri., €3). The tour lasts about an hour, and pre-booking is essential.

Activities and Recreation

In fine summer weather, there's no better diversion than a leisurely garden stroll. **Beaulieu House and Gardens** (Beaulieu, Drogheda, 5 km east of town on the Baltray road, signposted off the R167, tel. 041/983-8557, www.beaulieu.ie, 11am-5pm Mon.-Fri. May-mid-Sept., garden €5, house and garden €12) was erected on the site of a Plunkett castle in the 17th century. The admission price includes a guided tour (departing on the hour) of the big house in all its Georgian splendor. The walled garden dates from 1732, and there's also an early-19th-century church on the grounds that features some spooky tomb effigies. June and July are the best times to visit, as the roses are in full bloom.

Established in 1892, the **County Louth Golf Club** (Baltray, 7 km east of Drogheda on the R167, tel. 041/988-1530, www.countylouthgolfclub.com) is rated in the top six courses on either side of the border.

The more ambitious can cycle to nearby attractions—Mellifont Abbey and Monasterboice (both about 8 km), the Battle of the Boyne site (5.5 km), or Brú na Bóinne (11.5 km).

Food

Drogheda has never enjoyed a reputation for fine dining, though fortunately that's beginning to change with all the ongoing hubbub of "urban renewal." The pub at the **Westcourt Hotel** (West St., tel. 041/983-0965, www.westcourt.ie, food served noon-9pm daily, 3 tapas plates for €11.50) used to be old school, but they've recently remade it into **West 29,** a stylin' spot for tapas and cocktails.

For something a bit more traditional, head to the **Black Bull Inn** (1 km outside the city center on the Dublin road, tel. 041/983-7139, www.blackbullinn.ie, food served noon-10pm daily, €10-14), which is on every local's list of favorites. Asian-inspired dishes are a specialty, and all the burgers are made with local beef.

Two of the most popular eateries in town are Italian: **La Pizzeria** (15 St. Peter's St., www.pizzeriadrogheda.ie, 12:30pm-10pm or later daily, €10-15) and the more upscale **Sorrento's** (41 Shop St., tel. 041/984-5734, 6:30pm-11pm Tues.-Sun., €12-20). As with most Italian eateries in this country, keep low expectations and you may be pleasantly surprised!

With a great location right on the Boyne, ★ **Brú** (The Haymarket, Unit 8, North Bank, tel. 041/987-2784, www.bru.ie, 1pm-10pm or later daily, lunch €7-10, dinner €12-23, 3-course meal €24) would get the business even if the food were only half as nice as the view (and the floor-to-ceiling panoramic windows take full advantage). The Continental fare is excellent, however, and the sticky toffee pudding's the best in the county. Perhaps surprisingly for a place this chic, the waitstaff let you linger for as long as you like. All in all, no one would disagree with the owners that "a new era in urban dining has arrived in Drogheda."

Entertainment and Events

Drogheda has a pretty happenin' arts scene, the prime venue being the **Droichead Arts Centre** (Stockwell St., tel. 041/983-3946, www.droichead.com, €7-20). This is the place for film screenings, plays, concerts, and art exhibitions. The city hosts a few festivals throughout the year, the most popular being the **Drogheda Arts Festival** (tel. 041/987-6100) in April. The arts fest is a feast for the eyes and ears, with plenty of street theater, concerts, comedy acts, film screenings, dance performances, and visual art and crafts exhibits. (The Drogheda Samba Festival in July was another event locals got really excited for, though its future is uncertain since the 2015 festival was cancelled due to lack of funding.) There's also the **Irish Steel Guitar Festival** (tel. 041/984-5684, www.steelguitarireland. com), which attracts musicians from Nashville and the United Kingdom, in October.

Many of Drogheda's hip young things can be found at **Brú** (The Haymarket, Unit 8, North Bank, tel. 041/987-2784), a posh riverside bistro, which has a DJ on Friday and Saturday nights. Another hot spot is the chic bar at **The d Hotel** (Scotch Hall, tel. 041/987-7700), which also has a DJ on the weekends.

Not into "hot spots"? Fair enough. Far and away the best pub in town is **Tí Chairbre,** better known as **Carberry's** (North Strand, tel. 041/983-7409). With a fire burning brightly in the grate, layer upon layer of concert posters pasted to the walls and ceiling, and scratchy old recordings of American "Memphis blues" on the stereo, the atmosphere here is second to none—all in all, one gets the impression that very little has changed here since even your granddaddy was in diapers (or "nappies," as the Irish call them). The drinks are relatively cheap, the bartender's friendly, and the trad sessions are wonderful (*sean nós* Tuesday night, traditional music Wednesday, and another trad session on Sunday afternoon around 2pm-4pm). Come even if it isn't a music night—the locals are great fun.

If you're not in the mood for trad, you can catch an outdoor jazz session starting at 4pm on Sunday at the **Black Bull Inn** (Dublin Rd., tel. 041/983-7139, blackbullinn@eircom. net). Another worthwhile watering hole is the family-run **Sarsfield's** (Cord Rd., near St. Laurence's Gate, tel. 041/983-8032, www. sarsfieldsbar.com), which sponsors several local sports teams. In decades past several Drogheda pubs would open at 7:30am so dock and factory workers could have a pint before work, and until quite recently Sarsfield's was continuing that tradition.

Shopping

The best place for high-quality gifts is the **Millmount Design Store** (Millmount Craft Centre, tel. 041/984-1960, elainejewel-design@eircom.net), featuring work coming out of the Millmount Centre craft studios: knitwear, quilts, ceramics, silver, glassware, and suchlike.

Accommodations

Budget travelers' only option is **Spoon and the Stars** (13 Dublin Rd., tel. 087/970-9767, www.spoonandthestars.com, large dorms €18, private rooms €30 pp), but it's a good one. The management is easygoing and helpful and the proximity to the train station is a definite plus, though being on such a busy road doesn't make for a quiet night.

There aren't many bed-and-breakfasts in the area, but one to try is **Roseville Lodge** (Georges St., tel. 041/983-4046, www.rosevil-lelodge.com, €40 pp), an ivy-clad Victorian with genuinely welcoming proprietors a few minutes' walk northwest of the center of town. Coming from points south, you'll continue on the R132 to the right as it crosses the River Boyne, and the bed-and-breakfast is several blocks up this road on the left.

For an even more central location, try the **Westcourt Hotel** (West St., tel. 041/983-0965, www.westcourt.ie, €60 pp, s €65, weekend discounts available). The rooms and atmosphere are standard business class, though the staff are friendly and the bar food is a pretty good value for all its fanciness. On the weekends this hotel isn't a good choice for the early-to-bed set, as the bar and nightclub noise seeps up into most of the bedrooms.

With all the trimmings of a four-star cosmopolitan establishment, **The d Hotel** (Scotch Hall, south of the Boyne, tel. 041/987-7700, www.thedhotel.com, €95-130 pp) offers mod-yet-comfy bedrooms, a trendy bar with plenty of fun cocktails to choose from, complimentary laundry service, friendly staff, and an awesome breakfast menu. The d Hotel is part of a slick shopping complex, Scotch Hall—all of which exemplifies the city's mostly admirable push for redevelopment and renewal. Check the website for special deals.

Information and Services
The very helpful **tourist office** (Mayoralty St., tel. 041/983-7070, www.drogheda.ie, 9am-5:30pm Mon.-Sat.) is just off the North Quay, behind the Sound Shop.

You'll find plenty of ATMs and bureaux de change along Drogheda's main drags: **Bank of Ireland** (14 St. Laurence St., tel. 041/983-7653), **Ulster Bank** (104 West St., tel. 041/983-6458), or **AIB** (Dyer St., tel. 041/983-6523). **Hickey's Pharmacy** (10-11 West St., tel. 041/983-8651) is open Sundays and holidays.

Getting There
Drogheda is on Ireland's east coast between Dublin (50 km south) and Belfast (120 km north), reachable by the M1 motorway (which becomes the A1 in the U.K.) linking those two cities.

Drogheda is on the main Belfast-Dublin bus route (#1, 7/day Mon.-Sat. from both cities, 6/day Sun.). The Dublin-Dundalk route (#100 or #101, departures from Drogheda every 30 minutes, popular with commuters, is the quickest way to get back to Dublin. Other direct routes include Athlone and Galway (#70, departing Galway 12:30pm Mon.-Sat., and Fri. and Sun. at 6pm), and Slane (#188, 6/day Mon.-Sat.). You can also reach Drogheda from Kells (#188, 3/day Mon.-Sat., transfer at Navan). Beware that the **Bus Éireann** station

(John St. and Donore Rd., tel. 041/983-5023) is popular with pickpockets.

If you haven't purchased a Rover pass, however, you might want to take a slightly less expensive coach service: **Matthews Coaches** buses (tel. 042/937-8188, www.matthews.ie, single/return ticket €10/15) depart Parnell Street in Dublin 22 times a day Monday-Friday, 10 times on Saturday, and 9 times on Sunday, with equally frequent return service.

Drogheda is also on the Belfast-Dublin **Irish Rail** line (Dublin Rd., about half a kilometer east of the city center, tel. 041/983-8749, at least 5 express departures daily, frequent local service), which is perhaps the country's most popular commuter service.

Getting Around
Drogheda is small enough to walk everywhere; if driving, prepare yourself for considerable congestion and pay-and-display parking. There are taxi ranks on West Street at Duke Street and just opposite St. Laurence's Gate. Or ring **East Coast Cabs** (tel. 041/981-1198 or 086/838-4444).

For bike rental, contact **Quay Cycles** (11 N. Quay, tel. 041/983-4526, €14/day) or **P.J. O'Carolan** (77 Trinity St., tel. 041/983-8242, €15/day).

MELLIFONT ABBEY
Ireland's first Cistercian monastery, **Mellifont Abbey** (from *mellifons,* Latin for "honey fountain"; Tullyallen, 1.5 km off the R168, the main Drogheda-Collon road, tel. 041/982-6459 or 041/988-0300 for info in winter, www.heritageireland.ie, 10am-6pm daily May-Oct., €4, accessible without charge in winter) was established in 1142 by St. Malachy, the Archbishop of Armagh. Malachy planned with St. Bernard of Clairvaux to open a stricter, more rigorous religious order, a community made up of both French and native monks. Though the French and Irish failed to gel, the Cistercian ideology (and architecture) caught on in this country, and Mellifont became the "mother house" for many smaller monasteries.

The abbey's most unusual feature is its lavabo, an octagonal building used as a communal washing-place before meals, which was completed in 1157 (or nearer to the year 1200, depending on whom you ask). Otherwise, stumps of arches are most of what remains here, but never fear—if you can't restore this place in your imagination, there are several artists' renderings that can do it for you.

The focus of the visitors center is an exhibition on medieval masonry, but otherwise it's a bit short on the features one expects from Dúchas sites (no audiovisual, and no tearoom). Visit Mellifont before Monasterboice, because the abbey ruins aren't all that impressive compared to the exquisite high crosses at the latter site. Also note that in low season there won't be anyone to charge you an admission fee (but then again, you won't get the guided tour).

Unfortunately, there is no public transportation to Mellifont, but it's worth hiring a taxi from Drogheda to take you to both monastic sites. Biking it is also an option.

Mellifont Abbey, established in the 12th century

★ MONASTERBOICE

Established in the 6th century by St. Buite, a disciple of Patrick, **Monasterboice** (Mainistir Bhuithe, signposted off the M1 10 km north of Drogheda, tel. 041/982-6459, always accessible, free) is the only Irish monastery to bear the name of its founder. This secluded site in lovely pastoral surroundings consists of an incomplete round tower (now 33.5 meters high), two small churches (built in the 14th or 15th century), and, most important, a group of absolutely breathtaking 10th-century high crosses. These were no doubt used to teach the Gospel at a time when only scholars and holy men could read.

The 5.5-meter-high **Muiredach's Cross,** named for an abbot who died in the year 923, is widely considered the finest high cross in all Ireland, and it features both Old and New Testament scenes. It must have been carved before his death, however, as an inscription on the base reads, "a prayer for Muiredach, under whose auspices the cross was made." On the

eastern face, the Last Judgment is the central panel, with St. Michael weighing souls toward the bottom and St. Paul on the smaller panel above. On the shaft are the Adoration of the Magi, Moses striking the rock (to bring water to the Israelites), David and Goliath, Cain and Abel, and Adam and Eve. The central scene on the western face is of the Resurrection, with Moses and Aaron on the smaller panel above; Christ's mission to the apostles, doubting Thomas, and Christ's arrest are on the shaft. Though the carvings on the base are more difficult to discern, they are probably the signs of the zodiac. The cross is topped with a miniature church, the scenes with St. Paul and Moses comprising its sides.

The carvings on the other two high crosses, designated North and West, were surely just as magnificent at one time, but these two have suffered the weather more acutely. Of the 50 panels on the **West Cross,** only a dozen are still discernible. In the lee of the tower, the West Cross is one of the tallest in the country at 6.5 meters high (some say it's as tall as

7 meters), and its central panels also depict the Crucifixion and Last Judgment. Flanking this Crucifixion scene, however, are two small scenes showing sheep-shearing and -milking—allusions to Christ's traditional role as the "Good Shepherd." The shaft's eastern face depicts scenes from the Old Testament (David killing a lion, the sacrifice of Isaac, David with the head of Goliath, and David and Samuel), just as the western face is devoted to scenes from the Gospels (Christ's baptism, the ear-cutting scene in the garden of Gethsemane, and the kiss of Judas); like the Muiredach Cross, the West Cross also has a "house cap" on top.

Damaged by Cromwell's troops, the **North Cross** isn't quite as remarkable as the others; it features another Crucifixion scene on the western face and an abstract geometric design on the eastern face.

Monasterboice is about a 10-minute drive north of Drogheda. If you don't have a car, the best thing to do is to hire a taxi, as there is no public transportation to the site.

CARLINGFORD

The substantial seaside village of Carlingford (Cairlinn), a listed medieval heritage town in the shadow of Slieve Foy (a.k.a. Carlingford Mountain), is the focal point of the Cooley Peninsula in northern Louth. The locals take tremendous pride in the romantic stone ruins that make a ramble down the main streets so enjoyably atmospheric, and ongoing development on the outskirts of town hasn't so far diminished that laid-back medieval vibe. Various seafood, music, and sporting festivals transform this quiet place during the summer, but the fun is thoroughly infectious—even if you don't like oysters.

Most of Carlingford's shops, pubs, and eateries are on the Market Square and the Dundalk road on its southern side. Walking past the 15th-century, weed-dappled Taaffe's Castle from the tourist office and bus stop by the water will bring you to Newry Street; turn right at the Carlingford Arms pub and you've found the square. To your left is the atmospheric Tholsel Street, and through the arch in the gate tower you'll come to the old Holy Trinity Church, now the town's heritage center.

Sights

Carlingford's medieval architecture is unsurpassed in any other Irish town of its size. On the aptly named Tholsel Street you'll find the **Tholsel,** the gate tower, which was used by customs officials to monitor the influx of goods in medieval times. Just up that cobblestoned lane is **The Mint,** established in the mid-15th century by royal charter (though no coins ever came out of it). Pause to check out the small but elegant ogee arches flanked by intricately carved Celtic motifs.

The town center is dominated by the 15th-century **Taaffe's Castle,** a tower house chock-full of interesting architectural features: Note the murder holes, crenellated battlements, and slit windows used by archers all those centuries ago.

As far as monastic ruins go, the early-14th-century Dominican **Carlingford Friary** (Dundalk Rd., signposted from the heritage center) isn't terribly remarkable. The OPW takes good care of these ruins, but the graffiti and mold-speckled masonry create an air of neglect that will attract the romantically inclined.

On a rocky cliff overlooking the harbor on the western end of town, the eerie and imposing early Norman **King John's Castle** is so named for the king's visit to Carlingford in 1210—though building had commenced about 20 years before that, under the auspices of Hugh de Lacy (who, rather ironically, King John was heading off to fight at Carrickfergus Castle in Antrim). The castle's interior is closed off because it's no longer structurally sound, though hopefully conservation work will commence soon. In the meantime it's still worth climbing the steps for a brief walk-around and a peek through the barred doors.

Go for a one-hour walking tour covering Carlingford's medieval history, a worthwhile alternative to wandering around the town's ruined castles and monastery learning only what's on the OPW signposts; call **Carlingford Walks** (tel. 086/352-2732, tours at 11am, 2pm, and 5pm Wed., Thurs., and Sat., 11am and 2pm Fri. and bank holidays, 2pm and 5pm Sun. Apr.-Sept., appointments available Oct.-Mar., 4-person minimum, €5).

If you're interested in learning more on Carlingford's medieval history but can't make the walking tour, head to the **Holy Trinity Heritage Centre** (tel. 042/937-3454, www.carlingfordheritagecentre.com, 10am-12:30pm and 1:30pm-4:30pm Mon.-Fri., noon-4:30pm weekends, free).

Activities and Recreation

The 40-kilometer **Táin Way** walking route encircles the peninsula and the Cooley mountains, including plenty of scenic forest paths. Pick up an OS map at the tourist office before you leave. There's also a more adventurous 500-kilometer cycling route, the **Táin Trail,** which takes you through five counties, taking in all the legendary sites mentioned in *Táin Bó Cúailnge* ("The Cattle Raid of Cooley").

The **Carlingford Adventure Centre** (Tholsel St., tel. 042/937-3100, www.carlingfordadventure.com) offers a dizzying variety of day and weekend activities for all age groups—rock-climbing, archery, sailing, kayaking, volleyball, and plenty more—and packages include meals and housing in the center's hostel.

If you've ever wanted to learn how to sail, contact the **Carlingford Sail Training Centre** (tel. 042/937-3879, www.carlingfordsailtrainingcentre.com). The **Carlingford Sailing Club** (tel. 042/937-3238, www.carlingfordsailingclub.net) also offers sailing lessons and boat hire on weekends March-November. But if you feel like kicking back and watching it all go by, you can take an hourlong cruise on the lough with County Down-based **Castle Cruises** (tel. 028/4175-3425, daily departures June-Aug. subject to weather, €15).

Or would you rather be playing golf? The **Greenore Golf Club** (signposted off the R175, tel. 042/937-3212) is an 18-hole championship course five kilometers east of Carlingford, on the northern tip of the peninsula.

Food

Your best option for lunch or tea is **Dan's Stonewall Café** (The Square, tel. 042/938-3797, 9am-6pm daily, €8-15). The menu is on the pricey side for a small-town coffee shop, but at least the waitstaff are friendly.

Carlingford is darn near heaven for seafood lovers. Tucked at the back of a charming courtyard in an old stone edifice off the Dundalk road, **Kingfisher Bistro** (McGees Court, tel. 042/937-3716, www.kingfisher-bistro.com, 6:30pm-9pm Tues.-Fri., 6:30pm-late Sat., 5:30pm-8:30pm Sun., €15-29) offers the most adventurous menu in town and is also the best choice for vegetarians. But ask a random local for a recommendation, and more often than not you'll be told to go to **Magee's Bistro** (Tholsel St., tel. 042/937-3751, www.mageesbistro.com, 10am-4pm and 6pm-9pm weekdays, 6:30pm-9pm or later Sat., noon-4pm and 6:30pm-9pm or later Sun., €16-25, 2/3-course Sun. lunch €18/22 12:30pm-3:30pm). You can't beat the medieval ambience on the patio out front when the weather's good. Ring for a reservation on summer weekends.

If neither of these eateries is open (hours can be irregular in low season), try the pub food at the **Carlingford Arms** (Newry St., just off Market Sq., tel. 042/937-3418, food served noon-9pm daily, €14-24)—it's pretty good, if pricey. The portions are generous, however, and the barstaff are quite pleasant. Another option in the dead of winter is the restaurant at **McKevitt's Village Hotel** (Market Sq., tel. 042/937-3116, www.mckevitts.ie, food served noon-9pm daily), which usually has a three-course €25 menu on offer 7pm-9pm.

Entertainment and Events

The **Carlingford Arms** (Newry St., tel. 042/937-3418) and **McKevitt's** (Market

Sq., tel. 042/937-3116) are both sure bets for live music in summer. Otherwise, pop in for a pint at the delightfully old-fashioned **P.J. O'Hare's** (Tholsel St., the Square, tel. 042/937-3106).

The **Oyster Festival** (mid- to late August, ring the tourist office for details) is the biggest event on the Carlingford social calendar: live bands, oyster-tastings, kiddie amusements, and plenty more. Needless to say, book your accommodations well in advance. The **Carlingford Maritime Festival** in June is another big draw, with a regatta and boat races, walking tours, and seafood cookery demonstrations. Contact the tourist office or the **Carlingford Marina** (North Commons, tel. 042/937-3073, www.carlingfordmarina.ie) for more information.

Accommodations

Since the IHH **Carlingford Adventure Centre and Holiday Hostel** (Tholsel St., tel. 042/937-3100, www.carlingfordadventure.com, dorms €17-22, private rooms €30-35 pp) exists primarily to house people going windsurfing and whatnot, you may feel out of the loop if you aren't participating. You can expect clean dorms and en suite private rooms.

There are several rather posh bed-and-breakfasts along Ghan Road (in full view of Carlingford Lough and County Down beyond), but the stylishly designed and lavishly landscaped ★ **Shalom** (Ghan Rd., signposted on the R173 opposite the tourist office, tel. 042/937-3151, www.jackiewoods.com, €40-45 pp, s €55) is recommended for its accommodating proprietor and electric heating pads. All in all, it's a good value even if you're traveling on your own. Self-catering apartments are also available in the adjacent building.

With lots of Georgian character, a picturesque setting, and a top-notch restaurant and cookery school, 18th-century **Ghan House** (tel. 042/937-3682, www.ghanhouse.com, €75-125 pp, 4-course evening meal €45) is arguably Carlingford's classiest accommodation. Just be forewarned that the housekeeping isn't

always on par with the food. Book a B&B-plus-dinner package online for the best value.

There's also the **Four Seasons Hotel and Leisure Club** (just east of the village on the R173, tel. 042/937-3530, www.4seasonshotelcarlingford.ie, rooms €180-220), startlingly out of place in a town with such a low-key medieval character. It's your typical hotel, right on down to the overpriced bar and restaurant food, though the pool, sauna, and other leisure facilities are certainly a plus.

Information and Services

For pointers, postcards, and plenty more, head to the **Cooley Peninsula Tourist Office** (Old Dispensary, on the water, tel. 042/937-3033, www.carlingford.ie, 10am-5pm Thurs.-Mon. Nov.-Mar., 10am-5:30pm Mon.-Sat. and 11am-5:30pm Sun. Apr.-Oct.).

There's an **AIB** ATM on Newry Street, directly opposite the Carlingford Arms pub and restaurant, but no bank as such. Get cough drops at **Bradley's Pharmacy** (Market Sq., tel. 042/937-3259).

Getting There and Around

Carlingford is 24 kilometers east of Dundalk on the R173, just 10 kilometers southeast of the border with County Down in Northern Ireland and 108 kilometers north of Dublin. **Bus Éireann** offers a Monday-Saturday service on the Dundalk-Newry route (#161), with five departures from Dundalk but only two from Newry. For departure times, ring the bus station in Dundalk (tel. 042/933-4075) or Newry (tel. 028/3062-3531).

Need a lift? Call **Carlingford Taxis** (tel. 086/332-2256).

RAVENSDALE

Inland, the Cooley Peninsula is surprisingly developed, and the hamlet of Ravensdale (on a minor road, signposted off the R173 about 10 kilometers east of Dundalk) isn't a real tourist attraction as such. Ravensdale is on the **Táin Way** walking route, and there are a couple of other diversions to note. The grounds of the mansion of the Earl of Clermont are now part of the lovely **Ravensdale Forest Park,** the "big house" in question having burned like so many others in the Irish Civil War. Those interested in going horseback riding through these woods should contact **Ravensdale Lodge Equestrian & Trekking Centre** (Ravensdale, signposted off the N1, tel. 042/937-1034, www.ravensdalelodge.com).

Wicklow

There's something for everyone in County Wicklow (www.visitwicklow.ie), especially outdoor enthusiasts. The **Wicklow Way** is the most popular walking trail in the country, so there are plenty of accommodation and dining options along the route. You'll not have to sacrifice comfy mattresses and scrummy steak dinners for this weeklong adventure! Even the less-athletic visitor will enjoy a stroll through the gardens at Powerscourt, Kilruddery, or Avondale. Idyllic Glendalough, one of the country's most important monastic sites (just behind Clonmacnoise, in fact), offers at least nine different trails, whether you're out for a casual ramble or an all-day mountain climb.

ENNISKERRY

Just 18 kilometers south of Dublin, **Enniskerry** (Áth na Sceire, "Ford of the Reef") is a charming planned village, a perennial favorite with Dublin day-trippers for one reason: the magnificent **Powerscourt House and Gardens.** This tiny, tidy town—essentially just the one central square, marked with a small clock tower and lined with houses and a smattering of shops—was designed by the Earl of Powerscourt in the mid-18th century to house his staff. Most visitors just pop by for the afternoon, but several fine accommodation options make it worth an overnight stay, especially if you're planning on heading farther south into the vales of Wicklow.

★ Powerscourt House and Gardens

No one could argue that **Powerscourt House and Gardens** (signposted from the village, tel. 01/204-6000, www.powerscourt.

com, 9:30am-5:30pm daily, €9.50) isn't the finest estate in the country. The 19 hectares include a breathtaking Italianate garden designed in the early 19th century; the terraces were laid in the 1840s using granite and pebbles from the beach at Bray, and took more than 100 men a dozen years to complete. Lovely mid-19th-century garden sculptures—Apollo, Diana, cherubs, and so forth—bear obvious Italian and French influence. Indeed, it's easy to forget you aren't taking a ramble through some Florentine villa; only the temperature and Great Sugarloaf Mountain (501 meters) looming beyond remind you that the Mediterranean is a plane ride away. Beyond the terrace is a large lake guarded by a pair of fantastic winged horses cast from zinc in 1869.

There's more: a Japanese garden teased out of old boglands; winding paths flanked by rhododendrons and towering trees of North American origin; a tower shaped like a pepper urn, built in 1911 in anticipation of a royal visit, which you can climb for a fairly panoramic view; a huge walled garden with resplendent gates and an ivy-covered memorial to the seventh Viscountess of Powerscourt, which incorporates busts of four Renaissance masters; and a pet cemetery including some strangely poignant epitaphs ("faithful beyond human fidelity").

The house itself has been transformed into the classiest sort of mall: There's an Avoca shop (including delectable, if pricey, foodstuffs for takeaway), an interior design gallery, and a huge conservatory offering more practical souvenirs in addition to the usual potted plants. And of course, you can have

Wicklow and Kildare

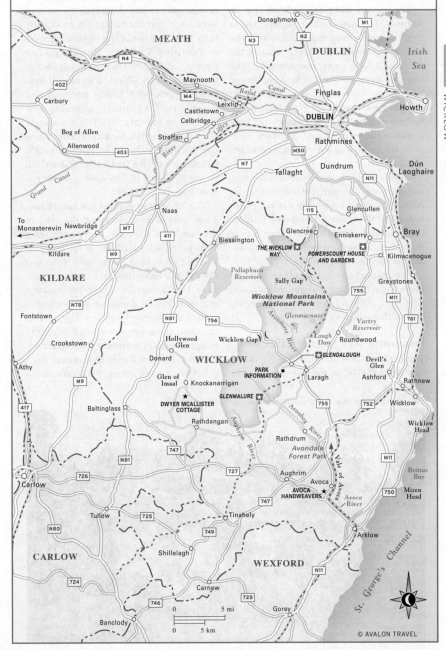

MEATH

Donaghmore

M1

N3

N2

DUBLIN

Irish Sea

N4

Maynooth

Royal Canal

Finglas

Howth

402

Carbury

M4

Leixlip

DUBLIN

Castletown

Celbridge

Rathmines

Straffan

River Liffey

Dún Laoghaire

Bog of Allen

403

N50

Allenwood

Grand Canal

N7

Tallaght

Dundrum

N11

Naas

115

Glencullen

To Monasterevin

Newbridge

M7

Blessington

Glencree

Enniskerry

Bray

411

THE WICKLOW WAY

POWERSCOURT HOUSE AND GARDENS

Kilmacanogue

Kildare

M9

Pollaphuca Reservoir

Sally Gap

Greystones

KILDARE

N78

Fontstown

N81

756

Wicklow Mountains National Park

Glenmacnass

755

M11

Vartry Reservoir

761

Crookstown

Hollywood Glen

Wicklow Gap

Avonmore River

Lough Dan

Roundwood

Athy

Donard

WICKLOW

GLENDALOUGH

Devil's Glen

M9

Glen of Imaal

Knockanarrigan

PARK INFORMATION

Laragh

Ashford

Rathnew

417

GLENMALURE

755

752

Wicklow

Baltinglass

DWYER MCALLISTER COTTAGE

Avonbeg River

Wicklow Head

Rathdangan

Aughrim River

Rathdrum

Avondale Forest Park

Vale of Avoca

M11

Brittas Bay

747

N81

727

Aughrim

Avoca

AVOCA HANDWEAVERS

Avoca River

750

Mizen Head

Carlow

726

Tullow

725

Tinahely

747

N80

749

Shillelagh

WEXFORD

N11

CARLOW

724

746

Carnew

725

Gorey

St. George's Channel

Banclody

0   5 mi

0   5 km

© AVALON TRAVEL

lunch here, too—on a patio overlooking the Italian garden.

The famous **waterfall** (9:30am-7pm in summer, 10:30am-dusk in winter, €6) is five kilometers away (signposted from the Enniskerry square), and, cheekily enough, the €9.50 ticket doesn't cover your admission. The cascade was created in 1821 for King George IV's visit to Powerscourt, but it was a lucky thing he never made it out of the house to see it; the bridge built to view it was washed away as soon as the waterfall was "turned on." Even today it's the highest waterfall in the country at 121 meters.

Powerscourt House and Gardens is one of the most popular tourist attractions in the country, so you'd better skip it if you prefer to keep off the beaten track—Secret Garden, this isn't. And gorgeous as they are, the only things Irish about these gardens are the labor and rain that nurture them daily.

Powerscourt also has a **golf club** (signposted from the house and gardens entrance, tel. 01/204-6033) with two different courses, both of them ultra-scenic.

Food and Accommodations

The **Terrace Café** (tel. 01/204-6070, 10am-5pm daily, €10-16) on the mansion's ground floor offers a fantastic view and sophisticated, high-quality lunch fare—quiches, salads, and the like. Alternatively, you can head back into the village for an equally tasty (and somewhat less expensive) meal at **Poppies Country Cooking** (The Square, tel. 01/282-8869, www.poppies.ie, 8am-6pm daily, €7-10), a warm, always-bustling café with hearty portions and friendly staff. Enniskerry's evening dining options are surprisingly not-awesome given Powerscourt's popularity; make lunch your big meal of the day and go for a simple pub dinner at **The Old Forge** (Churchill, on the R760, tel. 01/286-8333, food served 3pm-9pm daily, €11-16).

The **Knockree Hostel** (Lacken House, 7 km west of Enniskerry on the road to the hamlet of Glencree, signposted from Enniskerry, tel. 01/286-4036 for info, tel. 01/830-4555 to book, www.anoige.ie, dorms €18-22) has lovely pastoral and mountain views. Unlike other An Óige hostels in remote locations, this one doesn't do evening meals, so stock up on groceries at the village store on the main square. For accommodations in the village proper, try **Ferndale** (The Square, tel. 01/286-3518, www.ferndalehouse.com, Apr.-Oct., €40 pp, singles charged at double rate), a

the Italianate gardens at Powerscourt House, elegant and precise

★ The Wicklow Way

The country's most popular walking route, the 132-kilometer Wicklow Way, begins in Marlay Park in suburban Dublin and winds south into Wicklow Mountains National Park, passing through Glendalough and down the western flank of the monster-mountain Lugnaquilla in Glenmalure, and ending just over the Wicklow-Carlow border in Clonegal. The Wicklow Way walking trail info site (www.wicklowway.com) is by far the best resource in planning your hike: scope out the route, book accommodations and evening meals, arrange luggage transfer, and plan for appropriate clothing and equipment.

The way is dotted with original An Óige hostels (www.anoige.ie), some of which have been around since the 1940s, and plenty of B&Bs that cater especially to walkers. The route is less frequently traveled south to north, so if you're planning to walk it in high season it's worth considering starting off in Carlow instead of Dublin. In general, expect plenty of company if you're walking it in June, July, or August. Those who only have time to walk part of it generally start in Roundwood and walk south to Glendalough, a distance of approximately 12 kilometers. St. Kevin's Bus Service (tel. 01/281-8119, www.glendaloughbus.com) can get you back to Dublin from either place.

To get to Marlay Park (also known as Marley Grange) in Dublin, take the Ballinteer-bound Dublin Bus (tel. 01/873-4222, www.dublinbus.ie, #16, 3/hour) from O'Connell Street. If starting in Carlow, take the Dublin-Waterford Bus Éireann (tel. 01/836-6111, #5, 2/day Mon.-Sat. at 9am and 5:30pm, 3/day Sun. at 11am, 4:30pm, and 6pm) to Kildavin (3 km southwest of Clonegal on a local road, request stop) or, if you need to do any last-minute shopping, the larger town of Bunclody (5 km south of Clonegal on the R746); there is no bus service to Clonegal.

cheerful, immaculately maintained Victorian townhouse.

For something much grander, book a room at the **Summerhill House Hotel** (half a km south of the village, signposted off the N11, tel. 01/286-7928, www.summerhillhousehotel.com, rooms €90-175), with extensive and perfectly manicured grounds in the shadow of Sugarloaf Mountain. There's a posh "cocoon spa" here too.

Information and Services

Enniskerry doesn't have a tourist office, but the Powerscourt staff can answer any questions on the surrounding area. Check out the helpful community website (www.enniskerry. ie) before you go.

There is an **ATM** (but no bank) on the square.

Getting There and Around

Enniskerry is 18 kilometers south of Dublin. Traveling by car, take the M11 out of the city and take the Enniskerry exit onto the R117;

both house and waterfall are clearly signposted from the square.

Day excursions to Powerscourt as well as Glendalough are available through **Bus Éireann** (tel. 01/703-2574, departing Busáras 10:30am daily mid-Mar.-Oct., returning 5:45pm, €27.50, including admission fees). This tour doesn't include the waterfall, so if you'd like to see everything, spring for a tour with **Norman Dowling** (tel. 01/451-7877, www.dowlingcoachdrive.com, €33, includes all entry fees). This tour includes Glendalough, Avoca, and Mount Usher Gardens as well as Powerscourt, and you can arrange for pickup from your accommodation in Dublin.

From the Bray DART station, you can also reach Enniskerry via Dublin Bus #184 or #185 (3/hour daily). A slower but less convoluted way to go (to the house and gardens only) is a 60-minute ride on **Dublin Bus** (tel. 01/873-4222, www.dublinbus.ie, 3/hour) #44 or #44C from Townsend Street in Dublin.

WICKLOW MOUNTAINS NATIONAL PARK

Much of northern Wicklow has been designated a national park, approximately 20,000 hectares (or 200 square kilometers)—that's 10 percent of the county in all. The park is a delight whether you're walking the **Wicklow Way** or just driving through, with a load of astonishingly isolated glens and hollows; the views from the Sally Gap, the lofty intersection of the R759 and Military Road (the R115), are splendid, as is the view from the road that bends around the Glenmacnass Waterfall on the Military Road just north of Glendalough. These gorse-dappled hills also include sizable tracts of mountain blanket bog and a wealth of indigenous flora, fauna, and birdlife. Though **Glendalough** is the best-known hamlet within the park, there are other villages in which you could base yourself: **Laragh** is just a kilometer and a half east of Glendalough, and there's also **Roundwood** 11 kilometers up the road. Also inside the park, **Glenmalure** is popular with hikers on the Wicklow Way.

For tidbits on local geography and botany as well as navigational advice, head to the national park **information office** (Bolger's Cottage, tel. 0404/45656, tel. 0404/45425 for guided walks, off-season tel. 0404/45338, www.wicklowmountainsnationalpark.ie, 10am-6pm daily May-Aug., weekends in Apr. and Sept., free), which is at Glendalough, 100 meters west of the Upper Lake car park and two kilometers west of the Glendalough Visitor Centre. The info office hosts a summer lecture program and "sensory garden" as well.

TOP EXPERIENCE

★ GLENDALOUGH

Perhaps Ireland's most famous monastic site, **Glendalough** (Gleann dá loch, "Glen of the Two Lakes") is an utterly enchanting spot—no less so, miraculously enough, for all the coach buses and cheesy food and souvenir stands clustered outside the stone gateway to the old monastery and modern graveyard.

This is a lush, glacier-carved valley dotted in yellow gorse, with walking trails skirting two placid lakes and the substantial remains of a holy community founded by St. Kevin in the 6th century: a 10th- or 11th-century **round tower,** one of the tallest in the country at 30 meters, with a cap rebuilt from fallen stones in 1876; a badly weathered high cross; and the ruins of seven churches. By the 9th century Glendalough was second in size and prestige only to Clonmacnoise in County Offaly. (There are several illuminated manuscripts associated with Glendalough housed at Oxford and the British Library. Most interesting is the passage in the 11th-century Book of Glendalough that tells of a UFO sighting in unequivocal terms.)

One of Ireland's most beloved saints (after Patrick and Brigid, of course), Kevin's life is shrouded in intriguing (and sometimes dark) legends. It's said that after Kevin cured the high king's pet goose, he asked for the land under the bird's flight path as a reward. Many stories tell of his love of animals: Once, while he was praying with arms outstretched, a bird laid an egg in his open palm, and Kevin remained stock-still until it hatched. Another legend claims a local woman became smitten with Kevin and visited him in his cliff-top cave, known as **St. Kevin's Bed;** angered by her advances, he pushed her off the ledge and she drowned in the lake below. (That place is now known, rather inaccurately it seems, as **Lady's Leap.**) This much is true, however: Once word got around of an extraordinary hermit in an idyllic situation, other monks were joining him in droves, and a community was formed.

You can take in most of the monastic ruins (aside from **Temple na Skellig** on a ledge over the Upper Lake, accessible only by boat—though you can't hire one!) on a leisurely walk along the south shore of the Lower Lake. The old monastery grounds hold a small priest's house in the shadow of the round tower, the **Cathedral of Saints Peter and Paul** (dating from the 10th and 12th centuries), and the 12th-century **St. Kevin's Church**—this one is

St. Kevin's Church in Glendalough

later folklore claimed rainwater collected in the bullaun had curative properties—warts, of course.)

You can also pick up a scale map of the nine Glendalough **walking trails** (2-11 kilometers in length, from easy strolls to hill walks requiring navigational skills) for 50 cents. A walk in any direction is glorious, though the path along the Upper Lake at sunrise or sunset offers the most breathtaking views of all (and you'll enjoy them in utter solitude). An easy climb to **Poulanass Waterfall** begins at the national park information office on the eastern shore of Upper Lake, as does a far more strenuous hike up **Spinc Mountain** (490 meters). Alternatively, the fit and adventurous can scale **Camaderry Mountain** (700 meters) on the northern side of Upper Lake; the path begins at the Upper Lake car park. The **Wicklow Way** also skirts the eastern flank of Spinc Mountain.

For more information on outdoor activities and other topics, check out the Glendalough community website (www.glendalough.connect.ie).

Accommodations

You'll find more accommodation options in nearby Laragh than around Glendalough proper, though if you're of a romantic persuasion, consider spending the night at the hostel or hotel (which are right on the edge of the park) and taking a moonlit ramble through the ruins.

It's big enough to attract a lot of school groups, but the **Glendalough International Youth Hostel** (The Lodge, on the Upper Lake road, signposted off the R756, tel. 01/882-2563, www.anoige.ie, dorms €16-21) is still adequate for the backpacking set. All the rooms are en suite. As for bed-and-breakfast, you'll find a gorgeous view from the bedrooms at **Pinewood Lodge** (signposted on the Upper Lake road, tel. 0404/45437, www.pinewoodlodge.ie, €40-50 pp, s €60). You can rent bikes through the B&B and chill out in the garden after a long day's pedal.

It's on the stodgy side, and the food won't

quite unusual, having its original stone roof. The miniature round tower in the west gable resembles a chimney, which is why it's better known as "Kevin's Kitchen."

A visit to the Dúchas-run **Glendalough Visitor Centre** and **tourist office** (tel. 0404/45325, www.glendalough.ie, 9:30am-6pm daily mid-Mar.-mid-Oct., 9:30am-5pm mid-Oct.-mid-Mar., €4) isn't tremendously informative if you've been to other monastic sites, since the exhibit (including the 15-minute audiovisual) covers early Irish monasteries in general—the construction and function of round towers, manuscript illumination, everyday life, and so forth. There's not a lot of info about St. Kevin, and the legends told in an automated storytelling nook for the kiddies are 100 percent sanitized. That said, it's a worthwhile stop if the weather's bad, especially if you've purchased the Dúchas Heritage Card. The exhibit also includes a collection of early grave slabs and a bullaun stone, a primitive crucible carved out of a larger rock. (Initially used for crushing grain and herbs,

wow you, but the family-run **Glendalough Hotel** (tel. 0404/45135 or 0404/45391, www.glendaloughhotel.com, €65-95 pp) is situated right outside the old monastery gate. Between the location and the size (with 44 rooms, it's on the large side for a rural inn), it's a very popular wedding venue, so consider yourself warned. (If you stay here, consider walking down the road to Laragh to eat at the Wicklow Heather.)

Getting There

Glendalough is 60 kilometers south of Dublin; you can take the M11/N11 out of the city as far as Ashford before turning away from the coast (onto the R763), though the route south from Enniskerry (on the R755), passing Great Sugar Loaf to the east, is far more scenic. **St. Kevin's Bus Service** (tel. 01/281-8119, www.glendaloughbus.com, single/return €13/20) operates a daily bus service from Dublin to Glendalough via Bray and Roundwood, departing St. Stephen's Green North (at Dawson St., opposite Mansion House, at 11:30am and 6pm Mon.-Sat. and 11:30am and 7pm Sun. Sept.-June, 11:30am and 6pm Mon.-Fri. and 11:30am and 7pm Sat.-Sun. July-Aug.). There are at least two daily return buses from Glendalough (three on weekdays in July and Aug.).

LARAGH

A hamlet less than two kilometers east of Glendalough, Laragh is a vital stop for eats (whether dining out or stocking up on groceries) and gas (but no ATM). There are a few bed-and-breakfasts in and around the village, but the views just can't measure up to those in Glendalough proper. One to try is the relatively new **Trooperstown Wood Lodge** (on the R755, the Roundwood/Annamoe road, 2.5 km north of the village, tel. 0404/45312 or 086/263-1732, www.trooperstownwoodlodge.com, €40 pp). While the rooms are fairly standard, you can expect an old-fashioned welcome in the form of a tea-and-biscuit tray, and the owners (who also run the grocery-slash-gas station in

the village) will be a big help in getting your bearings in the area.

Pilgrims may want to stay in one of the self-catering *cillíns* (small churches) at the **Glendalough Hermitage** (signposted from the R756 just west of Laragh village, tel. 0404/45777, www.glendaloughhermitage.ie, twin room €40 pp, s €50), a prayer retreat run by St. Kevin's Parish Church. Each cottage (the architecture inspired by the Glendalough church ruins) has its own kitchenette, bathroom, sitting area, and open fireplace.

Open for breakfast, lunch, and dinner, the ★ **Wicklow Heather** (on the main road, the R756, tel. 0404/45157, 8am-10pm daily, dinner €16-24) serves up a refreshingly eclectic menu (and good coffee) in a romantic, if slightly quirky, dining room (the pitched wood roof with head-bangingly low crossbeams is decked out in white lights and bric-a-brac: kettles, farm implements, even lacrosse sticks). The service is pleasant, too—and you might even get a free half shot of Bailey's with your check. There's also nice-if-standard bed-and-breakfast available a couple doors down at **Heather House** (tel. 0404/45236, www.heatherhouse.ie, €40 pp), with breakfast served at the restaurant.

St. Kevin's Bus Service (tel. 01/281-8119, www.glendaloughbus.com, single/return €13/20) passes through Laragh en route to Glendalough. For a taxi, ring **John Preston** (tel. 087/972-9452).

ROUNDWOOD

There's not a whole lot going on in Roundwood, which advertises itself as the highest village in the county. The **Wicklow Way** passes less than two kilometers west (by the shore of Lough Dan, which unfortunately is surrounded by private land), accounting for most of the buzz in this sleepy one-street village on summer afternoons. Tired walkers doff their boots at the **Wicklow Way Lodge** (4 km southwest of the village off the R755, tel. 01/281-8489, www.wicklowwaylodge.com, Feb.-Nov., €50-55 pp). The walking route passes right in front of the B&B, and while no

Go for a long ramble through the isolated Glenmalure Valley.

stop on the **St. Kevin's Bus Service** Dublin-Glendalough route (tel. 01/281-8119, www.glendaloughbus.com).

★ GLENMALURE

Ireland's longest glacial valley, **Glenmalure** will probably remind Pennsylvanians of the Poconos. Between the hills clad in evergreens and yellow gorse, the nonexistent cell-phone service, the horse-drawn caravans on shady backroads, and the mobile library in the parking lot of the Glenmalure Lodge, you might be forgiven for thinking you've entered a time warp (in the very best sense). **Glenmalure Lodge** (11 km west of Rathdrum on a local road, tel. 0404/46188, glenmalurelodge@yahoo.com, food served noon-9pm, meals €10-20, B&B €35-40 pp, s €40-55) was established in 1801 and has a really cozy, amiable vibe; even if you're just passing through, do stop by for a pint at one of the picnic tables out front. (Too bad that time warp doesn't cover the drink prices.)

Pass the lodge, and after five or six kilometers the road terminates at a car park beside the River Avonbeg, where you'll find a modern monument to those patriots who perished in the 1798 rebellion. Just cross the small cement bridge and take off in either direction for a scenic ramble. The more ambitious can climb **Lugnaquilla,** the tallest mountain outside County Kerry at 924 meters. Approaching the mountain from Glenmalure (on the eastern side) is the easiest route; provided you're in good shape, the return trip will take about six hours. Glenmalure is also halfway along the **Wicklow Way.**

Public transport is nonexistent in this area, and even getting here by car can be tricky; the winding, pothole-riddled local roads aren't as well signposted as they could be. The surest way to reach the Glenmalure Valley is via Rathdrum, which is 11 kilometers east. From Laragh, the village just east of Glendalough, take the R755 south to Rathdrum (also 11 kilometers), or take the M11/N11 south out of Dublin and pick up the Rathdrum road (the R752) from the town of Rathnew. Then from

evening meals are provided, the owners will happily drive you into the village.

A unique fusion of Irish and German cuisine makes the **Roundwood Inn** (Main St., tel. 01/281-8107, bar food served noon-8:45pm daily, €12-20) a favorite with locals, and it should be your top choice for dinner if you're spending the night in Glendalough (though the Wicklow Heather in Laragh comes a very close second). Reservations are required at the adjoining restaurant (tel. 01/281-8107, 7:30pm-9:30pm Fri.-Sat., 1pm-2pm Sun., €15-25), though fortunately the full menu is available in the pub. Meat-lovers are expertly catered to here—enjoy your venison, local lamb, or suckling pig with a bottle of obscure German wine—though the quality of the seafood dishes can be a bit inconsistent. (Vegetarians are better off dining at the Wicklow Heather.) The inn dates from the 1750s, and the decor is an odd mix of hunting lodge and mock Tudor.

Roundwood is nine kilometers north of Laragh on the R755 and is clearly signposted from the eastern end of the village. It's also a

Rathdrum, Glenmalure is clearly (and correctly) signposted at a T junction beside the town square.

THE GLEN OF IMAAL

The **Glen of Imaal** (Gleann Ó Máil), named after the brother of a 2nd-century high king, is the prettiest part of western Wicklow—though the area doesn't attract many visitors because the northeastern section is blighted by a (however clearly marked) military firing range. Unfortunately, since the closing of the An Óige hostel five kilometers south of the village of Donard in 2006, backpackers have no place to spend the night (and after all, who in their right mind would open a B&B near an artillery range?). If by chance you find yourself driving down a shady backroad west of Glenmalure, however, you might want to stop at the Dúchas-run **Dwyer McAllister Cottage** (Derrynamuck, on the local Knockanarrigan-Rathdangan road, signposted from Knockanarrigan, tel. 0404/45325, 2pm-6pm daily mid-June-mid-Sept., free), a small folk museum in a thatched cottage of historical importance. During the 1798 rebellion several Irish leaders were surrounded in this cottage by British troops, and one of them, Samuel McAllister, burst out of the cottage to meet his death so his comrade Michael Dwyer could escape out the back.

AVOCA

A darling little village just beyond the southeastern border of the national park, **Avoca** (Abhóca) was put on the map by the popular BBC television series *Ballykissangel,* which ran six seasons between 1996 and 2001.

Based on writer and creator Kieran Prendiville's childhood memories of holidays in County Kerry, pretty much all of "Bally-K" was filmed here in real-life shops and pubs (well, *pub*). Just north of the village, the **Meeting of the Waters** is a verdant spot immemorialized in a sentimental poem by Thomas Moore. Here the Avonbeg and the Avonmore merge to form the River Avoca, making it a popular hangout for local anglers.

Avoca Handweavers

"Bally-K" aside, most visitors are here for **Avoca Handweavers** (Old Mill, up Main St. just beyond the village, tel. 0402/35105, www.avoca.ie, 9:30am-6pm daily), a craft complex that includes Ireland's oldest working mill (opened in 1723). This is where the Avoca mohair-tweed-and-gourmet-goodies empire

Avoca

began—or began again, to be more precise—in the 1970s, when a couple of Dublin businesspeople reinvested and reopened the mill. Today you can still pop into the weaving shed and watch the artisans at their looms. The shop isn't as spacious as you would expect, but the prices are a bit better than in the gift shops, and there's also an upstairs bargain room worth checking out. You can expect a gourmet meal at the ★ café (mains €10-13)—savory tarts, Guinness pie, and some of the most delicious brown bread you'll find anywhere to go along with your vegetable soup. Indeed, it's by far the best lunch spot in the area.

Food

Get your fill of traditional pub grub (shepherd's pie, fried cod, and suchlike) at **Fitzgerald's** (Main St., tel. 0402/35108, food served noon-8:30pm daily, €10-15), where the two televisions alternate between sport and soap. (There's a decent vegetarian option, too.) The *Ballykissangel* pub scenes were filmed here; check out the cast photos on the walls. There's live folk and trad on weekends year-round. Another option for hearty lunch or dinner grub, and live trad on Friday and Saturday nights in the summer, is **The Meetings** (4 km north of Avoca on the R752, tel. 0402/35226, www.themeetings.ie, food served noon-9pm daily, €12-18), a mock-Tudor pub so named for its location at the Meeting of the Waters. April-October you might also find an outdoor ceilidh—a rollickin' music and dance session—on Sunday afternoons starting around 4pm.

Accommodations

At ★ **Ashdene** (Knockanree Lower, less than 1 km from the village past the Avoca Handweavers shop, tel. 0402/35327, www.ashdeneavoca.com, Apr.-Oct., €38-40 pp, s €40-45), proprietor Jackie Burns greets you with tea and apple pie with fresh cream. This B&B is exceptionally homey, with plenty of pink and tranquil, unspoiled views of the surrounding hills and forest, along with

thoughtful touches like Q-tips in the bathroom and herbal teas on the hostess tray. The breakfast is as outstanding as the welcome: real brewed coffee, freshly squeezed orange juice, deluxe fruit salad, and Nutella for your toast (ah, heaven!). Another option is **Rockfield** (2.5 km southeast of Avoca, signposted off the R754, tel. 0402/35273, www.accommodationavoca.com, €38-43 pp, s €55), which also has lovely views of the surrounding countryside.

The Old Coach House (Meeting of the Waters, 4 km north of Avoca on the R752/Rathdrum road, tel. 0402/35408, www.avocacoachhouse.com, €35-40 pp, s €45-60), built in 1840 to accommodate coaches traveling from Dublin to Wexford, is a two-minute drive, is open year-round, and provides excellent value across the board.

Information and Services

You'll find the library and tourist office in one teeny building: the **Avoca I.T. Centre** (Main St., tel. 0402/35022, www.avoca.com, 9am-1:30pm and 2pm-5pm Mon.-Fri., 10am-2pm Sat.).

Getting There and Around

Avoca is 65 kilometers south of Dublin, with various possible routes; you could take the M11/N11 and turn off for Avoca at Rathnew, though the routes through the national park (the R115 or the R755) are, of course, much more scenic. Avoca is 23 kilometers south of Glendalough on the R755 (picking up the R752 in Rathdrum). The Dublin-Arklow route (#133) of **Bus Éireann** (tel. 01/836-6111) stops in Avoca as well as the Meeting of the Waters twice a day (once on Sunday), the two departures being at 9am and 5:30pm Monday-Saturday (arriving 11:05am and 7:35pm) and 2pm on Sunday (arriving 4:20pm). Note that this bus departs the Connolly Luas station on the eastern side of the city center during the week, and from Busáras on Sunday. Return buses pass through Avoca at 8:15am and 1:15pm Monday-Saturday and 5:45pm Sunday.

THE WICKLOW COAST

The gardens and mountains of Wicklow generally attract more attention than the county's beaches. There's little to bring the visitor to **Wicklow Town** (the beach is rocky and littered with broken beer bottles), though the tourist office tries its darnedest with the Wicklow Gaol; the exhibition is downright cheesy, and not worth your time. All things considered, Wexford's seaside towns— Kilmore Quay, Duncannon, and Arthurstown in particular—are quite a bit nicer, though the coastal walk from Bray to Greystones and the pristine strand at Brittas Bay are well worth stopping for.

Bray

Though this seaside town 20 kilometers south of Dublin has certainly spiffed itself up in recent years, Bray's ongoing shortage of quality cafés, restaurants, and accommodations puts a damper on any plans for an overnight visit. If, when walking the streets here, you get the sense that this isn't the best the east coast has to offer, you'd be hitting the nail on the head.

Having said all this, the **coastal walk** from the Bray promenade eight kilometers south to Greystones is a deservedly popular activity with Dublin day-trippers, and it's easy as pie to get down here on the DART, walk the route, and then return on the DART from Greystones. Bray itself is small enough to get the hang of in a few minutes; Strand Road hugs the promenade (or "esplanade," as it's locally known), to which Main Street runs briefly parallel; continuing down the main drag will eventually get you to Glendalough (30 km southwest). Turning off the northern end of Main Street onto Sea Point Road or Quinsborough Road will get you to the seafront the quickest.

Bray has its share of cultural attractions, namely **Kilruddery House & Gardens** (3 km south of town on the Greystones road/ R761, tel. 01/286-3405, www.killruddery.com, gardens 1pm-5pm Sat.-Sun. in Apr., 1pm-5pm daily May-Sept., house 1pm-5pm May, June, and Sept., gardens/combined €7.50/16),

a late-17th-century manor with a stunning domed greenhouse and Elizabethan-style architectural detail (all of which was added in the 19th century). The estate has been in the family of the earls of Meath since 1618, and the formal garden, laid out in the 1680s, is one of the oldest in the country. There's also an aquarium on the waterfront, **National Sealife** (Strand Rd., tel. 01/286-6939, www.visitsealife.com/bray, 9:30am-6pm Mon.-Sat., €12), which places as great an emphasis on marine conservation as it does on entertaining the kiddies. Book online for discounted tickets.

The town's best pub, for live music and general *craic,* is the **Harbour Bar** (Seapoint Rd., tucked away on a side road just north of the promenade, tel. 01/286-2274). This pub-cum-lounge is popular with all sorts, from hardcore sea anglers to the town's small "alternative" population. It's also worth stopping by the **Mermaid Arts Centre** (Main St., tel. 01/272-4030, art gallery 10am-6pm Mon.-Sat.) to see what's playing in its theater and art house cinema.

FOOD AND ACCOMMODATIONS

The menu at the ever-busy **Box Burger** (7 Strand Rd., tel. 01/538-1000, www.boxburger. ie, 5pm-10pm Wed.-Thurs., 5pm-11pm Fri., noon-11pm Sat., noon-10pm Sun., €8-12) includes a very tasty seitan burger with vegan cheese, and folks on a gluten-free diet can get their burger on a deluxe quinoa or avocado salad—so there really is something for everyone. You'll find this restaurant inside a Victorian railway building just down the street from the DART station. Next door is **Platform Pizza** (7 Strand Rd., tel. 01/538-4000, www.platformpizzabar.ie, noon-10pm Sun.-Wed., noon-11pm Thurs.-Sat., €8-22), owned by the same couple. Both eateries are local favorites.

Bray's B&Bs have a time-warp feel to them—clean, tidy, and otherwise adequate, but depressingly in need of an interior facelift. If you're determined to spend the night here, it's worth springing for a hotel. Try

The Martello (Strand Rd., tel. 01/286-8000, www.themartello.ie, rooms €100-120, s €90), which also has one of the town's most popular nightclubs Friday through Sunday nights (until 2:30am).

PRACTICALITIES

The **tourist office** (Main St. at Seapoint Rd., tel. 01/286-7128, www.bray.ie, 9:30am-1pm and 2pm-5pm Mon.-Sat. June-Sept., 2pm-4:30pm Mon.-Sat. Oct.-May) is in the town's old courthouse.

Getting to Bray from Dublin is easy, with frequent service from Pearse and Connolly Stations on the DART. The **Irish Rail** station (tel. 01/236-3333, trains every 5 minutes at peak, 2-3 off-peak departures/hour, single/return ticket €3.80/6.85) is off Quinsborough Road, about 500 meters east of Main Street. From here you can travel farther south to Wexford and Rosslare Harbour, or north to Dublin and Howth. If driving, you have a choice between the M11 motorway and the coastal road, the R119, though both get congested at peak periods.

Greystones

The eight-kilometer Bray coastal walk will leave you off in Greystones, another fishing village-turned-resort town-turned-commuter suburb. After that windswept jaunt, reward yourself with lunch at ★ **The Happy Pear** (Church Rd., less than a two-minute walk up the main street from the DART station, tel.

01/287-3655, http://thehappypear.ie, 9am-6pm Mon.-Sat., 10am-6pm Sun., €8-12). Everything about this vegetarian café is a delight, from the hearty hot meals and fresh salads (served with a genuine smile) to the pay-it-forward coffee option (at time of writing there were 45 coffees purchased for anyone in need, whether they forgot their wallet or are just having a bad day). Enjoy your mushroom chowder and coconut cappuccino upstairs in the bright and relaxed seating area, then pick up a snack for later in the small whole-foods grocery downstairs. Dinner service is available on Friday and Saturday evenings 6-10pm.

Though Greystones boasts a Blue Flag beach, there's not a whole lot going on otherwise, so you're best off heading back to Dublin on the **Irish Rail** (Church Rd., tel. 01/888-0343, 2-3 departures/hour, single/day return €5.90/10.80) suburban service.

Brittas Bay

A pristine five-kilometer Blue Flag strand, Brittas is the county's nicest beach. Located 18.5 kilometers south of Wicklow Town on the R750, it's predictably popular with Dublin day-trippers. There isn't anyplace to stay or eat in the area, though, strangely enough, so it makes the most sense to pack a picnic lunch in the morning and spend the afternoon before driving down to Wexford (or to the lovely hamlet of Avoca, 18 kilometers southwest) in the evening. Oh yes—and beware that cheeky €4 parking fee!

Kildare

Traveling through County Kildare feels a bit like walking a treadmill in purgatory. The landscape is flat and uninteresting (and presently treeless, despite the name Kildare, which means "Church of the Oak Wood"), dominated by sprawling suburban commuter estates. Kildare is also the center of Ireland's horse industry.

Flat fertile farmland aside, Kildare's

principal geographical features are an enormous peat bog (950 square kilometers) in the county's northern reaches, known as the **Bog of Allen,** which spreads into Counties Laois, Offaly, and Westmeath; the bog surrounds the **Hill of Allen** (200 meters), a scenic viewpoint topped by a lookout tower and rich in folklore (it's said the Irish hero Fionn mac Cumhaill lived here and buried his treasure somewhere along its slopes). In recent years the hill has been badly scarred by quarrying and pollution. Two canals cross the Bog of Allen: The 212-kilometer **Grand Canal,** used to transport both cargo and passengers from Dublin to points west, is still open for recreational vessels; and the less commercially successful **Royal Canal,** closed in 1961, nevertheless traces a 144-kilometer walking route known as the **Royal Canal Way** (www.irishtrails.ie).

CASTLETOWN

Yet another ho-hum commuter suburb, **Celbridge** is on the map for Ireland's largest, most glorious Palladian country house: the unimaginatively named **Castletown** (tel. 01/628-8252, www.castletown.ie, 10am-6pm Mon.-Fri., 1pm-6pm weekends Easter-Sept., 10am-5pm Mon.-Fri. and 1pm-5pm Sun. in Oct., €7). It was built in the 1720s for William Conolly, Speaker of the Irish House of Commons, a Donegal man of humble beginnings who was eventually considered the wealthiest man in the country. Construction was ongoing for decades after Conolly's death under a veritable parade of architects. The Guinness family purchased the house in the late 1970s and began the arduous restoration process. Now the estate is run by Dúchas, and the hour-long tour of Castletown is well worth the schlep out of Dublin. As a general rule, if you've toured one "big house" you've toured them all—grand sweeping staircases, intricate plasterwork, marble busts, and gilt furniture don't seem quite so splendid after a while—but if you visit only one Irish manse, let it be this one.

Castletown is 20 kilometers from Dublin; if driving, begin on the N4 west and take the Celbridge exit (putting you on the R403 for a few more kilometers). Otherwise, the **Dublin Bus** (tel. 01/873-4222, www.dublinbus.ie, #67 or #67A, 2-3 departures/hour Mon.-Sat., hourly on Sun.) will get you here from either the Pearse Street or Wood Quay stop in the city center.

MAYNOOTH

Considering the presence of a national university, one might expect **Maynooth** (Maigh Nuad, "New Plain") to be full of hot-and-happenin' cafés and bars. Not quite. Perhaps the seminary—Ireland's largest—has something of a dampening effect on even ordinary students' social aspirations. That said, the pleasant tree-lined Main Street has a few shops and pubs worth checking out, and the National University of Ireland (NUI) Maynooth campus boasts some stunning neo-Gothic architecture. All in all, it's the most worthwhile stop in County Kildare.

Sights

Now a branch of the National University of Ireland, **NUI Maynooth** (tel. 01/708-6000, www.nuim.ie) was opened as a seminary at the close of the 18th century. From a humble inaugural class of 40 aspiring priests, Maynooth prospered into the world's largest seminary by the year 1895.

The seminary is still here, surrounded by all the trappings of a modern university in the age of technology. NUIM is divided into north and south campuses, though everything to interest the visitor is on the south campus.

The most important building on campus is the cavernous **college chapel.** With its elaborate frescoes, stained glass, and miserichordia, this grand and somber church is truly awe-inspiring. The chapel is clearly signposted from the university's front gate at Parson Street, a two-minute walk.

Guarding the entrance to the south NUI campus, the 13th-century Anglo-Norman **Maynooth Castle** (tel. 01/628-6744, 10am-6pm Mon.-Fri. and 1pm-6pm weekends June-Sept., 1pm-5pm Sun. in Oct., free), once the primary residence of the earls of Kildare, has been in a state of ruin since the 17th century. The castle is now administered by Dúchas. Seeing as it's free, you might as well take a few minutes to check out what's left of the keep and gatehouse.

There is an **information point** on the NUI campus (tel. 01/708-3576, 9am-5pm and 6pm-10pm daily).

Food

The cafeteria-style **Coffee Mill** (Mill St., tel. 01/601-6594, 8am-5pm weekdays, 8:30am-4pm Sat., under €8) is your average student hangout, offering basic sandwiches and salads. In fair weather you can sip your coffee on a pleasant stone patio out back. Easily the best restaurant in town, **Stone Haven** (1 Mill St., tel. 01/601-6594, www.stonehaven-restaurant.com, 5pm-9:30pm Tues.-Sun., €13-25, 3-course dinner €20) offers an eclectic menu in a romantic ambience.

Getting There and Around

Maynooth is 26 kilometers west of Dublin, just off the M4 motorway. **Dublin Bus** (tel. 01/873-4222, www.dublinbus.ie, #66, #66X, #67A, #67N, or #67X, frequent daily departures, 1-hour journey) can get you here from Wellington Quay in downtown Dublin. A quicker option is **Irish Rail** (Leinster St., tel. 01/836-6222, Dublin Connolly-Sligo line, at least 8/day Mon.-Sat., 4/day Sun., 25-minute journey).

Maynooth Express Cabs (tel. 01/628-9999) offers 24/7 service, with both cabs and minibuses.

The Southeast

Wexford 125
Kilkenny 138
Tipperary 148
Waterford 153

F or Ireland at its friendliest and most workaday, you'll want to explore the rolling green hills and bright coastlines of the southeast.

To describe Counties Wexford (Loch gCorman, "Corman's Lake"; from Weiss Fjord, "White Ford") and Kilkenny (Cill Chainnigh, "Church of St. Canice") is an exercise in superlatives. The former is Ireland's sunniest county (just ask any meteorologist!), the latter its most medieval. Kilkenny in particular has a rich monastic history; aside from the substantial ruins at Jerpoint and Kells, the countryside is sprinkled with splendid high crosses and the remains of smaller abbeys and churches. Carlow (Ceatharlach, "Four Lakes"), on the other hand, is one of those nondescript counties with little to divert the tourist (the gigantic Browne's Hill Dolmen being one exception).

Heading a little farther west, you'll come to the fertile farmlands of Counties Tipperary (Tiobraid Árainn, "The House of the Well of Ara") and Waterford (Port Láirge, "Bank of the Haunch"; from the Danish Vadrefjord), nourished by the River Suir and occasionally broken by mountain ranges—the Comeraghs and the Galtees, the Monavullaghs and the Knockmealdowns, the Slievefelim and the Silvermines. Natives of landlocked Tipperary can still go boating on Lough Derg at the county's western boundary, and Waterford's pretty coastline is nearly as sunny as Wexford's. These counties have their primary attractions—Tipperary the Rock of Cashel, a medieval ecclesiastical complex on the site of a pre-Christian fortress, and Waterford its world-renowned crystal factory. The Rock is indeed Tipperary's most arresting sight, but Waterford's is the hilltop St. Declan's Oratory and round tower, with its breathtaking position overlooking Ardmore Bay.

HISTORY

St. Declan was making converts in County Waterford in the mid-5th century, several years before Patrick's arrival. Originally a Celtic settlement, Waterford City was resettled by the Vikings in 853. They built the city walls around their new base and regularly traveled north into Tipperary to raid (and terrorize) smaller native farming settlements

---

Previous: St. Declan's Well in Ardmore; Tipperary's quiet country roads and pretty pastoral views. **Above:** Jerpoint Abbey.

The Southeast

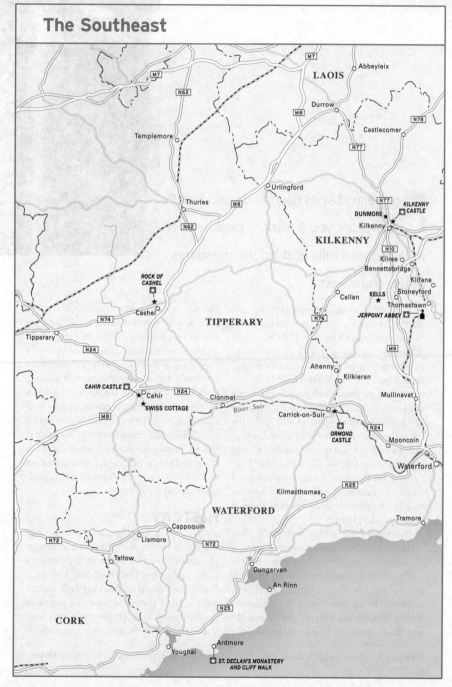

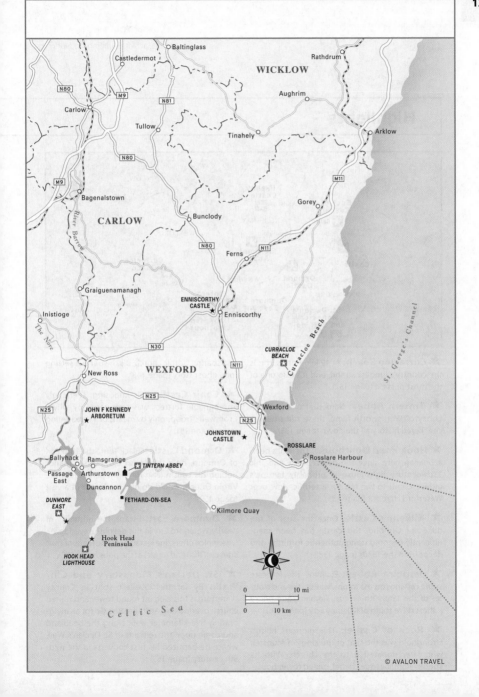

Look for ★ to find recommended
sights, activities, dining, and lodging.

Highlights

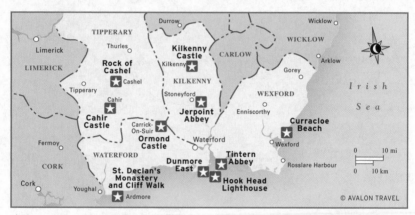

★ **Curracloe Beach:** At 19 kilometers, this is the country's longest strand, and it's also one of the most pristine (page 132).

★ **Tintern Abbey:** Named after the Welsh abbey of Wordsworth fame, these ruins have a checkered history all their own (page 135).

★ **Hook Head Lighthouse:** There has been a beacon here since the 6th century, and this 13th-century lighthouse is probably Europe's oldest. Climb to the top for a terrific view over Waterford Harbour (page 135).

★ **Kilkenny Castle:** Once the seat of the dukes of Ormond, this castle has been magnificently restored using authentic furniture and decor from the 1830s (page 138).

★ **Jerpoint Abbey:** Examine the intricate stone carvings on the tombs, walls, altar, and cloister of this late 12th-century Romanesque priory a short drive south of Kilkenny City (page 146).

★ **Rock of Cashel:** This glorious hilltop stronghold was the seat of the kings of Munster, who later donated it to the church. With its spooky Romanesque chapel, ruined tower house,

and soaring Gothic church, it's the perfect setting for a ghost story (page 148).

★ **Cahir Castle:** This imposing, seemingly impregnable fortress was conquered by Oliver Cromwell's troops only by means of a threatening letter (page 151).

★ **Ormond Castle:** "Black Tom," the 10th Earl of Ormond, built this lavish Elizabethan manor hoping his cousin (and rumored paramour), the Virgin Queen, would do him the honor of a visit (page 152).

★ **Dunmore East:** Escape the grittiness of nearby Waterford City in this delightful seaside village, which offers fine restaurants and loads of *craic agus ceol* (fun and music) at the pubs (page 158).

★ **St. Declan's Monastery and Cliff Walk:** By far the loveliest spot in County Waterford is this elegant round tower and ruined church overlooking Ardmore Bay. Go for an invigorating five-kilometer walk along the headland and come upon the remains of St. Declan's Well, where he baptized his first converts in the mid-5th century (page 159).

along the Suir. The Irish lived in fear of the Norsemen, yet they banded together to fight the Norman invaders in 1170. Their defeat was inevitable, and Waterford became the stronghold of Strongbow and his successors. Like the earlier invaders, they prized Tipperary's rich farmlands, which were later carved into plantations for English colonists.

Written in the "Marble City" in 1366 and passed the following year, the **Statutes of Kilkenny** were intended to segregate the Anglo-Norman colonists from the native Irish, banning intermarriage and the adoption of native customs, dress, and language. These laws were ultimately unsuccessful, as the Normans assimilated so well they became "more Irish than the Irish themselves," and though these laws predated the Reformation by nearly two centuries, they were nevertheless the ominous forerunner of the Penal Laws.

Of course, the Irish (inevitably outmanned and outgunned) rose against their oppressors time and again across the centuries, and when you travel through County Wexford, you might almost forget we're well over two centuries removed from the 1798 rebellion. Memorials are seemingly everywhere. Though it ended in bloody defeat, the memory of the **Battle of Vinegar Hill** (just outside Enniscorthy) in June 1798 would inspire the 1916 Easter Rising and the subsequent IRA guerrilla activity that led to the Anglo-Irish Treaty.

PLANNING YOUR TIME

Unless you have loads of time, you might want to choose between Wexford and Kilkenny. Want nightlife and fine grub in a quaint atmosphere? Do Kilkenny. Would rather bypass the tour buses? Go for Wexford, Hook Head especially.

The Rock of Cashel is Tipperary's crown jewel—and it should be at the top of your list when planning a tour of Ireland's southeast. If you must come in summer, spend the previous night in Cashel and arrive first thing in the morning.

Waterford City has dispensed with much of its dreariness in recent years, thanks in large part to an ambitious community street art project, but don't linger for more than lunch and 20 minutes or so admiring the murals (yes, even if you're into glassware—most "Waterford crystal" is now manufactured abroad). Travel onward to the coast, immersing yourself in the seaside loveliness of Ardmore, with its truly stunning monastic ruin and scenic cliffside walk. Dunmore East is another good option, if you'd like to base yourself on the coast for a leisurely night or two.

Wexford

Aside from the Blackstairs Mountains on the western border, Wexford is a flat and lowlying county with a pretty but undramatic coastline. While you're here, sample the local strawberries and order a cup of coffee with crème fraîche (instead of milk)—that's the way they traditionally like their java down here.

ENNISCORTHY

Site of the biggest battle of the 1798 rebellion, Enniscorthy (Inis Córthaidh) is fairly attractive as far as market towns go, though there's more nightlife to be found in Wexford. Make an afternoon of it on your way south to Wexford Town—unless, of course, you're here in late June or early July, when you'll want to spend your time gobbling juicy berries and fresh cream at the annual **Strawberry Fair.**

The town layout is a bit confusing, so pick up a copy of the Town Trail map from the **tourist office** (Castle Hill, tel. 054/923-4699, www.enniscorthytourism.com, 10am-1pm and 2pm-5:30pm Mon.-Sat. mid-June-Aug.,

South Leinster Sports

You can go hang gliding in the Blackstairs Mountains (along the Carlow-Wexford border) in the summer; Mount Leinster, the range's tallest peak at 795 meters, is particularly popular. For details, visit the **Irish Hang Gliding and Paragliding Association** online (www.ihpa.ie). The **Irish Parachute Club** (based in Edenderry, County Offaly, 61 km west of Dublin off the N4, tel. 1850/260-600 or 046/973-0204, www.skydive.ie, tandem dive €280) offers a significantly discounted rate for those wishing to jump for charity. Beginners' trips are available, as is an Accelerated Freefall certification course conducted on the weekends over a monthlong period. Experienced skydivers can take a tandem jump from an elevation of up to 4,000 meters!

Or if you prefer to keep your feet planted firmly on solid ground, there's always the 102-kilometer, infrequently traversed **South Leinster Way**, which begins in tiny Kildavin in County Carlow and ends at Carrick-on-Suir, County Tipperary. The walking route passes through the Blackstairs as well as the lovely village of Inistioge in County Kilkenny. For details on the route, accommodations, and other practical matters, check out the **South Leinster Way Walking Trail** website (www.irishtrails.ie).

2pm-5:30pm Sun. Sept.-mid-June); if it's closed, check out the map posted on Abbey Quay.

Sights

There's a fair bit to see here, including the early-13th-century **Enniscorthy Castle** housing the **Wexford County Museum** (Castle St., tel. 054/923-5926, 10am-1pm and 2pm-6pm Mon.-Sat., 2pm-5:30pm Sun. June-Sept., 2pm-5:30pm daily Oct.-Nov. and Feb.-May, Sun. only Dec.-Jan., €4). Another attraction is the Pugin-designed Catholic **St. Aidan's Cathedral** (Cathedral St.) in the town center.

Make the most time, however, for the **National 1798 Centre** (Mill Park Rd., signposted from the town center, tel. 054/923-7596, www.1798centre.ie, 9:30am-6pm Mon.-Sat., 11am-6pm Sun., €7); spend an hour and a half or so learning about the failed uprising that nevertheless inspired subsequent generations of patriots.

Afterward, take a walk up **Vinegar Hill** (Cnoc Fíodh Na gCaor, 2 km southeast of town, signposted from the center, always accessible, free), where the rebels lost control of County Wexford. That day, June 21, 1798, there were 1,000 Irish casualties (and 100 British). Writing just over a century after the

rebellion, William Bulfin mused: "Looking down from Vinegar Hill on the open country below, you could not help wondering how the Wexfordmen of '98 kept up the fight so long . . . there is no protection from infantry or artillery fire . . . had there been even a few barrels of gunpowder on Vinegar Hill the day of the battle, the two thousand rifles of the Wexfordmen would alone have sufficed, without artillery, to change the course of history." To get there, you'll walk up a street of ugly pebbledashed houses; at the top is a small car park, a modern memorial, the ruin of a signal tower, and a panoramic view of the River Slaney and a mix of countryside and suburban sprawl.

Activities and Recreation

Go quad-biking in all weather with the **Quad Attack Adventure Centre** (Clonroche, 13.5 km west of town on the N30, tel. 053/924-4660, www.quadattack.ie), which also has an indoor amusement ring complete with bungee jumps and sumo suits.

Food and Accommodations

On your way into **The Antique Tavern** (14 Slaney St., tel. 054/923-3428, food served noon-4pm Mon.-Sat., under €12), take a moment to read the amusing "hear ye" plaque

Wexford

© AVALON TRAVEL

posted by the innkeeper, which proclaims its hospitality "will not be extended to Highwaymen, Raperees, Bandits, Footpads, Thimblemen, Three-card trickers, Persons of no fixed abode, or persons whose appearance, manner or conduct might rise to offence." Provided that none of this applies, you can take your pint up to the cute-but-tiny Plexiglas-enclosed terrace pretty nearly overlooking the river. Another lunch option—quaint and cozy in a more modern sense—is the **Cotton Tree Café** (Slaney Pl., on the river, tel. 053/923-4641, 8:30am-5pm Mon.-Sat., 10am-5pm Sun., under €10). The menu happily abounds with hearty vegan and gluten-free options.

If you'd like to spend the night in Enniscorthy, try **Lemon Grove House** (Blackstoops, 1 km north of town off the N11, signposted from the center, tel. 054/923-6115, www.lemongrovehouse.ie, €40 pp) for B&B or the modern three-star **Riverside Park Hotel** (the Promenade, tel. 054/923-7800, www.riversideparkhotel.com, rooms €55-150), which has a new leisure center with exercise pool and all the usual facilities.

Browne's Hill Dolmen

The dolmen's capstone alone weighs over 100 tons.

If you're traveling from Dublin to Kilkenny or Waterford, you might want to stop in County Carlow to visit **Browne's Hill Dolmen** (Hacketstown Rd., 3 km east of Carlow Town on the R726, always accessible, free), one of Ireland's most important megalithic monuments.

The largest in Ireland, Browne's Hill Dolmen is more than 4,000 years old and has a capstone weighing a staggering 100 tons. Surrounded by pastures (and a string of car dealerships across the road), this awesome megalith is said to mark the grave of a prehistoric chieftain. Nowadays local hoodlums discard their beer cans in the low and spooky space beneath the capstone—sadly, even the cows show more respect. Spend a while between the grassy pastures, speculating how these Neolithic people could possibly have contrived to move such a gargantuan capstone into place.

Getting here from Carlow Town is a bit tricky, as the site isn't signposted from the town center. Head east on the main drag, Tullow Street, and at the end of it you'll come to a fork in the road: You'd go left for the M9 and the train station, but keep straight through the intersection—this is Pollerton Road. You'll soon come to a roundabout where the dolmen is signposted.

Ireland's second-smallest county, Carlow boasts few attractions for the visitor beyond Browne's Hill Dolmen, but the Blackstairs Mountains on the Wexford border make for a pretty drive (the scenic route, the R702, goes from Borris in Carlow to Kiltealy in Wexford), and on summer weekends it's even possible to hang glide from Mount Leinster, the highest peak in the province.

Practicalities

Enniscorthy is 20 kilometers north of Wexford Town on the N11. **Bus Éireann** stops here on the Dublin-Wexford-Rosslare Harbour (#2, 13/day Mon.-Sat., 10/day Sun.) and Dublin-Waterford (#5, 5-6/day daily) routes.

WEXFORD TOWN

With its medieval layout, wickedly narrow Main Street, and abundance of cozy pubs,

Wexford has a certain timeless quality. This is the kind of place where you might overhear one local say to another, "I'm sorry for your troubles, Jim," then turn a corner onto a residential street to find a couple of 10-year-olds swinging their hurling sticks in the gathering twilight. Unlike many other Irish towns, Wexford changes little from one visit to the next—and that's just the way it should be.

The town center is laid out along the

west bank of the River Slaney, which empties into Wexford Harbour. The railroad line runs between the river and the quay (which changes names, northwest to southeast, from Wellington Place to Commercial Quay, then to Custom House Quay, and finally to Crescent Quay). Crescent Quay is presided over by a statue of Commodore John Barry, Wexford native turned American revolutionary, a gift from President Eisenhower. One block west, Selskar Street, changing to North Main Street and then South Main Street, runs parallel to the quay, and the more residential John Street/School Street/Roches Road is another long block west, up an incline. At the top of Selskar Street is tidy, green Redmond Square, named for conservative nationalist Wexford MP John Redmond; roughly three blocks west is the Bull Ring, the town's historical nexus. Notice Diana Donnelly's boutique across the way? That building is on the site of the home of Oscar Wilde's mother, Jane Francesca Elgee Wilde—an accomplished pro-Ireland political commentator in her own right. (She used the pen name "Speranza.")

Sights

To get yourself oriented, you might want to spring for the 30-minute audiovisual on the town's medieval history at the **Westgate Heritage Centre** (8a Westgate, tel. 053/915-2900, 10am-5:30pm Mon.-Sat. Feb.-Dec., €7). The building incorporates a section of the original town wall. There are also a couple of cheesy folk parks in the area, but you'll learn more of local history by simply walking the streets. The **Bull Ring** has served many quotidian purposes over the years—marketplace, bull-baiters' arena—but it's also figured in every pinnacle (or low point) of Wexford's history. Here Cromwell slaughtered two-thirds of the town's population; here the 1798 rebels declared an Irish republic (and the Lone Pikeman statue is a tribute to those who died in the subsequent battle); here Daniel O'Connell and later Eamon de Valera took to the podium.

Like so many other friaries, **Selskar**

Abbey (Westgate St., beside the heritage center, 10am-5:30pm Mon.-Sat. Feb.-Dec., free) has Cromwell to thank for its present state. But the present maintenance of the old graveyard is an utter disgrace, too: grass as tall as your hips and rubbish everywhere (even inside a lidless tomb resting on the floor of the old church!). Not that they care much, wherever they are, but you can't help feeling sorry for the folks buried here.

It's said the first-ever treaty between the English and the Irish was signed on this site in 1169. The abbey itself was established in 1190 by Alexander de la Roche, who had just returned from the Crusades—and according to legend, there was a distraught element to this benefaction—as his sweetheart, fearing him dead, had locked herself in a convent.

The town's most interesting church is the Anglican **St. Iberius** (N. Main St., tel. 053/914-3013, 10am-5pm Mon.-Sat., free), built in the mid-17th century and extended in the 1760s. The dignified Georgian interior is dotted with eloquent wall memorials; the altar rail, moved here from St. George's in Dublin, saw the marriage of the Duke of Wellington in 1806. The caretaker has plenty more interesting stories about St. Iberius's history; supposedly there's been a church on this site since the 5th century, and at one time, when the water level was much higher, the river flowed up to the back door.

History-wise, Wexford's Catholic "twin churches" can't compete, but the neo-Gothic **Church of the Immaculate Conception** (Lower John St. at Rowe St., tel. 053/912-2055) and **Church of the Assumption** (Bride St., off School St.) are worth a peek if you find yourself ambling down the western end of town. In the latter church, there's a WWI memorial window by none other than the great Harry Clarke.

Activities and Recreation

Ireland's longest strand, the 19-kilometer **Curracloe Beach,** is only 8 kilometers north of town, and the nearly-as-lovely **Rosslare Strand** is 15 kilometers south. Rosslare is

Wexford Town

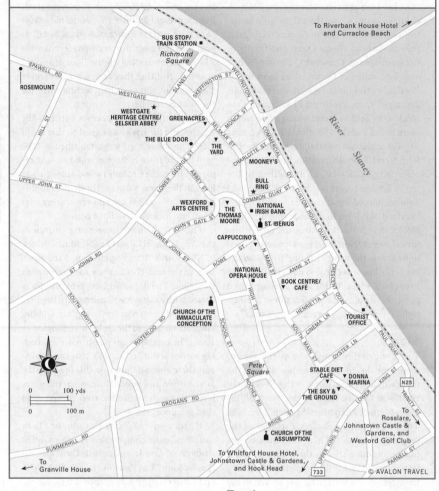

To Riverbank House Hotel and Curracloe Beach

BUS STOP/ TRAIN STATION

Richmond Square

SPAWELL RD

ROSEMOUNT

WESTGATE

SLANEY ST

SKEFFINGTON ST

WELLINGTON PL

River Slaney

WESTGATE HERITAGE CENTRE/ SELSKER ABBEY

GREENACRES

MONCK ST

COMMERCIAL QY

HILL ST

THE BLUE DOOR

SELSKAR ST

THE YARD

CHARLOTTE ST

MOONEY'S

LOWER GEORGE ST

ABBEY ST

BULL RING

UPPER JOHN ST

CUSTOM HOUSE QUAY

COMMON QUAY ST

WEXFORD ARTS CENTRE

THE THOMAS MOORE

NATIONAL IRISH BANK

ST. IBERIUS

JOHN'S GATE ST

CAPPUCCINO'S

ROWE ST

N MAIN ST

LOWER JOHN ST

ST JOHNS RD

NATIONAL OPERA HOUSE

ANNE ST

HIGH ST

BOOK CENTRE/ CAFÉ

CRESCENT QUAY

SOUTH DAVITT RD

HENRIETTA ST

CHURCH OF THE IMMACULATE CONCEPTION

SOUTH CINEMA LN

TOURIST OFFICE

PAUL QUAY

WATERLOO RD

SCHOOL ST

SOUTH MAIN ST

OYSTER LN

KING ST

Peter Square

STABLE DIET CAFÉ

DONNA MARINA

N25

ROCHES RD

THE SKY & THE GROUND

LOWER KING ST

TRINITY ST

0 100 yds
0 100 m

GROGANS RD

BRIDE ST

To Rosslare, Johnstown Castle & Gardens, and Wexford Golf Club

SUMMERHILL RD

CHURCH OF THE ASSUMPTION

UPPER KING ST

PARNELL ST

To Granville House

To Whitford House Hotel, Johnstown Castle & Gardens, and Hook Head

733

© AVALON TRAVEL

easier to get to by public transport, however. Equestrian centers near both Curracloe and Rosslare offer beach treks. Or go for a paddle down the River Slaney with **Wexford Kayak Safari** (Murrintown, tel. 087/673-9357, www.wexfordkayaksafari.com).

The 18-hole, par-72 course at the **Wexford Golf Club** (Mulgannon, 5 km south of town on the N25, tel. 053/914-2238, www.wexford-golfclub.ie) features views of the Blackstairs, Wexford Harbour, and the Saltee Islands.

Food

Get your caffeine fix at **Cappuccino's** (25 N. Main St., tel. 053/912-4986, 8am-6pm Mon.-Sat., 10:30am-6:30pm Sun., €6-9) or the new mod-and-airy café upstairs at the **Book Centre** (5 S. Main St., tel. 053/912-3543, 9am-5:30pm Mon.-Sat.). Cappuccino's has a range of breakfast and lunch options, and the bookstore café does prepackaged, though fresh, Italian gourmet sandwiches for around €6. For a more sit-down enjoy-your-meal kind of place, try the (however oddly named) **Stable Diet Café** (100 S. Main St., tel. 053/914-9012, www.stablediet.com, 8:30am-5pm Mon.-Sat., until 5:30pm Fri.-Sat., under €10), which does excellent gluten-free home baking—everything from scones to cakes to granola and flapjacks—along with soups, salads, and veg or chicken tagine.

The perfect combination of kitschy and romantic, ★ **Donna Marina** (106 S. Main St., tel. 087/394-1875, 6pm-10pm Tues.-Sat., from 5:30pm Sat., small plates €4-10) has Mediterranean-inspired menu options that are quite large and filling for tapas style—so anything you order is a very good value—and there's a separate (excellent) vegan menu, too. The owners, a friendly Italian couple, encourage their satisfied diners to scrawl their names on the orange walls. There's lounge music on the antique stereo and the place is lit with fairy lights, making Donna Marina the most delightful restaurant in Wexford, no doubt about it.

But if you're looking for something more upscale-modern-Irish, try **The Yard** (3 Lower Georges St., tel. 053/914-4083, www.theyard.ie, 9am-10pm Mon.-Sat., lunch €10-14, dinner €17-30), which transforms itself into a tapas-style wine bar on Thursday, Friday, and Saturday nights; or **Greenacres** (7 Selskar St., tel. 053/912-2975, www.greenacres.ie, 9am-10pm Mon.-Sat., lunch €9-12, 3-course dinner €33), a gourmet grocery-turned-restaurant with a top-notch wine selection. Both are solid choices for a special-but-not-*too*-pricey night out.

Entertainment and Events

Wexford's best watering hole is **The Sky & the Ground** (112 S. Main St., tel. 053/912-1273), the place to go for live trad, but pay no attention to the chalkboard out front advertising music at 9pm. The musicians seem to wander in when they feel like it, and not a moment before, so the session doesn't actually start until after 10pm. On Friday night you'll find another band, playing, weirdly enough, anything from Sinatra to Incubus.

The **Wexford Trad Trail** has organized local pub sessions so that you can sit in for one or more each night of the week; for full details, visit the website of **The Thomas Moore** (Cornmarket, between Abbey St. and N. Main St., tel. 053/917-4688, www.thomasmooretavern.com), which offers sessions on Tuesday nights. Or if you're here on a Wednesday, you might try **Mooney's** (12 Commercial Quay, tel. 053/915-5456), although they're trying to attract a younger crowd with karaoke and DJ nights on the weekends.

As for theater, the town's got two venues: The **Wexford Arts Centre** (Cornmarket, tel. 053/912-3764, www.wexfordartscentre.ie, €10-20) has the standard lineup of plays, concerts, and art exhibitions, while the **National Opera House** (27 High St., tel. 053/912-2144, www.nationaloperahouse.ie) offers classical concerts. Otherwise this is the prime venue for the town's most important annual event, the **Wexford Opera Festival** (tel. 053/912-2400, www.wexfordopera.com). Book your accommodations well in advance if you plan to attend, as Puccini-lovers from all over the globe flock here come late October. Tickets go on sale in June.

Shopping

You'll find plenty of boutiques and gift shops along Main Street, and there's a **market** on Fridays and Saturdays (9am-5pm) in the Bull Ring.

Root through the secondhand stacks at **Reader's Paradise** (19 Selskar St., tel. 053/912-4400) or stop by the **Book Centre** (5 S. Main St., tel. 053/912-3543), which has a nice café upstairs.

Accommodations

With a beautiful front garden on a plot the size of a postage stamp, **Rosemount** (Spawell Rd., tel. 053/912-4609, www.wexfordbedandbreakfast.ie, €30-50 pp, s €50-65) is equally classy and immaculate on the inside. It's right beside Redmond Memorial Park—within easy walking distance of the pubs, yet far enough outside the center for peace and quiet on a weekend evening. The gated private car park makes this a good option if you're driving. Closer to the action is another recommended B&B, **The Blue Door** (18 Lower Georges St., tel. 053/912-1047, www.bluedoor.ie, €35-45). This elegant Georgian townhouse does a fine breakfast, with smoked salmon, thoughtful meat-free options, and Fair Trade tea and coffee.

Not planning to spend the evening at The Sky & the Ground? A few minutes' drive from town is the lovely **Granville House** (1.5km west of town on the Clonard road, tel. 053/912-2648, www.granvillehouse.ie, €50 pp, s €55). This place may feel a tad stuffy at first, what with all that pristine white linen, but the electric heating pads guarantee a cozy night, and the kindly owners really bend over backwards to give you exactly the breakfast you want. It's worth paying the extra 10 or so euros for that attention to detail, and the immaculate gardens outside your window are a nice bonus.

The best (and best-value) hotel in Wexford is the family-run **Whitford House Hotel & Leisure Club** (New Line Rd., 3 km south of town off the N11, tel. 053/914-3444, www.whitfordhotelwexford.ie, rooms €100-140). Deluxe rooms have private balconies, huge bathrooms, and in-room safes (and the "superior deluxe" have king-size beds). The leisure facilities include a 20-meter pool, hydro-massage pool, sauna and steam room, gym, and day spa with massage and aromatherapy treatments available. The bar and restaurant fare is excellent, and there's live trad in the pub three or four nights a week.

Information and Services

The **tourist office** (tel. 053/912-3111, www.wexfordtourism.com, 9:30am-1pm and 2pm-5pm Mon.-Fri. Nov.-Mar., 9am-1pm and 2pm-6pm Mon.-Sat. Apr.-Oct.) is in an ugly new glass-and-concrete edifice right on the waterfront, within spitting distance of its former location on Crescent Quay opposite the Commodore Barry statue. **Wexford Hub** (www.wexfordhub.ie) is another good source of events information and resources.

You'll find ATM and bureau de change facilities at the **AIB** and the **National Irish Bank** on North Main Street. **McCauley's Pharmacy** (4/6 Redmond Sq., tel. 053/912-2422) is open daily.

Getting There

Wexford is 138 kilometers south of Dublin on the N11 and 59 kilometers east of Waterford on the N25. Buses and trains arrive at O'Hanrahan Station at Redmond Square on the quay (tel. 053/913-3114). Wexford is a stop on the **Irish Rail** Dublin-Rosslare Harbour line (3/day), and **Bus Éireann** offers direct service from Dublin (#2, 13/day Mon.-Sat., 10/day Sun.), Rosslare Harbour (#2, 13/day Mon.-Sat., 11/day Sun.), and Tralee via Cork and Waterford (#40, 4/day Mon.-Sat., 1/day Sun.).

Getting Around

Bike hire is available from **Haye's** (108 S. Main St., tel. 053/912-2462, €12/day) and the **Bike Shop** (9 Selskar St., tel. 053/912-2514, www.thebikeshop.ie, €12/day), both Raleigh dealers.

Call **T&J's** (tel. 053/912-8168 or 087/630-1360) for a cab. There's also a taxi rank outside Dunnes Stores at the Bull Ring.

NORTH OF WEXFORD TOWN
★ Curracloe Beach

No visit to Wexford is complete without a leisurely walk along the 19-kilometer Curracloe Beach, the longest strand in Ireland—and arguably the loveliest. Remember the Normandy invasion scene at the beginning of *Saving Private Ryan*? Filmed here!

How about an early-morning canter down the strand? Contact the **Poulregan Equestrian** (Castlebridge, 5.5 km north of Wexford off the R741, tel. 053/915-9667, www.poulreganequestrian.ie).

On the way to Curracloe, devoted birdwatchers should stop by the **Wexford Wildfowl Reserve** (North Slob, 8 km northeast of Wexford Town on the Castlebridge road/R741, tel. 053/23129, www.

wexfordwildfowlreserve.ie, 9am-5pm daily, free), which hosts as many as 10,000 wintering white-fronted geese from Greenland per year. Jointly administered by Dúchas and IWC BirdWatch Ireland, the visitors center offers a 15-minute audiovisual on the history of the Wexford Slobs.

Curracloe is eight kilometers north of Wexford on the R742. Upon entering the village, make a right immediately after the Curracloe Roadhouse and bear left to reach the strand. There's Bus Éireann service on Monday and Saturday only (#379, 1/day Mon., 2/day Sat.).

SOUTH OF WEXFORD TOWN
Johnstown Castle

Though the interior serves as Irish Environmental Protection Agency HQ, the grounds of the 19th-century neo-Gothic **Johnstown Castle** (6 km southwest of Wexford Town, signposted off the N25, 9am-5:30pm daily, €3, gardens free Oct.-Apr.) are open to the public: 20 hectares of gardens, woods, and pretty (artificial) lakes. There's also a sizable walled garden and conservatory, and the sunken garden is an ideal picnic spot. Fortunately, the grounds' popularity with young families doesn't detract from their tranquility in the slightest. Be on the lookout for peacocks!

The manor itself was built on the site of a medieval tower house, which was incorporated into a three-story castellated mansion in the 17th century. This manor, in turn, became a portion of the current structure through decades of construction from the 1820s onward. There's also the ruin of a medieval tower house, Rathlanon Castle. If the weather turns, you can head for the **Irish Agricultural Museum and Famine Exhibition** (tel. 053/917-1247, www.irishagrimuseum.ie, 9am-5pm Mon.-Fri. and 11am-5pm Sun. June-Aug., 9am-12:30pm and 1:30pm-5pm Mon.-Fri. and 2pm-5pm weekends Apr.-May and Sept.-Oct., closed weekends Nov.-Mar., €6), which offers a collection of Irish country furniture, replicas of artisan workshops and farmhouse kitchens, and a historical analysis of the famine—all worthwhile, though not while the sun's shining!

There is no public transportation to Johnstown, but it's an easy bike ride from Wexford Town.

Rosslare
The golden strand at Rosslare, 15 kilometers

Johnstown Castle and one of its resident peacocks

south of Wexford Town, attracts droves of young families in the summer. There are a few rather stodgy hotels and B&Bs within short walking distance of the beach, but frankly it makes more sense to do Rosslare as a day trip from Wexford Town (especially since decent seaside dining options are all but nonexistent), picking up provisions for a picnic lunch at the Tesco grocery store on the Crescent Quay before you go.

Rent a surfboard and wet suit from the **Rosslare Windsurfing Centre** (tel. 053/913-2101), May-September. **Loisin Riding Centre** (Kilrane, 7 km south of Rosslare, tel. 053/913-3962 or 086/609-2809, liosincentre@ocean-free.net) offers beach treks along Rosslare Strand, and accommodations are provided.

Rosslare is 15 kilometers south of Wexford off the N25, but you could also take **Irish Rail** (tel. 053/913-3114, 3/day) from O'Hanrahan Station.

Rosslare Harbour

Doing the European tour? Then you might find yourself leaving for Cherbourg in France via the ferry from Rosslare Harbour. The town itself is not a pleasant place, so many travelers stay over in Wexford and take the train down in the morning—the food and nightlife are pretty sad, as are the local hotel standards, although there are several good B&Bs. If you want to spend the night, there're a few nice B&Bs within one kilometer of the ferry port; an early breakfast option is standard. Try **Clifford House** (off St. Martin's Rd., tel. 053/913-3226, www.cliffordhouse.ie, €35-40 pp), a Victorian set on a cliff overlooking the sea; or on the way into town, **Cranny's** (on the N25, tel. 053/916-2800, www.crannysofrosslare.com, €30 pp) or **Anchor House** (on the N25, St. Patrick's Rd., tel. 053/913-3366, €35 pp).

Ferry operators include **Irish Ferries** (tel. 053/913-3158, www.irishferries.com), which sails to Cherbourg (3/week, 18-hour trip, car and driver €93, pedestrian €43) and Roscoff (3-6/week Apr.-Sept., 16-24-hour trip, similar fares) in France, as well as Pembroke in

Wales (2/day, 4-hour trip, car and driver €150-160, passenger/pedestrian €40); **Stena Line** (tel. 053/931-3997, www.stenaline.ie) sails to Fishguard in Wales (6/day, 3.5-hour trip, car and driver €135-185, pedestrian/passenger €40).

Rosslare Harbour is 156 kilometers south of Dublin and 18 kilometers south of Wexford on the N11 to the N25. This is the last stop on the **Irish Rail** (tel. 053/913-3114) lines from Dublin (3/day) and Waterford (1/day), and it's only a half-hour trip from Wexford (on the Dublin line). Or get here via **Bus Éireann** (tel. 01/836-6111) from Dublin or Wexford (#2, 13/day Mon.-Sat., 10/day Sun.) or Tralee, Cork, or Waterford (#40, 2/day Mon.-Sat., 1/day Sun.).

KILMORE QUAY

The road is still lined with whitewashed cottages in the fishing village of Kilmore Quay (Cé na Cille Móire). There's not much to do here aside from taking a walk along the harbor and chowing down on über-fresh seafood, but it's enough to occupy you for one glorious afternoon. You can also hop a boat to the Saltee Islands, a must for bird-watchers. Ring **Eamonn Hayes** (tel. 053/912-9723 or 087/213-5308, www.kilmoreangling.com) or **Declan Bates** (tel. 053/912-9684) for departure info.

The great thing about **Quay House** (on the R739 on the northern end of the village, tel. 053/29988, www.quayhouse.net, €35-50 pp) is that it's large enough to provide that ideal degree of anonymity. The bedrooms are bright and airy, and the comfortable and well-appointed guests' sitting room is an ideal spot for planning your itinerary for the following day. The four en suite rooms at **Mill Road Farm** (on the R739, tel. 053/912-9633, www.millroadfarm.com, €40 pp, s €50) have sea views, and there are self-catering cottages available as well (sleeping 2-4 people for €200-530 per week).

Look forward to dinner at **Kehoe's Pub and Parlour** (on the left-hand side of the R739 as you approach the harbor, tel. 053/29830, www.kehoes.com, food served noon-8:30pm daily, €10-25), whose nautical theme is amusingly over-the-top: There are two mannequins in old-fashioned scuba-diving gear, one of which is suspended from the ceiling. It's a great old pub, with amiable bartenders, a lively local crowd, music Friday through Sunday, and a perfectly adequate vegetarian option. Save room for the blackberry crumble.

Kilmore Quay is 20 kilometers south of Wexford Town on the R739. **Bus Éireann** provides infrequent service from Wexford Town (#382, 2 buses on Wed. and Sat.).

THE HOOK HEAD PENINSULA

Known to Wexford folk as simply "the Hook" (www.hookpeninsula.com), this 10-kilometer-long, low-lying peninsula forms the eastern boundary of Waterford Harbour and affords the county's finest scenery by far. The downside of this laid-back, untouristy atmosphere and a string of tiny, tranquil seaside villages is a dearth of public transportation—the **Bus Éireann** Wexford-Waterford route (#370) passes through on Monday and Thursday only. You'll find the area's best accommodations in Arthurstown. There's an ATM a few miles away in Ramsgrange, but be on the safe side and withdraw what you'll need before leaving Wexford.

The way south to Hook Head passes the vast, spooky, privately owned Loftus Hall; legend has it that in 1765 the devil (in the form of a handsome young man, naturally) courted Anne Tottenham, a relative and guest of Baron Loftus, and she wasted away after glimpsing his cloven feet under the card table one night. Her ghost is said to haunt the manor to this day. On the east side of the peninsula is Bannow Bay, where the Normans, led by Strongbow, first put boot to ground in 1169.

The tiny village of **Slade** is of interest for its ruined tower house and scuba-diving opportunities; contact the **Hook Sub-Aqua Club** (tel. 051/388-302 or 087/286-0648, www.divewexford.org) for more information.

★ Tintern Abbey

Named after the Welsh abbey immortalized by Wordsworth, the Dúchas-run **Tintern Abbey** (Saltmills, 16 km south of New Ross off the R734, tel. 051/562-650, 10am-6pm daily May-Sept., 10am-5pm daily Oct., €4) has a long and checkered history. Founded by William Marshal (Strongbow's son-in-law) at the turn of the 13th century, it was the third-richest Cistercian abbey in Ireland at the time of Henry VIII's suppression in the late 1530s. Afterward, Tintern was given to an English soldier, Anthony Colclough ("COLE-klee"), who converted it into a castle. His ancestors—a colorful lot, by all accounts—occupied Tintern continuously into the 1960s. Most colorful of all was "Sir" Vesey Colclough, who locked his wife in the tower and had five mistresses on hand at a time in the mid- to late 18th century. The exhibition on the top floor of the tower house is hilariously cheesy, and excellent guided tours are available as well. The most remarkable feature of the abbey architecture is the corbel tables high on the exterior chancel walls—individualized grotesque heads that could've inspired some of the creatures in Jim Henson's *Labyrinth*. There are (often muddy) walking trails beyond the abbey, one of which leads past an old lime kiln to the Colclough family graveyard.

Tintern is 30 kilometers southwest of Wexford on the R733, and unfortunately bus service is too infrequent to be of use.

★ Hook Head Lighthouse

Take in Wexford's best view atop the **Hook Head Lighthouse** (tel. 051/397-055, 9:30am-5:30pm daily, €6), probably the only secular medieval building still serving its original function. It's also the oldest operational lighthouse in Ireland or Britain, and one of the oldest in the world.

Built of local limestone by Anglo-Norman adventurer William Marshal in 1240, it was originally manned by monks from nearby St. Dubhan's Abbey (who had been lighting beacons back in the 6th century), and it still stands 36.3 meters high. A 20-minute guided tour takes you up the lighthouse's 115 steps, where you can see the Saltee Islands to the east, the Blackstairs and Comeragh Mountains to the north, and County Waterford across the harbor. It's really windy up here, and exhilarating indeed.

The lighthouse is south of Churchtown, at the very end of the peninsula. There's a Friday-only bus service from Wexford, but as there's only one bus it's of no use to tourists—you need a car.

Duncannon

A surprisingly quiet seaside town, **Duncannon** (Dún Canann, "Fort of Conan") offers a long white strand and the 16th-century, star-shaped **Duncannon Fort** (tel. 051/389-454, 10am-5:30pm daily June-Sept., guided tours at 10:30am, 12:30pm, 2pm, 3pm, and 4:30pm, €5). It also boasts the top restaurant on the Hook, **Squigl** (Quay Rd., tel. 051/389-188, 7pm-10:30pm Tues.-Sat. and noon-2:30pm Sun. all year, 7pm-9:30pm Sun. July-Aug., €12-24)—a bit on the trendy side, but the seafood is divine. Other dishes have a French/Mediterranean twist, and the veggie options are ample. The best accommodation options are in Arthurstown, however—just 3.5 kilometers north on a local road.

Arthurstown

There's not much going on in Arthurstown either, but it does have the Hook's best guesthouses. ★ **Marsh Mere Lodge** (on the R733 on the north side of Arthurstown, 1 km south of the ferry dock at Ballyhack, tel. 051/389-186 or 087/222-7303, www.marshmerelodge. com, €50 pp) is an absolute delight, filled with gorgeous antique furniture, artwork, books, stained glass, even a vintage hat collection flanking the hall mirror—and you might find a set of silver-backed brushes on your Victorian dressing-table. The upstairs sitting room offers a harbor view and a baby grand piano, and the bedrooms bear whimsical names ("Poor Poet" or "Passing Glances") instead of numbers. Best of all is the welcome: (loose-brewed) tea, delectable home-baked goods, and a friendly chat.

Another four-star guesthouse is an elegant, ivy-covered Georgian, **Glendine Country House** (on the R733, tel. 051/389-258, www. glendinehouse.com, Feb.-mid-Nov., €50-55 pp, 10% discount for two or more nights), surrounded by 50 acres of peaceful pastures. In addition to six commodious rooms overlooking Waterford Harbour, two self-catering cottages each sleep up to five (low/high season €300/550 per week). Though they don't

Hook Head Lighthouse

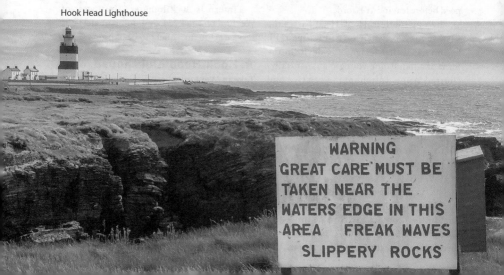

do dinner, Mr. and Mrs. Crosbie will feed you soup and sandwiches in the afternoon.

Both guesthouses offer consistently better breakfasts (and value in general) than the Georgian **Dunbrody Country House Hotel** (signposted off the R733 on the east end of Arthurstown, tel. 051/389-600, www.dunbrodyhouse.com, dinner and B&B €130-230). Some of the rooms are in need of maintenance and refurbishment and the food quality is strangely uneven—sometimes excellent, sometimes downright poor—so you have to wonder how much you can learn in the hotel cookery classes. At least the spa gets top marks.

Arthurstown is 17 kilometers north of Hook Head on a local road and 38 kilometers west of Wexford Town on the R733. There is no bus service.

Ramsgrange

Staying in Arthurstown, and prefer to eat someplace more relaxed than the hotel restaurant (or Squigl in Duncannon)? There's a very good gastropub, **The Hollow** (Ramsgrange, 2 km east of Arthurstown on the R733, tel. 051/389-230, www.thehollow.ie, food served 10:30am-9pm daily, €10-24) in the nearby village of Ramsgrange. Aside from a few surprises like a scrummy fried halloumi salad, the menu is fairly standard, with steak and seafood predominating. This place has been spiffed up—it used to be even less pretentious, with bare cement floors and 1970s-era wallpaper. Pass through the village on the Wexford-bound R733 and you'll see the pub less than a kilometer down on the right-hand side.

Need cash? There's an **ATM** at the Centra (open until 10pm) on the Arthurstown end of the village.

Ballyhack

Heading west to Waterford? Save time, gas, and aggravation by taking the **Passage East Ferry** (tel. 051/382-480, www.passageferry.ie, frequent departures 7am-10pm Mon.-Sat. and 9:30am-10pm Sun. Apr.-Sept., until 8pm Oct.-Mar., single/return fare €8/12 per car) across Waterford Harbour. Overlooking the tiny ferry terminal is a relatively unremarkable 15th-century tower house, **Ballyhack Castle** (tel. 051/389-468, 10am-6pm daily mid-June-mid-Sept., free). Ballyhack is just one kilometer north of Arthurstown on the R733.

NORTH OF THE HOOK

A somewhat grim and mostly uninteresting town 34 kilometers west of Wexford and 20 kilometers north of Arthurstown, New Ross is perhaps best experienced through your rearview mirror. There's a noteworthy attraction just south of here, however: The JFK memorial gardens will be of particular interest to American visitors. They're a nice afternoon stopover when traveling to or from the Hook Head Peninsula.

The John F. Kennedy Arboretum

Go for a leisurely stroll through the Dúchas-run **John F. Kennedy Arboretum** (10 km south of New Ross, signposted 1 km off the R733, tel. 051/388-171, 10am-5pm daily Oct.-Mar., 10am-8pm daily May-Aug., 10am-6:30pm daily Apr. and Sept., €4), opened in 1968 through the contributions of several Irish-Americans. The park comprises 623 acres skirting the 270-meter Slieve Coillte, and the 15-minute audiovisual tells you more than you need to know about the arboretum's design, botany, and animal life. The visitors center's "period" architecture seems downright quaint; check out the Wicklow granite fountain in the courtyard, which has JFK's most famous words—"Ask not what your country can do for you"—inscribed in Irish as well as English. Enterprising old chaps are on hand with their pony traps, and the grounds are abuzz with local families on weekend afternoons; the children's playground even has a small hedge maze.

The arboretum is signposted on the R733, 10 kilometers north of Arthurstown and 10 kilometers south of New Ross.

Kilkenny

Sure it's landlocked, but Kilkenny's still the most charming county in Ireland's southeast. The River Nore turns its sleepy villages into postcard-perfect scenes: 12-arched bridges, young couples walking hand-in-hand down tidy waterside paths, and local anglers casting their lines, looking like they haven't a care in the world. The county has wealth of monastic sites, from the famous (Jerpoint) to the small and secluded (Kells, Kilfane, and Kilree)—not to mention the Gothic splendor of its capital city.

Since there isn't much in terms of budget accommodation elsewhere in the county, backpackers are best off basing themselves in the city and renting a bike to explore the surrounding small towns and sights. (You could also travel by bus, but the service is infrequent enough to pose a few logistical challenges.)

KILKENNY CITY

With its winding medieval streets, narrow lanes, and ever-sociable spirit, Kilkenny is an utter delight. Its castle is magnificent, the pubs and music unsurpassed. Like the Jimmy Stewart flick you watch again and again, this city only gets better with age.

You may find yourself wondering what the deal is with all these cats—the local sports teams, the Cat Laughs Comedy Festival, the sign above Kyteler's pub. It was said that the witch of Kilkenny, Alice Kyteler, used to turn herself into a cat. The 18th-century **Tholsel** on High Street, built from the black marble from which Kilkenny gets its "Marble City" moniker, stands on the site where Kyteler's loyal maid was burned at the stake in 1324.

The city is more a large town, easily walkable. As Irish streets are wont to do, the main thoroughfare changes names from Patrick to High to Parliament Street, and it's called Irishtown after that. Hang a left at the end of this main street and you'll come to St. Canice's Cathedral on a small hill. High and

St. Kieran's Streets form an isosceles triangle with Rose Inn Street at the base; head east from Rose Inn and you'll cross the bridge onto John Street. Off Rose Inn is the Parade, where you'll find Kilkenny Castle and the city's prime boutique galleries in the old stables across the street.

★ Kilkenny Castle

Its grand hallways may often be gorged with tour groups, but you can't leave this city without visiting **Kilkenny Castle** (tel. 056/772-1450, www.kilkennycastle.ie, 10:30am-5pm daily Apr.-May, 9:30am-7pm daily June-Aug., 10am-6:30pm daily Sept., 10:30am-12:45pm and 2pm-5pm daily Oct.-Mar., €7). You won't find text-laden interpretive panels or artifacts under glass in this castle; the Office of Public Works (OPW) has carefully restored its principal rooms to their full 1830s grandeur, though unfortunately only 5 percent of the furniture is original to the house. The gallery and decorated rooms are accessible by guided tour only, which lasts about 50 minutes. There's also a 12-minute audiovisual you don't want to doze through—it has one or two scandalous anecdotes to share. Tuck your camera away before you enter the vestibule; otherwise, the staff will ask you to surrender it for the duration of the tour. Tours commence every half hour (beginning one-half hour after opening), but you may have to buy your ticket and wander the grounds for a bit first. There's more lawn than garden, though the rose garden is laid out in the shape of a Celtic cross, with a fountain at the center; a shady, secluded path follows the Nore.

From the 1390s to 1935 Kilkenny Castle was the principal seat of the Butler family. Their ancestor, James Butler, was a true-blue royalist who gained a nifty title—first Duke of Ormond—upon the restoration of Charles II to the English throne in 1660. It was he who reimagined this early-13th-century

Kilkenny

© AVALON TRAVEL

Butler family to quit their ancestral home for good. Thirty years of neglect ensued, and in 1967 Arthur Butler bequeathed the castle to the state for the nominal sum of £50.

The skylit Long Gallery, the last room on the tour, has tapestries on one wall, a poignant collection of Butler family portraits on the other (some clearly idealized, some clearly *not*), and wooden ceiling beams painted with colorful and intricate motifs inspired by the Book of Kells. Over the centuries the Butlers amassed a phenomenal international art collection, including works by Correggio, Tintoretto, Murillo, and Van Dyck, and it's a shame the collection is long since dispersed (at the auction in 1935). The Butler Art Gallery (free) in the old servants' quarters is a fitting legacy, though like all contemporary art, perhaps the exhibitions won't appeal to everyone.

In the courtyard, note the wonderfully vivid soldiers' heads (carved in stone, that is) flanking the Parade Tower doorways, as well as the balconies on the castle's original northern wall—all of which were added to soften the severity of the facade.

Other Sights

Kilkenny owes its medieval flavor to 13th-century, Anglican **St. Canice's Cathedral** (the Close, on the north end of town off St. Canice's Place/Dean St., tel. 056/776-4971, www.stcanicescathedral.ie, 9am-6pm Mon.-Sat. and 2pm-6pm Sun. June-Aug., 10am-1pm and 2pm-5pm Mon.-Sat. and 2pm-5pm Sun. Apr.-May and Sept., until 4pm Oct.-Mar., tower/church/combo €3/4/6), "Canice" being the Irish version of Kenneth. You'll find brilliant stained glass, tomb effigies and wall memorials, intricate choir-stall carvings—all the usual features of a Gothic cathedral. If you've been to others (like Dublin's Christ Church), a visit to St. Canice's shouldn't be a top priority. You can see five counties from the top of the 9th-century round tower, though the climb is not for the faint-hearted and the view is disappointingly industrial.

There are plenty more medieval churches in this town, including the Dominican **Black**

Anglo-Norman fortress as a French chateau, having spent a decade in exile there in the company of the king. Long before this, though, the site had been occupied by an early Norman motte-and-bailey erected by the infamous Strongbow in 1172. Because Kilkenny was the second-most important city in 13th- and 14th-century Ireland, the Irish Parliament often convened at the castle, and in 1366 the Statutes of Kilkenny, presage of apartheid, were written there. Fast-forward to 1935: The combination of genteel poverty and the new Irish Free State encouraged the

Kilkenny City

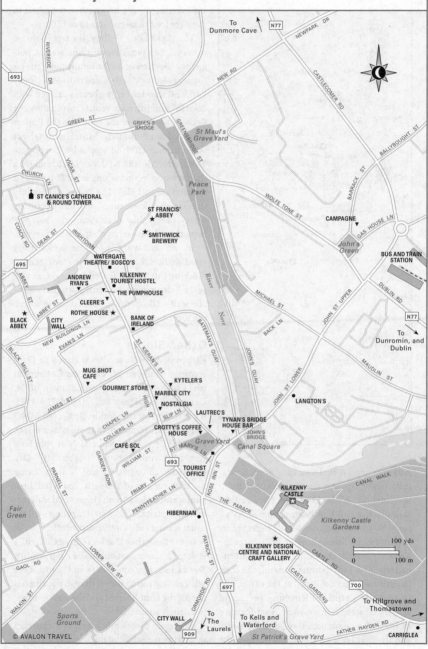

To Dunmore Cave
N77
NEWPARK DR
RIVERSIDE DR
693
NEW RD
CASTLECOMER RD
GREEN ST
GREEN'S BRIDGE
St Maul's Grave Yard
GREENSBRIDGE ST
BALLYBOUGHT ST
BARRACK ST
CHURCH LN
VICAR ST
Peace Park
WOLFE TONE ST
GAS HOUSE LN
ST CANICE'S CATHEDRAL & ROUND TOWER
CAMPAGNE
COACH RD
DEAN ST
IRISHTOWN
ST FRANCIS' ABBEY
SMITHWICK BREWERY
John's Green
BUS AND TRAIN STATION
695
WATERGATE THEATRE/ BOSCO'S
ANDREW RYAN'S
KILKENNY TOURIST HOSTEL
THE PUMPHOUSE
River Nore
MICHAEL ST
JOHN ST UPPER
DUBLIN RD
ABBEY ST
CLEERE'S
ROTHE HOUSE
BANK OF IRELAND
N77
To Dunromin, and Dublin
BLACK ABBEY
CITY WALL
NEW BUILDINGS LN
EVAN'S LN
BATEMAN'S QUAY
BACK LN
MAUDLIN ST
BLACK MILL ST
MUG SHOT CAFE
ST KIERAN'S ST
KYTELER'S
JOHN'S QUAY
JOHN ST LOWER
GOURMET STORE
MARBLE CITY
LANGTON'S
JAMES ST
HIGH ST
NOSTALGIA
SLIP LN
LAUTREC'S
TYNAN'S BRIDGE HOUSE BAR
CHAPEL LN
COLLIERS LN
CROTTY'S COFFEE HOUSE
JOHN'S BRIDGE
Canal Square
CAFÉ SOL
WILLIAM ST
ST MARY'S LN
Grave Yard
CANAL WALK
GARDEN ROW
693
TOURIST OFFICE
ROSE INN ST
PARNELL ST
FRIARY ST
PENNYFEATHER LN
KILKENNY CASTLE
Kilkenny Castle Gardens
Fair Green
HIBERNIAN
THE PARADE
0 100 yds
0 100 m
GAOL RD
PATRICK ST
KILKENNY DESIGN CENTRE AND NATIONAL CRAFT GALLERY
CASTLE RD
CASTLE GARDENS
700
WALKIN ST
LOWER NEW ST
ORMONDE RD
697
To Hillgrove and Thomastown
Sports Ground
CITY WALL
To The Laurels
909
To Kells and Waterford
St Patrick's Grave Yard
FATHER HAYDEN RD
CARRIGLEA
© AVALON TRAVEL

The Witch of Kilkenny

Easily the most colorful character in the city's history, Dame Alice Kyteler was a businesswoman in the early 14th century who gained more money and power with each husband she acquired. There were four in all, and since each died under mysterious circumstances it was inevitable that Dame Alice should be accused of witchcraft. (Why didn't they just charge her with poisoning them? One suspects her wealth and cleverness were perhaps her greater crimes.) Though she was formally charged in 1324, her influential friends (her brothers-in-law, mostly) had the offending bishop, Richard de Ledrede, imprisoned for 17 days. The trial commenced upon his release, however, and Dame Alice and her servant girl, Petronella (or Petronilla), were sentenced to burn at the stake. Dame Alice fled the country the night before the execution, leaving loyal Petronella to her fiery fate on November 3, 1324. Alice Kyteler's firstborn son, William Outlawe, agreed to give alms to the poor and reroof the choir stalls at St. Canice's Cathedral to avoid the gallows. Dame Alice was never seen or heard of again.

If you're of a literary bent, pick up a copy of award-winning *Room* author Emma Donoghue's fantastic book of "true fictions," *The Woman Who Gave Birth to Rabbits;* the final story in the collection, "Looking for Petronilla," is told from Alice Kyteler's point of view.

Abbey (Abbey St., off Parliament St., tel. 056/772-1279, free), now a Catholic church. Aside from an ugly altar window dating from its most recent renovation in 1976, the abbey retains much of its Gothic flavor. Built in the 13th century, it was used as a courthouse after Henry VIII's dissolution of the monasteries, laid to ruin by Cromwell's troops in 1650, and rebuilt in the 1860s.

Established in 1710, the **Smithwick Brewery** (Parliament St., tel. 056/778-6377, www.smithwicksexperience.com, 10am-6pm daily Mar.-Oct., 11am-5pm Nov.-Feb., €13, 10% online discount) is still brewing some of the country's best ale, though it's now owned by Guinness. (Tip: The W is silent in "Smithwick's.") The ruin of **St. Francis' Abbey** behind the brewery owes its present condition to—you guessed it!—Oliver Cromwell. The Franciscans were renowned brewers in their day; it's no coincidence that Edmund Smithwick set up shop here! Tours take place at 3pm weekdays May to September, but be sure to call ahead.

If you have time left over, spend an hour at the Tudor-era **Rothe House** (Parliament St., tel. 056/772-2893, www.rothehouse.com, 10:30am-5pm Mon.-Sat. and 3pm-5pm Sun. Apr.-Oct., 1pm-5pm Mon.-Sat. and 3pm-5pm Sun. Nov.-Mar., €5.50), the former home of a wealthy Kilkenny merchant who lost everything in 1690 after backing James II during the Williamite war. Now under the auspices of the Kilkenny Archaeological Society, it houses a modest collection of Celtic and Viking artifacts and 16th-century costumes. A 15-minute audiovisual is included in admission.

Jonathan Swift, philosopher George Berkeley, and dramatist George Farquhar all attended Kilkenny College on John Street, which is now the county hall.

Activities and Recreation
TOURS

Since there's a lot to see here, you might want to go on an hour-long walking tour so you don't miss anything. **Pat Tynan** (tel. 087/265-1745, www.kilkennywalkingtours.ie) is the Marble City's undisputed number one expert—and he's entertaining, too; tours depart from the tourist office (3/day Mon.-Sat., 2/day Sun. Mar.-Oct., €6).

OTHER ACTIVITIES AND RECREATION

Go for a stroll through the 50-acre **Kilkenny Castle gardens,** free of charge and open until 8:30pm in the spring and summer. Or rent a bike to explore all the peaceful villages along the River Nore. Looking for something a bit more unusual? Go for a round of clay pigeon-shooting, archery, or quad-biking at the **Countryside Leisure Activity Centre** (Bonnettsrath, 2 km northeast of the city, signposted off the N77, tel. 056/776-1791).

Golfers and horse riders are catered to locally as well, at the **Kilkenny Golf Club** (2 km north of the city on the N77, tel. 056/776-5400, www.kilkennygolfclub.com) and the **Warrington Top Flight Equestrian Centre** (Warrington, 5 km south of the city, signposted off the R700/Bennettsbridge road, tel. 056/772-2682, www.warringtonec.ie).

Food

Kilkenny has loads of quality cafés and restaurants, some of which may even send you over the moon. For scrummy (and very reasonably priced) sandwiches you can take on a long cycle, stop by the tiny **Gourmet Store** (56 High St., tel. 056/777-1727, 9am-6pm Mon.-Sat., under €8). **Crotty's Coffee House** (St. Kieran's St., tel. 056/776-4877, 9am-5:30pm Mon.-Sat., under €10) is a favorite with the locals, owing to homebaked apple pie and plentiful outdoor seating. Another option for prime people-watching out-of-doors (not to mention pure kitsch) is **Nostalgia,** also known as **M.L. Dore** (entrances at 65 High St. and St. Kieran's St., tel. 056/776-3374, 8am-9pm Mon.-Sat., 9am-7pm Sun., under €12).

The café at the Watergate Theatre, **Bosco's** (Parliament St., tel. 086/123-2462, www.boscos.ie, noon-6pm or later Tues.-Sun., €5-8), is all vegetarian, with fresh produce and locally roasted coffee. You might find something to the effect of "deviants welcome" scrawled on the chalkboard, which gives you a good idea of the place—funky and relaxed. Bosco's stays open later when there's a show on. Another good option for vegetarians is the **Mug Shot Café** (25 James St., tel. 056/777-7798, 8:30am-5:30pm Mon.-Sat., €8), which offers a meat-free menu every Wednesday, plus good coffee.

Kyteler's (27 St. Kieran's St., tel. 056/772-1064, food served noon-9pm daily, €12-23)

may seem like the obvious choice for pub grub—and it's very good indeed—but for something a bit less pricey, check out **Marble City** (entrances at 66 High St. and St. Kieran's St., tel. 056/776-1143, food served noon-10pm daily, €10-14) just across the way. Unsurprisingly, groups of local students hog the outdoor tables at this one. The **Hibernia Hotel** (1 Ormonde St., tel. 056/777-1888, food served noon-8pm Sun.-Thurs. and noon-5pm Fri.-Sat., €12-18) has an utterly delectable array of desserts to accompany your afternoon tea—spiced ginger pudding, anyone?

Café Sol (William St., tel. 056/776-4987, www.restaurantskilkenny.com, 11:30am-10pm Mon.-Sat., noon-9pm Sun., lunch €7-15, dinner €16-29) is a rather small, bustling spot with the sunny Mediterranean decor you'd expect with such a name. The waitstaff are quite accommodating when it comes to veg and gluten-free diets. If you're in the mood for pizza or tapas, go for **Lautrec's** (9 St. Kieran's St., tel. 056/776-2720, www.lautrecs.com, 12:30pm-10pm daily, until 11pm Fri.-Sat., €8-25, €24 3-course early bird special 5pm-7pm). The menu doesn't jive with the Frenchness of the name, but the ambience is quite romantic.

Before or after your visit to Kilkenny Castle, you might want to head across the street for any of the restaurants at the **Kilkenny Design Centre:** the **Foodhall** (Castle Yard, tel. 056/772-2118, 8:30am-6pm daily, under €10) for coffee and something sweet, the **Kilkenny Design Centre Restaurant** (10am-6pm daily, under €12) for breakfast or lunch, or the more formal **Anocht** (5:30pm-9:30pm Thurs.-Sat., €19-27), which means "tonight," for dinner. Modern Irish cuisine using local produce, meats, and seafood plus gluten-free bread options and attentive table service—a memorable meal is guaranteed.

One of Kilkenny's best restaurants is the Michelin-starred **Campagne** (5 The Arches, Gashouse Lane, tel. 056/777-2858, www.campagne.ie, 12:30pm-2:30pm Fri.-Sun., 6pm-10pm Tues.-Sat., 3-course lunch or early bird

€33, dinner €29-33), serving up posh French fare in modern decor. The menu includes a couple of vegetarian (but not vegan) options, and the staff (pleasant and efficient as they may be) aren't super helpful when it comes to gluten-free diets.

Entertainment and Events
ENTERTAINMENT
Kilkenny has a marvelous live music scene. The folks at **Cleere's** (28 Parliament St., tel. 056/776-2573, www.kilkennycomedyclub.com or www.cleeres.com) claim their Sunday night trad session is the longest running in the city—and it's also the best venue for comedy shows, open mics, blues, and rock. Or if you can elbow your way past the chain-smoking young ne'er-do-wells loitering outside, **Andrew Ryan's** (3 Friary St., tel. 056/776-2281) also does trad sessions worth coming out for on Thursday and Friday nights.

Tired of trad? Popular with a young crowd for its pool table, dartboard, and cheap sandwiches, **The Pumphouse** (26 Parliament St., tel. 056/776-3924) has live blues, rock, and folk acts on Sunday nights from 9:30pm.

Or for a nice quiet pint in a quaint Victorian pub, gaslights and all, step inside the sympathetically renovated **Tynan's Bridge House Bar** (2 Horseleap Slip, at St. John's Bridge, tel. 056/772-1921). And it may be touristy, but you've just got to have a pint at **Kyteler's** (27 St. Kieran's St., tel. 056/772-1064); the home of the city's infamous witch hasn't changed all that much since the day she skipped town on a flying broomstick.

Whatever dramatic or musical act's touring the country is sure to play at the **Watergate Theatre** (Parliament St., tel. 056/776-1674, www.watergatekilkenny.com, €12-20). The Watergate is one of the primary venues for the city's top two festivals—the Cat Laughs Comedy Festival and the Kilkenny Arts Festival.

FESTIVALS AND EVENTS
Sponsored by Smithwicks, the **Cat Laughs Comedy Festival** (Parliament St., tel. 056/776-3837, www.thecatlaughs.com) in late May/early June is the best known on the city's calendar, attracting some of the funniest performers on the planet. The well-established **Kilkenny Arts Festival** (9-10 Abbey Business Centre, Abbey St., tel. 056/775-2175, www.kilkennyarts.ie) in mid-August offers a marvelous program of jazz and classical concerts, film screenings, art exhibitions, book readings, and street theater. There's also the **Carlsberg Kilkenny Rhythm and Roots Weekend** (29 Parliament St., tel. 056/779-0057, www.kilkennyroots.com), a music festival focusing primarily on bluegrass and American country/western. Rhythm and Roots usually takes place the last weekend in April or first weekend in May.

Book your room well in advance even if you aren't planning to attend any events, as everyone and their uncle descends upon this little city for these three big festivals (the arts festival alone draws as many as 70,000 out-of-towners). For more info, check out **KilkennyCity.net** (www.kilkennycity.net).

Shopping
Kilkenny has a reputation for fine shopping thanks primarily to the flagship **Kilkenny Design Centre** (Castle Yard, tel. 056/772-2118, www.kilkennydesign.com), which is still selling the cutting edge of modern Irish design, be it jewelry, fashion, homewares, or cuisine. This upmarket store-cum-café is housed in the erstwhile stables of the castle directly across the street, where you'll also find the **National Craft Gallery** (Castle Yard, tel. 056/776-1804, www.ccoi.ie), which showcases the work of eminent Irish textile artists, woodturners, potters, silversmiths, and others.

Rightly described by its sweet-tempered shopkeeper as "a bit of a wonderland," **Butterslip** (Butterslip Ln., tel. 056/770-2502, www.butterslip.com) is a girlie paradise of French soaps and perfume, chic jewelry and handbags, and ultra-feminine garb. Ladies, don't miss this one.

Pick up paperbacks, OS maps, and maybe

even a bit of lunch at the **Kilkenny Book Centre** (10 High St., tel. 056/776-2117), which has an upstairs café.

Accommodations

You'll sleep well here no matter your budget. The **Kilkenny Tourist Hostel** (35 Parliament St., tel. 056/776-3541, www.kilkennyhostel.ie, dorms €14-20, private rooms €20-26 pp) is a great spot—central, friendly, laid-back, bohemian yet clean.

But not all B&Bs are created equal, especially in the city center; some are overpriced, run-down, or (often) both. One safe bet within a five-minute walk of the center is cheerful ivy-covered **Carriglea** (Archers Ave., Castle Rd., tel. 056/776-1629, www.carrigleakilkenny.com, Feb.-Nov., €30-38 pp), with fabulous pancake breakfasts and an incredibly kind and helpful proprietor. Another good choice is **The Laurels** (College Rd., tel. 056/776-1501, www.thelaurelskilkenny.com, €40-45 pp), with charming yet modern gabled rooms. It's a 10-minute walk southwest from the center of town.

If you have a rental car, consider staying at a truly superlative B&B, **Lawcus Farm** in Stoneyford, south of Kilkenny City.

Two of Kilkenny's best hotels are also the most central: **Langton's** (69 John St., tel. 056/776-5133, www.langtons.ie, rooms €115-145, s €75) and the ultra-classy Victorian **Hibernian** (1 Ormonde St., tel. 056/777-1888, www.kilkennyhibernianhotel.com, rooms €80-100). With its nightclub and modern bars, Langton's attracts a younger clientele (though one of the bars hosts trad sessions most nights of the week), and the Hibernian has a quieter, more reserved ambience (possibly to the point of stodginess, depending on your taste). Both offer good food and top-notch service at every turn.

Information and Services

The **tourist office** is housed in the city's 16th-century poorhouse (Shee Alms House, Rose Inn St., tel. 056/775-1500, www.kilkennytourism.ie, 9am-5pm Mon.-Sat. Nov.-Mar., 9am-6pm Mon.-Sat. Apr.-Oct., 11am-1pm and 2pm-5pm Sun. May-Sept., until 7pm July-Aug.).

There are several banks with ATMs and bureaux de change at the Parade and High Street intersection, and at the **Bank of Ireland** on Parliament Street. **O'Connell's Pharmacy** (tel. 056/772-1033) has two branches (4 Rose Inn St. and 89 High St.).

Getting There

Kilkenny City is 123 kilometers southwest of Dublin (on the M9) and 48 kilometers due north of Waterford (on the M9, picking up the N10 in Knocktopher). Buses and trains pull into MacDonagh Station (on the Dublin road, tel. 056/772-2024), just under half a kilometer east of the city center, over the bridge. **Bus Éireann** passes through on the Dublin-Cork (#7, 9/day Mon.-Sat., 7/day Sun.) and Waterford-Athlone (#73, 2/day Mon.-Sat., 1/day Sun.) routes; from Athlone you can change buses for Galway and other points north. **Irish Rail** stops here on the Dublin-Waterford line (4-5 trains/day).

Getting Around

Driving in Kilkenny can be a real pain in the you-know-what. Free parking is nearly impossible to come by, though you can find some beside the public library on John's Quay (on the east bank of the River Nore). There's also free parking along Ormonde Road, a five-minute walk from the town center.

For bike rental, stop by **J.J. Wall** (88 Maudlin St., tel. 056/772-1236, www.wallscycles.ie, €14/day).

The taxi rank is at the Patrick Street car park beside the castle. Or phone **Kilkenny Taxis** (tel. 087/225-5333).

NORTH OF KILKENNY CITY

Dunmore

The Irish words for **Dunmore Cave** (Ballyfoyle, 10 km north of Kilkenny, signposted off the N78, tel. 056/776-7726, €4) are Dearc Fearna—"Cave of the Alders"—a poetic name for one of Ireland's darkest places. Hours vary seasonally (9:30am-5pm daily mid-Mar.-mid-June and mid-Sept.-Oct., 9:30am-6:30pm daily mid-June-mid-Sept., 10am-5pm weekends the rest of year). Note that you can only visit the caves on a guided tour, and unfortunately you aren't allowed to take pictures.

SOUTH OF KILKENNY CITY
Stoneyford

How'd you like to take your breakfast in an old-fashioned greenhouse? ★ **Lawcus Farm** (Lawcus, near Stoneyford, 16km south of Kilkenny City on the N10 and R713, 086/603-1667, www.lawcusfarmguesthouse.com, €50 pp, s €80) is truly one of the most special accommodations anywhere on this island. The farmhouse itself has been lovingly restored, and there are plenty of adorable farm animals to coo over. Couples can fulfill a childhood dream by staying in an absolutely beautiful tree house partially constructed from salvaged materials (two-night stay €250, additional nights €100, rate includes breakfast in the main guesthouse). Set in the woods above the River Kings, the treehouse features a king-size bed and all mod cons excepting television and reliable Wi-Fi. So long as you've rented a car, Lawcus Farm is the ideal base for exploring Kilkenny City and all the county's delightful villages—Kells Priory is only a mile from the guesthouse.

Bennettsbridge

Quiet **Bennettsbridge** (Droichead Bineád) is on the tourist map for **Nicholas Mosse Pottery** (on the far side of the bridge, signposted, tel. 056/972-7105, www.nicholas-mosse.com), open Monday to Saturday all year, plus Sunday afternoons in July and August. There's a tearoom and do-it-yourself studio, too. Souvenir-hunters can make this a nice day trip out of Kilkenny, but there's not much of interest otherwise.

Bennettsbridge is 8.5 kilometers south of Kilkenny on the R700.

Kilfane

An early 14th-century church ruin outside the village of **Kilfane** (Cill Pháin, "Church of Pan," signposted 600 m off the M9) contains a truly stunning knight's effigy known as the **Cantwell Fada,** or "Long Cantwell"—most likely Thomas de Cantwell, the Welsh adventurer turned Lord of Kilfane. Complete with chain mail, sword, shield, and coat of arms, Tom's tall, skinny effigy is attached to the wall, unusually enough; the church has a castellated Norman tower as well.

One kilometer south is the **Kilfane Glen & Waterfall** (signposted off the M9, tel. 056/792-4558, www.kilfane.com, 11am-6pm daily July-Aug., 2pm-6pm Sun. Apr.-June and Sept., €7), with a 15-acre garden dating to the late 18th century and several shady walking trails.

Kilfane is three kilometers north of Thomastown off the M9, and you can request a stop on the **Bus Éireann** Waterford-Dublin route (#4, 10/day Mon.-Sat., 7/day Sun.).

Thomastown

Quiet as can be, **Thomastown** (named for Thomas de Cantwell) is a pleasant market town full of hardware stores and farm suppliers. This is the kind of place where a truckload of pigs (their rear ends wiggling through the side-slats) could back up traffic for several minutes as the driver negotiates a sharp bend in the narrow street. You'll pass through Thomastown on your way to the magnificent Jerpoint Abbey just south of town.

Though there are a couple of nice B&Bs in the area, the dearth of cafés and restaurants in town used to necessitate a trip into Kilkenny City for dinner. Fortunately, the friendly, Mediterranean-inspired Kilkenny City restaurant **Café Sol** (Low St., tel. 056/775-4945, www.restaurantskilkenny.com, 5:30pm-10pm Wed.-Sun., also noon-4pm Fri.-Sun., lunch €7-15, dinner €16-29) has opened a sister restaurant on the main street.

For the romantic Georgian farmhouse experience, look no further than **Ballyduff House** (5 km south of town off the R700, tel.

056/775-8488, €50 pp)—classy antiques, fire-places (nonworking, but they add to the at-mosphere), and commodious bedrooms and bathtubs. The house is a bit drafty (aren't they all?), but you've got an electric heating pad on that big comfy bed. Ballyduff House caters to wedding parties as well, so book in advance. Or try **Abbey House** (on the R448, 2.5 km south of town, tel. 056/772-4166, www.abbey-housejerpoint.com, €45 pp), directly across the road from Jerpoint. Built in 1750, the grounds (with well-kept gardens and a small river) are delightful, and you'll receive an old-fashioned welcome of tea and scones.

Thomastown is 18 kilometers south of Kilkenny on the R700. **Bus Éireann** passes through on the Athlone-Kilkenny-Waterford route (#73, 2/day Mon.-Sat., 1/day Sun.), as well as the Dublin-Waterford route (#4, 10/day Mon.-Sat., 7/day Sun.). The bus can drop you off at Jerpoint.

★ Jerpoint Abbey

Established by the Cistercian order in the late 12th century, **Jerpoint Abbey** (on the R448, 2.5 km southwest of Thomastown, tel. 056/24623, 10am-5pm daily Mar.-May and mid-Sept.-Oct., 9:30am-6pm daily June-mid-Sept., 10am-4pm daily Nov., €4) con-tains some of Ireland's most exquisite tomb and altar carvings in its Romanesque church. There are more effigies to be found along the early 15th-century cloister, including those of St. Christopher and various knights (or mer-cenaries). You can climb upstairs to the old dormitory to observe the cloister and its trim green lawn from above.

The visitors center has on display an early 16th-century double tomb effigy (of a harper and his wife) as well as a few fragments of a high cross from Kilkieran. Unfortunately, you aren't likely to get the 45-minute guided tour unless you tag along with a larger group. If you have time to see only one abbey ruin in the southeast, let it be Jerpoint.

Inistioge

Known as one the country's most charming

picturesque St. Mary's church in the riverside village of Inistioge

riverside villages, **Inistioge** (Inis Tíog, "in-ish-TEEG") has hosted several film crews over the years, most famously for *Circle of Friends*. It's as quiet and timeless as it looks in the movie, with just a few pubs around a small central green and an Anglican church, **St. Mary's,** with a small clock tower dressed in ivy. Inistioge is also on the 102-kilometer **South Leinster Way,** but those not so ath-letically inclined can go for a walk through the nearby **Woodstock Gardens** (1 km south of the village off the R700, signposted, tel. 056/775-8797, www.woodstock.ie, 9am-8pm daily May-Sept., 10am-4:30pm daily Oct.-Apr., €4 parking fee)—once the demesne of a big house (burnt during the Civil War in 1922), now a state park in the lee of 520-meter Brandon Hill, with shady walking trails and picnic areas.

After your ramble, stop by the predictably quaint **Old Schoolhouse River Café** (op-posite the riverside picnic green by the bridge, tel. 056/775-8723, 11am-6pm daily June-Sept., 11am-6pm Sat.-Sun. mid-Mar.-May and

Oct.-mid-Nov., €8) for tea and apple pie. (The outdoor seating would be even more pleasant were the main road not separating the café from the picnic green.)

The Irish-German family that runs **The Otter** (High St., tel. 087/622-3758, lunch served 1pm-5pm daily, under €12) has a delightfully mischievous sense of humor—take as evidence the sign on the windowsill proclaiming this pub a "husband crèche" (i.e., daycare center). The outdoor tables are a great spot to hang out with a pint of Guinness or Krombacher on a sunny afternoon.

The dearth of accommodations in and around Inistioge is surprising given its popularity with film producers. Your best option in town is upstairs at the **Woodstock Arms** (The Square, tel. 056/775-8440, www.woodstockarms.ie, €35-40 pp), which offers tidy (if small and Spartan) en suite rooms overlooking the square. The Woodstock Arms is also your best bet for dinner, and the front beer garden is the happeningest spot in town.

Outside the village is the wonderfully atmospheric, slightly quirky **Cullintra House** (The Rower, 7 km southeast of Inistioge, signposted off the R700, tel. 051/423-614, www.cullintrahouse.com, €60 pp), an 18th-century farmhouse with 230 acres of gardens and walking trails. If you're looking for a romantic getaway, you'll find no better place, what with the tranquil, verdant setting, optional candlelit dinners, and rooms authentically furnished with big brass beds (two in a converted barn with A-frame ceiling and exposed wood beams). One catch: There's a two-night minimum stay.

Inistioge is 26 kilometers southeast of Kilkenny on the R700, and Bus Éireann service is too infrequent to be of use (one bus, Thursday only).

Kells

There's not much of architectural interest in the sprawling ruin of the Augustinian **Kells Priory** (600 meters north of Kells village on the R697, always accessible, free), yet this place is majestic all the same. Seven towers punctuate a fortified wall featuring gates complete with murder holes, inside the high walls a vast lawn. Daisies and buttercups dapple the unmown grass. Most of what you see dates to the 15th century, though the oldest buildings are from the late 12th.

There are picnic tables just outside the gate, beside the car park, or you might rather take your lunch inside among the ruins. Kells is 13 kilometers south of Kilkenny off the N10 (the signposted turnoff at Stoneyford will take you west down a local road), and there is no public transportation.

Kilree

In an out-of-the-way spot in a small glen, **Kilree Church** features a roofless 28-meter round tower and a 9th-century high cross in the field beyond, said to mark the grave of a pagan chieftain. Hop the stone wall for a closer look at its carvings—Jacob and the angel, Daniel in the lions' den—and you'll soon have plenty of bovine company. For those interested in monastic ruins, tranquil Kilree is definitely worth the detour.

Kilree is two kilometers south of Kells, signposted off the R697.

Tipperary

Tipperary is the island's largest landlocked county, and one of its most fertile. In fact, the center of the county (within the basin of the River Suir) is called the "Golden Vale" for its high-yield farmlands, bounded by the Glen of Aherlow and the Galtee and Comeragh mountain ranges. From the lumpy Knockmealdowns to the aptly named Silvermines (which have the Shannon region's highest peak, the 694-meter Keeper's Hill), Tipperary's mountains and valleys provide plenty of hill-walking opportunities. On the whole, the county's towns are refreshingly business-as-usual, even in Cashel.

CASHEL

Aside from its magnificent hilltop fortress-cum-cathedral, there's not much going on in Cashel (Caiseal Mumhan, "Stone Fort of Munster"), though a few authentically traditional pubs, one excellent restaurant, and a touristy-but-fun ceilidh show warrant an overnight stay.

Most of what you'll need is located on or just off Cashel's Main Street, and it's easy to orient yourself since the Rock is visible from any place in town.

TOP EXPERIENCE

★ Rock of Cashel

One of Ireland's most spectacular ruins, the hilltop **Rock of Cashel** (500 m from town center off the M8, tel. 06 2/61437, 9am-7pm June-mid-Sept., 9am-5:30pm mid-Mar.-May and mid-Sept.-mid-Oct., 9am-4:30pm mid-Oct.-mid-March, €7) dominates the surrounding landscape—so much so that the breath catches in your throat when you first spot it on your way into town. Walking through the ruins is just as overwhelming—not just because of the crowds, but because there's so much to see, so much medieval history to absorb. From the mid-4th century

the Rock served as the seat of the kings of Munster, and Patrick baptized King Aengus here in 448 (why this place is often called "St. Patrick's Rock"). Much later, in 1101, another king donated the fortress to the church, and the 28-meter round tower, high cross, and Romanesque **Cormac's Chapel** all date from this early period.

The small, dark, spooky chapel is the Rock's most remarkable edifice. Carvings of individualized heads lining the walls are typical of the Romanesque style, but many of these faces belonged to real people: It's said the stoneworkers made likenesses of all the people who owed them money. The original wall frescoes were painted over in 1647 at Cromwell's command, and the remnants you see now were all that could be salvaged when the layers were carefully removed by modern technicians.

But the most dramatic building on the Rock is the 13th-century Gothic cathedral. At its western end is a 15th-century tower house built for the archbishop's residence, but it was so cold and damp that it wasn't used for long. A 19th-century lightning storm left a chunk of the castle wall on the grass outside, and it hasn't been moved since; you can gauge the wall thickness from the sheer size of this fragment. (By the way, "the Rock" refers to the whole medieval compound, not this particular "rock.")

The restored **Hall of the Vicars Choral** serves as the visitors center, where you can watch the 17-minute audiovisual and dutifully read the exhibition panels before the 45-minute guided tour begins. It's worth waiting for, as the guides have plenty of intriguing stories to tell. The most outrageous of these is about Miler McGrath, who served as Protestant archbishop here between 1571 and 1621—and simultaneously as a Catholic bishop near Belfast. At the time of his death no one had any idea that he'd embezzled from

Tipperary

GALWAY

353

352

463

OFFALY

N52

Birr

Kinnitty

LAOIS

N65

Lough Derg

421

440

Borrisokane

N62

Mountrath

M7

N52

Dromineer

Roscrea

Borris-in-
Ossory

495

Aghaboe

434

Garrykennedy

Durrow

494

Nenagh

M7

Rathdowney

Ballina

500

499

Silvermines

Templemore

Silvermine Mountains

Johnstown

Birdhill

497

TIPPERARY

M8

M7

KILKENNY

503

Rear Cross

503

Thurles

N75

LIMERICK

Hollyford

Holy
Cross

N62

689

Callan

N24

497

660

River Suir

Killenaule

513

Cashel

N74

ROCK OF
CASHEL

692

Tipperary

M8

Fethard

Garryspillane

663

N76

Galtee Mountains

Cahir

Carrick-
on-Suir

KNOCKMEALDOWN SCENIC ROUTE

CAHIR
CASTLE

671

Clonmel

ORMOND
CASTLE

Mitchelstown

668

The Vee
Mountains

Ballymacarbry

0   5 mi

N73

Knockmealdown

0   5 km

M8

CORK

669

WATERFORD

N25

N72

Fermoy

Lismore

672

© AVALON TRAVEL

both churches *and* had two wives (one of each denomination) and several children by each. The truth came out only when they read his epitaph, in which he boasted he was able to exist in two places at once.

Other Sights

Across the street (and a dung-dotted pasture) from the Rock is **Hore Abbey** (always accessible, free), built by the Cistercians around the same time as the **Dominican Friary** you'll pass on the way up to the Rock. There may not be a whole lot to see among these ruins, but they can offer a bit of quiet should the crowds at the Rock overwhelm you.

Bibliophiles should make time for the 12,000-volume **Bolton Library** (John St., tel. 062/61944, boltonlibrary@gmail.com, open by appointment, €2), which houses the world's smallest book as well as a collection of priceless first editions of works by Dante, Machiavelli, Swift, Newton, and others.

Food

Many of Cashel's pubs offer an all-day bar menu, but if you're looking for an extraordinary lunch you'll have to eat at **Café Hans** (Moor Ln., tel. 062/63660, noon-5:30pm Tues.-Sat., €12-18). Prepare to be astonished at the cosmopolitan feel of this always-crowded eatery, as well as the seemingly bottomless portions of fresh, inventively prepared pastas. Annoying as it is, it's worth waiting 15 or 20 minutes in the tiny vestibule beside the restrooms for food this good.

★ **Chez Hans** (Moor Ln., up the street from the café and closer to the Rock, tel. 062/61177, www.chezhans.net, 6pm-10pm Tues.-Sat., €25-38), Café Hans's sister restaurant, takes care of dinner—in a converted church with original stained glass, no less!—but it's quite a bit pricier. If you're trying to scrimp, do the café for lunch and have a simple bar meal for dinner.

Vegans beware: Sadly, your pickings are slim anywhere in this town. For wholesome snacks and other picnic supplies, stop by **Horan's Health Store** (29 Main St., tel. 062/62848, www.horanshealthstore.com, 9am-6pm Mon.-Sat.).

Entertainment and Events

Two of Cashel's best watering holes are **Feehan's** (105 Main St., tel. 062/61929) and **T.J. Ryan's** (46 Main St., tel. 062/62956).

For something more formal, catch the traditional song and step-dancing show at the **Brú Ború Cultural Centre** (on the R660 near the entrance to the Rock, tel. 062/61122, www.bruboru.ie, shows 9pm Tues.-Sat. July-Aug., €20, reservations not necessary).

Accommodations

The IHH, family-run **Cashel Holiday Hostel** (6 John St., tel. 062/62330, www.cashelhostel.com, dorms €15-18, private rooms €20-25 pp) offers excellent facilities (including laundry, real hot showers, and bike hire) without sacrificing the building's Georgian character—there's even a piano in the common room.

Cashel has several friendly, atmospheric Georgian townhouse B&Bs. Just 50 meters from the Rock of Cashel is **Joy's Rockside House** (Rock Villas, tel. 062/63813, www.joyrockside.com, mid-Feb-Oct., €40-50 pp), where many of the homey rooms have a scenic view. The helpful proprietors of **Ashmore House** (John St., tel. 062/61286, www.ashmorehouse.com, €35-40 pp, s €50) do a great morning fry. Both Joy's and Ashmore have private parking. **Ladyswell House** (Ladyswell St., tel. 062/62985, www.ladyswellhouse.com, €40-50 pp) rents four smallish but elegant rooms, and the owners offer their own "chauffeured" sightseeing tour.

The **Cashel Palace Hotel** (Main St., tel. 062/62707, www.cashel-palace.ie, rooms €195-275, s €150-180, suites €300-370), built for a Protestant archbishop in the 1730s, is the town's snazziest accommodation. It's worth paying a €30 supplement for stunning nighttime views of the floodlit Rock.

Information and Services

Both the **tourist office** (tel. 062/61333, www.

Cahir Castle

tipperary.ie and www.cashel.ie, 9:15am-6pm Mon.-Sat. May-Sept., daily July-Aug.) and **heritage center** (tel. 062/62511, 9:30am-5:30pm daily Mar.-Oct., Mon.-Fri. Nov.-Feb., free) are located in Cashel's Town Hall on Main Street.

For an ATM or bureau de change, visit the **AIB** or **Bank of Ireland,** both on Main Street, as are a couple of pharmacies, **Kennedy's** (tel. 062/61066) and the **Friary** (tel. 062/62120).

Getting There and Around
Cashel is 160 kilometers southwest of Dublin and 97 kilometers northeast of Cork on the M8. **Bus Éireann** stops here on the Dublin-Cork (#8, 6/day daily) and Athlone-Cork (#71, 2/day Mon.-Sat., 1/day Sun.) routes. Rent a bike from **McInerney TV** (Main St., tel. 062/61225, €12/day), or ring **Cashel Cabs** (tel. 087/203-6766) for a taxi.

CAHIR
Overshadowed by the magnificent hilltop castle-cum-church at Cashel, the robust fortress at workaday **Cahir** ("CARE"; An Cathair, "The City") is a destination in its own right.

★ Cahir Castle
The 15th-century **Cahir Castle** (Castle St., tel. 052/744-1011, 9:30am-5:30pm daily mid-Mar.-mid-June and mid-Sept.-mid-Oct., 9am-7pm daily mid-June-mid-Sept., 9:30am-4:30pm daily mid-Oct.-mid-Mar., €4) is on the site of a mid-12th-century stronghold belonging the O'Brien clan. The Butlers acquired it during the 14th century and made extensive additions, including the great hall overlooking the River Suir, and at the time it was the largest castle in Ireland. An illustration from the turn of the 17th century shows the castle essentially as it appears today, thanks to the prompt surrendering of the Baron of Cahir to Cromwell's forces in February 1650. Though the castle was clearly built to be defended, it seems Cromwell's "letter of threat" left the guardian of the underaged baron quaking in his boots. Today you can wander through the feudal-style courtyard and ascend (with due caution) a narrow staircase to the old ramparts. The exhibition features an impressively detailed model of the castle and battle stages during the siege of 1599.

Swiss Cottage
Cahir's other attraction is the **Swiss Cottage** (Kilcommon, 1.5 km south of Cahir, signposted off the R670, tel. 052/744-1144, 10am-1pm and 2pm-6pm Tues.-Sun. mid-Mar.-mid-Apr., 10am-6pm daily mid-Apr.-mid-Oct., 10am-1pm and 2pm-4:30pm Tues.-Sun. mid-Oct.-mid-Nov., €4), reachable from the castle by a shady pathway through Cahir Park. This thatched-roof "cottage orné"—a mansion by most people's standards—was designed by John Nash and built at the start of the 19th century for the first Earl of Glengall, Richard Butler. Access is by 40-minute guided tour only.

Practicalities
The **tourist office** (tel. 052/744-1453,

9am-5:15pm Mon.-Sat. Mar.-Sept.) and the **AIB** (with ATM) are both on Castle Street.

Cahir itself isn't a very interesting place, so just stop here for an hour or two between Cashel (15 km north on the M8) and Cork (80 km south on the M8). **Bus Éireann** passes through on its Dublin-Cork (#8, 6/day daily), Athlone-Cork (#71, 2/day Mon.-Sat., 1/day Sun.), and Limerick-Waterford (#55, 6-7/day daily) routes.

CARRICK-ON-SUIR

The otherwise unremarkable riverside town of Carrick-on-Suir ("SHOOR") means "Rock of the Suir" in Irish, for the presence of Ormond Castle.

★ Ormond Castle

Now Dúchas-run, **Ormond Castle** (Castle Park, off Castle St. on the east end of town, tel. 051/640-787, tel. 056/24623 in winter, 9:30am-6:30pm daily mid-June-early Sept., free) is the best Irish example of an Elizabethan manor house, though it's unique for several other reasons: The manor, built in the 1560s, integrates the ruins of the original towers from the previous century, and it is also Ireland's only unfortified castle from the 16th century. The state rooms offer some of the best examples of decorative plasterwork—which might sound stuffy but is actually well worth a few minutes' study. "Black Tom," the 10th Earl of Ormond, had Elizabeth's crown portrait done, flanked by figures representing Justice and Equity; there is another plasterwork portrait of the Virgin Queen beside one of the earl in the entrance passage, which is an inadvertent reference to the persistent rumor that Elizabeth bore him a child in 1554. As Brian de Breffny notes in his book on Irish castles, the earl spent many years at the English court and was "steadfastly devoted" to the queen, who reportedly referred to the "dark, amorous Irishman" as "my black husband." After all, Black Tom built this place hoping she'd someday honor her promise to visit him in Ireland. The 40-minute guided tour will provide you with plenty more interesting tidbits.

one of the superb high crosses at Ahenny

Getting There

Carrick-on-Suir is 27 kilometers northwest of Waterford City on the N24, and is served by **Bus Éireann** on the Dublin-Cork (#7, 6/day daily) and Limerick-Rosslare Harbour (#55, 6-7/day daily) routes.

Ahenny and Kilkieran

The magnificent **high crosses** at Ahenny—and their not-so-well preserved counterparts at Kilkieran—are well worth a detour as you're passing through Carrick-on-Suir. Both sites are clearly signposted off the R697 north of Carrick. To get to Ahenny, you'll drive five kilometers north of town, turning left onto a local road and following the signposts for a further two kilometers. Both the north and south crosses at Ahenny are well over three meters high, and both are made of sandstone and decorated with intricate geometric patterns (there are Old Testament scenes carved on both sides of each base, though you'll have to take the archaeologists' word for it!). These crosses are downright stunning to behold.

For Kilkieran, you'll retrace your route, turning left onto the R697 before making a right onto the R698; the site is about 300 meters down this road on your right. At the Kilkieran graveyard there's a holy well along with three crosses (plus the remnants of a fourth). On a hill overlooking the graveyard is the ultra-cozy **Kilkieran Cottage** (tel. 051/645-110, www.kilkierancottage.ie, 5pm-9:30pm Fri.-Sun., also noon-3pm Sun., €12-22), serving up fresh but unpretentious modern Irish fare (with a very good vegetarian option).

Waterford

Wedged between Tipperary to the north and Wexford just east of the estuary, County Waterford features the fertile farmland of the former and the sunny coastline of the latter. Tramore may be Waterford's best-known resort town, but it's desperately overdeveloped—and though it's not as tacky a place as reputed, it's still far from the best the county has to offer. For pretty sea views, pristine beaches, and water-sporting opportunities, head for Ardmore or Dunmore East instead. The stretch between Tramore and Dungarvan is known as the **Copper Coast**—a name devised for tourism purposes, but fitting enough for its smattering of 19th-century copper mines.

WATERFORD CITY

A bustling commercial port on the River Suir, workaday Waterford was founded by the Vikings in 853, making it Ireland's oldest city. Its reputation for fine crystal began when the first factory opened in 1783. Stiff British taxes led to its closing in 1851, but it reopened in 1947, and the current factory dates to 1971. Frankly, were it not for the factory Waterford wouldn't see much in the way of tourist activity; it can be downright depressing when the weather's gray, although the **Waterford Walls** (37 Mayor's Walk, tel. 087/762-4397, www.waterfordwalls.ie) project has done much to brighten things up. In 2015, a team of local and international artists painted some seriously gorgeous murals on 25 derelict buildings across the city center. This vibrant new street art is, hands down, the most worthwhile and inspiring thing here.

Sights

Pert as a pepperpot, the fully restored **Reginald's Tower** (The Quay, tel. 051/304-220, 10am-5pm daily Easter-May and Oct., 10am-5pm Wed.-Sun. Nov.-Easter, 10am-6pm June-Sept., €4) was erected in the 12th century and is now run by Dúchas. It was built by the Normans to defend their newly acquired city, and it's said that Strongbow and Aoife held their wedding feast here. In later centuries the tower was used as a mint, prison, and arsenal. Today it houses a historical exhibit, charters and swords and whatnot—worth a visit if you're a history buff. From the top floor of the tower you can spy the 13th-century **French Church** on Greyfriars Street. There are other medieval holdovers, scattered gates from the original city walls as well as the **Blackfriars Abbey** from the same time period, covered in blooming weeds and tucked behind a tall iron fence on Conduit Lane, just off High Street.

It's best known for the gruesome 15th-century cadaver tomb (the effigy on the lid depicts the deceased in a decomposed state) of Lord Mayor James Rice, but the Anglican **Christ Church Cathedral** (Cathedral Sq., tel. 051/874-119, www.christchurchwaterford.com, 10am-5pm daily, tours at 11:30am and 3pm, free but donations appreciated), built on the site of a Viking church, has a few other things worth checking out. There is only one stained-glass window, but it's surely a masterpiece: A. E. Child's *Joy and Sorrow* from 1930, which depicts a line from the Revelations: "Sorrow may endure for a night, but joy cometh in the morning." The magnificent Elliott

THE SOUTHEAST
WATERFORD

153

Waterford

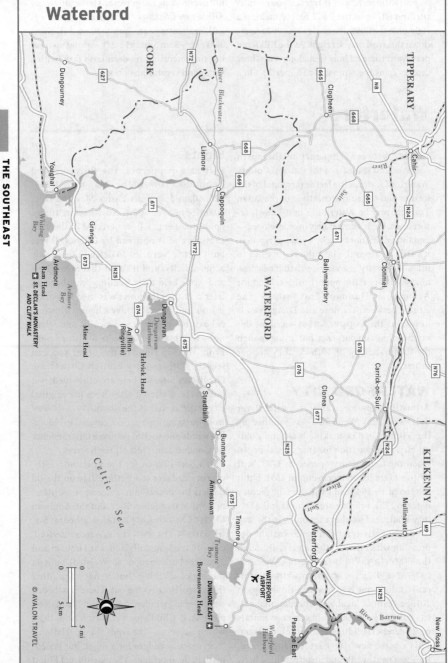

CORK

TIPPERARY

Dungourney

N72

627

River Blackwater

665

Clogheen

N8

668

Cahir

Lismore

668

669

River

Cappoquin

N72

671

665

671

Clonmel

N24

WATERFORD

Ballymacarbry

Youghal

Whiting Bay

Grange

671

673

N25

678

N76

Ardmore
Ram Head
✚ ST. DECLAN'S MONASTERY
AND CLIFF WALK

Ardmore Bay

674

Dungarvan
Dungarvan Harbour

675

676

Clonea

Carrick-on-Suir

N24

Mine Head

An Rinn
(Ringville)

Helvick Head

677

Stradbally

KILKENNY

Mullinavat

M9

Bunmahon

N25

Annestown

675

River Suir

Celtic Sea

Tramore

New Ross

Tramore Bay

WATERFORD
AIRPORT

Waterford

N25

Brow'stown Head

DUNMORE EAST
✚

Waterford
Harbour

Passage East

River Barrow

0 ____ 5 km
0 ____ 5 mi

© AVALON TRAVEL

Waterford City

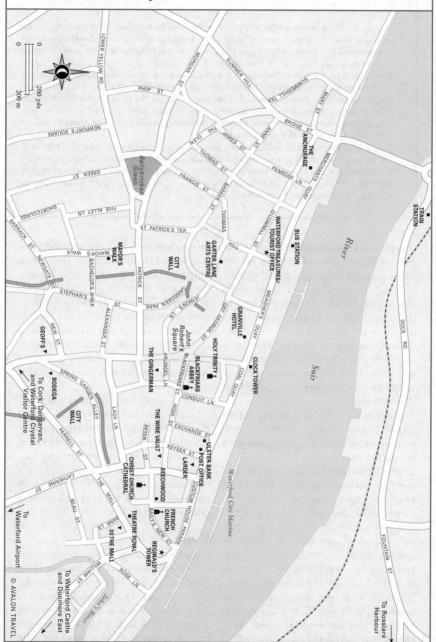

0
200 yds

0
200 m

LOWER YELLOW RD

PHILIP ST

NEWPORT'S SQUARE

GREEN ST

Ballybricken
Green

SHORTCOURSE

FIVE ALLEY LN

BARRACK ST

NEWGATE ST

MAYOR'S WALK

BACHELOR'S WALK

STEPHAN'S WALK

NEW ST

GEOFF'S

SPRING GARDEN ALLEY

BODEGA

To Cork, Dungarvan,
and Waterford Crystal
Visitor Centre

CITY WALL

LADY LN

PARNELL ST

CATHERINE ST

THE MALL

To
Waterford Airport

BEAU ST

WILLIAM ST

To Waterford Castle
and Dunmore East

© AVALON TRAVEL

MORGAN ST

MARY ST

SUMMER HILL

THE GLEN

JAMES ST

ANNE ST

THOMAS ST

FRANCIS ST

BARKER ST

THOMAS ST

ST PATRICK'S TER

PATRICK ST

ALEXANDER ST

CARRIGEEN PARK

JENKIN'S LN

GRT GEORGE ST

BLACKFRIARS LN

ARUNDEL LN

CONDUIT LN

HIGH ST

EXCHANGE ST

PETER ST

KEYSER ST

ULSTER BANK

POST OFFICE

LARDER

BEECHWOOD

CHRIST CHURCH CATHEDRAL

THE GINGERMAN

THE WINE VAULT

CUSTOM HOUSE PARADE

BAILY'S NEW ST

FRENCH CHURCH

THEATRE ROYAL

33 THE MALL

BANK LN

ROSE LN

REGINALD'S TOWER

JOHN'S RIVER

John Robert's
Square

HOLY TRINITY

BLACKFRIARS ABBEY

GRANVILLE HOTEL

CITY WALL

GARTER LANE ARTS CENTRE

CLOCK TOWER

COAL QUAY

MEAGHER'S QUAY

GREY FRIARS ST

O'CONNELL ST

HILL

WATERFORD TREASURES/
TOURIST OFFICE

BUS STATION

PENROSE LN

BRIDGE ST

SUMMERHILL TER

MERCHANT'S QUAY

THE ANCHORAGE

River

Suir

Waterford City Marina

DOCK RD

FOUNTAIN ST

TRAIN STATION

To Rosslare Harbour

Tipperary and Waterford Walks

You could pick up one of the country's shorter treks, the 70-kilometer **East Munster Way,** when you're done the South Leinster Way if you're feeling ambitious—the former begins where the latter ends, in Carrick-on-Suir, County Tipperary. You'll skirt the northern fringe of Comeragh Mountains on the East Munster Way, lots of heather-covered hills and eerily quiet evergreen forests. From Carrick-on-Suir, the route follows the River Suir, heading west through Clonmel and dipping into Waterford a couple of times before ending in the village of Clogheen (back in Tipperary). The route takes three days to walk. Then from Clogheen, the 185-kilometer **Blackwater Way** extends farther southwest through the lumpy Knockmealdown Mountains and the Boggeraghs of northern Cork, ending at Muckross in Killarney National Park. The whole Blackwater route will take nine days to walk.

As with all long-distance walking routes, your first stop should be the nearest tourist office to the starting point, where you can pick up a detailed guidebook and Ordnance Survey Discovery Series maps (the East Munster Way requires numbers 74 and 75). Don't have time for a long-distance route? A much shorter walk—only an hour long—is the exhilarating cliff walk just outside the village of Ardmore on the Waterford coast.

Organ, its rarity akin to the Stradivarius, was restored in 2003 at a cost of half a million euros. Notice that the intricate ceiling plasterwork in the antechamber and that in the church don't match—the former is done in the baroque style, the latter in rococo, owing to a fire in the organ loft in 1815. Also note the wall memorial for Susanna Mason, who opened the first girls' school in Ireland in the mid-1700s. A free summer concert series on Sunday mornings features top organists from all over Europe.

Waterford's Catholic cathedral, **Holy Trinity** (Barronstrand St., tel. 051/875-166, www.waterford-cathedral.com), was designed by John Roberts.

Now for the reason you're here: the factory tour and showroom at the **Waterford Crystal Visitor Centre** (Cork Rd., Kilbarry, 2 km south of town on the N25, tel. 051/332-500, www.waterfordvisitorcentre.com, retail store 9am-6pm Mon.-Sat. and 9:30-6pm Sun. Apr.-Oct., 9:30am-5pm Mon.-Sat. and noon-5pm Sun. Nov.-Dec., 9:30am-5pm Mon.-Sat. Jan.-Feb., 9am-5pm Mon.-Sat. and 9:30am-5pm Sun. Mar.). **Guided tours** of the factory floor (9am-4:15pm Mon.-Sat. and 9:30am-4:15pm Sun. Apr.-Oct., 9:30am-3:15pm Mon.-Fri. Nov.-Feb.,

9am-3:15pm Mon.-Sat. and 9:30am-3:15pm Sun. Mar., €13.50) start every 15 minutes, and it's best to ring ahead for a reservation in high season. Afterward you can take a walk through the historical exhibition—and do some shopping! But buyer beware: Much of Waterford crystal is now manufactured in Eastern Europe, some of which is for sale in the factory store, so before you buy, make sure your intended purchases were made on-site.

If it's pouring out, peruse the archaeological exhibits and slick interpretive displays at **Waterford Treasures** (Merchants Quay, tel. 051/304-500, www.waterfordtreasures.com, 9:15am-6pm Mon.-Fri., 9:30am-6pm Sat., 11am-6pm Sun., closing at 5pm Sept.-May, €7), housed in an old granary. The exhibition features everything from Viking baubles to 18th-century crystal.

Tours

If you have only an hour to spare on your way to the coast, spend it on a **historical walking tour** (tel. 051/873-711, www.jackswalkingtours.com, daily Mar.-Oct., one-hour tour €7). Tours depart the tourist office at 11:45am and 1:45pm; amiable local guide Jack Burtchaell breathes life into these old city gates and walls.

Food, Entertainment, and Events

Larder (111a Henrietta St., tel. 087/416-2401, 10am-5pm Mon., 9am-5pm Tues.-Thurs., 9am-6pm Fri., 9:30am-5:30pm Sat., light lunch under €6) does soups, wraps, and sandwiches on homebaked sourdough or spelt bread. This cute little café is on the main street facing the harbor.

You'll find good pub grub at **The Gingerman** (6 Arundel Lane, tel. 051/879-522, food served 10am-6pm Mon.-Sat., until 7pm Sat., 12:30pm-6pm Sun., €8-11), with traditional dishes like fish and chips and bacon and cabbage, or slightly quirkier fare (like shoestring potatoes) at **Geoff's** (9 John St., tel. 051/874-787, food served 10am-4pm daily, €9-14).

One of Waterford's best restaurants is fun and festive ★ **Bodega** (54 John St., tel. 051/844-177, www.bodegawaterford.com, noon-10pm Mon.-Sat., lunch €9-18, dinner €12-29), serving up modern-Irish favorites with Spanish panache. There are thoughtful, imaginative vegetarian and vegan options here as well, and the waitstaff are eager to help without being overbearing. You can have your lunch or dinner in a booth lined with dozens upon dozens of bottles of red. The early-bird menu (2/3 courses €21.50/26.50, 5pm-7pm Mon.-Fri.) is an awesome value.

Take in an opera, musical, ballet, or slick Shakespeare production at the **Theatre Royal** (The Mall, tel. 051/874-402, www.theatreroyal.ie, €20-30). The upstairs **café** is open daily (9am-4pm). The Theatre Royal also hosts the city's **Light Opera Festival** in late September and early October. Or catch a film, concert, or whatever play's making the rounds at the **Garter Lane Arts Centre** (22A O'Connell St., tel. 051/855-038, www.garter-lane.ie, €10-20).

Shopping

Don't get too hyped up about Waterford **crystal.** Much of it isn't even made in the local factory anymore—it's being outsourced to Slovenia, the Czech Republic, Hungary, and Germany. Instead, visit the smaller workshops of ex-Waterford craftspeople—they've got the skills, the prices are more reasonable, and you may even be able to meet the person who made your new purchase; try **Criostal na Rinne** (signposted off the R674, tel. 058/46174, www.criostal.com) on the Ring Peninsula (55 km southwest of Waterford) or **Kinsale Crystal** (Market St., tel. 021/477-4493, www.kinsale-crystal.ie) in Kinsale, County Cork.

Otherwise, Waterford has two weekly markets, the **city market** on Jenkin's Lane (10am-4pm Sat.) and the **country market** at St. Olaf's Hall (8am-1pm Fri.) across the street from Christ Church. Along with farmhouse cheeses and other comestibles, stalls sell locally made pottery, jewelry, and other lovely things.

Accommodations

There was no hostel in Waterford at time of writing, so budget travelers will need to spring for a B&B. Two of the most affordable are the homey **Mayor's Walk** (12 Mayor's Walk, tel. 051/855-427, www.mayorswalk.com, €30 pp) and **The Anchorage** (9 Merchant's Quay, tel. 051/854-302, www.anchorage.ie, €30 pp), which is more of a guesthouse.

The **Granville Hotel** (Meagher's Quay, tel. 051/305-555, www.granville-hotel.ie, €45-80 pp) is Waterford City's most historic. While the reception and bar areas are elegantly old-fashioned, the bedrooms can be a bit creaky. On the upside, the breakfast is fantastic—along with the full or vegetarian fry, you can get a shot of whiskey or Bailey's in your porridge.

And of course, **Waterford Castle** (The Island, Ballinakill, 5 km east of town off the R683, tel. 051/878-203, www.waterfordcastleresort.com, €120-200 pp) is one of the very finest accommodations in the country, in a restored 16th-century manor (incorporating a Norman keep built in 1190) on its own private island complete with golf course. The staff deliver on the king-and-queen-for-a-night promise, the food is tops, and the grounds are tranquil as can be. The only thing you can even begin to fault this place for is its slightly stodgy decor.

Information and Services

The **tourist office** (41 The Quay, tel. 051/875-823, www.discoverwaterford.com, 9am-5pm Mon.-Sat., until 6pm Apr.-Sept., 11am-5pm Sun. July-Aug.) shares the old granary with the Waterford Treasures museum.

There are plenty of banks with ATMs and currency exchange facilities in the city center, including **Ulster Bank** (97/98 Custom House Quay) and the **AIB** (72 The Quay). The local branch of **Boots** (Barronstrand St., tel. 051/872-255), the pharmacy, is on John Roberts Square.

Getting There

Waterford is 160 kilometers southwest of Dublin on the M9 and 122 kilometers east of Cork City on the N25. Plunkett Rail Station is on the far side of the Rice Bridge, north of the river; get here from Dublin (4-6/day daily) or Rosslare Harbour (2/day Mon.-Sat.) on **Irish Rail** (tel. 051/873-401); from Limerick, Ennis, Tralee, or Cork, change trains at Limerick Junction.

The **Bus Éireann** (tel. 051/879-000) station is on Merchants Quay, just east of the bridge. The Tralee-Cork-Rosslare Harbour route stops in Waterford (#40, 13/day Mon.-Sat., 10/day Sun.), and there is direct service from Dublin (#4 via Carlow, 10/day Mon.-Sat., 8/day Sun., #5 via Enniscorthy, 4/day daily) and Limerick (#55, 6-7/day daily).

You can also fly into **Waterford Airport** (Killowen, 7 km south of town on the R675, tel. 051/875-589, www.flywaterford.com) from London Luton or Birmingham.

Getting Around

There are several parking lots on the Waterford quay, generally with a daily rate of €5.50; the city itself is easily walkable. **Rapid Cabs** (tel. 051/858-585) offers 24-hour service. Rent a bike from **Waterford Greenway** (High St. at Henrietta St., tel. 085/111-3850, www.waterfordgreenway.com, €12/day), which also offers day tours.

PASSAGE EAST

The fastest way to get to County Wexford is on the **Passage East Ferry** (tel. 051/382-480, www.passageferry.ie, frequent departures 7am-10pm Mon.-Sat. and 9:30am-10pm Sun. Apr.-Sept., until 8pm Oct.-Mar., single/return fare €8/12 per car) across Waterford Harbour to Ballyhack. Passage East is 12 kilometers east of Waterford on the R683, and **Suirway** (tel. 051/382-209, www.suirway.com, 4/day Mon.-Sat., single fare €4) provides bus service from the city.

★ DUNMORE EAST

Easily the loveliest part of eastern Waterford, Dunmore East (Dún Mór, "Big Fort") is a popular weekend getaway for city folk. Dunmore is spread out along a kilometer or so, from the strand (the lower village) to the harbor (the upper village), with the post office, grocery stores, and ATM located in the latter. Take a leisurely stroll past rows of immaculately maintained thatched-roof cottages, chat with friendly locals, and drink in the gorgeous view of the bay and Hook Head beyond.

Activities and Recreation

You can tee off at the seaside **Dunmore East Golf & Country Club** (signposted from the lower village, tel. 051/383-151, www.dunmore-golf.com) or go sailboarding with the **Dunmore East Adventure Centre** (at the harbor, upper village, tel. 051/383-783, www.dunmoreadventure.com). The tennis court between the upper and lower villages has an awesome view of the Hook.

Food

The best eatery in town is a gastro-pub, ★ **The Spinnaker** (lower village, tel. 051/383-133, www.thespinnakerbar.com, food served noon-9:30pm daily, €9-25), with a nautical theme (that somehow manages to feel elegant) and amiable staff. Top-notch steaks and fresh seafood are on the menu, along with a few superb vegetarian dishes—so good, in fact, that the desserts are a letdown!

If you're in the mood for pizza or pasta

(including gluten-free options!), check out **Azzurro's** (Dock Rd., opposite St. Andrew's, between the villages, tel. 051/383-141, www. azzurro.ie, 5pm-11pm Mon.-Fri., noon-11pm Sat.-Sun., lunch €10, dinner €15-27). The wine list is as terrific as the food.

Entertainment and Events

Locals flock to the Tuesday night trad-and-folk sessions at **Power's** (upper village, tel. 051/383-318), where you can socialize and watch the musicians in the front room (there could be two or 10, depending on the week), or have a more intimate conversation in the dimly lit snugs in the back. The walls here are covered with witty (mostly nautical) epigrams like "marriages performed by the captain are valid only for duration of voyage."

Accommodations

For B&B, try **Brookside** (Ballymabin, signposted off the R684 1 km northwest of the village, tel. 051/383-893, www.brookside-bandblive.com, €37 pp, s €55), which offers even better rates for two- or three-night stays. The rooms are immaculate and the owners are genuinely friendly and welcoming, and you can order pancakes for breakfast. Another option, this one in the village proper, is **Creaden View** (Dock Rd., tel. 051/383-339, creadenvw@eircom.net, €35 pp). Ask for a room with a harbor view.

The Three Sisters Inn (upper village, near the harbor, tel. 087/786-3856, €50-60 pp sharing), under new management at time of writing and still working out a few kinks, is a good choice if you plan to soak up the local nightlife. **The Haven** (between the upper and lower villages, tel. 051/383-150, www.the-havenhotel.com, Mar.-Oct., €55-75 pp sharing) is older, grander, a bit on the quirky side, family-run, and child-friendly.

Getting There

Dunmore East is 17 kilometers southeast of Waterford on the R684. **Suirway** (tel. 051/382-209, www.suirway.com, 4/day Mon.-Sat., single fare €4) offers bus service from the city.

ARDMORE

The greatest delight in County Waterford is the seaside village of Ardmore (Áird Mhór), with its long sandy beach, spectacularly situated monastic ruins, and exhilarating clifftop walk. It may be a popular getaway for tourists and weekending Irish alike, yet Ardmore still manages to feel like a well-kept secret. No trip to Waterford is complete without at least one night here.

★ St. Declan's Monastery and Cliff Walk

Ardmore boasts some of Ireland's most beautifully situated monastic ruins. **St. Declan's Monastery** (signposted from Main St., a 5-minute walk uphill, always accessible, free) was founded in the 5th century. Surrounded by a modern cemetery, the ruins include an 8th-century oratory (the Beannchán, restored in the 18th century and said to mark Declan's grave), a complete 30-meter round tower built in the 12th century, and a Romanesque cathedral on the site of Declan's original church. Check out the stone carvings on the western wall exterior depicting both Old and New Testament scenes, which predate the building itself. Some of the scenes are still discernible: Adam and Eve, the Adoration of the Magi, and the Judgment of Solomon. There are two ogham stones inside the cathedral. The whole site overlooks Ardmore Bay, and there's no prettier place in Ireland when the sun's shining.

A five-kilometer, one-hour **cliff walk** begins at the monastery and loops around a pastoral headland, taking you past a couple of lookout posts, a rusted shipwreck from 1987, and **St. Declan's Well,** originally used to baptize the locals and later said to have curative properties. There's a church ruin nearby. From there it's a downhill walk back into town. Because most folks start from the cliff and walk clockwise, ending up at the monastery, you might want to walk it counterclockwise. Though you don't really need one, you can pick up a map at the tourist office or your B&B.

Shopping, Food, and Accommodations

Something else the town is known for is Mary Lincoln's pretty, pastel **Ardmore Pottery** (The Cliff, at the start of the scenic walk, tel. 024/94152, www.ardmorepottery.com), which sells locally made knitwear too. Also check out the thoroughly charming **Ardmore Gallery and Tea Room** (tel. 087/697-5014, 9:30am-6:30pm daily Apr.-Sept., 1pm-5pm Sat.-Sun. Oct.-Mar., lunch under €8).

You'd never know that Ardmore's one classy café-restaurant, **White Horses** (Main St., tel. 024/94040, 11am-11pm Tues.-Sun. May-Sept., 6pm-11pm Fri., 11am-11pm Sat., and noon-6pm Sun. Oct.-Apr., €9-24, 3-course lunch €25), is in the old police barracks. Come here for tea and a pastry, or a full meal featuring fresh local produce and inventively prepared seafood.

As for B&B, a few minutes' drive from the village is the tranquil **Newtown Farm** (Grange, 6.5 km northwest of Ardmore off the N25, tel. 024/94143, www.newtownfarm.com, €40 pp, s €48). On a working dairy farm, all the immaculate, country-style rooms offer sea and pastoral views. There's a tennis court, too, so bring your racket. Or try the 12-room **Round Tower Hotel** (College Rd., a few minutes' walk down the Youghal road, tel. 024/94494, www.roundtowerhotel.ie, food served until 9:30pm daily, B&B €45-55 pp). There's nothing fancy here, but the staff are affable and the seafood in the restaurant is worth writing home about.

If you *do* want the fancy, though, there's always the five-star **Cliff House Hotel** (Middle Rd., tel. 024/87800, www.thecliffhousehotel.com, rooms €230-370), complete with infinity pool and spa.

Practicalities

There's a seasonal **tourist office** (tel. 024/94444, 11am-4pm daily May-Sept.) in a

St. Declan's Monastery overlooking Ardmore Bay

small, strange-looking glass building on the strand. There was no ATM in Ardmore at time of writing, so be sure to withdraw funds before leaving Waterford or Cork.

Ardmore is 21 kilometers west of Dungarvan and 71 kilometers west of Waterford via the N25 and R673. Get here via **Bus Éireann** from Cork (#260, 2/day Mon.-Sat., 1/day Sun.) or from Waterford (#362, 2/day July-Aug. only).

LISMORE

A pleasant spot tucked between the Knockmealdowns and the River Blackwater, **Lismore** (An Líos Mór, "The Great Enclosure") draws tour buses for the three-hectare Elizabethan gardens at **Lismore Castle** (tel. 058/54424, www.lismorecastle-gardens.com, 1:45pm-4:45pm daily Easter-Sept., €8), though the castle itself is not open to the public. Owned by Walter Raleigh, later the earls of Cork, and now the dukes of Devonshire, perhaps the castle's claim to fame is the discovery of the Lismore Crozier along with the 15th-century, so-called Book of Lismore during a renovation in 1814. Part hagiography, part chronicle of the voyages of Marco Polo, the manuscript's proper title is the Book of Mac Cartach Riabhach. Both treasures are now in the National Museum of Archaeology and History.

For such a small town, Lismore's coffee shops have one or two surprises in store—take for example the "nipples of Venus" meringue cupcakes (€3) at the **Summer House Café** (Main St., tel. 058/54148, www.thesummerhouse.ie, 10am-5:30pm Tues.-Sun., under €8). Otherwise, nearly all Lismore's pubs have all-day bar menus; the best grub's at **Eamonn's Place** (Main St., tel. 058/54025, food served noon-9:30pm, €10-16), with an out-back beer garden.

There aren't many accommodations in this area, especially since several B&Bs have closed in recent years. Built in 1797, the **Lismore House Hotel** (Main St., tel. 058/72966, www.lismorehousehotel.com, €50 pp, s €60) isn't as grand as it used to be, but it will suffice.

You'll find both the **tourist office** (tel. 058/54975, www.discoverlismore.com, 10am-4pm daily Apr.-Oct.) and **heritage center** (tel. 058/54975, 9:30am-6pm Mon.-Sat., noon-6pm Sun., €5) in the old courthouse on Main Street. There's an ATM at the **Bank of Ireland** on West Street across the street from the public park.

Lismore is essentially one street, Main changing names to West Street. It's 68 kilometers west of Waterford via the N25 and N72. **Bus Éireann** provides infrequent service (#4/40, 1/day Mon.-Sat. leaving Waterford at 9pm; #41, 1/day Fri. and Sun. only, no Sun. service July-Aug.).

Cork

Cork City 167

Around Cork City 176

West Cork 182

The Mizen Head Peninsula 188

The Sheep's Head Peninsula . . . 190

The Beara Peninsula
   (Cork Side) 193

The postcard-perfect coastal scenery of West Cork's three peninsulas—Beara, Sheep's Head, and Mizen Head, from west to east—is the county's primary draw, though you'll find all three refreshingly untouristy in comparison to the Dingle and Iveragh Peninsulas of County Kerry.

Outside of the infamous Blarney Castle, the upscale harbor town of Kinsale is the most popular destination of all. West Cork is a haven for artists, and you'll find galleries full of intriguing contemporary works in even the most remote villages. The seafood is tops—you'll find fish caught here in Dublin's swankiest restaurants—and so are the opportunities for scuba diving and other water sports.

Many dismiss Cork City as excessively industrial, and though it's true the city can't compete with Dublin's sophistication or Galway's bohemian sparkle, it's still well worth a visit. You'll probably want to pass on through the relatively featureless farmlands of northern Cork, however.

Ireland's largest county, Cork (Corcaigh, "Marshy Place") has figured crucially in many of the nation's darkest chapters, particularly in the armed struggle for independence and subsequent Civil War of 1922-1923.

HISTORY

Dubbed the "City of Spires" for its distinctive skyline, Cork started out as a monastic settlement, founded by St. Finbarr (also spelled Finbar or Fin Barre) in the late 6th or early 7th century. But the city first prospered with the advent of the Vikings in the 1100s. The Normans took control of their trading settlement later on in the 12th century, and the city's dozen Anglo-Norman merchant families would prosper from its well-situated port in their trade with continental Europe. Cork's breweries, distilleries, woolen factories, and shipbuilders did a booming business in the 18th and 19th centuries.

After the Reformation, Cork was a predominantly Protestant city until the late 1840s, when the native Irish began moving in from the surrounding countryside hoping to escape the famine. Others would depart for North America from the nearby port of Cobh.

Previous: St. Finbarr's Oratory; the twin villages of Glandore and Union Hall. **Above:** 18th-century clock tower of St. Anne's Church in Cork City.

Cork

Map of the Cork region showing towns including Tralee, Killarney, Dingle, Kenmare, Bantry, and Skibbereen, with roads, lakes, and coastal features.

KERRY

Killarney National Park

Killarney

Killarney National Park
Upper Lake

Gougane Barra Forest Park

River Lee

Shehy Mountains

Gougane Barra

GLENGARRIFF WOODS NATURE RESERVE

GARNISH ISLAND

BANTRY HOUSE AND GARDENS

Glengarriff Harbour

Whiddy Island

Bantry

Lough Leane

Muckross Lough

Lough Guitane

Rathmore

Abbeyfeale

Castleisland

Ballydesmond

Castlemaine

Killorglin

Camp

Anascaul

Dingle

Cahersiveen

Derriana Lough

Cloonaghlim Lough

Lough Currane

Sneem

Cloon Lough

Kenmare

Cloonee Loughs

Caherdaniel

Kenmare River

Lauragh

Caha Mountains

Glengarriff

Ardgroom

Healy Pass

Adrigole

Eyeries

Rossmackowen

Cod's Head

Allihies

Castletownbere

Bere Island

Durrus

Garinish Point

Dursey Island

Cahermore

DZOGCHEN BEARA

Black Ball Head

Bantry Bay

Ahakista

Dursey Head

Crow Head

Kilcrohane

Sheep's Head

Dunmanus Bay

Toormore

Schull

Roaringwater Bay

Goleen

MIZEN VISION

Mizen Head

Brow Head

Crookhaven

Barley Cove

Cape Clear Island

Baltimore

Sherkin Island

Skibbereen

Glandore

Leap

Union Hall

DROMBEG STONE CIRCLE

Castletownsend

Whiddy Island

Fastnet Rock

Lough Caragh

Lough Currane

N69

556

551

N21

N86

561

N70

N23

577

N22

N70

N72

N71

569

N70

585

586

593

595

591

592

N71

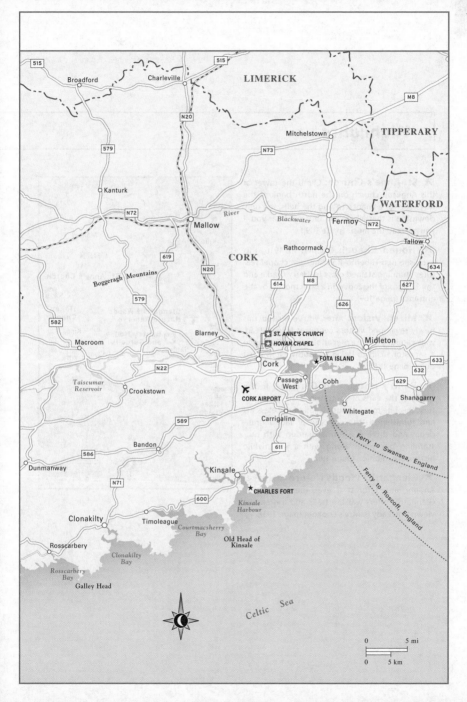

Look for ★ to find recommended
sights, activities, dining, and lodging.

Highlights

★ **St. Anne's Church:** Climb the tower of this Anglican church on the north bank of the River Lee for a chance to ring the bells; the only downside is that all of Cork City can hear you if you misread the music (page 169)!

★ **Honan Chapel:** Opened in 1916, this exquisite neo-Hiberno-Romanesque chapel features stunning stained glass by Harry Clarke and the 12 signs of the zodiac in a floor mosaic by the entrance (page 169).

★ **Mizen Vision:** After you've visited this newly revamped visitors center at Mizen Head, walk carefully down a precarious path clinging to a sandstone cliff to Ireland's southwesternmost point (page 188).

★ **Bantry House and Gardens:** In the family of the earls of Bantry since the 18th century, this fine manor house is full of priceless art and furnishings—the epitome of faded grandeur—and there is a formal garden with outstanding bay views along with a worthwhile historical exhibition (page 190).

★ **Glengarriff Woods Nature Reserve:** An enchanted forest if ever there was one, Glengarriff offers walking trails and a dramatic viewpoint, Lady Bantry's Lookout (page 193).

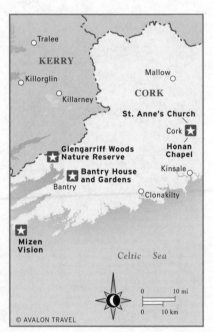

With this ethno-religious shift in the population, Cork became a staunchly nationalist city. Roughly 1,000 IRA members prepared for rebellion during the Easter Rising of 1916, as in Dublin, though unlike Dublin no blood was shed in Cork that day. The Black and Tans, those notoriously brutal and undisciplined British paramilitaries, wreaked violence on rebels and civilians alike, setting fire to much of downtown Cork. Two of the city's nationalist mayors met their ends through the Black and Tans: They executed Thomas MacCurtain at his home in March 1920, and in August of that year they imprisoned his successor, Terence MacSwiney, in London. MacSwiney went on a hunger strike, and when he died after 78 days the people of Cork regarded him as a martyr for their cause.

The violence continued after the truce and Anglo-Irish Treaty, when Irish nationalists split into pro- and anti-treaty factions. Civil war ensued in the summer of 1922, and initially Cork was dominated by anti-treaty forces. Michael Collins, the IRA leader who had gone to London to bargain for the Irish Free State, was ambushed and assassinated in West Cork on August 22, 1922, by the anti-treaty IRA, his former comrades. The fighting continued until April 1923, when the anti-treaty men finally gave up their arms.

By the 1980s many of Cork's traditional industries had bottomed out, and the unemployment rate soared. The economic boom of the mid-1990s brought new businesses to the area, however, and the city remains one of Ireland's busiest ports.

PLANNING YOUR TIME

Of Cork's three western peninsulas, the Beara is the most popular tourist destination (and the most picturesque). Those looking to get off the beaten track should visit Sheep's Head, which is more popular with Irish weekenders than international visitors. You could easily spend your whole vacation in West Cork, though many visitors just spend three or four days here before heading north to Killarney. Cork City merits one full day of sightseeing and two nights to sample its pubs, restaurants, and theaters.

Consider flying into Cork Airport from Dublin to save on gas and travel time, or at least flying one-way back to Dublin after a tour of Cork and Kerry (unless you have time to visit the Rock of Cashel, Kilkenny, and other places on the Dublin-Cork route).

Cork City

Dublin may seem increasingly like a generic European metropolis, but Cork still feels like a genuinely Irish city, industrial warts and all. This "changeling city" (so said Kate O'Brien) has an aura of confidence, a certain *je ne sais quoi*. You've probably heard otherwise, as even Cork natives have been known to badmouth their hometown, and it's true that to spend more than a couple of days here when you could be off frolicking in beautiful West Cork would be rather silly. But a vibrant nightlife (fueled by the presence of a national university), a few excellent restaurants, and a significant arts and theater scene plead a good case for spending the night here, if not two. After all, the Beara's not going anywhere.

The city center is wedged between two channels of the River Lee. You can often see flame-throwers and other performers at the small but always-jammin' **Bishop Lucey Park,** which is bordered by South Main Street on the west, the Grand Parade on the east, Tuckey Street on the south (which changes names to Oliver Plunkett to the east), and Washington Street one block to the north. St. Patrick's Street, lined with chain stores, curves like a smile a couple blocks northeast of the park. Immediately north of St. Patrick's Street, the artsier Huguenot Quarter is named

Cork City

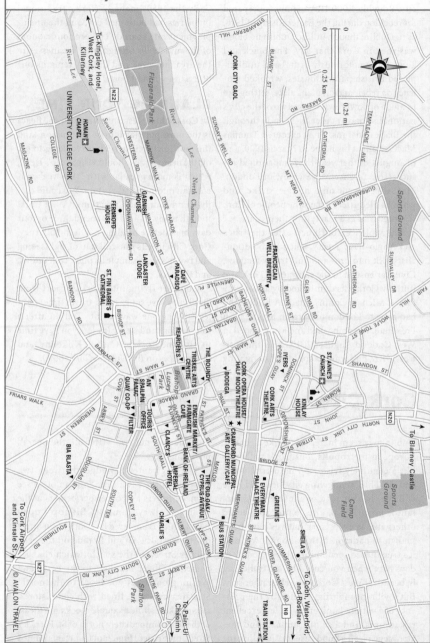

To Kingsley Hotel, West Cork, and Killarney

River Lee

Fitzgerald Park

N22

South Channel

UNIVERSITY COLLEGE CORK

HONAN CHAPEL

COLLEGE RD

MAGAZINE RD

FERNROYD HOUSE

GARNISH HOUSE

WASHINGTON ST

O'DONOVAN ROSSA RD

LANCASTER LODGE

ST. FIN BARRE'S CATHEDRAL

BANDON RD

BISHOP ST

BARRACK ST

FRIARS WALK

BIA BLASTA

DOUGLAS ST

EVERGREEN ST

ABBEY ST

COVE ST

S MAIN ST

QUAY CO-OP

COPLEY ST

SOUTH TER

SOUTHERN RD

N27

To Cork Airport and Kinsale St.

CORK CITY GAOL

STRAWBERRY HILL

BLARNEY ST

BAKERS RD

MARINA WALK

WESTERN RD

DYKE PARADE

River Lee

North Channel

SUNDAY'S WELL RD

MT NEBO AVE

CATHEDRAL RD

TEMPLEACRE AVE

GURRANABRAHER RD

Sports Ground

SUNVALLEY DR

FAIR HILL

WOLFE TONE ST

GLEN RYAN RD

CATHEDRAL RD

FRANCISCAN WELL BREWERY

GRENVILLE PL

NORTH MALL

BACHELOR'S QUAY

MILLERD ST

COACH ST

GRATTAN ST

N MAIN ST

POPE'S QUAY

BLARNEY ST

SHANDON ST

ST. ANNE'S CHURCH

IVERS

DOMINICK ST

KINLAY HOUSE

JOHN ST

ROMAN ST

CAFÉ PARADISO

THE ROUNDY

TRISKEL ARTS CENTRE

REARDEN'S

GRAND PARADE

Lucey Park

AN SPAILPÍN FÁNAC

TOURIST OFFICE

FILTER

BODEGA

ENGLISH MARKET

FARMGATE CAFÉ

CLANCY'S

ST PLUNKETT ST

SOUTH MALL

IMPERIAL HOTEL

BANK OF IRELAND

CORK OPERA HOUSE

HALF MOON THEATRE

PAUL ST

ST PATRICK'S ST

CRAWFORD MUNICIPAL ART GALLERY/CAFÉ

CORK ARTS THEATRE

DEVONSHIRE ST

NORTH CITY LINK ST

LEITRIM ST

N20

To Blarney Castle

CHARLIE'S

UNION QUAY

EGLINTON ST

ALBERT QUAY

ALBERT ST

CENTRE PARK RD

SOUTH CITY LINK RD

Shalom Park

To Páirc Uí Chaoimh

THE OLD OAK/ CYPRUS AVENUE

BUS STATION

MERCHANT'S QUAY

LAPP'S QUAY

BRIDGE ST

MAYOR ST

EVERYMAN PALACE THEATRE

GREENE'S

ST PATRICK'S QUAY

LOWER GLANMIRE RD

SUMMERHILL

SHEILA'S

Camp Field

Sports Ground

To Cobh, Waterford, and Rosslare

N8

TRAIN STATION

© AVALON TRAVEL

0 0.25 km
0 0.25 mi

for the influx of French Protestants who came to Cork to avoid religious persecution in the late 17th and early 18th centuries. And north of the Lee, the Shandon neighborhood is a quiet section—when the bells of St. Anne's aren't ringing, that is—with quaint rows of townhouses along narrow winding lanes, still the kind of place where the older locals greet you as you pass.

SIGHTS

There isn't a ton of stuff to see in Cork, but it's enough to keep you occupied for an afternoon.

★ St. Anne's Church

The clock tower at the 18th-century Anglican **St. Anne's Church** (John Redmond St., tel. 021/450-5906, www.shandonbells.ie, 9:30am-5pm Mon.-Sat., free, €5 to ring the bells) was traditionally known as the "four-faced liar" because each clock face read a different time. One of the coolest experiences you'll have in Cork is climbing the tower to play the eight "Bells of Shandon," memorialized in a popular early-19th-century song by a priest named Father Prout. You're even supplied with sheet music (the whole city's going to hear you, so you can't just ring them at random!). Afterward you can venture out onto the narrow balcony for a terrific view of the city.

★ Honan Chapel

Consecrated in 1916, the **Honan Chapel** (on the UCC campus, signposted, tel. 021/490-3088, 8am-8pm Mon.-Fri., 10am-6pm Sat., noon Mass Sun., free) is much more than the spiritual center of **University College Cork** (College Rd., southwest of the city center). With its intricate Hiberno-Romanesque doorway, funky floor mosaics, modern sculptures and wall hangings, and exquisite stained-glass windows by Harry Clarke and Sarah Purser, the chapel (named for the local family who funded it) stunningly exemplifies Celtic revival architecture as well as the Irish Arts and Crafts movement. You could spend a good hour admiring the windows alone, which depict several obscure Irish saints, like Ita (the

"Brigid of Munster") and one of her pupils, Fachtna, a bishop whom you might easily mistake for Patrick. With his craggy face and flowing white hair, it's hard to believe he lived only to the age of 46.

Other Sights

Art lovers should head to the **Crawford Municipal Art Gallery** (Emmet Pl., tel. 021/427-3377, www.crawfordartgallery.ie, 10am-5pm Mon.-Sat., free). Visiting exhibitions with historical themes complement a small but outstanding permanent collection of 18th- through 20th-century sculptures, paintings, and prints. Though most of the collection is of Irish provenance—don't miss the Harry Clarke room, with its gorgeous pen-and-ink illustrations, early stained-glass works, and preparatory drawings for *The Eve of St. Agnes* (on display at the Hugh Lane Gallery in Dublin)—you can also check out minor works by Picasso, Dali, Braque, and Miro. The gallery, which was once the Custom House, also houses one of the city's best eateries.

The exhibition at the early-19th-century **Cork City Gaol** (Convent Ave., Sunday's Well, tel. 021/430-5022, www.corkcitygaol.com, 9:30am-6pm daily Mar.-Oct., 10am-5pm daily Nov.-Feb., €8) does the whole wax-mannequins-and-sound-effects schtick, but it's still one of the city's top attractions.

The cavernous Anglican **St. Fin Barre's Cathedral** (Dean St., tel. 021/496-3387, http://corkcathedral.webs.com, 9:30am-5:30pm Mon.-Sat. and 12:30pm-5pm Sun. Apr.-Sept., 10am-12:45pm and 2pm-5pm Mon.-Sat. Oct.-Mar., €5) feels thoroughly Gothic, though it was built between 1865 and 1870 by the English architect William Burges (who designed all the stained-glass windows, mosaics, and sculptures, of which there are more than 1,260). The city's first bishop and patron saint, St. Fin Barre is said to have established a monastery on this site in the 7th century. The windows depict scenes from the New and Old Testaments—and the clerestory windows feature the signs

The Bizarre Brilliance of Harry Clarke

The Godhead Enthroned by Harry Clarke, on display at the Crawford Municipal Art Gallery

Ireland's greatest stained-glass artist (indeed, one of the world's finest), Harry Clarke, was born in 1889 in Dublin to an Irish mother and an English father, and he was educated by the Jesuits. Though Clarke was clearly influenced by Aubrey Beardsley, Gustav Klimt, and other romantic Nouveau artists, his stained-glass designs and "febrile, fantastical" illustration style (most famously exemplified in his superbly creepy watercolors and pen-and-inks for the stories of Edgar Allan Poe), his work is not derivative. Clarke's windows are informed by the classic "religious-sensual conflict," and though the artist was not a devout Catholic, his lingering guilt over his absence at his mother's death coupled with the Jesuits' fire-and-brimstone preachings contributed to a haunting, melancholy style that resonates with the viewer long after seeing his works. Clarke died in 1931 at the age of 42; he was so prolific during his relatively short career that one can only imagine how much more he might have accomplished had he lived a full life.

You'll find some of Clarke's finest work in the neo-Hiberno-Romanesque **Honan Chapel** at University College Cork (which also includes the work of a rival studio, that of Sarah Purser); in the **Hugh Lane Gallery** in Dublin *(The Eve of St. Agnes)*; and the absolutely magnificent three-light Last Judgment altar window at **St. Patrick's Church** in Newport, County Mayo. There are many smaller works in churches across Ireland, and a couple of small windows are on display at the **Crawford Municipal Art Gallery** in Cork City as well.

Stateside, you can see a series of nine windows commissioned during the last year of Clarke's life for the **Basilica of St. Vincent de Paul** in Bayonne, New Jersey. The *Geneva Window,* a series of illustrations of Gaelic revival works that was originally commissioned for the League of Nations, is on display at the **Wolfsonian Foundation** (www.wolfsonian.fiu.edu), a museum focusing on the "propaganda arts" at Florida International University in Miami.

For more information, check out *The Life and Work of Harry Clarke,* by Nicola Gordon Bowe, a professor at the National College of Art and Design in Dublin, and *Strangest Genius: The Stained Glass of Harry Clarke,* by Lucy Costigan and Michael Cullen.

of the zodiac. If you come later in the afternoon, you might be able to catch a rehearsal of the children's choir. Even if you don't want to pay the admission fee, you can sit on the small grassy knoll out front and admire the wonderful (life-sized) statuary tableaux inspired by that of Notre Dame. Gargoyles of every shape are perched high over the wise and foolish virgins (on opposite sides of the central door).

A side note for stout lovers: alas and alack, the venerable **Beamish and Crawford Brewery** on South Main Street closed its doors in 2009, though Beamish is still brewed at a Heineken facility on the Shandon side of the river. At time of writing the space was undergoing a €50-million redevelopment as an entertainment and conference venue.

ACTIVITIES AND RECREATION

Head west for excellent water-sporting opportunities in Kinsale, Schull, or Baltimore.

The **Pairc Uí Chaoimh** (Marina Walk, tel. 021/438-5876 or 021/496-3311, www.gaacork. ie), Cork City's hurling and Gaelic football stadium, was demolished in 2015, and the rebuild was ongoing at time of writing. When it does reopen for Sunday matches, you can get here via Bus Éireann local route #2 from Parnell Place.

FOOD

Cork has it all: character-filled gastro-pubs, chill cafés, and memorable gourmet restaurants. For the best coffee in town, drop by **Filter** (19 George's Quay, tel. 021/455-0050, 8am-6pm Mon.-Fri., 9am-6pm Sat., 10am-5:30pm Sun., under €8). This arty (if tiny) coffee shop does sandwiches and scrummy treats too, with vegan and gluten-free options. **Bia Blasta** (22 Douglas St., tel. 021/431-4560, 8am-4:30pm Mon.-Sat., cash only, under €10), which means "delicious food," even has a separate vegan menu.

Affiliated with the much-acclaimed Ballymaloe Cookery School, the **Crawford Gallery Café** (Emmet Pl., tel. 021/427-4415, 10am-4:30pm Mon.-Fri., 9:30am-4pm Sat., €10-20) is a perennial favorite with ladies-who-lunch (and pretty much everyone else in Cork, too). It's a perfectly classy (and convenient) spot to enjoy a gourmet quiche or salad after a morning of culture in the city art gallery.

With fresh meat, cheeses, and produce sourced from the downstairs farm market, the **Farmgate Café** (upstairs at the English

St. Fin Barre's Cathedral

Market, off Oliver Plunkett St. and the Grand Parade, tel. 021/427-8134, www.farmgatecork.ie, 8:30am-5pm Mon.-Sat., €11-14) offers hearty, great-value traditional dishes you won't find elsewhere nowadays: corned beef and cabbage, lamb stew, corned mutton, and drisheen (a kind of black pudding one customarily douses with mustard before sampling). There are a couple of terrific meat-free choices as well.

Clancy's (15-16 Princes St., tel. 021/427-6097, www.clancys-bar.com, food served 8am-midnight weekdays, 10:30am-midnight Sat., 12:30pm-4:30pm Sun., €8-20) is one of Cork's most popular gastro-pubs, with a reputation for very spicy buffalo wings and other good-value Mexican and Italian-inspired dishes. For funky atmosphere *and* scrummy eats, try **Bodega** (46 Cornmarket St., tel. 021/427-2878, www.bodegacork.ie, food served noon-9pm daily, until 10:30pm Wed.-Sun., lunch €7-15, dinner €15-25). Vegetarians have a choice as well.

Part of Isaac's Hotel, the wonderful **Greene's** (48 MacCurtain St., tel. 021/450-0011, www.greenesrestaurant.com, 12:30pm-3pm Mon.-Sat. and 12:30pm-4pm Sun., 6pm-10pm daily, 2/3-course lunch €22/25, 3-course early-bird special €32.50 6pm-7pm, €26-30) is reached through an atmospheric stone archway and a courtyard with a waterfall floodlit by night. The modern Irish fare is top-notch, and the desserts are to die for. While there are no vegan options on the menu, the chef will accommodate with something way more imaginative than a stir-fry, and gluten-free choices are abundant. Be sure to get here by 7pm for the early bird, which is a far better value than the à la carte.

Cork has three vegetarian restaurants: one small Indian café, one cafeteria-style above a whole-foods store, and the last a gourmand's delight. **Iyer's** (38 Popes Quay, tel. 087/640-9079, noon-5:30pm Tues.-Sat., plus 6pm-9pm Fri.-Sat., €8-15, cash only) is your place if you're hankering for homemade samosas and a hot chai on a chilly day. The **Quay Co-op** (24 Sullivan's Quay, tel. 021/431-7026, www.quaycoop.com, 9am-9pm daily, under €12) does hearty great-value meals—lasagna, chickpea burgers, savory tarts, and heaping salads. Be sure to work up an appetite before you arrive, because the portions are gigantic, and the desserts, though nothing fancy, hit the spot too. Though the same can't be said of ★ **Café Paradiso** (16 Lancaster Quay, tel. 021/427-7939, www.cafeparadiso.ie, 5:30pm-10pm Mon.-Sat., 2/3 courses €33/40), you'll more than forgive the daintiness. This is undoubtedly one of the best restaurants in the country, vegetarian or otherwise (and it's better than all Dublin's veggie eateries put together); owner-chef Denis Cotter has elevated meatless cuisine to an art form. The fantastically inventive menu changes regularly; expect to spend at least half an hour deciding on a main course. The lengthy, well-chosen wine list can present a dilemma as well, and any dessert you choose will send you swooning. Though the food is heavenly, what's even better about this place is the surprisingly relaxed atmosphere with attentive, down-to-earth service.

ENTERTAINMENT AND EVENTS
Entertainment

Founded in 1998 on the site of the 13th-century Shandon Friary, the **Franciscan Well Brewery** (14b North Mall, tel. 021/439-3434, www.franciscanwellbrewery.com) has quickly become Ireland's foremost craft brewery. The pub isn't quite as atmospheric as Cork's older watering holes, but it's still a fun spot to while away an evening sampling the Jameson Aged Pale Ale, Jameson Aged Stout, the Rebel Red, and other house brews.

The name means "The Wandering Migrant Worker," and fittingly enough, **An Spailpín Fánac** (S. Main St., tel. 021/427-7949) hosts the occasional socialist meeting. This pub might be on the grungy side, but it's still a local favorite for rollickin'-good trad sessions nearly every night of the week. **Rearden's** (26 Washington St., tel. 021/427-1969, www.reardens.com), a popular UCC hangout, hosts

LGBTQ Cork

After Dublin, Cork is the island's most gay-friendly city. Over August bank holiday weekends in the past, **Cork Pride** (www.corkpride.com) has put up a series of athletic races, film screenings, and even a formal ball. It doesn't happen every year, but it's worth looking up as you plan your trip.

You might want to make your first stop **The Other Place** (8 S. Main St., tel. 021/427-8470, noon-10pm Mon.-Sat., noon-6pm Sun.), a resource center, bookstore, and café. In addition to a calendar of social events and classes, The Other Place runs the Southern Gay Health Project, which educates local gay men on HIV/AIDS and so forth. The Other Place also offers a nightclub on weekend nights. Other resources include **L.Inc** (11A White St., tel. 021/480-8600, www.linc.ie, 8pm-10pm Thurs. and noon-3pm Tues.), short for "Lesbians in Cork," and the **Cork Gay Community Development Company** (4 S. Terrace, tel. 021/430-0430, www.gayprojectcork.com).

Gay-friendly pubs include **The Roundy** (Castle St., tel. 021/427-0433) and **Bodega** (46 Cornmarket St., tel. 021/427-2878). For clubbing, your best bet is The Other Place Friday-Sunday. There are a few other monthly clubs around town though; check out **GayCork.com** (www.gaycork.com) for the lowdown.

Same-sex couples might want to stay at **Emerson House** (2 Clarence Terrace, Summer Hill N., tel. 021/427-1087 or 086/834-0891, www.emersonhousecork.com, €40-80 pp sharing), an exclusively gay B&B.

bands or singer/songwriters Wednesday and Friday through Sunday nights. Across the way, the live acts at **Charlie's** (2 Union Quay, tel. 021/496-5272, www.charliesbarcork.com) are generally more Jerry-Garcia-lookalike than ambitious up-and-comer. There's trad on Sunday afternoon starting around 3pm. Charlie's is also noteworthy because you can start boozing it up from 7am every day but Sunday (when the bar opens at 12:30pm).

Or would you rather just chill out someplace hip-but-not-*too*-hip? Try **The Roundy** (Castle St., tel. 021/427-0433, www.theroundy.com), a smart and stylish bar (with windows all around a circular room, as you no doubt surmised) attracting an equally smart and stylish after-work crowd. DJs in the upstairs bar play Thursday, Friday, and Sunday nights. Some locals might tell you **Bodega** (46 Cornmarket St., tel. 021/427-2878) isn't quite as cool as it used to be, but don't pay them any mind. This converted warehouse has a soaring ceiling, whitewashed brick walls, two-story mirrors behind the bar, and bountiful outdoor seating (under festive canopies), all of which makes for a refreshingly laid-back atmosphere. The bar food's very good, too.

Cork's top venue for live pop/rock is **Cyprus Avenue** (Caroline St., tel. 021/427-6165, www.cyprusavenue.ie, €8-20), which has hosted the likes of Luka Bloom, Saul Williams, and Claire Sproule along with plenty of up-and-coming local bands. You can buy tickets for Cyprus Avenue gigs at the bar downstairs, the **Old Oak** (113 Oliver Plunkett St., tel. 021/427-6165), which also hosts live bands Sunday-Wednesday and DJs Thursday-Saturday. This is a spacious, classy, comfortable old pub where you can kick back in a leather booth with a pint in the late afternoon in relative peace and quiet, your old pal Van on the stereo.

This city has a thriving drama scene as well. See whatever theater company's making the rounds at the old-fashioned, pleasantly worn **Everyman Palace Theatre** (15 MacCurtain St., tel. 021/450-1673, www.everymancork.com, €10-30). There are generally more experimental dramas on the calendar at the **Cork Arts Theatre** (Carrolls Quay, tel. 021/450-8398, www.corkartstheatre.com, €12-25), in a newish building (on the site of the old theater) with a cozy 100-seat auditorium. Incorporating an 18th-century deconsecrated church, the **Triskel Arts Centre** (Tobin St., tel. 021/427-2022, www.triskelartscentre.ie,

€10-20) puts on film screenings, plays, photography exhibits, and international, sometimes-quirky musical acts.

As you'd expect, the **Cork Opera House** (Emmet Pl., tel. 021/427-6357, www.corkoperahouse.ie, €10-50) does much more than opera, and it's not all on the conservative side: Along with ballet, classical music, Shakespeare, and suchlike, you'll find the occasional black comedy or laugh-a-minute musical. Part of the opera house, the **Half Moon Theatre** covers the lighter stuff, pop/folk/rock concerts and comedy shows mostly.

Festivals and Events

Cork's festival calendar isn't quite as busy as Dublin's or Galway's, but there's still plenty to write home about.

Founded in 1954, the five-day **Cork International Choral Festival** (Festival House, 15 Grand Parade, tel. 021/422-3535, www.corkchoral.ie) straddles April and May with a busy lineup of competitions and concerts. Listening to a visiting children's choir perform some afternoon at St. Fin Barre's Cathedral might just be the highlight of your Cork sojourn.

Over 12 days at the end of June, the **Cork Midsummer Festival** (Civic Trust House, Popes Quay, tel. 021/421-5131, www.corkmidsummer.com) offers a program of park, street, and traditional theater; family-oriented recreation, like boat trips on the Lee; art exhibitions; comedy shows; and concerts from opera to pop/rock to cabaret.

Jazz and stout might not sound like the most natural combination, yet the ever-popular **Cork Jazz Festival** (www.guinnessjazzfestival.com, €15-40) is sponsored by Guinness. The four-day festival takes place at the end of October and features everything from swing bands to gospel choirs at the Everyman Palace Theatre, the Opera House, the Gresham Metropole Hotel, and many other venues. Contact individual box offices to book. Murphy's, the local stout, sponsors the weeklong **Cork Film Festival**

(tel. 021/427-1711, www.corkfilmfest.org) in October or November.

SHOPPING

The city's largest mall is the **Merchant's Quay Shopping Centre** near the bus station, but you'll only find the usual chains. Be sure to check out the **English Market** (Mutton Ln., off St. Patrick's St., tel. 021/492-4258, www.englishmarket.ie, 8am-6pm Mon.-Sat.) for pottery, art, and confectionary along with the usual fresh foodstuffs. This market has been going strong since 1788.

St. Patrick's Street is Cork's commercial thoroughfare, though you'll find smaller and more atmospheric shops on the side streets and lanes between St. Patrick's and Paul Streets. Secondhand **Connolly's Bookshop** (Rory Gallagher Pl., Paul St., tel. 021/427-5366), in the Huguenot Quarter, is good for an extended browse.

ACCOMMODATIONS

The dorms are on the cramped side, but IHH, family-run ★ **Sheila's** (4 Belgrave Pl., Wellington Rd., tel. 021/450-5562, www.sheilashostel.ie, dorms €16-25, private rooms €25-28 pp) is still the friendliest hostel in town. Sheila's has a sauna, bureau de change, and bike rental, and the staff are an excellent source of information. Another safe bet is **Kinlay House** (Bob & Joan's Walk, Shandon, tel. 021/450-8966, www.kinlayhousecork.ie, dorms €16, private rooms €25-28 pp)—clean and spacious, with good facilities, just like its sister hostels in Galway and Dublin.

Most of Cork's B&Bs are dotted along Western Road near the university, all with small car parks out front. Renowned for its deluxe breakfasts (smoked salmon, pancakes, porridge with a generous dollop of Bailey's) and well-appointed rooms, **Garnish House** (Western Rd., tel. 021/427-5111, www.garnish.ie, €50-70 pp, s €80-123) has acquired a reputation as the city's top guesthouse. Rates rise considerably at peak times (bank holiday and festival weekends in particular), and single travelers will certainly find better value elsewhere. Try **Fernroyd House** (4 O'Donovan Rossa Rd., off Western Rd., tel. 021/427-1460, www. fernroydhouse.com, €45-50 pp, s €70), an excellent choice for its airy and immaculate rooms, genuinely kind and accommodating proprietors, and lovely garden out back. The breakfast is top-notch, with homebaked breads and scones and ample vegetarian options. Western Road can be fairly noisy, but Fernroyd is off the main drag in a relatively quiet cul-de-sac.

Vegetarians will be thrilled to know that ★ **Café Paradiso** (16 Lancaster Quay, tel. 021/427-7939, www.cafeparadiso.ie, d €220, s €180) is now offering accommodations above the legendary restaurant. The three en suite double rooms are individually designed and furnished with such care that you feel like you're staying in the guest room of your (very hip) best friend. And of course, breakfast is divine (and divinely healthy—no rashers or black pudding in sight!).

Directly across the street, right on the River Lee, is the excellent business-class **Lancaster Lodge** (Lancaster Quay, tel. 021/425-1125, www.lancasterlodge.com, rooms €120-130, 10% senior citizen discount). Here you can expect friendly and professional staff, comfortable queen-size beds, plasma TVs, and soundproof walls and windows. Suites with Jacuzzi are available at a higher rate (€170). Breakfast is included in the room price, with a buffet as well as smoked salmon and omelets cooked to order.

The five-star **Kingsley Hotel** (Victoria Cross, past Western Rd. on the west end of the city, a 25-minute walk into town, tel. 021/480-0555, www.thekingsley.ie, rooms €150-310) was built on the site of the old Lee Baths, an open-air public pool that kept generations of Cork schoolchildren cool on those (albeit rare) dog days. The deluxe-grade rooms feature espresso machines, minibars, LCD televisions, CD and DVD players, down quilts, bathrobes and slippers, in-room safes, and "walk-in" showers along with bathtub. The spa offers a range of Ayurvedic treatments, and the leisure center has a huge pool, Jacuzzi, steam room, and sauna. Best of all, the all-around service lives up to the five-star rating. Check out the website for good-value B&B and dinner packages.

With a more central location, the **Imperial Hotel** (South Mall, tel. 021/427-4040, www. flynnhotels.com, rooms €150-190, penthouse €770) has a similarly high standard of service (and an Aveda salon and spa). All rooms feature Aveda toiletries and complimentary mineral water, and the superior-grade rooms have queen- and king-size beds, digital interactive television, and bathrobes and slippers. Breakfast isn't included in the room price, however.

INFORMATION AND SERVICES

Stop by Cork's **tourist office** (Grand Parade, tel. 021/425-5100, www.cork.ie, 9am-6pm Mon.-Fri. and 9am-5:30pm Sat. June-Aug., 9:15am-5:30pm Mon.-Sat. Sept.-May) for leaflets on upcoming events. You may find the staff are more helpful at the seasonal **Cork City Information Booth** (corner St. Patrick's St. and Winthrop St., daily June-Sept.), however.

For ATMs or bureaux de change, visit the **Bank of Ireland** or **AIB,** both on St. Patrick's Street. For a pharmacy, your best bet (it's open Sunday) is **Boots** (Merchant's Quay Shopping Centre, tel. 021/427-2230).

GETTING THERE

The Parnell Place Bus and Train Station is at Merchant's Quay. **Bus Éireann** (tel. 021/450-8188, www.buseireann.ie) provides regular service to Cork from Galway, Ennis, and Limerick (#51, 14/day daily), Dublin (#8, 6/day daily), Cashel (#8 and #71, 9/day Mon.-Sat., 7/day Sun.), Waterford (#40, 13/day daily), Tralee and Killarney (#40, 14/day daily), Kilkenny (#7, 4/day Mon.-Sat., 3/day Sun.), and many other places. Another option for Limerick and Galway is **Citylink** (tel. 091/564-163, www.citylink.ie, single fare €17/21).

It's faster to travel from Dublin via **Irish Rail** (tel. 021/450-6766, www.irishrail.ie, 9/day daily, single/open return €66/87), and you can snag a lower fare by booking online.

Fly into **Cork International Airport** (6 km south of the city on the N27, tel. 021/431-3131, www.corkairport.com) from Dublin (on Aer Arann or Ryanair), Belfast (on Aer Arann), Edinburgh, London (Heathrow on Aer Lingus, Stansted on Ryanair, and Gatwick on Ryanair or Easyjet), Rome, Barcelona, Amsterdam, and several other European cities. The most frequently traveled airlines are **Aer Arann** (tel. 0818/210-210, www.aerarann.ie), **Aer Lingus** (tel. 0818/365-000, www.aerlingus.ie), **Ryanair** (tel. 01/609-7800, www.ryanair.com), and **Easyjet** (tel. 1890/923-922, www.easyjet.com). Bus Éireann operates a shuttle between the airport and city center bus station (single fare €5.60), or a taxi will run you €20.

GETTING AROUND

You can get all over the city by foot, but if you don't feel like schlepping back to the B&B there's always the local bus service. Route #208 links Western Road with St. Patrick's Street in the city center (fare €2.10).

For a cab, ring the **Cork Taxi Co-op** (6 Washington St. W., tel. 021/427-2222) or **Shandon Taxi Cabs** (tel. 021/450-2255).

Hire a bike from **Rothar Cycles** (55 Barrack St., tel. 021/431-3133 or 087/217-1752, www.rotharcycletours.ie, closed Sun., €20/80 per day/week, €100 deposit, one-way service €30). *Rothar* means "wheel," by the way.

Around Cork City

BLARNEY

Built in the 15th century, **Blarney** (tel. 021/438-5252, www.blarneycastle.ie, €13) is Ireland's most infamous castle—and its biggest tourist trap. Hours vary seasonally (9am-sunset Mon.-Sat. and 9:30am-sunset Sun. Oct.-Apr., 9am-6:30pm Mon.-Sat. and 9:30am-5:30pm Sun. May and Sept., 9am-7pm Mon.-Sat. and 9:30am-5:30pm Sun. June-Aug.). During the reign of Elizabeth I the chatelain of Blarney Castle, Cormac MacDermot MacCarthy, was a veritable master of unfulfilled promises, and his smooth talk infuriated the old Virgin Queen. A legend arose from a priest's song-poem published in 1860, which promised that whoever kissed the now filthy-black stone, located along a parapet high above the castle floor, would be infused with MacCarthy's gift for honey-tongued BS.

So you can smooch the stone, a gruff elderly man lowers you, backward and head-first, down a gap at the edge of the wall. Many tourists find the experience exciting and count it a must-do while in Ireland, but from an anthropological standpoint it's all rather inexplicable, not to mention undignified. It's not just a rumor that British soldiers used to relieve themselves on that stone, and according to a few of the locals, disgruntled castle employees continue the tradition after hours.

Outside of that notorious stone, the castle ruins are picturesque and would be worth a visit were it not for the crowds. With so much company, it makes little sense to come here when you could enjoy a placid stroll among any of the other charmingly secluded ivy-clad ruins in this country.

Blarney is eight kilometers northwest of Cork off the N20. **Bus Éireann** (tel. 021/450-8188, #215, 25-minute trip, return fare €7.50) provides frequent service from Parnell Station.

FOTA ISLAND

Featuring walled and Italianate gardens dating to the first half of the 19th century, the **Fota Arboretum and Gardens** (Fota Island, Carrigtwohill, 8 km north of Cobh on the R624 and 14 km east of Cork City off the N25, tel. 021/481-2728, free) is laid out over 11 hectares. Hours are shorter in winter (9am-6pm Mon.-Sat. and 11am-6pm Sun. Apr.-Oct., 9am-5pm Mon.-Sat. and 11am-5pm Sun. Nov.-Mar.). If the weather turns, you can take a self-guided tour through the Regency-style **Fota House** (tel. 021/481-5543, www.fotahouse.com, 10am-6pm Mon.-Sat., 11am-6pm Sun., €8).

But the island's biggest draw, for families especially, is the 28-hectare **Fota Wildlife Park** (tel. 021/481-2678, www.fotawildlife.ie, 10am-5pm Mon.-Sat. and 11am-5pm Sun. mid-Mar.-Oct., 10am-3pm Mon.-Sat. and 11am-3pm Sun. Nov.-mid-Mar., €15.50). The wildlife park is much better than a zoo because there are no cages.

There is a €3 parking fee for both wildlife park and arboretum; Fota actually makes a better day trip from Cork City via **Irish Rail,** as there is a train an hour pulling into Fota Station.

COBH

Once the port of Cork City, **Cobh** ("Cove") was the *Titanic*'s final port of call in 1912 (a fact rather tackily milked by the local tourist office), and was also a common departure point for those immigrating to America and Australia. In a cringe-worthy twist of irony, Cobh was renamed Queenstown in 1849 after Victoria, who in the words of William Bulfin "never did anything for Ireland but preside over more than three-score years of its most disastrous history." After the Irish Free State was formed in 1921, the town council's first act was to change the name back again.

Frankly, Cobh is far too industrial-feeling—the row of huge and hideous factories on the far side of the estuary makes the "harbor view" boast pretty near laughable; nor are its cultural attractions quite interesting enough to merit a stopover. That said, if the Cork coast was the last your ancestors saw of Ireland, you might find the heritage center, **Cobh, The Queenstown Story** (in the old railway station, adjacent to the new one, tel. 021/481-3591, www.cobhheritage.com, 10am-6pm daily May-Oct., 10am-5pm

daily Nov.-Apr., €9.50), worth a visit. Situated on a hill overlooking town and harbor is the Catholic **St. Colman's Cathedral** (Cathedral Pl., tel. 021/481-3222, daily, free) in all its hyper-elaborate neo-Gothic glory. Designed by Pugin the Younger and associates, it was built over a period of 47 years (1868-1915). Much of the funding came from America and Australia.

Cobh's layout is a bit confusing at first, with narrow crisscrossing streets wedged between the harbor and the hill on which St. Colman's stands. Running west to east, the waterside main drag changes names from Lower Road to Westbourne Place to West Beach to East Beach. Everything you'll need is located on (or just off) this main drag.

Food and Accommodations

An immaculate B&B in a handy location a block from the town center is **Ard na Laoi** (15 Westbourne Pl., tel. 021/481-2742, www.ardnalaoi.ie, €40 pp). Ask for a room with an ocean view. **Knockeven** (Rushbrooke, off the R624/High Rd. less than 2 km west of the train station, tel. 021/481-1778, www.knockevenhouse.com, €50 pp, singles charged at double rate) is another good choice for its home-baking and jams, amiable owners, and electric heating pads on the comfy beds.

Cobh's best hotel is the **Watersedge** (Westbourne Pl., tel. 021/481-5566, www.waters-edgehotel.ie, rooms €120, suites €160-240); some of the rooms have balconies overlooking the water, and the hotel restaurant, **Jacob's Ladder** (food served 12:30pm-9pm daily, €14-24), is one of the town's best eateries. Another (less formal) pub-cum-restaurant, **The Quays** (Wellington Pl., tel. 021/481-3539, food served noon-9:30pm daily, €12-25) also has good food (the portobello mushroom burger hits the spot)—and a younger, hipper crowd on the harbor-facing deck.

Information and Services

The **tourist office** (tel. 021/481-3301, www.visitcobh.ie, 9:30am-5:30pm Thurs.-Tues., 1pm-5pm Wed.) and **Sirius Arts Centre** (tel.

021/481-3790, www.siriusartscentre.ie) are located in the old yacht club on the harbor. There's an ATM and bureau de change at the **AIB** on West Beach, just north of Kennedy Park, where there's a romantic old bandstand and a small farmers market on Friday mornings (selling mostly prepared foods, a nice option for an alfresco lunch on a bench overlooking the water).

Getting There

Cobh is 24 kilometers southeast of Cork City off the N25 (picking up the R624 before Carrigtwohill) and is a cinch to get to by **Irish Rail** (tel. 021/450-6766, hourly departures, single/day return €6.05/9.70).

MIDLETON

A humdrum town 20 kilometers east of Cork City, Midleton (Mainistir na Corann, "Abbey of the Choir") is only worth a stop for the **Jameson Heritage Centre** (signposted from the main street, tel. 021/461-3594, www.jamesonwhiskey.com, 10am-6pm daily, frequent tours Mar.-Oct., tours at 11:30am, 2:30pm, and 4pm daily Nov.-Feb., €16), a must for whiskey drinkers. The old distillery dates from the 1820s (though the buildings themselves date from the 1790s, as this complex was originally a woolen factory) and was turned into a tourist attraction when the new one opened in 1975. Here you'll find the world's largest pot still (with a capacity of 32,000 gallons). A 45-minute guided tour consists of an introductory audiovisual; a comprehensive tour of the old distillery with all its mills, stills, and warehouses (you'll practically be able to make whiskey at home after this); and a tasting in the bar afterward. Two volunteers in each group get to sample other Irish and Scotch varieties for comparison.

Midleton is 20 kilometers east of Cork on the N25, and there is frequent **Bus Éireann** service from the city (tel. 021/450-8188, #40 or #41, 18/day Mon.-Sat., 13/day Sun.). There is hourly **Irish Rail** service as well (single/day return €6.25/9.90).

KINSALE

When William Bulfin characterized the Battle of Kinsale as a "disastrous epoch" in Irish history, he might have been referring to either of the two conflicts that left the native Irish in even worse straits than before: in 1601, when the Gaelic earls of Tyrone and Tir Conaill (now part of Donegal) fought in vain to rid Ireland of the English imperialists; or in 1689, when the forces of William of Orange resoundingly defeated the Jacobites. Other local tragedies included the *Lusitania,* which sank 20 kilometers south of **Kinsale** (Cionn tSáile, "Head of the Sea") in May of 1915; nine of the survivors landed here.

Kinsale's food is as rich as its history; the town has declared itself Ireland's gourmet capital, and this is only a minor exaggeration. Between all the fancy eateries and its popularity with wealthy golfers and yachters, the budget-conscious visitor can feel out of place here; that said, good-value early-bird menus abound, and though you may pay five or ten quid more for a B&B than you would elsewhere, you'll find it's money well spent.

Though the layout is medieval, Kinsale is still pretty easy to get the hang of. The town wraps itself around the harbor inlet, bordered by Pier Road to the west, Emmet Place to the north, and Pearse Street to the east. Turn north off Emmet Place onto Market Quay (not on the water, despite the name), which will lead you to the Market Square. Cork Street is another block north of the square. On the west side of the town center, Main Street and O'Connell Street run parallel to Market Quay.

Sights

Built to be Kinsale's Custom House at the turn of the 16th century, Dúchas-run **Desmond Castle** (Cork St., tel. 021/477-4855 or 021/477-2263 in winter, 10am-6pm daily mid-Apr.-Oct., €4) later served as a French prison and famine workhouse. Today this tower house on the north side of town features a modest museum on the history of wine.

Built in 1677, the star-shaped **Charles Fort** (Summer Cove, 2 km east of town, tel.

021/477-2263, 10am-6pm daily mid-Mar.-
Oct., 10am-5pm daily Nov.-mid-Mar., €4)
was named in honor of Charles II. James II
"kept court" here before the disastrous Battle
of Kinsale in 1689 (during the Williamite war,
as opposed to the Battle of Kinsale in 1601 that
precipitated the event known as the Flight of
the Earls). The site is run by Dúchas, which
offers the usual exhibition and 45-minute
guided tour.

A freely accessible (and very picturesque)
ruin built in 1603 on a small peninsula in
Kinsale Harbour, **James Fort** offers a serene view of the town, bay, and surrounding
hillside. To get here, follow Pier Road (on the
west side of the harbor) south out of town and
make a left when you reach the bridge; the fort
is beyond the Castlepark Marina.

Activities and Recreation
TOURS
Don Herlihy's Historic Walking Tour (tel.
021/477-2873, www.historicstrollkinsale.
com, €7) offers a dynamic introduction to
the town's crucial role in Irish (and English)
history. The 90-minute guided walk departs
the tourist office at 11:15am daily mid-March
to mid-October.

OTHER ACTIVITIES
AND RECREATION
An easy two-kilometer walk takes you south
of town and over a bridge to **James Fort,** a
romantic old ruin overlooking the harbor. Or
pass the fort by boat on **Kinsale Harbour
Cruises** (tel. 086/250-5456 or 021/477-8946,
www.kinsaleharbourcruises.com, hourly
sailings in high season, 60-minute trip
€12.50). Cruises depart from the Kinsale
Marina, 300 meters south of the tourist office on Pier Road.

Kinsale is a golfer's haven, though the €240
high-season greens fee for 18 holes at the **Old
Head of Kinsale Golf Club** (8 km southwest of town, tel. 021/477-8444, www.old-
head.com) is beyond most folks' budgets. It
may not be quite as sought after (or scenic),
but an alternative is the **Kinsale Golf Club**

(Farrangalway, 3 km northwest of town on the
R607, tel. 021/477-4722, www.kinsalegolf.ie).

The **Oysterhaven Activity Centre**
(Oysterhaven, 10 km southeast of town on
a local road, signposted from the R600, tel.
021/477-0738, www.oysterhaven.com) offers
sailing and windsurfing courses as well as
canoe and kayak rental.

Food
Kinsale has many fine restaurants, but don't
let its gourmet reputation fool you into thinking you can get a great meal any old place. And
some highly praised restaurants are nevertheless overpriced; go for the early-bird special
if you can. (Also note that some eateries here
have an unwritten dress code even for lunch,
so you'd best leave the windpants and ball-
caps at the B&B.) For more info before you go,
take a look at **Kinsale's Good Food Circle**
website (tel. 021/477-4026, www.kinsaleres-
taurants.com).

On Tuesday the **farmers market** (Market
Sq., 9am-1:30pm) has stalls selling baked
goods, chocolate ice shakes, gourmet Fair
Trade coffee, and other ready-to-eat goodies.

For Irish-French fusion and daily seafood
specials, try **Max's** (48 Main St., tel. 021/477-
2443, www.maxs.ie, 6pm-9:30pm Tues.-Wed.
and Fri.-Sat., 2-course early-bird special
€25 served 6pm-7pm, dinner €16-27), where
rough stone walls and wide wooden tables add
to the laid-back, unpretentious atmosphere.
Another Kinsale mainstay is **Jim Edwards'**
(Market Quay, tel. 021/477-2541, www.jimed-
wardskinsale.com, bar food served 12:30pm-
10pm, restaurant 6pm-10pm daily, bar €12-18,
restaurant €18-30), which serves up the best
steaks in town.

Toddie's (Eastern Rd., just south of town
on the east side of the harbor, tel. 021/477-
7769, www.thebulman.ie, 6pm-10:30pm
daily in summer, closed Mon. in low season
and Jan., €18-30) offers inventively prepared
seafood in a stylish gallery-cum-dining room.
But Kinsale's most beloved seafood restaurant
is the **Fishy Fishy Café** (Crowleys Quay, tel.
021/470-0415, www.fishyfishy.ie, noon-9pm

daily Apr.-Sept., closed Sun. Oct.-Mar., but hours vary, €20-30), which has the best mussels you'll ever eat. You can have the catch of the day prepared however you like it, along with the requisite glass of white.

With all this hoopla around the local seafood, vegetarians and vegans can feel quite out of the loop. You definitely want to stay at **Gort Na Nain** (Ballyherkin, Nohoval, 10 km northeast of Kinsale, tel. 021/477-0647, www.gortnanain.com), which offers evening meals in high season. Otherwise, if you don't feel like taking your chances on the token vegetarian option, try **Malay Kitchen** (Short Quay, off Market Lane one block west of the tourist office, tel. 021/477-4937, 4pm-10pm Thurs.-Sun., €9-12, cash only), a friendly, mostly takeaway joint with delicious tofu fried rice and many other meat- and fish-free options.

Entertainment and Events

Calling all foodies: Be sure to time your arrival for the **Kinsale Gourmet Festival** (tel. 021/477-9900) in early October. Tickets for the various parties and tastings sell for as much as €75, though other events are free. The autumn bank holiday weekend (usually the last weekend in October) is another great time to be here, for the **Kinsale Jazz Festival.** Check out www.kinsale.ie for more festival info. Another longstanding event, the **Kinsale Arts Festival** (mid-July, www.kinsaleartsfestival.com), was taking a break at time of writing, but will hopefully be back up and running again in 2017.

If what you're looking for is a good old-fashioned trad session, head for the **Spaniard** (Scilly, follow Pearse St. south out of town and around the harbor, tel. 021/477-2436, www.thespaniard.ie), with sessions Wednesday all year and Friday night and Sunday afternoon in high season. **The Bulman** (Eastern Rd., just south of town on the east side of the harbor, tel. 021/477-7769, www.thebulman.ie) offers trad Thursday through Saturday nights as well as Sundays at 5pm. **Dalton's** (3 Market St., tel. 021/477-7957) does trad on Monday nights (more often in high season, along with other styles), and **The Tap** (Guardwell, at Church Square, a 5-minute walk northwest of the pier, tel. 021/477-3231) occasionally offers sessions as well. This is the only family-run watering hole left in Kinsale, four generations and counting. The owner's son runs the **Kinsale Ghost Tour** (tel. 087/948-0910, departing 9pm, €10), serving up spine-chilling tales with theatrical flair. The hour-plus tour

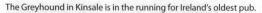

The Greyhound in Kinsale is in the running for Ireland's oldest pub.

begins at the pub every night but Saturday in high season.

The Greyhound (Market Sq., tel. 021/477-2889) is yet another pub claiming to be Ireland's oldest, and while there's no live music here, the atmosphere is curmudgeonly perfection.

Shopping

There are loads of opportunities for retail therapy in Kinsale (just take a stroll from the Market Square south along Main Street), but the two shops you shouldn't miss are **Kinsale Crystal** (Market St., tel. 021/477-4493, www.kinsalecrystal.ie), the workshop of a former Waterford master-cutter, and **Kinsale Silver** (Pearse St., tel. 021/477-4359, www.kinsalesilver.ie), a family-run workshop that produces beautifully handcrafted, one-of-a-kind Celtic designs.

Accommodations

This upscale town has plenty of upscale accommodations. Be sure to ask about discounts in the off-season.

Everything's as comfortable as home at **The Olde Bakery** (56 Lower O'Connell St., one block west of the Pier Rd. on the west side of the harbor, tel. 021/477-3012, www.theoldebakerykinsale.com, €40-50 pp): There are real quilts on the beds, an open fire in the cozy sitting room, and hearty food and friendly banter around the communal breakfast table.

Less than a 10-minute walk from the town center, **Woodlands House** (Cappagh, tel. 021/477-2633, www.woodlandskinsale.com, Mar.-mid-Nov., €35-50 pp, s €60-80) has a nice situation overlooking the harbor, lovely gardens, and king-size beds in its six immaculate rooms. There are in-room safes, and CD and DVD players are available if you ask. You'll be greeted with tea and cookies. To get here, head up O'Connell Street and make a left onto Church Street, passing St. Multose's Church (on your left) before bearing right; then follow the sign for Bandon, and you'll see the B&B up the road on your left.

A handsome ivy-clad Georgian, the **Old Presbytery** (43 Cork St., tel. 021/477-2027, www.oldpres.com, €60-80 pp) is one of Kinsale's most popular B&Bs for its equally atmospheric yet modern rooms (some with balconies and Jacuzzis) and deluxe breakfasts (crepes, smoked salmon, cheese plates, and suchlike). There's also a charming "penthouse suite" with fireplace, perfect for honeymooners.

Another top-notch guesthouse is **Friar's Lodge** (Friar's St., off Cork St., tel. 021/477-7384, www.friars-lodge.com, €55-60 pp, s €70-80), quite a good value considering how large, comfortable, and well-appointed the rooms are: DVD, radio, chocolates, in-room safe—even a pillow menu so you can choose your favorite type of pillow. You can pour yourself a complimentary drink in the sitting room, too. This B&B is canine friendly.

Kinsale's best hotels are boutiques. The carefully restored, well-maintained **Blue Haven Hotel** (3 Pearse St., by the harbor, tel. 021/477-2209, www.bluehavenkinsale.com, rooms €100-140) has lavishly decorated rooms featuring flat-screen TVs, and pillow menus, and the hotel restaurant can more than compete with Kinsale's finest eateries. A more modest option is the 10-room **White Lady Hotel** (Lower O'Connell St., one block west of Pier Rd., tel. 021/477-2737, www.whiteladyhotelkinsale.ie, rooms €150), with a great small-town feel (and the personal, friendly service to go along with it). The food's good, and the rooms are comfortable but no-frills. The White Lady has Kinsale's most popular nightclub, so this isn't your place if you're planning on an early night.

Vegetarians absolutely must plan on a night (or two, or three) at ★ **Gort Na Nain** (Ballyherkin, Nohoval, 10 km northeast of Kinsale, tel. 021/477-0647, www.gortnanain.com, d €85, s €60). Lucy and Ultan run this thoroughly wonderful mostly vegan B&B along with supplying organic produce to several Cork city restaurants (including Café Paradiso). The farmhouse is eco-friendly new construction, but it's been designed to feel cozy and old-fashioned, and the rooms all come with thoughtful touches like a selection of Pukka teas on the hostess tray, a stereo with a shelf of great music, and books besides the usual mass-market romances. Breakfast includes vegan sausages and tomato chutney (both made from scratch), homefries, gingerbread, and other delights. Of all the B&Bs you'll pass through on this trip, this is the one you'll be most likely to write home about. The route from Kinsale (via Belgooly) is a bit twisty-turny, but Lucy will send you detailed driving directions when you book your room.

Information and Services

The local **tourist office** (on the harbor, Pier Rd. and Emmet Pl., tel. 021/477-2234, 9:15am-1pm and 2:15pm-5:30pm Mon.-Sat. Mar.-mid-Nov., daily July-Aug.) is jointly run by the Irish Tourist Board and the Kinsale Chamber of Tourism (www.kinsale.ie). Also check out the *Kinsale Advertiser* (www.kinsaleadvertiser.com), a free weekly available at most newsagents.

The **Bank of Ireland** (Emmet St.) and the **AIB** (Pearse St.) each have an ATM and bureau de change; the **post office** on Pearse Street also changes money. Neither the **Collins Kinsale Pharmacy** (12 Market St., tel. 021/477-2077) nor **Moloney's** (Emmet St., tel. 021/477-2130) is open Sunday.

Getting There and Around

Kinsale is 23 kilometers south of Cork City on the R600. Rather than use the pay-and-display lot near the pier, turn right and make like you're leaving town, but following the water; you'll find plenty of free parking along this eastern side of the harbor, and it's only a two-minute walk back into town. **Bus Éireann** (tel. 021/450-3399, #249, 30-minute trip, 10/day Mon.-Sat., 5/day Sun.) offers frequent service from the city via the airport.

Need a lift? Ring **Kinsale Cabs** (tel. 021/470-0100 or 021/477-2642). Bike rental is available from **Mylie Murphy** (14 Pearse St., tel. 021/477-2703, €15/day), also open Sunday afternoons (noon-4pm) in high season.

West Cork

TIMOLEAGUE

A sleepy little town on a back road to Clonakilty, **Timoleague** (Tigh Molaige, "House of Molaga") is worth a stop for its splendid churches as well as **Timoleague Abbey.** Still standing imposingly over Courtmacsherry Bay, this Franciscan abbey was built around 1240 on the site of the hermitage of Molaga, an obscure 7th-century saint. Though these pigeon-infested ruins are worth ambling through, there isn't much of architectural interest. Take a peek through the altar window for a nice view of the bay.

Timoleague's churches are actually neater than the abbey ruins. The Anglican **Church of the Ascension** (one block east of the friary ruins), which dates from the early 19th century, features gorgeous wall mosaics completed over a period of 30 years (1894-1926),

a Crucifixion scene in the east window, and a life-size angel font, a copy of a Renaissance statue in Rome. Fortunately, unlike most Church of Ireland buildings, this one is open during the day. Timoleague's Catholic church, the Hiberno-Romanesque **Church of the Nativity of Our Lady** (a 2-minute walk up the hill, tel. 023/46185), features a three-light Harry Clarke window (from 1931) above the choir loft with scenes from the life of Jesus and the Ascension and the Coronation of Mary.

Timoleague is 10 kilometers east of Clonakilty on the R600 and 45 kilometers southwest of Cork City (from the N71, picking up the R602 west of Bandon). **Bus Éireann** (tel. 021/450-8188) route 238 from Cork City passes through Timoleague twice a day, Monday to Friday, and it is possible to reach Timoleague from Clonakilty, via Bandon, on route 47. That said, if you don't have wheels, it makes more sense to travel the 10 kilometers by bike from Clonakilty (as the connection in Bandon is very inconvenient).

CLONAKILTY

Best known as the birthplace of IRA military leader Michael Collins, Clonakilty (Cloich na Coillte, "Castle of the Woods") is a delightful market town with a friendly, easygoing vibe and a well-earned "Ireland's Tidiest Town" distinction. (It's also Ireland's first official "Fair Trade Town.") With its fun pubs and handful of great restaurants, this is an excellent place to base yourself when exploring West Cork.

Clonakilty's main street, the N71, changes names from Pearse to Ashe to Wolfe Tone from west to east, with the small Asna Square (with 1798 monument) marking the change from Pearse to Ashe. Bridge Street intersects Pearse Street on the west end of town, leading south past the church, post office, and a statue of Michael Collins to the pretty Georgian Emmet Square.

Sights

There's not much to see in Clonakilty, though the **West Cork Model Railway Village** (Inchydoney Rd., tel. 023/883-3224, www.modelvillage.ie, 11am-5pm daily Feb.-Oct., 10am-5pm daily July-Aug., noon-4pm weekends Nov.-Jan., admission with/without train ride €11/8) is a popular draw for families with children.

The Catholic, neo-Gothic **Church of the Immaculate Conception** (Bridge St.) features splendid wall mosaics and a rather disconcerting near-life-size wooden crucifix positioned right between the pews.

Activities and Recreation

How about a pony trek along sandy **Inchydoney Strand,** four kilometers south of town? Ring the **Clonakilty Equestrian Centre** (Inchydoney Rd., signposted from town, tel. 023/883-3533).

The nine-hole **Dunmore Golf Club**

(Muckross, tel. 023/883-4644, www.dunmoregolfclub.ie) is adjacent to the Dunmore House Hotel. The **Lisselan Golf Course** (4 km east of town off the N71, tel. 023/883-3249, www.lisselan.com) also has nine holes and is equally scenic (set within mature gardens along the Argideen River).

Food

Clonakilty is awash in quality eateries. On the café side of things, you can order a freshly squeezed pear-apple-lime juice to wash down your ciabatta at **Hart's** (8 Ashe St., tel. 023/883-5583, www.hartscafeclonakilty.com, 10am-5pm Tues.-Sat., under €8). Serving up gourmet takeaway meals using gorgeously fresh produce, the ★ **Lettercollum Kitchen Project** (22 Connolly St., tel. 023/883-6938, www.lettercollum.ie, 10am-6pm Tues.-Fri., 10am-5pm Sat., lunch under €10) also has a few stools available if it's definitely not picnic weather—it's a good spot to perch with the arts section of the *Irish Times* and a cup of first-rate coffee. This specialty grocery-cum-deli offers a full calendar of daylong cooking classes, from curries to Lebanese to gluten-free baking. A one-day course costs €95 and includes a hearty lunch.

One of Clonakilty's most beloved restaurants is **An Súgán** (41 Wolfe Tone St., tel. 023/883-3719, www.ansugan.com, food served 12:30pm-10pm daily, bar meals €6-12, mains €12-24), with a heavy seafood emphasis along with a couple of steak and duck dishes. **Scannell's** (5 Connolly St., tel. 023/883-4116, food served noon-3pm Mon.-Fri., until 4pm Fri., €8-14) is another mainstay, a cozy gastropub with an ultra-charming nautical ambience. A slightly less fish-heavy option is the classy **Farm** (30 Ashe St., tel. 023/883-4355, www.farmrestaurant.ie, 5pm-9:30pm Wed.-Sat., 12:30pm-3pm and 5pm-9pm Sun., €18-26), offering simple yet gourmet fare. (The veg option is, thankfully, not so traditional—it'll be something like beetroot risotto cakes.) The wine list is small but well chosen, the service prompt and polite.

The swanky-but-comfortable ★ **Richy's**

Bar and Bistro (Wolftone St., tel. 023/882-1852, www.richysbarandbistro.com, 9am-10pm daily, €27.50 3-course early bird 5pm-7pm Mon.-Thurs., dinner €17-28) provides that elusive combination of great food, laid-back atmosphere, and cordial and efficient service. The Mauritian owner-chef, Richy, describes his marvelously inventive cuisine as "West Cork fusion," but however you categorize the menu, there's something for everyone on it. There are even separate vegetarian *and* vegan menus.

And if all else fails, you can dine with confidence at **O'Keefe's** (Emmet Sq., tel. 023/883-3394, www.emmethotel.com, restaurant 6:30pm-9:30pm daily, bar food served noon-9:30pm daily, bar €12-22, restaurant €15-30), the restaurant at the Emmet Hotel, where the bar and restaurant fare is surprisingly high quality.

Entertainment and Events
When in Clonakilty, there's no better place to pass the evening than **Tigh De Barra** ("tee deh-BUR-ruh," 55 Pearse St., tel. 023/880-33381, www.debarra.ie), a veritable smorgasbord for the ears. There's live folk music every night of the week—though Monday is trad night, and other times you might find a tribute band paying homage to some rock legend (often Jimi Hendrix). Aside from these informal "sitting room sessions," bigger gigs have featured the likes of Christy Moore, Sharon Shannon, and Luka Bloom (€10-40).

But if it's just trad you're after, try "The Little House," **An Teach Beag** (5 Recorder's Alley, off Pearse St., tel. 023/883-3883), with sessions nightly July to mid-September. In low season there's music on Tuesday and Friday through Sunday.

Shopping
Clonakilty has its share of chintzy souvenir emporia, but some really nice boutiques dot the main drag. An upscale craft shop and contemporary art gallery, **Etain Hickey** (40 Ashe St., tel. 023/882-1479) stocks ceramics and other homewares, jewelry, framed prints, and stained-glass pieces. For delightfully old-fashioned eco-friendly playthings for the kiddos in your life, stop by **Little Green Dot** (7 The Belfry, Old Chapel Ln., tel. 087/130-2307, www.littlegreendot.ie).

Accommodations
Several B&Bs are signposted off the main N71 road on either end of Clonakilty, around a five-minute walk into town. The rooms at **Bay View** (Old Timoleague Rd., signposted off the N71 just east of town, tel. 023/883-3539, www.bayviewclonakilty.com, Mar.-Oct., €35-40 pp, s €55) have very comfortable (if very pink and frilly) beds and beautiful views of sea and gardens. **Glendine** (Tawnies Upper, just north of the town center, signposted from Pearse St., tel. 023/883-4824, www.glendine.com, Feb.-Nov., €45-50 pp) offers commodious rooms, accommodating owners, and an extensive breakfast menu with scrummy home-baked goods. The stiff single supplement's a bummer, though.

The most family-friendly B&B in town is **Melrose** (The Miles, signposted off the N71 on the western end of town, tel. 023/883-3956, www.melrosewestcork.com, closed Dec., €35-38 pp, s €40-55), with a back garden and patio with play area and barbecue, so you can self-cater here in the evenings if you don't feel like eating out. The showers are excellent, the rooms homey, the breakfasts delish (you'll sample the local black pudding), and the owners genuinely friendly and welcoming.

The **Emmet Hotel** (Emmet Sq., tel. 023/883-3394, www.emmethotel.com, €60-75 pp) has been offering "Georgian elegance since 1785," and though it's not posh it's friendly and well maintained, with spacious bedrooms and comfortable mattresses. Ask for a room overlooking the small town green. There's no private car park, but parking on the square is free. But if you don't need "character," then by all means stay at the **Quality Hotel & Leisure Centre** (on the N71, Skibbereen Rd., 1.5 km west of town, tel. 023/883-6400, www.qualityhotelclon.com, rooms €70-150). The 20-meter pool and other fitness facilities are fine, but forgo the bar and restaurant for dinner and drinks in town. Better yet, try the **Dunmore House Hotel** (Muckross, 5 km south of town, tel. 023/883-3352, www.dunmorehousehotel.ie, €95 pp sharing) for its country-house charm, gorgeous sea views from every bedroom, and cordial, can-do reception.

Information and Services
The **tourist office** (25 Ashe St., tel. 023/883-3226, www.clonakilty.ie, 9am-6pm daily June, 9am-7pm daily July-Aug., 9:30am-5:30pm Mon.-Sat. Sept.-May) can give you info for anywhere you're headed in West Cork.

The **AIB** at the corner of Pearse and Bridge Streets has an ATM and bureau de change. There are several pharmacies in town, including **Harrington's** (1 Ashe St., tel. 023/883-3318).

Getting There and Around
Clonakilty is 52 kilometers southwest of Cork City and 56 kilometers east of Bantry on the N71. **Bus Éireann** (tel. 021/450-8188, www.buseireann.ie, #47 or #236, 7/day daily) links Cork City with the towns on the Mizen Head Peninsula, stopping at Clonakilty en route.

Rent a bike from **MTM Cycles** (33 Ashe St., tel. 023/883-3584, €10/50 per day/week). For a cab, ring **Clonakilty Hackneys** (tel. 023/883-4130).

GLANDORE AND UNION HALL
Linked by a causeway over a tidal estuary, the darling twin fishing villages of Glandore (Cuan Dor, "Harbour of the Oaks") and Union Hall (Bréantrá, "Foul Beach"—an entirely inaccurate assessment!) are all abuzz with visiting yachters on warm summer evenings.

Just off the R597 three kilometers east of Glandore is the Bronze Age **Dromberg Stone Circle** (always accessible, free), with a dramatic situation among the fields overlooking Glandore Harbour. Nine meters in diameter, the circle consists of 17 upright stones, and archaeological evidence indicates that alterations were made to the original stone arrangement during the Iron Age. Also dating from that period is a nearby *fulacht fiadh,* a cooking site where piping-hot stones dropped into this trough from a nearby fire would have slow-cooked the night's repast.

You'll definitely want to book a boat with **Atlantic Sea Kayaking** (trips leave from Reen Pier, tel. 028/21058, www.atlanticseakayaking.com, 3-hour trip €50). By day or night, this paddle trip is a must-do for anyone "from nine to 98." Reen Pier is clearly signposted from the village center (take the road uphill to the church and bear right at the Y junction).

There are several nice beaches in the area, but the prettiest of all is also the most out-of-the-way. Following the same route to the pier, you'll come to a 19th-century schoolhouse (which used to be a wonderful hostel run by the owners of Atlantic Sea Kayaking), and there's a narrow, unpaved, uphill road immediately opposite. Turn onto this road, follow it for a couple kilometers, make a left at the T junction, and follow the steep downhill switchbacks, which lead to a small but delightfully secluded beach, just the kind of place the locals don't want you to find out about. The small grassy cliff above the tiny car park is perfect for sunbathing on sunny August afternoons.

Food and Accommodations
For steaks and seafood, try **Casey's Bar** (Main St., tel. 028/33590, www.caseysofunionhall.ie, food served 12:30pm-9:30pm in summer only, €12-20). On the Glandore side is the canary-yellow **Glandore Bistro** (tel. 083/469-4442, 6pm-10pm Mon. and Fri.-Sat., 1pm-9pm Sun. Mar.-Nov., €15-30), known for its mouthwatering seafood dishes and desserts. Reservations are a very good idea. Unfortunately, the future of the Marine Hotel next door to the bistro is in flux, and the Glandore Inn was also out of business at time of writing. Hopefully some enterprising spirit will rehab and reopen this lovely old pub.

Most accommodations are on the Union

Hall side. A short walk outside the village is **Lis-Ardagh Lodge** (less than 1 km northwest of the village on the L4227, tel. 021/34951, www.lis-ardaghlodge.com, €33-37 pp, s €40-50), which has spacious yet cozy rooms, a sauna, a mini-gym, and locally smoked salmon on the breakfast menu. It's a great value. Self-catering cottages rent for €250-350 per week in shoulder season, €450 in July and August. Another option for B&B is **Shearwater** (signposted from Union Hall town center, tel. 028/33178 or 086/314-1818, www.shearwaterbandb.com, Apr.-Oct., €35 pp, s €50), up the hill overlooking Glandore Harbour, where you'll have a view from every room.

Practicalities

There's a Bank of Ireland **ATM** at the Centra on Lisarken Road on the Union Hall side.

Glandore is 3.7 kilometers off the N71 (on the R597), with Union Hall one kilometer farther west across a one-lane causeway. If driving, make the turnoff at Leap; if traveling via **Bus Éireann** (tel. 021/450-8188, #47, at least 7/day Mon.-Sat., 5/day Sun.), you'll have to disembark at Leap and make the (albeit pleasant) walk down to Glandore.

SKIBBEREEN

A workaday, slightly rough-around-the-edges market town between Bantry and Clonakilty, **Skibbereen** (An Sciobairín) is worth a stop for its **tourist office** in the town hall on North Street (tel. 028/21766, 9am-6pm Mon.-Sat. June and Sept., 9am-7pm Mon.-Sat. July-Aug., 9:15am-1pm and 2pm-5:30pm Mon.-Fri. Oct.-May). The **Skibbereen Heritage Centre** (Old Gasworks Building, Upper Bridge St., tel. 028/40900, www.skibbheritage. com, 10am-6pm Tues.-Sat. mid-Mar.-May and Oct., daily June-Sept., 9:30am-5:30pm Mon.-Fri. Nov. and Feb.-mid-Mar., €6) is also worth a look for its in-depth Great Famine exhibition. You might also check out whatever visual art exhibition is on at the **West Cork Arts Centre** (North St., tel. 028/22090, www.westcorkartscentre.com, 10am-6pm Mon.-Sat.).

Make a withdrawal at the **AIB** ATM on Bridge Street before heading on to greener, bluer parts.

CASTLETOWNSHEND

When you pull into the sleepy and utterly charming seaside village of Castletownshend, you'll feel a strange urge to double-check that you're still in Ireland. The distinct English flavor, 18th-century stone townhouses and all, is mainly thanks to **Castle Townshend** (signposted just off Main St., tel. 028/36100, www. castletownshend.net, rooms €90-110, s €70). Originally built in the 17th century, the castle is still owned and run by the Townshend family as a surprisingly unpretentious B&B. Though much of the furniture is original, the rooms all have mod cons, and deluxe breakfasts are served in the marvelously old-fashioned dining room. Self-catering cottages are also available to let.

If you'd like to spend the night here, plan on dinner at **Mary Ann's** (Main St., tel. 028/36146, www.maryannesbarandrestaurantcork.com, food served 11am-9pm daily, dinner €17-27). This cozy gastro-pub specializes in seafood, and the wine list is superb. (Note that Mary Ann apparently spells her name both with and without an E on the end.)

While you're here, be sure to visit the very picturesque **St. Barrahane's Church**. Situated on a hill overlooking Castlehaven Harbour, it boasts three exquisite Harry Clarke windows, including the *Adoration of the Magi*. Unlike many Anglican churches, this one is open during the week.

Castletownshend is eight kilometers southeast of Skibbereen on the R596, and there is no Bus Éireann service.

BALTIMORE AND CAPE CLEAR ISLAND

A heck of a lot prettier than its Maryland namesake, **Baltimore** (Dún na Séad, "Fort of the Jewels") is at the tip of its own little peninsula, punctuated by two islands to the southwest: **Sherkin** and **Cape Clear,** the latter being a Gaeltacht region of 150 people.

Board a **ferry** from the Baltimore pier to either island (tel. 028/39159 or 086/346-5110, www.capeclearferry.info, 3-4/day daily May-mid-Sept., 1-2/day daily in low season, return fare €16). When you arrive on Cape Clear, you can go "glamping" in a yurt or tipi at **Chleire Haven** (Knockanamorough, 1 km due south of the pier, tel. 086/197-1956 or 028/39982, www.yurt-holidays-ireland.com, Apr.-Oct., €20 pp).

Though Baltimore means "Town of the Big House" (Baile an Tighe Mhóir), its official Irish name refers to the ruins of an O'Driscoll castle overlooking the harbor. Unsurprisingly, this little town is a beloved haunt of yachters, scuba divers, and sea kayakers; for more info on diving excursions, contact John Kearney at the **Baltimore Diving & Watersports Centre** (tel. 028/20300, www.baltimorediving.com), which also offers hostel and self-catering accommodations, a restaurant, bike hire—even a sauna. Beginning divers are welcome, as the center specializes in PADI courses. Another diving center is **Aquaventures** (Lifeboat Rd., tel. 028/20511, www.aquaventures.ie); for sailing lessons, contact the **Baltimore Sailing School** (tel. 028/20141, www.baltimoresailingschool.com). Five-day courses run May-September. If you'd rather keep your feet on solid ground, you can always go for a stroll out to the Baltimore Beacon, better known as **Lot's Wife,** which was built by the British after the 1798 rebellion.

Food, Accommodations, and Entertainment

It used to be one of Cork's best hostels, and now **Rolf's Country House** (500 meters off the R595, signposted on the north side of the village, tel. 028/20289, www.rolfscountryhouse.com, €40-50 pp, s 60-80) has revamped itself as a deluxe B&B. The situation is idyllic all-around, with mature well-tended gardens and gorgeous views from the flagstoned terrace and dining room. Airy, well-appointed two-bedroom cottages are available for weekly rental (low/high season €450/750). Best of all

is the adjoining café/wine bar/art gallery, **Café Art** (8am-11am and 6pm-9pm daily, plus 12:30pm-2:30pm June-Aug., dinner €25-30).

Baltimore is surprisingly short on B&B accommodations, but one to try is **Channel View** (half a km north of Baltimore on the R595, tel. 028/20440, www.channelviewbb.com, Mar.-Oct., €30-45 pp), with private gardens, colorful and comfortable rooms, and fresh fish for breakfast. Planning to stay a while? Look into renting one of eight well-appointed self-catering **Inish Beg Cottages** (Inish Beg Island, tel. 028/21745, www.inish-beg.com), part of a restored 39-hectare estate on its own island, accessible via bridge from Baltimore. Facilities include an indoor heated 13-meter pool, steam room, and gym. Rates vary from €50-70 per night for a one-bedroom cottage or "gypsy caravan" to €300-425 per night for the three-bedroom boathouse.

There are other hotels in and near Baltimore, but **Casey's of Baltimore** (on the R595 on the north end of the village, tel. 028/20197, www.caseysofbaltimore.com, €40-90 pp) is far and away the best in terms of service, food, maintenance, and atmosphere. Many of the spacious, homey rooms come with sea views and/or king-size beds. Casey's also has one of the friendliest, liveliest bars in Baltimore—you're sure to catch a trad session on summer weekend evenings, and the pub grub is faultless.

There's plenty of harborside pub action too; all the bars have picnic tables out front overlooking the bay. Aside from Casey's, you'll find the best bar meals in town at **Bushe's** (The Square, on the harbor, tel. 028/20125, www.bushesbar.com, food served 9:30am-8pm Mon.-Sat., 12:30pm-8pm Sun., under €12), a Baltimore institution. Sailors regularly stop in to pick up their newspaper subscriptions, shower, and grab a pint and an open-faced crab sandwich. Francophile fish-lovers will devour the shellfish platter (€50) at **Chez Youen** (on the quay, tel. 028/20136, 6pm-10pm daily, closed Nov. and Feb., 3-course dinner €30-40), another local favorite.

Practicalities

There is no tourist office in Baltimore, so ask for info in **Skibbereen** (13 km north on the R595), which you'll pass through on the way down. There's an **ATM** in Cotter's Gala grocery shop on the main drag.

Baltimore is 46 kilometers southwest of Clonakilty and 98 kilometers southwest of Cork City off the N71 (via Skibbereen). **Bus Éireann** (tel. 021/450-8188) route #47 (8/day Mon.-Sat., 6-7/day Sun.) will get you from Cork to Skibbereen, where you can change buses (#251, 4/day Mon.-Fri., summer-only service Sat.) for Baltimore.

The Mizen Head Peninsula

Not as well traveled as the Beara, the Mizen ("MIZZ-en") isn't quite as spectacular either. The Mizen Head warrants one full day, and you'll want to end it in Schull, the peninsula's most substantial town. Divers and anglers come here to spend the day in the water. On summer evenings the pleasant, tidy main drag hums with animated conversation from a line of picnic tables outside all the pubs.

Toward the very edge of the peninsula, **Crookhaven** is a nightmare on sunny summer weekends, when the main street is full of shirtless unsavories kicking footballs and sticky-faced children darting into oncoming traffic. You're coming here to relax (and load up on the fresh seafood), but the irony is that this place is so popular there's no peace and quiet to be found. **Schull** is touristy too, but it's also a whole lot classier (and it's never as crowded as that). It's certainly worth seeking out the lovely **Barley Cove** west of Crookhaven (signposted from the R591), though you'll have plenty of company.

★ MIZEN VISION

A highlight of any trip to West Cork is an exhilarating (if wind-tossed) walk around Mizen Head, the island's most southwesterly point, and a visit to **Mizen Vision,** the **visitors center** (at the end of a local road, signposted off the R591, tel. 028/35115, www.mizenhead. net, 10:30am-5pm daily mid-Mar.-May and Oct., 10am-6pm daily June-Sept., 11am-4pm Sat.-Sun. Nov.-Mar., €6) at Mizen Head. The lighthouse was built at Fastnet Rock in the early 1850s after an American ocean liner sank near Crookhaven, claiming 92 lives. A sturdier replacement tower was built at the turn of the 20th century. A walk down to the signal station is as memorable for the view as it is the exhibition inside, and there are bird-watching opportunities aplenty.

If you haven't rented a car, you can get here via day tour out of Cork City with **O'Brien Coaches** (tel. 021/454-5903, www.obrien-coachtours.com, Tues., Thurs., and Sat. Apr-Sept., Sat. only in winter, €35). Tours depart the tourist office on the Grand Parade at 9am and return between 6:30pm and 7pm.

SCHULL

Nestled between Roaringwater Bay and the 408-meter Mount Gabriel, **Schull** ("SKULL"; An Scoil, "The School") is the largest town on the Mizen Head Peninsula—but fortunately it doesn't feel like it. This one-street fishing village is a haven for scuba divers and yachting enthusiasts, as the busy harbor attests. In high season Schull is touristy but not overwhelmingly so; on summer bank holidays there are just as many Irish out-of-towners as there are international visitors, making for quite a festive atmosphere. The week after the August bank holiday brings the **Schull Regatta,** the most important event on the local calendar since its first race in 1884.

Sights

The **Schull Planetarium** (Schull Community College, Colla Rd., on the west side of the harbor, tel. 028/28552 or 028/28315) is the only one in the Irish Republic, with an eight-meter dome and a 70-seat auditorium. Opened in 1989 through the generosity of Josef Menke, a German industrialist who spent many holidays in Schull, the planetarium offers 45-minute "starshows" of the night sky in the Northern Hemisphere. Opening hours and showtimes vary during the summer (3:30pm-5pm Sun. mid- to end of May and first two Sun. in Sept., show at 4pm; 3:30pm-5pm Tues., show at 4pm, and 7:30pm-9pm Sat., show at 8pm in June; 3:30pm-5pm Tues., Fri., and Sat., show at 4pm, and Mon. and Thurs. 7:30pm-9pm, show at 8pm July-Aug.; €5).

Activities and Recreation

Waterbabies are well catered to here. **Schull Watersports Centre** (at the pier, tel. 028/28554) offers lessons and equipment rental, whether you want to go kayaking, sail-boarding, deep-sea angling, or scuba diving. **Divecology** (Cooradarrigan, tel. 028/28946 or 086/837-2065, www.divecology.com) is another option, and **Blue Thunder Charters** (tel. 086/804-5351) does sea angling excursions. Though there aren't any beaches in Schull itself, you can drive farther west to **Ballyrisode Strand** in Toormore (9 km) or **Barley Cove** near Crookhaven (23 km). There's a **surf camp** at Barley Cove (tel. 087/153-2248).

Tee off at the nine-hole, par-30 **Coosheen Golf Club** (signposted off the R592 3 km east of town, tel. 028/28182) overlooking Schull Harbour, or rent a pony from the **Ballycummisk Riding School** (tel. 087/765-5993, www.schullriding.com).

For many more options, check out the listings on the Schull tourism website (www.schull.ie/all-activities).

Food and Accommodations

Pop into **Café Cois Cuan** (Main St., East End, tel. 028/27005, www.cafecoiscuan.ie, 10am-6pm Mon.-Tues., 10am-8:30pm Fri.-Sat., 10am-4pm Sun., under €10) for anything from a bowl of chowder to a gluten-free brownie. Another good lunch option is the cheerful, airy **Newman's West** (Main St.,

tel. 028/27776, www.tjnewmans.com, food served 9am-midnight Mon.-Sat., until 11pm Sun., under €10). The sandwich menu features fresh local ingredients and is very reasonably priced, and the nutella crepes are scrummy. This café-winebar adjoins the town's most beloved watering hole, **T.J. Newman's.**

Grove House (Colla Rd., tel. 028/28067, www.grovehouseschull.com, 12:30pm-3pm and 6pm-10pm Mon.-Sat., 3-course set menu €30-35) is arguably Schull's best restaurant, serving up rather posh seafood dishes in a classy Georgian dining room. The restaurant remains open for tea and snacks between lunch and dinner service. You can stay here as well, in one of five stylish yet ever-so-slightly funky bedrooms (B&B €35-45 pp, s €40-65). **Stanley House** (signposted off the western end of town, a 2-minute walk up a local road, tel. 028/28425, www.stanley-house.net, Mar.-Oct., €38 pp, s €50), is one kilometer outside town. The views over Roaringwater Bay from every room are incomparable—as is the welcome—and there's a carefully tended garden out back perfect for relaxing in. On a quiet residential cul-de-sac just off Main Street is **Glencairn** (Ardmanagh Dr., tel. 028/28007, www.glencairnschull.com, €35 pp, s €40)—no view, but the location is handy.

Those with wheels should consider staying at **Fortview House** (on the R591 9 km west of Schull, signposted from the R592/Schull-Goleen road, tel. 028/35324, www.fortviewhousegoleen.com, Apr.-Oct., €50 pp, self-catering cottages low/high season €350/750 per week), a farmhouse built in 1913 with fine antiques (wrought-iron bedstands, the lot) but all mod cons, a genuinely friendly welcome, and a top-notch breakfast menu featuring eggs laid just out back.

The newish **Schull Harbour Hotel** (Main St., tel. 028/28801, www.schullharbourhotel.ie, rooms €120-180, s €75-90) features sea views from many of the rooms as well as a swimming pool, Jacuzzi, and sauna.

Information and Services

Schull doesn't have a tourist office, but check

out **Schull.ie** (www.schull.ie) before you go. The **AIB** on Main Street has an ATM and bureau de change; you can also withdraw funds from the ATM at the Centra supermarket across the way (open until 10pm).

Getting There and Around

Schull is 55 kilometers west of Clonakilty (from the N71 to the R592) and 105 kilometers west of Cork City by the same route. Public parking (in three different lots off the main street) is free and ample. **Bus Éireann** (tel. 021/450-8188, www.buseireann.ie, #47 or #236, 7/day daily) links Cork City with the towns on the Mizen Head Peninsula, including Schull, via Clonakilty.

For a cab, ring **J.P. Taxis** (tel. 086/121-2999). Rent a bike from **West Cork Bike Hire** (Brosnan's Eurospar, Main St., tel. 028/28236 or 087/233-0824, www.westcorkbikehire.com, €20/100 per day/week).

The Sheep's Head Peninsula

The least traveled of Cork's western peninsulas is Sheep's Head, a bucolic (and blissfully undeveloped) finger of land 26 kilometers long and only 4 kilometers wide. This is your best bet for getting off the beaten track in West Cork. Pick up maps for the 88-kilometer **Sheep's Head Way** or 100-kilometer **Cycle Route** from the tourist office in Bantry.

Accommodations are sparse on the peninsula; most visitors use Bantry as a base. The folks at **Seamount Farm** (Glenlough West, 12 km west of Bantry on Goat's Path Rd., signposted, tel. 027/61226, www.seamount-farm.com and www.sheepshead.ie, €35-45 pp) not only cater to long-distance walkers, they organize hill-walking holidays on Sheep's Head. This is a great-value B&B with terrific home-baked goods (tea and fresh-out-of-the-oven scones served on arrival), cozy rooms with electric blankets, and lovely sea and garden views.

Fortunately, it's possible to get out here without a rental car, even though **Bus Éireann** route #255 runs only on Saturday. **Bantry Rural Transport** (5 Church St., Bantry, tel. 027/52727, www.ruraltransport.ie, usually 2/day daily Mon.-Sat., single/return ticket €4/6) serves Durrus and Kilcrohane (on the south side of the peninsula) via Goat's Path Road; check the website for complete timetable.

BANTRY

The sizable harbor town of **Bantry** (Beanntraí), the gateway to the Sheep's Head, is quickly losing whatever charm it possessed to a row of luxury harborside condominiums and other new construction. The town also has more than its share of seedy-looking grog-houses, which doesn't exactly encourage one to venture down the main drag by night with an ear cocked for the strains of traditional music. That said, **J. J. Crowley's** (The Square, tel. 027/50029) is a nice old pub with traditional music, ballads, or set dancing on Wednesday, Friday, and Saturday nights and Sunday afternoons.

The town itself is easy to get the hang of, with Wolfe Tone Square (shaped more like a narrow rectangle) just east of the pier, Marino and New Streets heading east from the square's end, and Main Street (which becomes Church Road) branching off New Street (at the intersection where New Street turns into Bridge Street). Marino Street turns into the Glengarriff road.

★ Bantry House and Gardens

Come to Bantry for the stunning Italianate gardens at **Bantry House** (1 km southwest of town on the N71, the Skibbereen road, tel. 027/50047, www.bantryhouse.ie, 10am-6pm daily Mar.-Oct., house, gardens, and Armada center €11, gardens and center €5), which has been in the same family (the descendants of the earls of Bantry) since the 18th century. The house itself is a veritable museum of art and antiques, and admission includes a guided tour. On a fine day you might want to stick to the garden, though, which has a grand staircase of 99 steps offering a beautiful panoramic view of Bantry Bay. The French Armada exhibition focuses on a historical episode preceding the 1798 rebellion, in which a French fleet sailed to Ireland intending to overthrow the British; raging storms ruined their plans before the British could, and 10 of the 50 French warships were lost. One of them lies at the bottom of Bantry Bay, though it was only discovered in 1981.

Bantry House is also a hotel (but with the faded-grandeur routine you've got to expect occasional maintenance issues). B&B room rates start at €170.

Food

Bantry has a few nice coffee shops, but the most gourmet is **Organico Café** (2 Glengarriff Rd., tel. 027/51391, www.organico.ie, 10am-6pm Mon.-Fri. and 10am-5pm Sat., under €12), an inventive mostly vegetarian café, Fair Trade grocery, bakery, takeaway, and art gallery all in one. For the fresh Bantry Bay seafood you've been hearing about, head to the super-stylish, family-run **O'Connor's** (Wolfe Tone Sq., tel. 027/50221, www.oconnorseafood.com, 12:15pm-5pm and 6pm-10pm daily, lunch under €12, dinner €18-28)—the best restaurant in town.

Accommodations

Bantry's hostel and hotels are of a disappointingly low standard; you're better off at a B&B. Two fine ones are within easy walking distance of town. The first is **The Mill** (Newtown, 1 km north of town on the N71, tel. 027/50278, www.the-mill.net, Easter-Oct., €35-40 pp, s €50), a lovingly maintained chalet-style place with lush gardens; homey but character-filled sitting, dining, and bedrooms; laundry service; and deluxe breakfasts. The other is **Atlantic Shore** (Newtown, tel. 027/51310, www.atlanticshorebandb.com, €32-37 pp), where you can savor the home baking at the communal dining table.

Practicalities

You'll find the **tourist office** (tel. 027/50229, 9:30am-5pm Mon.-Sat. mid-Mar.-Oct., daily July-Aug.) on Wolfe Tone Square. There's an ATM and bureau de change at the **Bank of Ireland,** also on the square.

pastoral scenery near Bantry

Bantry is 44.5 km south of Kenmare and 14 kilometers southeast of Glengarriff on the N71, and 91 kilometers west of Cork on the R586. **Bus Éireann** can get you here via the Cork-Castletownbere route (#46, 4/day Mon.-Sat., 3/day Sun.). Rent a bike from **Nigel's Bicycle Shop** (the Glengarriff road/N71, on the north end of town, tel. 027/52657, €15/70 per day/week).

AHAKISTA

Another blink-and-you'll-miss-it village on the south side of the peninsula, **Ahakista** (Átha an Chiste) has the best watering hole on Sheep's Head, the **Tin Pub** (on the local Durrus-Kilcrohane road, tel. 027/67337, food served noon-9pm daily in high season, under €12). Named, laconically, for its corrugated tin roof, there's a pleasantly rustic atmosphere, indoors as well as in the rambling beer garden—a real garden!—out back. The bar menu consists of savory pies (shepherd's, chicken, salmon, or "superior fish") supplied by Ballymaloe Cookery School alumni Cully and Sully. The Tin Pub has a longstanding reputation for great music, with trad sessions here on Tuesday and Sunday nights along with the occasional karaoke or samba show. More formal gigs feature some pretty high-profile musicians (like The Bridies, formerly the lead fiddlers in Michael Flatley's *Lord of the Dance*).

NORTHEAST OF BANTRY
Gougane Barra Forest Park

By far the loveliest section of inland Cork is the four-square-kilometer **Gougane Barra Forest Park** (Gúgan Barra, always open, free) tucked in the Shehy Mountains on the Cork-Kerry border. Looking at all the thick swaths of pine and spruce covering these hillsides, it's difficult to believe this area was once pretty much treeless (until the forestation program commenced in 1938). Gougane Barra's wooded walking trails have a vaguely magical feel, like you're venturing into a world where banshees and other preternatural creatures still exist. There's a tearoom and hotel overlooking the dark, glassy Gougane Barra

Lake at the park entrance, and not much else. Before you enter the park, turn off onto an artificial causeway to a tiny island with a tiny chapel, **St. Finbarr's Oratory,** featuring stained-glass windows of obscure Irish saints. This is a popular pilgrimage site come September, as St. Finbarr lived a hermit's life on this little island in the 6th century; you can still see a holy well at the end of the causeway, as well as a complex of eight monks' cells just beyond the restored 18th-century Catholic chapel. The park entrance is 700 meters beyond the island causeway. In high season the park gets crowded with coach tours, so get here early in the day.

All the bedrooms at the family-run Óstan Gúgan Barra, or **Gougane Barra Hotel** (signposted 2 km off the R584 west of Ballingeary, tel. 026/47069, www.gougane-barrahotel.com, mid-Apr.-mid-Oct., €55-75 pp) offer lake and/or mountain views. This is the kind of place you might hesitate about—after all, it's got no competition, and a lack of competition usually breeds mediocrity in the hotel business—but fortunately that's not the case here. Though the restaurant is fine, the fresh-and-simple bar meals are a much better value, and breakfast comes with plenty of home-baked goods (bar food served noon-9:30pm Mon.-Sat., restaurant 5:30pm-9:30pm daily and noon-4pm Sun., set dinner €37, Sun. lunch €25, bar meals €10-20). A pleasant tearoom just across the car park, **Cronin's,** is named for the hotel's original owners.

For more information on the forest park, hotel, and recreational activities, visit the **Gougane Barra website** (www.gougane-barra.com). The park doesn't have a visitors center, so the hotel is also your best source of info once you're there.

Gougane Barra is 26 kilometers northeast of Bantry off the R584 and 71 kilometers west of Cork City on the N22, picking up the R584 a couple kilometers before Macroom. A Saturday-only **Bus Éireann** service (#255) links Bantry with the Gougane crossroads; the bus departs Bantry at 4pm, arriving outside the forest park at 4:40pm.

The Beara Peninsula (Cork Side)

The "Ring of Beara" is Cork's prettiest peninsula, though the northeast section belongs to County Kerry. If driving, you can take the longer coastal route through the sleepy pastel-hued villages of Eyeries, Ardgroom, and Allihies before reaching the Beara's de facto capital, Castletownbere; or you can cut through the Caha mountains from Lauragh (in Kerry) to Adrigole via the gorgeously scenic Healy Pass. Bus Éireann serves the Beara only as far west as Castletownbere, and though private bus services are available they're too infrequent to be much help to the visitor who has only a couple days to spare; if you want to do the Beara right, you're best off with a rental car. The 197-kilometer **Beara Way,** Cork's longest walking route, loops from Kenmare to Glengarriff to Castletownbere.

The nearest official Irish Tourist Board offices are in Kenmare and Glengarriff, though there's a kiosk on the square in Castletownbere, and you can visit the **Beara Tourism** website (www.bearatourism.com) before you go.

GLENGARRIFF

Popular for its enchanted-forest nature reserve, quality gift shops, friendly pubs, and speedy ferry to the garden isle of Ilnacullen, **Glengarriff** (An Gleann Garbh, "The Rugged Glen") is the southern gateway to the Beara. It also makes a far more pleasant base than Bantry for exploring the Sheep's Head Peninsula.

Glengarriff is a one-street town, and the fork in the road on the west end of Main Street will lead to Castletownbere if you go left and Kenmare (and the nature reserve) if you go right.

Garnish Island

Take the ferry to **Garnish Island** (also spelled Garinish) to visit the Dúchas-run **Ilnacullin** (1.5-km boat trip from Glengarriff

pier, tel. 027/63040, €4), a lovely 15-hectare Italianate garden designed by Harold Peto in the 1910s for British MP Annan Bryce, then-owner of Garnish. It's open 10am-4:30pm Monday-Saturday and 1pm-5pm Sunday March and October, 10am-6:30pm Monday-Saturday and 1pm-6:30pm Sunday in April, 10am-6:30pm Monday-Saturday and 11am-6:30pm Sunday May-June and September, 9:30am-6:30pm Monday-Saturday and 11am-6:30pm Sunday July-August (closed in winter). Bryce's dream of transforming this rocky little island into a paradise of flowers and shrubbery from all over the world might have seemed crazy at the time, but the dream came true after decades of nurturing his exotic plant menagerie. Ilnacullin, or Illaunacullin, means "Island of Holly," but it's the azaleas and rhododendrons that bloom the brightest in May and June. You can also watch seals sunning themselves on the rocks on the island's southern shore.

The garden is the only thing to see on the island, though there's a tearoom at the visitors center. Note that there's a charge to reach Garnish via the **Blue Pool Ferry** (tel. 027/63333, return trip €12) in addition to the gardens' admission. The pier is signposted next to Murphy's Village Hostel on Main Street.

Glengarriff Bamboo Park

There's another garden in Glengarriff you don't need a ferry to get to: **Glengarriff Bamboo Park** (signposted off Main St., tel. 027/63570, 9am-7pm daily, €6) hosts 30 bamboo and 12 palm tree species on five hectares; all of the species can flourish in West Cork's frost-free Gulf Stream climate.

★ Glengarriff Woods Nature Reserve

Three square kilometers of enchanting sylvan landscapes comprise the **Glengarriff Woods**

Long-Distance Walks in County Cork

Cork's longest walking route is the 197-kilometer **Beara Way,** which loops from Kenmare to Glengarriff to Castletownbere; at Allihies a path diverges toward Dursey Island, and there is also a section on Bere Island (accessible by ferry from Castletownbere). Walking the Beara Way and including this portion of the route will take approximately 10 days; without Dursey and Bere Islands, it can be completed in one week. The terrain is relatively easy, the scenery pretty but not quite as breathtaking as Dingle or the Ring of Kerry.

The Beara is much less popular than the Kerry Way, and quieter still is the 89-kilometer **Sheep's Head Way.** This route loops around the narrow Sheep's Head Peninsula, beginning and ending in Bantry, and can be completed in three days.

Visit **Irish Trails** (www.irishtrails.ie) for comprehensive information and resources on both these long-distance walks.

Nature Reserve (entrance on the N71 1 km north of town, dawn-dusk daily). For a 6.5-kilometer walking route that takes in all the park's highlights, pick up a *Slí Na Slainte* route map from the tourist office. There's also a list of suggested routes on a billboard by the car park. Whichever route you take, don't miss climbing the steps to **Lady Bantry's Lookout.** The hike is short (2-3 minutes) but steep; it's well worth the effort for a fantastic panorama of the forests of the nature reserve, the village of Glengarriff, Bantry Bay, and the Sheep's Head Peninsula on the horizon.

Activities and Recreation

It may only have nine holes, but the views at the **Glengarriff Golf Club** (2 km east of town on the N71, tel. 027/63150 or 087/246-8071, www.glengarriffgolfclub.com) are as beautiful as you'd expect.

Food, Entertainment, and Accommodations

Due in part to its ample outdoor seating, the **Blue Loo** (Main St., tel. 027/63167, food served 9am-6pm daily, under €12) is the most popular pub in town. Fill up on hearty grub here or at **Johnny Barry's** (Main St., tel. 027/63315, food served 12:30pm-9:30pm daily, under €12). Both pubs do reliably good steaks and seafood, and offer trad sessions on summer evenings.

And on your way to Bantry, be sure to stop at the **Old Church Café** (on the N71 just east of the village, by the harbor, tel. 027/63663, opening hours vary, under €10) for a cup of java and yummy baked goods in an atmospheric Protestant church-turned-tearoom, stained-glass windows and all. (There's also a lunch menu, though the food quality is uneven.)

Up a long, steep, switchbacked driveway is a beautifully situated B&B, **Oakfield** (on the eastern end of the village, tel. 027/63371, www.oakfieldbedandbreakfast.com, €40 pp). From up here you have a stunning view of Garnish Island beyond the perfectly manicured public park across the road. The rooms are comfortable, simple, and unpretentious, and Ann Barron is a genuinely kind and very helpful hostess. Be sure to ask for one of the front-facing bedrooms. Another B&B with lovely bedroom-window vistas is **Island View House** (signposted off the N71 just east of the village, tel. 027/63081, www.islandview-house.net, €35-45 pp, s €50), which also has self-catering accommodations available in a new four-bedroom holiday home with Jacuzzi, DVD, and Playstation (€550-900 per week).

Casey's Hotel (Main St., tel. 027/63010, www.caseyshotelglengarriff.ie, €40-70 pp) boasts the distinction of having hosted Eamon de Valera. It's a typical small-town, two-star establishment in every respect, with friendly staff and quaint reception rooms but rather smallish bedrooms. The quality of the

Go for an afternoon stroll through the tranquil Glengarriff Woods Nature Reserve.

10:15am-6pm Mon.-Sat. June-Aug.). The staff are far more friendly and helpful than the average Oifig Fáilte employee, so stop in if you have questions about any place at all in West Cork.

There was no ATM in Glengarriff at time of writing. If you need cash, plan to stop in Bantry or Kenmare.

Getting There and Around

Glengarriff is on Bantry Bay on the south side of the Beara Peninsula, 30 kilometers south of Kenmare and 14 kilometers northwest of Bantry on the N71. The Cork-Castletownbere **Bus Éireann** route (tel. 021/450-8188, www.buseireann.ie, #46, 3-4/day Mon.-Sat., 2/day Sun.) stops in Glengarriff.

For bike rental, stop by **Jem Creations Art Gallery** (just off Main St., Castletownbere Rd., tel. 027/63113, €12/72 per day/week). For a taxi, ring **Donal Harrington** (tel. 027/63564 or 086/105-0828, www.westcorkcoaches.com); **Glengarriff Cabs** (tel. 027/63060, www.glengarrifftours.ie) does guided tours as well.

ADRIGOLE

The southern terminus of the spectacular Healy Pass through the Caha mountain range, the widely scattered (along 10 kilometers!) village of **Adrigole** (Eádargoil) makes a nice base, what with its water-sporting opportunities, quality hostel and guesthouse, and charming café/gift shop/art gallery. Nearby **Hungry Hill** (685 meters) has the country's highest waterfall, dubbed the Mare's Tail.

The **West Cork Sailing Centre** (signposted off the R572, tel. 027/60132, www.westcorksailing.com) offers sailing courses and powerboat training, or you can just rent a kayak or canoe for €12-20 per hour.

Looking for a nice souvenir? You'll find contemporary oils, watercolors, and prints as well as giftier things (jewelry, knitwear, pottery, and such) at the **Adrigole Arts Centre** (signposted on the R572 just west of the village, tel. 027/60234, 10am-6pm Mon.-Sat. Mar.-Oct. and 11am-6pm Sun. May-Sept., snacks under €6). The staff are genuinely

restaurant and bar food is hit or miss, but unfortunately there aren't too many other options for dinner in Glengarriff.

Shopping

Looking for a pullover to bring home to Aunt Edna? You've got several quality craft emporia to choose from, all on the main street: **Quills Woolen Market** (tel. 027/63488), the **Glenaran Irish Market** (Killarney headquarters tel. 064/662-3102, www.glenaran.com), and **The Spinning Wheel** (tel. 027/63347, www.thespinningwheel.ie).

In keeping with West Cork's reputation for contemporary visual art, the **Catherine Hammond Gallery** (Main St., tel. 027/63812, www.hammondgallery.com) showcases exciting work by emerging and established painters from Ireland and America. No bland landscapes here, that's for sure.

Information and Services

On the Bantry end of the village is a small, seasonal **tourist office** (tel. 027/63084,

friendly and the coffee and baked goods are delish—plus there's a front terrace with a sea view on which to enjoy them.

Whether you want a campsite, dorm bed, double room, or self-catering cottage, the **Hungry Hill Lodge** (Adrigole Harbour, signposted on the R572, tel. 027/60228, www.hungryhilllodgeandcampsite.com, small dorms and doubles €19, s €28 pp, 2-person campsite €19-23) can accommodate. There's an adjoining pub/coffee shop serving breakfast and lunch (as well as real ground coffee), and dinner is available on request.

You'll find top-quality seafood at the überclassy **Mossie's** (Ulusker House, Trafrask, signposted off the R572 on the eastern side of the village, tel. 027/60606, www.mossiesrestaurant.com, €50-65 pp, s €70-85, restaurant noon-6pm and 7pm-9:30pm daily in summer, closed Mon.-Tues. in low season, lunch €12, dinner €18-23), where afternoon tea is served in the garden on sunny summer days. Given the elegant surroundings, the menu is surprisingly unpretentious. The bedrooms are wonderfully decorated, full of antiques (some with clawfoot tubs and balconies overlooking the bay), but not at all stuffy. Rates vary by the room; for instance, the deluxe Russian Room is nearly twice as much as a smaller double room with shower instead of bath.

Adrigole is 14.5 kilometers south of Lauragh on the R574 (the Healy Pass), 17 kilometers east of Castletownbere, and 19 kilometers west of Glengarriff. **Bus Éireann** (tel. 021/450-8188) stops in Adrigole on the Cork-Castletownbere route (#46, 4/day Mon.-Sat., 3/day Sun.).

EYERIES

This colorful-but-sleepy village is mainly on the map for its excellent restaurant, **Rhonwen's** (on the R571 just north of the main street, tel. 027/74884, www.eyeriesbistro.ie, 5pm-8:30pm Thurs., 12:30pm-8:30pm Fri.-Sun., lunch €8-15, dinner €14-24). Seafood chowder, local craft beers, friendly and efficient service, generous and imaginative options for vegetarians, vegans, and

celiacs—this place is bound to be one of your most memorable dining experiences on your Irish holiday.

CASTLETOWNBERE

By far the busiest town on the Beara, **Castletownbere** (Baile Chaisleáin Bhéarra) is something of a disappointment. You might sit for 20 minutes with your engine running on the ridiculously narrow main street, and the lack of quality restaurants is surprising considering the town has one of Ireland's largest fishing fleets (there are plenty of the Irish equivalent of a greasy spoon, though). Granted, tourism isn't a high priority, and some folks may actually find the town's indifference rather refreshing. The town's name originated from a MacCarthy stronghold that no longer exists.

"Castletown" is the place to be for water sports. Based in Castletownbere, Frank Conroy at **Sea Kayaking West Cork** (tel. 027/70692 or 086/309-8654, www.seakayakingwestcork.com, half-/full-day trips €40/70) offers kayaking trips off the Beara Peninsula from a half day to three days' duration; prices include an organic picnic lunch (generally free-range pork or seafood, but vegetarians need only ask to be accommodated), and beginners are welcome. Same goes for **Beara Diving & Watersports** (The Square, tel. 027/71682 or 087/699-3793, www.bearadiving.com, 3-hour beginner's dive €75), which caters to rookies and experienced divers alike.

A couple of art galleries are worth seeking out: the **Sarah Walker Gallery** (at the pier, tel. 027/70387, www.sarahwalker.ie), which offers landscapes and natural images that are easy on the eye, and the **Mill Cove Gallery** (3 km east of town on the R572, tel. 027/70393, www.millcovegallery.com), which has abstract sculptures and landscapes on display.

Food

It's worth driving the eight kilometers to **Eyeries** for Rhonwen's Bistro for your dinner. Otherwise, you can go for dinner at the

The Wild Atlantic Way

Officially "opened" in 2014, the 2,500-kilometer (1,553-mile) **Wild Atlantic Way** stretches from Malin Head on the Inishowen Peninsula in County Donegal all the way down to Kinsale in County Cork. This driving route is essentially a tourist-board marketing tactic, though it can be useful when planning a tour of the west coast. Highlights include **Connemara,** the **Cliffs of Moher,** the **Dingle Peninsula,** and the **Ring of Kerry,** as well as equally worthwhile places you may not have heard of yet. There are many quieter towns and villages along Ireland's west coast that could certainly use the extra tourist euros; in County Cork, for example, you could have dinner at O'Neill's pub in **Allihies** after a blissful afternoon at **Ballydonegan Strand,** or ride the cable car to **Dursey Island,** or explore the seldom-traversed **Sheep's Head Peninsula.** For more information, visit the official Wild Atlantic Way website (www.wildatlanticway.com).

Olde Bakery (112 Main St., West End, tel. 027/71832, 5pm-9pm Wed.-Sat., noon-9pm Sun., closed Dec.-Jan., €12-24), a chill, cordial, if bland place for a steak or pizza. Another option is **Murphy's** (East End House, tel. 027/70244, 9am-9pm daily, €10-18) for burgers, quiche, or scallops.

For picnic fixings, pop into **Loop de Loop** (Bank Place, on the main street, tel. 027/70770, 10am-5pm Mon.-Sat.), a friendly health-foods shop with a good variety of wholesome snacks and staples.

Accommodations

Castletownbere has a few good B&Bs. Try **Island View House** (Knockanroe Heights, signposted from the pier, a 3-minute walk uphill, tel. 027/70415, www.islandviewhouse. com, €46 pp, s €55-70, discounts for more than one night), which offers fantastic breakfasts of fresh grilled seafood (cod, hake, mackerel, or whatever's come off the boats that morning), omelets, and porridge with Bailey's. **Realt na Mara** (1 km east of town on the R572, tel. 027/70101, www.realtnamara.org, €32-36 pp, s €40-45), a modern bungalow set high above the road, has bay views from the front rooms. **Summerhill** (Droum North, on the R572 just southwest of town, tel. 027/70417, www. summer-hill.com, €35 pp, s €40-50) is another good-value B&B with an extensive breakfast menu a five-minute walk from town.

Practicalities

The **AIB** on the square has an ATM.

Castletownbere is 36 kilometers west of Glengarriff on the R572. This is the end of the line on the **Bus Éireann** route from Cork City (tel. 021/450-8188, #46, 4/day Mon.-Sat., 3/day Sun.).

DZOGCHEN BEARA

A Tibetan Buddhist retreat in an absolutely idyllic location overlooking the sea, **Dzogchen Beara** (Garranes, near Allihies, 8 km southwest of Castletownbere, signposted off the R572, tel. 027/73032, www.dzogchen-beara.org) offers spiritual retreats lasting a weekend or longer, and accommodations are available in the converted 18th-century farmhouse **hostel** (dorms €17, private rooms €35) or one- and three-bedroom self-catering cottages (€500-750 per week, €400-520/week in low season) as well as the **care center** (€35-45 pp including continental breakfast). You can involve yourself in the meditation classes and prayer services as much or as little as you like. This is a fantastic option for those looking for a relaxing space and time for reflection—but be sure to book ahead by phone or email. The sea-facing vegetarian **café** and **shop** (10am-5pm daily) are well worth a leisurely visit.

There is no bus transport along this stretch, though you can get a taxi from Castletownbere; try **Shanahan's** (tel.

027/70116) or **Beara Cabs** (tel. 087/649-4796). The fare should be about €15.

ALLIHIES

Come to tiny **Allihies** (Na hAilichí) for a romp on the lovely **Ballydonegan Strand,** no less enchanting for its popularity with local families. A quiet, unspoiled, one-street village once known for its copper mines, Allihies is a fine alternative to bustling Castletownbere. Another draw for international college students is the **Allihies Language & Arts Centre** (on the main street, tel. 027/73154, www.allihies.ie), housed in the old village schoolhouse.

There's no hotel in Allihies, but you have a choice of B&Bs: **Sea View** (on the R575, tel. 027/73004, www.allihiesseaview.com, Mar.-Oct., €35-40 pp) is in the village center, a five-minute walk from the beach; closer still is **Beach View** (on the R575, tel. 027/73105, www.beachviewbandb.com, €30-35 pp, s €35-45), a cheerful white bungalow perched right above the strand.

Your only dining option is **O'Neill's** (Main St., tel. 027/73008, www.oneillsbeara.ie, food served 12:30pm-9pm daily, €10-15), offering the standard fare (paninis, steaks, and whatnot) in a standard pub atmosphere, along with a spiffier restaurant upstairs (2/3-course dinner €20/25). It doesn't start serving lunch until 12:30, yet you can order a pint here at 11am. There's live trad weekends in high season.

Allihies is 18 kilometers west of Castletownbere on the R575 and 58 kilometers southwest of Kenmare in County Kerry. Unfortunately, there is no Bus Éireann service beyond Castletownbere, and private buses run too infrequently to be of use to tourists.

DURSEY ISLAND

Only a quarter of a kilometer off the peninsula's edge, 6.5-kilometer-long **Dursey Island** (www.durseyisland.ie) is connected to the mainland by the country's only **cable car** (runs 9am-11am, 2:30pm-5pm, and 7pm-8pm Mon.-Sat., 9am-10am, noon-1pm, 4pm-4:30pm, and 7pm-7:30pm Sun. all year, return fare €8). This is the only means of transport for Dursey's 60-odd inhabitants, who regularly send their terrified market-bound sheep and cattle across. Aside from bird-watching (there's a sanctuary), there's not much to see on the island itself, nor are there any B&Bs, although a couple of self-catering cottages are available. Check the website for details.

Kerry

The Dingle Peninsula 204

The Iveragh Peninsula 217

The Beara Peninsula
  (Kerry Side) 240

North Kerry 241

Look for ★ to find recommended sights, activities, dining, and lodging.

Highlights

★ **The Harry Clarke Windows at Díseart:** There are many fine stained-glass windows by Harry Clarke and his workshop all over the country, but the six windows in this neo-Gothic chapel are among his most exquisite (page 204).

★ **Slea Head Drive (Dingle Peninsula Loop):** This is one of the country's most dramatic scenic routes, leading you west from Dingle Town to the village of Dunquin, Europe's most westerly point (page 212).

★ **Ring of Kerry:** With sublime mountain and sea views, this is Ireland's most iconic scenic drive (page 217).

★ **The Skellig Ring:** A short detour off the well-traveled Ring of Kerry gets you great views of St. Finian's Bay and the Skellig Islands via the Coomanaspig Pass—not to mention far less traffic (page 223).

★ **The Skellig Islands:** Early Christian monks had it tough, but none so much as the holy men of Skellig Michael off the coast of the Iveragh Peninsula (page 226).

★ **Killarney National Park:** Even the droves of tourists in July and August can't detract from the fantastic scenery of Killarney's lakes, glens, and mountains (page 231).

★ **Macgillicuddy's Reeks:** A daunting sight even for experienced climbers, these mountains include Corrán Tuathail, the country's tallest peak (page 234).

A trip to Ireland customarily includes a few days in Kerry (Ciarraí), whether you're backpacking or on a golfing holiday. Many consider the landscapes in this county the loveliest on the island, and it's true that Killarney National

Park, the Ring of Kerry driving route (which loops the Iveragh Peninsula), and the Dingle Peninsula are all deservedly popular.

Therein lies the paradox: You are a tourist annoyed by the presence of many other tourists. Come to Kerry expecting otherworldly scenery but plenty of company.

There are a few opportunities for escaping the well-worn tourist track, however: The Kerry Way walking route is the country's longest at 215 kilometers, taking you through the astonishingly remote highlands, and the Beara Peninsula (most of which belongs to Cork) is another fine choice for a taste of peace and solitude even in the summer.

HISTORY

The history of County Kerry commenced with the plodding of a lizardlike creature 365 million years ago, whose fossilized footprints can be seen on the eastern edge of Valentia Island. There human activity has been traced as far

back as 4560 BC. Copper mines in the Kerry highlands date to the Bronze and early Iron Ages, and attracted entrepreneurial settlers from mainland Europe; the remains of another ancient mine can be seen on the eastern shore of Killarney's Lower Lake.

Kerry's early Christian heritage is rich; some of the country's earliest monasteries were founded at Inisfallen (on Killarney's Lower Lake), Ardfert, Kilmalkedar (on the Dingle Peninsula), and Skellig Michael.

In the 15th century the county was ruled by the earls of Desmond (the Fitzgerald family), who were of Norman origin but became, as the saying goes, "more Irish than the Irish themselves." They were great patrons of the Gaelic bards and poets. Better known locally as the knights of Kerry, the Fitzgeralds—never loyal to the British crown—rebelled in the late 16th century and lost their lands, title, and lives in a massacre at the northwestern tip of the Dingle Peninsula in 1580. The county was

---

Previous: tranquil Lough Caragh off the bustling Ring of Kerry; Cahergall ring fort. **Above:** *The Agony in the Garden,* one of Harry Clarke's six windows at Díseart in Dingle Town.

Kerry

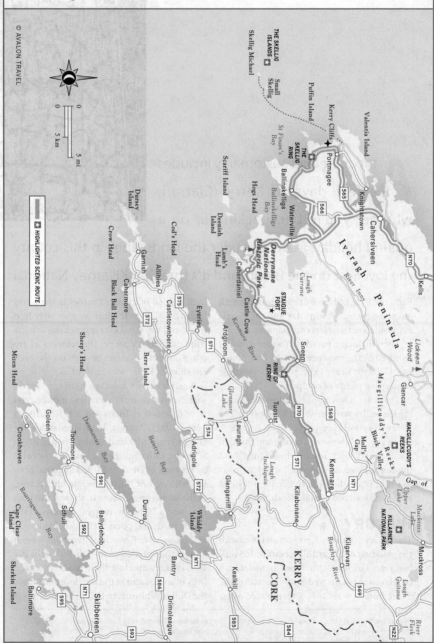

© AVALON TRAVEL

HIGHLIGHTED SCENIC ROUTE

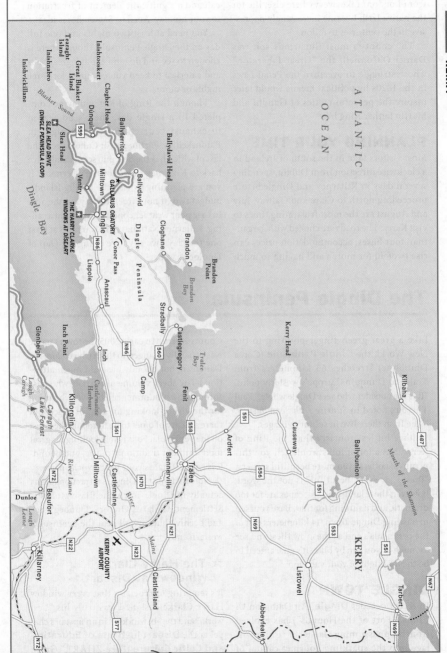

colonized anew with loyalist Protestants fresh from London. Like everywhere else, life for the native Irish became increasingly oppressive in the centuries to follow.

The county's most illustrious son was Daniel O'Connell, the "Great Liberator," whose struggle to overturn the Penal Laws in the 1820s by political means would later inspire the peaceful tactics of Gandhi and Martin Luther King Jr.

PLANNING YOUR TIME

Most visitors take in the south of Ireland in a clockwise direction from Dublin, spending several days in Killarney and Dingle before proceeding north to Clare and Galway. July and August are the most frustrating times to visit Kerry: The roads are choked with gargantuan tour buses, accommodation prices can rise twofold (or more), and having so much company at sites best experienced in solitude can add a significant element of frustration to your holiday. April or September is ideal.

You need at least two nights and one full day on the Dingle Peninsula, though there is enough to see and do (and enough great pubs and eateries) to keep you occupied for three nights or more.

Though the Ring of Kerry may be completed in a single day, there's no reason to exhaust yourself. Spend the night in Ballinskelligs, Portmagee, or Cahersiveen (the last of which has the best pub scene) and drive back to Killarney the following afternoon. If you are planning to visit the Skellig Islands, budget two (if not three) full days in the area in case poor weather conditions prevent a sailing. Killarney National Park warrants at least one full day, two if you're doing the Gap of Dunloe as well.

The Dingle Peninsula

Like a great green finger pointing to the New World, the **Dingle Peninsula** (Corca Dhuibhne) stretches 65 kilometers from Tralee to Dunquin, Europe's westerly point. "It is the outsider who sees Dingle whole," Paul Theroux noted in *Sunrise with Seamonsters.* "The Irish there live in solitary villages."

It's a bit less touristy than the Ring of Kerry, but a lot of folks would tell you this peninsula offers even more beautiful scenery. "Pretty" or even "beautiful" is not the word, however; these land- and seascapes are far too dramatic and haunting for that. Base yourself in bustling Dingle Town, 14 kilometers east of the peninsula's end as the crow flies, and see as much as you can by bike. It's guaranteed to be the highlight of your vacation.

DINGLE TOWN

In recent decades **Dingle** (An Daingean Uí Chúis, "Fort of the Hounds") has evolved from an unassuming Gaeltacht fishing village into the sparkling gourmet capital of County Kerry. (In early 2005 the town's name was officially changed to the Irish version, An Daingean, but nobody has paid much attention.) The sheer volume of tourists who pass through every summer can be overwhelming for the visitor looking for a bit of peace, but there's plenty of quiet to be found farther west on the peninsula. For visitors looking for great food, brilliant traditional music, and boundless *craic,* Dingle's your new favorite place.

Note that most of Dingle's attractions aren't actually in Dingle Town: the Riasc Monastic Settlement, Gallarus Oratory, Dunbeg Fort, and beehive huts are all near the peninsula's western end.

★ The Harry Clarke Windows at Díseart

It's tempting to proclaim that *every* window Harry Clarke designed was truly his "best work," and the six windows in an upstairs chapel at the **Díseart Institute of Education and Celtic Culture** ("dee-ZHART," Green

St., tel. 066/915-2476, www.diseart.ie, 9:30am-1pm and 2pm-5pm Mon.-Fri., €3) are no exception. Until June of 2001 only the nuns of St. Joseph's Convent could view these scenes from the life of Christ in this glorious neo-Gothic chapel, but the nuns of the Presentation order are no longer here, and the Díseart Institute has generously opened the chapel for public viewing. Commissioned in 1922, these six two-light mullioned windows—from the Gifts of the Magi to the Risen Christ and Mary Magdalene—are newly cleaned and renovated. And each one is utterly breathtaking. Before heading upstairs to the chapel, pick up a leaflet from the hall table—it lists the biblical excerpts corresponding to each window—and pop by the reception room if you have any questions. The Díseart staff are tremendously friendly and helpful, and the modest admission fee includes a postcard.

Other Sights

The town's most popular attraction is a dolphin named **Fungie** (with a hard "g") who's been shadowing the fishing boats since early 1984. He's Dingle's most popular personality, and you can either swim or motor out to greet him with **Dingle Dolphin Boat Tours** (the pier, inside the tourist office, tel. 066/915-2626, www.dingledolphin.com, 1-hour cruise €16). You can also catch the resident dolphin on video at the cool (but overpriced) **Oceanworld** (Strand St., on the west side of town, tel. 066/915-2111, 10am-8:30pm daily July-Aug., 10am-6pm daily May-June and Sept., 10am-5pm daily Oct.-Apr., €9). There are more than 300 fishy species at this aquarium, nearly all of which are native to these waters.

Outside **St. Mary's Church** on Green Street (not of much interest in itself) is the weird-but-wonderful **Trinity Tree**, a three-trunked wooden column—a dead sycamore—carved up and down with biblical characters in a funky, South American tribal style. This is the work of Chilean wood carver Juan Carlos Lizana, who was recruited by the parish priest, Monsignor Padraig Ó Fiannachta,

in 2001. At time of writing the sculpture had been removed for preservation using wax and olive oil.

Activities and Recreation

No trip to Dingle is complete without cycling **Slea Head Drive (Dingle Peninsula Loop)**, a roughly 47-kilometer loop that offers otherworldly vistas and archaeological treasures in equal measure. A shorter cycle (sans most archaeological sites) would take you out to Slea Head, but turning east in Dunquin, after a steep climb, will send you on an exhilarating downhill ride before rejoining the R559 a couple of kilometers west of Ventry.

For scuba diving in the bay and around the Blaskets, contact the **Dingle Marina Diving Centre** (Strand St., at the harbor, tel. 066/915-2422); the **Leisure Centre** (tel. 066/915-1066) at the marina rents fishing tackle. For your best chance of a face-to-face meeting with Fungie the famous dolphin, get in touch with **Dingle Dolphin Boat Tours** (the pier, inside the tourist office, tel. 066/915-2626, www.dingledolphin.com, 1-hour cruise €16).

The peninsula's mountains and beaches make for some unforgettable pony trekking. To book, contact **Dingle Horse Riding** (Ballinaboola, Dingle, signposted on the west end of Main St., tel. 066/915-2199 or 086/813-7917, www.dinglehorseriding.com) or stop in at the **Mountain Man** (Strand St., tel. 066/915-2400, www.themountainmanshop.com). This shop also organizes guided walks, as does **Con Moriarty** (tel. 087/221-4002, www.hiddenirelandtours.com).

Food

Dingle is a gourmand's joy. This is the place to break out the plastic for a truly memorable meal. For a simple, cheap, but tasty lunch, though, try the wonderful hole-in-the-wall ★ **An Café Liteártha** (Dykegate St., tel. 066/915-2204, 9am-6pm Mon.-Sat., later summer hours, lunch under €6), with a bookshop in front. For java done right along with delicious baked goods, plan on a leisurely half hour at **Bean in Dingle** (Green

The Dingle Peninsula

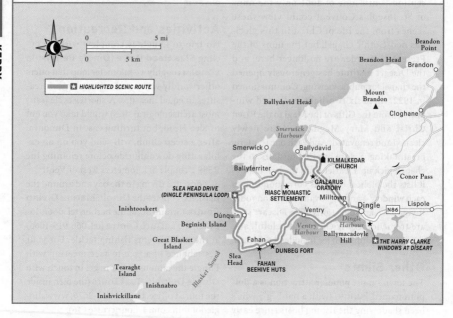

0   5 mi
0   5 km

★ HIGHLIGHTED SCENIC ROUTE

Brandon Point

Brandon Head

Brandon

Mount Brandon ▲

Cloghane

Ballydavid Head

Smerwick Harbour

Smerwick

Ballydavid

🏛 KILMALKEDAR CHURCH

Ballyferriter

Conor Pass

★ GALLARUS ORATORY

SLEA HEAD DRIVE (DINGLE PENINSULA LOOP) ★

★ RIASC MONASTIC SETTLEMENT

Milltown

Inishtooskert

Dúnquin

Beginish Island

Ventry

Dingle   N86   Lispole

Dingle Harbour

Great Blasket Island

Fahan

Ventry Harbour   Ballymacadoyle Hill

★ THE HARRY CLARKE WINDOWS AT DÍSEART

Tearaght Island

Slea Head

★ DUNBEG FORT

★ FAHAN BEEHIVE HUTS

Blasket Sound

Inishnabro

Inishvickillane

St., tel. 087/299-2831, www.beanindingle.com, 8:30am-5pm Mon.-Sat., under €5). The ambience is ever so slightly hipster, to which older locals are happily oblivious.

And on a warm summer day, make straight for **Murphy's Ice Cream** (Strand St., tel. 066/915-2644, www.murphysicecream.ie, 11am-6:30pm daily, €4-8). It may be pricey, but you get what you pay for: heaven by the scoopful. Even if you're vegan, there's chocolate sorbet and soy milk for your hot chocolate.

Adh Danlann Café (Dykegate Ln., tel. 087/773-5815, www.adhgallery.com, Mon.-Sat., hours vary, under €10) adjoins a small wonderland of toys, clocks, and musical instruments. The simple menu (curries and so forth) is 100 percent vegetarian, with plenty of gluten-free options. As for Dingle's other beloved veg cafe, **Cul Gairdin** (Main St.), its future was uncertain at time of writing. Give it a Google before you go. The specialty at the **Chowder Café** (Strand St., the Mall, tel. 086/236-0634, 10am-4pm daily, €9-15) may be

self evident, but they do have a very nice vegan chickpea burger on the menu as well.

Most of the pubs do food. Some of the best grub can be found at the cozy **James Ashe** (Main St., tel. 066/915-0989, food served noon-3pm and 6pm-9pm, €8-18) and **Adams** (Main St., tel. 066/915-1231, food served noon-4:30pm daily, €8-12).

With romantic mood lighting and friendly service, **Grey's Lane Bistro** (Grey's Lane, tel. 066/915-2770, www.greyslanebistro.com, 11am-9pm Mon., 10am-4pm Tues.-Thurs., 10am-9pm Fri.-Sat., 11am-5pm Sun., lunch €10-13, dinner €17-24, 2/3-course early bird €22/25 6pm-7:30pm) is a solid choice for lunch or dinner, and while the food may not completely dazzle you like Dingle's very best restaurants, Grey's Lane tends to be open in low season when most of those other eateries have closed for the winter. There's sometimes live jazz too.

There is no one "best" seafood restaurant in Dingle. Try the bright and airy **Out of the**

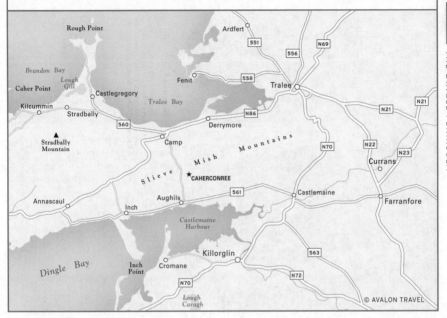

© AVALON TRAVEL

Blue (Strand St., tel. 066/915-0811 or 086/169-9531, www.outoftheblue.ie, 5pm-9:30pm daily, closed Nov.-Feb., lunch €10-17, dinner €25-40), with an astonishingly extensive wine list, or the equally marvelous **Fenton's** (Green St., tel. 066/915-2172, www.fentonsrestaurantdingle.com, noon-2:30pm and 6pm-10pm Tues.-Sun., closed Dec.-Feb., €15-30, 2/3-course dinner menu €22/25). At Fenton's there are lamb and chicken dishes as well as freshly caught fish, and as at all fine restaurants, the lone vegetarian option is well worth the lack of choice. Out of the Blue, on the other hand, sometimes doesn't open (or closes early) if there isn't fresh fish available.

For awesome Continental fare in a swanky-yet-cozy candlelit room, try **The Chart House** (Mail Rd., tel. 066/915-2255 or 085/122-1604, www.thecharthousedingle.com, 6:30pm-10:30pm daily, closed Mon.-Tues. in low season as well as Jan.-mid-Feb., €18-28, 3-course "value menu" €32.50). The only downside is the staff; though mostly cordial, they can be borderline snooty at times. Make a reservation.

But of all the top-notch restaurants in Dingle, ★ **The Global Village** (Main St., tel. 066/915-2325, www.globalvillagedingle.com, 5:30pm-10:30pm daily, €19-39, 2/3-course early-bird menu €28/32 5:30pm-6:45pm) is the least pretentious. The staff are lovely, the atmosphere relaxed, the modern-Irish (yet internationally inspired) fare terrifically inventive—and the early-bird special is a very good value given the memorable excellence of this place.

Entertainment and Events

Lookin' for trad? You're in for a treat no matter where you go. **An Droichead Beag** ("The Small Bridge," Main St., tel. 066/915-1723) and **O'Flaherty's** (Bridge St., tel. 066/915-1205) both have rollickin'-good trad sessions, but they're also quasi-tourist traps. Fewer people know about **An Conair** (Spa Rd., tel. 066/915-2011), which is just around the corner from

Dingle Town

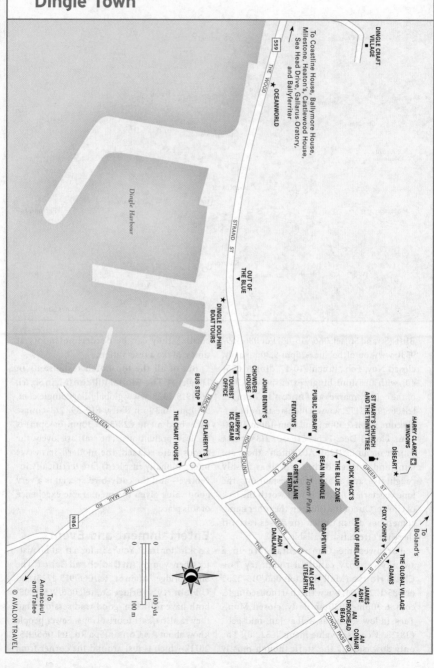

DINGLE CRAFT VILLAGE

559 THE WOOD

★ OCEANWORLD

To Coastline House, Ballymore House,
Milestone, Heaton's, Castlewood House,
Sea Head Drive, Gallarus Oratory,
and Ballyferriter

Dingle Harbour

STRAND ST

OUT OF THE BLUE

★ DINGLE DOLPHIN BOAT TOURS

BUS STOP ■

TOURIST OFFICE ■

CHOWDER HOUSE ▼

JOHN BENNY'S ▼

THE TRACKS

MURPHY'S ICE CREAM ▼

O'FLAHERTY'S ▼

HOLY GROUND

PUBLIC LIBRARY ■

FENTON'S ▼

ST MARY'S CHURCH AND THE TRINITY TREE ★

HARRY CLARKE WINDOWS ★

DISEART ★

COOLEEN

THE CHART HOUSE ▼

GREY'S LN

GREY'S LANE BISTRO ▼

BEAN IN DINGLE ▼

THE BLUE ZONE ▼

DICK MACK'S ▼

GREEN ST

FOXY JOHN'S ▼

Town Park

GRAPEVINE ▼

BANK OF IRELAND ■

THE MALL RD

N86

To
Annascaul,
and Tralee

DYKEGATE ST

ADH DANLANN ▼

AN CAFÉ LITEARTHA ▼

THE MALL

AN CONAIR

AN DROICHEAD BEAG ▼

JAMES ASHE ▼

ADAMS ▼

THE GLOBAL VILLAGE ▼

MAIN ST

To
Boland's

CONOR PASS RD

0   100 yds
0   100 m

© AVALON TRAVEL

The Small Bridge. All three have sessions nightly in high season. Another possibility is **John Benny's** (Strand Rd., tel. 066/915-1215, www.johnbennyspub.com), with a range of live entertainment on Monday (trad with set dancing), Wednesday and Friday (just trad), and Saturday (blues and folk).

Two "novelty pubs" are **Dick Mack's** (Green St., tel. 066/915-1070) and **Foxy John's** (Main St., tel. 066/915-1316), both full of crusty old locals. Dick Mack's, half boot repair and leather workshop, has attracted loads of celebrities over the years (just check out the star-studded walk of fame on the sidewalk outside), and Foxy John's is half hardware store. Not only is **James Ashe** (Main St., tel. 066/915-0989) the coziest spot in town to soak up a pint, but the pub grub is second to none.

The **Hillgrove Hotel** (www.hillgrovedingle.com) on Spa Road has the town's only nightclub—ideal for observing the mating habits of rural teenagers and bachelor farmers alike—but your choices are limited if you're looking for something more along the lines of a swanky late-night wine bar. **The Blue Zone** (Green St., tel. 066/915-0303, 6pm-1am or later daily, pizzas €11-16) fits the bill—and the pizzas are scrummy!—but it's not technically supposed to be open past 1am, which means the *gardaí* sometimes come a-knocking on a Saturday night. You'll find live jazz on Tuesday and Thursday.

Fancy Irish traditional music but don't like the 10pm starting time of most pub sessions? There's an excellent thrice-weekly **folk concert** at the Anglican **St. James' Church** (Main St., tel. 087/982-9728, performance at 7:30pm Mon., Wed., Fri. May-Sept., €15) featuring some of the best musicians in the country, let alone Dingle. Be sure to book ahead at the tourist office.

Shopping

Dingle has plenty of opportunities for top-notch retail therapy. The brightly painted **Ceardlann na Coille,** the **Dingle Craft Village** (The Wood, just off Strand St., tel. 066/915-1778) on the western fringe of town has a range of studios, from pottery to knitwear, woodworking, and leather goods.

Renowned goldsmith **Brian de Staic** (Green St., tel. 066/915-1298, www.briandestaic.com) has a studio and shop here; another jeweler with more innovative designs is **Niamh Utsch** (Green St., tel. 066/915-2217, www.nugoldsmith.com). Also drop by the studio-cum-shop of weaver **Lisbeth Mulcahy** (Green St., tel. 066/915-1688, www.

Dick Mack's is one of the quirkier pubs in Dingle Town.

The Dingle Way

If you have the time and the stamina, the 179-kilometer **Dingle Way** is the ideal way to experience the otherworldly Corca Dhuibhne. The route begins at Tralee, heading west to the village of Camp on the north side of the peninsula; from Camp the path becomes a loop that skirts the coast. This loop is traditionally traversed in a clockwise direction, which means you'll pass through Annascaul, Dingle Town, Ventry, and Dunquin before reaching the formidable Mount Brandon on the peninsula's northwest tip. The clockwise route is easier the first few days, allowing you to prepare yourself for Brandon (of course, if you are *extremely* fit and looking for more solitude along the trail, you'd probably want to walk it counterclockwise, tackling Mount Brandon toward the beginning). The whole hike, beginning and ending in Tralee, should take about eight days, though if you start and finish in Camp you can do it in six and a half (with a total distance of 136 kilometers).

For travel advice, maps, details on hiker-friendly B&Bs, and suchlike, visit the excellent **DingleWay.net** (www.dingleway.com).

lisbethmulcahy.com), whose husband Louis has a much-celebrated pottery farther west on the peninsula.

The **Greenlane Gallery** (Holy Ground, tel. 066/915-2018, www.greenlanegallery.com) has some pretty fun avant-garde sculpture in addition to the requisite landscape paintings. **Commodum Design** (Main St., tel. 066/915-1380, www.commodum.ie) has a gorgeous selection of hand-knit sweaters and Avoca blankets (and plenty more great gift ideas). **An Gailearaí Beag** ("The Little Gallery," Main St., tel. 066/915-2976, www.angailearaibeag.com) has locally made pottery, knitwear, stained glass, and cute little children's chairs made of traditional *súgán* rope.

Bibliophiles, don't miss **An Café Liteártha** (Dykegate St., tel. 066/915-2204). Opened in 1979, this small Gaeilge-speaking café-bookshop serves up cheap and tasty lunches behind a terrific selection of Irish-interest books. It's a Dingle institution. The friendly proprietors of the **Dingle Bookshop** (2 Green St., tel. 066/915-2433, www.dinglebookshop.com) promise you "the book you never knew you wanted," and they deliver. While you're here, pick up a copy of *The Dingle Peninsula* by Steve MacDonogh (and updated by Camilla Dinkel, the owner of the bookshop). This book is an excellent and very readable overview of the region's archaeology and culture.

Accommodations

Backpackers have several hostel choices in Dingle. The central **Grapevine** (Dykegate St., tel. 066/915-1434, www.grapevinedingle.com, dorms €17-24) is the place to stay if you're planning on a pub crawl. The dorms are cramped but clean, the sitting room is wonderfully cozy, and the place attracts hikers and bohemians in equal measure. Confirm your reservation the day before in high season, lest your bed be given away.

The rooms are immaculate and the showers excellent at **Coastline House** (The Wood, a 5-minute walk west of town on the R559, tel. 066/915-2494, www.coastlinedingle.com, €35-45 pp). Ask for a front-facing room for a view of Dingle Bay. The B&Bs along this stretch are ideal because you're guaranteed a quiet night, yet you're still close enough to town to walk home from the pub. Another nice B&B a short walk from town is **Milestone** (Milltown, 1 km west of town on the R559, tel. 066/915-1831, www.milestonedingle.com, €40-50 pp, s €60-75), an extraordinarily friendly and accommodating place named for the Bronze Age standing stone in the front garden.

If you've rented a car, consider staying at **Ballymore House** (3 km west of Dingle on the R559, tel. 066/915-9736, www.ballymorehouse.com, €35-40 pp), which offers a peaceful night's rest and proper vegan breakfast options.

The Archaeology of the Dingle Peninsula

The Irish name for the Dingle Peninsula, **Corca Dhuibhne,** means "The Seed of Duibhne"—Duibhne being a goddess worshipped by the Celtic settlers who arrived here a few centuries before Christ. Human habitation goes as far back as 4000 BC, however. There are more than 2,000 extant archaeological sites on the peninsula, including Iron Age forts; the foundations of Bronze Age farmhouses, particularly in the **Loch a'Dúin Valley** near the village of Cloghane, on the northern end of the Conor Pass; Europe's most substantial collection of prehistoric *clocháin,* or beehive huts; early Christian monastic ruins at Gallarus and Riasc; and 60 **ogham stones** ("OH-um"), so named for their inscriptions using an old Celtic script with an alphabet of 25 characters, consisting of tick marks across (or above, or below) a continuous line.

Traveling Slea Head Drive will take you by the principal sights, though enthusiasts might want to sign up for a specialized tour. **Sciuird Archaeological Tours** (Holy Ground, tel. 066/915-1606 or 066/915-1937, archeo@eircom.net, tours at 10:30am and 2pm daily, €20) jams 6,000 years' worth of information into a 2.5-hour minibus trip. Tim Collins can pick you up at your lodging.

But if a night at the pubs is what you've come for, **Boland's** (Goat St., tel. 066/915-1426, www.bolandsdingle.ie, €40-60 pp) is a good option—the location is more central and the owners are accommodating. You might want to ask for a room at the back of the house if you're staying at the weekend, though.

Dingle's posh guesthouses tend to look and feel vaguely like classy-but-bland American hotels; then again, it's nice to have hotel amenities along with an owner who remembers your name and appreciates your business. At each of these guesthouses you can expect awesome gourmet breakfasts (smoked salmon with your scrambled eggs, fresh porridge with cream and whiskey or Bailey's, an array of pastries, all that sort of thing). The first is **Heaton's** (The Wood, 600 m west of the marina, tel. 066/915-2288, www.heatonsdingle.com, closed Jan., €45-75 pp, s €60-90, suites €60-90 pp), which has Jacuzzi bathtubs and spacious rooms with French furniture and white decor that feels peaceful rather than excessively minimalist. Five-star **Castlewood House** (The Wood, west of town just before the Milltown roundabout and bridge, tel. 066/915-2788, www.castlewooddingle.com, Feb.-Dec., €50-80 pp, s €75-110) offers CD/DVD players, whirlpool bathtub-shower combos, and individually designed and decorated bedrooms.

If you generally stay in hotels, you might consider a guesthouse while in Dingle, as the town's hotels can be disappointing in terms of service and value.

Information and Services

The ever-busy **tourist office** (Strand St., tel. 066/915-1188, www.dingle-peninsula.ie, 9am-6pm daily June-Sept., 9am-1pm and 2pm-5pm Mon.-Sat. Oct.-May) is at the harbor. Before you go, check out **Dingle Post** (www.dingle-post.com) for more info on upcoming events.

O'Keefe's Pharmacy (tel. 066/915-1310, open Sun.) as well as **AIB** and the **Bank of Ireland** (both with ATMs and bureaux de change) are all on Main Street.

Getting There

Dingle is 49 kilometers southwest of Tralee, 70 kilometers northwest of Killarney, and 346 kilometers southwest of Dublin. **Bus Éireann** (tel. 066/712-3566) can get you from Tralee to Dingle, dropping you off at the pier (#275, at least 4/day Mon.-Sat., 3/day Sun., 6/day Mon.-Sat. and 5/day Sun. in summer). A less frequent summer service links Killarney with Dingle via Inch and Castlemaine (#281, 1-2 buses a day June-Sept.). You could also ride **Irish Rail** (tel. 066/712-3522, 2/day Mon.-Sat. from Dublin Heuston) to Tralee and then transfer to Bus Éireann.

Getting Around

Dingle Town can be traversed end-to-end in under 15 minutes. Planning to cycle Slea Head Drive? Rent a cycle from **Paddy's Bike Shop** (Dykegate St., tel. 066/915-2311, www.paddys-bikeshop.com), **Mountain Man** (Strand St., tel. 066/915-2400), or **Foxy John's** (Main St., tel. 066/915-1316). Rates are roughly €15/75 per day/week.

Need a taxi? Dial **Dingle Cabs** (tel. 087/218-9430).

WEST OF DINGLE

Locals claim they breathe the freshest air in Europe, and that's no idle brag. You'll look back on a cycling tour of west Dingle, a still-vibrant Gaeltacht (Irish-speaking region) as one of the most—no, *the* most—exhilarating experience of your vacation.

TOP EXPERIENCE

★ Slea Head Drive (Dingle Peninsula Loop)

Otherwise known as the R559, the **Slea Head Drive** loop takes you west from Dingle to the southern tip of the peninsula, Slea Head, and turns north, passing through several small villages before delivering you back to the hamlet of Milltown just over the bridge from Dingle Town. This route takes in some of the most incredibly beautiful scenery in Ireland.

Though it isn't signposted, Slea Head should be driven only in a clockwise direction, as the road clinging to the side of the cliff is too narrow for passing in several spots. Buses frequently get stuck on hairpin turns (one of which is crossed by a robust stream; prepare for soaked sneaks if cycling). The various sites and villages are listed in the order you will come upon them, the total distance from Dingle to Slea Head, Dunquin, Ballyferriter, and back to Dingle being just shy of 47 kilometers. To beat the tour buses, arrange to pick up your rental bike the evening before so you can make an early start.

It is also possible to reach the villages on the end of the peninsula via **Bus Éireann** (tel.

Slea Head Drive winds its way to the edge of the Dingle Peninsula.

066/712-3566), which runs a Dingle-Dunquin service (stopping in Ventry and Ballyferriter) on Monday and Thursday only (#276, 2/day Mon., 3/day Thurs.). Clearly you're better off biking or hiring a taxi from town!

Ventry

The first village of substance on Slea Head Drive is **Ventry** (Ceann Trá, 7 km west of Dingle), with a pretty Blue Flag strand, an adjacent caravan park, and not much else. If that sounds like heaven, though, you can always spend the night here: try **Ceann Trá Heights** (signposted from the village, tel. 066/915-9866 or 087/683-6945, www.ceanntraheights.com, mid-Mar.-mid-Nov., €30-38 pp, s €45-55), a bungalow overlooking Ventry Harbour offering sea and mountain views from bedrooms and a "sun lounge," and a veggie-friendly breakfast menu.

West of Ventry

As you approach Slea Head you'll see signs for the Neolithic **Fahan beehive huts** and the Iron Age **Dunbeg Fort.** Admission fees are about €3 for each, provided someone is around to collect them. Dunbeg isn't anywhere near the best example of a promontory fort, the cliffside setting isn't as dramatic as it sounds, and even a careful visit will take you well under 10 minutes. The beehive huts are roofless, so it's their age (four millennia plus) more than their appearance that is noteworthy. In other words, these ruins would be worth seeing so long as you didn't have to pay for the privilege.

What is worth paying for, however, is a meal at the **Stone House** (directly across the R559 from Dunbeg Fort, tel. 066/915-9970, www.stonehouseventry.com, 12:30pm-3:30pm and 6:30pm-10pm Wed.-Mon., lunch €9-14, dinner €17-25, dinner reservations required), in a striking building modeled after the Gallarus Oratory (and built with local stone). Enjoy your meal of fresh steak or seafood and local produce in the simple, cheery dining room, or at a picnic table out front.

Dunquin

The peninsula's westernmost village, **Dunquin** (Dún Chaoin) is scattered for a couple of kilometers along the R559. The village's much-ballyhooed pub, Kruger's (once a favorite haunt of bad-boy playwright Brendan Behan), isn't actually all that great: The grub is mediocre and the atmosphere provokes a vague and inexplicable sense of unease. The real reason to linger, besides the view of course, is the Dúchas-run **Blasket Centre** (tel. 066/915-6444, 10am-6pm Easter-June and Sept.-Oct., 10am-7pm July-Aug., €4), for an introduction to the culture and strife-strewn history of those islands in the distance. Be sure to visit before you hop the boat for Great Blasket (which departs from the village pier, signposted off the R559). Backpackers on their way to or from the Blaskets stay at the An Óige **Dunquin Hostel** (on the R559 on the northern end of the village, tel. 066/915-6121, www.anoige.ie, Feb.-Nov., dorms €15-17, doubles €20-21 pp)). Unfortunately, meals are only available for groups.

Dunquin is 20 kilometers west of Dingle on the Slea Head road, and is served by **Bus Éireann** route #276 (2/day Mon., 3/day Thurs.).

The Blasket Islands

Europe's most westerly islands are the **Blaskets** (Na Blascaodaí), five kilometers off the Dingle coast. They are inhabited today only by the staff of a small café and visitors center on the largest of these seven lonesome isles, **Great Blasket.** All seven were once inhabited, and many bear archaeological evidence of Iron Age and early Christian settlements. In the early decades of the 20th century the savage weather conditions often prevented contact with the mainland—to the point of near-starvation—and the last inhabitants, native Irish speakers with a formidable literary tradition, finally quit these islands in 1953.

Great Blasket is only six kilometers long and just over a kilometer wide, but there is still plenty to see and do: Incredibly scenic walking routes take you by the melancholy ruins of many old cottages, opportunities for bird- and seal-watching abound, and there's a long, lovely strand as well. The regular Blasket Island ferry service wasn't running at time of writing, but **Marine Tours** (Ventry Harbor, tel. 086/335-3805, www.marinetours.ie) lands on Great Blasket as part of their all-day **Eco Marine Tour** (€55). Note that this tour company operates out of Ventry, not Dunquin.

Clogher

Along with more ordinary milk jugs and dinner plates, the potters at **Louis Mulcahy's workshop** (Clogher, 4 km west of Ballyferriter on the R559, tel. 066/915-6229, www.louismulcahy.com) produce huge (four- or five-foot) brightly glazed urns fit for an Etruscan funeral. Mulcahy ships worldwide.

Ballyferriter and Around

The pleasant, compact village of **Ballyferriter** (Baile an Fheirtearaigh) is 10 kilometers west of Dingle on the R553. From here you can continue north on a local road to scenic Smerwick Harbour, with its small sandy strand and a few pubs with outdoor picnic tables overlooking the water. Sadly, the wonderfully atmospheric pub-cum-shop, petrol station, and B&B Tig Bhric closed its doors in 2014, but it's worth doing a bit of Googling before you arrive to see if someone else has taken it over. An alternative accommodation is a spiffy (but tasteful) hotel, **Óstán Ceann Sibéal** (Main St., tel. 066/915-6433, www.ceannsibealhotel.com, Mar.-Nov., rooms €90-130, bar food served 12:30pm-5:30pm and 6pm-9pm daily, until 9:30pm weekends, €10-18), whose staff are very accommodating for those walking the Dingle Way.

Heading east from Ballyferriter, you'll find two of the most important archaeological sites on the peninsula: the Riasc Monastic Settlement and the Gallarus Oratory.

Riasc Monastic Settlement

About 1.5 kilometers east of Ballyferriter, look for the turnoff (an old-fashioned signpost) to the **Riasc Monastic Settlement** on your left; the site is about 300 meters down a narrow bumpy side-road. This 5th- and 6th-century monastic site includes the stone foundations of several *clocháin* (beehive huts) as well as an exquisitely carved standing stone dating somewhere around 500 BC (the cross at the top was added by the first monks). The location is splendid, a placid daisy-dappled enclosure surrounded by sea and mountain vistas. If you've brought a picnic lunch, this just might be the spot for it.

Gallarus Oratory

It looks like an overturned boat made of stone, and the 8th-century **Gallarus Oratory** (signposted off the R559 3 km northeast of Ballyferriter, tel. 066/915-5333, www.gallarusoratory.ie, 9:30am-8pm daily Apr.-Oct., though site freely accessible all year) is just as watertight. The walls of this tiny (8-by-5-meter) church are unmortared—and more than 1 meter thick—though there are remnants of plaster on the interior walls. The oratory was

built on an east-west axis to allow morning light through the round window on the eastern wall.

A €3 admission fee gets you a parking space and an informative 12-minute audiovisual on the peninsula's archaeology. But as with Dunbeg Fort and the beehive huts, one gets the distinct impression this visitors center is more a business venture than a conservation effort. You can keep walking up the lane (instead of making a left into the visitors center car park) to see the oratory on your own.

Nearby **Gallarus Castle** (tel. 066/915-6444, June-Aug., grounds free) is Dúchas-maintained, however. Built by the Fitzgerald family sometime during the 15th century, this four-story tower house retains its original vaulted ceilings.

Ballydavid

Return to the R559 and head about 3.8 kilometers north toward **Ballydavid** (Baile na nGall, "Town of the Foreigner") for the 12th-century Hiberno-Romanesque **Kilmalkedar Church** (Cill Maolchédair, "Church of St. Maolcethair"). This four-hectare site is associated with St. Brendan, and the ruin of a two-story edifice—thought to have housed the clergy—bears his name. Kilmalkedar marks the start of the **Saint's Road,** the traditional pilgrimage route up Mount Brendan.

The church has a typically decorated chancel doorway, and an alphabet stone bearing Latin script has been resurrected inside (in its broken state, it's just over 1.2 meters high). There's also a decorated sundial on the grounds, also 1.2 meters in height. Notice the hole at the top of the pre-Christian ogham stone (1.8 meters high) at the start of the lane, which was chiseled later on; when locals wanted to seal a deal or renew a marriage vow, they'd come here, stand on opposite sides of the stone, and touch fingers through the hole.

Ballydavid is another stop on the Dingle Way. Stay at the IHH **Tigh an Phóist** (An Bóthar Buí, beside the Carraig Church in Ballydavid, 12 km west of Dingle Town, tel. 066/915-5109, www.tighanphoist.com, mid-Mar.-Oct., dorms €13-18, private rooms €16-28 pp), which has an adjoining grocery, bike rental, and bureau de change, as well as two spiffy new self-catering apartments (sleeping 4-5); the weekly rate starts at €150 and climbs to €550 in July and August.

While you're in the neighborhood, treat yourself to a seaweed bath (€25/40 per 30/60 min.) or massage (€50/hour) at **Spa Atlantach** (on the local sea-facing road northwest of Murreagh, Ballydavid, via the R559, tel. 083/443-7322, www.spaatlantach.com).

NORTH OF DINGLE

The lush green fields east of Dingle give way to a stark and often surreal landscape as you head north out of town for **Conor Pass,** the highest in the country at 456 meters. Even in shoulder season there's often an ice cream truck at the car park near the summit, from where you can see Mount Brandon to the north, Dingle Bay to the south, and a lot of bleak and rocky slopes in between.

Castlegregory

The town itself isn't of much interest, but **Castlegregory** (Caislean an Ghraire) offers extraordinarily clear waters for **scuba diving** around the privately owned **Maharees Islands.** Divers (beginners included) can arrange accommodations, equipment, and boat hire through **Harbour House** (Scraggane Pier Rd., Kilshannig, 7 km north of town on the Fahamore road, tel. 066/713-9292, www.maharees.ie, €40-45 pp, s €45-50), which also sports an indoor pool, sauna, and deluxe exercise room as well as pilates and aqua aerobics lessons in high season. Weekend break packages include dinner in the adjoining restaurant (which is also open for lunch).

Surfers should contact **Jamie Knox Watersports** (Maharees, the Fahamore road, 4 km north of town, tel. 066/713-9411, www.jamieknox.com) for lessons and equipment rental.

A Friday-only **Bus Éireann** (tel. 066/712-3566) service links Tralee with Camp,

Castlegregory, and Cloghane (#273, departs Tralee at 8:55am and 2pm, departs Cloghane at 10:05am and 3:10pm).

Mount Brandon

Ireland's second-highest peak, **Mount Brandon** (Cnoc Bréanainn, 950 meters), was once a well-traveled pilgrimage, second only to Croagh Patrick in popularity. The ruins of St. Brendan's oratory top the summit; the seven-kilometer round-trip takes about 6-7 hours, and navigational skills are essential.

At the northern terminus of the Conor Pass, follow the signs for Brandon Point (12 km); you'll pass through the village of Cloghane and a couple of sandy beaches, Ballyquin and Brandon Bay, before the steep uphill road ends at the small Brandon Head car park. The worn grassy mountain path begins here.

EAST OF DINGLE

The second- and third-highest peaks on the peninsula, **Caherconree** (827 meters) and **Baurtregaum** (852 meters), are on the eastern side, and the Dingle Way walking route passes along their northern flanks. If you take the Caherconree Pass, from Camp south to Aughils Bridge, on your left you'll pass the turnoff for an Iron Age promontory fort that was supposedly built by an ancient king of Munster, Curaoi Mac Daire (The mountain's Irish name, Cathair Conraoi, means "Cú Roí's Stone Fort.") The views from the top of the pass are bleak but stunning, and seeing as fewer people know about this than about Conor Pass, there aren't nearly as many cars competing for road space.

Annascaul

When Antarctic explorer Tom Crean returned to his childhood home, Annascaul, to run a pub in his retirement, he put this sleepy one-street village on the map (he came home after World War I and opened the pub several years later, in 1927). Painted in predictable ice blue and white, the rough stone walls inside at **The South Pole Inn** (Main St., tel. 066/915-7388, food served €12:30pm-8pm daily, €8-16) are covered in framed photos and news clippings. Not at all a tourist trap, it is certainly the coziest pub in town, with open fires, an amiable bartender, and hearty no-frills grub. Be sure to stop in for a pint if you're passing through; if you're spending the night, note there are trad sessions Wednesday and Friday-Sunday nights.

There isn't much here otherwise, though Annascaul is on the 179-kilometer Dingle Way. Also, you might stop by the long-established **Annascaul Pottery** (Main St., tel. 066/915-7505, www.annascaul.ie/annascaul-pottery). Niall Phelan's work is quietly whimsical, and definitely worth an extended browse.

For B&B, try **Four Winds** (Main St., tel. 066/915-7168, www.thefourwindsbb.com, Mar.-Nov., €30-32 pp, s €37-40), an unpretentious bungalow on the western edge of town with lovely mountain and bay views (but no TVs in the bedrooms, though there's a guest lounge). There are several townhouse B&Bs along Main Street as well.

Annascaul is 18 kilometers east of Dingle on the N86. The Tralee-Dingle **Bus Éireann** (tel. 066/712-3566) route stops in Annascaul (#275, at least 4/day Mon.-Sat. and 3/day Sun. year-round, 5-6/day daily in summer).

Inch

You'll find the best beach in County Kerry at **Inch** (Inse), a tiny hamlet 25 kilometers east of Dingle tucked beneath the Slieve Mish Mountains. The pale golden sand stretches for nearly five kilometers, and though it's popular with **surfers** there's no place to rent equipment. Pop by **Sammy's** (on the R561, tel. 066/915-8118, www.sammysinchbeach.com, 9:30am-10pm daily, meals €5-22, B&B €40-60 pp) for tourist info.

Shanahill East

Aside from the lovely strand at Inch, there's not much along the south coastal road between Annascaul and Castlemaine—though no self-respecting vegetarian should pass **The Phoenix** (6 km west of Castlemaine on the R561, tel. 066/976-6284, www.thephoenixrestaurant.com, 11am-6pm Mon.-Wed., 11am-8pm Thurs.-Sun., rooms €40 pp, s €35-40, camping €12 pp, self-catering chalet for 2-4 people €450/week). It's a delightfully bohemian farmhouse B&B and organic vegetarian restaurant (lunch €12-20, dinner €20-30). "Glamping" in brightly painted Romany wagons (or gypsy caravans, for the less politically correct) is an option for €60 pp including breakfast and dinner, as are three-hour cookery classes for €150/200/250 (for 1/2/3 people), including lunch. The food is terrific and bountiful, if slightly overpriced; you'll enjoy your meal (be it a quinoa and spinach bake topped in pesto or the signature "firebird curry") on a rustic flagstoned patio with colored lights and all sorts of Eastern whirligigs suspended from the corrugated plastic roof. The restaurant opening times vary, so call ahead even if you aren't looking for accommodations.

In summer, **Bus Éireann** stops right outside the Phoenix on the Killarney-Dingle route (#281, 1-2/day daily June-Sept.).

The Iveragh Peninsula

Looped by the famous Ring of Kerry, the Iveragh Peninsula has a few hidden places you'll want to seek out, from the Skellig Ring to the quiet highlands. The 215-kilometer **Kerry Way** walking route also loops the peninsula.

★ RING OF KERRY

One of Ireland's top three tourist destinations, the **Ring of Kerry**—the N70 on your road map—makes a 180-kilometer loop of the lovely Iveragh Peninsula, crowned in the west by the breathtaking Skellig Islands. Though it's possible to complete the ring in a single day, try to make a more leisurely two-day trip of it if your itinerary allows. You can also cycle it over three or so days, but it's wise not to attempt this in July or August.

Since you're driving on the left and the coach buses always travel counter-clockwise, it makes sense to start the Ring of Kerry at Kenmare and proceed in a clockwise direction to Killarney: This way there'll be no buses obscuring your view or slowing you down. Drive with great caution, as you'll be meeting those coaches at blind curves instead!

The primary sights along the route are the late Iron Age **Staigue Fort, Derrynane House** (ancestral home of Daniel O'Connell), and the **Skelligs** (reachable by ferry from Portmagee, Caherdaniel, or Cahersiveen). If you're looking to dip out of the well-worn tourist track, make a detour off the N70 onto the scenic **Skellig Ring,** or **Glencar** and **Caragh Lake** in the Kerry highlands farther along the N70. Traffic is delightfully sparse along the narrow local roads skirting the mountains.

Avoid any roadside inn along the way that has parking spaces marked for tour buses. The only thing this kind of place usually has going for it is the view—but why stop when you can just pull off the road and savor it for free?

Bus Éireann (tel. 064/663-4777) runs a Ring of Kerry service. Route #279 goes from Waterville to Killarney via Cahersiveen (1/day Mon.-Sat., departing Waterville at 7:30am; another bus originating at Cahersiveen departs at 12:15pm). Summer-only route #280 makes the whole circuit, stopping in Cahersiveen, Waterville, and Caherdaniel (departing Killarney at 8:30am daily late June-early Sept., 1:45pm daily early June-mid-Sept.).

KENMARE

Situated at the southern end of the Ring of Kerry on the shores of an eponymous bay, **Kenmare** (Neidín, "Little Nest," or Ceann Mara, "Head of the Sea") is a pleasantly bustling town, laid out in the 17th century, with a slew of great restaurants. The lovely shady park at the town square is a popular spot on sunny afternoons, with hardly any green visible between all the locals starved for some vitamin D! Kenmare makes a far nicer base than Killarney Town for the national park; while it's still a touristy location, Kenmare is never gaudily or overwhelmingly so. It's also a "gateway" to the Beara Peninsula, most of which belongs to County Cork—and so makes a feasible base for both Beara and Iveragh.

The town is compact and easy to get the hang of. A triangle of streets—Henry on the west side, Main to the northeast, and Shelbourne on the south leg—is crowned by the town square and park. Proceed past the park for Holy Cross Church (and free parking), or turn onto Market Street from the square to reach the Druid Stone Circle, Kenmare's primary sight.

Sights

You come to Kenmare more for the food and general atmosphere, though there are a few attractions of note. The first is the whimsically

The Iveragh Peninsula

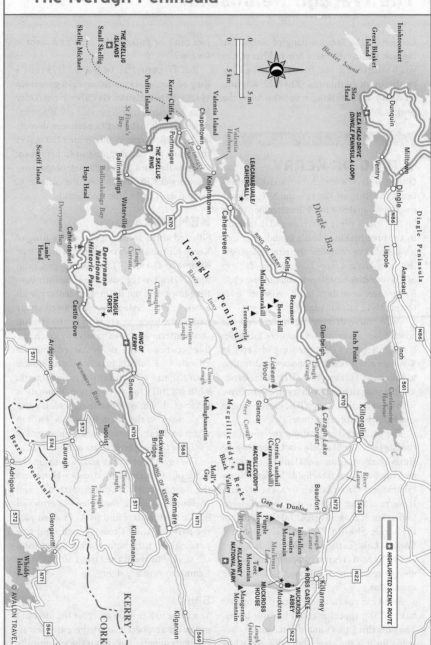

Inishtooskert
Great Blasket Island
Blasket Sound
Slea Head
SLEA HEAD DRIVE (DINGLE PENINSULA LOOP)
Dunquin
Ventry
Dingle
Milltown
Lispole
Anascaul
Inch
Inch Point
Dingle Bay

Dingle Peninsula

N86
N86
561
N70

Castlemaine Harbour

Skellig Michael
Small Skellig
THE SKELLIG ISLANDS
Skellig Islands
Puffin Island
St Finan's Bay
Kerry Cliffs
Chapeltown
Valentia Island
Valentia Harbour
Portmagee
THE SKELLIG RING
Portmagee Channel
Knightstown
LEACANABUAILE/CAHERGALL
Cahersiveen
Kells
RING OF KERRY
Mullaghnarakill
Beenmore
Been Hill
Teeromoyle
Glenbeigh
Lickeen Wood
Caragh Lake
Lough Caragh
Killorglin
River Laune
River Maine
Glencar
Caragh River Forest
Corrán Tuathail (Carrauntoohil)
MACGILLICUDDY'S REEKS
Macgillicuddy's Reeks
Molls Gap
Black Valley
Gap of Dunloe
Beaufort
Lough Leane
N72
563
N70

Scariff Island
Hogs Head
Ballinskelligs
Ballinskelligs Bay
Waterville
Lough Currane
Cloonaghlin Lough
Derriana Lough
Cloon Lough
Mullaghanattin
Derrynane National Historic Park
Caherdaniel
Lamb' Head
Derrynane Bay
Castle Cove
STAIGUE FORTS
RING OF KERRY
Sneen
Kenmare River
Iveragh Peninsula
Inny River

N70
N70

Ardgroom
571
Lauragh
573
574
Tuosist
Cloonee Loughs
Lough Inchiquin
Blackwater Bridge
Kenmare
RING OF KERRY
568
571
N71
N71

Beara Peninsula
Adrigole
Glengarriff
572
N71
Whiddy Island

KERRY
CORK

Killabunane
Kilgarvan
584
569
N22

Killarney
N22

Purple Mountain
Tomies Mountain
Torc Mountain
KILLARNEY NATIONAL PARK
Upper Lake
Muckross Lake
Innisfallen
MUCKROSS HOUSE
Muckross
ROSS CASTLE
MUCKROSS ABBEY
Mangerton Mountain
Lough Guitane

HIGHLIGHTED SCENIC ROUTE

© AVALON TRAVEL

0   5 mi
0   5 km

but inaccurately named **Druid Stone Circle,** a collection (15 meters in diameter) of 15 rocks around a small dolmen with a large boulder for a capstone. In peaceful suburban surroundings, this circle dates to the early Bronze Age (before 1000 BC) and may have been used to mark the solstices. The dolmen may cover a burial, though the site has not been excavated. To get here, walk from Main or Henry Street onto the square and turn left onto Market Street, and after five minutes or so you'll come to a fork in the road. Bear right and the site is straight ahead.

Erected in 1864, **Holy Cross Church** (Old Killarney Rd.) is well worth a visit for its exquisite angel spandrels carved out of wood from the Black Forest in Germany. Somewhat unusually, the altar window depicts the Crucifixion, and the Stations of the Cross were donated by the infamous Nun of Kenmare (presumably before she converted back to Protestantism).

On a rainy day, check out the **heritage center** (The Square, tel. 064/714-1233, 9am-1pm and 2pm-5:30pm Mon.-Sat. May-June, 9am-6pm Mon.-Sat., 10am-5pm Sun. July-Oct., free), which includes exhibits on the local lace industry in the mid- to late 19th century as well as the woman who helped develop it: Margaret Anna Cusack, the "Nun of Kenmare," a renegade proto-feminist who converted from Protestantism to Catholicism and back again.

Activities and Recreation

The 215-kilometer Kerry Way passes through Kenmare en route west to the southern side of the Ring of Kerry, and north to Killarney. Casual walkers can take to the trail at **Gleninchaquin Park** (signposted off the R571, 13 km west of Kenmare, tel. 087/712-8553, www.gleninchaquinpark.com, daily year-round, €6), which culminates in a waterfall overlooking Kenmare Bay and the Caha Mountains on the Beara Peninsula. In fine weather you can swim in the rock pools beneath the cascade.

Seafari River Cruises (Kenmare Pier, follow Henry St. south just out of town, tel. 064/664-2059, www.seafariireland.com, 2-hour cruise €25) can take you on a dolphin-, whale-, and seal-watching trip on Kenmare Bay; you can also rent watersporting equipment. Or try the **Starsailing & Adventure Centre** (Dauros, 12 km west of Kenmare on the R571, tel. 064/714-1222, www.staroutdoors.ie), a five-minute drive west of town. (No wheels? No problem—the owners will pick you up and drop you off.) Here you can sign up for a sailing course, sea kayaking, canoeing, or a hill-walking excursion.

The **Ring of Kerry Golf & Country Club** (Templenoe, 6.5 km west of Kenmare on the N70, tel. 064/714-2000, www.ringofkerrygolf.com) offers a par-72 championship course in an exquisite location. **Kenmare Golf Club** (on the R569/Cork road just east of town, tel. 064/714-1291, www.kenmaregolfclub.com) is more convenient, though not as scenic.

Food

Kenmare lives up to its reputation for fine dining in every price range. It only opened in 2015, but ★ **Mick and Jimmy's** (36 Henry St., tel. 064/664-2820, www.mickandjimmys.com, 8am-10pm daily, lunch €8-12, dinner €12-20) has very quickly established itself as one of Kenmare's most beloved hangouts. Coffee shop by day, winebar by night, the food is always gourmet caliber. Even a simple breakfast of avocado toast and coffee is mouthwateringly memorable. The mood is chill and cheerful, and the service is kind and attentive.

Another terrific lunch option is the all-vegetarian **Bookstop Café** (Bridge St., tel. 064/667-9911, 9:30am-4pm Mon.-Sat., until 5:30pm in high season, under €8), serving up yummy plates of beet burgers, crepes, and deluxe salads along with abundant vegan and gluten-free dessert options. Browse the shelves of secondhand paperbacks once you've finished your lunch. Small-town grocery meets organic whole foods at **The Pantry** (30 Henry St., tel. 064/664-2233, 9am-6pm Mon.-Sat.,

11am-4pm Sun.), the perfect place to stock up for a healthy picnic lunch.

"Pub grub" isn't quite the term—the food's too sophisticated for that—but stop by **P.F. McCarthy's** (14 Main St., tel. 064/664-1516, www.pfskenmare.com, food served 10:30am-3pm Mon.-Sat., 5pm-9pm Tues.-Sat, lunch €7-12, dinner €12-20) anyway for a terrific falafel pita, a hearty steak sandwich, or a "posh nosh nibble platter." For a fantastic omelet or salad, eat at the **Purple Heather** (Henry St., tel. 064/664-1016, www.thepurpleheatherkenmare.com, 11am-6:30pm Mon.-Sat., €8-18). This daytime eatery, a local favorite, is surprisingly publike in decor and atmosphere, and the food is super-fresh and creatively prepared. The only downside is the lackluster service.

Sample the inventive Continental fare at **Packie's** (Henry St., tel. 064/664-1508, 6pm-10pm Mon.-Sat. mid-Mar.-Oct., open weekends and the week before Christmas Nov.-Dec., closed late Dec.-mid-Mar., €17-33), a bustling bistro the owner converted from her (eponymous) uncle's old grocery. Or try the trendier, Asian-tinged **Mulcahy's** (36 Henry St., tel. 064/664-2383, 6pm-10pm daily, closed Tues.-Wed. in low season, €18-30), whose owner is the brother of famous Dingle potter Louis Mulcahy. "Best Restaurant" status is up for debate, of course, but lots of people would give the award to **The Lime Tree** (Shelbourne St., tel. 064/664-1225, www.limetreerestaurant.com, 6:30pm-10pm daily Apr.-Oct., €19-30). In a quaint stone cottage that was once part of the Lansdowne Estate, you'll find incredibly fresh, out-of-this-world seafood (or local lamb or beef) and lots of art on rough whitewashed walls.

Entertainment and Events

Unlike those in Killarney, Kenmare's music pubs don't adhere to the frolicking-leprechaun kitsch-fest. You'll find trad at the small-but-jumpin' **Crowley's** (26 Henry St., tel. 064/664-1472) on Monday and Tuesday nights all year, and nearly nightly in high season. Other laid-back watering holes that have live music most nights in summer are **Davitt's** (Henry St., tel. 064/664-2741, www.davittskenmare.com) and **Foley's** (Henry St., tel. 064/664-1379, www.foleyskenmare.com).

Shopping

You could spend the better part of a day shopping in Kenmare—and fortunately, there are proportionally fewer tourist traps here than in Killarney. Most shops are flush with swaths of crisp linen, sometimes finished off in intricate handmade lace or crochet. One shop to check out is **The White Room** (21 Henry St., tel. 064/664-0600), which has reasonably priced country-chic homewares on offer as well.

Cleo (2 Shelbourne St., tel. 064/664-1410) stocks Irish-made tweed, linen, and knitwear (some produced locally). Most beautiful of all are the alpaca wool sweaters hand-knit on Inis Meáin. They're very expensive (more so than if you bought one on the island), but considering the quality and work involved, they're worth every cent.

For local OS maps—or nearly any book ever written about Michael Collins—head to the **Kenmare Bookshop** (Shelbourne St., tel. 064/664-1578).

There's an outdoor **market** outside the park at the town square, with antiques and local produce on daily offer in the summer.

Accommodations

The owner of the IHH **Fáilte Hostel** (Shelbourne at Henry St., tel. 064/664-2333, www.kenmarehostel.com, mid-May to mid-Oct., dorms €18, private rooms €20-26 pp) prides herself on running a spotless-yet-comfortable establishment. The kitchen facilities are excellent, the sitting room is cozy, and the 1:30am curfew is pretty much a nonissue.

A restored period bungalow with gingerbread trim, **Whispering Pines** (Bell Height, Glengarriff Rd., tel. 064/664-1194, www.whisperingpineskenmare.com, Mar.-Nov., €32-40 pp, s €42-45) is as cheerful as the exterior, with that increasingly rare traditional welcome of tea and fresh scones. It's only a three-minute walk south of town, yet this B&B (with only four rooms) is much quieter than those in the center.

It's room only (no breakfast), and the town center location isn't a plus if it's a bank holiday weekend, but **Virginia's Guesthouse** (Henry St., tel. 064/664-1021, www.virginias-guesthouse.com, €35-40 pp, s €50-60) has good showers and helpful owners. With so many excellent eateries in town, you won't mind having to go out for your morning meal.

The nicest hotel in town is the **Lansdowne Arms** (corner of Main St. and Shelbourne St., tel. 064/664-1114, www.lansdownearms. com, €120-150 pp), with kindly, nothing's-too-much-trouble service and above-average bar and restaurant fare. (Fair warning though: The showers are old-school.)

There are larger, more upscale hotels on the outskirts of Kenmare, but consider staying instead at **Sallyport House** (Glengarriff Rd., tel. 064/664-2006, www.sallyporthouse.com, mid-Mar.-Oct., rooms €110-150), a tranquil country manor with extensive gardens and orchard. It's still owned by the Arthurs, the family who built the house in 1932. Many of the rooms boast four-poster queen- and king-size beds and other beautiful antiques, though the bathrooms all have modern bath-and-shower combos. The breakfast is as tasty as the rooms are luxurious. One caveat: Sallyport isn't kid- or dog-friendly (though children 13 and up are welcome).

Information and Services

The **tourist office** (The Square, tel. 064/664-1233, www.kenmare.com, 9am-6pm Mon.-Sat. and 10am-5pm Sun. May-Oct.) is closed in low season.

The **Bank of Ireland** (on the square) and **AIB** (corner of Henry and Main) both have ATMs and bureaux de change. For a pharmacy, try **Brosnan's** (Henry St., tel. 064/664-1318).

Getting There

Kenmare is at the southeastern terminus of the Ring of Kerry, 32 kilometers south of Killarney on the N71. **Bus Éireann** (tel. 064/663-0011) services Kenmare on the Sneem-Killarney route (#270, at least 4/day daily June-Sept.). For buses to Dingle, Tralee, Cork, and Kinsale, you'll have to transfer in Killarney.

Getting Around

Driving in Kenmare's congested one-way traffic system can be a real nightmare. Park your rental car in the spacious free lot across the street from Holy Cross Church on the old Killarney road (and beside the public toilets).

Rent a cycle from **Finnegan's Corner** (38 Henry St., at the corner of Shelbourne, tel. 064/664-1083, closed Sun., €15/day).

For a taxi, ring **Declan Finnegan** (tel. 064/664-1491, www.kenmaretaxis.com) or **Denis Griffin** (tel. 087/614-7222, www.drive-kenmare.com), both of whom also do day tours of Beara, Dingle, and the Ring of Kerry.

STAIGUE FORT

Sheep frolic in the heathery hills around **Staigue Fort** (4 km north of the N70, sign-posted from the village of Castle Cove), a remarkably well-preserved ring fort with a commanding view of Kenmare Bay. In the centuries before the advent of Christianity, a minor chieftain would have lived here (in long-gone wooden edifices within the fort) with his family and servants. Thirty meters in diameter, the fort features mortarless walls six meters high and four meters thick. The site is certainly worth a brief detour, though a cheeky notice at the entrance proclaims that "all visitors are to pay one euro land trespass charge."

CAHERDANIEL

The village of Caherdaniel is just large enough for a hostel, a couple of B&Bs, a petrol station, and a great pub, the Blind Piper.

Caherdaniel is on the Kerry Way walking route, though there are other recreational opportunities. Whether you need a lesson or just want to rent the equipment, **Derrynane SeaSports** (Derrynane Harbour, 3 km west of Caherdaniel, tel. 066/947-5266 or 087/908-1208, derrynaneseasports@eircom.net, 10am-dusk June-Sept.) has the goods for canoeing, windsurfing, surfing, sailing, and waterskiing. **Eagle Rock Equestrian** (Caherdaniel, off the N70, tel. 066/947-5145) can set you up for a one- or two-hour beach, forest, or mountain trek.

Derrynane National Historic Park

Six kilometers west of the Staigue Fort turn-off is Derrynane National Historic Park, which includes the ancestral home of Daniel O'Connell, **Derrynane House** (2.5 km off the N70, turnoff signposted at the Blind Piper pub, tel. 066/947-5113, www.derrynanehouse. com, 1pm-5pm weekends Nov.-Mar., 1pm-5pm Tues.-Sun. Apr. and Oct., 9am-6pm Mon.-Sat. and 11am-7pm Sun. May-Sept., €4). Built by O'Connell's uncle, Maurice "Hunting Cap" O'Connell, with the proceeds of a booming smuggling business, the house features ornate original furniture, family portraits, and plenty of personal effects, from snuff boxes to the pistols O'Connell used in his duel with John D'Estene in 1815; the tour is self-guided. In the coach house you'll find the gloriously restored chariot on which O'Connell

rode through Dublin after his release from prison in 1844; unfortunately, the space is far too small to admire it properly. An excellent 20-minute audiovisual clearly explains the historical impact of O'Connell's law career.

Admission to the demesne is free of charge, with expansive, exotic gardens dotted with tiny moss-covered grottoes and wooded walking trails. Look out for the **summerhouse**, the ruin of a small tower house O'Connell used as a study. There's also beach access, and you can reach the small monastic ruin at **Abbey Island** at low tide.

Food and Accommodations

At the **Blind Piper** (just off the N70, tel. 066/947-5126, food served noon-8pm daily, until 10pm June-Sept., until 4pm Mon.-Thurs. in low season, €11-20), the service can be infuriatingly slow, but the grub is marvelous (with a fairly good vegetarian option). Outside there's a picturesque riverside green where children frolic as their parents enjoy their pints at nearby picnic tables.

A charming and well-maintained hostel, **Traveller's Rest** (on the N70, tel. 066/947-5175, www.hostelcaherdaniel.com, Feb.-Nov., dorms €18-19, double €21-22 pp) is popular with activity groups. There are only eight

The Iron Age Staigue Fort was built without mortar.

beds, so booking ahead is essential. Inquire at the petrol station directly across the road if no one answers the door. An option for B&B is **Derrynane Bay House** (1 km west of the village on the N70, tel. 066/947-5404, www. ringofkerry.net, €38-40 pp, s €50-60), a modern bungalow with splendid bay views (ask for a front room) and an outstanding breakfast array.

Getting There

Caherdaniel is on the N70 47 kilometers west of Kenmare, and is served by the Bus Éireann Ring of Kerry route (#280).

BALLINSKELLIGS

A scattered seaside hamlet at the start of the scenic but less-traveled Skellig Ring, **Ballinskelligs** (Baile na Sceilge, "Town of the Rocks") makes for a quiet stopover if you're doing the Ring of Kerry over more than one day. Overlooking the beach are the remains of the Augustinian **Ballinskelligs Priory** (signposted off the Skellig Ring 1 km north of the village, always accessible). It's said the monks of Skellig Michael moved here after quitting the island in the 12th century. What's left of the monastic buildings probably dates from the 15th century, and they have suffered the erosive effects of the sea. There's not much to see, but the windswept, somewhat melancholy locale is perfect for a contemplative stroll. Across the strand are the very scant remains of a tower house built by the MacCarthy clan in the 16th century.

No doubt the best gallery/café on the Ring of Kerry is **Siopa Cill Rialaig** (on the R566 just east of the village, tel. 066/947-9324, cillrialaig@esatclear.ie, 10:30am-7pm daily Easter-Sept., 11am-5pm Thurs.-Sat. low season), which is also an international artists' retreat of some renown (painters trade one or more of their works for food and board).

Skellig Lodge (signposted from the R566, 500 m up a local road, tel. 066/947-9942, www.skelliglodge.com, private rooms €24-28 pp) is essentially a hostel with only private rooms. The facilities are pretty good—there's

a pool table in the common room—but note that reception is only open 3pm-7:30pm. If you're arriving later, ring ahead. There are surprisingly few B&B options in this area, the best being **Beach Cove** (6.5 km south of Portmagee, tel. 066/947-9301 or 087/202-1820, www.stayatbeachcove.com, €43 pp) midway between Ballinskelligs and Portmagee on the Skellig Ring road.

The 14-room, 19th-century **Ballinskelligs Inn** (on the R566, tel. 066/947-9106, www.ballinskelligsinn.com, B&B €45 pp, food served noon-9pm daily, €10-16) won't cost you much more than a B&B. This no-frills hotel has a delightfully friendly and helpful staff—and the beach is just beyond the grounds. The hotel pub, **Cable O'Leary's,** is the locals' watering hole of choice.

In addition to trips to Skellig Michael, **Sean Feehan** (tel. 066/947-9182 or 086/417-6612, www.skelligboats.com) also does sea fishing and diving excursions.

Ballinskelligs is 16 kilometers south of Cahersiveen (from the N70, turn right onto the R566) and just under 13 kilometers west of Waterville (turn left onto the R567 from the N70). There is no public transportation.

★ THE SKELLIG RING

From Ballinskelligs, follow the signs for the **Skellig Ring,** a 19-kilometer loop (32 kilometers from Waterville) that takes you up a local road north through the Coomanaspig Pass before depositing you in Portmagee. From there, you proceed east on the R565 to rejoin the Ring of Kerry south of Cahersiveen. There are plenty of layabouts along these narrow hill-hugging roads to provide panoramic views of the Skellig Islands and St. Finian's Bay. This detour provides a welcome break from the perennial Ring of Kerry madness, especially since the tour buses can't travel down these narrow lanes.

The Kerry Cliffs

The enterprising O'Donoghue family has recently opened its coastal land for tourism, and the thousand-foot **Kerry Cliffs** (on the R566

1 km south of Portmagee, tel. 066/948-0985, www.kerrycliffs.com, 9am-8pm daily, €4 pp) are possibly even more breathtaking than the Cliffs of Moher in County Clare. Pass on by the ridiculous "replica" beehive huts—complete with gannet and puffin statues creaking in the wind—for some actual bird-watching. From the railings, the view across the ocean to the Skellig Islands on the western horizon is dramatic, to say the least. On a changeable day (which is most days, of course), the shifting light on the jagged rocks and frothing waves can leave even the accountants and actuaries among us feeling like Romantic poets. There's a tearoom and restrooms, too. You'll have no trouble finding it; the site is clearly and repetitively signposted all up and down the Skellig Ring road. Some visitors have complained about price gouging, which is understandable (and it's true the signposts have been sneakily designed to look like official tourist-board signage), but in fairness, the views are every bit as gorgeous as the Cliffs of Moher (and you'll pay €6 per person to park there). Free viewing points elsewhere along the Skellig Ring are simply not comparable, although if you have time to visit Valentia Island, you'll get a great view of the Skelligs from the western tip, at Bray Head.

Portmagee

Besides fishing, and lots of it, there's not a whole heck of a lot going on in the tidy seaside hamlet of **Portmagee** (An Caladh, "The Ferry"). If you're determined to get to Skellig Michael (and you should be!), you may need to put down here for more than one night if the weather's too iffy to sail.

For **sea angling** excursions, contact **Nealie Lyne** (tel. 087/687-1261, www.valentiaangling.com), who operates the *Mary Frances* out of Portmagee and Valentia.

Portmagee has one friendly bakery-café, **Skellig Mist** (on the main street, tel. 066/947-7250, 9:30am-6pm daily, under €8), where you can pick up a sandwich for your picnic lunch on Skellig Michael. The desserts are tasty too, rhubarb pie and suchlike, and there's more

seating on a terrace out back overlooking the harbor.

It's got a posh reputation, but the atmosphere at **The Moorings** guesthouse (the pier, tel. 066/947-7108, www.moorings.ie, Mar.-Dec., restaurant 6pm-10pm Tues.-Sun., €19-35, reservations recommended) is actually quite relaxed. The seafood doesn't get any fresher (seeing as the harbor is all of two feet away), and you might describe the cuisine (fish and otherwise) as gourmet comfort food. The vegetarian lasagna is heavenly, and the service is friendly too. Slightly less expensive pub fare is available next door at the **Bridge Bar** (food served noon-8pm daily, €10-23), under the same ownership; they do breakfast for nonresidents as well. There's live trad on Friday and Sunday nights. Or you could opt for the more traditional grub (no veggie options) at the **Fisherman's Bar** (on the pier, tel. 066/947-7103, food served 10am-9:30pm daily, €11-20).

The Moorings (the pier, tel. 066/947-7108, www.moorings.ie, Mar.-Dec., standard room €38-40 pp, s €53-55, room with view €45-70 pp, s €60-100) is the village's top accommodation (with excellent dining), but there are other options. Formerly the Portmagee Hostel, **Skellig Ring House** (on the Skellig Ring road just south of the village, tel. 066/948-0018 or 087/962-8100, www.skelligringhouse.com, €20-30 pp) is now operating as a no-frills guesthouse; bring groceries and cook your own breakfast in the communal kitchen.

For B&B in an idyllic location right on the strand at St. Finian's Bay, make a reservation at **Beach Cove** (on the Ballinskelligs road 6.5 km south of Portmagee, tel. 066/947-9301 or 087/202-1820, www.stayatbeachcove.com, €43 pp). The very helpful owner will arrange your Skelligs trip for you. Definitely ask for one of the upstairs bedrooms. A self-catering cottage nearby sleeps four.

Portmagee is on the R565, 11 kilometers off the Ring of Kerry (the N70) and 15.5 kilometers west of Cahersiveen. Unfortunately, there is no public transportation to Portmagee. If you want to get to the Skelligs but don't have wheels, plan to leave from Cahersiveen.

VALENTIA ISLAND

The first transatlantic cable was run from Valentia Island ("vah-LEN-see-uh"), just off the Iveragh Peninsula, to New York in 1857. Another claim to fame transpired five years later, when the **Altazamuth Stone** in Knightstown, on the eastern side of the island, was used to determine the size of the world, along with its lines of longitude and latitude. Valentia also boasts Europe's westernmost harbor, which was established to export stone materials from the slate quarry on the northeastern side of the island.

The afternoon before your trip to Skellig Michael, visit the **Skellig Experience** (just over the bridge from Portmagee, tel. 066/947-6306, www.skelligexperience.com, 10am-6pm daily Apr.-May and Sept.-Nov., 10am-7pm daily June-Aug., €5), a grass-roofed interpretive museum on everyday life for both the monks of Skellig Michael and the lighthouse keepers and their families who came long after them. The smallish exhibition also covers local bird- and waterlife, and includes model beehive huts and a 16-minute audiovisual. Since the guided tour of the island is extremely informative in itself, though, it's no biggie if you can't make it here. From here you can also book a two-hour **cruise** around the islands (€30), an alternative for those not feeling up for that vertiginous climb to see the monastic ruins.

Another option, if you're feeling energetic, is the scenic **Bray Head Loop walk** on the western tip of the island. From the Bray Head car park (four kilometers west of the bridge), it's a five-kilometer circular hike along a grassy clifftop with a marvelous view of the Skellig Islands if conditions are clear. It'll take you an hour and a half, two hours tops.

Valentia has yet another claim to fame: North of the slate quarry, off the road to the coast guard station at Reenadrolaun Point (the island's northernmost tip), the fossilized footprints of a primordial amphibian, a creature about one meter long, were discovered by a Swiss geology student (an undergrad, no less!) in 1992. Newly exposed by tidal erosion, the **Tetrapod Trackway** is by far the oldest set of footprints in Europe at 370 million years. The island is also dotted with holy wells, ogham stones, and souterrains, mostly on the island's northern and western sides. None of these sites are properly signposted, though, so it's worth asking at the **Valentia Heritage Centre** (Jane St., on the north side of Knightstown, tel. 066/947-6411, daily Apr.-Sept., €3.50) for detailed directions. There's more information on the Valentia-U.S. transatlantic link here as well.

Christened after (and planned by) the local landlord, the "knight of Kerry," **Knightstown** is a delightful village with two bustling pubs, a diving center, and a ferry to Renard Point (5 km from Cahersiveen). The dearth of accommodations no doubt keeps the place relatively untouristy.

Valentia Island Sea Sports (on the pier, tel. 066/947-6204 or 087/242-0714, www.valentiaislandseasports.com, 9am-8pm daily May-Aug., by appointment Sept.-Oct.) offers weeklong **diving** courses as well as full equipment and boat rental for experienced divers.

For **sea angling** excursions, contact **Nealie Lyne** (tel. 087/687-1261, www.valentiaangling.com), who operates the *Mary Frances* out of Valentia and Portmagee.

Food and Accommodations

The service might be on the slow side, but **Boston's** (Jane St., perpendicular to the pier, tel. 066/947-6140, food served noon-9:30pm daily, €9-19) serves great pub grub. Nonsmokers can also savor the irony in all those vintage tobacco ads on the walls.

A huge, rambling Victorian (formerly a hostel), the **Royal Hotel** (on the pier, tel. 066/947-6144, www.royalvalentia.ie, €40-80 pp) is very convenient for divers and drinkers alike (as Knightstown's most popular pub is here too). You'll get basic en suite B&B at **Spring Acre** (on the west end of the village, tel. 066/947-6141, www.springacrebb.com,

Mar.-Oct., €40 pp, s €50), which is right on the promenade (just across the road from the car ferry to Renard Point). There are beautiful views of sea and peninsula from the front bedrooms, and the mattresses are comfortable.

Getting There

Valentia Island is off the Ring of Skellig via a bridge at Portmagee, and Knightstown is on the island's eastern end (7 km from the bridge); there is no public transportation. Taking the **car ferry** (runs 8:15am-10pm Mon.-Sat. and 9am-10pm Sun. Apr.-Sept., single/return €7/10 cars, €2/3 cyclists, €1.50/2 pedestrians) from Knightstown to Renard Point will save you time and gas if you're headed to Cahersiveen and other points east; the passage is less than five minutes.

★ THE SKELLIG ISLANDS

George Bernard Shaw described these islands—**Skellig Michael** (Sceilig Mhichíl, "Michael's Rock," after the archangel) and **Small Skellig** (Sceilig Beag), a UNESCO World Heritage site—as "an incredible, impossible, mad place. I tell you the thing does not belong to any world that you and I have lived and worked in; it is part of our dream world." No visit to Ireland is quite complete without experiencing the breathtaking precariousness of the 6th-century monastery on Skellig Michael, perched on a crag 180 meters above the waves, with a long ascent on true "stairway to heaven" rock steps that are more than 1,400 years old. The Skellig Islands have been inhabited mainly by birds since the last monks departed in the 12th century. (Way more recently, the closing scene of *Star Wars* VII was filmed here!) Small Skellig is a designated bird sanctuary, and from the larger island it resembles the mother of all pillow fights.

Once ashore on Skellig Michael, you'll begin a long ascent of the island, climbing the same steps used by the monks for six centuries. (It's astonishing to remind oneself that none of this existed when the monks

The Skellig Islands are home to puffins, gannets, petrels, and many other bird species.

first arrived in the 6th century AD. Talk about penitential works!) The monastery consists of six beehive huts used for sleeping and living quarters, an oratory, a high cross, and a very small graveyard. A dozen monks would have lived here at a time. While their life was arduous, it wasn't unbearable: They fished, gardened, and kept livestock. Rainwater was collected in cisterns under the courtyard; the cisterns are still there, though the water is definitely not potable!

The monastery survived many attacks over the centuries. The monks finally left in the 12th century, but not because the rough, secluded lifestyle became too difficult; the Normans were moving in, along with a more modern religious organization that had everlessening respect for ascetic ideals and the "spiritual warfare" the monks believed was necessary to preserve the souls of those on the mainland.

In the 19th century, lighthouse keepers and their families lived on Skellig Michael and used the oratory as their church, whitewashing its interior. At the turn of the 20th century it was decided that the structure should be conserved. Today a very smart and engaging guide lives on the island during the tourist season—a population of one.

All ferry operators let you have two hours on the island, which is enough time for an uphill hike, a lecture on the history of the monastery, a picnic lunch (there are no facilities on the island), and lots of picture-taking. Don't eat in the monastery (you can eat anywhere outside it). Skellig Michael hosts around 15,000 annual visitors, so it's best to visit in April, early May, or late September.

Getting There

Skellig Michael is 12 kilometers off the coast of the Iveragh Peninsula; be forewarned that the 45-minute boat trip (as long as 90 minutes from Caherdaniel) can be rough, so bring your motion-sickness medicine. The round-trip ferry passage costs €40/50 in shoulder/high season, and all operators run April or May through September.

If you're staying at Portmagee, try **Brendan Casey** (tel. 066/9472437 or 087/239-5470, www.skelligislands.com, departure from Portmagee Pier 10am daily), who will also steer you around Small Skellig for better bird-watching. **Sea Quest** (Valentia Island, tel. 066/947-6214 or 087/236-2344, www.skelligsrock.com, departing Portmagee 9:45am) is another option.

Another ferry operator leaves from Caherdaniel: **John O'Shea** (tel. 087/689-8431 or 087/964-6325, departs Bunavalla Pier in Caherdaniel 11am daily), who also does fishing trips.

If you prefer to leave from Ballinskelligs, contact **Sean Feehan** (tel. 066/947-9182 or 086/417-6612, www.skelligsboats.com, departs Ballinskelligs Pier between 10am and noon daily), who also runs weekend diving excursions.

CAHERSIVEEN

The "capital" of the Ring of Kerry, **Cahersiveen** (Cathair Saidhbhín, "Fort of Little Saidhbh," also spelled Cahirciveen, Cahirsiveen, or Caherciveen) is a small and surprisingly untouristy market town with an earthy, unselfconscious charm. Cahersiveen's claim to fame is the "Great Liberator" and uncrowned king of Ireland, Daniel O'Connell, who was born just outside town. This place is rich in history in other ways, too, with several Iron Age ring forts (only two of which have been reconstructed; the others are so ruinous you might not even notice them) and eerie Ballycarbery Castle on the far side of the River Fertha estuary, which is spanned by a 289-meter, late-19th-century railway bridge. For a generous helping of local history, don't miss the museum at the Old Barracks Heritage Centre.

Cahersiveen's primary street changes names several times, West Main (or New) to Main to Church to New Market to East End as you move west to east.

Sights

The Old Barracks Heritage Centre

(Bridge St., tel. 066/947-2777, 10am-5:30pm Mon.-Sat. and 1pm-5:30pm Sun. June-Sept., 10am-4:30pm Mon.-Fri., 11am-4:30pm Sat., 1pm-5pm Sun. Oct.-May, €4) is housed in the erstwhile Royal Irish Constabulary barracks, which were built between 1869 and 1871, burned in 1922 by anti-treaty forces, and rebuilt in 1991. With its slender turrets and sickly hued facade, the building itself seems amusingly out of place in this workaday town; the story goes, of course, that the British mixed up the building plans with those for another barracks on the northwest Indian frontier. The museum relies heavily on exhibition boards to tell the stories of Daniel O'Connell and many lesser-known local luminaries, like Monsignor Hugh O'Flaherty, a.k.a. "the Scarlet Pimpernel of the Vatican," and playwright Sigerson Clifford (whose exhibit includes a copy of his hilarious funeral instructions). This might not sound very exciting, but for a lover of history the sheer analysis and frank insight on these panels is entirely worth the price of admission. (The downside of this kind of presentation is that the museum isn't especially kid-friendly.)

It's so cold, cavernous, and gloomy, you might be forgiven for thinking the 19th-century **O'Connell Memorial Church** (Main St.) is *real* Gothic. As far as anyone knows, it's one of only three churches in the world named after a layperson.

Cahersiveen's most important historical sights are over the River Fertha bridge at a distance of about 2.5 kilometers; all are clearly signposted. There isn't much to see at the spooky, ivy-choked **Ballycarbery Castle,** and technically you aren't supposed to hop the fence to check it out. Built in the 15th century by the MacCarthy clan, the castle was later occupied by the O'Connells until the advent of Cromwell in 1652.

After the castle turnoff (about three kilometers from town) you'll pass a reconstructed Iron Age ring fort, **Cahergall,** and another called **Leacanabuaile** situated on a neighboring hill. Keep going until you reach the small car park, from where the separate paths to both forts begin. (The access road for Leacanabuaile is marked "private road—no cars.") Cahergall features an amphitheater-like interior with a grassy rampart about two meters wide, which you can walk all around, as well as the walls of a central beehive hut; this was excavated in 1991, the yield a small trove of metal tools in fragments.

To get to the castle and ring forts, turn onto Bridge Street, pass the barracks, and follow the signposts. On this same road, before you reach the forts, you'll come upon the ruinous **Abbey of the Holy Cross,** the final resting place of Daniel O'Connell's parents, Morgan and Catherine.

Activities and Recreation

Walk or bike to the sights on the far side of the Fertha estuary, or to **White Strand** (5 km from town across the bridge, clearly signposted), a pretty beach with a view of Valentia Island. Pick up a free list of short walking routes (3-5.5 km long) at the Old Barracks Heritage Centre.

For fishing excursions, contact **Kerry Sea Angling Charters** (tel. 066/947-2244 or 087/260-0748, www.kerryseaanglingcharters. com). Boats depart the Cahersiveen Marina.

Food

Even if you're just passing through, be sure to stop for lunch at ★ **Cafésiveen** (11 Main St., tel. 066/401-0404, 9am-5pm Mon.-Fri., 9am-4pm Sat., under €10), a warm and friendly coffee shop that manages to feel hip and country-kitchen at the same time. The salads, soups, and sandwiches are fresh, imaginative, and delicious, with abundant veg and gluten-free options. This is certainly one of the very best eateries on the Ring of Kerry. **Helen's** (Main St., tel. 066/947-2056, hours vary, under €8) is more of a small-town coffee shop, a good option if you're looking for the full fry. The roasted potatoes are thoroughly delish. For hearty, great-value pub grub with a few surprises (like a vegetarian cutlet!), try **O'Driscoll's** (8 New Market St., tel. 066/947-2531, food served 12:30pm-9pm daily, €6-15), a delightfully unassuming "old man's pub."

The fanciest eatery in town is **QC's** (3 Main St., tel. 066/947-2244, www.qcbar.com, noon-3pm Mon.-Sat. and 6pm-9:30pm daily May-Oct., open for dinner Fri.-Sun. Nov.-Apr., bar €11-16, restaurant €17-28), a classy but relaxed pub-cum-restaurant rightly renowned for its über-fresh seafood dishes. Everything is caught that morning by the owners' fisher kin. The place itself is dimly lit, with a more formal elevated dining area in the rear, but you can get less pricey, fish-and-chips kind of bar food up front. Exposed stone walls back gorgeous landscape paintings by local artists (many of which are for sale). And as with all top Irish restaurants, the lone vegetarian option is an excellent one; in fact, the only downside is the slow service.

Entertainment and Events

If telling your life story to a bunch of crusty old Irishmen you've known for five minutes sounds like fun, head to **Mike Murt's** (East

End, tel. 066/947-2396), which sells hardware and farming equipment on the side . . . or is a hardware store pulling pints on the side, depending on how you look at it.

The best spot for music sessions is **The Shebeen** (East End, tel. 066/947-2361)— nightly in summer and Wednesday-Sunday in low season. Otherwise, the pool table and dartboard will keep you occupied. Other live trad venues include the **East End Bar** (East End, tel. 066/947-2361), with music on Fridays, and the **Skeilig Rock** (New St., tel. 066/948-1567), with trad almost nightly.

The most happenin' time of the year is the weekend in August when the **Cahersiveen Festival of Music & the Arts** (tel. 066/947-2589, www.celticmusicfestival.com) draws an international crowd for art and music workshops, free concerts, street performances, lectures, art exhibitions, and guided walks.

Shopping

At **Gallery One** (Church St., tel. 066/947-2346), the local arts and crafts cooperative, you'll find woolen goods, landscape paintings, pottery, woodwork, and plenty more. In a deconsecrated Anglican church, the **Old Oratory** (Church St., tel. 066/947-2996) is primarily a wedding and concert venue these days, but they sometimes host a crafts market.

Accommodations

There aren't quite as many accommodations as you might expect, being on the Ring of Kerry and all. Proprietors will generally be delighted to arrange a trip to the Skelligs for you.

Backpackers should head for the 30-bed IHH **Sive Hostel** (15 East End, tel. 066/947-2717, www.sivehostel.ie, dorms €20, private rooms €24 pp), an immaculate townhouse with comfortable beds and a very helpful and informative owner. Also in the town center is **O'Shea's** (Church St., tel. 066/947-2402, www.osheasbnb.com, €35 pp, s €40-45), a spacious 18th-century home across the street from the bus stop. This should be your top choice if you're planning to spend the night in the pubs.

It means "Magic Nook" in Irish, and **Cúl Draíochta** (Points Cross, 1.5 km west of town on the N70, tel. 066/947-3141, www. Culdraiochta.ie, €33-39 pp, s €40-45) won't disappoint, what with sea and mountain views from the bedrooms in this cheerful, purpose-built, well-maintained bungalow set back from the main road. The welcome is a traditional one (with tea and fresh homemade scones), and a four-course dinner (€20) is served with advance notice. (Note that there's a guest lounge with television rather than sets in the rooms.)

The **Ring of Kerry Hotel** (Valentia Rd., 1 km west of town on the N70, tel. 066/947-2543, www.ringofkerryhotel.com, €55 pp), sister of the Ballinskelligs Inn, offers the same friendly, nothing's-too-much-trouble management style and smallish-but-comfortable rooms.

Information and Services

The Old Barracks Heritage Centre also dispenses **tourist information** (Bridge St., tel. 066/947-2777, 10am-5:30pm Mon.-Sat. and 1pm-5:30pm Sun. June-Sept., 10am-4:30pm Mon.-Fri., 11am-4:30pm Sat., 1pm-5pm Sun. Oct.-May). There's an ATM at the **Bank of Ireland** on Main Street beside the church.

Getting There and Around

Cahersiveen is 62 kilometers west of Killarney on the N70 (picking up the N72 from Killarney to Killorglin). **Bus Éireann** (tel. 064/663-4777) runs a Ring of Kerry service, stopping at Cahersiveen and other towns along the N70 (#279 and #280, 2/day Mon.-Sat. all year, 3-4/day Mon.-Sat. and 2/day Sun. June-Sept.).

You can reach Knightstown on Valentia Island by **car ferry** (runs 8:15am-10pm Mon.-Sat. and 9am-10pm Sun. Apr.-Sept., single/ return €7/10 cars, €2/3 cyclists, €1.50/2 pedestrians) from Renard Point (5 km west of Cahersiveen off the N70).

Bike rental is available from **Eamonn Casey** (New St., tel. 066/947-2474, www. bikehirekerry.com, €16/80 per day/week).

The Kerry Way

At 215 kilometers, the Kerry Way is the republic's longest walking trail, and it's also the best way to experience the Kerry highlands—a region far less traveled than Killarney or the coastal Ring of Kerry but every bit as scenic. Beginning and ending in Killarney, the path winds along the eastern shores of the national park's famous three lakes, forking just south of the Upper Lake to form a great loop that mostly follows the coastline of the Iveragh Peninsula. Most hikers turn right at this fork to proceed in a counterclockwise direction: through the Black Valley, Macgillicuddy's Reeks (along the flank of Corrán Tuathail, Ireland's loftiest peak), and pretty wooded Glencar to Glenbeigh on the northeast of the peninsula; west to Cahersiveen; south through Waterville to Caherdaniel; then east to Kenmare before heading back north to Killarney. The whole route will take 10-12 days, though many travelers choose to walk only a portion of it and return to Killarney by bus. The three-day stretch from Killarney to Glenbeigh is the most challenging, and arguably the most visually rewarding.

For everything else you need to know—where to sleep, travel tips and caveats, what to expect along the trail—check out the helpful Kerry Way.com (www.kerryway.com).

For a taxi, ring **McCarthy's** (Church St., tel. 066/947-2249).

GLENCAR

The scattered and delightfully isolated region of Glencar lies at the western foot of **Corrán Tuathail,** and it's possible to base yourself here to scale it; the **Kerry Way** also meanders through. Even if you're just doing the regular Ring of Kerry route, take an hour or two to get off the N70 and dip into these Kerry highlands east of Glenbeigh. A local road encircles the placid **Lough Caragh,** ringed in gorse bushes and thick evergreen forests over hefty hills.

The few B&Bs cater to long-distance walkers and mountain climbers. **Stepping Stone** (Maghanlawaun, 26 km south of Killorglin via the Ballaghbeama Gap, tel. 066/976-0215, www.steppingstonebandb.com, closed Nov., €12/20 for 1/2 people camping, B&B €38 pp, s €65) has an adjoining café (preposterously named "Cooky Monsters") with a reputation for the island's most delicious hot chocolate. Note that there's only one seating for dinner, at 7pm (3-course meal €28.50). A package deal (B&B, dinner, and a packed lunch) is the best value. Stepping Stone is a little less than 10 kilometers southeast of Glencar on a local road.

A spacious, charming old farmhouse in a truly lovely location overlooking the Caragh River, **Blackstones House** (15 km off the N70 on a local road just south of Lough Caragh, clearly signposted, tel. 066/976-0164, blstones@iol.ie, Apr.-Oct., €33 pp, s €45) offers four-course evening meals with advance notice (usually salmon or local lamb, and wine is included) and two self-catering cottages. After turning off the N70 for Caragh Lake (the turnoff is opposite the Bianconi Inn), just follow the signposts for the B&B.

GLENBEIGH

This village is the standard first stop on the Ring of Kerry coach tours, complete with Irish coffee and a quick walk-around at the overpriced **Kerry Bog Village** (on the N70, tel. 066/976-9184, www.kerrybogvillage.ie, 9am-6pm daily, €6.50). That said, Kerry Way walkers might want to stay at the curiously named **Sleepy Camel Hostel** (on the N70, tel. 066/976-8660, www.thesleepycamel.com, dorms €20, d €23-25 pp), which earns top marks for cleanliness and hospitality (and the price includes continental breakfast). Even if you're just driving through, you might want to make a detour for a walk (or icy swim) at the Blue Flag **Rossbeigh Strand** (3.5 km west of the village on the R564).

★ KILLARNEY NATIONAL PARK

Designated a UNESCO Biosphere Reserve in 1981, the glorious Killarney National Park comprises 102 square kilometers of lakes, mountains, and forest teeming with both indigenous and exotic plant- and wildlife. Killarney is also Ireland's oldest national park, established in 1932 with the bequest of Muckross Estate from the Bourn family and their son-in-law, Irish Senator Arthur Vincent. The adjacent lands of the former Kenmare Estate, most recently owned by an Irish-American businessman named John McShain, were added to the park in 1989.

Whether you just want a leisurely stroll, an afternoon biking excursion, a paddle to an uninhabited island, or a hardcore mountain-climb, Killarney has boundless opportunities for outdoor recreation. The park encompasses three lakes and four mountains—Torc (535 meters), Mangerton (840 meters), Purple (832 meters), and Shehy (570 meters)—as well as Muckross House and Gardens, Muckross Abbey, and Ross Castle.

The Lower Lake

Lough Leane (or Lower Lake) means "Lake of Learning," a reference to the 7th-century monastery founded by St. Finian the Leper on **Inisfallen Island.** The 11th- to 13th-century *Annals of Innisfallen* have provided much of what we know of early monastic Ireland; the manuscript is now in the Bodleian Library at Oxford (along with the *Book of Glendalough* and loads of other Irish biblio-treasures). You can rent a rowboat at the pier at **Ross Castle** (2.5 km west of the pedestrian entrance opposite the cathedral, on the lake's eastern shore, tel. 064/663-5851, 9:30am-5:30pm daily mid-Mar.-May and Sept.-mid-Oct., 9am-6:30pm daily June-Aug., 9:30am-4:30pm Tues.-Sun. mid-Oct.-mid-Nov., €4) to reach the ruins, which include a 12th-century oratory with a remarkable Romanesque doorway.

The castle itself was erected in the late 15th century by the O'Donoghue Ross chieftains, and in 1652 Cromwell's forces circumvented a prophecy that the castle would never be taken by land—by having a boat anchored in Castlemaine Harbour transported down the River Laune and set afloat on the Lower Lake. Seeing that the prophecy was about to be ful-filled, the castle's Irish defenders waved the white flag without further ado. Ross Castle is now furnished with 16th- and 17th-century furniture, and the 40-minute guided tour em-phasizes the unhygienic conditions of medieval life. There isn't so much to see that you should waste an hour inside on a sunny day, but if storm clouds are looming, it's worth a visit.

Another site of note on the eastern shore of the Lower Lake is the **copper mine** on a small peninsula just south of the castle (in-aptly known as Ross Island), which dates to the early Bronze Age (c. 2000 BC).

Near the park entrance is **Knockreer House and Gardens** (about half a kilometer west of the cathedral entrance, clearly signposted), former home of the last Earl of Kenmare. The original Victorian manor was destroyed in a fire, and the current edifice dates to the 1950s. It now serves as the **National Park Research and Education Centre** (tel. 064/663-5960, killarneynationalpark@ealga.ie), which puts on conservation and ecology workshops for students and groups. It isn't generally open to the public, though the gardens are.

Muckross

Killarney's **Middle Lake** is also known as **Muckross Lake.** "Muckross" derives from the Irish for "Pig Peninsula" (Muc Rois), so named for the area's former population of wild pigs. Muckross Lake is encircled by a bike path, but it is essential that you ride in a counterclockwise direction.

An ancient yew tree grows in the cloister of 15th-century **Muckross Abbey** (4 km south of town off the N71/Kenmare road, 7-minute walk from the parking lot and jaunting car depot, tel. 064/663-1440, 10:30am-5pm

Killarney National Park

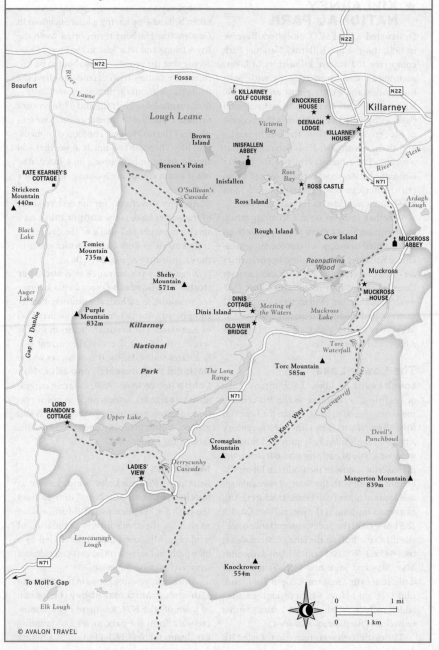

mid-June-Aug., free), a romantic sight. It's possible that the tree predates the monastery, and the cloister was built around it. The abbey has the nefarious Oliver Cromwell—who else?—to thank for its ruined state.

The most popular attraction in the park is the splendid Victorian **Muckross House and Gardens** (6 km south of town off the N71/Kenmare road, 15-minute walk from the parking lot and jaunting car depot, tel. 064/663-1440, www.muckross-house.ie, 9am-5:30pm daily Nov.-mid-March, 9am-6pm daily mid-Mar.-June and Sept.-Oct., 9am-7pm daily July-Aug., open for tourist info all year, €9, joint ticket to house and farms €15), country manor of the Herbert and Vincent families. In anticipation of a visit from Victoria in 1861—and hoping for a title—the Herberts spent most of their fortune doing up the house to impress the queen and her entourage, but the visit lasted only two nights, Albert died a few months later, Herbert never got his title, and they went bankrupt soon afterward. The Vincent family donated the house and grounds to the state in 1932, and it's been impeccably restored and maintained with 70 percent of the house's original furniture. Every room is full of stunning art and antiques, with the requisite portraits of anemic white-wigged magistrates and elaborate silver tea services—not to mention the frighteningly vast collection of mounted deer heads (most of them in skeletal form). Admission is through an excellent 45-minute guided tour.

In addition to a deluxe craft emporium downstairs (there are potters, bookbinders, and weavers with workshops on the premises), there's also a rather posh restaurant with a wine license and views of Torc Mountain and the gardens.

And here's a fun time-warp experience for the kiddies: **Muckross Traditional Farms** (1pm-6pm weekends mid-Mar.-Apr. and Oct., 1pm-6pm daily May, 10am-7pm daily June-Sept.) has three separate, fully functioning farms using technology (if you can call it that) from the 1930s.

West of here, the three lakes converge at the

Meeting of the Waters, a popular spot with local anglers. **Dinis Cottage** (at the Meeting of the Waters, signposted, tel. 064/663-1954, 9am-6pm daily May-Sept.), a turn-of-the-19th-century hunting lodge, serves tea and light snacks.

Also clearly signposted across the N71 from Muckross Lake is **Torc Waterfall.** Tourists frequently brave these slippery rocks in questionable footwear for a snapshot.

The Upper Lake

Smallest of the three and dappled with "fairy islands," the **Upper Lake** lies just west of the Kenmare road (N71), and there is a small car park just south of **Ladies' View.** This lookout over Macgillicuddy's Reeks, Purple Mountain, and the lake below was so named because Victoria's ladies-in-waiting paused here during the queen's tour of Killarney in 1861. A walking trail west along the lake's southern shore leads to **Lord Brandon's Cottage,** another über-touristy 19th-century hunting lodge turned restaurant, which is also signposted just before the southern terminus of the Gap of Dunloe.

Information

The national park **visitors center** (tel. 064/663-1440 or 064/663-5960, www.heritageireland.ie, 9am-6pm daily mid-Mar.-June and Sept.-Oct., 9am-7pm daily July-Aug., free) is at Muckross House. There is also an information office at the **Torc Waterfall** near the eastern shore of Muckross Lake (9:30am-6:30pm daily June-mid-Sept.).

For a guided walk, contact **Richard Clancy** (Currach, Aghadoe, tel. 064/663-3471 or 087/639-4362, www.killarneyguidedwalks.com, 2-hour walk €9), whose guided tours (mostly two-hour walks, but half- and full-day trips can be arranged) cover the history and botany of the park. Tours depart from the gas station opposite the cathedral at 11am daily all year.

Getting There and Around

There are **two entrances** to the park: one

opposite St. Mary's Cathedral at the end of New Street and the other east of Muckross Lake on the Kenmare road. If you want to see Ross Castle, take the cathedral entrance; otherwise, head down the N71 (a distance of five kilometers, certainly walkable, but get an early start if you want to get as far as the Torc Waterfall).

Cycling is the best way to see the park; rent a bike in Killarney Town. You can also hire a **jaunting car** with a crusty old local (a "jarvey"), though you'll cover far more ground hiking or biking. Frankly, this horse-drawn option is the lazy man's way to see the park, and walkers don't appreciate having to step around the horse dung all over the roads. All that said, it's actually the most practical option for families with small children; a one-hour tour for four people will run you roughly €40, €60 for two hours, though the price is negotiable. There's a depot at Kenmare Place in the center of town and another on the N71 at the Muckross entrance to the park (where you can also park your car).

WEST OF KILLARNEY NATIONAL PARK
The Gap of Dunloe

A marked contrast to the lushness of the national park, the glacier-carved Gap of Dunloe cuts south through a string of stark, ominously beautiful mountains: Macgillicuddy's Reeks to the west and the Tomies and Purple Mountains to the east.

Cars are forbidden in the gap in high season, and though it's possible to drive through in the off-season, this is not recommended—you'll get caught behind every jaunting car and hiking group on your way south (not to mention the scornful looks you might receive from said parties!). Walking and cycling are the best ways to see the gap; you can hire a jaunting car outside **Kate Kearney's Cottage** (a tourist-trap tearoom and restaurant), but the pony-trap route just dips into the mountains before returning you to the cottage, so you won't get to see more than a mile or two of dramatic scenery.

A 1.5-hour ride will run you about €20 per person.

To get to the Gap of Dunloe entrance from Killarney Town, take the Beaufort road (N72) and you'll see it clearly signposted on your left 10 kilometers west of town. If you follow the gap's full length, roughly 11 kilometers, you'll come to the junction of the R568 and the N71, also known as **Moll's Gap,** offering another stark and scenic panorama.

Those walking the Kerry Way—and/or tackling Corrán Tuathail, Ireland's highest peak—will probably need to pass the night at the An Óige **Black Valley Hostel** (13 km south of Beaufort Town along the Gap of Dunloe, also accessible from Moll's Gap on the Kenmare end of the N71, tel. 064/663-4712, www.blackvalleyhostel.com, Mar.-Sept., dorms €18-19, 11am-5pm lockout), but be forewarned that you've no hope of a hot shower. There is an adjoining grocery store though.

★ Macgillicuddy's Reeks

Ireland's highest mountain range, **Macgillicuddy's Reeks** (or Na Cruacha Dubha, "The Black Tops"), looms west of the national park. These glacier-carved, mist-shrouded sandstone peaks were named for a local landowning family and are joined by ridges with colorful names like "Hag's Tooth" and "Devil's Ladder." King of the Reeks is **Corrán Tuathail** (sometimes anglicized "Carrauntoohill"), the country's tallest mountain at 1,040 meters. A trip to the summit takes at least four hours round-trip, and most climbers leave in the late morning to avoid the early-morning cloud cover. Corrán Tuathail aside, "the Reeks" offer the only other two Irish peaks over 1,000 meters in their 20-kilometer stretch: 1,010-meter **Beenkeragh** (Binn Chaorach, "Mountain of Sheep") and 1,001-meter **Caher**.

Unless you're a seasoned climber, consider a guided hike (since there are no well-trod paths on Corrán Tuathail, orienteering experience is a must); try **Con Moriarty** (tel. 087/221-4002, www.hiddenirelandtours.com), who provides tidbits of archaeology, folklore, flora, and fauna along with the requisite navigational skills.

KILLARNEY TOWN

You'd be smart to avoid Killarney, as it is garishly overcommercialized; it may not be as convenient, but Kenmare makes a much more pleasant base for exploring the national park. Most of Killarney's restaurants are mediocre and overpriced, many of the pubs push the old stage-Irish kitsch (some even charge a cover for their music sessions), and a sprawling indoor shopping mall adjoining the bus and rail stations dominates the eastern end of town. Droves of eager tourists keep on spilling out of those jumbo charter buses.

If you want to experience the national park but don't have wheels, though, you're going to have to spend a bit of time in town. Consider coming in the off-season; iffy weather for a blissful absence of charter buses is a worthwhile trade-off. (Whatever you do, don't come in July or August.)

Sights

National park aside, Killarney's primary sights are mostly ecclesiastical. The awe-inspiring **St. Mary's Cathedral** (Cathedral Pl. at the western end of Lower New St., tel. 064/663-1014) is a cavernous neo-Gothic edifice built between 1842 and 1855. The unfinished church was used as a hospital during the famine, and victims often gathered on the lawn outside.

A highlight in Killarney is a typically superb five-light Harry Clarke window (designed by apprentice Richard King) that features the Seven Joys of the Blessed Virgin as well as St. Francis's stigmata; above these scenes are three rosettes, each depicting one element of the Holy Trinity. The window is above the organ gallery at the 19th-century **Church of the Holy Trinity** at the still-active **Franciscan Friary** (Fair Hill, tel. 064/663-1334), which also features an elaborate Flemish-style altarpiece.

Activities and Recreation

What are you waiting for? Get thee to Killarney National Park!

There are plenty of golf courses in the area, chief of which is the **Killarney Golf and Fishing Club** (4 km west of town on the N72/Killorglin road, tel. 064/663-1034, www.killarney-golf.com). Founded in 1893, it offers a championship course on the Lower Lake with stupendous views of the national park and Macgillicuddy's Reeks.

It's possible to fish in the national park; stop by **O'Neill's** (6 Plunkett St., tel. 064/663-1970) for permit and equipment.

Equestrians should head on over to the **Killarney Riding Stables** (Ballydowney, signposted on the N72 2 km west of town, tel. 064/663-1686, www.killarneyridingstables.com), which hosts one- to six-hour treks through the national park. Beginners are welcome.

Food

Nearly all the pubs do food at lunchtime, but you'll want to be off walking or pedaling around the park. Pick up fixings for a picnic lunch at the Tesco grocery store on Beech Street, or get sandwiches (on freshly baked bread) for takeaway at **Cathleen's Country Kitchen** (17 New St., tel. 066/663-3778, 8am-10pm daily, under €10). Another good spot for a hearty lunch or delectable home-baking is **Noelle's Retro Café** (Old Market Ln., off New St., tel. 087/687-3364, 9am-8pm Mon.-Sat., under €12), which offers gluten-free (though not vegan) options. Enjoy your tea and daintily frosted cupcake in one of the comfortable nostalgia-themed rooms.

For two scoops of freshly made Bailey's ice cream or a cup of gourmet coffee, turn the corner for **Murphy's** (37 Main St., tel. 066/915-2644, www.murphysicecream.ie, 11am-6:30pm daily, €5-8). Tucked down a quiet lane off High Street, **Stonechat** (Fleming's Ln., tel. 064/663-4295, www.stonechatkillarney.ie, 10am-10pm Mon.-Sat., 2/4-course early-bird menu €20/24 6pm-7:30pm, €12-20) is a romantic, low-key,

Killarney Town

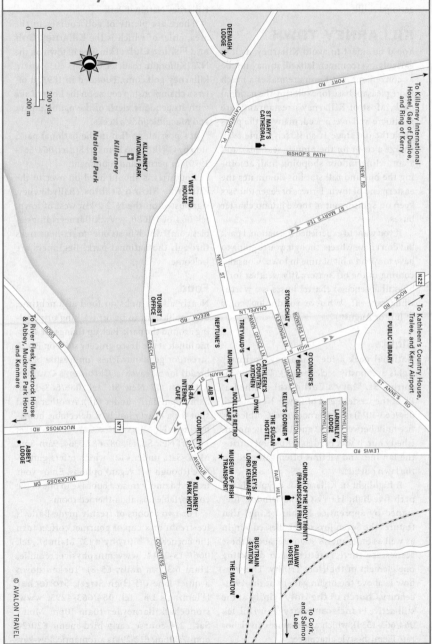

0
0

200 yds
200 m

National Park

KILLARNEY NATIONAL PARK
Killarney

DEENAGH LODGE ★

PORT RD

To Killarney International Hostel, Gap of Dunloe, and Ring of Kerry

CATHEDRAL PL

ST MARY'S CATHEDRAL ✝

BISHOP'S PATH

NEW RD

ST MARY'S TER

▼ WEST END HOUSE

NEW ST

N22

ROCK RD

To Kathleen's Country House, Tralee, and Kerry Airport

■ PUBLIC LIBRARY

ST ANNE'S RD

BEECH RD

▲ TOURIST OFFICE ■

CHAPEL LN

STONECHAT ▼

FLEMINGS LN

PAWN OFFICE LN

BOWERS LN

HIGH ST

O'CONNOR'S ▼

▼ BRICIN

HILLIARD'S LN

▼ NEPTUNE'S

TREVAUD'S ▼

CATHLEEN'S COUNTRY KITCHEN

DYNE

MAIN ST

MURPHY'S ▼

BEECH RD

MANGERTON LN

KELLY'S CORNER

SUNNYHILL VIEW

SUNNYHILL UPR

LARKINLEY LODGE

SUNNYHILL LWR

LEWIS RD

ROSS RD

To River Flesk, Muckrock House & Abbey, Muckross Park Hotel, and Kenmare

N71

MUCKROSS RD

RI-RA INTERNET CAFÉ ■

AIB ■

▼ NOELLE'S RETRO CAFÉ

THE SUGAN HOSTEL

COURTNEYS ▼

EAST AVENUE RD

MUSEUM OF IRISH TRANSPORT ★

BUCKLEY'S/ LORD KENMARE'S ▼

FAIR HILL

CHURCH OF THE HOLY TRINITY (FRANCISCAN FRIARY) ✝

MUCKROSS DR

● ABBEY LODGE

● KILLARNEY PARK HOTEL

COUNTESS RD

THE MALTON ●

BUS/TRAIN STATION ●

RAILWAY HOSTEL ●

To Cork, and Salmon Leap

good-value alternative to Killarney's plethora of pretentious eateries; though the menu is relatively unadventurous, vegetarians (and vegans) are well catered for.

But the most veg-friendly restaurant in Killarney is **DYNE** (New Market Ln., off High St., tel. 087/190-2567, 6pm-10pm Thurs.-Sat., noon-10pm Sun., €10-16), offering deluxe salads as well as pizzas and pastas in a chill and pleasantly quirky space. Sunday brunch options include pancakes, eggs Benedict, and Turkish *saksuka*.

If you're in the mood for French twists on the standard steak or seafood, try bustling **Treyvaud's** (62 High St., tel. 064/663-3062, www.treyvaudsrestaurant.com, noon-11pm Tues.-Sun., lunch €8-14, dinner €18-27, 2/3-course early bird €25/29). The desserts are scrummy and the lone vegetarian option is *très bon*. Treyvaud's is also a safe bet if you're visiting in low season.

If gourmet boxties (traditional potato pancakes) and fresh seafood sound like just the thing, plan on dinner at **Bricín** (26 High St., tel. 064/663-4902, www.bricin.com, 6pm-9:30pm Tues.-Sat., closed Jan.-Feb., €19-26, 2/3-course early bird €23/26 6pm-6:45pm). With exposed stone walls, romantic lighting, and friendly waitstaff and owners, the ambience is warm and festive. Vegetarians will be thrilled with the deluxe nut roast and mushroom gravy. Desserts (fruit crumble or chocolate cake) are simple but scrummy.

Serving delicious modern Irish fare to the strains of flamenco, **Lord Kenmare's** (College St., above Murphy's pub, tel. 064/663-7245, www.lordkenmares.com, 6pm-10pm daily, €17-29) is refreshingly unpretentious. Some mains are better than others—the corn-fed chicken and the vegetarian pasta dish are safe bets—but the desserts truly put the sparkle on your dining experience; the "real" Bailey's cheesecake is second to none. Reservations are recommended, as the place buzzes with locals any night of the week.

Entertainment and Events

The least touristy music pub in town is **Buckley's** (College St., tel. 064/663-1037), with nightly sessions in high season; the downside of a relatively unselfconscious place like this is that the musicians can be more lax in their performance—showing up a bit later and interspersing more chitchat with their buddies. Just give them an audience and they'll rise to the occasion. Cozier **Courtney's** (Plunkett St., tel. 064/663-2689, www.courtneysbar.com) also offers live trad and folk in the upstairs bar, though not on a regular schedule as such. Courtney's is the only pub in the country licensed to serve Guinness in jam jars. More touristy, but still tolerable, is dim-and-dusty **O'Connor's** (High St., tel. 064/663-1115), which offers nightly sessions.

Shopping

Most of the gift shops in Killarney carry cringe-inducing Irish kitsch, but some stores are worth seeking out. Those visitors looking for cutting-edge Irish fashion and homewares should stop by the local branch of **Kilkenny Design** (3 New St., tel. 064/662-3309, www.kilkennydesign.com). **Quill's Woollen Market** (1 High St., tel. 064/663-2277) has a branch here. And if you need to pick up some new underwear or something, you can always make for the monstrous **Killarney Outlet Centre** (Fair Hill, tel. 064/663-6744, www.killarneyoutletcentre.com).

Bookstores in town include the **Killarney Bookshop** (32 Main St., tel. 064/663-4108), good for picking up OS maps for your hike, and the secondhand **Dungeon Bookshop** (99 College St., 2nd floor, tel. 064/663-6536).

Accommodations

Needless to say, there's no shortage of beds in this town—but it's still not wise to leave it to chance in summer. Two clean, central budget options are the **Railway Hostel** (Fair Hill, tel. 064/663-5299, www.killarneyhostel.com, dorms €14-19, d €22-28 pp, s €32-45) and **Neptune's** (New St., tel. 064/663-5255, www.neptuneshostel.com, dorms €14-22, d €18-27 pp, s €20-35). Bed prices at both hostels include a light continental breakfast.

Outside of town is the An Oige **Killarney International Hostel** (5 km west of town on the N72, Aghadoe House, Fossa, tel. 064/663-1240, www.anoige.ie, year-round, dorms €16-18, d €20-22 pp), an immaculate converted 18th-century hunting lodge set in 75 acres of gardens. It's highly recommended for its clean and spacious kitchen facilities and common areas (often buzzing with school groups), but the location is majorly inconvenient if you're not driving. Though it's just outside the park, you can't actually access the park from anywhere nearby—you've got to walk, pedal, or drive to the entrance in town, opposite the cathedral. A full cooked breakfast is available for €8 (€5 continental), and they'll pack a lunch for you (€7).

Between seen-better-days B&Bs over pubs and guesthouses ostentatiously displaying their five-star AA ratings, quality "budget" B&Bs can seem a bit difficult to come by. Many undistinguished places are positively overpriced. An excellent choice is **Larkinley Lodge** (2 Lower Lewis Rd., tel. 064/663-5142 or 087/238-9537, www.larkinley.ie, €45-60 pp)—unscramble the letters—an immaculately kept townhouse a couple minutes' walk from the College Street roundabout. The rooms are small but comfortable, with stylish bedspreads, a sprinkling of antiques, and real art on the walls. You'll find other townhouses along Lewis and St. Anne's Roads advertising lower rates (just look for the shamrock seal of approval!).

If you have a rental car, consider basing yourself at ★ **Salmon Leap** (Glenflesk, 14 km southeast of town on the N22, tel. 066/775-3005, www.salmonleapfarm.com, €35-55 pp), an 18th-century farmhouse B&B that takes sustainability seriously, with solar panels and biodegradable toiletries. Five minutes in the eco-friendly shower-dome is like spending an hour in a steam room; you'll emerge feeling awesomely refreshed. There's also an early-Christian burial site on the grounds, which could be up to 1,500 years old; ask kindly owner Sean O'Donoghue to take you out back for a quick tour. Heading south toward Cork;

the B&B signpost and turnoff come up quite suddenly on the right (especially in the dark), so drive carefully.

Brick-and-stone, tastefully faux-Gothic **Abbey Lodge** (Muckross Rd., tel. 064/663-4193 www.abbey-lodge.com, €40-55 pp, s €55-95) is easily the most attractive guesthouse along the N71 south of town. It's every bit as nice on the inside, with comfortable rooms furnished with lovely antiques and excellent showers, not to mention the ultra-helpful proprietors, Mr. and Mrs. King. The whole house is a veritable art gallery. And with 15 rooms, it's also large enough to guarantee a greater degree of privacy. You can expect all the same on the other side of town at **Kathleen's Country House** (Tralee Rd., 1 km north of town, signposted on the N22, tel. 064/663-2810, www.kathleens.net, €55-65 pp, s €70): comfy rooms, helpful proprietors, an admirable art collection, more than a hectare of carefully manicured gardens, and greater anonymity (as there are 17 rooms). Kathleen's is ideally situated for golfers, as there are five courses within a five-minute drive (no children under five, though).

Situated directly opposite the Muckross Abbey car park, the ★ **Muckross Park Hotel** (on the N71 5 km south of town, tel. 066/662-3400, www.muckrosspark.com, rooms €140-390, s €70-90) offers a rare combination of elegance and friendliness, old (classic furnishings) and new (pool and spa). If you want to stay in a hotel but aren't too keen on the Killarney town tourist parade, this is an excellent choice. The bartenders at the adjoining Monk's pub are really kind and helpful, too.

There are loads of hotels in and around Killarney, many of which are overwhelmingly ostentatious (and those with park views all too often rate poorly in every other respect). For the height of Victorian elegance with all mod cons, you've got to stay at **The Malton** (East Avenue Rd., tel. 064/663-8000, www.themalton.com, rooms €170-260), gorgeous inside and out—and just as important, the staff are admirably efficient and courteous.

If the gilt-and-marble lobby is too over-whelming, you can always kick back with a pint in a leather armchair by the (albeit gas-lit) fireplace in the classy-yet-atmospheric pub. Be sure to book a spa treatment while you're here.

Another establishment that won't disap-point is the five-star **Killarney Park Hotel** (Kenmare Pl., tel. 064/663-5555, www.killar-neyparkhotel.ie, rooms €270-320), set back from the street for a bit of quiet in the heart of town. Deluxe pool and spa, complimentary DVD rental at reception for the big-screen television in your room (which you'll find to be the antithesis of anonymous corporate chic), fluffy slippers and bathrobes, open fires in the elegant library and other sitting rooms, superb pub and restaurant food, refreshingly unpretentious staff—a room at this top-notch place is worth every euro.

Information and Services

The **tourist office** (Beech Rd., tel. 064/663-1633, www.killarney.ie, 9am-6pm Mon.-Sat. and 10am-6pm Sun. June-Sept., 9:15am-5:30pm Mon.-Sat. Oct.-May) is bustling yet efficient.

You'll have no trouble finding an ATM in this town. The **AIB** (Main St.), **Bank of Ireland** (New St.), and **TSB** (New St.) all have cash machines as well as bureaux de change. There are plenty of pharmacies in town, in-cluding **Shanahan's** (19 Plunkett St., tel. 064/663-2630).

Getting There

Killarney is 33 kilometers south of Tralee and 87 kilometers northwest of Cork City on the N22, and 305 kilometers southwest of Dublin on the N7, picking up the N21 in Limerick and the N23 in Castleisland.

Bus Éireann (Park Rd., behind the out-let center, tel. 064/663-0011) can get you here from Dingle (#281, 1-2 early departures Mon.-Sat. June-mid-Sept., all other times via Tralee), Tralee (#14 or #40, at least 11/day daily), Cork (#40, at least 11/day daily), Kenmare (#270, at least 4/day daily June-Sept.), and most towns on the Ring of Kerry (#279 and #280, 2/day Mon.-Sat. all year, 3-4/day Mon.-Sat. June-Sept. and 2/day Sun.).

From here you can board a direct train ser-vice to Cork, Dublin, or Limerick via **Irish Rail** (off Park Rd., near East Ave. Rd. across from the Malton Hotel, tel. 064/663-1067, at least 4/day daily to each city). There is no quick route from the bus depot to the train station; you have to walk around the outlet mall to get from one to the other.

You can also reach County Kerry by air. The tiny **Kerry Airport** (Farranfore, 15 km north of Killarney on the N22, tel. 066/976-4644, www.kerryairport.ie) has frequent flights from Dublin (4/day Mon.-Fri., 2/day Sat., 3/day Sun. on Aer Arann, tel. 081/821-0210, www.aerarann.com) and London Stansted (1-2/daily on Ryanair, tel. 081/830-3030, www.ryanair.com).

Getting Around

Killarney is eminently walkable; it'll take you less than 15 minutes to foot it from end to end, and most accommodations are within easy walking distance from the center. Rent a cycle from **David O'Sullivan's Bike Shop and Outdoor Store** (49 High St., tel. 064/663-1282, www.killarneyrentabike.com, €15/80 per day/week). O'Sullivan's has outposts all over town (Beech Rd. opposite the tourist of-fice, College St., and Muckross Rd.), so you needn't go out of your way to visit the main shop.

Free parking? No such luck. Ask when booking your room if you'll be able to park your car before you check in. There's a taxi rank on College Square, but you could also ring **John Burke** (tel. 064/663-2448 or 087/263-0323), who has a minibus.

The Beara Peninsula (Kerry Side)

Though "the Beara" is often synonymous with West Cork, the north side of the peninsula is actually part of County Kerry. Of all Kerry's coastline it's the least traversed, a prime opportunity for a bit of peace and quiet just off the tourist merry-go-round. Glenmore Lake in particular is a haven of tranquility, though the lack of amenities necessitates a fair bit of advance planning.

LAURAGH

A scattered hamlet 23 kilometers west of Kenmare, Lauragh (An Láithreach) is the starting point for the stunning, vaguely Alpine Healy Pass through the Caha Mountains south to the hamlet of Adrigole in County Cork, a journey of 11 kilometers. The views farther west along this peninsula are lovely, but not nearly so dramatic as this.

But before turning on to the Healy Pass, pause at Derreen Gardens (signposted on the R573, tel. 064/668-3588, www.derreengarden.com, 10am-6pm daily Apr.-Sept., €7), renowned for Tasmanian tree ferns, gargantuan rhododendrons, camellias, and red cedars. The garden was designed by the fifth Lord Lansdowne when he inherited his title in 1866, and work continued up until the 1950s; the house isn't open to the public.

There aren't many accommodation options in the immediate area, and many visitors choose to see Derreen Gardens as an afternoon trip from Kenmare. A bungalow farmhouse on the northern end of the Healy Pass (translation: an awesome view from your bedroom window), Mountain View (on the R574, tel. 064/668-3143, www.staybeara.com,

Easter-mid-Oct., off-season by arrangement, €35 pp, s €50) offers evening meals featuring fresh seafood.

And in terms of "nightlife," you'll often find live music and set dancing sessions at An Sibin (signposted from the R571, tel. 064/668-3941), a rather self-consciously rustic (and slightly twee) pub that's good fun nevertheless.

The summer-only Killarney-Castletownbere route on Bus Éireann (tel. 064/663-4777) passes through Lauragh (#282 from Castletownbere, #270 from Killarney, 2/day Mon.-Sat.) from late June to the beginning of September.

GLENMORE LAKE

A placid lake nestled in the low Caha Mountains south of Lauragh (and just west of the Healy Pass), Glenmore (also spelled Glanmore) is ringed with evergreens and splashes of purple rhododendrons in early summer. There's next to nothing out here—just one memorable restaurant—but that may be just the reason to go.

For lunch, tea, or dinner, try the ideally situated Josie's Lake View House & Restaurant (clearly signposted off the R574, tel. 064/668-3155, www.josiesrestaurant.ie, hours vary, but generally 11am-9pm or later daily all year, €10-24), with a truly awesome vantage overlooking the lake and surrounding mountains. The bright, airy restaurant itself has a cordial staff and good food—good, not great, but it truly doesn't matter with a view like this!—and the vegetarian options are surprisingly bountiful. Make a reservation for a table with a view.

North Kerry

Most visitors just pass through inland Kerry, with its workaday towns and villages, en route to Dingle, Killarney, and the Ring of Kerry. That said, Tralee makes a good stopover on the way to Dingle.

TRALEE

Some folks seem to want to visit **Tralee** (Trá Lí, "Strand of the Lee") just because it's the location of the annual Rose of Tralee pageant, which is open to girls of Irish heritage as well as native lasses. Though it's a pleasant enough town—the largest in the county—there's little cause to linger, what with all the dramatic landscapes of the Dingle Peninsula and Killarney National Park awaiting you. That said, public transportation connections might necessitate a stopover for the night. The town is north of the slender River Lee, the main street being the Mall, Lower Castle Street, Upper Castle Street, and Boherboy as it proceeds west to east. On a south perpendicular is Denny Street, which culminates in the Kerry County Museum and entrance to the carefully manicured town park; from the main drag, turn north onto Edward Street for the train and bus station. The town's square is one block south of the Mall.

Fans of sport and local Antarctic adventurer Tom Crean will find a fair bit of diversion at the **Kerry County Museum** (Ashe Memorial Hall, Denny St., tel. 066/712-7777, www.kerrymuseum.ie, 10am-4:30pm Tues.-Fri. Jan.-Mar., 9:30am-5:30pm Tues.-Sat. Apr.-May and daily June-Aug., 9:30am-5pm Tues.-Sat. Sept.-Dec., €5). On your way out of town on the Dingle road, you'll spot the restored **Blennerville Windmill** (on the N86 1 km west of town, tel. 066/712-1064, 9:30am-5:30pm Apr.-Oct., €5), which is the largest working windmill in Ireland or Britain. The price of admission gets you an eight-minute audiovisual, a one-room exhibition, and a half-hour guided tour of the windmill itself.

For mostly traditional pub fare, head over to **Kirby's Brogue Inn** (Rock St., tel. 066/718-1998, www.thebrogue.ie, food served 9am-9:30pm daily, €10-24). To get here, head west down the Mall, bear right onto Russell Street, and you'll see Kirby's on your left. Located in the wine cellar of a Georgian townhouse that incorporated the ruins of Tralee Castle, **Finnegan's Cellar Restaurant** (17 Denny St., tel. 066/718-1400, www.finneganswinecellar.com, 5pm-10pm daily, €15-27, 3-course menu €23) serves up reliably good modern Irish (using local meat and seafood, with a couple of veggie options) in the most romantic ambience in town—checkered tablecloths, open fires, rough stone walls, candlelight, the whole shebang.

Siamsa Tíre ("SHAHM-sah TCHEE-reh," Ivy Terrace, west of the county museum and park, tel. 066/712-3055, www.siamsatire.com, €25), Ireland's "national folk theater," hosts film screenings, comedy shows, drama, and concerts, but the primary draw is a series of dance-and-theater performances interpreting the finest tales in the canon of Irish folklore (starts at 8:30pm Mon.-Sat. Apr.-Oct., €18).

Backpackers stay at the pleasingly quirky, IHH **Finnegan's** (17 Denny St., tel. 066/712-7610, www.finneganshostel.ie, dorms €17, d €50 pp), a rambling Georgian townhouse in a central location. On the far side of Tralee's lovely town park is **Green Gables** (1 Clonmore Villas, Ballymullen Rd., tel. 066/712-3354, www.greengablestralee.com, mid-Feb.-mid-Dec., €27-35 pp, s €37-45), a well-kept Victorian townhome painted a handsome olive. The rooms are smallish but full of genuine character (that's no euphemism), and the communal breakfast table is endowed with plenty of fresh fruit. For more upscale Victorian glamour, book a room at the aptly named **Grand Hotel** (Denny St., tel. 066/712-1499, www.grandhoteltralee.com, €45-50 pp, s €60-70), though the bar and reception rooms are more old-fashioned than the rooms are. This is the most popular hotel with Irish weekenders, so be forewarned that the nightclub noise can seep up into some of the rooms on Friday and Saturday nights.

The **tourist office** (Ashe Memorial Hall, tel. 066/712-1288, www.tralee.ie, 9am-5:15pm Mon.-Sat.) is around the corner at the Kerry County Museum, opposite the entrance to the town park on Denny Street.

Two banks with ATMs and bureaux de change are **AIB** (Denny St. and Castle St.) and the **Bank of Ireland** (Castle St.).

Tralee is 32 kilometers north of Killarney on the N22 and 104 kilometers southwest of Limerick on the N21. **Bus Éireann** (John Joe Sheehy Rd., tel. 066/712-3566) offers frequent service to Killarney (#14 or #40, at least 11/day daily), Cork (#40, at least 11/day daily), Galway and the Cliffs of Moher (#50, 2 direct services/day daily), and Dublin and Limerick (#13, 12/day daily). You can also ride **Irish Rail** (John Joe Sheehy Rd., tel. 066/712-3522, at least 2/day Mon.-Sat. from Dublin Heuston).

ARDFERT

In the sleepy village of **Ardfert** (Ard Fhearta, "The Height of the Burial Mounds") are the awe-inspiring remains of **Ardfert Cathedral** (signposted from the R551, in the village center, tel. 066/713-4711, 9:30am-6pm mid-Apr.-Sept., €4). The Dúchas-run site dates from the 6th century (and is associated with St. Brendan the Navigator, who supposedly reached the New World in a curragh at least 800 years before Columbus), though most of the present architecture dates from the 13th century onward. The cathedral is in the English and Gothic styles, with a striking restored Romanesque west doorway made of sandstone (dating to the 12th century); it also boasts the tallest lancet windows in the country, a dozen in all. The round tower was destroyed in 1771, and the stones may have been used to build the site's low surrounding wall. There are two smaller churches on the site: the 15th-century **Temple na Griffin,** so named for an effigy of that mythical beast (also known as a "wyvern"), and the late 12th-century **Templenahoe** ("Church of the Virgin").

The old chancel (reroofed and used for Anglican services in the 17th century) has been converted into a visitors center with a small but informative exhibition that includes two late-13th-century effigies of local bishops anchored to the visitors center wall (one of which has been incorrectly identified as St. Brendan). Though there isn't much else of interest in the vicinity, those who enjoy wandering through monastic ruins will find the cathedral well worth a visit.

Ardfert is nine kilometers northwest of Tralee on the R551 (the Ballyheigue road). The Tralee-Ballybunion **Bus Éireann** (tel. 066/712-3566, #274) service passes through Ardfert, with at least four buses a day late June-early September. Service in the off-season is too infrequent to be of use.

Clare and Limerick

Eastern Clare 248

The Clare Coast 257

The Burren 268

Limerick City 276

Look for ★ to find recommended sights, activities, dining, and lodging.

Highlights

★ **The Cliffs of Moher:** No postcard can convey the misty magnificence of these dramatic cliffs standing sentinel over the waves (page 262).

★ **Gus O'Connor's Pub:** Kick back with a pint and savor a live trad session in Doolin, the mecca of Irish traditional music (page 265).

★ **The Burren Way:** Hike 45 kilometers across a craggy limestone plateau dotted with fragrant wildflowers and prehistoric monuments (page 270).

★ **Dysert O'Dea:** Examine the high crosses, round tower, and intricate Romanesque doorway at Clare's most important monastic site (page 275).

★ **St. Mary's Cathedral:** This spooky 12th-century church contains medieval tombs behind the altar. Its black-oak misericords are unique in Ireland (page 279).

★ **Hunt Museum:** Don't miss Ireland's finest collection of antiquities outside Dublin. Treasures include the 17th-century Galway Chalice and a da Vinci bronze (page 279).

★ **Lough Gur:** Cycle around this picturesque lake and examine its Neolithic wedge tombs,

stone circle, *crannóg,* and other remains (page 282).

C lare and Limerick are the northwestern counties in the province of Munster, demarcated from one another by the River Shannon on the south and east of County Clare. Many tourists head straight for County Clare (An Clár) to

see the dramatic Cliffs of Moher, which are beseiged by coach buses year-round.

Relatively few of those visitors stick around to wander through Clare's wealth of monastic ruins, prehistoric sites, and castles, though some take part in pricey, kitschy-but-fun medieval banquets at Bunratty and Knappogue (where everyone's a lord or lady for an evening). There's also much to be said for the Burren's breathtaking, deceptively barren limestone peaks and plateaus, as well as the county's pretty coastline with its green cliffs and sandy beaches.

The terrain of County Limerick (Luimneach, "Bare Spot") is relatively featureless—mostly flat green farmland—until you reach the Galtee and Ballyhoura mountain chains slipping over the Tipperary and Cork borders. Situated on the River Shannon, Limerick City is still struggling to dispel a reputation for violence and poverty; when you say you've been there many Irish will ask you why.

Yet 21st-century Limerick has a thriving arts scene, as exciting after dark as any other university town. (Many of Ireland's most successful fashion designers, like Merle O'Grady and Laura Kinsella, honed their skills at the city's School of Art and Design.) Suffice it to say this is no longer the Limerick of Frank McCourt's bestselling memoirs, though if you enjoyed *Angela's Ashes* you might want to raise a glass to his memory at South's Pub on O'Connell Avenue, McCourt's favorite watering hole whenever he came home for a visit.

HISTORY

The earliest evidence of human habitation in County Limerick dates to 3500 BC, with the stone remains at Lough Gur dating 500 years later. Clare's megalithic tombs—Poulnabrone and 130 others—are all at least 5,000 years old, and archaeological digs in the Burren have revealed a Neolithic society nourished by the earliest hunters and fishermen, a society that

---

Previous: Doonagore Castle; the Cliffs of Moher. **Above:** one of Kilfenora's 12th-century high crosses.

Clare and Limerick

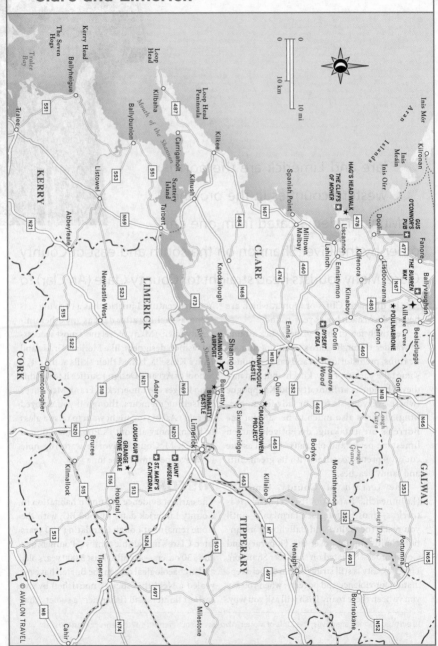

© AVALON TRAVEL

eventually evolved into complex farming and animal husbandry. It's hard to imagine now, but the Burren's limestone plateaus were once covered in soil and light forest. It was those first farmers who cleared the trees for their fields, enabling the gradual soil erosion that resulted in this rocky landscape.

The first missionaries introduced Christianity in the 5th century, and the new religion spread as quickly in Clare and Limerick as it did elsewhere in Ireland. Evidence from early Christian and medieval ring forts shows many farmers lived and worked with their extended families in and around these ring forts, which may have functioned as a method of quarantine against the plague as much as for protection from invaders. Today there are remains of 2,300 stone and earthen forts in County Clare alone, as well as 150 early churches, eight monasteries, three cathedrals, 10 stone crosses, five round towers, and 190 castles.

Though the county was divided into small baronies ruled by several prominent families (the O'Deas, the McNamaras, and others)—an arrangement dating back to the advent of the Celts around 400 BC—it was the O'Brien clan, the kings of Thomond (from "Tuath-Mumhan," meaning North Munster), that dominated Clare for centuries. The Danish Vikings raided the county many times over the 9th and 10th centuries, but Brian Boru, the most famous of the O'Briens, defeated them at the beginning of the 11th, and again at the Battle of Clontarf near Dublin in 1014.

Limerick City was founded on the site of an earlier Viking settlement dating to 922. In 1194 the death of Donal Mór O'Brien, the king of Munster—who had funded the establishment of dozens of monasteries in these counties—enabled the invading Normans to seize control of Limerick, and King John commanded a castle be built on the Shannon at the turn of the 13th century. The city enjoyed ongoing prosperity under Norman control.

Being a staunchly Catholic city, Limerick eagerly threw its support behind the Jacobite cause during the rebellion of 1691—known as Cogadh an Dá Rí, the War of the Two Kings. Defeat was inevitable, however, and the terms Jacobite general Patrick Sarsfield secured in the Treaty of Limerick were thrown out by the Irish Parliament. Hundreds of years of redoubled Catholic oppression were to follow.

PLANNING YOUR TIME

All told, you could easily spend your entire vacation in County Clare. With so much variety, several excellent child-friendly museums, and plenty of visitor amenities, Clare makes an especially good choice for families. The Burren can be done in a day, but hill-walkers and other nature-lovers should plan for a visit of at least three days. The sights of southeastern Clare—Ennis, Quin Friary, Dysert O'Dea, or Bunratty Castle—make a good last-day excursion, if you are flying out of Shannon. To do Clare thoroughly, from Hook Head to the Cliffs of Moher to the Burren to Killaloe, would take the better part of a week. Though a fine day in low season is the ideal time to visit the Cliffs of Moher (when there are fewer coach buses and visitors in general), keep in mind that many attractions (Ennis Friary, the Craggaunowen Project, Scattery Island, and so on) are closed between November and February, and in some cases October and March as well.

You can cover County Limerick's primary points of interest—Lough Gur, King John's Castle, the Hunt Museum—in just a day (or two, very leisurely). Some visitors will want to pause in Limerick on the way to or from Killarney, the Dingle Peninsula, or County Cork.

Eastern Clare

ENNIS

If you plan to spend any time in the Burren or along the Clare coast, you'll likely pass through Ennis, the county capital, which straddles the River Fergus. Its medieval flavor is highlighted by the quaintly narrow main drag and picturesque ruins of the 13th-century Ennis Friary, and there's some fine traditional music to be heard in and around town. This old market town can seem a little bit drab when the sun's not shining, though. You may want to linger just long enough to take in the friary and the ruins at nearby Quin before you head out west to the wilder, rockier, more scenic parts of the county. That said, its proximity to the Shannon Airport makes Ennis a good place to spend your last night in Ireland.

Ennis's town square features an extremely tall pedestal topped by a statue of the "Great Liberator," Daniel O'Connell. The primary streets—High, Abbey, O'Connell—extend from here. The tourist office is just east of the square, down Arthur's Row.

Sights

Seven hundred years ago, a community of 1,000 men—400 friars and 600 pupils—lived a life of reflection and asceticism at the **Ennis Friary** (Francis St., tel. 065/682-9100, 10am-5pm daily Apr.-Oct., closed Nov.-Mar., €4). Now managed by Dúchas, the friary was established by Donough Cairbreach O'Brien for the Franciscans around 1240, though most of the ruins date from the 15th century (including most of the nave, south wing, tower, and decorated windows). The lovely five-light east window in the choir was erected in the late 13th or early 14th century, however. The friary's most fascinating features are its old family tombs (particularly the MacMahons', which dates to 1460 and features alabaster panels carved with scenes from the Passion) and wall carvings, including one depicting St. Francis with the stigmata and another of the Crucifixion. The guided tour is optional, though highly recommended.

Housed in the tourist office, the **Clare Museum** (Arthur's Row, tel. 065/682-3382, www.clarelibrary.ie/eolas/claremuseum, 9:30am-1pm and 2pm-5:30pm Mon.-Sat., 2pm-5pm Sun., closed Mon. Oct.-May, free) offers a perspective on 6,000 years of local history and is certainly worth a visit, especially on a rainy day.

One of Clare's most important monastic sites, Dysert O'Dea, is nine kilometers north of Ennis. Quin Abbey, Knappogue Castle, and the Craggaunowen Project are all within 16 kilometers.

Activities and Recreation

Outdoor enthusiasts will want to continue through Ennis to the Burren region (Ballyvaughan, Corofin, Carron, and Doolin all make good bases from which to explore it). Alternatively, you can rent a bike, pack a picnic lunch, and pedal out to Quin Abbey (8 km), Knappogue Castle (10 km), and the Craggaunowen Project (14 km).

Food

There isn't an astounding selection of great eateries in Ennis, but neither is a hearty meal tricky to come by.

In addition to an impressive variety of gift baskets (wine, cheese, jam, chocolate, you name it), the **Ennis Gourmet Store** (1 Barrack St., tel. 065/684-3314, www.ennisgourmetstore.com, 9am-7pm Mon.-Sat., lunch €8) does a brisk salad and sandwich business. Another good choice for an inexpensive (Hungarian-inspired) lunch is **Souper Café** (10 Merchants Sq., tel. 065/682-3901, 9am-5pm Mon.-Sat., €7-10). Locals recommend the goulash in particular.

The atmospheric **Old Ground Hotel** on O'Connell Street operates two eateries, the **O'Brien Room** (tel. 065/682-8127,

Ennis

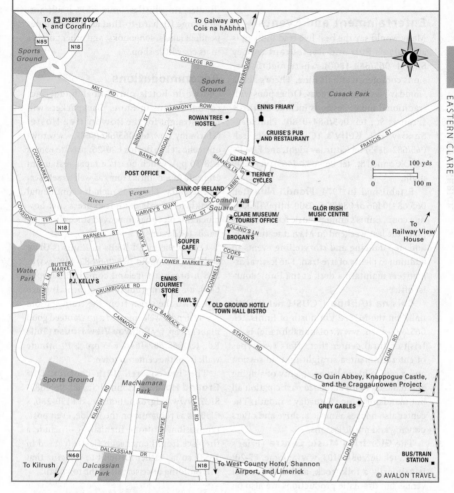

© AVALON TRAVEL

noon-2:30pm and 6:30pm-9:15pm daily, €14-22) and the less formal **Town Hall Bistro** (tel. 065/682-8127, 10am-5pm and 6pm-10pm daily, lunch €12, dinner €15-25). The former offers a gourmet menu with an emphasis on local meats and produce, and the latter is a solid choice for lunch or afternoon tea; vegetarians will be well catered for as long as they ask when making a reservation. A third option at the Old Ground is the pub grub at the **Poet's Corner,** served noon-9pm.

If you want it all—a delicious meal, a pint of stout, a rollicking-good trad session, and an authentic medieval atmosphere—then head to **Cruise's Pub and Restaurant** (Abbey St., tel. 065/684-1800, 6pm-10:30pm daily, €14-22). You might be surprised to learn that the building dates from 1658—it feels even older. The service isn't nearly as good as the food, however. **Brogan's** (24 O'Connell St., tel. 065/682-9859, www.brogansbarandrestaurant.com, 10am-11:30pm daily, lunch €7-14, dinner €13-23) is another Ennis mainstay, offering hearty traditional Irish dishes.

Entertainment and Events

Many would say the best live trad in town is at **Cruise's Pub and Restaurant** (Abbey St., tel. 065/684-1800), where nightly sessions commence at half-nine. There's also a "midday" session on Sunday. Other pubs with traditional music sessions include **Ciaran's** (Francis St., tel. 065/684-0180) Thursday-Sunday, **P.J. Kelly's** (Carmody St., tel. 065/682-8155) on Saturday night, and **Fawl's** (69 O'Connell St., tel. 065/682-4463) on Friday night.

Established in 1974, **Fleadh Nua** (tel. 065/684-0406 or 086/826-0300, http://fleadh-nua.com), Ennis's annual music festival, takes place the last weekend in May; it features set and step dancing and storytelling events in addition to plenty of live trad. The festival organizers maintain a desk at the Ennis tourist office.

Cois na hAbhna ("CUSH nah HOW-nah," on the M18, 2 km north of Ennis, tel. 065/682-4276, www.coisnahabhna.ie) is an Irish cultural center that offers two types of entertainment: a straight-up trad session and a *céilí*, which also has plenty of singing and dancing (with audience participation all but mandatory), one Saturday a month. The center also houses a music archive and offers dancing and music lessons.

The **Glór Irish Music Centre** (Friar's Walk, tel. 065/684-3103, www.glor.ie, €7-20) is primarily a folk, rock, and trad concert venue, but dramatic productions are also on the schedule. Performances usually take place at 8pm. Glór (Irish for "sound") is a safe option if you're looking for a more formal setting in which to enjoy good music.

Shopping

Ennis does have a shopping center on O'Connell Street, but there aren't really any shops of special interest to the visitor. If you're interested in traditional music, however, there's a shop you shouldn't miss: **Custy's**

Music (Cookes Lane, tel. 065/682-1727, www.custysmusic.com) has plenty of instruments (fiddles, tin whistles, bouzoukis, bodhrans, you name it), hard-to-find albums on independent labels, songbooks, and other goodies in its cozy little shop.

Accommodations

Old-world hotels outnumber budget accommodations in Ennis. Backpackers will head straight for the **Rowan Tree Hostel** (Harmony Row, tel. 065/686/8687, www.rowantreehostel.ie, dorms €20-26, private rooms €28-30 pp), which boasts a tapas restaurant and café (open until 11pm) as well as self-service laundry. The price includes continental breakfast. Words cannot express just how much this place has improved since changing hands (and names)!

One of the nicest B&Bs in Ennis is **Grey Gables** (Station Rd., tel. 065/682-4487, www.bed-n-breakfast-ireland.com, €32.50 pp, s €40), an elegant (but not too formal) place just down the street from the train station. For a friendly welcome and a guaranteed good night's sleep, try **Railway View House** (Tulla Rd., tel. 065/682-1646, €35 pp), a 10-minute walk from the center of town.

The ivy-covered 18th-century **Old Ground Hotel** (O'Connell St., tel. 065/682-8127, www.oldgroundhotel.ie, d €130-250, s €110) is as romantic on the inside, even post-renovation. Antique furnishings include a fireplace from Lemaneagh Castle (carved in 1553), so it's rather difficult to imagine that this building once served as the town jail!

Information and Services

Before heading out to the Burren or the coast, stop by the Ennis **tourist office** (O'Connell Sq., tel. 065/682-8366, 9am-9pm daily June-Sept., 9am-6pm Mon.-Sat. and 10am-6pm Sun. Oct.-May) to pick up maps, walking guides, and other info.

ATMs and bureaux de change are located at the **Bank of Ireland** (O'Connell Sq., tel. 065/682-8615) and **AIB** (Bank Pl., off O'Connell Sq., tel. 065/682-8089). The Dunnes

Stores on O'Connell Street also houses a pharmacy, **Michael McLoughlin** (tel. 065/682-9511); another option is **Duffy's Pharmacy** (inside the Tesco Shopping Centre, Francis St., tel. 065/682-8833).

Getting There

Ennis is on the M18, which runs north to Galway (66 km) and southeast (the N18/M18) to Limerick (37 km). From Dublin, take the M7 to Limerick (198 km), then the N18/M18 up to Ennis (235 km total).

Ennis is serviced by both **Bus Éireann** (tel. 065/682-4177) and **Irish Rail** (tel. 061/315-555, call the Limerick station for departure times). Buses depart for west Clare at least four times a day (the Liscannor-Cliffs of Moher-Doolin route is #337; Ballyvaughan requires a change of bus, usually at the cliffs); you can catch a direct bus to Ennis from the Shannon Airport, Limerick, Galway, and Cork (all on route #51, at least 14 buses/day). Change at Limerick for the Dublin bus (#12). Departure times are clearly posted outside the station office.

Eastbound trains run direct to Limerick (7-8/day daily), or you can change at Limerick Junction to get to Dublin (4-5/day Mon.-Sat., 3/day Sun.) and Waterford (2-3/day Mon-Sat.).

Getting Around

Ennis is a small town and can be traversed end to end on foot. Bike rental is available from **Tierney's Cycles** (17 Abbey St., tel. 065/682-9433, www.clarebikehire.com, 9:30am-6pm Mon.-Sat., €20/day, €80/week, helmet rental €10).

Need a ride? Ring **Joe Barry Taxicabs** (tel. 065/682-4759) or **Burren Taxis** (tel. 065/682-3456).

QUIN AND VICINITY

Eight kilometers southeast of Ennis is a tiny village, **Quin** (Chuinche), renowned for its castle and monastic remains, as well as a preserved castle offering medieval banquets and an excellent outdoor museum of both reconstructed and original prehistoric architecture. In 1854 a trove of golden torcs and other ancient jewelry was discovered here during the Limerick-Ennis railway construction, though few pieces made it to the National Museum.

Quin Abbey (10am-4pm Tues.-Sat., 9am-3pm Sun., free) was erected in the 1430s on the ruins of a castle built in the late 1270s. The abbey ruins are not easily distinguishable from those of the earlier castle, and in this respect the friary is quite unique. There are several tombs of note within the church, the

First a castle, then a monastery, Quin Abbey still offers the sprawling ruins of both.

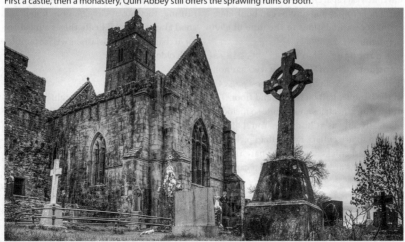

most interesting of which is the MacNamara tomb niche (dating to the mid-15th century) beside the altar stone. It was the MacNamaras who founded the abbey on the foundations of Richard de Clare's late 13th-century castle, and their tombs feature the family's leonine coat of arms. You can enter the old sacristy and look up the stairs that used to lead to one of the monks' dormitories. An arcade surrounds the well-preserved cloister on three sides, and you can climb the belfry for an aerial view.

Visible from the abbey across the stream is **St. Finghin's Church** (east of the R469, always accessible), a diminutive Gothic 13th-century nave-and-chancel edifice you can reach on foot from the primary ruin.

Knappogue Castle

Knappogue Castle (3 km southeast of Quin, signposted from the R469, tel. 061/368-103), a three-story tower house, was erected by the MacNamara clan in 1467. Cromwell seized Knappogue ("Hill of the Kiss" in Irish) to use as a base, which is why it's so well preserved, though it was returned to the MacNamaras after the Restoration. The castle was converted into an aristocratic residence in the 19th century and restored again in the 1960s. Sadly, Knappogue is not currently open for daytime visits apart from the Victorian walled garden. Families and groups can book stateroom accommodations to the tune of €900 per night.

Knappogue also does **medieval banquets** (tel. 061/360-788, www.shannonheritage.com, 6:30pm nightly Apr.-Oct., €48) in the banquet hall on the ground floor. The dinnertime theatrics aren't quite so melodramatically silly as at Bunratty. You'll also be allowed to use cutlery rather than picking at the roasted chicken with your bare fingers. Reservations are required, but you can book online.

Craggaunowen Project

The third sight in the Quin area is the **Craggaunowen Project** (6 km southeast of Quin, signposted off the R469, tel. 061/360-788, www.shannonheritage.com/craggaunowen, 10am-5pm daily late Mar.-Sept., €9), a fascinating outdoor museum established by John Hunt on the grounds of Craggaunowen Castle, another MacNamara tower house dating to the mid-16th century. The castle has been restored, and its ground floor houses medieval artifacts from the Hunt family's extensive collection.

Outside, you'll find a series of reconstructed Iron Age and early Christian sites: a ring fort enclosing circular thatched huts, a souterrain (an underground passage used mainly for food storage), kilns, a prehistoric *crannóg* (or man-made island), and an open-air cooking site (or *fulacht fiadh*) where heated stones would have been used to boil water in a wooden trough. One original artifact is a *togher*, or wooden track, pulled from a bog and at least 2,000 years old.

Craggaunowen also houses "the Brendan Exhibition," which displays the leather curragh used successfully by explorers in 1976 to demonstrate the possibility that St. Brendan the Navigator could've beat Columbus to the New World by more than nine centuries.

Besides the reconstructions, there are walking trails through the surrounding forest and around nearby Lough Cullaun, and plenty of good spots for a picnic lunch. If it's raining, the café at Craggaunowen makes a good alternative. All in all, this is a must-see for archaeology enthusiasts as well as families with older children.

Getting There

Quin and its surrounding sights make an easy day trip from Ennis, though Bus Éireann doesn't stop here. Cyclists can rent a bike in town and head out on the R469, the road past the bus and train station.

BUNRATTY

Bunratty is often called a medieval Irish Disneyland, and it's true the place is tourist central in high season. The nightly medieval banquets at Bunratty Castle are the village's primary draw, and though they're extremely kitschy, they can be a lot of fun. The majority of attendees are on coach tours, and most of the crowd is older, along with a few families with small children. Those who would bypass Bunratty because of its crowds are encouraged to visit in the off-season, however, for Bunratty Castle is a delight in itself—not to mention its friendly tour guides, who turn the hefty admission price into a good value with their knowledge and genuine enthusiasm.

Bunratty Castle

From the Middle Ages onward the site of **Bunratty Castle** (tel. 061/361-511, 9am-4pm daily, €15) offered a strategic position on the river, for its occupants could monitor the water traffic to and from the port of Limerick. The first stone castle on the site was built in the late 13th century by Sir Thomas de Clare, and a town populated by English settlers soon grew up around it. Clashes between the English gentry and the Irish rebels throughout the 14th century meant that the castle didn't remain in either side's hands for long, though by the mid-1400s the MacNamara clan was firmly established there. Through marriage the castle eventually passed to the O'Briens, one of whom surrendered it to Henry VIII in 1542. The castle was abandoned during the English Civil War, and afterward only a small portion of it was lived in by the next owners, the Studderts, who soon built a Georgian mansion on the far side of the demesne.

Bunratty Castle eventually fell into terrible disrepair, making it a popular mischief-making spot with the local hooligans. In 1956 it was purchased by Lord Gort, who set about carefully restoring it with the support of the Office of Public Works. The new timber roof was modeled after that of Dunsoghly Castle in County Dublin (the only castle in the country to retain its original medieval roof).

Today the castle houses an impressive collection of tapestries, sculpture, and furniture, including a series of bizarre horned-mermaid chandeliers called *leuchterweibchen*. (Needless to say, they are of German origin.)

The antlers predate the carved chandeliers by thousands of years, having been preserved in the bogs.)

The castle is best known, however, for its nightly **medieval banquets** (tel. 061/360-788, www.shannonheritage.com, seatings at 5:30pm and 8:45pm nightly year-round, €54 pp), a kitsch-filled evening of songs, storytelling, and surprisingly good food for which you must forgo eating utensils. Mostly middle-aged tour groups greatly enjoy the songs and antics of several talented young performers in motheaten velvet garb. If you purchase banquet tickets, you are entitled to a discounted admission to the castle and folk park. Reservations are required, but you can book online.

A reconstructed village on the castle demesne, the 26-acre **folk park** is less interesting than the castle itself; it includes furnished one- and two-room cottages, a smithy and forge, a National Schoolhouse, and several gift shops offering woolen goods, hand-thrown pottery, and other quality stuff.

A slightly less expensive alternative to the medieval banquet is **traditional Irish night** (tel. 061/360-788, 7pm nightly Apr.-Oct., €44 pp), held in the folk park. As you would expect, this version is meant to show you how the *peasants* ate and entertained themselves.

There's a cozy pub called **Mac's** inside the folk park, offering live traditional music on Wednesdays and weekends during the summer, and weekends only in low season. It has a less touristy atmosphere than you would expect, making it one of the more popular spots with the locals once the folk park has closed for the night. (It's still accessible, and you don't have to pay to get in.) Mac's has a less touristy feel than **Durty Nelly's** (tel. 061/364-861), a pub dating to 1620 located right beside the castle. Locals still hang out there despite the hokey decor.

If you can, visit Bunratty in the off-season, as the castle and folk park are overwhelmed by charter buses all filled to capacity April-September. If you are actively interested in medieval castles and antiques,

Bunratty is definitely worth a visit. Those who are not quite as enthusiastic about museums and drafty stone fortresses, however, will most likely pass on Bunratty in view of the steep admission price and touristy atmosphere.

Food and Shopping

If you're opting out of the medieval banquet, Durty Nelly's is one dinner option, or you could try **Kathleen's Irish Pub** inside the Bunratty Castle Hotel. Another possibility for lunch is the café inside the **Blarney Woolen Mills** (tel. 061/364-321, www.blarney.com, 9:30am-6pm Mon.-Sat., 10am-6pm Sun., €10-12), which also offers a huge inventory of crystal, sweaters, linens, porcelain, jewelry, and so forth.

Accommodations

Shoestring travelers should stay elsewhere (or splurge on B&B). There are many guesthouses along the main road (the N18) within a stone's throw of the castle, in addition to upscale hotels, the most established of which is **Bunratty Castle Hotel** (tel. 061/478-700, www.bunrattycastlehotel.com, €70-150 pp, €20-40 single supplement), on a hill right across the street from the castle (behind the shopping complex).

Perhaps the nicest B&B, **Headley Court** (tel. 061/369-768, www.headleycourt.net, €35 pp), is a five-minute drive outside Bunratty proper at Minister's Cross. Headley Court boasts exceptionally comfortable rooms, good breakfasts, renovated bathrooms with spacious showers (a definite plus), and a sitting room with lovely Gothic-inspired pointed-arch windows and a crystal collection on display.

Information and Services

A very helpful information office is located at **Bunratty Village Mills** (tel. 061/364-321, 9am-5:30pm Mon.-Fri. Oct.-mid-May, 9am-5:30pm daily mid-May-Sept.), the small shopping complex across the road from the castle. There you'll find an ATM.

Getting There and Around

Bunratty is on the Newmarket road, the N18, between Ennis (24 km) and Limerick (13 km). The **Shannon Airport** is only 10 kilometers west of Bunratty, and it's the **Shannon taxis** you'll be calling should you need one (tel. 061/471-538). The fare from Shannon to Bunratty will run you about €22.

Bus Éireann buses run between Shannon and Limerick, passing through Bunratty up to 17 times a day. There are also plenty of southbound buses from Ennis; check the times posted at the bus stop (in front of the Fitzpatrick Bunratty Shannon Shamrock Hotel, a couple minutes' walk from the castle), or call the Ennis (tel. 065/682-4177) or Limerick (tel. 061/313-333) station for bus times.

SHANNON AIRPORT

The republic's second-largest airport, **Shannon Airport** (tel. 061/712-000, www.shannonairport.ie) allows for a less stressful entry into Ireland than Dublin. Shannon was once an important refueling stop on trans-Atlantic flights, and the Irish coffee (with whiskey and cream) was invented in the airport bar.

Since the town of Shannon exists only because of the airport (and the town center consists solely of a shopping center with no free parking or worthwhile dining options), it doesn't make much sense to spend your last night here. Galway is best. Ennis and Bunratty are other popular options for your last night in Ireland, and if you're renting a car you have even more places to choose from (Corofin, 12 km north of Ennis, is recommended).

Food and Services

The airport itself is quite small, but the duty-free shops offer plenty of last-minute gifts, and the upstairs **Estuary Café** does decent à la carte meals, including a hearty vegetarian-friendly cooked breakfast for around €7. The **Bank of Ireland** (tel. 061/471-100, 6:30am-5:30pm daily) is next to the information desk in the arrivals hall. There are ATMs outside.

Remember to drop the rest of your postcards in the mailbox outside Hughes & Hughes, the bookshop between the check-in desks and the arrivals hall; you can purchase stamps from a kiosk at the adjacent convenience store.

Accommodations

In case you are one of those unfortunate souls who have missed your flight, the most convenient place to spend the night is the **Radisson Park Inn** (in front of the airport, tel. 061/471-122, rooms €90-200). Discounts are often available, especially in the off-season. The food's not great, but you'll be home soon enough! Otherwise, it makes the most sense to stay in Ennis or Bunratty and take a taxi back to Shannon in the morning.

Getting There and Around

The bus stop is just to the left of the arrivals hall as you exit the airport. **Bus Éireann** buses leave frequently for Limerick (#51, 8/day Mon.-Sat., 10/day Sun.); Ennis and Galway (#17 or #51, up to 12/day daily); and Cork, Killarney, Waterford, and Dublin (#16, at least 12/day Mon.-Sat., at least 6/day Sun.). Destinations on the #16 route often require a transfer at Limerick. Purchase tickets on board, or stop by the ticket desk (tel. 061/474-311, 7am-5pm daily) in the arrivals hall. There is also a bus service between Shannon, Limerick, and Dublin (including Dublin Airport) through **J.J. Kavanagh** (tel. 056/883-1106, www.jjkavanagh.ie, single ticket €18), but it is not especially punctual.

The airport is at the end of the N19, which you can pick up from the M18 coming south from Galway and Ennis or the N18 northeast from Limerick. **Air Canada** (tel. 888/247-2262, www.aircanada.com) offers direct flights from Toronto to Shannon. **Delta** (tel. 800/221-1212, www.delta.com) and **Aer Lingus** (tel. 800/474-7424, www.aerlingus.com) are other options.

KILLALOE

Hardcore anglers and boaters tend to dominate the Lough Derg area in eastern Clare,

and most visitors bypass it entirely for the more dramatic scenery of the Burren. But the charms of **Killaloe** ("kill-ah-LOO," Cill Da Lúa), a small town nestled between the hills of Slieve Bernagh and the River Shannon on the Clare-Tipperary border, merit a day at least. Here the Shannon draws from Lough Deirgeirt, which in turn opens into the vast Lough Derg. There are lovely views of the lough as you drive north out of Killaloe; about four kilometers up the R463 is the **University of Limerick Activity Centre,** a great resource for anyone interested in water sports on the lake.

Killaloe and the village across the bridge in County Tipperary, **Ballina,** essentially function as one town. The Clare side is certainly more picturesque, not least of all for the medieval **Killaloe Cathedral** and the boats bobbing gently in the dark waters below. A scenic overlook at the end of Ballina's main street provides a fine opportunity for picture-taking.

Sights

At the bottom of Church Street stands the 12th-century, now-Anglican **Killaloe Cathedral,** whose finest feature is its Hiberno-Romanesque south doorway, a strange and ornate combination of chevrons, zigzags, and individualized human and animal heads. It's possible this doorway was moved here from another church. The cathedral is bisected by a wood-and-Plexiglas wall that separates the renovated church from the artifacts (a high cross taken from Kilfenora, an 11th-century ogham stone that also has a Scandinavian runic inscription, and the south doorway) in the cold, spooky, whitewashed antechamber. Among the gravestones outside is **St. Flannan's Oratory** with its steep pitched roof, also dating to the 12th century, which features a simpler Romanesque doorway on its western side.

On the opposite end of Church Street is the 10th-century **St. Molua's Oratory,** beside St. Flannan's Catholic Church. What's so unusual about this oratory is that this is not its original location: It once stood on Friar's Island on the River Shannon, and was disassembled and reconstructed here in 1929 and 1930 after the damming of the river (at which point the island was submerged) as part of a new hydroelectric scheme. St. Flannan's has a rather creepy proliferation of painted plaster statues but is worth a peek for its three marvelous Harry Clarke windows, two flanking the altar and one on the southern wall.

Activities and Recreation

Killaloe is a great spot for water sports and horseback riding. For windsurfing, kayaking, sailing, and canoeing on Lough Derg, head up to the **University of Limerick Activity Centre** (Two Mile Gate, 4 km north of Killaloe on the R463, tel. 061/376-622, www. ulac.ie).

Those who'd like to fish for brown trout, pike, and bream on Lough Derg or along the Shannon should stop by **T.J.'s Angling Centre** (Main St., Ballina, tel. 061/376-009). The **Lough Derg Equestrian Centre** is on the Tipperary side (10 km south of Ballina, signposted on the R463, tel. 061/376-144 or 086/263-1361).

Two long-distance walking trails also pass through the town: the 180-kilometer circular **East Clare Way,** which passes through Mountshannon and other villages near Lough Derg's western shore, as well as the 65-kilometer **Lough Derg Way** from Limerick to Dromineer, of which Killaloe is the midway point. If a short leisurely stroll is more your thing, there are lovely paved paths along both sides of the river.

Food and Entertainment

Dining options are surprisingly good for such a small place. As friendly as it is colorful, **The Wooden Spoon** (Bridge St., tel. 061/622-415, 9am-5pm daily, under €10) brews an excellent coffee, and for lunch you can order a frittata, salad, or wrap. The scrumptious dessert offerings include carrot cake and banoffee pie, and if you have time you may be able

to take part in a cooking class on-site. **Wood Brothers** (Main St., tel. 061/376-230, www. woodbrothers.ie, 9am-4pm daily, for dinner Fri.-Sat., lunch €8-14) boasts the best breakfast in town, and you can savor your meal in the courtyard out back during the summer. If both these cafes are too crowded, try **Derg House** (Bridge St., Killaloe, tel. 061/375-599, 8am-5pm Mon.-Sat., 9am-4pm Sun., under €10), a good-enough spot for breakfast (served all day), lunch, or tea.

Most of the pubs in Killaloe and Ballina serve good pub grub. Particularly popular with the locals are the thatched-roof, super-cozy, somewhat pricey **Gooser's** (Main St., Ballina, tel. 061/376-792, 10:30am-10:30pm daily, pub meals €12, dinner €15-35) and **Molly's** (Main St., Ballina, tel. 061/376-632, food served noon-9pm, €10-20), which also has a nightclub downstairs on the weekends. **Crotty's** (Main St., Killaloe, tel. 061/376-965, €11-23) has an ivy-clad beer-garden entryway and a seafood-heavy menu. All three of these pubs offer live trad (usually on weekends), but they're not as formally scheduled as at **The Anchor Inn** (Bridge St., Killaloe, tel. 061/376-108), which has a regular session on Wednesday night.

Accommodations

Killaloe is popular with weekenders as well as tourists, and there isn't much in the way of accommodations, so it's wise to book ahead even in the off-season. Most central is **Kincora House** (Church St., tel. 061/376-149, www. kincorahouse.com, €40 pp, s €45), a beautifully maintained Georgian townhouse with a warm and helpful owner. If Kincora House is fully booked, **Gooser's** (Main St., Ballina, tel. 061/376-792, €33-40 pp, s €40-50) also offers accommodations. A few minutes' walk up a side road from Gooser's is **Lakeland House** (Boher Rd., Ballina, tel. 061/375-658, www. lakeland-killaloe.com, €33-40 pp, s €40-49), which offers excellent alternatives to the full breakfast fry, including homemade granola and jams.

Information and Services
The **tourist office** (tel. 061/376-866, 10am-6pm daily mid-May-mid-Sept.), **Heritage Centre** (tel. 061/376-866, same hours, €2), and **public library** are all housed in the same building, The Lock House, on Bridge Street.

There's an ATM at the **AIB** (at the southern end of Church St., Killaloe, tel. 061/376-115). **Collins' Pharmacy** (tel. 061/375-505) is on Ballina's Main Street.

Getting There and Around
Killaloe and Ballina are only 23 kilometers northeast of Limerick City on the R463. The Limerick-Birr **Bus Éireann** route (#323, tel. 061/313-333) passes through both towns, with at least four daily in each direction. It is necessary to take the bus back to Limerick for all other destinations.

If you need a taxi, ring **Reddans** (tel. 061/376-146).

MOUNTSHANNON
On the western shore of Lough Derg 26 kilometers north of Killaloe is the pleasant village of Mountshannon, where white-tailed eagles have recently nested for the first time in more than a century (for more information, visit www.mountshannoneagles.ie). The nesting site on Lough Derg is viewable from the harbor. Bird-watching aside, the tourism here is geared toward serious boaters

and anglers, and those whose interests lie elsewhere might feel pretty well out of the loop. Anglers should note the row of boat rental kiosks at the Mountshannon pier; if unattended, there will be a contact number posted on the door. Alternatively, you can contact **Michael Waterstone** (tel. 061/921-328), a local guide who also hires boats. Mountshannon does have one site of general interest, however: **Holy Island,** two kilometers out on Lough Derg, on which lie the remains of a monastic settlement founded by yet another obscure saint, Cáimín, in the 7th century. Its ruined round tower, four churches, and medieval graveyard are worth a visit. If you're interested in making a day trip out to Holy Island, contact **Ger Madden** (tel. 061/921-615, www.holyisland.ie, Apr.-Sept., €10). It's a 15-minute ride and you'll have an hour to explore the island.

After your trip, you *must* go for dinner at **The Snug** (Main St., tel. 061/926-826, thesnugpizzeria@gmail.com, 4pm-9pm Wed.-Fri., 6pm-9pm Sat., 4pm-9pm Sun., €12-14), where you can wash down your pizza or tapas with a glass of cabernet on a lovely patio in the summer. (Gluten-free pizza is available.) And if you'd like to spend the night, try **Sunrise** (300 m up a local road, signposted off R352, tel. 061/927-343, www.sunrisebandb.com, €55 pp), which offers three rooms with views of either Lough Derg or Arra Mountain.

The Clare Coast

The Clare coastline is less haunting—but no less lovely—than the shores of Dingle or Connemara. Kilrush is an excellent spot for water sports, and Loop Head to the west affords tremendous views of both the Galway and Kerry coasts. Walking the periphery of Clare's westernmost tip is cold, windy, and truly exhilarating, especially since there aren't many others to have to share it with.

Driving north from Loop Head, you'll pass the super-touristy sea resort of Kilkee;

the musical Miltown-Malbay; another resort town, Lahinch, slightly unappealing due to a proliferation of fast-food joints and identical pastel holiday homes, but a mecca for surfers; the fishing village of Liscannor; the famous Cliffs of Moher; and Doolin, whose pubs offer great traditional music, still sublime for all its popularity. There isn't too much—people-wise, that is—when you get north of Doolin, but it's an awfully scenic drive through the tiny village of Fanore up to craggy Black Head on the R477 before turning southeast toward the pleasant harbor town of Ballyvaughan, "Gateway to the Burren."

KILRUSH

Situated on the Shannon estuary in southwestern Clare, Kilrush (Cill Rois) is a pleasant town whose scenic harbor fills with boaters and sailboarders in the summer. People are friendly here, and resources for tourists are more than adequate, but its laid-back, workaday atmosphere makes Kilrush an especially appealing destination. The tourist office doesn't go overboard advertising the town's virtues, a refreshing change from the resort towns on Clare's west coast. Because water sports are its primary draw, Kilrush is actually something of a ghost town in the fall and winter. Once you've dolphin-watched, windsurfed, and taken a stroll through the "lost" gardens on the old Vandeleur estate, you can use Kilrush as a base for exploring the delightfully remote Loop Head.

The town hub is **Market Square,** with a roundabout encircling the 19th-century Town Hall. From the west, the N67 drops you into Henry Street, which leads down to the square; broad Frances Street leads you from the bottom of the square out to the marina.

Sights

Two hundred years ago the Vandeleur family dominated every aspect of life in Kilrush. In the post-famine era, Hector Vandeleur treated his tenants without mercy, forcing 20,000 out of their homes onto boats bound for the New World. Today the late-18th-century **Vandeleur Walled Garden** (the Killimer road, tel. 065/905-1760, www.vandeleurwalledgarden.ie, 10am-5pm Mon.-Fri., noon-5pm Sat.-Sun. Apr.-Sept., 9:30am-4:30pm Mon.-Fri. Oct.-Mar., free), just over two acres, is newly restored and open to the public. Surrounded by 420 woodland acres, this garden with its high stone wall features tousled flowerbeds of white poppies and purple daisies, a beech maze, and a new glasshouse for the nurturing of young specimens.

If gardens and tearooms are your thing, you shouldn't miss this. And if you're interested in the garden's historic importance, check out the "Kilrush in Landlord Times" exhibit at the Heritage Centre.

Kilrush's Catholic church, **St. Senan's** (Toler St., off Frances St., tel. 065/905-1093), is known for its Harry Clarke windows.

Activities and Recreation

April-October, you can go **dolphin-watching** (Scattery Island Ferries, Kilrush Creek Marina, tel. 065/905-1327, www.discoverdolphins.ie, 2-hour trip €245) on the Shannon Estuary, which is home to more than 100 of our lithe flippered friends. The boat is pretty high-tech—there's even a hydrophone through which you can hear the dolphins underwater, clucking their tongues at you. In high season there are four trips a day.

Kilrush Wood is just east of town on the Killimer road, surrounding the Vandeleur Walled Garden. It's a tranquil spot for short walk and a picnic lunch.

Food and Entertainment

The coffee shop at the **Vandeleur Walled Garden** (Killimer Rd., tel. 065/905-1760, 10am-5pm Mon.-Fri., noon-5pm Sat.-Sun. Apr.-Sept., 9:30am-4:30pm Mon.-Fri. Oct.-Mar., lunch under €10) is a nice spot for tea or a light lunch, and **The Potter's Hand** (3 Vandeleur St., tel. 086/880-4946, 9am-5pm Mon.-Sat., until 8pm Wed., under €8) is the very best spot in the center of town, a cheerful, friendly, bright café with great coffee, superb baked goods, and light meals like soup and sandwiches.

The best pub-cum-restaurant in town is **Kelly's Steak and Seafood House** (26 Henry St., tel. 065/905-1811, food served 11am-9:30pm Mon.-Sat., 12:30pm-9:30pm Sun., lunch €10, dinner €10-24), with hearty, unpretentious fare and friendly service in a warm atmosphere. Despite the name, Kelly's does offer a few decent vegetarian options. There's live trad Saturday nights starting at 10pm.

Another option is the comparable pub grub a few doors down at the **Haven Arms** (Henry St., tel. 065/905-1267, food served noon-9:30pm, lunch €8-16, dinner €10-24).

Other pubs with live music on the weekends include **O'Looney's** (John St., tel. 065/905-1349) and **Percy French** (Moore St., tel. 065/905-1615).

The Saturday **farmers market** (Market Sq., 10am-2pm) provides healthy snacks as well as atmosphere.

Accommodations

Budget travelers should stay at the IHH-affiliated **Katie O'Connor's Holiday Hostel** (49/50 Frances St., tel. 065/905-1133, www.katieshostel.com, dorm beds €20), a central family-run townhouse with 28 beds. Quarters are close but cozy, and the owners provide thorough information on every imaginable activity in Kilrush.

Kilrush B&Bs ★ **Hillcrest View** (Doonbeg Rd., tel. 065/905-1986, www.hillcrestview.com, €33-40 pp, s €50) and **Innwood House** (Killimer Rd., tel. 065/906-2724, www.westclare.net/innwoodhouse, €30-35 pp, s €40-50), a Georgian-style house directly opposite the Vandeleur Walled Garden, are both a two-minute drive outside town and are open year-round (unlike many other B&Bs in the area). They are immaculate family homes, elegantly but comfortably furnished, with excellent breakfasts and all the little amenities you would expect at a hotel. Proprietors Ethna Hynes and Helen and Terry (respectively) are kind and full of helpful information.

Information and Services

The Kilrush **tourist office** (tel. 065/905-1577, www.kilrush.ie, 10am-1pm and 2pm-6pm Mon.-Sat. late May-Aug.) and the mildly interesting **Heritage Centre** (tel. 065/905-1596, 10am-6pm Mon.-Fri., noon-4pm weekends June-Aug., €3) are both in the Market House on Market Square. Two tourism websites, **Irish Heritage Towns** (www.heritagetowns.com/kilrush.html) and the **Kilrush**

Chamber of Commerce (www.westclare.com), are loaded with useful information.

ATMs are available at the **Bank of Ireland** (corner of Francis St. and Toler St., tel. 065/905-1083) and **AIB** (Francis St., tel. 065/905-1012). If you need a pharmacy, try **Malone's** (Frances St., tel. 065/905-2552).

Getting There and Around

Kilrush is on the N67, 44 kilometers southwest of Ennis. Bus Éireann routes #15 and #336 go from Limerick to Kilrush and Kilkee via Ennis (at least 7 daily). In summer, route #50 between Galway and Cork passes through Kilrush and other coastal towns (2 daily).

A handy shortcut, if you want to get from Clare to Kerry without driving back through Shannon and Limerick, is the **Killimer Car Ferry** (Killimer, tel. 065/905-3124, www.shannonferries.com, single/return €18/28 with car, €5 pedestrians and cyclists), which connects Killimer (8.5 km east of Kilrush) with Tarbert in northern Kerry. Sailings are hourly in winter and more frequent in high season, and the trip takes only 20 minutes (and saves you 137 km).

For a taxi, ring **Joe Cropera** (tel. 087/252-8888).

You can rent a bicycle from **Gleeson's** (Henry St., tel. 065/905-1127, gleesonfort@tinet.ie, €20/day, €80/week, €40 deposit).

SCATTERY ISLAND

Home to the remains of St. Senan's 6th-century monastery as well as a host of birds (at least 31 species have been counted), wildflowers, rabbits, goats, and gray seals, treeless Scattery—just a kilometer or so long—is an otherwise uninhabited island three kilometers out from the Kilrush pier. Legend has it that a sea serpent called the Cathach terrorized the locals until Senan banished it, miraculously, to a lake far north in County Mayo. The only trace left of the monster is the island's name, Inis Cathaigh, "Island of the Cathach" (sometimes mistranslated as "Island of the Battles," which is still accurate in light of the bloodthirsty Vikings' 9th-century raids). Today,

Scattery makes a lovely afternoon trip from Kilrush and is a must-see for avid bird-watchers (the 31 species include oystercatchers and ringed plovers, both of which breed on the island) as well as those looking for a beautiful escape from the Cliffs of Moher-Doolin-Bunratty tourist circuit.

Ruins

The monastic ruins include five churches, an 24-meter round tower with conical stone roof intact (and, unusually, a ground-level doorway, which allows you to see all the way up to the roof). The most intriguing of the five churches is the Romanesque cathedral east of the round tower, which features antae projecting from the west wall. The other four are the part-early-Christian, part-medieval Church of the Hill of the Angel (southwest of the cathedral and round tower); the 14th-or 15th-century Church of the Dead, toward the eastern side of the island; Senan's Temple, medieval and much ruined; and a nameless smaller Romanesque nave-and-chancel oratory, just north of the round tower, mostly dating to the 1100s (though, as you can see, it was partially rebuilt in the 19th century).

There are also ruins of a Napoleonic-era battery, a holy well, and the village of the island's last inhabitants, who left Scattery for good in 1978.

Getting There

Passage is available only in summer through **Scattery Island Ferries** (tel. 065/905-1237, €12), which operates from the Kilrush Creek Marina. The trip out to Scattery takes only 20 minutes, but the sailing schedule is unfixed, so it's essential to ring ahead or at least stop by the ferry office at the marina.

Before you depart, check out the **Scattery Island Interpretive Centre** (Merchants Quay, Kilrush, tel. 065/905-2144, scatteryisland@ealga.ie, 10am-1pm and 2pm-6pm daily June-Sept., free). The Dúchas-run interpretive center offers an informative exhibit on the island's ruins and wildlife.

THE LOOP HEAD PENINSULA

County Clare's westernmost tip makes a splendid afternoon drive, dotted with quiet hamlets and placid ocean panoramas, and punctuated by the lighthouse at Loop Head. "Loop" is actually a corruption of "Leap": One legend says the warrior Cuchulainn jumped from the cliff at the end of this peninsula to dodge Mal, the frightening and powerful beldam-goddess (who also inspired "Malbay" and "Hag's Head"); the other legend says it was Diarmuid and Gráinne who leaped while escaping her vengeful husband.

The nearest town is Kilkee, but unfortunately this resort town's old Victorian charms have given way to perpetual construction sites. Kilrush's tourism is more discreet, making it a nicer base.

Kilkee

Divers may want to visit Kilkee, 13 kilometers northwest of Kilrush on the N67, for its splendid sea caves. There are arches and stacks along this stretch of coast, and explorers will find plenty of geological interest beneath the waves as well. There's not a whole lot in terms of underwater life, however, though you may be able to spot a lobster or eel. **Kilkee Dive Centre** (the pier, tel. 087/641-3413, www.diveireland.com) can take you out to the caves on a rigid inflatable boat. Sailors, dolphin-watchers, and sea-anglers are also catered to.

Carrigaholt

The tiny village of Carrigaholt on the peninsula's southern side offers **dolphin-watching** excursions out at sea (Dolphinwatch, www.dolphinwatch.ie, tel. 065/905-8156, 2-3 hour trip €35). There's also a swimmable beach just east of the village.

Kilbaha

The last village on the peninsula, Kilbaha, has a fascinating and unique piece of history within its small church: a "little ark" built by an intrepid priest named Michael Meehan in the mid-1850s to circumvent the Penal Laws (some Protestant landowners evidently paid no attention to the Catholic Emancipation Act of 1829). Celebration of the Mass was still forbidden by the local landlord, but when Father Meehan brought this tiny floating church just a few yards out at sea to say Mass for a few parishioners at a time, the landlord couldn't touch him. **The Church of the Little Ark,** clearly signposted from Keating's pub on the main Kilbaha street, has the floating ark on display in a side room. The altar and bible stand remain, and there's even a bit of patterned wallpaper still stuck to the back wall. If you're doing Loop Head Drive, you should definitely make a brief stop here.

Loop Head

Loop Head is crowned by a lighthouse that isn't open to the public. There is, however, an unpaved path from a car park beside the lighthouse around the edge of the peninsula that makes for a short but exhilarating walk of half an hour. You'll enjoy mist-swathed views of the Dingle Peninsula (the tallest peak is Mount Brandon) and the Blaskets to the south, and Connemara and the Aran Islands to the north. Approach the cliff edge with caution, as the winds can be gusty.

CENTRAL CLARE COAST
Miltown Malbay

Can't get enough of that trad? Miltown Malbay, an erstwhile Victorian resort town 32 kilometers south of Doolin (now with a slightly run-down air), hosts a tremendously popular **traditional music school and festival** called the **Willie Clancy Summer School** (tel. 065/708-5107, www.scoilsamhraidhwillieclancy.com, early July), in honor of Willie Clancy, a native of the town and one of the country's best-ever uilleann pipers. There's good music and *craic* to be had in the pubs year-round, especially at **O'Friel's** (The Square, tel. 065/708-4275). This fine old-fashioned pub was once the home of Willie Clancy himself.

If you're passing through Miltown Malbay, a good spot for lunch is **The Old Bake House**

Restaurant (Main St., tel. 065/708-4350, www.theoldbakehouse.ie, noon-3pm daily, 6pm-9pm Tues.-Thurs., 6pm-10pm Fri.-Sat., noon-8pm Sun., lunch €10-12, dinner €13-22). The walls at this laid-back eatery feature photography and oil paintings by local artists. The menu is diverse, the portions large, and the service excellent.

Lahinch

Twenty kilometers southeast of Doolin, Lahinch is Clare's most popular resort town. Like Kilkee, the place is extremely overdeveloped, far from the best the Clare coast has to offer. **Surfers** will disregard this advice, however, as the best waves are here. Rent a surfboard and hire an instructor (if necessary) at the **Lahinch Surf Shop** (on the promenade, tel. 065/708-1543, www.lahinchsurfshop.com). Horse lovers should contact **Daly's Equestrian Centre** (Ballingaddy, 7 km northeast of Lahinch off the N67, tel. 086/307-7142, www.dalysequestriancentre.com) for beach rides.

If you do want the resort experience, the best place to indulge yourself is the newly renovated, four-star **Lahinch Golf & Leisure Hotel** (Main St., tel. 065/708-1100, www.lahinchgolf.com, €80-130 pp), which offers sleek, modern bedrooms and a 17-meter swimming pool and gymnasium—though contrary to the name, there isn't actually a golf course on site; it's a few minutes' drive out of town. Most surfers stay at the clean and sociable (read: noisy) **Lahinch Hostel** (Church St., tel. 065/708-1040, www.lahinchhostel.ie, dorm beds €18), within a few minutes' walk of the beach.

Liscannor

Liscannor (Lios Ceannúir) is a small fishing village just south of the Cliffs of Moher on the R478, at the end (or start) of the Burren Way. There are a couple of reasons to linger here for an afternoon in the summer: the safe and sandy beach, Clahane, just west of the village, and, for equestrians, the **Cliffs of Moher Pony Trekking Center** (tel. 065/708-1283).

The best lodging in this area is the **Moher Lodge Farmhouse** (tel. 065/708-1269, www.cliffsofmoher-ireland.com, Apr.-Oct., €40 pp, s €50), three kilometers north of Liscannor on the road to the Cliffs of Moher; it offers the traditional Irish welcome (tea on arrival, open turf fire) along with amazing sea views.

The village itself is rather featureless, though it does boast an outstanding seafood restaurant, **Vaughan's Anchor Inn** (Main St., tel. 065/708-1548, www.vaughansanchorinn.com, food served noon-9:30pm daily, lunch €9-13, dinner €18-23, B&B rooms €90-100). There isn't even one vegetarian option, unfortunately.

On your way up to the cliffs from Liscannor, you'll see a tall stone pillar on the left side of the road. This marks **St. Brigid's Well,** a local pilgrimage site.

Ennistymon

Located at the junction of the N67 and the N85 in western Clare, **Ennistymon** (Inis Díomáin) is a pleasant little town and well worth a stop for lunch. **The Cascades,** a rather breathtaking row of waterfalls on the River Inagh, are the town's prime diversion, reachable through an archway at the end of the town's main street. Once you've had your

fill of picture taking, head for lunch at the utterly delightful ★ **Ginger Lou's** (Main St., tel. 065/707-2370, 9am-5pm Mon.-Sat., 11am-4pm Sun., under €10). The food is hearty and delicious, using local produce when possible, and the full vegetarian fry comes with falafel and roasted eggplant. The folks who work here offer traditional Irish hospitality with a wry 21st-century sensibility. Oh, and the coffee's very good too.

Because Doolin, Lisdoonvarna, and other popular destinations don't have banks, you should probably make a withdrawal from the ATM at the **Bank of Ireland** (Parliament St., tel. 065/707-1036). Note that the **AIB** (Main St., tel. 065/707-1018) closes for lunch, and the ATM is inside.

★ THE CLIFFS OF MOHER

This world-famous sight is a series of dramatic, mist-shrouded cliffs rising as high as 200 meters above the waves. The Cliffs of Moher are one of Ireland's loveliest natural wonders. From the car park and visitors center a stone walkway leads out to the cliffs, where you can continue on a short walk pretty

The Cascades, just off the main street, are Ennistymon's loveliest feature.

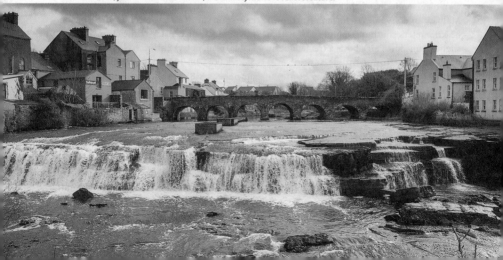

darn near the edge, looking south to the cliffs themselves and out at the glittering sea. It's not wise to hop the railings, as tourists have been blown off the edge. And expect crowds even in low season and foul weather—and in the fog and rain keep in mind that you may not be able to see much. If the weather report is hopeless, consider visiting the cliffs another day. Regardless of the time of year, you'll have fewer fellow tourists if you arrive before 9am.

As you finish your walk up the main pathway toward the cliff edge, you'll spot **O'Brien's Castle** (9:30am-6pm daily Mar.-Oct., €2). This small round tower may look medieval, but it was built in 1835. The view's just as good from the ground, so you might want to save that two-euro coin for the busker on the banjo braving the chilly winds.

Hag's Head Walk

From the Cliffs of Moher you can take the six-kilometer **Hag's Head Walk** south to the end of the Hag's Head peninsula, 134 meters above the waves at its pinnacle. It's a windy hike on an unpaved path, but the view of the cliffs and ocean is well worth the three-plus hours there and back, especially since you'll meet very few people along the way. A ruined signal tower on the head was erected by the Brits in the early

19th century (fearing an attack by Napoleon); it lies on the site of a prehistoric promontory fort called **Mothar.** Now you know how the cliffs got their name.

Information and Services

The new Cliffs of Moher **visitors center** (tel. 065/708-6141, www.cliffsofmoher.ie, 9am-5pm daily, until 6pm Mar., Apr., Oct., until 7pm May-Jun. and Sept., and until 9pm Jul.-Aug.) is a circular, ultramodern structure built into one of the hills so as to better integrate with the landscape, and there is an ATM along with an information desk. The café/restaurant boasts dramatic floor-to-ceiling windows looking out on Liscannor Bay, and though there is an interpretive exhibition, it's primarily of interest to families with small children.

Getting There

Doolin makes the best base when visiting the Cliffs of Moher. From the village it's a brisk eight-kilometer uphill bike or walk and no more than a 10-minute drive. The tour buses start pulling in around 9am, so try to arrive at least half an hour earlier to enjoy the view in peace and quasi-solitude. The first public bus of the day (#350) leaves the Doolin Hostel for

the Cliffs of Moher

the cliffs at 8:12am (arriving at 8:25). Those driving will pay €6 per person (not per car) to park in the lot, and while this is intended as the official Cliffs of Moher entrance fee, there is no one charging admission or collecting tickets if you come by bus, bike, or on foot. On your way from Doolin up to the cliffs you'll spot the 15th-century **Doonagore Castle,** built by the O'Briens and privately owned.

Not satisfied with the view from the summit? One-hour cruises on the **O'Brien Line** (the pier, tel. 065/707-5555, www.obrienline. com, €15 if purchased online) leave Doolin at least three times daily between St. Patrick's Day and the beginning of November. You can also book a combo ticket for any one of the Aran Islands.

DOOLIN

It might seem strange at first, flocking to a small village in rural County Clare to listen to world-class musicians, but once you've arrived you'll forget your skepticism. Music-makers from other countries often come to **Doolin** (Duláinn) with their guitars or fiddles in tow, spending every night in the pubs joining in the trad session. Even if you're not a musician, there's something exciting about watching a new friend you've just shared a pint with open her fiddle case and, after a warm invitation, start playing right alongside the regulars. Purpose-built B&Bs and holiday cottages were sprouting up like dandelions in the years before the economic downturn, yet Doolin seems to have retained much of its charm despite its burgeoning popularity (the ugly new mini-strip mall between the villages being the only real exception).

Doolin comprises two villages: **Fisherstreet,** the lower village, and **Roadford,** the upper village. The lower village is closer to the harbor (about a kilometer and a half), and the upper village is across the Aille River bridge, on the way to Black Head and the village of Fanore. It takes 10-15 minutes to walk from one village to the other. Be sure to pack a flashlight (or "torch," as the Irish and Brits say)—at night that road is darker than pitch. On a clear evening, though, all the constellations twinkle brilliantly.

Doolin is technically inside the Burren and is on the Burren Way, but the land is lush. Travel north or east, though, and you'll see that fissured limestone landscape—or is it moonscape?—tumbling out almost as far as the eye can see.

Activities and Recreation
Doolin is roughly midway along the 45-kilometer Burren Way.

Several hidden spots in the vicinity are suitable for diving and caving. The University of Bristol Speleological Society first explored the Doolin cave system in 1953, noting its length of 10.5 kilometers and network of rivers worn through the limestone. Access is via the **"Fisherstreet Potholes"** in an inconspicuous location near the Aille River Hostel; ask at your hostel or B&B for precise directions. Sea-wise, there's a network of undersea caves called the **Green Holes of Doolin,** beneath the rocks just to the north of the harbor. As there are no commercial caving or diving outfits in the area, the potholes and undersea caves should only be attempted by experienced spelunkers. There is, however, the **Doolin Activity Lodge** (nearer the Fisherstreet end, on the left side as you head toward the pier, tel. 065/707-4888, www. doolinlodge.com), which offers caving excursions in addition to horseback riding, guided walks and bike trips, kayaking, and deep-sea and lake angling. It's part of a tourist complex offering B&B and a not-awesome restaurant, however, so backpackers and other independent types might want to avoid it. It's a good choice for families, though.

Food
Outside of the pubs there aren't many options for food, but there are a couple of good restaurants if you want something besides pub grub. The ★ **Doolin Café** (Roadford, near McDermott's and McGann's, tel. 065/707-4795, www.thedoolincafe.com, breakfast/lunch €6-10, dinner €15-22, hours vary,

Mar.-Dec., no credit cards) is a relaxed little place offering everything from pancakes and the full fry to a five-course dinner menu featuring organic produce. This café is many locals' favorite spot, although the opening hours can be maddeningly inconsistent. A newer but equally beloved eatery is **The Riverside Bistro** (Roadford, tel. 089/985-0979, 5pm-11pm daily), where seafood is, unsurprisingly, the specialty.

★ Gus O'Connor's Pub

Hands down, **Gus O'Connor's Pub** (lower village, tel. 065/707-4168, www.gusoconnors-doolin.com) offers the best traditional music sessions in the county (and the best pub grub, too). Founded in 1832, it's also the oldest of Doolin's four watering holes. West Clare has always been especially known for its musical heritage—many of its natives, like whistler Micho Russell (from Doolin) and piper Willie Clancy (from Miltown Malbay), came from "musical families" and became internationally revered (and today, annual music festivals celebrate their legacies). The village is even home to its own trad record company.

At O'Connor's, the circle of musicians in the back of the pub can swell to over a dozen, and many of these music-makers have come here on vacation (because they've heard Doolin, and specifically O'Connor's, is the place to join in on a session). Other fiddlers and guitarists are well known among the regulars. With its low ceilings and open fires, the place still feels cozy and welcoming no matter how crowded it gets at night (and the owners have provided microphones for the performers so you can enjoy the music even if you can only find a table in the front room). Even in winter, you can find at least one talented guitar-strumming ballad singer every evening. In sum, you'll meet people from all over Europe, Australia, and the Americas while listening to some of the best live music Ireland has to offer.

Other Entertainment

There are two other well-established pubs in Doolin (we're not bothering with the new pub in the aforementioned strip mall!), and both offer food and nightly traditional music sessions in high season. In all the pubs, a main course at lunch will run you €12 or less, dinner €12-24.

McGann's (upper village, tel. 065/707-4133, www.mcgannspubdoolin.com) is good for a hearty meal—and note that if you are looking for a late dinner, McGann's is the safest bet, as it continues serving food a little past 9:30pm. (If you go to O'Connor's hoping for a meal at half-nine, they'll charge you an exorbitant amount for an undelectable toasted cheese sandwich.)

Many locals prefer the third pub, **McDermott's** (upper village, tel. 065/707-4328, www.mcdermottspubdoolin.com), which has more of a "corner bar" feel than the others. It also offers good pub grub, nightly trad sessions in high season, and weekend sessions in the winter.

Shopping

Doolin has an excellent crafts store and tearoom, the **Doolin Craft Gallery** (the Lisdoonvarna road, tel. 065/707-4309, www.doolincrafts.com, 10am-6pm Tues.-Sun., café open Easter-Christmas), filled with gorgeous sweaters, jewelry, and other fine souvenirs. The pottery selection is particularly noteworthy.

No self-respecting musician will pass up an extended browse at the **Traditional Music Shop** (Fisherstreet, tel. 065/707-4407, www.irishmusicdoolin.com), which stocks recordings, sheet music, and instruments (bodhrans, flutes, fiddles, concertinas, and so on), many of which are locally made. They ship worldwide, so if you were thinking of learning the harp now's the perfect chance!

Accommodations

There's no shortage of accommodations here, but it's still wise to book well in advance.

The backpacking set's favorite place to crash is the ★ **Aille River Hostel** (tel. 065/707-4260, www.ailleriverhosteldoolin. ie, mid-Mar.-Dec., dorms and private rooms

€17-18 pp, camping and tipis €9), a converted 17th-century farmhouse with a cozy sitting room by the open turf fire (and plenty of board games and paperbacks), free laundry, bike rental, and decent beds. Another highly recommended place is the cozy, family-run ★ Rainbow Hostel (tel. 065/707-4415, www.rainbowhostel.net, dorms €15-19, private rooms €20-25), on the Roadford side of the bridge (near McDermott's and McGann's). The Rainbow also offers bike rental, nice beds, and a cozy skylit sitting room with a turf fire. The Doolin Hostel (tel. 065/707-4006, www.doolinhostel.com, Feb.-Oct., dorms €14-15, private rooms €19-20), right across the street from the bus stop, is better than adequate (and so convenient), but the other hostels are cozier and more atmospheric (with turf fires and so forth). It does have a good coffee shop though.

The following guesthouses have all been around a while, so their atmospheres are quite homey. The Rainbow's End (tel. 065/707-4415, rainbowhostel@eircom.net, €36 pp, room-only rate €28), next door to the Rainbow Hostel and owned by the same friendly couple, Carmel and Mattie, offers comfortable rooms (some with skylights) and gorgeous handcrafted woodwork designed and installed by the owner. Furthermore, Mattie offers a slide show for interested hostel and B&B guests. His photographs are outstanding, and his knowledge exceeds that of many professional tour guides. Mattie also does Burren walks free of charge in the summer.

Another cozy choice is Daly's House (lower village, tel. 065 7074242, www.dalys-doolin.com, €50-60 pp), which sometimes hosts visiting musicians. The owner, Susan, will welcome you with an Irish or Bailey's coffee, and you can have your breakfast in the garden on sunny summer mornings. To get here, turn right after O'Connor's pub; you can't miss it. Also recommended is nearby Atlantic View (tel. 065/707-4189 or 065/707-4980, www.atlanticviewdoolin.ie, €43 pp, s €50), which is less than a 10-minute walk past the lower village down toward the pier. There's a lovely little library upstairs tucked into an alcove, and the views from the bedrooms are incomparable.

Done with hostelling, but still on a budget? Try Doolin Cottage (tel. 065/707-4762, €33 pp, Mar.-Nov.), a cozy, unpretentious little place behind the Aille River Hostel between the upper and lower villages. The cottage's proprietor welcomes drop-ins for breakfast along with its own guests (a fine option for hostellers) and is very accommodating for vegetarians.

Information and Services

There is no bank in Doolin, so hit the ATM in Ennis, Ennistymon, or Galway first. There is a new tourist information point (adjoining the Doolin Hotel, tel. 065/707-5649, hours vary) in the aforementioned unsightly strip mall, but as always, if you have any questions—about the Burren, the Cliffs of Moher, the pubs, or anything else—just remember that your B&B or hostel hosts are nearly always fonts of useful information. Before you go, check out the helpful Doolin Tourism website (www.doolin-tourism.com).

Getting There and Around

Buses stop outside the Doolin Hostel in the lower village several times a day (the schedule is posted at the stop); most continue to either Ennis or Galway City. From Galway, the #50 bus will take you directly to Doolin, and from Ennis and Limerick it's #337. Those coming from Dublin on the #12 bus will change at Limerick.

Beginning at 8:12am, buses stop outside Paddy's Doolin Hostel before continuing on to the Cliffs of Moher. This is your best bet if you'd rather not hike, bike, or drive it. Do try to catch the first bus of the morning so as to beat most of the tour buses—you'll be glad you set your alarm.

Get your wheels from Doolin Rent-a-Bike (lower village, 086/109-1850, www.doolinrentabike.ie, €15/day, €90/week), which offers friendly and efficient service.

Doolin Ferries (the pier, tel. 065/707-4455 or 065/707-4466, www.doolinferries.com, €25 return to Inis Oírr, €35 return to Inis Mór) can take you to the Aran Islands between Easter and September (though sailings are more subject to weather conditions than the ferries out of Rossaveal in County Galway). If the kiosk at the pier is closed, call or stop in at the nearby Atlantic View B&B (tel. 065/707-4189)—it's run by the same owners.

In need of a cab in or around Doolin? Call **Sean Cullinan** (tel. 086/402-9997) or **Joe Burke** (tel. 086/370-2652).

NORTH OF DOOLIN

The road north out of Doolin to the tiny village of **Fanore** offers a fabulous view of the sea on the left and the rocky Burren landscape on the right; it makes for an excellent bike ride, about 32 kilometers round-trip. On your way there, you'll spot privately owned 15th-century Ballinalacken Castle.

Black Head looms above sleepy Fanore, crowning the northwesternmost part of the county. Serious climbers will want to hike up the head to **Cathair Dhún Iorais,** an Iron Age fort. Needless to say, the view from the summit is incomparable, but note that there is no actual path up the hill. Tackle it only with the proper footwear and only if the weather is clear.

The Fanore area is also popular with sea anglers, as the shore teems with cod and sea bass, and the village's beach is the only safe one along the northern coast of Clare. From Black Head it's a short drive east to the town of Ballyvaughan. Bus Éireann operates a service to Fanore only two times a week, so you do need a set of wheels.

LISDOONVARNA

Renowned for its annual **matchmaking festival** (tel. 065/707-4405, late Sept.), Lisdoonvarna is essentially a one-street town

16 kilometers southwest of Ballyvaughan on the N67 and 8 kilometers east of Doolin on the R478. The festival has traditionally drawn bachelor farmers from the county and beyond, but in recent years it's attracted fun-seeking gay men from all over Europe.

The other attraction in "Lisdoon" is the Victorian-era **Spa Wells Centre** (Kincora Rd., tel. 065/707-4023, 10am-6pm daily June-Sept., sulfur bath €25), which offers hot and cold mineral baths (doctor-recommended for those with arthritis and several other physical complaints), aromatherapy, and massage. This is the only true spa in Ireland.

You can use Lisdoonvarna as a base for visiting the Cliffs of Moher, but Doolin is much more scenic (and the pubs are more fun, too).

The best bets for food in town are the **Irish Arms** (tel. 065/707-4207) and the **Royal Spa Hotel** (tel. 065/707-4288), both on Main Street, with good pub grub in the €10-15 range. There are two nice restaurants in the bright and airy **Imperial Hotel** (Main St., tel. 065/707-4042, www.theimperial-hotel. com, €11-24).

The excellent Galway-based Sleepzone franchise has recently opened a hostel here, **Sleepzone Burren** (signposted on Main St., tel. 065/707-4036, www.sleepzone.ie/burren, dorm beds €15, d €25 pp). Another accommodation option is **O'Neill's Town Home** (St. Brendan's Rd., tel. 065/707-4208, May-Oct., €30-40 pp). O'Neill's is home to **The Burren Painting Centre** (www.burrenpaintingcen-tre.com), which offers two- to six-day painting courses May-October.

Lisdoonvarna is on the Bus Éireann route (#337) from Limerick through Ennis to Doolin (Mon.-Sat.) and the #50 or #423 route from Galway to Doolin (Mon.-Sat. in high season). Limerick- and Galway-bound buses stop four or more times a day.

The Burren

This rocky limestone plateau is Clare's true treasure, stretching for nearly 300 square kilometers in the northwestern part of the county. The land preserved within the Burren National Park is less than 17 square kilometers, however, centered around the limestone peak of Mullaghmore just north of Corofin. The Burren—from *boireann*, "a rocky place"—may seem a harsh and desolate region at first look, but these rain-carved crevices are teeming with strange and beautiful flora and fauna.

The Burren shelters a greater variety of plants than any other region in Ireland. Cross-pollination, the absence of trees and shrubs (any incipient growth is usually eaten by wild animals), and a unique soil composition of dried algae and rabbit dung allow Alpine, Arctic, and Mediterranean flowers to grow like little miracles in the soil between the limestone slabs. There are more than 30 varieties of orchids here, which serious botanists, photographers, and watercolor artists delight upon every summer. Wildlife abounds, too: feral goats, rabbits, pine martens, stoats, badgers, foxes, birds galore, as well as seven bat species and 28 species of butterfly.

Nature lovers of all stripes will find much to inspire and intrigue. Though you can drive past the Burren's principal sights in a single day (or take a day tour on a coach bus out of Galway), it's well worth spending two or three days here on your own. Take part in a guided nature walk, bike part or all of the Burren Cycleway, or wander through the remains of several early Christian ring forts dotted around the area.

For more information before you go, visit **Burrenbeo** (www.burrenbeo.com), a great "one-stop information resource." Burrenbeo is far more substantive than the official Tourist Board sites because it's run by a journalist and an academic (Ann O'Connor and Brendan Dunford, respectively). Don't miss the excellent photo gallery.

BALLYVAUGHAN

A pleasant little harbor town situated between Galway Bay and the northern edge of the Burren, **Ballyvaughan** (Baile Uí Bheacháin) is home to the **Burren College of Art,** established in 1993, which uses the restored 16th-century **Newtown Castle** nearby as a gallery space. Many of the Burren's most important sights are within easy driving or cycling distance, including Poulnabrone, the Aillwee Caves, Dysert O'Dea, and several early Christian ring forts. A village eight kilometers east of Ballyvaughan on the N67, **Bealaclugga** (also known as **Bellharbour**), offers the substantial and picturesque ruins of the Cistercian Corcomroe Abbey. Guided Burren walks and other outdoor activities are readily available, making Ballyvaughan an ideal base for exploring the lunar-limestone landscape.

Sights

If Ballyvaughan is your entry into the Burren, you might want to visit **Burren Exposure** (in the village, tel. 065/707-7277, 9am-6pm daily Mar.-Nov.), which offers an outstanding audiovisual introduction to the area's botany and geology.

Founded by Donal Mór O'Brien in 1194, most of what remains of **Corcomroe Abbey** (1.5 km southeast of Bealaclugga, signposted from the N67, free) dates to the early 13th century. The church's transverse wall was erected in the 15th century, just after the Black Plague; the lay brothers had fled the monastery, and apparently the remaining monks wanted a smaller house of worship to suit their diminished community.

There's a second morbid tale attached to this monastery. In 1317, two branches of the O'Brien clan (led by Dermot and Donough) were about to do battle near the abbey for dominion of the county. The evening before the battle, Donough O'Brien encountered a

The Burren

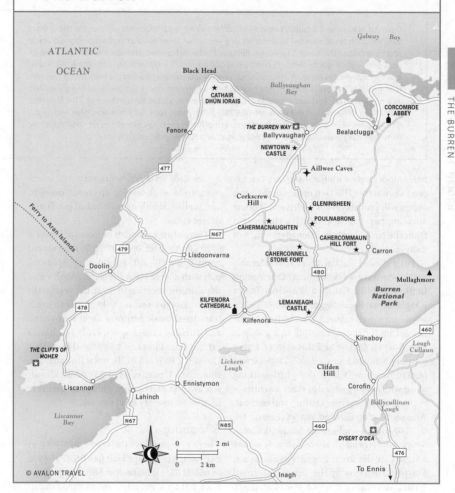

specter doing her washing among a mess of bloody limbs and severed heads in a stream near the abbey—one of which was Donough's. The Morrigan (a Celtic war goddess who often appeared in this form) told the chieftain that this would be his fate if he went ahead into battle. Donough ignored her warning, and by the following night he and all his warriors were lying lifeless in the abbey.

The abbey is in a secluded spot, surrounded by farmlands, and like other monastic ruins, its land serves as a modern graveyard (which the local farmers' dogs have been known to desecrate on occasion).

Activities and Recreation

The 69-kilometer signposted **Burren Cycleway** connects Ballyvaughan with Doolin and Lisdoonvarna. For travel tips and detailed information on the terrain, visit the tourist office in the village center. The 45-kilometer **Burren Way** also begins

★ The Burren Way

Devoted hill-walkers shouldn't miss the **Burren Way,** a 45-kilometer signposted route from Ballyvaughan southwest to Liscannor (or vice versa) that takes you across the limestone plateau and down along the coast. The walk is designed to be self-guided, though you can join a group walk with a local guide through **Burren Guided Walks** (Fanore, tel. 065/707-6100, www. burrenguidedwalks.com). **Walk Ireland** (www.walkireland.ie), part of the Irish Sports Council, recommends you break it down into four half-day segments; check out the website for detailed info on the terrain and recommended maps, which are available for purchase at **The Burren Centre** in Kilfenora (on the R476, tel. 065/708-8030, 10am-5pm daily mid-Mar.-May and Sept.-Oct., 9:30am-6pm daily June-Aug.) or the tourist office in Ennis (O'Connell Sq., tel. 065/682-8366, 9am-9pm daily June-Sept., 9am-6pm Mon.-Sat. and 10am-6pm Sun. Oct.-May).

here. Moderately ambitious walkers can ascend **Corkscrew Hill** (180 meters high); most others will probably want to drive it. It offers amazing panoramic views. It's signposted from the N67, about six kilometers south of Ballyvaughan.

For a guided walk with a knowledgeable local, you have a few choices. One option is **Burren Wild Guided Walking Tours** (Oughtmama, Bealaclugga, tel. 087/877-9565, www.burrenwalks.com, 3-hour walks €20 pp). An option for those traveling in a group is **The Burren Outdoor Education Centre** (Turlough, Bealaclugga, tel. 065/78033, www. burrenoec.com), which does hill-walking along with a smorgasbord of other activities—rock climbing, caving, sailing, you name it. Also see **Burren Guided Walks** (Fanore, tel. 065/707-6100, www.burrenguidedwalks.com).

As for "strands," there are a few fine beaches in the area: Popular with locals, **Flaggy Shore** is at the tip of the small Finavarra Peninsula, which opens up north of Bealaclugga. Flaggy Shore and nearby New Quay village are signposted from the N67. There are also sandy beaches at Fanore and Bishop's Quarter, which is about three kilometers east of Ballyvaughan off the Kinvara road.

Food
Burren Exposure (in the village, tel. 065/707-7277, 9am-6pm daily Mar.-Nov.) has a nice café attached, good for a light lunch. Another option is the **Soda Parlour** (Main

St., tel. 065/708-3999, hours vary, mid-Mar.-Nov., under €12), serving up crepes, omelets, and sandwiches along with baked goods and decent coffee.

There's fine seafood to be found at **Monk's** (The Old Pier, tel. 065/707-7059, food served noon-8pm, €10-20), a light, airy, spacious pub with a large open fireplace. Monk's also has a decent selection of meat and vegetarian dishes, lasagna and suchlike. You can catch traditional music Saturday night year-round and Tuesday June-August. Or if you have a car, consider **Linnane's Seafood Bar** (New Quay, tel. 065/707-8120, www.linnanesbar. com, noon-11pm daily, €10-25), which also offers a vegetarian option. This place gets rave reviews from every local you ask.

Shopping
There's a worthwhile **craft market** at Ballyvaughan Village Hall (tel. 065/707-8955 or 086/811-1511, 10am-6pm Sun. Easter-Oct.). Look out for watercolors by talented botanical artist **Leueen Hill** (tel. 065/707-8955 or 086/811-1511). Otherwise, have a look inside **Quinn's Craft Shop** (Main St., tel. 065/707-7052).

Accommodations
Though Ballyvaughan is a natural base for Burren exploration, budget travelers should probably stay in Carron or Doolin, as there are no hostels. Pauline and Gerry, the supremely helpful owners of **Ballyvaughan Lodge** (on

the N67 just east of the village, tel. 065/707-7292, €40-48 pp, s €50-58), will tell you everything you need to know to find your way around the Burren. Those with a car—and a New Age bent—should consider staying in Fanore, at the **Rocky View Farmhouse** (14 km west of Ballyvaughan, signposted off the R477, tel. 065/707-6103, www.rockyviewfarmhouse.com, €35 pp, s €45). Not only are vegetarian, vegan, and other special diets catered for to a far greater extent than at the average B&B, but also there's a holistic healing center on the premises.

Information and Services
Ballyvaughan has no bank or ATM, so make your withdrawal before leaving Ennis, Galway, or Ennistymon. The **tourist office** (tel. 065/707-7077, www.ballyvaughantourism.com, 9am-5pm Mon.-Sat.) is inside **Linnane's Village Stores** in the center of town.

The **Burren Pharmacy** (tel. 065/707-7029) is on Main Street.

Getting There and Around
Ballyvaughan is at the intersection of the N67 and R477 in northern Clare, 38 kilometers northwest of Ennis and 49 kilometers south of Galway. Bus Éireann routes #50 and #423 go from Galway to the Cliffs of Moher, stopping in Ballyvaughan (at least 3/day Mon.-Sat., 1/day Sun. year-round, at least 8/day Mon.-Sat., 2/day Sun. June-Sept.). The bus stop is right outside Linnane's Village Stores. For a taxi, ring **Tom Connolly** (tel. 087/698-7470).

SOUTH OF BALLYVAUGHAN
Newtown Castle
Like so many other castles in Clare, **Newtown Castle** (3 km south of Ballyvaughan, signposted off the N67, tel. 065/707-7200, www.burrencollege.ie, 10am-6pm daily, free) was built by a branch of the O'Brien clan, and it has quite a unique shape—"a cylinder impaled upon a pyramid." It later belonged to the O'Loughlin family, who proclaimed

themselves "princes of the Burren." The last of the O'Loughlins lived there in the late 19th century, and the tower house had fallen into ruin before the newly established Burren College of Art restored it in the early 1990s. The castle has five floors, the top of which serves as an exhibition space—quite dramatic with the new conical oak roof overhead. This room was originally a bedchamber.

Outside the castle, a 1.3-kilometer **nature trail** will lead you through the northern Burren.

Aillwee Caves
Few Irish tourist attractions are as thoroughly advertised as the **Aillwee Caves** (signposted from the N67 3.5 km south of Ballyvaughan, tel. 065/707-7036, www.aillweecave.ie, 10am-5:30pm daily Nov., 10am-6:30pm daily July and Aug., €9)—there are billboards dotted all over the county. Retreating glaciers at the end of the Ice Age carved these caves from the same limestone that covers the Burren, and you can see stalagmites that are thousands of years old along the 1.3-kilometer floodlit pathway. The visitors' experience of the caves is as touristy as the advertising would suggest, and it's by no means a must-see if you've been inside other caves. Admission is by 40-minute guided tour only.

Poulnabrone
Keep heading south for Ireland's best-known (and most-photographed) Neolithic portal tomb, **Poulnabrone** (signposted and visible from the R480 between Ballyvaughan and Corofin, 8 km south of Aillwee, always open). It's usually called a dolmen, but this is inaccurate—a dolmen consists of two standing stones and a capstone, but Poulnabrone has three standing stones, and its capstone weighs five tons. Picture this 5,400-year-old monument filled in with smaller stones and soil, as it would have been originally. Archaeologists found 22 skeletons buried underneath the stones in 1986. Six were children, none were over the age of 30, and all suffered from severe malnutrition.

It's best to visit early or late in the day, at sunrise or sunset ideally; the site will be deserted, and in the changing light, your view of the portal tomb will be rather dramatic.

Historic Forts

One kilometer south of Poulnabrone on the R480 is the early Christian **Caherconnell Stone Fort** (signposted and visible from the road, tel. 065/708-9999, www.burrenforts. ie, 10am-5pm daily Mar.-Oct., 9:30am-6pm daily July-Aug., €7). This ring fort probably dates to the 5th century and protected a prosperous farmer and his family. Archaeological evidence says it may have been inhabited as late as the 17th century. It's not a must-see, though, especially given the steep admission price.

Another fort with even greater historical significance is **Cahermacnaughten** (12 km south of Ballyvaughan, signposted from the N67 and visible from the minor road to Kilfenora, free), the site of a Brehon law school that flourished here until the end of the 17th century. This fort is 30 meters in diameter, and at its west end are the foundations of another building most likely used by the school. Because the fort was occupied for so long, the interior ground level is nearly flush with the surrounding wall.

CARRON

The delightfully remote village of **Carron** (An Carn) may best be known for the **Burren Perfumery and Floral Centre** (Carron, tel. 065/708-9102, www.burrenperfumery.com, 9am-5pm Mon.-Fri., until 7pm June-Sept., free). The only handicraft perfumery in the country distills the scents of Burren wildflowers. There's also a lovely tearoom, an organic herb garden, and a short movie on the local botany.

Three kilometers south of Carron is the cliff-facing **Cahercommaun Hill Fort,** one of 45,000 medieval Irish ring forts that archaeologists believe may have been designed to prevent the plague from afflicting its inhabitants. Others think the fort may date to the Iron Age. Either way, the fort was last occupied in the 9th century. Note the triple-walled construction and the souterrain leading from the interior to the outer face of the rampart. The uphill path to the fort is steep and rocky, but the climb is well worth the effort for breathtaking panoramic views of the rocky Burren landscape.

Accommodation and food options in Carron are very slim, but of good quality. Popular with families and groups, **Clare's Rock Hostel** (Carron, tel. 065/708-9129, www.claresrock.com, May-Sept., only group bookings in off-season, dorms €15, en suite doubles-quads €25 pp, bike rental €10) enjoys a scenic location in the mountains overlooking the largest disappearing lake (or *turlough*) in western Europe. The hostel also rents out bikes. The pub next door, **Cassidy's** (Carron, tel. 065/708-9109, www.cassidyspub. com, Apr.-Oct., food served noon-9pm Mon.-Sat., noon-8pm Sun., €9-20) is a pleasant, slightly quirky place (alluding, in decor and dish names, to the building's former uses as a British Royal Irish Constabulary station and subsequently a police barracks). Cassidy's has trad sessions on Friday and Saturday nights, with set dancing on Friday.

Carron is not served by Bus Éireann or any private buses, so unfortunately it's not a viable destination if you don't have a car.

KILFENORA

A sleepy little place between Lisdoonvarna and Corofin on the R476, **Kilfenora** (Cill Fhionnúrach) offers both a Burren information center and the remains of an important cathedral. Despite its remote location, the parish prospered so much during the medieval period that it was made its own diocese in 1152. Because Kilfenora currently has no bishop, the title officially belongs to the pope. Driving south from Lisdoonvarna, you'll pass through a lovely evergreen forest, leading you to forget you're in the Burren. Kilfenora is best done as a day trip, since there's a greater choice of accommodations in Doolin, Ballyvaughan, or even Corofin.

St. Fachnan's cathedral in Kilfenora

Sights

Kilfenora's modest 12th-century cathedral, **St. Fachnan's,** is renowned for its high crosses. The cathedral stands on the site of St. Fachnan's 6th-century monastery. Though the nave is still used (for Protestant services) and is closed during the week, the ruined chancel is always open. It features a triple sedilia on the north wall, a delightfully creepy effigy of a medieval bishop opposite, and a dramatic three-light east window.

In the adjacent room, fitted with a new pitched glass roof, are two 12th-century high crosses. The most famous, the Doorty Cross, was "re-used" to mark the Doorty family grave in the 18th century, subsequently broken in two, and finally restored in 1955. It depicts a bishop, perhaps St. Fachnan, with mitre and crozier and four birds perched on his shoulders. The opposite face is carved with the Crucifixion. The North Cross, shorter and better preserved, features abstract Celtic designs. An unnamed ringed cross from the same period stands tall in the adjacent field,

clearly visible from the gravel track that leads to the cathedral itself. This last cross is also carved with the Crucifixion, along with intricate interlacing.

The Burren Centre (Kilfenora, tel. 065/708-8030, www.theburrencentre.ie, 10am-5pm daily mid-Mar.-May and Sept.-Oct., 9:30am-6pm daily June-Aug., €6) offers a detailed topographical model of the Burren as well as a short audiovisual and a 15-minute lecture on the region's geology, botany, archaeology, and history. Those planning to explore the Burren in depth should definitely stop here first. It has the usual tearooms and craft shop.

On the way south from Kilfenora to Kilnaboy and Corofin on the R476, you will pass the 15th-century, O'Brien-built **Lemaneagh Castle.** It is privately owned and not open to the public, but it bears mentioning for its intriguing history. Conor O'Brien, who built the mid-17th-century mansion facade with the mullioned windows, married the wild Máire Rua. After Conor died in battle, she refused to allow his corpse back into the castle, and later on she even married one of Cromwell's soldiers in order to retain the estate.

Food and Accommodations

For a traditional pub lunch, try **Vaughan's** (tel. 065/708-8157, www.vaughanspub.ie) or **Linnane's** (tel. 065/708-8157), both on Main Street. Vaughan's does more elaborate dishes (mains €8-12) and hosts set dancing sessions in the back barn from 9:30pm on Sunday evenings.

Backpackers can rest their weary heads at the brightly painted **Kilfenora Hostel** (Main St., tel. 065/708-8908, www.kilfenorahostel.com, dorm beds €20-24, d €26 pp). The owners can help you arrange for any outdoor activity you feel like.

COROFIN

An utterly peaceful village less than 20 minutes from Ennis, Corofin has rolling green farmlands that give way to a few rocky peaks on the northern horizon, reminding the visitor that they're still on the fringes of the Burren. **Corofin** (Cora Finne) is relatively quiet even in July and August, since visitors often make only a brief stop before heading out to Doolin or other points along the coast. There are enough worthwhile sights within a few kilometers to keep you here for at least a day and night, however, and Corofin's tranquil setting may convince you to dally even longer.

Sights

Housed in a deconsecrated Protestant church, the **Clare Heritage Centre** (Church St., tel. 065/683-7955, 10am-6pm daily mid-May-Oct., €4) offers a trove of historical information. There are scale models and artifacts illustrating everyday life in the 19th-century, as well as exhibits on the famine, emigration, and traditional music. The center's Dr. George McNamara Gallery holds a collection of Neolithic stone ax heads, 17th-century chalices, and other treasures. The **Genealogical Centre** (tel. 065/683-7955, www.clareroots.com, 9am-5:30pm Mon.-Fri.), catercorner across Church St., is the place to visit if you're tracing your heritage in County Clare.

Activities and Recreation

The nearby loughs (Inchiquin, Atedaun, Ballycullinan, and others) and the River Fergus are very popular with anglers, and there is boat hire available in season. The Wood Road around Lough Inchiquin is a nice place for a quiet ramble on a sunny afternoon. The lake and road, just west of Corofin, are signposted from the village.

Those with proper footwear can tackle the Burren's southern peaks, **Clifden Hill** (west of the village, off the Ennistymon road) or **Mullaghmore,** north of Kilnaboy, reachable by the road beside the old church (where the Kilnaboy church and school are signposted). The path is about four kilometers down on the right side of the road.

If you are visiting Dysert O'Dea, you may want to bring a picnic lunch to pretty **Dromore Wood** (Ruan, 8 km southeast of Corofin on the R476 to a regional road, tel. 065/683-7166, dawn-dusk, free). This Dúchas-run nature reserve encompasses several medieval ruins, including two ring forts and a castle built by the O'Brien clan.

Food

Corofin is long on charm and short on eateries, alas. In addition to fine trad, **Bofey**

Lemaneagh Castle near Kilfenora

Quinn's (Main St., tel. 065/683-7321, noon-11pm or later daily, €8-18, full Irish breakfast €8.50) is good for hearty traditional dishes, pizza, or an old-fashioned ice cream sundae. Otherwise, you might want to head into Ennis for dinner.

Entertainment and Events

The cozy, unpretentious **Bofey Quinn's** (Main St., tel. 065/683-7321, noon-11pm or later daily) hosts trad sessions on Wednesday and Saturday nights in winter and on Monday, Wednesday, and Friday in high season (un-scheduled sessions often happen other days of the week). The food's good, too. There's music almost 24/7 here during the **Corofin Traditional Music Festival** in early March.

Shopping

Corofin can boast one of the finest potter-ies in Ireland, **The Pottery Shop** (Church St., tel. 065/683-7020, 9:30am-6pm daily). Yvonne McEnnis's work is lighter and more elegant than most of what comes out of the larger workshops, though her prices are comparable. Being able to meet the potter herself is a great experience, especially since Yvonne is so friendly, kind, and helpful. Once you've stepped inside this wonderful little shop, you'll never again be tempted to buy Nicholas Mosse or any other assembly-line pottery.

Accommodations

One outstanding B&B in the area is ★ **Fergus View** (3 km outside town in Kilnaboy, across the street from the church, tel. 065/683-7606, www.fergusview.com, €36 pp, s €48-52), with a peaceful, bucolic view from every window. The Kellehers' gorgeous family home was built at the turn of last cen-tury as a teacher's residence for none other than Declan Kelleher's grandfather. (Fittingly enough, Mr. Kelleher now serves as princi-pal of the Corofin school.) The welcome is a warm one, with tea (brewed the old-fashioned way, from loose leaves) and homemade raisin bread. Mary's breakfasts are absolutely out of

this world. The firm, comfortable beds also come with electric blankets!

Another recommended B&B, the **Corofin Country House** (Ennistymon Rd., tel. 065/683-7791, €35 pp), is run by Mary Kelleher's sister-in-law, Mary Shannon. The elegant landscaping and decor of this mod-ern home will make the place seem like more of a splurge than it actually is. It has only four bedrooms, and Fergus View six, so be sure to book ahead in high season. Corofin may be a remote spot, but both B&Bs are flourishing with repeat business.

Services

There is no bank or ATM in Corofin, so make your withdrawal before leaving Ennis or Galway. Corofin has one pharmacy, **Rochford's** (Main St., tel. 065/682-7932).

Getting There and Around

Mid-May through September, a **Bus Éireann** service (tel. 065/682-4177, #337) to Corofin departs from Ennis once a day in the early afternoon. That bus continues to Doolin and Lisdoonvarna. Returning to Ennis, the #333 bus passes through Corofin around 9am Monday-Friday, and the #337 bus comes by around 7pm daily.

Corofin is only 12 kilometers northwest of Ennis, so even if you aren't renting a car, you could easily take a taxi from the princi-pal town.

★ Dysert O'Dea

Corofin is the closest town to one of Clare's most important monastic sites, **Dysert O'Dea** ("desert oh-DEE," 1.5 km west of the R476, just south of Corofin, year-round), which includes a ruined church, round tower, and high cross. The church is a 17th-century reconstruction of a 12th- or 13th-century ed-ifice and features a remarkable Romanesque doorway with voussoirs of eerily individual-ized human and animal heads. What makes it even more noteworthy is that this door-way is a composite of the original arch and one from another unidentified site. The

famous high cross here, east of the church (in the pasture beyond the enclosure wall), has the figure of a bishop carved on the east face, which is surmounted by a smaller effigy of the crucified Christ. The remains of the 12th-century round tower are about 15 meters high. A three-kilometer footpath takes you past dozens of ancient and medieval remains—ring forts, more high crosses, and so forth.

The very worthwhile **Archaeology Centre** (connected to the monastic site by footpath, tel. 065/683-7401, 10am-6pm daily May-Sept., €4) is within a four-story tower house that was built by the O'Deas in the late 15th century and trashed by the nefarious Cromwell in 1651. The collection includes Neolithic stone ax heads, Bronze Age spear and javelin heads, medieval and 18th-century swords, and IRA weapons used during the Civil War. A half-hour movie describes the local archaeology.

a Romanesque doorway at Dysert O'Dea

Kilnaboy

About four kilometers north of Corofin on the R476 is the tiny village of Kilnaboy. Its ruined church is known for the *sheila-na-gig* above the doorway. Carved in stone, this is a female effigy with exaggerated genitalia (the phrase literally means "Sheila of the teats"). Sadly, the stone is so worn that the figure is barely distinguishable, but the church is still worth a peek. Its haunting serenity has generations of romantic poets yet to inspire. The church is always open, accessible from a set of steep stone steps from the main road.

Limerick City

Limerick is no longer the crime-ridden "Stab City" out-of-towners made a point to avoid before the advent of the Celtic Tiger. On sunless days it can still be a vaguely drab place, but its fairly good arts scene and a prominent art and design school do much to counteract that sour vibe of yesteryear. What crimes do happen are almost always drug-related and do not affect upstanding citizens or visitors who exercise caution when out late at night, as in any city. Today, the republic's third-largest city is truly a working study in urban renewal.

Limerick doesn't have to be just a stopover on your way south to Killarney or west to rural Clare. **King John's Castle** and the spooky **St. Mary's Cathedral** are emblematic of the city's rich history and render the city worthy of an overnight visit. Limerick's Georgian architectural heritage is exemplified in landmarks like the Old Custom House and in the doorways of townhouses all over the city. And not only are the late Neolithic remains at nearby **Lough Gur** of tremendous archaeological importance, but the lakeside is splendid for a bike ride and picnic lunch.

Downtown Limerick is laid out in a simple

grid system, quite easy to navigate. O'Connell Street is the main drag, running parallel to the River Shannon, and becomes Patrick Street, then Rutland Street as it continues north to the Abbey River. Cross the Abbey River and you'll find the castle and cathedral. Colbert Bus and Train Station, the People's Park, and the municipal art gallery are on the south side of the city center. Everything you need is on the eastern shore of the River Shannon.

SIGHTS

There are enough worthwhile stops to keep you in Limerick for at least a full day.

King John's Castle and Vicinity

The keepless **King John's Castle** (Nicholas St., tel. 061/411-201, 9:30am-5:30pm daily May-Oct., 9:30am-4:30pm daily Nov.-Feb., 9:30am-5pm daily Mar.-Apr., €7) was erected on the banks of the Shannon between 1200 and 1207 at the command of the castle's namesake. It is one of Ireland's oldest intact examples of medieval architecture, though the expensive restoration effort of the 1990s had mixed results: The interpretive center looming out of the castle's center is downright hideous, but on the upside, visitors can now

descend into archaeological excavations dating to the Hiberno-Norse period (the 9th and 10th centuries), a truly fascinating experience.

There isn't much in the adjacent **Limerick Museum** (Castle Ln., Nicholas St., tel. 061/417-826, 10am-1pm and 2:15pm-5pm Tues.-Sat., free) to occupy you for more than half an hour, but it's still worth a look. Items include Bronze and Stone Age artifacts, antique silver and lace from the city's workshops, a few paintings, and official documents.

The **Bishop's Palace** (across the road from the castle), originally part of Cromwell's 1649 settlement, served as the grand residence of Limerick's Protestant bishops until 1784. After two centuries of neglect, the Limerick Civic Trust rescued the palace from demolition, and now, fully restored, it serves as Trust headquarters. Also directly across the street from the castle is a "Gothic folly" **toll house,** erected in 1840 by the architects of the Thomond Bridge.

Across the bridge from the castle and museum is the **Limerick Treaty Stone,** on which the Treaty of 1691, the surrender of Jacobite Patrick Sarsfield to the troops of William of Orange, is believed to have been signed. The treaty was also meant to provide protection for Irish Catholics, but it should

Limerick City and lights along the River Shannon

Limerick City

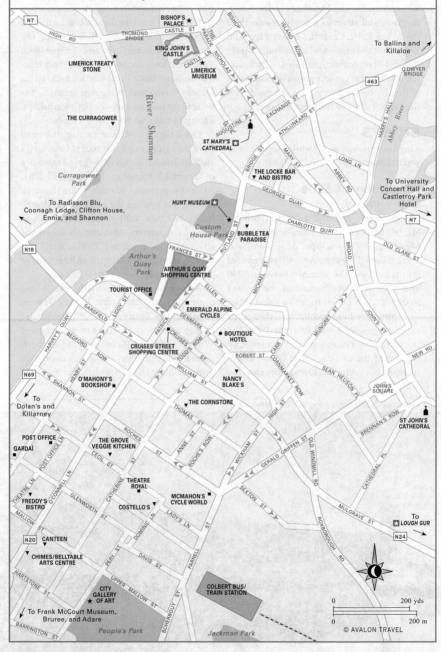

N7 HIGH RD

THOMOND BRIDGE
CASTLE ST
BISHOP'S PALACE ★
KING JOHN'S CASTLE
CASTLE LN
CASTLE ST
THE PARADE
BISHOP ST
ST NICHOLAS ST
ISLAND RD
ROW

To Ballina and Killaloe

463
O'DWYER BRIDGE

LIMERICK TREATY STONE ★

LIMERICK MUSEUM

EXCHANGE ST
ATHLUNKARD ST
HARRY'S HALL
Abbey River

THE CURRAGOWER ▼

ST AUGUSTINE PL
ST MARY'S CATHEDRAL ✚

MARY ST
LONG LN
ABBEY RD

River Shannon

Curragower Park

BRIDGE ST
THE LOCKE BAR AND BISTRO ▼

GEORGES QUAY

To University Concert Hall and Castletroy Park Hotel

To Radisson Blu, Coonagh Lodge, Clifton House, Ennis, and Shannon

HUNT MUSEUM ✚

Custom House Park

RUTLAND ST
CHARLOTTE QUAY
BROAD ST
OLD CLARE ST

N7

N18

Arthur's Quay Park
FRANCES ST
BUBBLE TEA PARADISE ●

ARTHUR'S QUAY SHOPPING CENTRE

ELLEN ST
MICHAEL ST

TOURIST OFFICE ■

SARSFIELD ST
LIDDY ST

EMERALD ALPINE CYCLES ■

DENMARK ST
PATRICK ST
CRUISES ST
TODD'S ROW

● BOUTIQUE HOTEL

CARR ST
CORNMARKET ROW

N69

HARVEY'S QUAY
BEDFORD ROW

CRUISES STREET SHOPPING CENTRE

WILLIAM ST
ROBERT ST
SEAN HEUSON PL

NEW RD

O'MAHONY'S BOOKSHOP ■

HENRY ST
SHANNON ST

NANCY BLAKE'S ▼

JOHN'S ST
JOHN'S SQUARE

To Dolan's and Killarney

THOMAS ST
THE CORNSTORE ▼

ANNE ST
HIGH ST

ROCHES ST
ROCHES ROW
WICKHAM ST
BRENNAN'S ROW

POST OFFICE ■
GARDAÍ ■

POST OFFICE LN

THE GROVE VEGGIE KITCHEN ▼

CECIL ST

ST JOHN'S CATHEDRAL ✚

CATHEDRAL PL

THEATRE LN
O'CONNELL LN

THEATRE ROYAL ▼

CATHERINE ST

MCMAHON'S CYCLE WORLD ■

GERALD GRIFFEN ST
OLD WINDMILL RD

FREDDY'S BISTRO ▼

GLENWORTH ST
COSTELLO'S ▼

LADY'S LN
SEXTON ST

MULGRAVE ST

To LOUGH GUR ✚

MALLOW ST

N20

CANTEEN ▼

PERY ST
DOMINIC ST
DAVIS ST
PARNELL ST
ROXBOROUGH RD

N24

CHIMES/BELLTABLE ARTS CENTRE ▼

HARTSTONE ST

CITY GALLERY OF ART ★

UPPER MALLOW ST
BOHERBUOY

COLBERT BUS/ TRAIN STATION

To Frank McCourt Museum, Bruree, and Adare

BARRINGTON ST

People's Park

Jackman Park

0   200 yds
0   200 m

© AVALON TRAVEL

come as no surprise that this particular clause was forgotten almost as soon as the treaty was signed.

★ St. Mary's Cathedral

It is ancient, dank, and cavernous—in other words, the perfect setting for one of Sheridan Le Fanu's scariest short stories. As Limerick's oldest edifice, **St. Mary's Cathedral** (Bridge St., tel. 061/416-238, 9am-5pm daily Oct.-May, 9am-1pm June-Sept., €4) is a must-see even if your taste doesn't veer toward the Gothic.

Parts of the original late-12th-century building survive in the nave, chancel, and restored Romanesque west doorway (visible from the outside). Items of interest include black-oak misericords (cheat-seats for standing choristers)—dating to 1489, they are unique in Ireland and are intricately carved with animal figures—and a stone reredos (an ornamental partition in front of the altar) carved by the father of patriot Patrick Pearse and installed in 1907. Also contributing to the sense that one has wandered into a Gothic tale are the medieval tombs behind the altar. One of these belongs to Donal Mór O'Brien, king of Munster, who donated the land to the church in 1180.

St. Mary's is part of the Church of Ireland. Be sure to pick up the brochure as you enter—the counterclockwise self-guided tour is full of strange historical tidbits.

St. John's Cathedral

The neo-Gothic Catholic cathedral, **St. John's** (Cathedral Place, tel. 061/414-624), was designed by the English architect Philip Charles Hardwick and built in the late 1850s. The cathedral is crowned with an ornate 85-meter spire, one of the three tallest in Ireland. The austerity of its facade isn't continued inside—it's certainly worth a look, though this church is inevitably less intriguing than St. Mary's.

★ Hunt Museum

No visit to Limerick would be complete without an afternoon at the marvelous **Hunt Museum** (Old Custom House, Rutland St., tel. 061/312-833, www.huntmuseum.com, 10am-5pm Mon.-Sat., 2pm-5pm Sun., €5), which offers the greatest collection of ancient and medieval artifacts outside of the National Museum in Dublin (though not all its treasures are of Irish origin). John and Gertrude Hunt, a couple of philanthropic art historians, donated their vast private collection to the state in 1974, though the museum was only opened in 1997 (the collection was housed at the University of Limerick in the interim); the oldest pieces are Neolithic tools as well as Bronze Age jewelry, funerary pottery, and cooking utensils. Religious artifacts include 8th- and 9th-century bronze monastic bells, a reliquary cross that belonged to Mary, Queen of Scots, and the 17th-century Galway Chalice. The prize of the small painting collection is a self-portrait of the neoclassicist Italophile Robert Fagan and his wife *à la grecque*, and in the same room you'll see a small bronze horse cast by Leonardo da Vinci.

Limerick City Gallery of Art

If the Hunt hasn't quite satisfied your love of fine art, head for the **Limerick City Gallery of Art** (Pery Sq., tel. 061/310-633, 10am-1pm and 2pm-6pm Mon.-Wed. and Fri., 10am-1pm and 2pm-7pm Thurs., 10am-1pm Sat., free), in the neo-Romanesque Carnegie Building (built at the turn of the 20th century). As is the case with many municipal art galleries, this one has many small treasures (landscapes and portraits mostly) but not enough space for them. The upper floor feels more airy and hosts rotating exhibitions that can be surprisingly postmodern.

The Frank McCourt Museum

This tribute to the life of the late Irish-American memoirist was opened by his brother Malachy in 2011 in the Tudor-style building where the McCourts attended grade school. The period-decorated rooms of the **Frank McCourt Museum** (Leamy House, Hartstonge St., tel. 061/319-710, www.frankmccourtmuseum.com, 11am-4:30pm

Mon.-Fri., weekends by appointment, €4) will appeal primarily to visitors who have read *Angela's Ashes* or his other books, though anyone with a keen interest in early 20th-century Irish history will find this little museum worthwhile.

ACTIVITIES AND RECREATION

Serious walkers will want to check out at least part of the 65-kilometer **Lough Derg Way,** which begins in Limerick City, heads up to Killaloe in eastern Clare, and continues north through the shale-flecked Arra Mountains to Dromineer in northern Tipperary, a pleasant resort town. Most walkers begin at Killaloe and walk either south to Limerick or north to Dromineer, though the way can be traversed in either direction, and lush countryside, lovely Shannon and lake views, and wildlife-watching opportunities abound along both sections. The signposted route begins at the Arthur's Quay tourist office, where you can pick up maps and guides on local flora and fauna.

Lough Gur is a popular cycling destination since it's only 20 kilometers southeast of the city (on the R512).

Limerick's nearest golf course is **Rathbane** (3.2 km south of town, signposted off the R512, tel. 061/313-655, www.rathbane-golf.com, open daily); advance booking is recommended.

FOOD

Limerick can boast several quality eateries, if not quite so many as you'd expect for a city of its size. Run by a mother-and-daughter team for more than three decades, **The Grove Veggie Kitchen** (11 Cecil St., tel. 061/410-084, 9:30am-4pm Mon.-Fri., under €10, cash only) dishes up hearty lunches like lasagna, chickpea curry, and stuffed tomatoes with gluten-free breadcrumbs. Dairy cheese is a common ingredient, however, so vegans might want to grab a falafel wrap and a smoothie at **Bubble Tea Paradise Healthy Café** (3 Rutland St., tel. 061/211-072,

8am-5pm Mon.-Fri., 10am-6pm Sat., €6-10). **Canteen** (20 Mallow St., tel. 085/215-3212, www.wearecanteen.com, 8am-4pm Mon.-Fri., 10:30am-4pm Sat., under €10) is the perfect option for meat-lovers who want a quick and relatively healthy meal, though the menu is quite veg-friendly too.

Limerick's most beloved gastro-pubs are known for their seafood. **The Locke Bar and Bistro** (3 Georges Quay, tel. 061/413-733, www.lockebar.com, meals served noon-10:30pm, lunch €8-12, dinner €17-26) offers an extensive beer menu as well as the nightly trad sessions. Or enjoy a bowl of award-winning chowder at **The Curragower** (Clancy Strand, tel. 061/321-788, www.curragower.com, noon-11pm daily, lunch €10-14, dinner €11-30).

It isn't a formal restaurant, but at **The Cornstore** (19 Thomas St., tel. 061/609-000, www.cornstorelimerick.com, noon-10pm daily, lunch €10, dinner €14-23, 3-course early bird €28) reservations are definitely recommended on weekend evenings. The cocktails are legendary, the menu includes plenty of gluten-free options, and the service is terrific.

For a special night out, make a reservation at cozy, family-run ★ **Freddy's Bistro** (Theatre Ln., Lower Glentworth St., tel. 061/418-749, www.freddysbistro.com, 6:30pm-10:30pm Tues.-Sat., 2/3-course menu €25/30), which seems to have garnered every culinary award it is possible to win! Irish beef dominates the menu, though the vegetarian options (like nut roast in a filo pastry) are equally thoughtful, and gluten-free and vegan diets are catered to upon request. Try to save some room for the lemon tart or sticky toffee pudding.

ENTERTAINMENT

The best pubs in Limerick City for live trad include **The Locke Bar** (3 Georges Quay, tel. 061/413-733, www.lockebar.com), established in 1724, with sessions Tuesday, Thursday, and Sunday nights; **Nancy Blake's** (19 Upper Denmark St., tel. 061/416-443) Sunday-Wednesday; and **Costello's** (4 Dominic St., tel. 061/418-520) for trad on the weekends. The Locke and Nancy Blake's offer a charming old-world ambience and popular outdoor beer gardens, and Costello's offers (relatively) cheap drinks and a somewhat arty crowd.

For rock shows, the place to go is **Dolan's Warehouse** (Dock Rd., tel. 061/314-483, www.dolans.ie, €7-20), adjoining the more traditional **Dolan's Pub** (which also has excellent live trad nightly). Featured bands at the warehouse run the gamut from indie pop/rock to "Irish metal," and Wednesday night is reserved for stand-up comedy.

The University of Limerick's **University Concert Hall** (University of Limerick campus, tel. 061/331-549, www.uch.ie, €8-30) is the place to go if you enjoy classical and choral music. More convenient than the UCH box office is the City Centre Ticket Desk, at the Limerick tourist office at Arthur's Quay (tel. 061/314-314, 9:30am-1pm Mon.-Sat.). You can also book online, though a €1 service charge applies. (Take a taxi to the campus, which is about 5 km east of the city off the R503.)

Another option is the dinner recital series at the **Hunt Museum** (Old Custom House, Rutland St., tel. 061/312-960, friends@hunt-museum.com, €50). On Sunday evenings, an intimate concert featuring top-notch classical artists is followed by a candlelight dinner in the museum restaurant.

SHOPPING

Limerick boasts the country's largest indie bookstore, **O'Mahony's** (120 O'Connell St., tel. 061/418-155, www.omahonys.ie). Established in 1902, it's more spacious than the Eason's on Cruises Street and offers a fine selection of Irish history and literature.

ACCOMMODATIONS

Unfortunately, at time of writing there were no hostels in Limerick, and there aren't as many B&Bs as you'd expect for such a large city. There are plenty of hotels, though, which mostly cater to business travelers.

Several B&Bs dot Ennis Road on the far side of the Sarsfield Bridge. With 16 bedrooms, **Clifton House** (Ennis Rd., tel. 061/451-166, €30-35 pp, s €40-45) is more a guesthouse than a B&B, though the owners are just as welcoming as if you were staying in their lone spare room. You'll find tea, coffee, and cookies in the guest lounge until 11pm. Or if you have a car, try **Coonagh Lodge** (Coonagh, 4 km west of town via the N18, tel. 061/327-050, www.coonaghlodge.com, €35-40 pp, s €50), an immaculately kept bungalow with tranquil garden views.

Budget hotels don't come much nicer than **The Boutique** (Denmark St., tel. 061/315-320, www.theboutique.ie, €40 pp, s €70), and for all that the furnishings aren't as luxurious as they're meant to look, a room here is still a good value. The only caveat is that the Boutique offers special packages for stag and hen parties, so if you book a room at the weekend just brace yourself for a noisy night.

If you have a rental car and are up for a splurge, try the **Castletroy Park Hotel** (Dublin Rd., 5 km east of town, tel. 061/335-566, www.castletroypark.ie, €80-230 pp, s €145-195), directly across the road from the University of Limerick main entrance—it's a four-star hotel with five-star service. It has a 20-meter pool and a gymnasium as well as a salon and spa. Castletroy Park is arguably the best hotel in town, though another option is the **Radisson Blu** (Ennis Rd., 3 km west of town, tel. 061/456-200, www.radissonblu.com, rooms €115-180), which is set on 20 acres of landscaped grounds and offers similar facilities to Castletroy Park (plus a special wing for female business travelers with rooms featuring extra girly comforts like lavender-scented cushions and deluxe bath products).

INFORMATION AND SERVICES

For guided walking tours, UCH concert tickets, and general sightseeing advice, visit the Limerick **tourist office** (Limerick Tourism Centre, Arthur's Quay, tel. 061/317-522, www.shannonregiontourism.ie, 9am-7pm Mon.-Fri. and 9am-6pm Sat.-Sun. July-Aug.; 9:30am-1pm and 2pm-5:30pm Mon.-Sat.

May-June and Sept.-Oct.; 9:30am-1pm and 2pm-5:30pm Mon.-Fri. and 9:30am-1pm Sat. Nov.-Apr.).

ATMs and bureaux de change are available at the **Bank of Ireland** (O'Connell St., tel. 061/415-055) and **AIB** (O'Connell St., tel. 061/414-388). If you need a drugstore, try **Charlotte Quay Pharmacy** (Charlotte Quay, tel. 061/400-722).

Limerick's **Garda Síochána headquarters** (Henry St., tel. 061/212-400) are on the southwestern end of town, one block west of O'Connell Street.

GETTING THERE

Limerick is 25 kilometers southeast of the Shannon Airport on the M18/N18, also the road to take if you're coming from Galway (103 km). Take the N24 from Waterford (126 km), the N20/M20 from Cork (100 km), the N21 from Tralee (105 km), and the M7 from Dublin (232 km).

Colbert Bus and Train Station (Parnell St., tel. 061/315-555) is catty-corner to the People's Park on the southern side of the city. You can reach Limerick by **Bus Éireann** (tel. 061/313-333) from Dublin (#12, 10/day); Galway, Ennis, Cork (#51, 13/day); the Shannon Airport (#343, 2/hour); Tralee (#14, 9/day); Athlone (#72, 10/day), or Waterford (#55, 8/day).

Direct **Irish Rail** service is available from Ennis (7-8/day). Other destinations are via Limerick Junction: Dublin (6/day), Waterford (3/day), and Cork (7/day). Ring the station for train times.

GETTING AROUND

Though Bus Éireann offers local service, Limerick is small enough that you can walk everywhere you need to go. Taxis line up outside Colbert Station and on two side streets off O'Connell Street (Thomas and Cecil); to ring for one, try **City Cabs** (74 Henry St., tel. 061/311-111) or **Munster Cabs** (78 O'Connell St., tel. 061/061/412-727).

Emerald Alpine Cycles (21 Roches St., tel. 061/416-983, www.irelandrentabike.com,

9:15am-5:30pm Mon.-Sat., €20/day, €80/week, €25 one-way fee) offers free luggage storage (or a one-way rental for an additional fee, alternatively). Given the city's size, you won't need a bike unless you're planning to explore the outlying countryside.

★ LOUGH GUR

The remains of a series of settlements between 3000 BC (the late Neolithic period) and the Middle Ages surround the small, picturesque Lough Gur, only 11 kilometers southeast of Limerick City. The **Lough Gur Interpretive Centre** (on the R514, tel. 061/361-511, www.loughgur.com, 10am-5pm Mon.-Fri., noon-6pm Sat.-Sun. mid-May-Sept., €5) is unique in that it's housed in a pair of replica Bronze Age thatched huts, the result of an archaeological dig led by John Hunt (of Hunt Museum renown). The admission fee is somewhat excessive for the amount of insight it contains. You may want to skip the center and explore the sites on your own.

Looking south from the interpretive center, you will see **Bolin Island,** which was originally a Bronze Age *crannóg* (man-made from rocks and other natural materials). From here you can spot the ruins of 15th-century Bourchier's Castle (to your left) and the 13th-century Black Castle on the far side of the lake; the former is inaccessible, but you can reach the latter by heading east on the lakeside path.

The Lough Gur periphery is dotted with standing stones, the ruins of millennium-old cottages, and burial mounds. The two most important sites, Grange Stone Circle and Giant's Grave, are slightly farther away.

Grange Stone Circle

The **Grange Stone Circle** (signposted on the left-hand side of the R512 from Limerick, just past the village of Grange, 3 km west of the interpretive center, €2 suggested donation) is at least 4,000 years old, putting it within the early Bronze Age. The circle—sometimes referred to as Ireland's Stonehenge—is 45 meters in diameter and comprises 113 boulders and cut stones, the tallest of which is 2.4

meters high. New Agey types flock here for the summer solstice, when a beam of light cuts through the circle's center at sunrise. Timothy Casey, the kindly farmer who owns the land, lets his newborn calves test their legs in the circle every spring. There's a smaller stone circle and a huge standing stone also on his land, both visible from the Grange.

Giant's Grave

The second monument is the **Giant's Grave** (signposted on the R512, 1.5 km southwest of the interpretive center), a Bronze Age wedge tomb at least 2,500 years old. Its double stone walls, in-filled with rubble, are topped with several capstones and bisected by a perpendicular slab, forming a low dual-chambered gallery about 3 meters wide and over 15 meters long. This was most likely a communal tomb, but "giant's grave" is certainly more poetic.

Getting There

Bus Éireann does offer a service through the village of Bruff near Lough Gur, but it's so limited that busing it just isn't a viable option. Driving or cycling out of Limerick City, take the Waterford-bound N24, and then pick up the R512 just outside of town.

ADARE

Sixteen kilometers southwest of Limerick City on the River Maigue, Adare is popular with the coach-bus set for its picture-perfection—the town's tourism promoters actually hype it as a "storybook village." Thatched-roof gift shops line the main thoroughfare,

and accommodations are disproportionately expensive. Some might say that Adare's charm is unabashedly contrived, but others will find reason to linger for a few hours. The town's exclusive golf course (the Adare Manor Golf Club, tel. 061/396-204) includes the splendid ruins of **Desmond Castle** and a **Franciscan Friary.** Obtain permission from the club before visiting them.

If churches are your thing, you shouldn't miss the **Trinitarian Friary Church** (Main St., beside the Heritage Centre), which now serves as Adare's Catholic parish church. The Trinitarian Friary was founded in the 13th century and is the only surviving church of this religious order in the country. There's also the 14th-century **Augustinian Friary** (on the Limerick road, on the right side as you enter Adare), founded by the first Earl of Kildare, which now serves as the Church of Ireland. Take a peek at the cloister and the restored domestic buildings, as well as the lovely switch-line tracery on the Gothic windows inside the church. In fine weather you can take the picturesque riverside walk originating at the friary gates.

For more information on medieval Adare, check out the **Adare Heritage Centre** (Main St., tel. 061/396-666, www.adareheritagecentre.com, 9am-6pm daily, free), which offers an audiovisual presentation along with a model of the town at the turn of the 16th century. Walking tours depart here July-September.

You can reach Adare from Limerick City on the N20, and Bus Éireann services Adare on the #13 or #14 route between Limerick and Tralee (at least 8/day out of Limerick).

Galway

Galway City. 288

The Aran Islands 300

Connemara. 311

Southern and Eastern Galway. . 323

Detour to Clonmacnoise 327

Ireland's second-largest county, Galway (Gaillimh) is the west at its best: a vibrant, bohemian capital city; wild, boggy, mountainous Connemara, dotted with lakes that look black in fog but shimmer brilliantly when the sun shines;

and islands crisscrossed in ancient stone walls, rich in pre-Christian and monastic heritage as well as traditional Gaelic language and culture.

Galway is a deservedly popular tourism base, since you can visit Connemara and the Burren in County Clare on easy day trips, but it's a bit easier to hop off the merry-go-round here than it is in County Kerry. Once you get outside Roundstone and Clifden, Connemara feels almost as lonely and remote as it would have a hundred years ago.

In contrast, the plains of eastern Galway offer little in the way of interesting scenery or tourist attractions, though there are a few sights worth a detour en route to Galway City from points east.

HISTORY

No one quite knows the origin of "Gaillimh"; some people say it was named for the daughter of an Iron Age chieftain who drowned in the River Corrib, which was originally known as the River Galway. At any rate, archaeological evidence indicates that the first settlement of Galway dates to Neolithic times, and there may have been an earthen fort erected in what would later become the city's Claddagh section. Though the Vikings pillaged the native Irish settlements here several centuries before the advent of the Normans, they did not found their own city here as they'd done in Wexford, Waterford, Dublin, and other places.

Galway is often called the "City of the Tribes" for the 14 Norman families who established themselves here from the 13th century on; the native Irish were forced to move to the Claddagh, a fishing village outside the city walls. The Normans had erected these walls to defend themselves against the O'Flaherty clan, from whom they had usurped the land. The Normans were loyal to the English crown, of course, and in the 15th and 16th centuries the port of Galway flourished with

Previous: the ruins of a 13th-century church on Inishbofin; boats on the Claddagh in Galway City. **Above:** Clonfert Cathedral.

Look for ★ to find recommended
sights, activities, dining, and lodging.

Highlights

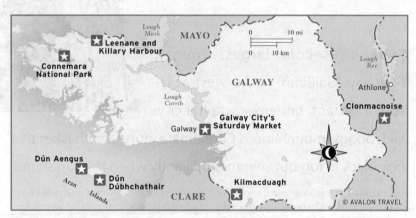

★ **Galway City's Saturday Market:** It's not just farm stands at the market outside St. Nicholas' Collegiate Church; shop for whimsical souvenirs and treat yourself to anything from vegetarian Indian grub to deluxe crepes, fresh bagels and doughnuts, chocolate-covered strawberries, and gourmet coffee (page 295).

★ **Dún Aengus:** This 2,000-year-old semicircular fort is stunningly situated atop a 90-meter sea cliff (page 302).

★ **Dún Dúbhchathair:** It's as quiet as Aengus is touristy, but the scant remains of this cliffside fort are just as breathtaking (page 302).

★ **Connemara National Park:** These 1,300 boggy, beautiful hectares include three peaks of the Twelve Bens mountain range (page 318).

★ **Leenane and Killary Harbour:** The hills bordering Ireland's only fjord have a haunting, almost supernatural atmosphere, and the village of Leenane makes a lovely base for exploring northern Connemara (page 320).

★ **Kilmacduagh:** The highlight of this off-the-beaten-track monastic ruin is a 34-meter round tower leaning 60 centimeters off-center, a truly arresting sight (page 324).

★ **Clonmacnoise:** Make a detour into the midlands to the country's most important monastic city, founded by St. Ciarán in the 6th century along the bank of the River Shannon (page 327).

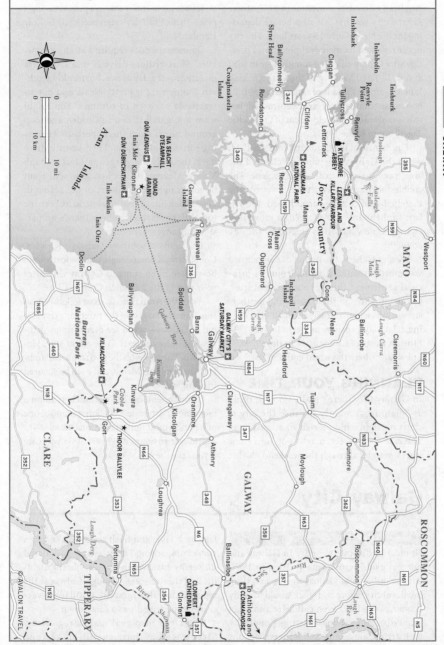

Galway

Inishbofin

Inishshark

Inishturk

Slyne Head

Ballyconneely

Cleggan

Renvyle Point

Tullycross

Renvyle

Doolough

355

N59

Croaghnakeela Island

Roundstone

341

Clifden

Letterfrack

KYLEMORE ABBEY

LEENANE AND KILLARY HARBOUR

Aasleagh Falls

Recess

340

CONNEMARA NATIONAL PARK

Joyce's Country

MAYO

Maam

N59

N59

Westport

Aran Islands

DÚN AENGUS

NA SEACHT DTEAMPAILL

Inis Mór Kilronan

DÚN DÚBHCHATHAIR

IONAD ARANN

Gorumna Island

Rossaveal

Maam Cross

Oughterard

Inchagoil Island

Cong

Neale

345

Lough Mask

N84

Inis Meáin

Inis Oírr

Doolin

N67

Ballyvaughan

336

Spiddal

Barna

GALWAY CITY'S SATURDAY MARKET

Galway

N59

Lough Corrib

Headford

334

N84

Claremorris

N60

N17

Ballinrobe

Lough Carra

N85

Burren National Park

KILMACDUAGH

Coole Park

Kinvara

460

N18

Galway Bay

Kinvarra Bay

Kilcolgan

Oranmore

Claregalway

N17

Tuam

N83

Dunmore

CLARE

THOOR BALLYLEE

Gort

N66

Athenry

347

GALWAY

Moylough

N63

Roscommon

N60

352

353

Loughrea

348

358

ROSCOMMON

N61

352

Lough Derg

Portumna

N65

M6

Ballinasloe

River Suck

357

Lough Ree

N63

N5

TIPPERARY

N52

356

River Shannon

CLONFERT CATHEDRAL

Clonfert

357

To Athlone and CLONMACNOISE

N61

© AVALON TRAVEL

0   10 km
0   10 mi

trade from Spain and Portugal. It's even said that Columbus stopped here for Mass at the Anglican Cathedral sometime in 1477; others say the city was his last stop before departing for the New World 15 years later. The city never regained its medieval power and prestige after Cromwell's nine-month siege in 1652 and its ill-fated backing of the Catholic king James against William of Orange in 1691; its bohemian vitality may feel deep-rooted, but this is truly more a development of the "Celtic Tiger" boom of the 1990s.

The demise of the Claddagh came in 1934, when the Galway Corporation claimed the area was a threat to health and hygiene. The cobblestoned streets were tarred over and the thatched-roof cottages demolished; the village's inhabitants were forced to move into charmless new buildings erected by the city council.

West of Galway, the region of Connemara was mostly isolated from the county's principal settlement throughout the centuries; the farming life on these rock- and heather-strewn hills was extremely difficult even during relatively prosperous periods. As H. V. Morton wrote of Connemara in the 1920s, "I know now where the world ends."

PLANNING YOUR TIME

In Galway City there's really no such thing as "planning," mainly because the city is short on sights and so rich in atmosphere. Traverse Shop Street, maybe pop into a few stores, wander through the weekend market outside the cathedral and down to the Spanish Arch on the River Corrib, and wind up at a streetside table at Neachtain's pub, savoring a pint—that's a full day's sightseeing by Galway standards.

Connemara does require a strategy, however. Most visitors drive it in a clockwise direction over a day or two, but frankly southern Connemara is pretty bleak, and not attractively so, even in summer. You might want to hightail it west to Clifden and loop around north from there, perhaps venturing into County Mayo. Then savor a drive back through the gorgeous Lough Inagh Valley. Meanwhile, backpackers will want to get straight to the heart of the action in Letterfrack (for the national park) or Leenane (on Killary Harbour, where there's an outstanding adventure center).

The sights of southern Galway—Kinvara, Coole Park, Kilmacduagh, and so forth—are best taken in en route to Galway City after your tour of the Burren in County Clare.

As for the Aran Islands, most folks just visit Inis Mór, the largest of the three, as a day trip out of Galway—yet to see everything worthwhile requires at least a one-night stay, ideally two. The sights on the two smaller islands, Inis Oírr and Inis Meáin, can each be scoured in a single day.

If you've rented a car, definitely plan on a morning or afternoon at Clonmacnoise, one of Ireland's most important monastic sites. It's a little over an hour's drive east of Galway City if you take the M6.

Galway City

TOP EXPERIENCE

"It must be difficult to arrive in Galway and not feel glad," wrote Kate O'Brien in 1962. All the millions of visitors to this sparkling medieval city before and since would heartily concur. Some folks even call it Ireland's San Francisco. Its west-coast setting; popularity with artists, musicians, and writers; friendly, laid-back vibe; and fresh sea air make this a viable comparison. The presence of a national university enriches an already vibrant nightlife and theater scene. Though Galway is the republic's fourth-largest city, it still feels as accessible and friendly as a small town.

The city's medieval main drag, **Shop Street,** is always buzzing with buskers and other enterprising entertainers—puppeteers, flame-throwers, even the occasional didgeridoo. From the recently refurbished Eyre Square (where the bus and train station is), walk south, passing Eglinton Street on your right, and venture down the cobblestoned pedestrian thoroughfare: Like most Irish main streets, Shop Street starts out as William, then becomes Shop, then High Street, before splitting into Quay Street (on the left) and Mainguard (later Bridge) Street on your right. At the end of Quay Street you'll find the Spanish Arch, a popular hangout for the city's bohemian population in fine weather (while Eyre Square tends to attract all the terminally bored teenagers). Cross the Wolfe Tone Bridge and you're in the old Claddagh section of the city, which now offers some of Galway's best pubs and cafés.

SIGHTS

Noteworthy architecture can be spotted on the northwestern side of Eyre Square, at the 17th-century **Browne's Doorway** (as you can see, the doorway itself is all that remains of Browne's townhouse); at the 16th-century **Lynch's Castle** on Shop Street at Abbeygate Street, which has housed the main Galway branch of the Allied Irish Bank since the 1960s (look for the original stone carvings high on the exterior walls); and at the solid, 16th-century **Spanish Arch** at the bottom of Quay Street on the River Corrib, so named for the Spanish ships that sailed through the no-longer-extant city wall carrying cargoes of exotic spirits.

Cathedrals

Galway's two cathedrals, one Catholic and one Anglican, are both named for Santa Claus (who was also the patron saint of sailors) and thus are easily confused. In the center of town, just off Shop Street, the Protestant **St. Nicholas' Collegiate Church** (Lombard St., tel. 091/564-648, generally 9am-6pm Mon.-Sat. and 1pm-6pm Sun. in high season, 10am-4pm Mon.-Sat. and 1pm-5pm Sun. Oct.-Mar.,

free but donation appreciated) dates to the early 14th century. There are several medieval tombs and 19th-century stained-glass windows worth a short visit.

On the western side of the Protestant Cathedral churchyard is the **Lynch Memorial Window,** the horrible history of which is well documented. In 1493 the mayor of the city, James Lynch FitzStephen, invited a Spaniard into his home. A spat of jealousy between the visitor and FitzStephen's son Walter ended in murder, and the mayor found his son guilty of the crime. When all the usual hangmen (understandably) refused to tighten the noose around the neck of the mayor's own son, legend states that the just-to-a-fault FitzStephen did the deed himself, from the window of his house on Market Street. Now you know the probable origin of the word "lynch."

Built in the mid-1960s on the site of the old city jail, the cavernous, green-domed **St. Nicholas' Roman Catholic Cathedral** (University Rd. and Gaol Rd., tel. 091/564-648, free) features a mosaic portrait (in a side chapel) of John F. Kennedy, whom the Irish have all but canonized. This cathedral is on the west shore of the Corrib, just over the Salmon Weir Bridge.

Nora Barnacle House

Of primary interest to Joyce buffs, **Nora Barnacle House** (8 Bowling Green, tel. 091/564-743, 10am-1pm and 2pm-5pm daily mid-May-mid-Sept. and by appointment, €2.50) offers a trove of love letters, photographs, and other memorabilia on display in the childhood home of James Joyce's wife. This 19th-century townhouse is also the smallest museum in the country!

Galway City Museum

The **Galway City Museum** (Spanish Arch, tel. 091/532-460, 10am-5pm Tues.-Sat. all year, noon-5pm Sun. Easter-Sept., free) is in a sleek new building behind the quaint old museum. The temporary exhibitions complement a small permanent collection of art,

Galway City

To Marless House, Roncalli House, Salthill, Barna, Spiddal, and South Connemara

FATHER GRIFFIN AVE

ST MARY'S RD

RALEIGH ROW

ST HELENS ST

NEWCASTLE RD

CANAL RD LOWER

ELY PL

SEA RD

KAI

THE CRANE

PRAGUE HOUSE

MUNSTER AVE

336

THE BLUE NOTE

MASSIMO'S

FATHER GRIFFIN RD

ST DOMINICK'S RD

MONROE'S

RÓISÍN DUBH

FAIRHILL RD

To Claddagh Arts Centre

CLADDAGH QUAY

GOURMET TART COMPANY

NIMMO'S PIER

NIMMO'S PIER

WOLFE TONE BRIDGE

PARNABARA

NEW RD

MILL ST

NUNS ISLAND

GAOL RD

ANIAR

BRIDGE ST

BOWLING GREEN

NORA BARNACLE HOUSE

KIRWIN'S LANE CREATIVE CUISINE

SPANISH ARCH

McDONAGH'S

QUAY STREET KITCHEN

BUSKER BROWNES

ARTISAN

KIRWIN LN.

CROSS ST

THE PIE MAKER

TIGH COILI

LOMBARD ST

MARKET ST

COLLEGIATE CHURCH LYNCH MEMORIAL WINDOW

ST NICHOLAS'

MARY'S ST

JAVA'S

ABBEYGATE ST

SPANISH ARCH

QUAYS PUB

DRUID THEATRE

NEACHTAIN'S

CAVA BODEGA

MURPHY'S

THE DÁIL

HIGH ST

THE TAAFFE'S

FREENEY'S

MIDDLE ST

THE SATURDAY MARKET

SHOP ST

WILLIAM ST

McCAMBRIDGE'S

DOUGH BROS.

HALO! ELECTRIC GARDEN

THE LIGHT HOUSE

EGLINTON ST

THE CELLAR BAR

ARD BIA @NIMMO'S

GALWAY CITY MUSEUM

FLOOD ST

QUAYS

VIÑA MARA

HOUSE HOTEL

NEW DOCK ST

MERCHANTS RD

ST AUGUSTINES ST

LYNCH'S CASTLE

SKEFFINGTON ARMS HOTEL

EYRE SQUARE SHOPPING CENTER

KINLAY HOUSE GALWAY

BROWNE'S DOORWAY

HERON'S REST

LONG WALK

DOCK ST

DOCK RD

QUEEN ST

BÓTHAR NA LONG

Kennedy Park

FORSTER PARK

FORSTER ST

GREAT SOUTHERN HOTEL

BUS/TRAIN STATION

DÚN AENGUS DOCK

Galway Bay

To Lough Atalia

LOUGH ATALIA RD

To Lough Atalia

© AVALON TRAVEL

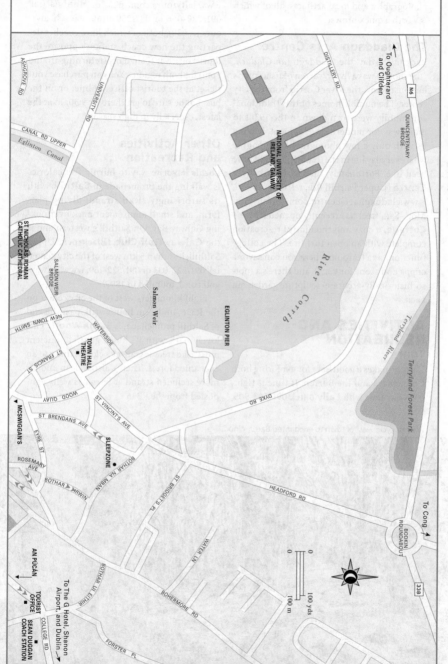

To Oughterard and Clifden

N6

DISTILLERY RD

QUINCENTENARY BRIDGE

ASHGROVE RD

UNIVERSITY RD

CANAL RD UPPER

Eglinton Canal

NATIONAL UNIVERSITY OF IRELAND, GALWAY

River Corrib

ST NICHOLAS ROMAN CATHOLIC CATHEDRAL

SALMON WEIR BRIDGE

NEW TOWN SMITH

WATERSIDE

Salmon Weir

EGLINTON PIER

Terryland River

Terryland Forest Park

ST FRANCIS ST

TOWN HALL THEATRE

WOOD QUAY

ST VINCENT'S AVE

ST BRENDANS AVE

MCSWIGGAN'S

EYRE ST

SLEEPZONE

BOTHAR NA MBAN

DYKE RD

ROSEMARY AVE

BOTHAR IRWIN

ST BRIDGET'S PL

HEADFORD RD

To Cong

BODKIN ROUNDABOUT

338

BOHERMORE RD

WATER LN

BOTHAR UÍ EITHIR

AN PUCAN

TOURIST OFFICE

To The G Hotel, Shanon Airport, and Dublin

SEAN DUGGAN COACH STATION

COLLEGE RD

FORSTER PL

0   0

100 yds

100 m

photographs, and local artifacts, all of which is worth a quick browse.

The Claddagh Arts Centre

Back in the day, the Claddagh (*an Cladach,* "the shore") was a lively warren of fishermen's huts just across the River Corrib from the city center. The humble homes of this traditional community were torn down in the 1930s to make way for modern development, leaving us with only a few photographs to imagine what everyday life in the Claddagh might have been like. Fortunately, the **Claddagh Arts Centre** (Upper Fairhill Rd., tel. 091/526-917, www.claddaghartscentre.com, noon-6pm Mon.-Sat., free) has recently opened **Katie's Cottage,** a cozy and thoughtful re-creation complete with an open turf fire. The cottage functions as a tearoom where you can savor a cuppa and scone for €3.50, and there's a (not-so-historically-accurate) sculpture garden out back.

ACTIVITIES AND RECREATION
Tours

Galway makes a good base for exploring both Connemara and the Burren. If time is tight, try a day tour with **Lally's** (tel. 091/562-905, www.lallytours.com, €25) or **Healy's** (tel. 091/770-066 or 087/259-0160, www.healytours.ie, €30), both of which have coaches departing the new coach station opposite the tourist office at 10am daily (returning around 6pm) for both regions. You can purchase your ticket at the tourist office, online, or on the bus, but be sure to get there by 9:30am at the latest, especially in high season.

Other Activities and Recreation

Locals' favorite way to burn a few calories is walking the promenade in **Salthill,** with its surprisingly clean strand, diving platform, and small amusement park overlooking Galway Bay. On Salthill's western end is the **Galway Golf Club** (Blackrock, Upper Salthill, less than 5 km west of the city center, tel. 091/522-033 or 091/522-169, www.galwaygolf.com), founded in 1895.

Eight kilometers west of the city center on the R336, under an hour's walk past the end of Salthill promenade, is **Barna Wood.** This lovely park with its huge, gnarled, ancient moss-clad trees is Galway's closest thing to an enchanted forest. There's also a clean and far more secluded strand at Barna as well, sign-posted from the R336.

Walk or cycle west of town to enchanted Barna Wood.

Corrib Canoe Courses (tel. 087/743-5644, www.corribcanoe.com, weeklong course €100) offers a five-day (two sessions per day) canoe course for all ages and experience levels.

FOOD

Downtown Galway is brimming with excellent eateries; just walk down Shop Street, the old medieval main drag, until it turns into Quay Street. There are so many memorable restaurants that you'll have a difficult time choosing between them. Seafood is the highlight of most menus, unsurprisingly, but there are restaurants to suit every taste.

Cafés

Given Galway's watch-the-world-go-by vibe, you're naturally spoiled for choice! **The Pie Maker** (10 Upper Cross St., tel. 091/513-151, noon-10pm daily, €10-12) does sweet and savory, and since they only use spelt flour everything is gluten free. It's a tiny shop with limited seating, but if the weather's fine you can always take your pastry outside for a picnic along the Corrib. The family-owned ★ **Gourmet Tart Company** (Upper Salthill, opposite Salthill Church, 091/861-667, www.gourmettartco.com, 7:30am-7pm daily, later in spring and summer, lunch €9-13, 3-course dinner €25) is another splendid choice: The cafe-restaurant is located in Salthill, but they have takeaway shops on Ravens Terrace, 7 Lower Abbeygate Street, and inside the Galway Shopping Centre on the Headford Road. You can also look for their stall at the Saturday market.

The Pie Maker and Gourmet Tart Company don't cater for vegans, but happily you can make straight for ★ **The Light House** (8 Upper Abbeygate St., no phone, 10:30am-6pm Mon.-Sat., noon-6pm Sun., under €10) for delicious dairy-free desserts along with hearty and flavorful lunches (some featuring homemade cashew cheese) and excellent coffee. The menu is mostly gluten-free, too. If there are no tables open in this sweet little café, it's definitely worth the wait. If you're in the mood for pizza, the much-ballyhooed

Dough Bros (24 Upper Abbeygate St., tel. 087/176-1662, www.thedoughbros.ie, noon-10pm Tues.-Sat., noon-9pm Sun.-Mon., €9) is just down the way.

It may have changed hands a few times over the years, but **Java's** (17 Upper Abbeygate St., tel. 091/533-330, 11am-midnight, until 1am Thurs.-Sat., under €10) is still a Galway institution for students and arty types. Here's the perfect spot for a rejuvenating afternoon cappuccino or a sweet or savory crepe after an evening at the pub.

Brought to you by one of Ireland's premiere wedding cake designers, **Goya's** (2/3 Kirwan's Ln., tel. 091/567-010, www.goyas.ie, 9:30am-6pm Mon.-Sat., lunch 12:30pm-3pm, €10) is the ideal spot for tea and a slice of freshly baked pear tart. You'll have a hard time deciding on a dessert—they're all scrumptious.

Casual Restaurants

You'll find the city's best pub grub at **The Dáil** ("doll," 42/44 Middle St., tel. 091/563-777, www.thedailbar.com, food served noon-9:30pm daily, lunch €8-12, dinner €11-18), with both hearty traditional dishes and healthier hummus-and-quinoa-type fare on the menu. It's a terrific value, and there's always something on in the way of entertainment—live music during the week and DJs on the weekends.

McDonagh's (22 Quay St., tel. 091/565-001, noon-10pm Mon.-Sat., 5pm-10pm Sun., under €12) is a Galway institution, serving up fresh battered fish-and-chips for four generations. There are three shops in one here: the chipper on the left with its long wooden tables, the full restaurant on the right (reservations accepted only in the off-season), and a fish-market around the back. Salmon, trout, cod, turbot, prawns, sole, silver hake, lobster—you name it, they've got it, and you can be certain it came off a local fishing boat that very morning. Too bad the chips are sold separately.

Viña Mara (19 Middle St., tel. 091/561-610, www.vinamara.com, 12:30pm-2:30pm and 6pm-10pm Mon.-Sat., opens at 5:30pm Sat.,

Traditional Music

Ireland's traditional music is a sound unto itself, by turns rollicking and otherworldly. The Celts brought an exclusively oral tradition to this island about 2,000 years ago, and back then the harp was the primary instrument of the genre. Bards composed vocal and harp music for their patrons, the kings of Ireland. The uilleann pipes, comparable to Scotland's bagpipes, were played almost as far back, though they were an instrument of the "common" people rather than the highly revered bards. After the Flight of the Earls in 1607 this musical heritage was suppressed, along with so many other aspects of Irish culture.

You might be surprised to learn just how recently other essential instruments of "modern" folk music were introduced; the fiddle we recognize didn't appear in Ireland until the 1720s, and now it is the most iconic instrument of all. (The Irish fiddle is identical to a classical violin, which is pretty astounding given how different the sound is!) The bodhrán, a goatskin drum struck by a wooden beater, was used in warfare and other non-musical purposes, only appearing in trad sessions starting in the 1960s. There was a flute-like instrument played in medieval Ireland, and the Irish flute is commonly heard in sessions today, though the modern tin whistle didn't show up until the early 19th century. Today guitarists sometimes join in, adding a flavor of international folk.

The old songs were gradually put to paper beginning in the 18th century. After a period of decline (apart from a recording project undertaken in the 1920s), the folk tradition saw a remarkable resurgence in the mid-20th century, thanks to Sean Ó Riada and many other dedicated musicians. Traditional music fostered close-knit immigrant communities in England, America, and Australia. Fortunately for us all, the Irish music revival continues to this day.

Passionate about folk music? You might want to plan your holiday around the annual Fleadh Cheoil na hEireann, a festival and competition established in 1951 that can attract upwards of 400,000 people. The event is usually held in August or September and the location changes each year, so visit Comhaltas Ceoltóirí Éireann online (www.comhaltas.ie) for full details on the next fleadh. Many more traditional music festivals worth planning an itinerary around are held in County Clare: the Doolin Folk Festival (www.doolinfolkfestival.com, June), the Feakle Festival (www.feaklefestival.ie, August), the Ennis Trad Festival (www.ennistradfest.com, November), and, if you're a musician yourself, the Willie Clancy Summer School (www.scoilsamhraidhwillieclancy.com, July) in Miltown Malbay. If you get up to Donegal, the Ballyshannon Folk Festival (www.fb.com/ballyshannonfolkfestival, July) is another long-running and very convivial event.

If your vacation is on the shorter side, Galway's pubs (see page 296) are an easy option for traditional music sessions. Tigh Coili and The Crane both offer excellent live music. Monroe's has nightly sessions as well as set dancing on Tuesday evenings, and you are more than welcome to join in! You have your pick of pub sessions in Dublin, too, of course, but the atmosphere in small-town pubs is much more workaday and relaxed.

lunch €8, 2/3-course dinner €20/24) offers excellent midweek specials (€10 main courses!) in low season. The atmosphere is warm, if a bit business-casual, and there are always proper vegan options on the menu since one of the chefs is vegetarian. Or if you're in the mood for Spanish tapas, try romantic, candle-lit Cava Bodega (1 Middle St., tel. 091/539-884, www.cavarestaurant.ie, 5pm-10pm Mon.-Fri.,

noon-late Sat.-Sun., small plates €6-14). Despite the cured meats strung around the bar, this place is actually quite veg-friendly, and the wine list is well curated.

Another vegan-friendly restaurant option is the Quay Street Kitchen (Quay St., tel. 091/865-680, 11:45am-10:30pm daily, €10-18), which always includes something like barbecue tofu or faux fish fingers on the menu along with the usual veg curry. It's an ideal spot for outdoor people-watching in the summer. Save room for the lemon tart.

It started off as a really excellent food hall, and now ★ **McCambridge's** (38/39 Shop St., tel. 091/562-259, www.mccambridges.com, 8am-7pm Mon.-Wed., 8am-9pm Thurs.-Sat., 10:30am-6pm Sun., €12-15) has expanded into a lovely upstairs café-restaurant with some of the best coffee and treats in town. The atmosphere hits that sweet spot between cozy and elegant, buzzing (for all the shopping going on downstairs) and chill.

Fine Dining

Note that "fine" is indicative of price, not atmosphere—don't worry about what you're wearing!

Many excellent restaurants have graced the space above Neachtain's pub over the years, but ★ **Artisan** (2 Quay St., tel. 091/532-655, www.artisangalway.com, noon-3pm and 5:30pm-10pm daily, lunch €11, dinner €17-29, 3-course early bird €25) seems to have real staying power. This is modern Irish at its finest, with fresh local beef and seafood along with a delectable vegetarian option. If you're dining in a larger group, be sure to ask for the stained-glass snug.

Once upon a time, there was a cozy and unpretentious restaurant with utterly gorgeous food in the old stone building in the shadow of the Spanish Arch. The happy evenings of classic Nimmo's are long past, but you can still go for a special meal at **Ard Bia @ Nimmo's** (Long Walk, Spanish Arch, tel. 091/561-114, www.ardbia.com, noon-3:30pm and 6pm-10pm Mon.-Fri., 10:30am-3:30pm and 6pm-10pm Sat.-Sun., lunch €8-12, dinner €19-27). The food is just as gorgeous as in the old days and the medieval digs are wonderful, but the atmosphere can feel a little too-cool-for-school. The diner is left with the impression, in the way they generally do business, that the owners are terribly impressed with themselves. Focus on the food, though, and you'll be well satisfied.

If the much-beloved Heneghan's flower shop-café *had* to close, at least a splendid new restaurant has taken its place in this atmospheric stone building with the spire of the neighboring church peeking through the pitched-glass roof: it's **Kai** (20 Sea Rd., 091/526-003, www.kaicaferestaurant.com, 9:30am-3pm and 6:30pm-10:30pm Mon.-Fri., 10:30am-3pm and 6:30pm-10:30pm Sat., noon-3pm and 6:30pm-10:30pm Sun., closed Mon.-Tues. in winter, lunch €12, dinner €18-26), with inventive modern-Irish fare garnished with an edible flower more often than not.

For a once-in-a-year kind of night out, try the Michelin-starred **Aniar** ("ah-NEER," 53 Lower Dominick St., tel. 091/535-947, www.aniarrestaurant.ie, 6pm-10pm Tues.-Thurs., 5:30pm-10pm Fri.-Sat., 6-course dinner menu €115/75 with/without wine). The owner-chefs are always coming up with new and clever ways to incorporate various kinds of Connemara seaweed into their gourmet dishes—*aniar* means "from the west." Needless to say, reservations are pretty much essential. Aniar also offers cooking classes, so if you (almost) die of happiness after a lavish and leisurely meal, there may be a daylong workshop happening while you're in town.

★ The Saturday Market

On Saturdays, don't miss the **outdoor market** (10am-6pm) along Churchyard Street outside St. Nicholas' Collegiate Church. A few stalls are also open on Sunday year-round, and there are loads of food and gift merchants open every day of the week in high season. You'll find plenty of terrific lunch and snacking options, but best of all is ★ **Govinda's** (tel. 087/680-4683, 10am-6pm Sat., noon-6pm Sun., lunches under €6), whose vegetarian Indian dishes and whole-wheat samosas are truly sublime. Definitely check out the pricey-but-worth-every-cent Mediterranean stall too, with divinely delicious olives, cheeses, and other picnic staples.

LGBTQ Galway

While Galway prides itself on its open-minded ethos, pun intended, it doesn't offer as many resources or meeting spots as Dublin or Cork. There's no resource center as such, though there is one switchboard: the **OutWest Gay Helpline** (tel. 094/937-2479, www.outwest.ie, 8pm-10pm Wed.). **Amach! LGBT Galway** (www.amachlgbt.com), established in 2010, is an active community working on opening a permanent resource center at time of writing. Check out their links page for more information on a broad spectrum of local social groups and meetups. These online resources are the best ways to find out about pubs and clubs, since they don't tend to stick around too long, unfortunately. You might want to time your visit for the annual **Pride Parade** (www.galwaypride.com) in mid-August—it's quite well established.

ENTERTAINMENT AND EVENTS
Entertainment

Galway entertainment offers something for everyone—good plays, live rock and traditional music, and a choice of nightclubs (though most of them are teeming with rowdy teenagers).

Galway boasts plenty of live trad, though **Monroe's** (Upper Dominick St., tel. 091/583-397) is the only pub in the city with set dancing sessions (on Tuesday night). It has traditional music sessions every night of the week and decent pizzas in the adjoining shop—recommended for the late-night munchies. Other spots for traditional music nightly include **The Crane** (2 Sea Rd., www.thecranebar.com, tel. 091/587-419), which also has a long-running Sunday session (starting 1pm) featuring Sean Ryan of Leap Castle; **Taaffe's** (19 Shop St., tel. 091/564-066); and **An Púcán** (11 Forster St., tel. 091/561-528). **Tigh Coili** (Mainguard St., tel. 091/561-294) has a rollickin' Wednesday-night (and occasional Saturday-night) session.

Two labyrinthine, multilevel pubs with fairly good food are the **Quays Pub** (Quay St., tel. 091/568-347) and **McSwiggan's** (3 Eyre St., Woodquay, tel. 091/568-917). The Quays is the more ancient and cavernous of the two, offering live music (trad on Mon.-Thurs. nights and Fri.-Sun. at 5pm, pop/rock on weekend nights) and a hearty, good-value buffet lunch upstairs on the weekends.

If you're looking for a change of pace—an unpretentious pub frequented by garrulous old Irishmen instead of busloads of tourists—try **Freeney's** (19 High St., tel. 091/562-609) or **Murphy's** (9 High St., tel. 091/564-589), across the pedestrian street from one another. **The Salt House** (Ravens Terrace, 091/441-550) draws a younger crowd for its chill vibe and extensive international beer selection, and the open fire counterbalances the latest sporting event on the television.

A perennial favorite with hip young Galwegians is **Neachtain's** (17 Cross St., entrance on Quay St., tel. 091/568-820), an exceedingly old-fashioned pub with outdoor seating in the summer (but good luck finding a table).

Róisín Dubh ("raw-SHEEN DOVE," "Black Rose," Upper Dominick St., tel. 091/586-540, tel. 091/589-202 for concert info, www.roisindubh.net, cover €7-15, sometimes free) is by far the best live music venue in Galway—and certainly one of the top venues nationwide. Artists like Warren Zevon, Christy Moore, Andy Irvine, Luka Bloom, and Karen Casey (formerly of Solas) have played there over the years, as have bands like Doves and The Frames—and plenty more fine musicians who may never be household names. Another solid venue for live rock is **Massimo's** (10 William St. W., tel. 091/582-239), or try **The Blue Note** (3 William St. W., tel. 091/589-116) for live jazz. All of these pubs are top picks even if you aren't interested in what's going on in the back room; Massimo's is trendy yet cozy, the Blue Note is dimly lighted and slightly seedy (in a basement jazz club kind of way), and Róisín Dubh is the most crowded of the three in the evenings.

You'll find two of the city's best nightclubs at the same address: **Halo** (36 Upper Abbeygate St., tel. 091/565-976, www.halonightclub.com, cover €5-12) is for "the over-23s" (but-under-30s), and **Electric Garden** (www.electricgalway.com) will make you feel like you're walking into a Spanish hacienda. It's a lot of fun. Two spacious pubs that also serve good food in the daytime but are better for students and young professional types at night are **The Cellar Bar** (Eglinton St., tel. 091/563-966, www.thecellar.ie) and **Busker Brownes** (Cross St., tel. 091/563-377, www.buskerbrownes.com), which was built as a Dominican convent in the 17th century.

The **Town Hall Theatre** (Courthouse Sq., tel. 091/569-777, www.townhalltheatregalway.com, €8-20) is the city's primary venue for traveling dramatic and musical productions. Some plays are better than others, but the congenial atmosphere in the upstairs bar makes for a worthwhile evening even if the play is mediocre (though fortunately most of the plays are very good). Town Hall also hosts a foreign film series on Sunday night in the spring and fall, as well as most of the readings during the Cúirt literary festival.

The **Druid Theatre** (Courthouse Ln., tel. 091/568-617, www.druid.ie, €15-20) is more avant-garde than Town Hall and showcases contemporary Irish playwrights.

Festivals and Events

Galway's busy festival calendar underscores the city's popularity with artists, poets, and dramatists. The biggest event is the **Galway Arts Festival** (tel. 091/566-577, www.galwayartsfestival.com, €7-35), which keeps the city humming with a marvelous smorgasbord of concerts, plays, avant-garde exhibits, and street performances during the last two weeks of July. The **Cúirt International Festival of Literature** is the city's literary festival, bringing together an international assortment of

distinguished and emerging writers around Eastertime, generally mid- to late April. The likes of Seamus Heaney, J. M. Coetzee, Maxine Hong Kingston, Rick Moody, and Chuck Palahniuk have all given readings over the years; most events take place at the Town Hall Theatre. For more information, contact the **Galway Arts Centre** (47 Dominick St., tel. 091/565-886, www.galwayartscentre.ie). And as you'd expect, the weeklong **Galway Film Fleadh** (tel. 091/751-655, www.galwayfilmfleadh.com) in mid-July offers a busy schedule of international film screenings.

As for music events, the **Galway Jazz Festival** (contact the Town Hall, tel. 091/569-777, www.galwayjazzfest.com) takes place over four days in mid-October, showcasing both local and American talent. Another four-day fest in early November is the **Spirit of Voice** (contact Mulligan Records, 5 Middle St., tel. 091/564-961, www.spiritofvoice.com), a reincarnation of the Galway City Festival of World Music. Proceeds benefit the Cystic Fibrosis Foundation.

None of that artsy-fartsy stuff for you? There's the **Galway International Oyster Festival** (tel. 091/522-066, www.galwayoysterfest.com), a four-day event at the end of September featuring lots of live music. Here's your chance to sample that ambrosial combination of oysters and Guinness. And no self-respecting horse-racing fan should miss the **Galway Races** (tel. 091/753-870, www.galwayraces.com), which often overlap with the Galway Arts Festival in late July. You can take a special Bus Éireann shuttle service (single/return €5/7) from Eyre Square East to the Ballybrit Racecourse five kilometers east of town. (Needless to say, you've got to book accommodations many months in advance if you'll be in the city around this time.) It also goes without saying that both these events are characterized by staggering amounts of drink!

SHOPPING

The **Saturday market** (10am-6pm, daily in summer) along Churchyard Street outside St. Nicholas' Collegiate Church is perfect for leisurely browsing: You'll find handmade silver and beaded jewelry, pottery, incense, artsy photos of the Connemara landscape, and plenty more. Great lunch options also abound at the market.

The Treasure Chest (31-33 William St., tel. 091/563-862, www.treasurechest.ie) stocks classy gifts (Avoca blankets, Galway crystal, and the like) along with the kitschy stuff. There's a choice of sweater stores along Shop Street, but most of the inventory is machine-knit. **Ó'Máille's** (16 High St., tel. 091/562-696, www.omaille.com) is your best bet for an authentic Aran jumper. And for children's souvenirs, head straight for the **Wooden Heart** (3 Quay St., tel. 091/563-542, www.wooden-heart.ie), which stocks a range of delightfully old-fashioned toys manufactured mostly in Europe.

The best bookshop in Galway is **Charlie Byrne's** (The Cornstore, Middle St., tel. 091/561-766, www.charliebyrne.com), which specializes in secondhand and overstock books. Charlie Byrne's is a Galway institution, so it's hard to believe it only opened in 1989. Helpful, laid-back staff, plenty of bargains on quality titles, the occasional reading and signing with a local author: For the bibliophile it's like Christmas every time you step inside.

ACCOMMODATIONS
Hostels

There's no shortage of budget accommodations in Galway, but a few places are sketchy, and others are downright cramped. The city has two very good hostels, my favorite being the relatively new **Sleepzone** (Bothar Na mBán, Woodquay, tel. 091/566-999, www.sleepzone.ie, dorm beds €19-22, private rooms €25-30 pp). The kitchens are spacious enough to accommodate everyone at mealtimes, and the spotless en suite rooms range from singles to four-, six-, and eight-bed dorms to long-term self-catering apartments. There's also a regular shuttle service to Sleepzone Connemara (5 km outside Leenane, 50 km from Galway City; ask at reception) and a Sleepzone Burren day tour-shuttle combo option.

The other recommended hostel, **Kinlay House Galway** (Merchants Rd., Eyre Sq., www.kinlayhouse.ie, tel. 091/565-244, fax 091/565-245, dorm beds €18-25, private rooms €35 pp), offers a convenient city center location, though it can be mobbed with school groups in high season. You can buy tickets to the Aran Islands at a kiosk on the ground floor, and the shuttle bus departs right outside the door. Very nice kitchen and common areas, and a light breakfast is included in the room price. Note that reception is on the fourth floor—and there is no elevator.

Bed-and-Breakfasts

If you have a rental car, it makes the most sense to stay a little ways out of town to avail of free parking at your B&B; Salthill is ideal. After all, nothing beats a seaside stroll first thing in the morning. (The promenade is a great place to watch the sunset, too, if the weather is clear.) A B&B just up from the waterfront on the west end of town is **Marless House** (Threadneedle Rd., tel. 091/523-931, www.marlesshouse.com, €33-36 pp, s €45-50), which also serves very good breakfasts. Closer to town is light and airy **Roncalli House** (24 Whitestrand Ave. at Lower Salthill Rd., tel. 091/584-159, www.roncallihouse.com, €30-33 pp, s €40-45), whose breakfasts fall into the near-legendary category. Located on the Salthill side of the city centre, **Prague House** (40 Father Griffin Rd., tel. 091/584-083, www.praguehousegalway.com, €40-45 pp) is fairly standard, but it makes a good base if you care for windy walks along the prom *and* the Quay Street pub scene.

Romantically situated on the Long Walk overlooking the Claddagh, ★ **Heron's Rest** (16a the Long Walk, tel. 091/539-574, www.theheronsrest.com, €70-80 pp, no single supplement) has cushy bedrooms and a divinely delicious breakfast menu served at a communal dining table (though room service is also an option). Kick back and watch the swans (and boats) sail by with a cup of tea before dinner. Not all rooms are en suite, but fluffy white bathrobes are a nice compensation!

Hotels

Galway offers a variety of fine hotels, the most posh being **The g Hotel** (Wellpark, old Dublin Rd., on the northeast fringe of town, tel. 091/865-200, www.theghotel.ie, rooms €280-400), a brand-new, five-star establishment with interior design by celebrated British accessory designer Philip Treacy and €19 cocktails in the unbelievably swanky hotel bar. The view isn't so posh, though—it overlooks the parking lot of the Eye Cinema.

But before The g Hotel opened, the Victorian **Hotel Meyrick** (Eyre Sq., tel. 091/564-041, www.hotelmeyrick.ie, d €180-280, off-season specials as low as €89) was the grandest in town; it has a pool, sauna, and steam room. A less opulent and slightly more relaxed choice on the square is the **Skeffington Arms** (south side of Eyre Sq., tel. 091/563-173, www.skeffington.ie, rooms €120-190). Special rates abound, so check the website. The televisions in the hotel pub, "the Skeff," are often tuned to American sporting events. Another atmospheric hotel with an excellent pub is the ★ **Spanish Arch** (Quay St., tel. 091/569-600, www.spanisharchhotel.ie, s €75-85, d €99-145). Erected in 1584, the building first served as a Carmelite convent. Or you might try the **House Hotel** (Spanish Parade, tel. 091/568-262, www.thehousehotel.ie, rooms €110-200), where visiting authors stay during the Cúirt International Festival of Literature each April. It's a lovely place, elegant and low-key.

INFORMATION AND SERVICES

The **tourist office** (Forster St., tel. 091/537-700, www.irelandwest.ie, 9am-5:45pm daily June-Sept., 9am-5:45pm weekdays and 9am-12:45pm Sat. Oct.-May) is between the old and new bus stations. Read up on city news and events in the *Galway Advertiser* (www.advertiser.ie, a free weekly) before you go.

Banks with ATMs and bureaux de change include **AIB** (Shop St.), **Bank of Ireland** (Eyre Sq.), and **Ulster Bank** (33 Eyre Sq.). Need a pharmacy? **Boots** (35 Shop St., tel. 091/561-022) is open daily.

GETTING THERE

Galway is 217 kilometers west of Dublin on the M6, 105 kilometers north of Limerick on the N18/M18, and 217 kilometers north of Killarney on the N23, N21, and N18/M18.

You can get here from Dublin Heuston via **Irish Rail** (Eyre Sq., tel. 091/561-444, www.irishrail.ie, 5 trains/day daily, single/5-day return fare €29/41) or **Bus Éireann** (Eyre Sq., tel. 091/562-000, www.buseireann.ie), which offers services from Dublin and Athlone (#20, 15/day daily), Killarney and Tralee (#54, 3/day daily, transfer at Limerick), Cork and Limerick (#51, 12/day daily), Belfast (#65, 4/day daily, transfers at Sligo and Enniskillen), Derry (#64, 5/day daily), and many other towns.

Private bus services stop at the **new coach station**, the Sean Duggan Centre (Fairgreen Rd.), as do many day tour buses. There's a fee to use the toilets, so if you have to go, pop into the loo at the old station (beyond the train platforms). **GoBus** (tel. 091/564-600, www.gobus.ie) offers reliable service to Dublin and Cork (single/return fare €12/20, €17/27 to Dublin Airport if purchased online). **Citylink** (tel. 091/564-163, www.citylink.ie) can take you to Clifden (in Connemara), Dublin, Cork, or Limerick for about the same prices. A one-way ticket to Dublin Airport will run you €18.

GETTING AROUND

Downtown Galway is easily walkable, though you might want to take the local bus (#1, 3/hour, fare €2.10) to Salthill. All local buses depart from the northern side of Eyre Square.

Rent a bicycle from **West Ireland Cycling** (Earls Island, signposted opposite the Catholic cathedral, tel. 091/588-830, €30/150 per day/week), which also organizes cycling trips in Connemara. You can even rent a tandem bike.

Taxi ranks are at Eyre Square and Bridge Street, or you can ring **Abby Taxis** (11A Eyre St., tel. 091/533-333) or **City Taxis** (tel. 091/525-252).

The Aran Islands

These three rocky islands seem far removed from the Burren region of County Clare, yet the sea has carved them out of the same limestone reef lurking beneath Galway Bay. The ubiquitous stone walls demarcating the farmers' fields on the largest island alone run 4,800 kilometers in total. The butcher pays a visit from the mainland two days a week, and the local priest is a very busy man: He performs Mass on all three islands. These are echoes of an old way of life, and yet no visitor is deprived of any modern convenience. Free Wi-Fi is almost as widespread as it is on the mainland, and you can book a room at even the quaintest B&B online with your Visa card.

The largest island, Inis Mór, also offers some of the most important archaeological sites in the country, the crown jewel of which is Dún Aengus. You will spend your first night on Inis Mór reworking your itinerary so you can stay twice as long as you'd planned—and if you can't, you'll be thinking well ahead to your next trip.

Though you'll be hard-pressed to find an islander in traditional garb, and only a couple of homes still have thatched roofs, the denizens of the Aran Islands usually speak English only in the presence of strangers. If you can, spend a few days before you arrive learning a few Irish words and phrases. It's the surest way to see a native smile, and you'll quickly distinguish yourself from the hordes of stereotypical vacationers.

GETTING THERE AND AROUND
Ferry from Galway (Rossaveal)
Island Ferries (4 Forster St., Galway, tel. 091/568-903 or 091/561-767, tel. 091/572-273 after hours, fax 091/568-538, www.aranislandferries.com, €25 return plus €7 for the bus) sails to all three islands year-round, operating a double-decker shuttle service from Queen Street off Eyre Square in Galway to the port at Rossaveal. Bus and ferry tickets may be purchased at the Kinlay House lobby or at any of the Island Ferries offices sprinkled throughout downtown Galway.

April-October, ferries leave for Inis Mór at 10:30am, 1pm, and 6:30pm. More sailings are added in July and August, so call or drop in for the high summer schedule. April-October, ferries leave Inis Mór for Rossaveal at 8:15am (9am Sun.), noon, and 5pm (and 6:30pm June-September). November-March, ferries depart Rossaveal for Inis Mór at 10:30am and 6pm, departing Inis Mór at 8:15am and 5pm.

The Inis Meáin/Inis Oírr ferry departs from Rossaveal at 10:30am and 6pm, leaving the islands at 8am and 4:30pm. Departure times are subject to change, especially the early sailings, so ring ahead for confirmation.

The Galway-Rossaveal bus departs one hour before sailing time. Allow yourself an extra half hour to purchase your tickets and use the restroom at Kinlay House—even in the early spring the shuttle bus is filled to capacity.

Those driving from Galway should take the R336 west to Rossaveal and park in the €5-per-day lot beside the dock. You can purchase ferry tickets at the office there. The ferry company is now allowing travelers to bring their bicycles, though limited space is available; if you're on a cycling holiday, call ahead and ask if there's room on the day you wish to sail.

Ferry from County Clare
If you want to reach the Aran Islands from County Clare, **Doolin Ferries** (The Pier, Doolin, tel. 065/707-4455 or 065/707-4466, fax 065/707-4417, www.doolinferries.com, €25 return to Inis Oírr, €35 return to Inis Mór) is an option, though the service isn't as reliable as the ferry out of Rossaveal. The

ride is about 10 minutes shorter, however, as Inis Oírr is only eight kilometers off the Clare coast. Boats leave Doolin for Inis Oírr daily March-November at 10am, 11am, 1pm, and 5:30pm, returning at 8:30am, 12:15pm, 2pm, and 4:45pm. The boat to Inis Mór departs Doolin at 10am and 1pm, departing Inis Mór at 11:30am and 4pm. For Inis Meáin, your departure options are 10am and 1pm, returning 11:45am or 4:15pm.

Air

The faint of stomach can fly to the islands via **Aer Arann** (tel. 091/593-034, www.aer-arannislands.ie, €49 return, €44 group rate of four or more, €25 one-way), also via shuttle bus from the Victoria Hotel off Eyre Square in Galway City. Flights depart Connemara Airport at Minna (35 km west of Galway) and last 10 minutes. Reserve your seats by phone or email well in advance during high season, as the planes carry only nine passengers. Scenic flights are also available for €60 per person in July and August, leaving at noon daily.

Flights depart Minna for Inis Mór at least three times daily year-round, with five or six departures in high season. The airstrip overlooks Killeany Bay, two kilometers southeast of Kilronan. There are two or three flights daily to each of the smaller islands; the Inis Meáin airstrip is on the northeastern end of the island a good two kilometers from the pier, and the Inis Oírr strip is more conveniently situated just east of the strand.

INIS MÓR

Inis Mór (Inishmore), the "Great Island," is 14.5 kilometers long and 4 kilometers at its widest point. Though the largest of the Aran Islands is also the most frequently visited, Inis Mór has a way of accommodating tourists without feeling the slightest bit commercial. Much has inevitably changed since the days of Aran fishermen going to work in their curraghs and reroofing their thatched cottages every six years, yet you'll be pleasantly surprised at how remote and

romantic this place still seems, especially at night. Even in Kilronan, the island's heavily touristed port town, the moon lends a preternatural aura as it illuminates the low stone walls and shimmers over the dark sea beyond.

Most visitors only spend the day here—they take the early ferry in, rent a bike or board a minibus just before noon, travel to the more prominent sights before a late lunch, and return to Galway on the last ferry at 5pm. Ideally, however, you should allow yourself at least two days to see everything in between **Dún Dúbhchathair** ("Black Fort") on the eastern side of the island to the quieter villages beyond **Dún Aengus** and **Na Seacht dTeampaill** ("The Seven Churches"), all of which are among Ireland's greatest archaeological treasures. It's best to spend the day of your arrival seeing the less touristy sights around Killeany, like the Black Fort, then rising early the following morning to beat the rush of day-tourists to Dún Aengus and the Seven Churches. Being able to walk through these ruins in relative peace and solitude is well worth the extra planning.

If you're especially interested in the islands' archaeology, geology, flora, and fauna, make your first stop at Ionad Árann, the Aran Islands Heritage Centre.

Ionad Árann

Ionad Árann, the **Aran Heritage Centre** in Kilronan (tel. 099/61355, www.visitaran-islands.com, 10am-7pm daily June-Aug., 11am-4pm daily Apr.-May and Sept.-Oct., €3.50, €5.50 for film and exhibition combination ticket), offers a worthwhile introduction on the history, culture, geology, and wildlife of the Aran Islands. The cost of admission used to include a screening of Robert Flaherty's 1934 film *Man of Aran,* but these days you'll have to purchase a combo ticket if you'd like to see it. Use your time wisely, however, and visit Ionad Árann on a foul-weather day. The center also has a small coffee shop and bureau de change.

★ Dún Aengus

Dún Aonghasa, or **Dún Aengus,** is a magnificent semicircular hill fort perched 90 meters above the ocean and flanked on the remaining sides by *cheveaux de frise,* which are stone spikes arranged to deter invaders. The site is about 2,000 years old, and despite the spikes and defensive walls (5.5 meters high and 4 meters thick), archaeologists are still unsure as to its precise function. Dúchas operates a small **exhibition** (tel. 099/61008, 10am-6pm Mar.-Oct., 10am-4pm Nov.-Feb., €4) at the base of the rocky uphill path to the fortress. Dún Aengus is the Aran Islands' prime tourist attraction, and with good reason: There are precious few thrills in the world as heady as this one. Pop your head over the stony brink to feel the spray from the water crashing on the rocks hundreds of feet beneath you.

Na Seacht dTeampaill

Na Seacht dTeampaill ("The Seven Churches") is an early Christian monastic site comprising two churches and the ruins of several other domestic buildings dating from the 8th century, with 19- and 20th-century gravesites covering the ground between them. Look closely and you can also spot what's left of a few penitential beds *(leapacha)* and 11th-century inscribed high crosses. St. Brendan the Navigator, the intrepid holy man who supposedly crossed the Atlantic in a curragh, is said to be buried here. To get to the Seven Churches, take the main road past the Dún Aengus turnoff; the Seven Churches signpost is down less than a kilometer on the right.

Na Seacht dTeampaill is a popular stop on the tourist circuit, so if you're cycling try to visit before the first ferry arrives (around 11:30am) or after the last one leaves at 5pm. If you go during the day, wait for a pause between the minivans—this place is best savored in relative solitude. (Both Dún Aengus and the Seven Churches can flood in the springtime, so bring a pair of waterproof boots. Some determined travelers have braved the cold waters in the Dún Aengus entryway with waterproof

a view over the Atlantic from Dún Aengus

sandals or even barefoot, but needless to say this isn't the best option.)

★ Dún Dúbhchathair

Dún Dúbhchathair ("Black Fort") is a gem: utterly breathtaking cliffs, and very few tourists with whom to share them. The actual fort is older and not as well-preserved as Dún Aengus is, but you can still spot some of the *cheveaux de frise,* and what's left of the spiraling dead-end corridors is well worth an extended visit. The fort and the cliffs surrounding it make the ideal spot for a picnic lunch. If you want to keep well away from the tourist track, the Black Fort is your new haven—just be careful not to walk too close to the edge. On the eastern end of the island, the Black Fort isn't an easy hike from the Killeany road (which is too rocky for cycling in some parts), but it's worth the time and effort.

Other Sights

Near the Seven Churches, **Dún Eoghanachta** is an inland ring fort housing the ruins of several *clocháin,* or beehive dry-stone huts. You can see another better-preserved *clochán* (known as **Clochan na Carraige**) on the north side of the main road, just before the Seven Churches turnoff. If you take a peek inside the little round hut you'll notice that the interior is actually rectangular.

Another ring fort with impressive walls and terraces near the highest point on the island, **Dún Eochla** offers a splendid panoramic view of the eastern side of the island. It's about 400 meters south of the main road about a kilometer outside Kilronan, a gentle uphill walk of 15 or 20 minutes.

Other less prominent sites south of the main road between Kilronan and Dún Aengus include the **Leaba Diarmuda agus Ghráinne** ("Bed of Diarmuid and Gráinne," a pair of doomed lovers in Irish mythology), a megalithic wedge tomb dating back to the time of Dún Aengus, and the probable burial site of several early farmers; and the **Teampall an Cheathrair Áileann,** the 15th-century "Church of Four Beautiful Saints" who were supposedly laid to rest beneath four nearby flagstones. Near these church ruins is a holy well that inspired John Millington Synge's play *The Well of the Saints.* Near the village of **Gort na gCapall,** off the walking route on the southern side of the island, is the **Poll na bPéist,** the "Serpent" or "Worm Hole." A rectangular pool in the old stone nourished by the ocean through an underground channel, it makes for an eerie but worthwhile detour.

There is more to see on the eastern end of the island. The Killeany road is dotted with queer vertical tombs, mostly from the early 19th century, which are dedicated to those fishermen whose bodies were never found. It's a tricky path up to **Teampall Bheanáin,** a tiny 6th-century church set on the north-south axis rather than the customary east-west. Just remember that there's no need to hop any stone walls—there is a set path uphill, so if you don't spot any weathered markers see if you can flag a passing local to ask for directions. Going the right way, you'll spot the remains of a round tower on your walk up, along with what's left of the 5th-century **monastery of St. Enda,** patron saint of the Aran Islands. Benin's church is a creepy site with a fine view over Killeany and the harbor, but it's not a must-see unless you're a pilgrim or archaeological enthusiast. The humbleness of this site belies its importance, for St. Benin succeeded St. Patrick at his monastery in Armagh, and in its heyday St. Enda's was an important center of learning. Historian Peter Harbison has called this place "a veritable nursery of saints."

On the northern coast road outside Kilronan are the ruins of **Teampall Chiaráin,** named for the St. Ciarán who later founded the magnificent monastery at Clonmacnoise in County Offaly. It's mostly notable for the high Celtic cross in the churchyard and is worth a peek if you're biking back from Dún Aengus on the quieter coast road.

Activities and Recreation
TOURS
Of all the tour operators clamoring for your attention as you disembark at the Kilronan pier at 11am, **Noel Mahon** (tel. 087/778-2775, www.tourbusaranislands.com, €10 for a 3-hour tour) is by far the least obnoxious, and arguably the most knowledgeable. After stops at Dún Aengus and the Seven Churches, he'll take you through the village of Bun Gowla at the far end of the island and back to Kilronan, offering plenty of interesting tidbits about life on the island as he drives. If you're lucky you'll sight a few seals bobbing in the waves off the north shore at **Port Chorrúch** on the return trip. Just ask if you'd like to be dropped off at the entrance to either the Black Fort or Dún Eochla, both of which are well worth the uphill hikes (though the latter is the only viable option if you're leaving on the evening ferry). If you don't feel up to biking the island, this is your best option for seeing the most in the least amount of time.

OTHER ACTIVITIES AND RECREATION

At **Ionad Árann** you can pick up a map detailing the various **walking routes** around the island. You can spend three full days sightseeing on foot without seeing everything, though, so you might want to hire a **bicycle** at the pier for at least a day (€10). Wear waterproof boots and clothing, unless by some freak chance you're visiting on a brilliant cloudless day (they do happen every once in a while), and pick up sandwich fixings at the Spar before you leave. Except for the government-handled Dún Aengus, several of the other ruins make great spots for a picnic lunch if the weather holds.

Plenty of cyclists brave the minibus-clogged main road—it is the most direct route to Dún Aengus—but to avoid most of the traffic on the way back, take the coast road on the north side of the island.

There's a terrific Blue Flag beach at **Kilmurvey,** though it's rarely warm enough to go for a swim. If you're not visiting in July or August and still want to go for a dip, come prepared with a wet suit. Equestrians can inquire about **pony-trekking tours** (tel. 087/982-8746, stiofankelly@eircom.net) in the afternoons during high season.

Food

As you would expect, seafood dominates the menus at the island's restaurants, and its small cafés offer simple but hearty fare. The pubs are always an option for dinner.

Excellent service, a nifty book-trading practice, and hearty, reasonably priced sandwiches, soups, and stuffed Rooster potatoes make **Lios Aengus** (Kilronan, tel. 099/61030, 10am-4pm daily, under €8) the ideal place for breakfast before a day of biking, or for an early supper afterward. The desserts are scrumptious, too (try a slice of banoffee pie or chocolate cake). Take the main road up from the pier about 150 meters and you'll see it on your right. Lios Aengus is next door to the **Spar** supermarket (9am-8pm Mon.-Sat., 10am-5pm Sun.), site of the island's lone ATM. There's a

good selection of frozen dinners and baked goods for hostellers, but beware the produce section, the contents of which hail from far-off lands and consequently may not be fresh.

Another good café option just across the road from the Spar is the whitewashed **An tSean Chéibh** ("The Old Pier," tel. 099/61228, 11am-8pm daily Apr.-Oct., under €12), popular for its fish-and-chip meals. Takeout is an option, but ask for "takeaway" instead.

If you find yourself at Dún Aengus around lunchtime, and it's more than likely you will, get thee to **Teach Nan Phaidi** (tel. 099/20975, 11am-5pm daily Apr.-Oct., lunch €12), a cheerful spot close to the main road with simple but filling soups and sandwiches.

A seat at the all-you-can-eat mostly vegetarian buffet at the **Mainistir House Hostel** (tel. 099/61169) will set you back €15, a humble price considering that dessert is included (and the rave reviews it's received in *The Irish Times*). Dinner is served at 8pm in summer and 7pm in winter, and it's BYOB. Do call ahead to reserve a spot, especially in summer. If it's seafood you're after, **The Pier House** (Kilronan, tel. 099/61811, www.pierhouse-aran.com, 11am-10pm, €10-20) will gladly accommodate.

Entertainment and Events

Finding live traditional music in the pubs of the Aran Islands is often a matter of luck, since there doesn't seem to be any sort of fixed performance schedule. Sometimes you'll find just two or three musicians playing as if for themselves, and other times you'll find something totally unexpected, like a troupe of Spanish bagpipers. Despite the Kilronan Hostel just up the stairs, the cozy **Tí Joe Mac's** (tel. 099/61248) seems to attract more weekending Irish than it does foreigners. Basic pub grub (soup and sandwiches), a crackling fire, and live "trad" (short for traditional music) most nights make it a fine place to pass a rainy evening. A few yards up the main Kilronan road on the right side is **The Bar** (Kilronan, tel. 099/61130), which used to be called "the

Aran Sweaters

In John Millington Synge's heart-wrenching one-act play set on the Aran Islands, *Riders to the Sea*, a young woman realizes that the clothes of a drowned fisherman (found on the shores of Donegal, and buried there) are those of her missing brother when she notices the stitch she herself dropped while knitting his socks. The powerful pathos of this scene is indicative of hand-knitting's central place in the history and culture of these islands. That said, the notion of a unique cabled pattern for each family is a myth created by the head of an Aran knitwear company back in the 1930s. It was simultaneously morbid and romantic, perhaps, to think of being able to tell which family a drowned fisherman belonged to by the design on his waterlogged jumper!

You almost certainly won't see any shawls, *crios* (woolen belts), *mairtíní* (stockings sans feet), or other traditional garb outside the Aran museum, though the scarves and gloves sold in the shops are no less cozy for their lack of authenticity. The most popular seller remains the fisherman's sweater, knit in the traditional unbleached wool (called *báinín*, "baw-NEEN") or a variety of jewel-toned yarns, but as Pat Boran wryly notes, Aran jerseys are "now worn almost exclusively by German hippies, University College Dublin science students, and on RTE soap operas."

American Bar" for the pool table in the back room and the '90s rock tunes on the speakers.

Farther up the road is the cozy **Joe Watty's** (tel. 099/61155). You can find live music here most nights, and this pub has the friendliest ambience of all those in Kilronan, though you may find better quality pub grub elsewhere.

If you'd care for a quieter place than Kilronan for a pint and a meal (and possibly a room for the night), **Tigh Fitz** in Killeany (tel. 099/61213, www.tighfitz.com) also offers pub food, set dancing, and live music in high season, and accommodations year-round.

Shopping

You're probably in the market for an authentic Aran sweater for yourself or a loved one back home, but don't waste your time inside the first shop you see. Local rumor has it that the Carraig Donn sweaters (at the Kilronan pier) are actually machine-knit in South America. Whether or not they're made in Ireland, you can tell on sight they aren't made by hand. Same goes for the merchandise at the Aran Sweater Market next door.

By the entrance to Dún Aengus, **Sarah Flaherty** (tel. 099/61233, 9am-5pm Mon.-Sat.) and other hand-knitters make their classic jumpers available at the **Kilmurvey Craft Village**. Mrs. Flaherty knits gorgeous sweaters, hats, and scarves in richly colored wool, chatting animatedly with her customers as her needles work their magic between her hands. She'll even whip up a pullover or cardigan especially for you if you call ahead with your chest and underarm-to-waist measurements. You'll pay upward of €100 for one of these sweaters, but they're worth it. Several other shops sell jewelry, handkerchiefs, and other souvenirs. For Celtic stonework, pop in to **Lia Arann** (tel. 099/61411, www.liaarann.com).

Accommodations

The **Kilronan Hostel** (tel. 099/61255, www. kilronanhostel.com, 4- and 6-bed dorms €22-25 pp), on the pier, is above Tí Joe Mac's, which is either convenient or noisy depending on your priorities. It's clean and otherwise adequate, and a continental breakfast is included in the price, but you may not receive as warm a welcome as you would at other hostels on the island (probably because this is the hostel of choice for the vast majority of backpackers arriving off the ferries, thus overwhelming the receptionist).

The great thing about **Mainistir House Hostel** (tel. 099/61169, mainistirhouse@eircom.net, 4-bed dorms €20 pp, doubles €25-35 pp) is its nightly mostly vegetarian buffet, so if you're interested in eating here it makes sense to stay here, too. The room prices include continental breakfast with freshly baked bread. It's a bit of a hike from the pier; the owners claim it's only a 10-minute walk, but expect to walk about 20. It's up the main road, past Joe Watty's, on the left-hand side. You may be able to get a ride from one of the hostel owners if you call. At least there are bikes to rent once you arrive.

Kilronan has a fair number of modest B&Bs. **Claí Bán** (tel. 099/61111, €35 pp, s €40-60) is perhaps the nicest in town, tucked down a path just beyond the Bank of Ireland. On your way up the main Kilronan road, you'll see a sign for Claí Bán on your left. You could also try **Pier House** (tel. 099/61417, €30-35, s €45-55), even closer to the dock, which is pricier for the convenience but offers a downstairs restaurant.

Or if you'd prefer to stay somewhere quieter, **Kilmurvey House** (tel. 099/61218, kilmurveyhouse@eircom.net, €40-45 pp) is an 18th-century stone home near Dún Aengus, with the Blue Flag beach a stone's throw away.

Information and Services

The wee tourist office, or **Oifig Fáilte** (tel. 099/61263 or 099/61420, 10am-1pm and 2pm-5pm daily Apr.-mid-Sept.), on the Kilronan pier, can provide you with maps, B&B accommodations, and the like. You can also drop your luggage here for a nominal fee.

The **Bank of Ireland** (tel. 099/61178) on the main road is open on Wednesday only (plus Thursday in July and August), so the best place to get cash is at the **Spar supermarket ATM.**

If you need medical assistance, call the island's **doctor** (tel. 099/61171) or one of two **nurses** (tel. 099/61165). There is no hospital on any of the islands, so emergency cases must be airlifted. There is a lone *garda* **(police officer)** assigned to all three islands (tel. 099/61102).

Getting Around

There's no doubt that biking this island is the best way to go, and renting one at the Kilronan pier is the easiest thing you'll ever do; the universal rate is €10 a day plus a deposit. There are plenty of bikes for all, but if you want to book ahead, try **Aran Bike Hire** (tel. 099/61132, www.aranislandsbikehire.com, €15 for 24 hours).

A **public minibus** serves the whole island. Ask for the schedule at the tourist office, but if that's closed, there's also one posted at the Lios Aengus café.

You could travel to Dún Aengus in a **pony trap,** which will run you about €40 for up to four people. There are plenty for hire down at the Kilronan pier.

INIS MEÁIN

The 225 natives of **Inis Meáin** (Inishmaan, the "Middle Island") have garnered a reputation for unfriendliness that may in small part explain why most tourists choose not to visit it. For every smileless islander there are plenty who'll welcome you, however. The landscape is somehow bleak and breathtaking at the same time, the stones of the endless dividing walls culled from the limestone beneath the shallow soil. Honeysuckle and orchids bloom all over the island, and the pollen of hundreds of other exotic flowers has been transported across the ocean from places as far off as the Mediterranean and the Arctic Circle. If the thought of elbowing your way through the summer crowds on Inis Mór doesn't appeal, take the ferry here instead. You'll be happy you did.

The Middle Island also offers plenty of activity for bird-watchers and other nature enthusiasts. Of the wealth of prehistoric and early monastic ruins, the most important is **Dún Chonchúir,** "Conor's Fort"—Conor being the brother of Aengus (as in Dún Aengus on Inis Mór).

Inis Meáin is only five kilometers wide and two and a half kilometers long, so you could certainly visit it on a day trip from Inis Mór or Inis Oírr (both of which offer more amenities for tourists). You'll have enough time to visit the principal ruins and enjoy a leisurely pint at Teach Ósta (provided it's reopened by the time you read this!) before heading back to the pier. Two main roads head west from the pier, a high road on your left (leading to the pub, church, and Conor's Fort) and a low road on your right that leads to the knitwear factory.

Sights

Though its three outer walls have crumbled, the fortress wall of the oval-shaped **Dún Chonchúir** remains almost completely intact, and it affords a tremendous view over the whole island: church and houses to the south, newfangled windmills to the north, and Gregory's Sound to the east. As with many other ruins on these islands, the age of this fort falls within a wide range of centuries—the 1st through the 7th AD, that is.

John Millington Synge, whose dramatic works dominated the calendar at the Abbey Theatre in Dublin during the Gaelic Literary Revival of the early 20th century, gleaned much of his inspiration from the Aran Islanders. *Riders to the Sea* is set on Inis Meáin, in fact. Synge spent his summers here between 1898 and 1902, and you can visit **Teach Synge** (tel. 099/73036, noon-2pm and 3pm-4pm Mon.-Sat. June-Sept., €3), the small thatched cottage where he stayed, just across

the road from the entrance to Dún Chonchúir. **Cathaoir Synge** ("Synge's Chair"), the playwright's favorite thinking spot, is just a rocky limestone promontory overlooking Gregory's Sound; you can even see the cliffs of the Black Fort on Inis Mór. Synge's Chair is marked on your right up the main road after the Dún Chonchúir turnoff.

On Inis Meáin there's another Neolithic wedge tomb known as **Leaba Diarmuda agus Ghráinne,** signposted from the low road (as you've no doubt surmised, the story of Diarmuid and Gráinne is one of the more lascivious in Irish mythology). This one has collapsed, however, so there's not too much to see.

Another stone fort on the eastern side of the island, **Dún Fearbhaí** (signposted off the high road, just up from the Tigh Chonghaille B&B) could be as old as the 1st century or as "new" as the 8th, and its square layout makes it peculiar. Climb onto the ramparts for an excellent view of the northern side of the island.

Though little remains of the **Teampall na Seacht Mac Rí** ("Church of the Seven Sons") near Conor's Fort, the nearby freshwater spring and holy well, **Tobar Chinndeirge,** is said to have restorative properties. The well is named for St. Cinndearg, who is supposedly

Teach Synge, where the playwright John Millington Synge stayed at the start of the 20th century

buried by the south door of the *teampall* (temple). In bygone centuries the Church of the Seven Sons was a popular pilgrimage site, and faithful islanders still flock here for the Stations of the Cross on the ides of August.

It seems St. Gregory spent much time in lonesome contemplation on this island, as several sites in addition to the sound on the west side of the island bear his name. Near Dún Fearbhaí on the eastern side of the island is the 8th-century **Cill Cean Fhionnaigh** ("Church of the Fairheaded One," an epithet for St. Gregory), which is one of the most perfectly preserved of the early Aran churches (though there is still not much to see). The people of Inis Meáin buried their dead here up until the mid-1950s, and there's another holy well nearby. On the opposite side of the island is **Uamhain Ghríora** ("Gregory's Cave"), on the strand facing Gregory's Sound.

Ready to visit a church with roof intact? The **Seipeal Eoin agus Naomh Mhuire gan Smal** ("Chapel of Saint John and Immaculate Mary"), built in 1939, features typically exquisite stained-glass windows by Harry Clarke's workshop: a three-light altar window of the Madonna and Child flanked by Saints Peter and John the Baptist, as well as four smaller windows on the north and south walls, the most striking of which depicts Mary Magdalene. Most churches in rural Ireland are painfully austere, so this *seipeal* (chapel) is a real gem.

Activities and Recreation

It may be too cold for a swim, but you can at least doff your boots and socks for a walk down the sand at **Trá Leirtreach,** a sheltered strand 500 meters north of the small pier. There's another beach on the far side of the island, facing Gregory's Sound, where you can see the cliffs on Inis Mór's southeast side.

Food and Accommodations

To be frank, budget and solo travelers might not have the best time of it here. The island's few B&Bs have raised their rates considerably in recent years, and the single supplement can

be rough on the wallet. You're better off staying at one of the hostels on Inis Mór or Inis Oírr and making a day trip of Inis Meáin.

B&Bs generally offer a handful of basic rooms with a shared bath along with evening meals. Two guesthouse-restaurant options are **Tigh Chonghaille** (tel. 099/73085, bbinismeain@gmail.com, €40 pp), a cheerful yellow bungalow just up from the pier at the fork in the road, and **An Dún** (tel. 099/73047, www.inismeainaccommodation.ie, €50 pp, B&B plus 3-course dinner €70 pp), which is up the main road about a kilometer and a half on the right-hand side, directly opposite Dún Chonchúir; this one also has a shop where you can throw together an impromptu picnic to bring up to the fort. With a coin-operated sauna and Jacuzzi, An Dún is the fanciest B&B on the island.

Alas and alack, at time of writing the island's only pub and affordable hotel, **Teach Ósta Inis Meáin** (high road, 3-minute walk west of the church, tel. 099/73003) was closed until further notice. Hopefully by the time you're reading this it'll be under new management and reopened, cozy as ever; when it does, you'll be able to get lunch or dinner (though they'll likely stop serving pretty early, like 7pm) and enjoy a traditional music session afterward (in high season).

Cleverly designed to blend into the landscape, **Inis Meáin Suites and Restaurant** (tel. 086/826-6026, www.inismeain.com, Apr.-Sept., two-night stay €900 and up) is hands-down Ireland's most perfect spot for a honeymoon—extravagant and remote—though calling it a splurge would be a bit of an understatement. Hotel staff will collect you at the pier, the lavishly appointed suites come equipped with bikes and fishing poles, and you're sent off on a day's exploring with a hotpot for an alfresco lunch. Breakfast is delivered to your room, and you'll likely be wanting the four-course dinner too (€65, special diets accommodated with advance notice). Some may find this juxtaposition of the luxe and the rustic a bit jarring—Aran Islanders are the least pretentious people in all the world, after all—but you have to hand it to the husband-and-wife team who built this place (one of whom *is* a native islander) for carrying out such an ambitious project.

Shopping

In the factory showroom at the Inis Meáin Knitting Company, **Cniotáil Inis Meáin** (on the low road about 1 km west of the pier, tel. 099/73009, fax 099/73045, www.inismeain.ie), you'll find hand-knit Aran sweaters at below-retail prices. (They're still considerably more expensive than Sarah Flaherty's on Inis Mór, though, so just think how much they cost at those exclusive shops in Paris, Tokyo, and New York!)

Information and Services

The island has no bank or ATM, so make your withdrawal before leaving Galway. The **Inis Meáin Island Cooperative** (tel. 099/73010, 9am-4pm Mon.-Sat.) serves as a tourist information point in high season. Take the low road from the pier and you'll see it past the knitwear factory on your left, on a side road that brings you up to the high road.

INIS OÍRR

The "Eastern Island," anglicized as "Inisheer," is just over three by three kilometers. Its population is greater than that of Inis Meáin, however. The rocky shore on the western side of the island makes for an awesome spot to watch the sunset, since the road back to the pier is perfectly safe to traverse in the twilight. Its three pubs are some of the warmest, friendliest spots anywhere in Ireland. Trad performances are on a rather spotty schedule in the off-season, but during the summer you're guaranteed live music at all three. There may only be enough on this island to occupy you for the day, but Inis Oírr's charming cottages, lonely ruins, and sandy lanes make for quite a serene afternoon.

Sights

The O'Briens were one of two ruling families on the Aran Islands until the late 16th century, and their three-story tower house (better known as **Caislean Uí Bhriain** or "O'Brien's Castle") was built in the 1400s within the ruins of another 1st-century ring fort, **Dún Fhormna.** The castle overlooks the pier on the north side of the island, and from that vantage you can spot the **wreck of the** *Plassey* off the eastern shore. A storm in 1960 threw that freighter onto the reef of **Carraig ná Finnise,** where it remains to this day.

On the western end of the harbor, past Tigh Ned and the Fisherman's Cottage restaurant, **Inis Oírr Heritage House** (tel. 099/75021, 10am-6pm Mon.-Sat. June-Aug., €1) offers a small museum, café, and craft shop. It's one of the few buildings left with a traditional thatched roof.

Also on the northwestern side of the island, a short walk from the Inis Oírr Heritage House, the 8th- or 9th-century **Cill Ghobnait** ("St. Gobnait's Church") was dedicated to a Cork-born nun-on-the-run who apparently had more than one enemy in County Clare (legend has it that she kept an army of bees with which to defend herself). Back then Gobnait was the only woman allowed on these islands. Continue two kilometers down that road on the western edge of the island and come to the holy well of St. Enda, **Tobar Éinne,** which is still as sacred to the islanders today as it was a millennium and a half ago. Enda is said to have lived for a time in a *clochán* near this well, though very little remains of it now.

Enda may be the patron of Aran, but Kevin is the patron saint of Inis Oírr. The 10th-century **Teampall Chaoimháin** ("St. Kevin's Church"), just southeast of the airstrip, seems to be drowning in the ever-shifting sands, but the denizens of Inis Oírr clear it out every year on St. Kevin's feast day, June 14. Note the more recent gravestones, the Gothic chancel, and the shells and other remnants of a medieval kitchen dump.

The lower level of **Cnoc Raithni,** a two-level burial mound, dates from the Bronze Age, making it the oldest ruin on the island by far. It was serendipitously uncovered after a storm in 1885 blew away the tons of sand hiding it. The tumulus is situated beside the campground overlooking the harbor.

Activities and Recreation

An Trá, "The Strand," makes for a pleasant stroll east of the harbor. The signposted **Inis Oírr Way,** 10.5 kilometers long, leads you through the uninhabited part of the island, where farmers have long demarcated their rolling fields. You'll meet more cows and horses than people there, however. An uninhabited **lighthouse** stands at the island's southern tip, and though visitors aren't allowed, the path that leads there (down the eastern side of the island) is more popular with tourists than the western road. You can rent a bike at **Rothair Inis Oírr,** by the pier.

Food

The Fisherman's Cottage, a.k.a. **South Aran Restaurant** (tel. 099/75073, www.southaran. com, Apr.-Oct., €12-22), which serves exceptionally good seafood and organic vegetables, is near the pier just past Tigh Ned pub and the bike-rental shop. Check out the website for upcoming cookery classes.

The restaurant at the family-run **Óstán Inis Oírr** (tel. 099/75020, www.hotelinisoirr. com, 4-course dinner €25) is open daily in July and August and on weekends April-June and September. If the restaurant is closed, there's always decent grub to be had on the pub side, where there's live trad every night during the summer.

Entertainment and Events

There are two pubs in addition to the bar at Óstán Inis Oírr: **Tigh Ruaírí** (tel. 099/75020) and **Tigh Ned** (tel. 099/75004), both of which are fun places to pass an evening. The walls of Tigh Ruaírí are peppered with rusted American license plates and other fun tchotchkes, and the live music is spirited even when only a couple of musicians show up. Tigh Ned is just as cozy but attracts a younger, rowdier crowd of dart-throwers, so

unless you're backpacking it you might want to stick with Tigh Ruaírí or the hotel pub. All three are very close to the Inis Oírr pier; when standing at the pier with your back to the island, the hotel lies straight ahead, with Tigh Ruaírí just beyond it and Tigh Ned to your right.

Inquire at the Inis Oírr Heritage House or tourist kiosk about the island's **boat-racing festival,** which is usually held in August. There's also **ceilidh dancing** in high season; ask for the particulars if you're visiting in summer.

Accommodations

The **Brú Radharc Na Mara** hostel (at the pier, tel. 099/75024, www.bruhostelaran. com, mid-Mar.-Oct., dorm beds €15-20, private rooms €20-30 pp) is exceptionally cozy, clean, and comfortable, so much so that to stay at the nearby hotel might even seem like a waste of money. There's a spacious self-catering kitchen, though the small grocery store beside the hotel doesn't offer much of a selection. There are 35 beds, so it's not necessary to book ahead in spring or autumn; there are only two private rooms, though, so reserve one in advance if that's your preference.

For B&B, look no further than **Radharc an Chláir** (near O'Brien's Castle, tel. 099/75019, bridpoil@eircom.net, €35 pp, s €40, dinner €20). Bríd Poil provides a traditional welcome of tea and scones fresh out of the oven (with homemade jams) in a warm and tranquil atmosphere. Book in advance, as this one deservedly draws loads of return visitors.

You can drink, sleep, and eat three meals a day at the island's sole hotel, the friendly, family-run **Óstán Inis Oírr** (tel. 099/75020, www.ostaninisoirr.com, €30-50 pp, s €60), where the price of a room includes a hearty breakfast.

Information and Services

There's a small stand right at the pier offering tourist information 10am-6pm daily in July and August, but in the off-season call the

Island Cooperative (tel. 099/75008) should you need assistance. The post office is inland, past O'Brien's Castle, and while you can change money there it makes more sense to take out as much as you'll need from the Spar ATM on Inis Mór.

Getting Around

Rothair Inis Oírr (tel. 099/75049, www.ro-thai-inisoirr.com, €13/day plus deposit, open daily) rents bicycles, but the island is so small you can definitely see everything in one afternoon on foot.

Connemara

Wild, wet, boggy, and mountainous, Connemara (Conmhaicne Mara, "Descendants of Con Mhac of the Sea") is still seen as a remote stronghold of traditional Irish culture despite ongoing development and exorbitant real estate prices in many parts. The name "Connemara" is generally used to describe the region west of Lough Corrib (the republic's largest lake), with the Atlantic forming a border on the north, west, and south. (Between northern Connemara and southern Mayo is Ireland's only fjord, the starkly beautiful, salmon-dotted Killary Harbour.) The region is also known for its production of whitish-green marble and strong-and-sturdy ponies.

Much of Connemara lies within the Gaeltacht, or Irish-speaking area, and many visitors come to learn the Connaught dialect at local summer schools. Others want to trample through the relatively small but utterly lovely Connemara National Park, and the most adventurous (not to mention experienced) of them all come to trek through the two mountain ranges forming the Lough Inagh Valley: the Maumturks to the east and the Twelve Bens (also called the "Twelve Pins") to the west. The Lough Inagh Valley shelters the loveliest of Connemara's many lakes, and many consider this scenic drive the finest in the region.

Most visitors experience Connemara in a whirlwind coach tour from Galway, but ideally you should spend at least two nights. Connemara's "capital," Clifden, may seem like the natural choice for a base, but keep in mind that this town was all but established for tourists, making it high on amenities but lacking "authenticity." The hamlets of Leenane and Letterfrack are much quieter, offering picturesque scenery and a sense of quotidian life in Connemara without all the harp-and-shamrock foolishness.

Regarding the stretch of Connemara west of Galway City, the novelist Kate O'Brien put it best when she wrote: "There are stretches of South Connemara that are terrifying, grey and as if denying life." This description is apt even in the summer. Eventually the inevitable suburban sprawl around Spiddal, depressing in itself, gives way to rock-and-heather-strewn desolation. You might want to skip this area altogether, cutting through Connemara via the N59 and heading north from Recess or Clifden into far lovelier parts, particularly the Lough Inagh Valley (the R334 from Recess north to Lough Fee, just east of Connemara National Park). Here you'll find the shimmering black lakes and evergreen-swathed mountains you've heard so much about.

GETTING THERE

All roads lead from Galway City: The N59 takes you west to Clifden and loops around for Letterfrack and Leenane before passing into County Mayo. The R336 will take you west from Galway into southern Connemara. Plan on 2.5 hours to reach Clifden or Letterfrack, longer if you're driving through south Connemara. Drive with especial caution, as the Connemara roads are narrow and full of dangerous hairpin curves.

You have a choice when it comes to bus transportation, though Bus Éireann

Connemara

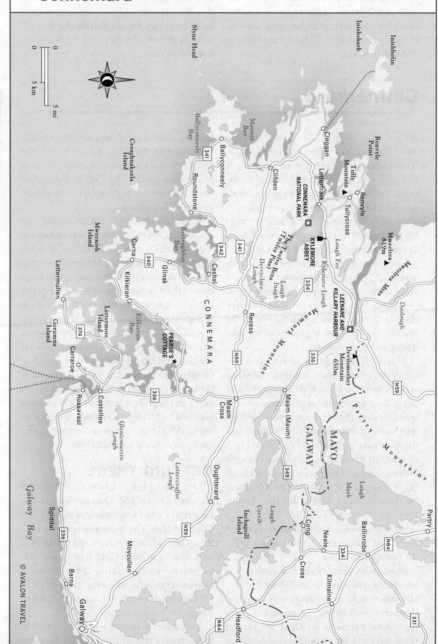

0
5 km

0
5 mi

Inishbofin

Inishshark

Slyne Head

Cleggan

Renvyle
Point

Inishbofin

Mannin
Bay

Ballyconneely
Bay

Ballyconneely

341

Croaghnakeela
Island

Roundstone

342

341

Clifden

Letterfrack

CONNEMARA
NATIONAL PARK

KYLEMORE
ABBEY

LEENANE AND
KILLARY HARBOUR

Tully
Mountain

Renvyle

Tullycross

Mweelrea
819m

Mweelrea Mts

Doolough

Mweenish
Island

Carna

340

Glinsk

Cashel

Bertraghboy
Bay

The Twelve
Bens (Twelve Pins)

Derryclare
Lough

Lough
Inagh

Kylemore Lough

Lough Fee

Lough
Killary

334

Lettermullen

Gorumna
Island

374

Kilkieran

Lettermore
Island

Kilkieran
Bay

PEARSE'S
COTTAGE

C O N N E M A R A

Recess

N59

336

Maumturk Mountains

Devilsmother
Mountain
650m

N59

Carraroe

Rossaveal

Costelloe

Glenicmurrin
Lough

336

Maam
Cross

Maam (Maum)

GALWAY

MAYO

Partry Mountains

Spiddal

Barna

336

Moycullen

N59

Oughterard

Letterecroffoe
Lough

345

Lough
Mask

Cong

Inchagoill
Island

Lough
Corrib

Neale

Cross

Kilmaine

334

Ballinrobe

N84

Partry

N84

Galway

Headford

N84

331

Galway Bay

© AVALON TRAVEL

service (tel. 091/562-000, #61 or #419, 3-4/ day Mon.-Sat., 1-2/day Sun.) in Connemara is disappointingly spotty. Route #61 links Galway City with Oughterard, Maam Cross, Recess, Roundstone, and Clifden between late June and early September (5/day Mon.-Sat., 3/day Sun.). September-June, route #419 leaves Galway for Oughterard, Maam Cross, Leenane, Kylemore, Letterfrack, Cleggan, Recess, Roundstone, and Clifden (3/day Mon.-Sat., 2/day Sun.).

A more reliable alternative is **Citylink** (tel. 091/564-164, www.citylink.ie, #923, single/return ticket €13.50/18 if booked online), which serves Maam Cross, Recess, Cashel, Clifden, Letterfrack, Tullycross, and Cleggan. Buses depart the new coach station in Galway five times a day. Visit the website for a full timetable.

SOUTHERN CONNEMARA
Rossaveal
Thirty-nine kilometers west of Galway City off the R336, the pier at Rossaveal is the departure point for the Aran Islands. There is a ticket office and car park for those who don't need the shuttle bus from outside Kinlay House off Eyre Square.

Pearse's Cottage
History buffs might want to pause in **Carraroe** to visit **Pearse's Cottage,** or **Teach an Phiarsaigh** (Inbhear, just west of Gortmore on the R340, signposted, tel. 091/574-292, 10am-6pm daily June-mid-Sept., weekends late Sept., €4), the restored summer home of Gaelic revivalist, poet, playwright, and Easter patriot Patrick Pearse (also spelled Pádraic or Pádraig). Born in Dublin in 1879 to an Irish mother and an English father, he began learning Irish as a young teen and became a devoted teacher of the language, establishing St. Enda's School in Dublin. It was to this cottage he brought his city pupils for summer classes. Pearse and his brother Willie were two of the 15 rebel leaders executed by the British after the Easter Rising of 1916, and the house was burned during the War of Independence. Fully restored, the house features a small exhibition and collection of personal memorabilia. A half-hour guided tour is available on request.

Roundstone
Dubbed "Galway 4" for its holiday-home popularity with well-heeled Galwegians (Dublin 4 is a swanky residential section), **Roundstone** (Cloch na Rón, "Stone of the Seals") is still a pretty low-key fishing village, drawing visitors for its proximity to pristine beaches: **Gurteen Bay** and **Dog's Bay** are two kilometers west of town. There are two more lovely strands at **Trá Mhóir** and **Mannin Bay** near the hamlet of Ballyconneely, 14 kilometers farther west on the R341. And even the most casual hikers can take a walk up **Errisbeg** (300 meters), which affords a postcard-perfect view of Bertraghboy Bay. A side road (beside O'Dowd's pub) heading west out of town will get you there.

Though Roundstone's shopping can't compare with Clifden's, the musically inclined will definitely want to stop by **Roundstone Musical Instruments** (signposted from Main St., tel. 095/35808, www.bodhran.com, Mon.-Sat. year-round, daily July-Aug.), located in an old Franciscan monastery, which specializes in the goatskin drum used in every proper traditional music session: the bodhrán.

Roundstone's most popular B&B is **St. Joseph's** (Main St., tel. 095/35930 or 095/35865, www.roundstonebandb.com, €30-37 pp, s €46), a cheerful 19th-century townhouse with comfortable rooms and ample breakfasts (and vegetarians are catered to). A spiffy hotel featuring locally made bedroom furniture and a cozy library/sitting room, **Eldon's** (tel. 095/35933, www.eldonshotel.com, Mar.-Oct., B&B €45-60 pp) has a fine adjoining restaurant, **Beola** (tel. 095/35871, 6pm-9pm daily Mar.-Oct., €15-25), where seafood is a specialty. For a more informal meal, opt for the **hotel bar** (food served noon-9pm daily, €12-20).

A delightful little one-stop spot is the **Bogbean Café** (Main St., 095/35825, www.

bogbeanconnemara.com, 9:30am-5pm Thurs.-Sun. mid-Mar.-Oct., Thurs.-Tues. June-Aug., under €10), especially if you're into water sports—they offer sea kayaking and paddleboarding excursions (€40/35 for a 2.5/2-hour trip) as well as B&B (€35-40 pp), not to mention some seriously good cappuccino and sweet treats. (The lunch menu has something for everyone, too—vegans are well taken care of.) Another dining option is the praiseworthy pub grub at O'Dowd's (Main St., tel. 095/35809, food served noon-9pm daily, €12-24), a local favorite. You'll find live trad in Roundstone's three pubs nightly in high season.

There is no tourist office here (the closest is in Clifden), but you can always visit the community website (www.roundstone.ie) before you go for more information.

Roundstone is 23 kilometers south of Clifden on the R341 and 77 kilometers west of Galway, and is served by Bus Éireann routes #61 and #419.

CLIFDEN

The "capital of Connemara," Clifden (An Clochán, "Beehive Hut") was laid out by local landlord John D'Arcy in 1819, and its long broad streets and tall church spires evoke a Victorian flavor. The area is historic for other reasons: Guglielmo Marconi chose Clifden for his first transatlantic wireless telegraphy station in 1907 (linking Clifden with Nova Scotia), and in June of 1919 John Alcock and Arthur Brown completed the first nonstop transatlantic flight when they crash-landed into a bog just six kilometers outside town.

The River Owenglen passes through the southern part of town before it empties into narrow Clifden Bay. Though the town isn't unpleasant, it's a bit too commercial for comfort. Clifden has the banks, shopping, and lunch options, but you're best off just passing through for such necessities en route to Renvyle or Leenane. There isn't much in the way of "sights" in Clifden, though you could use it as a base for Kylemore Abbey and the national park.

The central Market Square forms the west base of a triangle of streets, with Market on the south side, Main on the west, and Bridge on the east. Most of what you'll need is on these three streets. Church Street rises north from the square toward the Anglican Christ Church, and the Galway-bound N59 empties into the town center at the corner of Main and Bridge.

Activities and Recreation

Cycle down the wonderfully scenic Sky Road stretching west from town, which is signposted at the Market Square. Or go for a half-day hike with Michael Gibbons (Island House, Market St., tel. 095/21379, www.walkingireland.com), whose tours focus on the region's archaeology and botany.

Windsurfing and sailing lessons and equipment rental are available through the Clifden Boat Club (Coast Rd., tel. 095/21711 or 087/241-8569). Or go deep-sea angling with Blue Water Fishing (Sharamore House, Streamstown, tel. 095/21073, www.seafishingireland.net), which welcomes beginners.

Equestrians should contact the Cleggan Beach Riding Centre (tel. 095/44746 or 086/875-7333, www.clegganridingcentre.com) or the Errislannan Riding Centre (Ballyconneely Rd., 3.5 km south of town on the R341, tel. 095/21134, www.errislannan-manor.com), which also offers beach treks.

Designed by Eddie Hackett, Connemara Championship Golf Links (Aillebrack, Ballyconneely, tel. 095/23502, www.connemaragolflinks.com) is the finest course in the region.

Food

The bright and comfortable second-floor seating area at Upstairs/Downstairs (Main St., tel. 095/22809, 9am-6pm weekdays, 10am-6pm Sat., 11am-4pm Sun., under €8) is a perfect vantage for people-watching. It's a great spot for a simple, hearty, inexpensive sandwich, and the baked goods are delish.

Pretty much all the Clifden pubs do bar food, but Mannion's (Market St., tel.

095/21780, food served 12:30pm-8:30pm daily, under €15) offers the best value. The soups and paninis at **Lowry's** (Market St., tel. 095/21347, under €10) are also popular with the locals, as are the pizzas at **Guy's** (Main St., tel. 095/21130, www.guysbarclifden.com, €7-14), though vegans should note the dough is made with milk.

It's a bit self-consciously elegant, which is why **Mitchell's** (Market St., tel. 095/21867, www.mitchellsrestaurantclifden.com, noon-10pm daily Mar.-Oct., lunch €12, dinner €16-25), the best restaurant in town, attracts such a well-heeled crowd for lunch and dinner. The menu emphasizes local seafood, of course, though there are gourmet takes on traditional dishes and a veggie-dish-of-the-day as well. A more relaxed (and more veg-friendly) alternative a few doors down is the **Derryclare** (Market St., tel. 095/21990, www.derryclare. com, 11am-10pm Wed.-Sun., €12-15).

Entertainment and Events

Trad sessions take place at **Mannion's** (Market St., tel. 095/21780) every night in the summer starting at 10pm, and on weekends in the off-season. It's a nice spot for a pint despite all the televisions. **D'Arcy Inn** (Main St., tel. 095/21146) offers traditional music as well as open-mic guitar and poetry nights. **Lowry's** (Market St., tel. 095/21347) has ceilidh sessions almost nightly in high season.

Shopping

Clifden offers the usual cheesy souvenir stores, but fortunately it's not hard to find unique gifts elsewhere in town. For funky fused glassware, head for **Connemara Blue** (The Pink House, Market Sq., 95 30782, www. connemarablue.com). **Love Vintage** (Market St., 085/151-5879) is a delightful trove of clothing, jewelry, and doodads, both secondhand and new.

The courtyard at **The Clifden Station House** (on the southern end of town, at the end of Bridge St., tel. 1850/377-000, www. clifdenstationhouse.com) offers serious retail therapy, be it super-chic women's clothing,

19th-century antiques, or Connemara landscapes. The shopping courtyard is part of a larger complex converted from the town's old train depot that includes a hotel, bar, and restaurant.

Accommodations

Clifden's IHH hostel, the **Clifden Town Hostel** (Market St., tel. 095/21076, www.clifdentownhostel.com, dorms €19, private rooms €20-24 pp), is clean and central.

Many of the guesthouses in and around Clifden are pretty posh (aside from the multitude of rather worn B&Bs in the center of town). For something more rustic, stay at **Faul House** (signposted off the Ballyconneely road 1 km south of Clifden, 2 km down a winding road on the right, tel. 095/21239, www. faulhouse.com, Mar.-Oct., €35-45 pp). Connemara ponies are bred on this working farm in a serene, bucolic setting. The beds are supremely comfortable and the owners are delightfully warm and welcoming. On that same road, before you reach Faul House, is the more upscale **Mallmore House** (Ballyconneely Rd., tel. 095/21460, www.mallmore.com, Mar.-Oct., €40-45 pp sharing), a restored Georgian manor with spacious, comfy rooms sprinkled with antiques and a highly lauded breakfast menu that includes pancakes and smoked salmon.

The pick of the town-center hotels is the uniquely situated **Clifden Station House** (in the station courtyard off Hulk St. on the east side of town, tel. 095/21699, www.clifdenstationhouse.com, rooms €55-75 pp, s €85). This swanky-yet-atmospheric complex incorporates the old Clifden Railway Station, which stopped running in the 1940s, and offers a leisure center with pool and all other facilities, friendly and professional staff, and better-than-average bar and restaurant fare. Deluxe, modern, self-catering apartments are available as well, and they include leisure center privileges.

A four-star option one kilometer west of town is the **Abbeyglen Castle Hotel** (Sky Rd., tel. 095/21201, www.abbeyglen.ie,

€120-175 pp, 12.5% service charge). Built in 1832 by John d'Arcy, the local landlord (and founder of Clifden), this incomparably situated neo-Gothic hotel is small, fully renovated, family-run, and even has a resident parrot.

Information

The **tourist office** (Galway road, tel. 095/21163, www.clifden.ie, 10am-5pm daily July-Aug., 10am-5pm Mon.-Sat. Sept.-June) is on the N59, directly across the street from the Connemara coach bus stop.

Services

You'll find ATMs and bureaux de change at the **AIB** (on Market Sq.) and at the **Bank of Ireland** (Beach Rd., west of the Market Sq.). Do what you gotta at **Moran's Pharmacy** (Main St., tel. 095/21273) and **Shamrock Dry Cleaners & Washeteria** (Market Sq., tel. 095/21348), which offers same-day and delivery service.

Getting There

Clifden is 78 kilometers northwest of Galway City and 64 kilometers southwest of Westport on the N59. **Citylink** (tel. 091/564-164, www.citylink.ie, #923, single/return ticket €13.50/18 if booked online) passes through Clifden five times a day in either direction. This service is faster, less expensive, and more comfortable than **Bus Éireann** (tel. 091/562-000, #61 or #419, 3-4/day Mon.-Sat., 1-2/day Sun.).

Getting Around

Parking in the town center is pay-and-display April-September (€1.20/hour). Cycle rental is available from **Mannion Bike Hire** (Bridge St., tel. 095/21160, €15/day). For a taxi or tour of Connemara, ring **O'Neill Cabs** (tel. 095/21444 or 086/859-3939).

NORTHERN CONNEMARA

The **Connemara Loop** (www.goconnemara.com), which can be cycled or driven, takes in all the highlights of northern Connemara:

starting at Maam Cross, you're on the westward N59 before turning off for the scenic Lough Inagh valley drive (R334), getting back onto the N59 for Letterfrack and turning off again for the Renvyle Point loop. Back on the N59, Leenane is the next stop before taking the R336 south for a view of the Maumturks from their eastern sides, finishing back in Maam Cross 85 kilometers later. Ask in the tourist office in Galway for more info and a free map.

Inishbofin

Ten kilometers off Connemara's northwest coast, flat and low-lying **Inishbofin** (Inis Bó Finne, "Island of the White Cow") was the place to which Oliver Cromwell banished a group of Catholic priests in 1652. Actually, he went as far as to build a prison—on an island!—and even chained a bishop to a low-lying rock, leaving him to drown when the tide came in (hence a stone known as "Bishop's Rock" near the harbor). Long before this, however, St. Colman founded a monastery here in the 7th century, and the ruins of a 13th-century church are northeast of the harbor; in the 16th century the piratess Grace O'Malley used "Bofin" for her own strategic purposes. Because of the island's size (6 km by 3.5 km), Inishbofin's pristine beaches and seal- and bird-watching opportunities may only keep you occupied for a day, but it will be a day well spent; you can even swim out to **Inis Laighean** ("IN-ish LANE") off the eastern shore. There's a wonderful café, **The Galley** (East End, tel. 095/45894, hours vary, under €10) just up from the beach. The fare is hearty (and veg-friendly), and the owners are very kind and helpful.

You can rent a bike from a kiosk on the pier, but the island's small enough that you don't really need one. Once disembarked, most of the ferry traffic heads down the road to your right, which is where you'll find the **Inishbofin House Hotel and Marine Spa** (tel. 095/45809, www.inishbofinhouse.com, €50-65 pp, s €80). Also in this direction is the IHH **Inishbofin Island Hostel** (700 m up

Inishbofin are 1pm and 5pm daily, and 9am daily except Tuesday, Friday, and Saturday, when the early departure is at 8:15am. All times are valid mid-March to mid-October; check the website for low-season sailing times.

To learn more about Inishbofin before you go, visit www.inishbofin.com.

Letterfrack

The village of **Letterfrack** (Leitir Fraic, "Frac's Hillside"), founded by Quakers, is the obvious base for visiting the national park; it's no more than a crossroads with a few pubs and shops, but it's a quiet and picturesque spot to spend the night, and there's an ATM in the **Country Shop** (8am-10pm daily).

You'll find a dizzying array of seafood dishes on offer at **The Cloverfox** (Main St., tel. 095/41042, www.cloverfox.ie, food served noon-9pm in summer, until 6pm in low season, €10-20), formerly "The Bard's Den," which also has hostel accommodation (dorm beds €18-25, d €20-33). **Veldon's** (Main St., tel. 095/41042, food served noon-9pm, until 7pm in low season, under €15) has a more eclectic menu and live folk/rock music (think Van Morrison) on the weekends.

There's a wonderfully atmospheric hostel here, the **Old Monastery** (signposted at the Letterfrack crossroads, less than 500 m from the main road, tel. 095/41132, www.oldmonasteryhostel.com, dorm beds €20), whose name reveals the charming building's former function. Built in the 1840s, the Old Monastery is cozy in a bohemian way, if dusty, and breakfast consists of oatmeal and scones for breakfast (included in the price). There's also a three-course dinner for an unbelievable €10. It's a popular spot for campers, and the national park is literally in the backyard.

Another excellent budget choice is **Letterfrack Lodge** (200 m off the N59, signposted on the Clifden end of the village, tel. 095/41222, www.connemaranationalpark.com, mid-May-mid-Sept., dorms €18, private rooms €20-40 pp), a purpose-built hostel/guesthouse/restaurant clad in handsome stone, super clean and with a tremendously

the pristine beach at the eastern end of Inishbofin

from the pier, tel. 095/45855, www.inishbofin-hostel.ie, mid-Apr.-Sept., dorms €15-18, private rooms €20-25 pp), in a charming and well-run converted farmhouse.

Turn left from the pier for the unpretentious, somewhat less popular **Doonmore Hotel** (near the harbor, tel. 095/45804, www.doonmorehotel.com, Apr.-Oct., low/high season €45/60 pp, s €60/70, lunch €15, dinner €30). This hotel has few en suite rooms, leading you to feel a little bit like you're staying in a boarding house. Nevertheless, the views from the bedrooms are the best on the island, and the seafood in the restaurant is über-fresh.

Ferries to Inishbofin depart the Cleggan pier, 11 kilometers north of Clifden off the N59. Make a reservation on the **Island Discovery** (tel. 095/45819 or 095/45894, Cleggan ticket office 095/44878, www.inishbofinislanddiscovery.com, 30-minute ride, return fare €20). Ferries depart from Cleggan at 11:30am and 2pm daily, and 6:45pm daily except Tuesday and Friday, when the late ferry leaves at 7:30pm; departure times from

friendly and helpful staff and great facilities (including three kitchens and two dining rooms).

The Connemara Environmental Education & Cultural Centre gets up its annual **Bog Week** in late May and **Sea Week** in late October (tel. 095/41034 or 095/43443, www.ceecc.org), both of which feature conservation talks, sporting events, and loads of great trad.

Letterfrack is 14 kilometers north of Clifden on the N59, served by both Bus Éireann and Citylink.

★ Connemara National Park

You may be surprised to find that this national park, while full of beautiful vistas and well worth a visit, can be traversed in a single afternoon: Though it encompasses three of the Twelve Bens, the park is only 13 kilometers square. Three easy walking trails, none over an hour in duration, cover bog-and-heathered hills where you can often watch Connemara ponies grazing on the slopes; you might be surprised to find the ruins of 19th-century homes and outhouses that predate the park itself (most of this land once belonged to the Kylemore Abbey estate). A few scattered megalithic court tombs on the park grounds date as far back as 2000 BC. If you're up for a more strenuous hike, follow the signs for **Upper Diamond Hill**.

With time and patience, you might spot a stoat, shrew, badger, fox, or pine marten. Park **birdlife** includes skylarks, chaffinches, wrens, meadow pipits, kestrels, and peregrine falcons. The native red deer population was rendered extinct in the mid-19th century, though park officials have recently introduced a new herd from elsewhere in Ireland.

The mountain and blanket bogs give life to a surprising variety of flora. Orchids and purple moorgrass color the heathery slopes. The largely temperate plantlife includes insectivorous species like butterworts and sundews, though some Arctic plants (like mountain sorrel, roseroot, and purple and starry saxifrages) can also be found at higher altitudes.

The **visitors center** (signposted on the N59 just east of Letterfrack, tel. 095/41054 or 095/41006, www.connemaranationalpark.ie, 10am-5:30pm daily mid-Mar.-Oct., 10am-6:30pm June, 9:30am-6:30pm July-Aug., grounds open all year, free) offers the usual exhibition on local botany and geology and 15-minute audiovisual. Guided nature walks (2- to 3-hours long, included in admission price) depart the visitors center at 10:30am

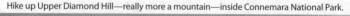

Hike up Upper Diamond Hill—really more a mountain—inside Connemara National Park.

on Monday, Wednesday, and Friday in June, and every weekday in July and August.

Kylemore Abbey

One of Connemara's prime attractions is **Kylemore Abbey** (signposted on the N59 3 km east of Letterfrack, tel. 095/41146, www. kylemoreabbeytourism.ie, 9am-5:30pm daily, €13), a neo-Gothic manor erected on the shores of Lough Kylemore in the 1860s. Originally known as Kylemore Castle, it was built by an English businessman, Mitchell Henry, for his wife, Margaret, who died in Cairo just a few years after its completion. Henry erected a lovely neo-Gothic chapel (with exquisite stained-glass windows) down a lakeside path to honor his wife's memory, and both are buried in a small brick mausoleum a little farther along the path.

Just after World War I, the manor was converted into an abbey by an order of Benedictine nuns (known in Belgium, their erstwhile home, as De Iersche Damen, "The Irish Dames"). The nuns of Kylemore Abbey were running it as a prestigious international boarding school for girls, though it came as a shock to parents all over Europe in early 2006 when they announced the school's impending closure in 2010 due to the order's dwindling numbers. Those who remain are shrewd businesswomen, however, exploiting (however tactfully) tourists' interest in their abbey on the lake with a café, an incredibly posh gift shop, and a steep entry fee to the manor (three downstairs rooms, only interesting enough for a quick peek), the Victorian gardens, and the lakeside walk leading to the neo-Gothic chapel.

Kylemore Abbey is a three-minute drive east of Letterfrack and the national park on the N59. **Bus Éireann** (#61 or #419, 3-4/day Mon.-Sat., 1-2/day Sun.) can drop you off at the Kylemore post office.

Tullycross

There's not much going on in this wee hamlet 4.5 kilometers north of Letterfrack on a local road, but **Tullycross** (Tulach Na Criose,

"Cross on the Hill") is well worth pointing out for **Paddy Coyne's** (tel. 095/43499). Established in 1811, this is quite possibly the coziest pub in all Connemara. It's a crime to pass through on your way to the beach without stopping for a pint here (not to mention the legendary Wednesday night trad sessions).

Just next door is the **Maol Reidh Hotel** (tel. 095/43844, www.maolreidhhotel.com, €45-65 pp, s €90-100). This is quite a nice establishment, with views of the Twelve Bens and the sea from many of the rooms—but as with all too many Irish hotels, the restaurant fare is a disappointment (especially considering the prices). The pub grub is also substandard and overpriced. It's worth driving to Letterfrack for dinner.

Also, those with an appreciation for stained-glass windows should check out **Christ the King Church,** which features three pieces by the brilliant Harry Clarke.

Renvyle

Remote **Renvyle** (Rinn Mhaol, "Bare Headland") is on a local road looping a peninsula of the same name, which makes for an excellent walk or bike ride (11 kilometers round-trip from Letterfrack); you can see the islands of Inishbofin and Inishturk from Renvyle Point.

A fair number of the guests at the **Renvyle House Hotel** (signposted off the N59, on a local road 17 km north of Clifden, tel. 095/43511 or 095/43444, www.renvyle.com, Mar.-Nov., €55 pp low season, €85 shoulder season, €120 July-Aug.) are returning customers. The former home of surgeon, writer, and wit Oliver St. John Gogarty, Renvyle House boasts a heated outdoor pool, private lake for trout fishing, and nine-hole golf course. The hotel has a lovely seaside setting, 80 hectares of landscaped grounds, and top-notch restaurant fare, but don't be surprised to find that the building itself is in considerable need of remodeling. It's also reputedly haunted.

Go diving in Killary Fjord with **Scuba Dive West** (tel. 095/43922, www.

scubadivewest.com), on pristine white **Glassilaun Beach.**

Renvyle is three kilometers north of Letterfrack (the N59) on a local road. There is no public transportation.

★ Leenane and Killary Harbour

Ireland's only fjord is the hauntingly lovely **Killary,** 16 kilometers long and 45 meters deep, which separates northern Connemara from the mountains of southern Mayo (the tallest of which is 814-meter Mweelrea, the "Bald King"); just east of the tip of the fjord is another bleakly intimidating peak, the 650-meter Devil's Mother (the original Irish name meant "devil's testicle," but the Brits declined to use the literal translation when they rejigged their maps).

In the 2005 novel *Notes from a Coma,* Mike McCormack captured Killary's mood to perfection:

"What no tourist bumf will tell you is that this inlet is suffused with an atmosphere of ineffable sadness. Partly a trick of the light and climatic factors, partly also the lingering residue of an historical tragedy which still resonates through rock and water . . . think of grey shading toward gunmetal across an achromatic spectrum; think also of turbid cumulus clouds pouring down five centimetres of rainfall above the national average and you have some idea of the light reflected within the walls of this inlet."

This is a land- and seascape both melancholy and enchanting, the sort of remote locale where you can still imagine wailing banshees and changelings wandering through the heather.

Base yourself near tiny **Leenane** (An Líonán, "The Fill") on the lip of the fjord, best known as the setting of Jim Sheridan's 1989 film *The Field,* starring John Hurt, Richard Harris, and Brenda Fricker. The village itself offers three pubs, a shop, a tourist office, and not much else (not even an ATM, though the post office has a bureau de change), but there are plenty of colorful characters in its two cozy Main Street pubs, **Hamilton's** (tel. 095/42234) and **Gaynor's** (tel. 095/42271), on any given evening (and both do soup and sandwiches during the day).

Killary Harbour is ideal for **water sports,** and there's an outstanding adventure center here to satisfy your thirst for action. **Killary**

the crook of Killary Harbour near the village of Leenane

Adventure Company (signposted off the N59 5 km south of Leenane, tel. 095/43411, www.killaryadventure.com), established in 1981, offers sea kayaking, canoeing, windsurfing, waterskiing, sailing, archery, clay-pigeon shooting, mountain biking, rock climbing, and plenty more. Congenial owner Jamie Young has rounded Cape Horn in a kayak (and that's only one on the Youngs' long list of feats), so you know you're in good hands! Accommodation (both hostel and B&B-style) is provided at "K2," a sleek new building across the N59 from the center. The 84-kilometer **Connemara Way** (part of the longer Western Way walking route) also converges briefly with the N59 at this point.

If you'd rather just kick back and enjoy the scenery, board a ship on **Killary Fjord Boat Tours** (tel. 091/566-736, www.killaryfjord. com, 4/day daily July-Aug., 3/day daily Apr.-June and Sept., 2/day daily Oct., 90-minute cruise €19, cruise plus lunch €24) for a tour of the fjord.

FOOD AND ACCOMMODATIONS

The only restaurant in town is, fortunately, a very nice one: The **Blackberry Café** (on the main street, tel. 095/42240, www.blackberryrestaurant.ie, 9am-4:30pm and 6pm-9pm daily May-Aug., closed Tues. Apr. and Sept., €16-23) serves up seafood, seafood, and more seafood in a cozy ambience. There isn't a vegetarian option on the menu, but if you ask the staff will do their best to accommodate.

Like its sister hostel in Galway City, ★ **Sleepzone Connemara** (6 km south of Leenane off the N59, tel. 095/42929, www. sleepzone.ie, weekends only Nov.-Mar., dorm beds €16, d €25 pp, s €35, campsites €10 plus €7 per extra person) has friendly staff and plenty of opportunities for socializing. No car? No worries: You can get a shuttle-Connemara-day-tour combo ticket via the **Galway Tour Company** (tel. 091/566-566, www.galwaytourcompany.com, €25), and there's usually someone around who can give you a lift down to the pubs. In fact, the only less-than-stellar thing about this hostel is that it often attracts large school groups. To get here, head south out of the village on the N59 (toward Letterfrack), and after five kilometers you'll see the hostel clearly signposted. Make that right, and it's another kilometer down a horribly potholed road.

Just a bit farther down the N59 is the turn-off for **Glen Valley** (www.glenvalleyhouse. com, €35-40 pp), a secluded farmhouse B&B with a kind reception and fabulous views from the bedroom windows. If you don't have a car, there are a few places within a few minutes' walk of the village, including **The Convent** (Leenane Hill, just outside the village on the Westport-bound N59, tel. 095/42240, www. connemara.net/convent, €40 pp)—which, despite the name, has been a B&B for quite a few years now and is far more comfortable than you might expect. The chapel-turned-dining room features original brilliantly colored stained-glass windows.

A 19th-century coaching inn overlooking the water, the **Leenane Hotel** (just south of the village, tel. 095/42249, www.leenanehotel. com, mid-Apr.-Oct., €50-60 pp, s €60-70) is delightfully old-fashioned, with claw-footed tubs in the bathrooms and open turf fires in the sitting rooms and bar; the restaurant menu features local meat, seafood, and produce, and it's as good as the grub available in town.

PRACTICALITIES

Be sure to withdraw funds before leaving Westport or Galway. For tourist information, head to the **Leenane Cultural Centre** (village center, tel. 095/42323, 10am-6pm daily Apr.-Sept.), which includes a small exhibit on the local wool industry (not really worth the admission price) as well as a gift shop and café.

Leenane is 32 kilometers south of Westport, 19.5 kilometers east of Letterfrack, and 34 kilometers northeast of Clifden on the N59. From Galway (64.5 km), take the N59 to Maam Cross and make a right onto the R336 (or continue on the N59 to Recess and take the R334 north through the Lough Inagh Valley).

Need a lift to or from the pub? There's a Leenane-based **24-hour taxi and minibus service** (tel. 087/204-8929).

Recess

Near the southern end of the lovely Lough Inagh Valley, **Recess** (Sraith Salach, "Dirty Line") is a popular stopover for anglers and hikers (though the village itself consists of a pub, shop, and gas station). The former stay at the stately Victorian **Lough Inagh Lodge** (7 km north of Recess on the R334, tel. 091/34706, www.loughinaghlodgehotel. ie, €115 pp, s €135) and spend a few days fishing in Lough Inagh or Lough Derryclare; the latter crash early at the old-school, idyllically situated An Óige **Ben Lettery Hostel** (8 km west of Recess on the N59, tel. 091/51136, www.anoige.ie, late May-Sept., dorms €15-17) and set off to conquer one of the Twelve Bens first thing in the morning.

Or what if you're looking for a fairy-tale getaway? Look no further than the Victorian **Ballynahinch Castle** (signposted off the N59 6 km west of Recess, tel. 095/31006, www.ballynahinch-castle.com, €120-200 pp sharing May-Sept., €105-170 pp sharing Oct.-Apr., s €150-230/135-200, 10% service charge), where even the "standard" rooms offer lavish extras like fluffy bathrobes and slippers. The 180-hectare estate, with its wealth of small lakes and the Ballynahinch River, is also a haven for serious anglers, but you could easily pass the afternoon in the terraced gardens or on wooded walking trails. The restaurant fare—using only local fish, meats, and produce—is certainly worth writing home about.

Backpackers can take **Citylink** (tel. 091/564-163, www.citylink.ie) to get to the An Óige hostel. **Bus Éireann** (tel. 091/562-000, www.buseireann.ie) is an option in high season.

Oughterard

A small, pleasant-enough town on the west shore of Lough Corrib, **Oughterard** ("OOK-ter-ard," Uachtar Ard, "High Top") is a popular stop for angling enthusiasts, as the lake is

Aughnanure Castle

rich in sea and brown trout as well as salmon. Just south of town are the ruins of a six-story tower house overlooking the Corrib, **Aughnanure Castle** ("The Field of the Yews," 3 km east of town, signposted off the N59, tel. 091/552-214, 9:30am-6pm daily Apr.-Oct., €4). Run by Dúchas, this 16th-century O'Flaherty fortress was built on a series of natural caves through which the River Drimneen still flows. The tower has a modern roof, and there's a detached banquet hall in an advanced state of ruin. This is a magically peaceful spot well worth stopping for on your way out to Connemara.

Farther south is a good diversion for families, **Brigit's Garden** (Pollagh, Roscahill, 9 km south of Oughterard off the N59, tel. 091/550-905, www.brigidsgarden.ie, 10am-5:30pm daily mid-Apr.-Sept., €8), with a series of themed gardens and nature trails, plus a calendar of cooking, weaving, and wine appreciation courses.

A three-star guesthouse with evening meals (with advance notice) and wine license, **Corrib Wave** (Portacarron, 3 km east of Oughterard, signposted off the N59, tel. 091/552-147, www.corribwave.com, Feb.-Nov., €39-45 pp, s €50-55, dinner €24) hires boats and fishing equipment, and boasts its own private jetty. Another B&B that caters to anglers, this one just outside the town center, is the stately Victorian **Waterfall Lodge** (Glann Rd., signposted from the town center, tel. 091/552-168, www.waterfalllodge.net, €40 pp, s €50), with mature gardens and an excellent breakfast menu.

The best eatery in town is **Connemara Greenway** (Main St., tel. 091/866-645, www.connemaragreenwaycafe.com, 9am-8:30pm Tues.-Sat., noon-4pm Sun. summer to autumn, 9am-6pm Tues.-Thurs. and 9am-8:30pm Fri.-Sat., noon-4pm Sun. in winter, lunch €8-13, dinner €13-22). The menu isn't terribly imaginative (nor particularly veg-friendly), but the fresh baking is delish and the service is genuinely friendly.

Oughterard is 27 kilometers northwest of Galway on the N59. **Bus Éireann** will get you here from Galway (tel. 091/562-000, summer-only #61 runs late June-early Sept., 5/day Mon.-Sat., 3/day Sun.; #419 runs Sept.-May, 3/day Mon.-Sat., 2/day Sun.).

Southern and Eastern Galway

KINVARA
A pretty little fishing village on the Burren's northern fringe, **Kinvara** (Cinn Mhara, "Headland of the Sea") offers small-town charm and plenty of peace and quiet despite its location on the busy N67. There isn't a whole lot to do, but Kinvara makes a good base for exploring the Burren and sights of southern Galway—Kilmacduagh, Coole Park, and Thoor Ballylee.

Sights
The name of restored 16th-century **Dunguaire Castle** (half a km north of the village on the N86, tel. 091/637-108, 9:30am-5pm daily Apr.-Sept., €6) is anglicized as "Dungory," and though you'll never see it spelled that way now, it sure helps with the pronunciation! Perched atmospherically on the lip of Kinvara Bay, the castle demesne harbors freshwater springs. This was the royal seat of the king of Connaught in the 7th century, a ruler renowned for his hospitality. (His name was Guaire Aidhneach, hence Dún Guaire, "Fort of Guaire.") The present structure once belonged to the surgeon and wit Oliver St. John Gogarty, who purchased Dunguaire for its proximity to other literati of the Irish renaissance: Edward Martyn (of Tullira Castle), Yeats, and Lady Gregory.

During the day you can check out the historical exhibition and admire the view, but most visitors experience the castle as the setting for a **medieval banquet** (tel. 1800/269-811 for reservations, 5:30pm and 8:45pm nightly Apr.-Oct., €48), on a smaller scale than the entertainment at Bunratty—fewer diners and entertainers, but the four-course meal (with silverware) and format are the same.

Activities and Recreation
You'll find a Blue Flag strand at **Trácht,** 6.5 kilometers west of the village (and signposted from the N67). Alternatively, the **Burren Nature Sanctuary** (Cloonasee, 1 km east of the village, turnoff at Sexton's pub, tel. 091/637-444, www.bns.ie, 10am-6pm daily, €4) is a very worthwhile diversion for families, showcasing local botany in a playful atmosphere. There's also a café.

Food
You'll have a view of the harbor at the **Strawberry Hedgehog Café** (The Quay, tel. 091/638-129, 9am-6pm Sun.-Thurs., 9am-10pm Fri.-Sat., under €10), which serves up

crepes, sandwiches, and quite good coffee. The decor is as whimsical as the name.

One safe bet for an evening meal is **Keogh's** (The Square, tel. 091/637-145, food served 10am-10pm daily, €8-18), renowned for its hearty seafood dishes and quaint atmosphere. Another well-established eatery is the **Pier Head** (on the harbor, tel. 091/638-188, food served 5pm-10pm Mon.-Sat., noon-8pm Sun. June-Oct., 5pm-8pm daily Nov.-May, €15-27), where you can order duck or quail if you're not in the mood for seafood; tables at the upstairs restaurant offer a better view of the bay. The Pier Head is also the (de facto) top choice for vegans, since the vegetarian dish of the day can generally be made sans cheese.

Entertainment and Events

If the medieval banquet and Dungaire Castle isn't your thing, there are a few good pubs in the village. Try **Connolly's** (The Quay, tel. 091/637-131, www.connollyskinvara.com), with its "real" beer garden (albeit made of potted plants); inside, an open fire burns in the grate. There's often traditional music here, though it isn't scheduled as such. **Keogh's** (The Square, tel. 091/637-145) has live trad on Monday and Thursday nights, and visiting musicians are always welcome to join in.

Annual festivals include **Fleadh na gCuach,** "The Cuckoo Festival," which offers a load of traditional music sessions over the May bank holiday weekend, and **Cruinniú na mBad,** the "Gathering of the Boats," when sails are raised in homage to the traditional Galway hooker every August.

Accommodations

Most of Kinvara's B&B accommodations are a few kilometers outside of town; if you're driving, try **Clareview House** (3 km east of the village on the R347, tel. 091/637-170, www. clareviewhouse.com, €35-38 pp, s €40-45, dinner €25), a working farm offering old-fashioned hospitality (complete with delightful home baking).

It may be rather oddly situated above the Londis supermarket, but the ★ **Kinvara**

Guesthouse (The Square, Main St., 091/638-562, www.kinvaraguesthouse.ie, €30-50 pp, single €50-85) combines the privacy and spaciousness of a hotel with a B&B's friendliness, attention to detail, and good value. The owners have made wheelchair accessibility a priority, and the breakfast spread isn't phoning it in like so many other places these days: You'll have a choice of fresh pineapple and strawberries, croissants, coffee cake, and suchlike, along with cooked meals for every taste, from pancakes and the full Irish fry to a hearty vegan version with fried mushrooms, tomato, and baked beans. If the guesthouse is booked up, try the **Merriman Hotel** (Main St., tel. 091/638-222, www.merrimanhotel. com, €60-80 pp). The staff aren't as friendly or accommodating, but it will do.

Information and Services

Kinvara does not have a tourist office, though there's plenty of info to be found at **Kinvara Online** (www.kinvara.com) before you go.

Kinvara's two supermarkets, Londis and McMahon's, have ATMs, and there's a bureau de change at Merriman Hotel—all on Main Street. The **Kinvara Pharmacy** (tel. 091/637-397) is also on Main Street.

Getting There and Around

Kinvara is 30 kilometers south of Galway on the N18, picking up the N67 in Kilcolgan. **Bus Éireann** (tel. 091/562-000) can get you there on the summer-only route from Cork and Tralee to Galway via the Burren and Cliffs of Moher (#50, 2-4/day daily June-Sept., 1-2/day Sun.). Route #423 from Galway to the Cliffs of Moher via Kinvara operates all year (3/day Mon.-Sat.).

For a taxi, ring **JF Cabs** (tel. 087/660-8551).

★ KILMACDUAGH

One of Ireland's most stunning monastic ruins is little-known even among many natives. The old churches may not offer much out of the ordinary, but the round tower at **Kilmacduagh** (5.5 km west of Gort, site always open, free) is Ireland's equivalent of the Leaning Tower of Pisa. Complete with conical roof, the tower—perhaps the tallest in the country at 34 meters—slants a full 60 centimeters to the south, and the visual effect is extraordinary (and strangely unsettling). Though most of the other ruins are locked, you can wander around them and poke your head through the gates for a peek at the interiors.

The monastery was founded by St. Colman MacDuagh (the name means "Church of MacDuagh") in the 7th century and patronized by the king of Connaught, Guaire Aidhne, who lent his name to Dunguaire Castle in Kinvara. Kilmacduagh was another important center of learning in medieval times and eventually received its own diocese, though it never quite attained the power or influence of Clonmacnoise or Glendalough.

Getting to Kilmacduagh can be downright tricky. Though it is possible to reach the site from Kinvara, the signposts can be inaccurate. It's easiest to approach Kilmacduagh from Gort, 37.5 kilometers south of Galway City. From the town square, follow the sign for Corofin. About a block off the square, make a right onto the road directly opposite the SuperValu (you'll see Kilmacduagh signposted there). Then it's a straightforward trip,

less than five minutes by car. There's no public transportation to the monastic site, though it's possible to ride **Bus Éireann** to Gort (tel. 091/562-000, route #51 or #55, 14/day daily) and walk or bike (if you've brought your own).

COOLE PARK

Lady Augusta Gregory, friend and patron of William Butler Yeats and cofounder of the Abbey Theatre, entertained most of Ireland's greatest writers at her estate at Coole Park from the 1890s until her death in 1932. In 1880 she had married William Gregory, member of Parliament and former governor of Ceylon, and made her home here; after his death in 1892—he was 35 years her senior—she devoted herself to literary pursuits, recording the folktales of the native Irish and writing several plays of her own. The house no longer exists, but **Coole Park** (3 km north of Gort, signposted off the N18, tel. 091/631-804, www.coolepark.ie, visitors center 10am-5pm Apr.-May and Sept., 10am-6pm June-Aug., park 8am-7:30pm daily year-round, free) now offers a historical exhibit, tearoom, and audiovisual along with a nature reserve with wooded lakeside walking trails. Don't miss the "autograph tree," carved by many of the turn-of-the-century literati: the Yeats brothers,

Kilmacduagh, with its leaning tower and extensive church ruins, is monastic Ireland's best-kept secret.

Synge, George Bernard Shaw, George Russell ("Æ"), Augustus John, Sean O'Casey, and Lady Gregory herself.

Coole Park is 35 kilometers south of Galway off the N18. The park is easiest to reach by car, though you can take **Bus Éireann** (#51 or #55, 14/day daily on the Galway-Shannon-Cork route) and ask to be dropped off at the Coole turnoff.

THOOR BALLYLEE

A tower house built by the de Burgo clan in the 16th century, Islandmore Castle is far better known as **Thoor Ballylee** ("Ballylee Tower," Peterswell, tel. 091/631-436, www.yeatsthoorballylee.org, 9:30am-5pm Mon.-Sat. late May-Sept., €6). It was purchased by William Butler Yeats for a whopping £35 in 1916, the bargain-basement price due to the castle's neglected state. The poet had chosen the tower for its romantic situation as well as its proximity to the home of his great friend and patron, Lady Gregory. After a period of restoration work funded by his lecture tours, Yeats moved there in 1919 with his wife and daughter, and the modest tower served as their summer home for the dozen years that followed. Yeats's new home inspired many of the poems in his aptly named collection, *The Tower.*

The Yeats family stopped coming here in the late 1920s, and the poet retreated there only sporadically during the 1930s. After another period of disuse, the Irish Tourist Board purchased and renovated the castle in 1965, turning it into a small Yeats museum with original furniture and the usual gift shop and tearoom. There's also a short audiovisual, but it (like the rest of the exhibition) covers only the tower's 20th-century history.

Thoor Ballylee is 47 kilometers south of Galway and is signposted off the N18 south of the village of Ardrahan (the tower is 1 km farther down a local road). There is no public transportation.

CLONFERT CATHEDRAL

Near the Galway-Offaly border, the sleepy hamlet of Clonfert is on the map for its small, 12th-century St. Brendan's Church of Ireland, better known as Clonfert Cathedral. Its six-arched, pedimented Romanesque doorway features limestone carvings of eerily individualized human and animal heads and plant motifs; it is absolutely exquisite and well worth a detour (despite a botched restoration attempt sometime in the 19th century).

The church itself was founded by St. Brendan the Navigator in the 6th century (before his epic voyage to the New World in a small curragh), and he is supposedly buried here (the site of Na Seacht dTeampaill on Inis Mór claims the same distinction, however). Though the building is generally locked except for Sunday services, what's inside pales in comparison anyway (if you do really want to get inside, knock at the house next door and ask for the key). Otherwise, just spend a while staring up at those faces carved above the doorway, wondering what they might tell you of the last 900 years if only they could speak.

Clonfert is 82 kilometers east of Galway City. It's most efficient to visit en route to Galway from Athlone, since the nearest town to Clonfert, Ballinasloe, is on the M6 between those two cities. From Ballinasloe, take the R355 south for Laurencetown; once there, you'll see Clonfert signposted on your left. The church is another 8 kilometers or so down a local road (follow the signs for "Emmanuel Providence House" if unsure). The journey from Ballinasloe is 20 kilometers altogether. Unfortunately, there is no bus service to Clonfert.

Detour to Clonmacnoise

Amid the midlands' vast swaths of bog and farmland you'll find the magnificent monastic city of Clonmacnoise in County Offaly, worth a detour when traveling between Galway and Dublin. If you need to spend the night in the area, Athlone (21 kilometers north) is the best choice in terms of amenities, nightlife, and quality eateries.

★ CLONMACNOISE

Along with Glendalough in County Wicklow, **Clonmacnoise** (21 km south of Athlone, signposted off the N62, tel. 090/967-4195, 10am-5:30pm daily Nov.-mid-March, 10am-6pm mid-Mar.-mid-May and Sept.-Oct., 9am-7pm mid-May-Aug., €7) is Ireland's most important monastic site, picturesquely situated right on the River Shannon. It's a strange irony that more than 100,000 visitors pass through this otherwise peaceful "monastic city" each year—then again, as William Bulfin noted sadly when he visited Cluain Mac Nois, these ruins attracted plenty of impious Victorian picnickers in his time, too. Get here first thing in the morning, before the advent of the coach buses, and you can almost hear echoes of laughter and tinkling teacups as you wander through the old graveyard.

The Irish name, meaning "retreat of the sons of the noble," probably refers to the monastic school's popularity with Gaelic princes. Founded by St. Ciarán in the 540s (less than a year before he died of yellow plague at the age of 33), Clonmacnoise flourished as a center of learning and scholarship for centuries, in part for its location at the crossroads of the island's two most popular travel routes: the River Shannon and the Eiscir Riada ("Highway of the Kings"), a ridge left by the ice age. The monastery was plundered repeatedly (and finally by the English in 1552 under Henry VIII) for its trove of jewel-encrusted reliquaries, book covers, croziers, and so forth. Many of the world's most important medieval manuscripts were produced here, including the 12th-century *Leabhar na hUidhre,* the "Book of the Dun Cow," which contains the earliest extant version of that great Irish epic, the *Táin Bó Cuailnge.*

The ruins include three high crosses (all

Clonmacnoise is charmingly (and strategically) situated on the River Shannon.

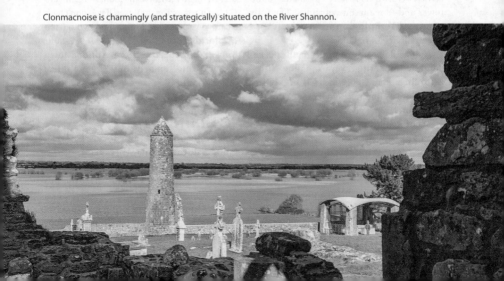

moved inside to the exhibition for preservation, but there are convincing replicas in their places), a cathedral, two round towers, and seven churches dating from the 10th to the 13th centuries. And on a small hill near the car park is the teetering remnant of an early-13th-century castle.

Trysting couples used to linger in the ornate doorway of **The Cathedral,** known as the **whispering arch** because a whisper carries from one side to the other. It is also said this acoustical marvel was used by priests to hear the confessions of lepers. This arch dates to the 14th or 15th century, and thus is not as old as the cathedral itself. You'll also find effigies of Saints Dominic, Patrick, and Francis above the doorway.

Another bit of folklore concerns the tiny **Temple Ciarán,** the saint's burial place: The earth from the church's interior is said to have miraculous properties, so for generations locals have been taking fistfuls to sprinkle on their fields for a successful crop, and on the floors of their homes to ward off sickness; this is why the church floor is on a much lower level than the surrounding ground. Temple Ciarán is the most sacred ruin at Clonmacnoise, but **Temple Finghin** (or Finian) near the Shannon's shore is the most attractive, with its restored 17-meter round tower and Romanesque carvings. The fully renovated **Temple Connor** nearby is used by the Church of Ireland.

Half a kilometer east of the main site, beyond the modern graveyard, is the **Nuns' Church,** built in 1180, which has an excellent example of a Hiberno-Romanesque doorway. This church was a gift to the monastery from Dearbhforgaill (or Dervorgilla), the "Irish Helen of Troy," who ran off with the king of Leinster (MacMurrough, the same king who invited in the Normans) during a raid in 1152. This incident doubtless contributed to the Norman invasion, as Dervorgilla's husband was one of the chieftains who subsequently drove MacMurrough into exile. Afterward the princess came here to repent, and she died at Mellifont Abbey in Louth at the age of 85.

Many people on the coach tours don't realize it's here, so if you find yourself in the midst of a noisy group outside the visitors center, you'll be relieved to find you have the Nuns' Church all to yourself.

The exhibition center offers a series of scenes illustrating the monastic city's history over time (including a scriptorium, a small wooden house where a monk would have copied and illuminated manuscripts). There's the usual 18-minute audiovisual, a collection of early Christian sandstone grave slabs, and the exquisitely carved high crosses brought indoors for preservation. The most famous of these, the **Cros na Scraeptra** (Cross of the Scriptures), has been hugged by thousands of superstitious visitors, as legend has it whoever can touch their fingertips on the far side will be blessed with healing powers.

Practicalities

Seeing as it's the closest town to Clonmacnoise, **Shannonbridge** (4 km southwest of the monastic site) might *seem* like the natural choice for a base. Not to malign the good people of Shannonbridge, but who wants to spend a night on vacation in the lee of the West Offaly Power Plant? You're best off staying in **Athlone** in County Westmeath (21 km north of the site), even if you don't have a car; you can get to Clonmacnoise with **Irish Midlands Tours** (tel. 087/092-9468, 2-hour tour €20), departing from Athlone town center. (Unfortunately, Bus Éireann offers bus service to Clonmacnoise only for school groups.)

ATHLONE

Most folks—natives and tourists both—know **Athlone** (Baile Átha Luain, "Town of the Ford of Luan") as the town midway between Dublin and Galway where the Bus Éireann bus makes a pit stop. Get off the bus, head into town, and you'll find it's actually a pretty cool place, mostly for its small but up-and-coming "Left Bank" quarter lined with neat little shops and cafés. There's not much

The Hauntings at Leap Castle

As you'd expect in the most haunted spot in the country (if not all Europe), **Leap Castle** ("LEP," Clareen, 16 km south of Kinnitty on the R421, tel. 057/913-1115 or 087/234-4064, seanryan@mail2web.com, open daily by request, €6) has a long and extremely violent history, starting with the priest murdered in the "Bloody Chapel" by his own brother in 1532. And then there's the spike-studded oubliette where people were said to have been pushed (and subsequently impaled).

What's that you say—you don't believe in all that hooey? Just *you* try to concoct a rational explanation for the horrible stench emanating from an uninhabited wing of the house (this odiferous brand of ghost is called an "elemental," and Leap's appears half-human, half-sheep) or the transparent old man sitting in a rocking chair by the fireplace.

The owner, a musician by the name of Sean Ryan, knows there's no such thing as a rational explanation for the spectral parade he finds in his living room on a daily basis (ghost hunters say there are 20 of them in all)—though he likes to think his family's music calms

Leap Castle, home to friendly musicians and not-so-friendly ghosts

the spirits. Mr. Ryan is an absolutely delightful man, willing to tell you as much about the castle's history as you dare to know, and if you're lucky you may get to hear him play a tune on his tin whistle. He's amazingly relaxed and gracious when it comes to planning your visit, but do be sure to email or ring ahead of time. You likely won't be able to visit on a Sunday, when Mr. Ryan drives to Galway to play at Crane's pub.

Leap Castle is 57 kilometers south of Athlone via the N62; the drive takes about an hour.

to see in Athlone, but it's definitely the best place to base yourself when planning a visit to Clonmacnoise.

The town straddles the River Shannon, with the late-1930s Catholic Church of Saints Peter and Paul and the massive early-13th-century Athlone Castle just over the Town Bridge on the Left Bank. From the castle, turn left onto Castle Street for Main Street and Fry Place, where you'll find the famous Sean's pub and delicious Left Bank Bistro. From there, turn left onto High Street (which becomes Bastion Street and then O'Connell Street) for more eats and shopping. Back on the right bank, the main drag (starting from the bridge) changes names from Custume Place to Church to Dublin Gate to Mardyke to Costello. Mostly everything you'll need is along this thoroughfare.

Food

There are plenty of passionate chefs in Athlone hoping to develop their town into a foodie mecca to rival Dublin itself, and in years to come it just might happen! The most exciting eateries are in the Left Bank. Two of Athlone's nicest, most laid-back cafés are **Slice of Life** (Connaught St., tel. 090/649-3970, www.sliceoflifeathlone.webs.com, 8:30am-6pm Mon.-Sat., €10) and **Beans & Leaves** (Lloyds Ln., tel. 090/643-3534, 9am-6pm Mon.-Fri., closed Sat., noon-5pm Sun., €10), which delivers on "simple ingredients, magical food" (though with pancakes and cinnamon buns on the menu, they're not promising it's healthy!) along with a pretty Shannonside view. Another great lunch option is the **Corner House Bistro** (Dublingate St., tel. 090/647-0077, www.cornerhousebistro.ie,

Detour to Clonmacnoise

© AVALON TRAVEL

sauce. The fare is top notch. Athlone's *other* best restaurant is **Thyme** (Custume Pl., tel. 090/647-8850, www.thymerestaurant.ie, 5pm-10pm Mon.-Sat., noon-10pm Sun., €16-26, 2/3-course dinner €25/30), which is a terrific option for those travelers on a gluten-free diet.

Entertainment

Many pubs claim to be Ireland's oldest, but only **Sean's** (Main St., in the Left Bank section, tel. 090/649-2358, www.seansbar.ie) is listed in the *Guinness Book of Records*. Supposedly there's been a pub on this site since the beginning of the 10th century. It's still the most happenin' spot in town, with live trad sessions in the front room on the weekends and a huge tented beer garden out back.

Accommodations

There aren't many B&Bs in Athlone, and most of them are either on the shabby side or were up for sale at time of writing. Just because ★ **The Bastion** (2 Bastion St., tel. 090/649-4954, www.thebastion.net, €35-45 pp) has virtually no competition doesn't lessen its excellence. A labyrinthine townhouse filled with antiques, exotic knickknacks, and potted plants, it's a delightfully quirky, bohemian spot—and Anthony and Vinnie, the owners, are exceptionally friendly and helpful. Come morning there's a smorgasbord of fancy breads and cheeses along with fruit, cereal, and Fair Trade coffee and herbal tea—a nice change from the usual greasy fried breakfast.

On the main drag, the **Prince of Wales** (Church St., tel. 090/647-6666, www.theprinceofwales.ie, €60-85 pp, s €85-105) has business-class rooms with DVD/CD players (and a selection of DVDs), radio, digital safes, and king-size beds in many of the rooms. There's also same-day laundry service. The four bars and nightclub downstairs attract a youngish local crowd.

It's not actually in town, but the **Wineport Lodge** (Athlone Relief Rd., 5 km north of town, just outside the village of Glasson off the N55, tel. 090/643-9010, www.wineport.ie, €65-140 pp) is generally considered Athlone's

9am-5pm Mon.-Sat., €9-16), offering gourmet versions of traditional dishes like boxties and the ploughman's lunch.

No doubt it's the finest restaurant in town—with a bright, airy, minimalist dining room and an Asian- and Australian-inspired menu—but consider yourself warned that the service at the **Left Bank Bistro** (Fry Pl., off Main St. in the Left Bank, tel. 090/649-4446, www.leftbankbistro.com, 10:30am-9:30pm Tues.-Sat., lunch €10-15, 3-course early-bird special €25 5:30pm-7:30pm Tues.-Fri., dinner €19-25) can be somewhat negligent. That said, you can have yourself an open-faced sandwich with exquisitely fresh goat cheese salad for lunch, or go all out for dinner with an Asian-marinated half-roast duck in apple-mint

best hotel-restaurant, in part for its great location right on Lough Ree. The carefully selected wine, champagne, and cocktail lists in the hotel lounge are worth the visit alone, but with spacious, swanky, lake-facing rooms (with balcony) and a top-notch room-service breakfast included in the price, this is *the* place to treat yourself when touring the midlands.

Information and Services

The **tourist office** (tel. 090/649-4630, 9:30am-5:30pm Mon.-Fri. Apr.-Oct., www.eastcoastmidlands.ie and www.athlone.ie) is at Athlone Castle. Just across the Town Bridge from the castle is a **Bank of Ireland** (31 Church St.) with ATM and bureau de change. **Boots the Chemist** (tel. 090/647-6997) is in the Golden Island Shopping Centre and is open on Sunday.

Getting There and Around

Athlone is roughly midway between Galway (93 km) and Dublin (123 km) on the M6. Get here from Dublin or Galway via **Irish Rail** (tel. 090/647-3300, www.irishrail.ie, 5/day Mon.-Sat., 4/day Sun., €20-25 each way). The other option is the **Bus Éireann** (tel. 090/648-4406, www.buseireann.ie) Dublin-Galway route (#20, 15/day daily). Direct service is also available from Cork, Cashel, and Cahir (#71, 2/day Mon.-Sat., 1/day Sun.) and Limerick (#72, 4/day Mon.-Sat., 2/day Sun.).

The bus and train stations are on the east side of the Shannon, a 10-minute walk from the town center. From Station Road, head east and bear right onto Ballymahon Road, which becomes Gleeson Street. Then turn right onto Mardyke, the east section of Athlone's main drag.

Bike hire is available from **D.B. Cycles** (23 Connaught St., tel. 090/649-2280, www.db-cycles.ie, €12/70 per day/week). Need a ride? Ring **Athlone Cabs** (tel. 090/647-4400) or **O'Neill Hackneys** (tel. 090/647-5765).

the Athlone skyline along the River Shannon

The Northwest

Mayo 337
Sligo 357

Donegal 369

You hear a lot about Ireland's west—its dramatic landscapes, its stubborn adherence to tradition, its blissfully slow pace—and this notion is most accurate in the counties of Mayo (Maigh Eo, "Plain of Yews"), Sligo (Sligeach, "Place of Shells"), Leitrim (Liatroim or Liath Druim, "Gray Ridge"), and Donegal (Dún na nGall, "Fort of the Foreigner").

Gorgeous (if sometimes bleak) sea and mountain landscapes are thoroughly worth the extra effort in getting up here, especially considering that your fellow travelers are more often weekending locals than stereotypical tourists. Lovely as it is, you can't say this of Connemara. And if you need a bit of nightlife along with your surfing or hill-walking, you'll find plenty of *craic* in Westport and Sligo Town.

There's a certain element of spin-doctoring to the pervasive "Sligo is Yeats country" catchphrase, since the poet never spent much time here after those childhood summers with his maternal grandparents; nevertheless, Irish literary buffs won't be disappointed with what there is to see at Drumcliffe and the Sligo County Museum.

Located between Sligo and Donegal and the source of the River Shannon, tiny Leitrim isn't a tourist destination as such. Like nearby Counties Cavan and Fermanagh, Leitrim is dotted with lakes, and it's a local joke that land here is sold not by the acre, but by the gallon; with Sligo the county shares Lough Gill.

An extended visit to the republic's northernmost county, wonderfully remote Donegal is an excellent way to get off the beaten tourist track. There are more weekending Northern Irish than international tourists at any time of year, but the relative lack of tourism is due to simple geography, not a lack of gorgeous landscapes.

HISTORY

Sligo and Donegal abound in prehistoric monuments; dating before the turn of the third millennium BC, the megalithic tombs at Carrowmore and Knocknarea are probably as old as Newgrange, the lesser-known Carrowkeel and Creevykeel sites date from

---

Previous: Streedagh Beach; Grace O'Malley's Rockfleet Castle. **Above:** the Italianate garden at Glenveagh Castle.

Look for ★ to find recommended
sights, activities, dining, and lodging.

Highlights

★ **Doolough Valley:** Take a long quiet drive up this lonely road to view some of the most stunningly isolated mountain scenery in the west (page 339).

★ **Croagh Patrick:** Generations of pilgrims and casual hikers alike have journeyed to the summit of "Ireland's Sinai," which offers beautiful vistas on clear days (page 346).

★ **Knocknarea:** This unexcavated megalithic tomb tops another hill, this one in Sligo, with an awesome panorama of sea and countryside (page 366).

★ **Kilcullen's Seaweed Baths:** Relax in a hot porcelain tub of saltwater and freshly gathered seaweed—which eases sore joints and gets your skin soft and glowing—in this delightful, authentic Edwardian bathhouse overlooking Killala Bay (page 367).

★ **Carrowkeel Passage Tomb Cemetery:** This prehistoric necropolis in the Bricklieve Mountains of southern Sligo is perhaps the spookiest spot in the country (page 368).

★ **Rossnowlagh Beach:** Rossnowlagh is one of Donegal's finest strands, popular with surfers yet far quieter than the overdeveloped resort of Bundoran to the south (page 373).

★ **Slieve League:** The muddy track along the ridge of Europe's tallest sea cliffs makes for a tough but very rewarding five-hour hike (page 377).

★ **Glenveagh National Park:** Take a walk

through the "Poisoned Glen," climb the quartzite-capped Mount Errigal, tour the Victorian Glenveagh Castle, and watch for the golden eagle in the country's northernmost national park (page 379).

★ **Grianán of Aileách:** This superbly situated Iron Age ring fort near the Donegal-Derry border offers a view of five counties as well as Loughs Swilly and Foyle (page 386).

The Northwest

somewhere in the third millennium, and archaeological evidence says human habitation in County Donegal goes back as far as 7000 BC. There was plenty going on in Mayo in the Stone Age, too, as the subterranean remains of a substantial farming settlement at Céide Fields attest. Local history in early Christian times centers around St. Patrick's sojourn on the summit of the mountain that bears his name, somewhere around AD 441. The snake-banishing bit may be more legend than truth, but his 40-day fast atop Croagh Patrick is probably based in fact.

In 1588, the ill-fated Spanish Armada (on its way to England with the rather optimistic hope of deposing the Virgin Queen, a Protestant) was wrecked off these shores; Broadhaven and Blacksod Bays in northern Mayo swallowed thousands of sailors, and the beaches north of Sligo Town were covered in casualties of the sea. Those who survived were slain by the English garrison.

The consequence of so much starkly beautiful scenery is a dearth of arable land, and the people of these northwestern counties had a more difficult time of it even before the Great Hunger. The Great Famine of 1845-1846 exacted a disproportionate number of casualties in this region; there were 100,000 dead in County Mayo, and another 100,000 emigrated.

As for the "foreigner" of Donegal's Irish name, it far predates the English or even the Normans—it refers to the Celts, though oddly enough it was the English who initiated use of the name in the late 16th century. Before this, the county was divided into smaller kingdoms, each with a ruling family. In the early 1590s the leaders of two of these local ruling families, "Red" Hugh O'Donnell and Hugh O'Neill, joined forces in an attempt to purge the English; they achieved initial victories in 1595 and 1598, but their disastrous defeat at Kinsale (in County Cork) in 1601, O'Donnell's hasty departure for Spain (whose waylaid Armada was not able to help them in battle at Kinsale), and O'Neill's eventual surrender and self-imposed exile allowed the subsequent English Plantation. The departure of O'Neill and O'Donnell and their families became known as the "Flight of the Earls" or "Flight of the Wild Geese," and their lands became forfeit to the English crown.

PLANNING YOUR TIME

Everywhere you travel along Ireland's west coast, you'll see signs for the **Wild Atlantic Way** (www.wildatlanticway.com). These northwestern counties—being less popular destinations than Kerry, Clare, and Galway—stand to benefit the most from this new marketing initiative from the Irish tourist board. Check out the website for more information and suggested itineraries.

County Sligo's smallish size means you can take in the principal sights—Drumcliffe, Knocknarea and a handful of other megalithic monuments, and the cultural attractions of Sligo Town—in a matter of two days. Westport is the tourist hub of County Mayo, a natural base for taking in Croagh Patrick, Achill Island, and the islands of Clew Bay. Northern Mayo is far more remote, though hill-walkers will find two or three days' diversion here. If you're planning to spend most of your time in Mayo, Sligo, and/or Donegal, it makes more sense to fly into Knock Airport.

Some visitors "do" Donegal while touring Northern Ireland, since it's easy to dip into the Inishowen Peninsula as a day trip out of Derry City. But Donegal's refreshing remoteness can be addictive, and those looking to veer off the beaten track should plan to spend the greater part of their vacation here. Consider flying into Donegal Airport, near Gweedore, via Dublin. It takes an extra effort to get here no matter how you come, but you'll be rewarded with otherworldly landscapes and few other visitors with whom to share them. Getting around Donegal without a rental car can be a real headache, though; those without wheels are best off choosing just one region to visit, since public transport within the county is downright poor. If you can, bring your own bicycle to cover more ground. Banking facilities are very limited outside Donegal's larger towns, so be sure to withdraw enough cash before leaving Donegal Town, Ardara, or Letterkenny; there's also an ATM at Bunbeg in Gweedore.

Mayo

County Mayo is Ireland at its wildest and most remote, particularly on Achill Island, the Nephin Beg mountains, and the Mullet Peninsula. Even the most isolated reaches of Donegal won't give you the almost frightening sense that you've arrived at the end of the world. Thanks to the Celtic Tiger, myriad other locales across the country can no longer offer such enchantment; though the forces of capitalist progress move at a slower pace up here, it's still only a matter of time.

That said, Mayo's largest towns, Castlebar and Ballina, are workaday places with very little to deter the visitor. You'll probably want to base yourself in or near the pleasantly bustling Westport; from here you can scale Croagh Patrick, the greatest pilgrimage in Irish Catholicism, or catch a ferry to Clare Island from nearby Roonagh Quay. If driving, approach Westport from Connemara via the Doolough Valley, which affords some of the most stunningly isolated mountain scenery in the west. The **Clew Bay Archaeological Trail** (www.clewbaytrail.com) is liberally signposted in this southwestern section of

the county and includes both monastic sites and prehistoric tombs of lesser importance.

Another route into Mayo from points south runs through Cong, a kitschy-yet-charming town just over the border from Galway, renowned for the filming of John Ford's film *The Quiet Man* in the summer of 1951.

CONG

A tidy little town between the northern shore of Lough Corrib and the southern shore of Lough Mask, just over the Galway-Mayo border, **Cong** (Conga Feichin, "Feichin's Narrows") draws visitors for one reason: Much of *The Quiet Man,* the 1951 film starring John Wayne and Maureen O'Hara, was shot in and around it. The movie was considered a technicolor marvel at the time, and the tourist trade is still selling the decades-old excitement over the arrival of a Hollywood crew. Movie aside, the lovely Cong Abbey and a walk along the Cong River will keep you occupied for an hour or so, and you can even sign up for a falconry lesson at the swanky Ashford Castle on the outskirts of town.

the Cong Abbey monks' fishing hut, perched above the Cong River

Cong is a snap to navigate: Main Street runs north-south; Abbey Street on the southern end loops north, following the River Corrib as the Circular Road, and meets Main Street again at O'Connor's grocery and gas station.

Sights

Forget all the *Quiet Man* hubbub. No, really. Many small businesses are still trying to cash in on the kitsch more than 65 years after the movie was made, and their tackiness is a blight on this otherwise charming riverside village. A tour of the original film locations is a disappointment: Many places no longer exist, and others aren't in or near Cong at all. Most tourists come to the **Quiet Man Heritage Cottage** (at the end of Abbey St., tel. 094/954-6089, 10am-5pm daily, €5) believing that the movie was actually filmed here, but it wasn't; this small building has no connection to the film whatsoever. The building features a wall of photocopied newspaper clippings from the summer of 1951, when *The Quiet Man* was being filmed in the area, as well as a bedroom furnished to look like that of the main character. The only authentic thing in it is a horse saddle, though, and who in their right mind would pay €6 to look at a saddle? Don't waste your time or money.

No, the best reason to visit is **Cong Abbey** (always accessible, free), refounded in the 12th century on the site of an earlier monastery established by St. Feichin, along with the marvelous Harry Clarke altar window at the adjacent **St. Mary's Church.** That this 1933 masterpiece could exist within such an architectural monstrosity is sadly amusing (more sad though, seeing as the window is now artificially lighted). The Virgin Mary of the left panel looks more like a flapper than the mother of God. (If you do end up watching *The Quiet Man* while you're here, look for this window in the early church scene.)

The abbey is a delight to wander through, with a late-Romanesque doorway, the substantial remains of a cloister, and an upstairs dormitory. (The magnificent gold Cross of Cong, which supposedly contained a splinter from the True Cross, is now in the National Museum of Archaeology and History in Dublin.) Follow the path west toward the stream, cross the small bridge, and you'll alight upon a striking pointed archway with the noseless face of Rory O'Connor, the last high king of Ireland, who spent his last days here at the abbey once he'd seen the proverbial writing on the wall. Through the archway, a path leads to the **monks' fishing hut** perched over the river, where a bell (attached to the net dropped through the slot in the floor) would ring every time a fish was caught. If you continue over the Cong River bridge, you'll find another regal countenance carved above a pointed archway: This is the face of Turlough O'Connor, father of Rory and patron of the abbey, which he reestablished in 1120. Continue through this arch on a tranquil stroll through the woods.

Activities and Recreation

You can make a half-hour visit to **Inchagoill Island,** which has monastic ruins dating to the 5th and 12th centuries, with **Corrib Cruises** (tel. 087/679-6470, www.corribcruises.com, departs Lisloughrey Pier at Ashford Castle, 1 km south of town, at 10:45am and 2:45am daily Apr.-Oct., €20). Anglers are well catered to in Cong; ring Frank at **Ashford Bay Boat Hire** (tel. 094/954-6348 or 087/252-4253, ashfordbay@hotmail.com).

The highly regarded **Ashford Equestrian Centre** (tel. 094/954-6507, www.ashford-equestrian.com) is on grounds adjacent to Ashford Castle (but no longer part of the estate). No prior experience is necessary for a lesson at **Ireland's School of Falconry** (Ashford Castle, tel. 094/954-6820, www.falconry.ie).

Food and Entertainment

The sandwiches and salads at the super-cheerful **Hungry Monk Café** (Abbey St., tel. 094/954-6866, www.hungrymonkcong.com, 10am-6pm daily July-Aug., 10am-6pm Tues.-Sun. mid-Mar.-June and Sept.-Oct., €7-11) are the tastiest in town. This should be your first choice for lunch. Otherwise, the **Crowe's Nest** pub at Ryan's Hotel (Main St., tel. 094/954-6243, www.ryanshotelcong.ie, food served 9am-7pm daily, €8-16) does good paninis, and for a more formal dinner there's the hotel restaurant, the **Fennel Seed** (7pm-9:30pm daily, €14-25). You can also find hearty (if unadventurous) pub grub at **Danagher's** (Abbey St., tel. 094/954-6028, meals served noon-9:15pm daily, €10-20). These two pubs are also sure bets for live trad in the summer.

Shopping

You won't find anything too far out of the ordinary at the **Cong Art Gallery** (Main St., tel. 094/954-5675 or 086/358-3468 for off-season inquiries, www.congartgallery.com), but there are plenty of oil paintings of local landscapes. The other shops in town are mostly of the cheap-and-cheesy variety.

Accommodations

Affiliated with both An Óige and IHH, the **Cong Hostel** (Lisloughrey, Quay Rd., turn left at the Ashford Castle gates onto the R345 and make the next right at the signpost, tel. 094/954-6089, www.quietman-cong.com, dorms €24, private rooms €32 pp) offers small dorms with comfy beds and clean facilities. You can also camp here for €12 per person, €13 for two or three people.

In the center of town, you can expect comfortable, no-frills bedrooms at **Lydon's Lodge** (Circular Rd., tel. 094/954-6053, Mar.-Oct., €50 pp), which also arranges boat hire, and at **Ryan's Hotel** (Main St., tel. 094/954-6243, www.ryanshotelcong.ie, Feb.-Dec., €40-60 pp, s €45-65). Both hotel pubs have live trad almost nightly in the summer.

Considering the lengthy list of politicians, entertainers, and royalty who have stayed here over the years, it should come as no surprise that both grounds and hotel at the sprawling, fairy-tale **Ashford Castle** (signposted from the southern end of town, tel. 094/954-6003, www.ashford.ie, rooms €550-785), erstwhile home of the Guinness clan, are as exclusive

as exclusive gets (if you're not staying here, prepare to be shooed out of the lobby without further ado). In summer, though, you can pay €5 to walk the grounds (9am-5pm daily), and there are often special room deals available in low season. The original castle was erected in the early 13th century by the O'Connors (the last Irish kings), and successive owners added a French chateau and two Victorian wings.

Information

The very helpful **tourist office** (Abbey St., tel. 094/954-6542, 10am-6pm Apr.-May and Sept.-Nov., 9:30am-7pm July-Aug., sometimes closed 1pm-2pm for lunch in low season) is in Cong's comically tiny old courthouse.

Services

Cong doesn't have a bank, but there's an **ATM** at O'Connor's, the shop-cum-gas station on Main Street, and a bureau de change at the **post office** (Main St., tel. 094/954-6001). Cong has a pharmacy, **Mary Daly** (Abbey St., tel. 094/954-6119).

Getting There and Around

Cong is 42 kilometers north of Galway City on the N84. The **Bus Éireann** (tel. 091/562-000) route from Galway passes through Cong en route to Ballina (#420, 4/day Mon.-Sat. June-Sept., additional Galway-Cong weekday service on route #432).

Rent a bike from the local gas station, **O'Connor's** (Main St., 954-6008, daily/weekly €20/80). For a taxi, ring **Marty Holian** (tel. 094/954-6403 or 087/238-6820).

★ DOOLOUGH VALLEY

The road from Leenane in northern Connemara up to Louisburgh and Westport winds around the end of Killary Harbour (the N59 to the R335 at Aasleagh); once you've passed the waterfall, a left turn onto the R335 will take you through the splendidly remote Doolough Valley—so named for Lough Doo, on your left as you traverse the narrow road that winds through heathered peaks and the occasional swath of evergreens. These are the

Mayo and Sligo

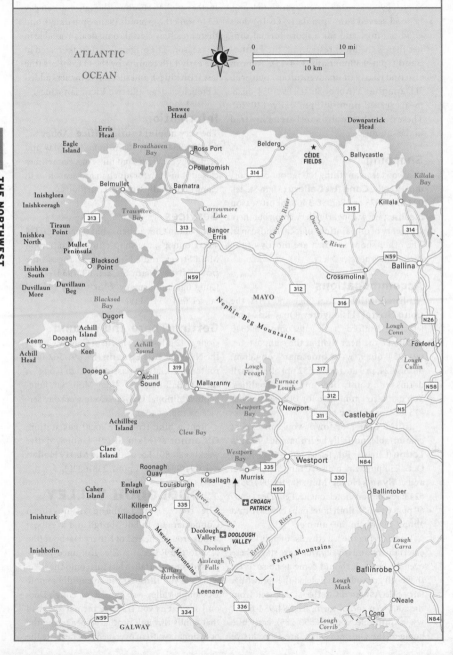

ATLANTIC

OCEAN

ATLANTIC OCEAN

Benwee
Head

Erris
Head

Eagle
Island

Downpatrick
Head

Broadhaven
Bay

Ross Port

Belderg

Ballycastle

CÉIDE
FIELDS

Pollatomish

Killala
Bay

Belmullet

Barnatra

314

315

Killala

Inishglora
Inishkeeragh

Trawmore
Bay

Carrowmore
Lake

313

314

Tiraun
Point

313

Inishkea
North

Mullet
Peninsula

Bangor
Erris

Owenduff River

Owenmore River

N59

Ballina

Blacksod
Point

N59

Crossmolina

Inishkea
South

Duvillaun
More

Duvillaun
Beg

Blacksod
Bay

312

MAYO

316

N26

Dugort

Achill
Island

Nephin Beg Mountains

Lough
Conn

Keem

Dooagh

Foxford

Achill
Head

Keel

Achill
Sound

319

Lough
Cullin

Lough
Feeagh

317

Dooega

Achill
Sound

Mallaranny

Furnace
Lough

N58

312

Achillbeg
Island

Newport
Bay

Newport

311

Castlebar

N5

Clew Bay

Clare
Island

Westport
Bay

335

Westport

N84

Roonagh
Quay

Kilsallagh

Murrisk

330

Caher
Island

Emlagh
Point

Louisburgh

N59

Ballintober

Killeen

335

CROAGH
PATRICK

River Bunowen

Inishturk

Killadoon

Mweelrea Mountains

Doolough
Valley

DOOLOUGH
VALLEY

River Erriff

Lough
Carra

Inishbofin

Doolough

Partry Mountains

Ballinrobe

Aasleagh
Falls

Killary
Harbour

Lough
Mask

Leenane

Neale

N59

334

336

Cong

Lough
Corrib

N84

GALWAY

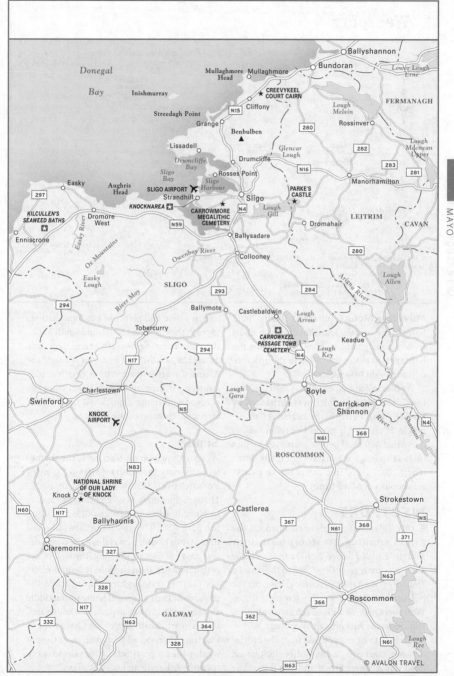

© AVALON TRAVEL

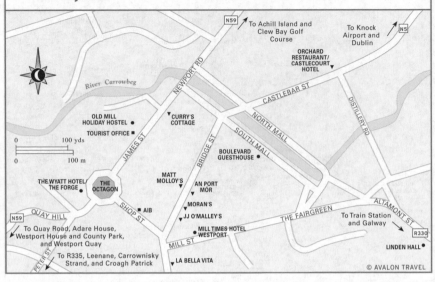

Westport

Mweelrea Mountains (Maol Réidh, "Bald King" very loosely translated); the highest (eponymously named) peak overlooking the Killary fjord is also the tallest in the province of Connaught (814 meters).

A place called Delphi, on this road just over the Galway-Mayo border, was christened by Lord Sligo after a trip to the infamous Grecian oracle. It was to his grand Georgian fishing lodge that 400 local people journeyed on foot in 1847 to beg for assistance, a futile death march that turned into one of the very darkest chapters of Mayo history.

WESTPORT

A tidy 18th-century planned town on the River Carrowbeg, **Westport** (Cathair na Mairt, "City of Cows") offers more visitor amenities than any other town in the county. Not only is it a handy (if touristy) base, but the pub scene in itself is worth a few nights' stay. Westport Quay, two kilometers west of town, features some fine upscale shopping.

It's easy to orient yourself from the central octagon, marked by a diminutive clock tower; head down James Street and you'll pass the

tourist office and plenty of accommodations to reach the tree-lined North and South Malls, the river running beneath them. Continue down the South Mall and you'll reach the Altamount Street train station after half a kilometer. Or turn onto Shop Street from the octagon and make a quick left onto Bridge Street, where most of the action is.

Sights

Westport's primary attraction is the shamelessly touristy **Westport House & Country Park** (tel. 098/25430, www.westporthouse.ie, 11:30am-5pm daily Mar.-Oct., weekends only in Nov., house and gardens €13, including fun park €21). The owners of this 18th-century manor house, who claim to be direct descendants of Grace O'Malley (the wife of the original owner, John Browne, was supposedly her great-granddaughter), have turned the grounds of their ancestral home into a kiddie amusement and caravan park. The house itself is only worthwhile if you don't have time to tour another restored Irish manor. At time of writing the property was up for sale, so check the website before making any plans.

One-hour guided historical tours by **Westport Walking Tours** (tel. 087/410-1363, www.westportwalkingtours.ie, €5) depart the octagon at 10am, noon, and 2pm daily, and admission includes a cup of tea at the end.

Activities and Recreation

There's a lovely Blue Flag beach, **Carramore,** within easy driving distance (28 km west on the R335, following the signs for Carramore from Louisburgh), though the strand at **Carrownisky** near Louisburgh is most popular with surfers. Lessons and board rental are available from **Surf Mayo** (on Carrownisky Strand, Louisburgh, tel. 087/283-4420, www.surfmayo.com).

The **Drummindoo Stud & Equitation Centre** (1.5 km east of Westport, follow signs for Knockranny village, tel. 098/25616, www.drummindoo.com, Mon.-Sat. Easter-Sept., only Sat. in low season) offers bay and backcountry rides as well as a foul-weather indoor arena. And you can't beat the vistas on the nine-hole **Clew Bay Golf Course** (Claggan, Kilmeena, signposted 6 km north of Westport on the N59 and a further 3 km west, tel. 098/41730 or 098/41739, www.clewbaygolf.com).

Electric Escapes (tel. 098/56611, www.electricescapes.ie, 9am-6pm Mon.-Fri.) offers a choice of cycling itineraries for six-hour (€95) and three-day (€250) tours. Your guide will meet you at your lodging in the morning.

The **Great Western Greenway** (www.greenway.ie) begins in Westport and runs 42 kilometers out to Achill Island on an old railway route (which closed in 1937). Check the website for the full scoop on walking or cycling this ultra-scenic track.

Food

Westport has a seemingly endless supply of cafés serving up the full fry, soups, and sandwiches, though on Sundays the town's pubs and hotels are your best bet for lunch or coffee.

Scrambled eggs meet Irish cottage kitsch at **Curry's Cottage** (Lower James St., tel. 098/25297, 10am-6pm Tues.-Sat., under

€8), where you can enjoy breakfast, a light lunch, or a frosted cupcake beside the open peat fire.

With minimalist decor and a carefully curated wine menu, **An Port Mór** (1 Brewery Place, tel. 098/26730, www.anportmor.com, 5pm-midnight Tues.-Sun., €15-28) is generally considered the finest restaurant in Westport. The modern-Irish menu has something to suit every palate—Clew Bay catch is a specialty—and the token vegetarian dish is inventive. The two-course early-bird menu (€24, 5pm-6pm daily) is the best value, and reservations are a good idea any night of the week.

If you're in the mood for Italian, try **La Bella Vita** (High St., tel. 098/29771, www.labellavitawestport.com, 5:30pm-10pm daily, €11-24), which also offers a great-value early-bird (3 courses for €19, 5:30pm-7pm daily). Another safe bet for a memorable meal is the **Orchard Restaurant** at the Castlecourt Hotel (Castlebar St., tel. 098/55088, www.castlecourthotel.ie, 6pm-9:30pm daily), with a two-course French-inspired menu available all night for €29. An Port Mór is the better option for vegans, though.

Entertainment and Events

You'll find no shortage of unselfconsciously old-school pubs in this town. A grocery in front and pub in the back, **Moran's** (15 Bridge St., tel. 098/26320) exudes a pleasantly old-fashioned atmosphere, with colorful football scarves festooned from the ceiling. Sports television aside, it's a nice spot for a quiet pint.

It may be a fire hazard by night (you can barely breathe, with all the trad lovers craning their necks for a view of the musicians), but during the afternoon there's no better spot than **Matt Molloy's** (Bridge St., tel. 098/26655, www.mattmolloy.com) for a Bailey's coffee with cream by a crackling open fire. Matt Molloy's the flutist for the celebrated trad-orchestral group The Chieftains (having previously performed with Planxty and the Bothy Band), so it's no surprise the walls are covered with framed photos of some of Ireland's most illustrious musicians.

Somewhat less crowded near-nightly trad venues include **Conway's** (Bridge St., tel. 098/26145), **J.J. O'Malley's** (Bridge St., tel. 098/27307), and **The Forge** (Wyatt Hotel, The Octagon, tel. 098/25027). Pretty much every pub in Westport has live music in the summer, though, so if all else fails just follow your ears.

If you're here around the end of September, see what's on the lineup for the **Westport Arts Festival** (1 James St., tel. 098/27375 or 087/054-8544, www.westportartsfestival. com, €5-12); generally there's a healthy dose of contemporary theater and opera, film screenings, art exhibitions, and jazz and trad sessions. Most performances take place in hotels and pubs around town. There should be a mobile box office on or around James Street (noon-2:30pm and 4:30pm-6:30pm during the festival).

And in the "touristy but fun" category, we have **Teach Ceoil** ("Music House," Mill St., tel. 087/232-7694, performances 8pm Wed., €8), a quasi-traditional ceilidh (music, song, and step dancing).

Shopping

Westport should be proud of its delightful little shops. An antiques store chock-full of deals is **The Long Acre** (in the courtyard off Bridge St. behind Gavin's Coffee Shop, tel. 087/206-6341, www.thelongacre.com). It's a true hodgepodge. Run out of leisure reading? Have a browse at **The Time Traveller's Bookshop** (James St., tel. 098/29465, www. timetraveller.ie). Though antiquarian books are the specialty, you also have your pick of quality secondhand paperbacks. **O'Reilly Turpin** (Mill St., tel. 098/28151, www.oreillyturpin.ie) is the best shop in town for upscale Irish-made jewelry, textiles, pottery, paintings, and sculpture. For cozy blankets and scarves, visit the **Foxford Woollen Mills** (Bridge St., tel. 098/27844, www.foxfordwoollenmills.com).

Accommodations

Westport accommodations can be overpriced; you have to look a bit harder to find good-value rooms.

The **Old Mill Holiday Hostel** (James St., beside the tourist office, tel. 098/27045, www. oldmillhostel.com, dorms €21-23) is the only hostel in Westport open year-round. Being along Westport's main drag, it's not quite as charming as the name suggests, though the kitchen facilities are good, the beds are comfortable, and the brisk but efficient management takes pains to prevent rowdiness.

There are several relatively modest B&Bs on Altamount Street, which leads to the train station—still only a five-minute walk from the center of town. The cream of these is **Linden Hall** (Altamount St., tel. 098/27005, www.lindenhallwestport.com, €40 pp), a beautifully maintained townhouse with exceptionally friendly and accommodating owners. You can expect the same at **Boulevard Guesthouse** (South Mall, tel. 098/25138 or 087/284-4018, www.boulevard-guesthouse.com, €40 pp, no single rooms), another immaculate townhouse (this one on the River Carrowbeg, on the quiet end of town); the breakfasts are well above average, the mattresses quality, the five rooms colorful yet tastefully decorated, and the cozy, light-filled upstairs sitting room is the perfect spot to decompress. There's even a game room (complete with snooker table) out back.

On the other end of town, the back bedrooms and dining room at **Adare House** (Quay Rd., tel. 098/26102, www.adarehouse. ie, €33-40 pp, s €50) offer splendid views of Croagh Patrick. This and other B&Bs on Quay Road are within a seven-minute walk of Westport proper and Westport Quay.

Of the hotels in town, the **Mill Times Hotel Westport** (Mill St., tel. 098/29200, www.milltimeshotel.ie, €55-65 pp) offers great value (especially on weekdays!) without sacrificing luxuries like canopy beds. Though the rooms have somewhat standard corporate furnishings, the **Wyatt Hotel** (The Octagon, tel. 098/25027, www.wyatt-hotel.com, €55-100 pp) still comes recommended—with rollickin'-good trad and folk sessions in the Forge pub and surprisingly good bar and restaurant fare, you might end up not leaving the hotel at all.

Information

If you're planning to head farther north, stop for advice before leaving town at the **tourist office** (James St., tel. 098/25711, www.irelandwest.ie, 9am-6pm Mon.-Sat. and 10am-6pm Sun. July-Aug., 9am-5:30pm Mon.-Sat. Apr.-June and Sept., 9am-12:45pm and 2pm-5pm weekdays Oct.-Mar.).

Services

You'll find ATMs and bureaux de change at the **Bank of Ireland** (North Mall, tel. 098/25522) and the **AIB** (Shop St., tel. 098/25466). The **Washeteria** (Mill St., tel. 098/25261) is self-service. One pharmacy is **O'Donnell's** (Bridge St., tel. 098/25163, tel. 098/27347 after hours).

Getting There

Westport is 270 kilometers northwest of Dublin on the N5 and 80 kilometers north of Galway on the N84 (picking up the N5 in Castlebar). A longer (108-km) but far more scenic alternative from Galway is via northern Connemara: Take the N59 west to Maam Cross, picking up the R336 there and heading north to Leenane. Get back on the N59 briefly, and once in County Mayo, turn left for the R335, the Doolough Valley route. It's well worth the extra mileage.

The **Bus Éireann** (tel. 091/562-000) stop is on the octagon. Direct routes to Westport include Galway (#52, 4/day daily), Dublin and Athlone (#21, 2/day daily at 2pm and 5pm Mon.-Sat., 8am and 8pm Sun.), and Sligo (#66, 3/day Mon.-Sat., 2/day Sun.). **Irish Rail** (Altamount St., tel. 098/25253, 3/day daily, ticket €29) can get you here from Dublin Heuston.

Getting Around

Westport is small enough that you can walk everywhere. For a taxi (or minibus), ring **McGing's** (Lower Peter St., tel. 098/25529 or 087/241-7466). Rent a bicycle from **Seán Sammon** (James St., tel. 098/25471, €12/56 per day/week).

MURRISK

A tiny hamlet in the shadow of Croagh Patrick, **Murrisk** (Muir Riasc, "Marsh by the Sea," or Muir Iasc, the name of a Celtic sea monster) is well worth an overnight stay for its utterly picturesque setting on Clew Bay, an outstanding pub-cum-restaurant, and a couple of lovely B&Bs. Have a memorable meal, get to bed early, and tackle "the reek" first thing in the morning.

There isn't much left of the Augustinian **Murrisk Abbey** (signposted on the R335 opposite the Croagh Patrick car park, always accessible, free), founded in 1457, but it's still worth the short stroll from the main road. The **National Famine Monument,** a metal sculpture of a "coffin ship" installed in 1997, is also directly across the road from the Croagh Patrick car park.

Several Murrisk B&Bs have closed in recent years; the accommodations there now are generally self-catering, which is only feasible if you're traveling in a large group (and if you are, see the community website at www.murrisk.ie for options). Otherwise, it makes the most sense to base yourself in Westport.

That said, after you climb Croagh Patrick you *must* have a celebratory meal at ★ **The Tavern** (on the R335, tel. 098/64060, www.tavernmurrisk.com, food served noon-10pm or later, €10-25) before heading back to town. Owner, chef, and bartender extraordinaire Myles O'Brien has put a lot of sweat, love, and savings into this place—and it shows. The Tavern is so popular with locals you'd be forgiven for thinking this place has been around for decades, but it only opened in 2001. Halfway decent modern Irish would have ensured the Tavern's popularity (seeing as you used to have to drive into Westport for any meal at all), so it's a delightful surprise to find it's good-value (a €48 dinner for two on Wednesday night includes a bottle of wine!), top-notch gourmet. Live trad plays on the weekends—and menus are posted inside the bathroom stalls.

Murrisk is just 10 kilometers west of Westport on the R335; drive north from Connemara through the Doolough Valley and you'll reach the village before you hit Westport. **Bus Éireann** can get you here from Westport (ring the Galway office, tel. 091/562-000, #450, 2/day Mon., Wed., and Fri., 3/day Tues. and Sat., 4/day Thurs., no Sun. service). If you need to get to Westport (or elsewhere), ring **Carrowkeel Cabs** (tel. 087/988-2267).

★ CROAGH PATRICK

A starkly beautiful mountain rising over Clew Bay, **Croagh Patrick** ("Patrick's Hill," 762 meters) was aptly described by H. V. Morton as "Ireland's Sinai." It's said that St. Patrick rang a bell on the summit, at which point all the snakes in Ireland threw themselves into the Atlantic—and the mountain, also referred to as "the reek," has been the ultimate pilgrimage destination ever since. As many as 40,000 people have climbed it in a single day, and the most devout of all do it sans shoes (when you climb it yourself in a pair of sturdy boots, you'll see why this act in itself merits beatification). Even the most bitter of lapsed Catholics should consider a climb, though,

as the views from every point on the way up are utterly incomparable on a clear day. In an admirable display of religious devotion, local men schlepped eight-pound bags of cement mix up the mountain to build a chapel at the summit in 1905; this edifice is typically hideous and creepy in the tradition of provincial Irish Catholic churches.

The climb is a challenging one, and the precarious scree-strewn path just below the peak will make you glad you brought a walking stick (you can borrow one from the owner of your B&B or purchase one at the visitors center). Even with frequent pauses for breath-catching and picture-taking, it should take you no more than two hours to reach the summit, and the descent takes a little less than an hour and a half. As always, bring raingear and a big water bottle, and wear at least a good set of running shoes.

There is a **visitors center** (signposted on the R335, tel. 098/64114, www.croagh-patrick.com, 10am-6pm daily Apr.-May, 10am-7pm daily June-Aug., 11am-5pm daily Sept.-Oct., irregular winter hours) at the foot of the mountain with the usual facilities—an information desk that organizes guided tours of the mountain, gift shop, and a tearoom that also sells packed lunches. Lockers and shower

It may be a popular pilgrimage, but climbing Croagh Patrick isn't for the faint-hearted.

facilities cost a couple of euros. The visitors center is just 10 kilometers west of Westport on the R335, in Murrisk; drive north from Connemara through the Doolough Valley and you'll reach Murrisk before you hit Westport. **Bus Éireann** can get you here from Westport (ring the Galway office, tel. 091/562-000, #450, 2/day Mon., Wed., and Fri., 3/day Tues. and Sat., 4/day Thurs., no Sun. service).

CLARE ISLAND

At only 16 kilometers square, **Clare Island** (Oileán Chliara) is still the largest of the 365 islands in Clew Bay. Most foreigners never make it out here—there aren't many "sights" as such, and it's more of a local getaway—but Clare is the perfect place to kick back and take it easy, going for long walks across Mayo's "green pearl" with a pair of binoculars strung around your neck (**birdlife** abounds—gannets, red-beaked choughs, and the like). There are three routes to the isle's highest point, **Knockmore** (461 meters), on the western side, between 90 minutes and four hours in length. (Your ferry passage includes a map of the island's walking trails.)

The locals place an emphasis on environmental responsibility (organic farming, solar energy, and New Agey pursuits like yoga and reiki are popular) and are very proud of their Blue Flag beaches.

History buffs will note that the pirate queen Grace O'Malley is buried in the churchyard of the 13th-century, Cistercian **Clare Island Abbey** (3 km down the south road from the pier, always accessible), and her eponymous **castle** still guards the harbor.

Frequent ferry service makes Clare an easy day trip from Westport, but there are a few accommodations on the island. Backpackers should book a bed at **Go Explore Hostel** (about 600 m north of the pier on the main road, tel. 098/26307, www.goexplorehostel. ie, dorms €20-24), which also has a pub and restaurant (it used to be the Bay View Hotel). The rate includes a light breakfast. Otherwise, **O'Grady's** (tel. 098/22991, www.ogradys-guesthouse.com, €40-45 pp, s €60, 2-night minimum stay) and **Granuaile House** (tel. 098/26250, granuailehouse.wordpress.com, €40-45 pp) are two friendly, comfortable B&Bs very close to the pier, both open May to September. Granuaile's has been a guesthouse under one name or other for well over a hundred years.

Or, if your eyes light up at the mention of the words "organic vegetarian" and you never turn on the television in your room, contact Ciara and Christophe at **Macalla Farm** (on the lighthouse road, 2.5 km from the pier, tel. 087/250-4845, www.macallafarm.ie). They no longer do B&B, but check out the website for a year-round schedule of yoga and meditation retreats. You can volunteer here, too.

The island's more-or-less official website (www.clareisland.ie) is another fine resource when planning your trip.

From Roonagh Quay, 28 kilometers west of Westport (take the R335 to Louisburgh and turn off onto the local road, pier signposted), you can board the **Clare Island Ferry** (tel. 098/28288, 098/26307, or 087/241-4653, www. clareislandferry.com, 4/day May, June, and Sept., 8/day July and Aug., return ticket €15). The passage takes about 15 minutes (the island's only 5.5 km from the mainland); once on the island, you can rent a bicycle from the ferry operator. Unfortunately, there is no public transport to Roonagh Quay. You can purchase tickets at the quay or at the **Westport tourist office** (James St., tel. 098/25711).

INISHTURK

Home to not even a hundred souls, **Inishturk** (Inis Toirc, "Wild Boar Island") is a delightfully unspoiled island on Clew Bay between Clare Island and Inishbofin off the coast of Galway. At only five kilometers long, the island is short on "sights" but rich in opportunities for bird-watching and long rambling walks in the hills or on two lovely sheltered strands (**Tranaun** and **Curraun,** both on the eastern coast). Inishturk is an even better opportunity for "getting away from it all."

The three B&Bs on the island all serve evening meals featuring locally caught seafood

Walking Routes in County Mayo

Mayo walking routes are more frequently traveled by local hill-walking groups than international walkers, which can be a great way to meet a few like-minded natives. The newest trail is the 42-kilometer **Great Western Greenway** (www.greenway.ie), along the old railway route between Westport and Achill Island.

The 48-kilometer **Bangor Trail** begins in Newport, stretching north to Bangor Erris through the extremely remote and boggy Nephin Beg mountain range. While the trail can be done in two days, there aren't any accommodations available at the midway point, so bring your camping gear and grub. In Newport, alas, the old An Óige hostel catering to walkers has closed its doors, but there are other accommodations. In Bangor Erris, **Hillcrest House** (Main St., tel. 097/83494, www.hillcresthousemayo.com, €30-35 pp, s €40) is a friendly B&B where an evening meal can be arranged. As with all walking routes, pick up the applicable Ordnance Survey Discovery Series maps—in this case, you'll need more than one (#23 and #31, available at tourist offices and bookstores).

A longer walking route that spans Mayo as well as Connemara is the 193-kilometer **Western Way,** which begins in Oughterard on the southern shore of Lough Corrib, heading through the Maamturk Mountains in northern Connemara and passing through Westport and Newport en route to Killala and Ballycastle on Mayo's north coast, near the Céide Fields site, and terminating at the Sligo border near Ballina. The Galway section of this route is 84 kilometers long and is often called the "Connemara Way," though it's more accurately known as "the Connemara section of the Western Way." Most folks walk only a portion of this route (which would take 10-12 days total), though the diversity of the landscape is remarkable—from lush forests to desolate boglands, the rocky southern flank of Croagh Patrick to the heathery hills near Downpatrick Head, and vistas studded with lakes of all sizes, their surfaces black and shimmering when the sun shines.

In addition to the OS Discovery Series maps, other materials for both walking routes are available from the tourist offices in Galway, Oughterard, and Westport.

and organic produce: **Ocean View House** (half a km north of the harbor, tel. 098/45520, oceanviewhouse.inishturk@gmail.com), **Teach Abhainn** ("River House," 1.5 km west of the harbor, tel. 098/45110, teachabhainn@hotmail.com), and the **Tranaun House** ("Beach House," on the harbor, tel. 087/761-6582 or 098/45641, tranaunhouse@gmail.com). B&B will run you €33-38 per person (s €40), with dinner an additional €15-25.

Inishturk is 14.5 kilometers off the coast of south Mayo. The island's sole ferry service is **O'Malley Ferries** (tel. 098/25045, www.omalleyferries.com, return fare €20), which operates from Roonagh Quay (2 departures per day Wed. and Fri.-Mon. May-Sept., once daily all year). There's no tourist office on the island (though there is a helpful website, www.inishturkisland.com). Otherwise, stop by the tourist office in Westport before you go.

NEWPORT

The starting point for the 48-kilometer **Bangor Trail,** Newport (Baile Uí Fhiacháin) is popular with anglers for its proximity to Clew Bay, Loughs Furnace, Beltra, and Feeagh, as well as the River Newport bisecting the town. You'll pass through on your way to Achill Island. The place itself has a slightly run-down feel, and as such is only worth a pause for the truly magnificent Clarke window inside the neo-Romanesque **St. Patrick's Church** (signposted from Main St., a two-minute walk uphill), erected in 1918. These three windows over the high altar feature an almost excruciatingly vivid Last Judgment scene, complete with damned grotesques lurking at the bottom of the right panel. It was Harry Clarke's last work—and could very well be his greatest.

Two sites west of Newport, en route to Achill Island, are worth a brief detour: the

Harry Clarke's Last Judgment window at St. Patrick's Church in Newport

produce, and all the commodious rooms are filled with gorgeous antiques.

For a lunch break, try **Kelly's Kitchen** (Main St., tel. 098/41647, 11am-9:30pm Mon.-Sat., 12:30pm-9:30pm Sun., €8-12), which does hearty, no-frills meat and pasta dishes in a cheerful spot that's humming with locals. The owners claim it's the oldest building in Newport.

Newport is 13 kilometers north of Westport on the N59. From Galway and Westport, take **Bus Éireann** (tel. 091/562-000) route #441 (or #440 from Westport only), which passes through town en route to Achill Island (2/day Mon.-Sat., 1/day Sun.).

MULRANNY

Nestled in the shadow of Claggan Mountain on an isthmus connecting the mainland with the Corraun peninsula, the tiny hamlet of Mulranny overlooks glittering Bellacragher Bay. From here you can hop on the 42-kilometer **Great Western Greenway** (www.greenway.ie), which runs from Westport to Achill Island on an old railway route (shut down in 1937). Even if you don't have time for the whole route, just a 20-minute stroll will afford you lovely views of forest, sea, and mountains—and then you've walked up an appetite for lunch at the **Mulranny Park Hotel** (on the N59, tel. 098/36000, www.mulrannyparkhotel.ie, B&B €120-220 pp, food served 1pm-9pm daily, bar €10-14, restaurant €28-30). The restaurant desserts may be pricey at €10, but they are worth every cent and then some. The Greenway is accessible via the car park of the apartment complex behind the hotel.

A delightful antiques shop, the **Old Thatch** (on the N59 east of the hotel, tel. 098/27823, www.vanessaparkerrarebooks.com, 2:30pm-6pm Sun.), is in an early 19th-century thatched cottage with a cozy sitting area heated by a real turf fire. The owner will offer you a cup of tea or coffee even if you're only casually browsing. Since regular opening hours are extremely limited, you might want to ring ahead.

scant remains of the 15th-century Dominican **Burrishoole Abbey** (signposted 2.5 km north of town on the N59, and another 1 km down a local road, always accessible, free), with a tranquil riverside setting; and a simple 16th-century tower-house set on a Clew Bay inlet, **Rockfleet Castle** (signposted from the N59, 5 km west of Newport). This tower house was the primary residence of the pirate queen Grace O'Malley after the death of her second husband in 1583. (Back then it was called Carraig an Chabhlaigh, or Carrigahowley, meaning "rockfleet" in Irish.) The sign on the castle door states the key is available from the neighboring garage, but seeing as there *is* no neighboring garage you'll just have to survey the castle on the outside.

Newport also has a genteel, ivy-clad Georgian hotel, **Newport House** (Main St., tel. 098/41222, www.newporthouse.ie, Mar.-Sept., €95-140 pp, s €120-165), popular with golfers and anglers. The renowned hotel restaurant emphasizes local seafood and

ACHILL ISLAND

At 147 kilometers square, **Achill Island** (Oileán Acla) is the largest island off the Irish coast, joined to the mainland by a 200-meter swing bridge named after 19th-century patriot and Land League founder Michael Davitt. Artists have found plenty of inspiration in this bleak and boggy landscape (87 percent of the island is blanketed in peat bog), among them the painter Paul Henry and the Nobel laureate Heinrich Böll, whose Achill Island passages are among the most poignant in his travelogue, *Irish Diary* ("Everything not made of stone eaten away by wind, sun, rain, and time, neatly laid out along the somber slope as if for an anatomy lesson, the skeleton of a village").

Roughly 24 kilometers long by 17 kilometers wide, the island looks like an inverted boot, with the R319 connecting its main villages—Dooagh and Keel on the western end and Achill Sound on the east, just beyond the mainland bridge (with Cashel in between, though there's nothing to note here besides the gas station and tourist office).

Frankly, you do not want to visit Achill in the fall or winter; grim landscape and weather aside (and it's pretty grim), there's next to nothing open.

Sights

Achill doesn't have any tourist attractions, per se. There's the **Slievemore Deserted Village,** in the shadow of the island's highest mountain—just the mortarless remains of a group of cottages carpeted in sheep pellets, a sad and lonely reminder of the famine. It's an appropriate spot for some quiet reflection. To get here from Keel, take Slievemore Road (the turnoff is beside the Achill Cliff House Hotel). The deserted village, beside a modern graveyard, is just over two kilometers down that road.

On the island's eastern coast, follow the local coast road 6.5 kilometers south of the village of Achill Sound to **Kildavnet Castle,** a tower house probably built by the O'Malley clan in the 15th century; in any case, it was frequented by the infamous Grace, the pirate queen.

Activities and Recreation

With a coastline of 127 kilometers, Achill has plenty of beaches, quiet and pristine. All are Blue Flag: **Trawmore Strand** at Keel; **Keem Bay,** at the western terminus of the R319; **Dooega** on the southern side; and two strands at **Dugort,** on the island's northeastern edge. Divers should contact

curious locals on Achill Island

Achill Island

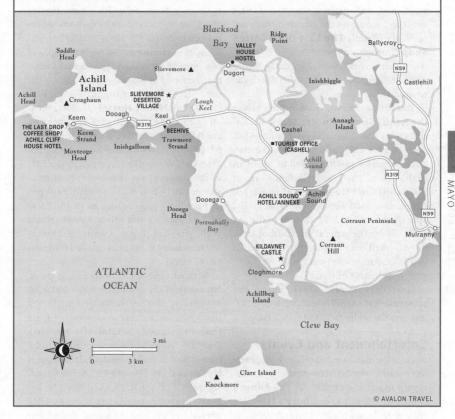

Achill Dive Centre (Purteen Harbour, just south of Keel village, tel. 087/234-9884, www.achilldivecentre.com), which can accommodate all experience levels. The **Achill Outdoor Educational Centre** (Keel, tel. 098/47253 or 098/47304, www.achilloutdoor.com) offers courses in windsurfing and mountaineering.

Achill's tallest peak, **Slievemore** (671 meters), makes for a very strenuous all-day hike (figure on 12 hours round-trip); the trail begins at the deserted village. A shorter option (about 6 hours round-trip) is second-tallest **Croaghaun** (668 meters) on the island's western edge; its northeast face is a nearly perpendicular sea cliff (600 meters), and

along its slopes there are five corrie lakes (i.e., small glacier-carved dips in the mountainside). Begin the Croaghaun hike at the Keem Bay car park. An OS map (pick up Discovery Series #30 at any Mayo tourist office) and all the usual gear (rainwear, boots, compass, etc.) are essential for both hikes.

Achill Seaweed Baths (Mulhollow B&B, Keel, tel. 087/717-1713, www.achillseaweed-baths.com) is the perfect way to relax after an outdoorsy day.

Food

Follow the old adage of the pessimist when it comes to dining on Achill: Don't expect much, and you won't be disappointed. The

Beehive (Keel, on the R319, tel. 098/43134, 10:30am-6pm daily Easter-Oct., under €12), a café and craft gallery, does the tastiest cakes and scones on the island; if that's not open, try friendly **The Last Drop Coffee Shop** (Dooagh, on the R319, tel. 098/43119, www.gieltys.com, 10am-7pm daily, under €8), adjoining Gielty's pub, which does basic soup and sandwiches.

You'll find decent, good-value grub at the **Achill Sound Hotel** (Achill Sound, tel. 098/45245, food served noon-8pm daily, under €12), and the **Annexe** pub does burgers-and-chips kind of meals in high season. The relatively fancy fare at the **Achill Cliff House Hotel** (Keel, tel. 098/43400, food served 7pm-9pm daily, 1pm-3pm Sun., €12-22, 3-course dinner €25) follows the general standard of Irish hotels—mediocre and overpriced—but if you're here in low season it's pretty much your only dinner option.

Hostellers should stock up at the **supermarket** (Achill Sound, tel. 098/45243) just over the bridge from the mainland.

Entertainment and Events

Many of the island's pubs host live trad, generally only on Saturday in low season and near-nightly in July and August. Try **The Annexe** (Keel, tel. 098/43268) or **Gielty's** (Dooagh, tel. 098/43119, www.gieltys.com), both along the R319. The best time to be in Achill is in late July or early August, when the annual weeklong summer school for language and music, **Scoil Acla** (tel. 098/43414, www.scoilacla.com), gets the island hopping with traditional sounds. Aspiring fiddlers and pipers flock here from all over the world to join in on the pub sessions.

Shopping

Achill is home to several potteries, one of which is the simply named **Achill Pottery** (Keel, tel. 098/43145, daily May-Sept., ring for appointment in low season). The **Beehive** (Keel, tel. 098/43134, daily Easter-Oct.) stocks a wide range of locally made crafts.

Accommodations

The island offers several good hostels. Stay at the cozy, clean, 16-bed **Rich View Hostel** (Keel, tel. 098/43462, richviewhostel@hotmail.com, dorms €16-18) is the ideal owner: friendly, ultra-informative, eager to help, and of a musical persuasion (he's in a trad band that performs in the pubs). Rich View is the only place open year-round. The family-run **Valley House Hostel** (Dugort, turn-off signposted at the village of Bunacurry on the R319, and a further 4 km to the hostel, tel. 098/47204, www.valley-house.com, mid-Mar.-Oct., dorms €16-22, private rooms €22-25 pp, camping €5 pp) has comfy beds, good showers, and—best of all—a pub with an open turf fire that's popular with locals and backpackers alike. It's also within a stone's throw of the strand at Dugort. Continental breakfast is included in the price of a bed (campers pay €5 extra).

Granted, nearly all B&Bs are family homes, but many of those on Achill can feel a bit *too* homey; in other words, you might feel like you're just staying in somebody's spare room (which, come to think of it, you are!). One to recommend for its sea views, helpful owner, and adorable resident dalmatian is **Hy Breasal** (St. Fionan's Rd., Achill Sound, signposted off the R319, tel. 098/45114, hybreasalmayo@hotmail.com, €35 pp). ("Hy Breasal," by the way, is a legend about a lost island and a preternatural stallion that comes galloping out of the sea.)

One of the most established B&Bs on the island is **Joyce's Marian Villa** (Keel, on the R319, tel. 098/43134, www.joycesachill.com, €45-60 pp), a spacious, immaculately kept place with a helpful proprietor, hearty breakfasts with homemade jam and other trimmings, and beach and cliff views (though rooms with sea views cost more than those without). Another option in Keel is **Mulhollow** (River, Keel, tel. 098/43324, www.mulhollow.com, €37.50 pp), which also offers seaweed baths.

Achill's hotels are all of the slightly stodgy, small-town variety. You'll receive a warmer reception at the **Ostan Ghob A'Choire,** a.k.a. the **Achill Sound Hotel** (Achill Sound, on the R319, tel. 098/45245, www.achill-soundhotel.com, €45-50 pp, s €55), which also rents bikes, but the 10-room, three-star **Achill Cliff House Hotel** (Keel, on the R319, tel. 098/43400, www.achillcliff.com, €45-70 pp) is a bit more posh, with bathtubs in all rooms (though there's an extra fee for use of the sauna).

Information and Services

The community-run **tourist office** (Cashel, tel. 098/47353, www.achilltourism.com, 9am-6pm weekdays July-Aug., 9am-5pm weekdays Sept.-June) is in a trailer beside the Esso station.

In addition to two "mobile banks" that pass through Keel, Achill Sound, and all points in between, there is an **ATM** and bureau de change at **Sweeney's Spar and Craft Shop** (Achill Sound, tel. 098/45243).

Getting There

Achill Island is midway along Mayo's west coast, south of the Mullet Peninsula and Blacksod Bay, and north of Murrisk and Clew Bay. The gateway village, Achill Sound, is 43 kilometers northwest of Westport, and the primary villages of Dooagh and Keel are 18.5 kilometers and 14.5 kilometers west of Achill Sound along the R319. From Westport, you can take **Bus Éireann** (tel. 096/78100) to Achill (#440 or #441, 2/day Mon.-Sat., 1/day Sun., departure times vary daily); the bus stops in each village along the main road.

Getting Around

For a taxi on Achill, ring **Michael Scanlon** (tel. 087/366-1422). Rent some wheels from **Achill Bikes** (Keel, tel. 087/245-7686, www. achillbikes.com).

NORTH MAYO

You want off the tourist merry-go-round—far, far off? You got it.

Driving north toward the Mullet Peninsula, where heaping piles of turf are drying on the side of the road, is a strange experience in itself. The bog-and-moorgrass landscape has a placid, color-bleached, on-and-on bleakness that—were it not for the smudgy hills of the Nephin Beg mountain range—would nearly remind one of Wyoming. The haze lingering on the horizon gives you a queer sensation, like a portal has opened to that fairy world of Irish folklore.

There's another reason for that ominous feeling. This region (particularly the villages of Rossport and Ballinaboy along the Broadhaven Bay inlet) has attracted attention in recent years for its battle against Shell, the oil conglomerate, which is preparing to open a gas pipeline on land owned by local farmers (five of whom have gone to prison for their protests): a classic David-and-Goliath tale with profound environmental consequences. For more information on the community's ongoing campaign, visit **Shell to Sea** online (www.shelltosea.com).

If traveling the R314, which follows Mayo's north coast, you may notice signposts for **Tír Sáile,** the **North Mayo Sculpture Trail** (tel. 098/45107 for more information). A group of native artists, along with several from the U.K., the U.S., Japan, and Denmark, installed 14 sculptures in 1993 that were intended to celebrate "the integral vitality of the landscape"—and as a consequence you might hardly notice some of them without the brown signpost pointing them out!

Public transport is scarce. If you don't have a car, you're better off sticking to Westport; while the renowned archaeological site at Céide Fields is worth a visit, most people wouldn't consider it a must-see. ATMs are still something of a rarity in these parts (though there are a couple of banks in Belmullet), so be sure to get to the bank before leaving Westport.

Bangor Erris

The barely-there hamlet of **Bangor Erris** (Beannchar Iorrais or Beann Géar, "Sharp Peak")—Bangor for short—warrants a mention because it's the start- or end-point of the

48-kilometer **Bangor Trail,** which ends (or begins) in Newport.

Not that you've much choice, but the most popular accommodation—whether you're finishing the trail, going fishing, or just passing through—is **Hillcrest House** (Main St., tel. 097/83494, www.hillcresthousemayo.com, €30-35 pp, s €40). Mrs. Cosgrove will bring you a proper tea tray in her comfortable sitting room, and she also serves evening meals in high season. Anglers are well cared for, with fishing permits, equipment, boat hire, and packed lunches all taken care of. Another option for B&B is **Ennisdrum** (signposted off the R313 just west of the village, tel. 097/83039, ennisdrum@gmail.com, €30-35pp), another modern bungalow with a friendly reception.

There are no respectable dining options in Bangor, just fast food. If you aren't planning on an evening meal at your B&B, drive 20 kilometers north to the Talbot or Broadhaven Bay Hotels in Belmullet. There's a Spar supermarket on Main Street with an **ATM.**

Bangor Erris is 62 kilometers north of Westport on the N59 and 49 kilometers north of Newport. In July and August only, **Bus Éireann** (#446, 1/day Sun.-Thurs., 2/day Fri.-Sat.) offers a service between Ballina and Blacksod Point on the Belmullet Peninsula, stopping in Bangor along the way.

The Mullet Peninsula

This Gaeltacht region, roughly 30 kilometers long, is possibly the least traveled of any place on the Auld Sod. The town of **Belmullet** (Béal an Mhuirthead, "Mouth of the Isthmus") is more substantial than you'd expect, but there's little to interest the visitor. The town's principal streets shoot out from the central Carter Square, where at the **Bank of Ireland** (tel. 097/81311) you can pad your wallet at the ATM. Then stop by the seasonal **tourist office** (Barrack St., tel. 097/81500, 9:30am-4:30pm weekdays Easter-Sept.) for help in getting your bearings in the area.

Continue on the R313 south another 20 kilometers to **Blacksod Point,** which affords a starkly beautiful view over the eponymous bay to Slievemore and Croaghaun, Achill Island's highest peaks. There are two splendid, oft-deserted strands along the peninsula's eastern edge, **Elly Bay** and **Mullaghroe Beach** a bit farther south.

Belmullet's hotels serve decent pub food; seafood predominates, naturally, though the menu at **The Talbot Hotel** (Barrack St., tel. 097/81007, www.thetalbothotel.ie, B&B €65-100, 12:30pm-7:50pm Mon.-Thurs., 12:30pm-9:30pm Fri.-Sat., 12:30pm-7:30pm Sun., €10-24) offers a few chicken and meat dishes as well. The other option is the surprisingly swanky restaurant at the **Broadhaven Bay Hotel** (on the R313, tel. 097/20600, www. broadhavenbay.com, B&B €40-50 pp, s €65, food served 12:30pm-8:30pm daily, €10-18), an inoffensively modern establishment with panoramic sea views from the platform seating area. The spacious, candlelit ambience, friendly barstaff, generous portions, and reasonable prices all make for a delightful evening.

Belmullet is 20 kilometers northwest of Bangor Erris on the R313. In July and August, **Bus Éireann** (tel. 096/71800) offers a service between Ballina and Blacksod Point via Belmullet (#446, 1/day Sun.-Thurs., 2/day Fri.-Sat.).

Pollatomish

A scattered and delightfully remote village on Broadhaven Bay, **Pollatomish** (Poll an tSómais, "Hollow of Comfort") is completely untouched by the Celtic Tiger: There are no restaurants, gift shops, nightclubs, or housing estates to be found. You can go for a long walk along the water to Benwee Head without meeting a soul for miles. In other words, it's heaven on earth for outdoorsy travelers looking to get well off the beaten track.

The area's sole lodging is the IHH ★ **Kilcommon Lodge** (signposted off the R314, Pollatomish, tel. 097/84621, www. kilcommonlodge.ie, dorms €16, private rooms €20 pp, laundry service €4), easily the best hostel in County Mayo. This clean, cozy,

25-bed hostel has been around for nearly 30 years; four out of five guests are repeat visitors, and aging backpackers often return with their own children. The kind and helpful owners, Betty and Fritz Schult, cook breakfast (€5-6.50), lunch (€8), and four-course dinner (€15) by prior arrangement. They can also make a reservation for you on one of the ferries to the **Inishkea Islands,** which you can spot from the large windows in the common room with its open peat fire and multitude of books and classic board games. If it's a private room you're after, ask for room 8—it's the coziest. And be sure to ask for a free copy of *A Guide to Walking in the Barony of Erris,* which details two dozen walking routes in the area.

There are two pubs in Pollatomish, **McGrath's** (by the pier) and **McGuire's** (signposted off the local Pollatomish road), which is the more popular, especially with the younger crowd. Neither pub serves food, but McGuire's does offer the occasional trad session. The village's lone grocery is sparsely stocked and rather pricey, so you're better off stocking up before leaving Belmullet, Ballina, or even Bangor.

Pollatomish is 16 kilometers east of Belmullet, signposted off the R314 and 6 kilometers farther down a local road. From that turnoff, it's 21 kilometers east to Céide Fields and 29 kilometers to Ballycastle. There is no public transportation.

Céide Fields

You may have heard that **Céide Fields** ("KAY-juh," on the R314 8 km west of Ballycastle, tel. 096/43325, ceidefields@opw. ie, 10am-5pm daily mid-Feb.-mid-Oct., €4) is one of Ireland's most important Stone Age sites, but don't expect anything dramatic and you won't be disappointed. Most of the evidence of an early Neolithic farming community remains beneath the bog, and only small white posts indicate the presence of ancient stone walls deep under the moor-grass. The interpretive center (a sleek but acutely out of place glass-and-steel pyramidal structure

poking up out of the hill) is certainly worth a visit—so long as you're in the mood for an archaeology lesson.

Admission to this Dúchas site includes a 20-minute audiovisual (very informative, but with some weirdly ominous background music) and a guided tour of the site. The center is dominated by a pillar-like pine tree trunk, thousands of years old, that was fished out of a nearby bog.

Céide Fields is eight kilometers west of Ballycastle on the R314, and there is no public transport.

Ballycastle

A one-street village along the R314, **Ballycastle** (Baile an Chaisil, "Townland of the Ring Fort") is a common stopover for visitors heading to or from Céide Fields, and the dramatic Downpatrick Head is only six kilometers away. Ballycastle's sole eatery is **Mary's Cottage Kitchen** (Main St., tel. 096/43361, 10am-4pm Mon.-Fri., 11am-3pm Sat., until 6pm Mon.-Sat. Apr.-Oct., €5-8), a lovely old-fashioned café with a cheerful fire and seating in the open loft beneath a pitched wood roof. You can also take your tea and tasty rhubarb pie in the garden out back when the weather's fine.

If you're spending the night in Ballycastle, either have an early meal at Mary's or eat in at Keadyville House. Sadly, there really aren't any other options besides the overpriced hotel fare at the Stella Maris, which is three kilometers outside town on the Belmullet road.

The rooms at the delightfully homey **Keadyville House** (Carrowcubbic, the first right outside the village off the Killala road, tel. 096/43288, www.keadyvillehouse.com, €35 pp, s €40), a working farm, feature window seats with views of Downpatrick Head and comfy beds with real quilts and electric heating pads. Continue to admire the sea view with an excellent, carefully prepared breakfast in the conservatory. Barbara Kelly, the nicest proprietor you'll find anywhere, also serves evening meals in high season.

Ballycastle is 53 kilometers northeast of

Bangor Erris via the N59 (picking up the R315 in Crossmolina). **Bus Éireann** operates a local Ballina-Killala-Ballycastle service on weekdays only (#445, 2/day Mon.-Thurs., 3/day Fri.); to get to Ballina, take route #52 from Galway and Westport (5/day daily) or #22 from Dublin (6/day daily).

Downpatrick Head

Don't pass through Ballycastle without making a detour for Downpatrick Head. The first sight you'll come to is the **Poll na Seantoine,** an eerie cavity beneath the cliff that's claimed dozens of lives over the centuries. No wonder there's a high fence around the circumference now. Beyond the blowhole is a statue of St. Patrick erected in 1993, and an ugly cement lookout station dates from World War II. Finally you come to the edge and a rock stack known as **Dun Briste** ("Broken Fort"). Even if you aren't a geology buff, you'll appreciate the 350 million years' worth of rock formations in this birds' haven separated from the mainland in the shifting of the continents. On the northwestern horizon you can see the Inishkea Islands.

Someday far in the future, the earth above the blowhole will collapse into the sea—and so will Dun Briste. The view seems even more dramatic when you consider this.

To get here, take the coast road turnoff opposite MacNamee's grocery on the Killala end of Ballycastle and proceed for about six kilometers. This quiet winding road makes for a pleasant walk or cycle, especially since the road after the final turnoff for Downpatrick is hideously potholed. If you're driving, you might want to park before the gravel gives way to trenches and walk the rest of the way.

If you turn left at the final Downpatrick turnoff instead of back toward Ballycastle, you'll eventually reach **Lacken Strand,** a golden, gorgeously expansive and sheltered beach.

Ballina

Mayo's biggest town, **Ballina** (Béal an Átha, "bah-lih-NAH," 56 km northeast of Westport

and 60 km southwest of Sligo) offers little to interest the visitor.

To get to those remote places in northwestern Mayo via Bus Éireann, you'll first have to switch buses in Ballina. Direct services to Ballina include Galway and Westport (#52, 5/day daily) or Dublin (#22, 6/day daily).

KNOCK

As many as 1.5 million people per year visit the little town of **Knock** (Cnoc Mhuire, "Hill of Mary") to pray at the **National Shrine of Our Lady of Knock** (tel. 094/938-8100, www. knockshrine.ie). One night in August 1879, 15 people claimed to have seen a trio of apparitions—the Virgin Mary, St. Joseph, and St. John the Evangelist—in the south gable of the parish church.

Today you'll find a sprawling religious complex on the site of the apparition, replete with larger-than-life statues, "confessions, this way" signs, and some of the most unsightly ecclesiastical architecture on God's green earth. Knock, its churches, and the **folk museum** (tel. 094/938-8100, 10am-6pm daily, €4) will appeal only to devout Catholics.

Food and Accommodations

On the shrine grounds, the three-star **Knock House Hotel** (Ballyhaunis Rd., tel. 094/938-8088, www.knockhousehotel.ie, May-Dec., restaurant 7:30am-10pm daily, hotel rates €70-95 pp) has 68 standard business-class rooms. A more economical B&B option just up the road from the hotel is **Drum Haven** (Ballyhaunis Rd., tel. 094/938-8046, www.drumhavenknock.com, €35-45 pp). The town doesn't have much in the way of proper dining options, so the Four Seasons restaurant at the Knock House Hotel is your best bet.

Getting There

Knock is signposted off the N17, 72 kilometers north of Galway and 71 kilometers southwest of Sligo, and 225 kilometers northwest of Dublin off the N5. **Bus Éireann** (tel. 096/71800) provides direct service from

Dublin and Athlone (#21, at least 2/day daily), Galway (#52 or #64, at least 4/day daily), Westport (#21, 3/day Mon.-Sat., 1/day Sun.), and Sligo and Derry (#64, at least 2/day daily). The **Irish Rail** station at Claremorris (tel. 094/71011, 3/day Sat.-Thurs. from Dublin Heuston, 4/day Fri.) is 9.5 kilometers southwest of Knock, and you can ring **Brendan's** (tel. 087/294-1227) for a taxi.

Locals regard **Knock Airport** (tel. 094/936-7222, www.knockairport.com) as their *other* miracle. From here you can fly to Dublin (Aer Arann, www.aerarann.ie, 1/day daily), London Stansted (Ryanair, www.ryanair.com, 1/day daily), London Luton (Ryanair, 1/day daily), and London Gatwick (Ryanair and easyJet, www.easyjet.com, 2/day

daily), and there's at least one flight a day to/from Manchester, Birmingham, and Durham Tees Valley (all on BMI Regional, www.bmiregional.com). Seeing as Knock and Shannon are nearly equidistant from Galway, you might consider leaving from here if you're heading for England. It's a tiny airport, though, so expect bare-bones amenities along with a €10 "development fee."

Knock Airport is 13 kilometers north of Knock and 89 kilometers north of Galway off the N17, and 63 kilometers east of Westport on the N5. There is only local bus service to the airport (not from the town of Knock, though, inexplicably), so if you don't have a rental car to return, it is much easier to catch a flight from Shannon or Dublin.

Sligo

Bordered by Mayo to the west, Roscommon to the south, Leitrim to the east, and the Atlantic to the north, County Sligo has the richest trove of prehistoric sites on the island. Sligo is popular with local golfers, and surfers will find some of Europe's best waves at Enniscrone and Easky along the county's western coast. The northern landscape is dominated by a limestone "table mountain" called **Benbulben** (530 meters), which appears in several Irish legends, including those of Fionn mac Cumhaill (who discovers his long-lost son wandering along the mountain's lonely plateau) and Diarmuid and Gráinne (though these star-crossed lovers have supposedly jumped off every cliff in the country).

But more than anything else, Sligo is synonymous with the nation's most beloved poet, William Butler Yeats. Though Yeats didn't actually spend much time here (he was born in Dublin, educated in London, bought a tower house in Galway, and spent his last years in France), his mother's home was obviously dear to his heart: He asked to be reburied 7.5 kilometers north of town in the Drumcliffe

churchyard, where his great-grandfather once served as rector.

SLIGO TOWN

Developers are still hoping **Sligo** (Sligeach), a bit gritty round the edges and delightfully workaday despite all the Yeats-centric tourism, is destined to be the "new Galway." Though that hasn't quite happened yet, it's certainly true that Sligo's nightlife and arts scene is on the upswing. Put it this way: If you want an (albeit small) taste of urban bohemia without all those fanny-packed, ballcap-wearing tourists gorging Galway's Shop Street, then Sligo's the spot for you.

The town straddles the River Garavogue, with an L-shaped bend at Rockwood Parade; the main drag, O'Connell Street, is one block west. Head south on O'Connell and you'll hit one of those streets that keeps changing names, this one from John to Grattan to Castle to Abbey Street (from west to east), and there are plenty of shops and pubs along this road. The bus and train stations are on the southwest of town.

Sligo's coolest attractions—namely,

Knocknarea and Carrowmore—are a pleasant bike ride out of town.

Sights

Locals will tell you of the days when **Sligo Abbey** (Abbey St., tel. 071/914-6406, 10am-6pm daily mid-Mar.-Oct., 9:30am-4:30pm Fri.-Sun. in winter, €4) lay weed-choked and derelict. Fortunately, Dúchas has conserved this 13th-century Dominican friary in recent years. It's well worth a wander for its solemn atmosphere and creepy monk and angel effigies. Look out for the burial marker "here lyeth the boby," with most of the deceased's identifying details scratched out. Whatever the poor man might have done to warrant this long-ago act of vandalism will remain a mystery.

Art lovers should head for the the **Model Gallery** (The Mall, tel. 071/914-1405, www.modelart.ie, 10am-5:30pm Tues.-Sat., 11am-4pm Sun., free) for its permanent collection of the works of Sean Keating and Jack B. Yeats, along with major traveling exhibitions, not to mention the Ping Pong table in the entry hall (hey, anything can be considered art!). If you dig the contemporary stuff (and might even want to take it home), stop by the **Sligo Art Gallery** (Yeats Memorial Building, Hyde Bridge, tel. 071/914-5847, www.sligoartgallery.com, 10am-5pm Mon.-Sat.), which usually has an exhibition on offer.

With the personal effects of the Yeats brothers and Easter rebel Constance Markievicz on display, the **Sligo Museum** (Stephen St., tel. 071/914-1623, www.sligolibrary.ie, 10am-noon and 2pm-4:50pm Tues.-Sat. June-Sept., 2pm-4:50pm Tues.-Sat. Apr.-May and Oct., free) should be another item on your rainy-day backup plan.

Activities and Recreation

With so many great sporting opportunities just outside town, you'll barely notice that Sligo doesn't have a park of its own. Don't leave without climbing **Knocknarea:** It's a 45-minute walk to the summit (becoming moderately difficult only at the end), and the views from the cairn are awesome. **Dooney Rock,** a scenic viewpoint seven kilometers east of town overlooking the famous Innisfree on Lough Gill, incorporates a nature reserve and a brief but tranquil walk through the woods.

For long walks on sandy shores, drive north to **Rosses Point, Streedagh,** and **Mullaghmore,** or west to **Strandhill.**

Excellent golf courses in the vicinity

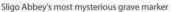
Sligo Abbey's most mysterious grave marker

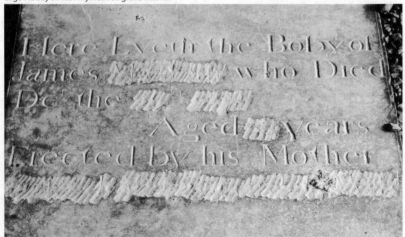

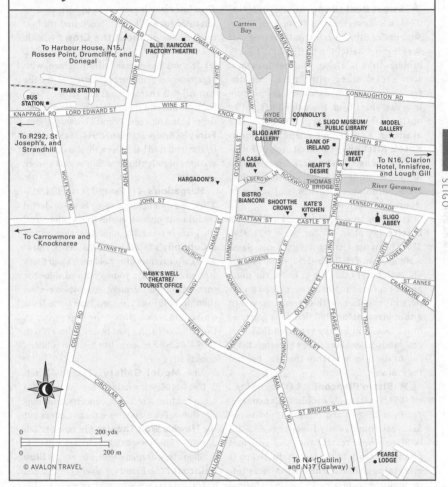

Sligo Town

To Harbour House, N15, Rosses Point, Drumcliffe, and Donegal

FINISKLIN RD

BLUE RAINCOAT (FACTORY THEATRE)

LOWER QUAY ST

Cartron Bay

MARKIEVICZ RD

HOLBORN ST

UNION ST

QUAY ST

FISH QUAY

CONNAUGHTON RD

TRAIN STATION

BUS STATION

WINE ST

KNOX ST

HYDE BRIDGE

CONNOLLY'S

SLIGO MUSEUM/ PUBLIC LIBRARY

MODEL GALLERY

KNAPPAGH RD

LORD EDWARD ST

To R292, St Joseph's, and Strandhill

O'CONNELL ST

SLIGO ART GALLERY

STEPHEN ST

BANK OF IRELAND

To N16, Clarion Hotel, Innisfree, and Lough Gill

ADELAIDE ST

A CASA MIA

SWEET BEAT

HEART'S DESIRE

River Garavogue

HARGADON'S

TABERGAL LN

ROCKWOOD

THOMAS BRIDGE

THOMAS BRIDGE ST

KENNEDY PARADE

WOLFE TONE RD

JOHN ST

BISTRO BIANCONI

SHOOT THE CROWS

KATE'S KITCHEN

GRATTAN ST

CASTLE ST

ABBEY ST

SLIGO ABBEY

To Carrowmore and Knocknarea

FLYNNS TER

CHARLES ST

CHURCH

HARMONY

W GARDENS

TEELING ST

CHARLOTTE

LOWER ABBEY ST

CHAPEL ST

ST ANNES

CRANMORE RD

HAWK'S WELL THEATRE/ TOURIST OFFICE

LUNGI

DOMINIC ST

MARKET ST

IS HIGH

OLD MARKET ST

PEARSE RD

CHAPEL HILL

COLLEGE RD

TEMPLE ST

MARKETYARD

CONNOLLY'S

BURTON ST

CIRCULAR RD

MAIL COACH RD

ST BRIGIDS PL

GALLOWS HILL

To N4 (Dublin) and N17 (Galway)

PEARSE LODGE

0   200 yds
0   200 m

© AVALON TRAVEL

SLIGO

THE NORTHWEST

include the **County Sligo Golf Club** (Rosses Point, tel. 071/917-7134, countysligogolfclub. ie) and the club at **Strandhill** (tel. 071/916-8188, www.strandhillgc.com).

Equestrians should contact **Island View** (Grange, 16 km north of Sligo on the N15, tel. 071/916-6156, islandviewridingstables.com), which offers rides on the beach, or the **Sligo Riding Centre** (Carrowmore, tel. 087/230-4828, http://irelandonhorseback.com). SUP

Sligo (The Back Avenue, Doorly Park, 3 km southeast of town via Cranmore Rd., tel. 087/996-8861, www.standuppaddlesligo. ie, €35-40 for a 1.5-hour session, €50 private session) offers stand-up paddling lessons on Lough Gill, the River Garavogue, or Half Moon Bay.

Go Skydive Ireland (tel. 087/279-2014, www.goskydive.ie, training course and first dive €320) operates out of Sligo Airport.

Food

Vegetarians should make straight for ★ **Sweet Beat** (Bridge St., tel. 071/913-8795, www.sweetbeat.ie, 10am-5pm Mon.-Sat., under €10), a bright and relaxing café serving up delicious coffee and hearty lunches, like falafel or chili with cashew sour cream along with juices, smoothies, and cookies or date bars. Everything is vegan apart from the dairy milk coffee option; otherwise all types of "mylk" are available. Another veg-friendly option is **Kate's Kitchen** (3 Castle St., tel. 071/914-3022, www.kateskitchen.ie, 8:30am-5:30pm Mon.-Sat., under €10), which stocks Irish-made hummus, chocolates, and sauces in its grocery section.

It may be in a parking lot, but **Heart's Desire** (Stephen St. car park, 071/914-3744, heartsdesiresligo@eircom.net, 9am-5:30pm Mon.-Fri., 10am-5:30pm Sat., under €8, cash only) takes the cake for the most perfect coffee-shop name ever. You can expect killer coffee (with espresso served in a shot glass, naturally), delicious gourmet loose teas, and hearty veg-friendly soups and sandwiches along with a generous helping of droll humor from the gent behind the counter.

★ **Bistro Bianconi** (44 O'Connell St., tel. 071/914-1744, www.bistrobianconi.ie, 12:30pm-2:30pm and 5:30pm-10pm Tues.-Sat. year-round, daily June-Aug., €13-25) is Sligo's best restaurant—the gourmet pizzas are truly to die for. (Actually, so is everything else on the menu; the sticky toffee pudding is amazing.) This isn't a formal eatery by any means, but reservations are essential on the weekends. If Bianconi's is booked up, try its sister restaurant, **A Casa Mia** (Tobergal Ln., tel. 071/914-1690, www.acasamiasligo.com, 10am-late daily, lunch €9-14, dinner tapas €4-10), which is also a good spot for a leisurely lunch. These eateries are part of what locals are now calling the "Italian quarter"—there's a French bakery and a Polish grocery shop in this neighborhood as well.

Entertainment and Events

ENTERTAINMENT

Sligo has enough great pubs to keep you entertained for a full week. You'll find the best *craic* by far at **Shoot the Crows** (Castle St., tel. 071/916-2554, www.shootthecrows.ie). "Shoots" is snug and dimly lighted, with creepy wood sculptures hanging above the bar. All this character attracts an arty, laid-back crowd, and there's live trad (and sometimes blues) on Tuesday and Thursday nights. **Furey's** (Bridge St., tel. 071/914-3825), owned by the Irish trad band Dervish, also does great sessions nightly (three or four nights a week in winter).

Hargadon's (4 O'Connell St., tel. 071/915-3709, www.hargadons.com) is a wonderful traditional pub with quaint snugs galore, and the grub is second to none. Another option is **Connolly's** (Markiewicz Rd., tel. 071/914-3340), a pleasantly dingy old man's pub that's started attracting a younger crowd since the turnover in management. Atmosphere-wise, though, nothing's changed here since Jesus walked on water. Notice the neat poster in the window listing pint prices from 1900 to 1995—€4.50 sure seems like highway robbery, doesn't it?

The **Model Gallery** (The Mall, tel. 071/914-1405, www.modelart.ie, events €7-15) often has film screenings, concerts, and comedy shows. For mainstream theater, check out the **Hawk's Well Theatre** (Temple St., tel. 071/916-1518, www.hawkswell.com, €10-20).

Sligo's true dramatic gem, however, is **Blue Raincoat** (The Factory, Lower Quay St., tel. 071/917-0431, www.blueraincoat.com, €10-15). Everyone thought artistic director Niall Henry was touched in the head for opening a mime-based theater company in little old Sligo Town—in an erstwhile slaughterhouse, no less—but since its inception in 1990 the troupe is flourishing. Blue Raincoat isn't for everyone, but if you enjoy experimental drama you'll find their plays an immensely satisfying way to pass an evening. They often take their shows to Westport, Galway, and a few other towns.

FESTIVALS AND EVENTS

The **Cairde Sligo Arts Festival** (www. cairdefestival.com, early July) offers a packed weeklong calendar of music, dance, visual art, and comedy, with plenty of kid-friendly activities as well. The **Sligo Jazz Project** (tel. 071/917-0431, www.sligojazz.ie, July) is a music school and jazz festival featuring teacher-performers from all over Europe and a couple from the United States. There are free gigs in pubs all over town, including Shoot the Crows and Hargadon's. Most of the events in the **Sligo International Choral Festival** (November, tel. 071/917-0733 or 086/259-2290, www.sligochoralfest.com), a four-day blitz of competitions and concerts, take place at the Aula Maxima at the Sligo Institute of Technology (entrance on Ash Ln., on the northern side of the city). The **Model Gallery** (tel. 071/914-1405, www.modelart. ie) hosts several international musical events, including the **Festival of Baroque Music** (late October) and the **New Music Festival** (late March).

Shopping

Sligo has a couple of shopping centers full of chains, including the new Quayside Centre off Wine Street, but the best shops are along O'Connell Street and the other main drag, Grattan-Castle-Abbey Street. The nicest sweater shop in town is **P.F. Dooney** (36 O'Connell St., tel. 071/914-2274), with a wide selection of warm and colorful pullovers. **The Cat & the Moon** (4 Castle St., tel. 071/914-3686, www.thecatandthemoon.com) does beautiful jewelry, crafts, and framed art.

Sligo has lost some of its excellent bookshops since the recession hit, but you can still browse for hours at **Liber** (35 O'Connell St., tel. 071/914-2219, www.liber.ie) or the quirky secondhand **Bookmart** (5 Lower the Mall, 083/361-3127, www.bookmart.ie), which regularly hosts poetry open-mic nights (sans mic).

For information on local artisans (ceramicists, goldsmiths, woodworkers, and more) and where to find their work, check out the **Sligo Craft Trail** (www.madeinsligo.ie).

Accommodations

The private rooms at the spotless IHH **Harbour House** (Finisklin Rd., tel. 071/917-1547, www.harbourhousehostel.com, dorms €18, d €20 pp, s €25) are B&B quality (TVs and towels included), and the whole place has a homey atmosphere few other hostels can match. DVD rental and a comfortable, character-filled common room make it an excellent choice, despite a less-than-ideal location in an industrial area.

Pearse and Mail Coach Roads on the south end of town are lined with B&Bs, one of which is **Pearse Lodge** (Pearse Rd., tel. 071/916-1090, www.pearselodge.com, €40-50 pp). It's a bit larger than the average Irish B&B, so it offers more of a sense of privacy, and there are vegetarian-friendly breakfast options. Another really nice B&B is **St. Joseph's** (Strandhill Rd., tel. 071/917-0655, gemma35@gmail.com, €40-50 pp), with a gorgeous stained-glass entryway that will catch your eye from the road. Pem O'Dowd is a jovial and very helpful and informative host. Both B&Bs are a 10-minute walk from the center of town.

Frankly, there are no outstanding hotels in Sligo; the occasional maintenance glitches and management slip-ups can plague even the newly renovated ones like the regal **Clarion Hotel** (Clarion Rd. on the northern edge of town, off Enniskillen Rd., signposted from the N4, tel. 071/911-9000, www.clarion-hotelsligo.com, rooms €200-275). The leisure center is second to none, with a pool, sauna, Jacuzzi, exercise room, the works (though the facilities can get crowded in the evenings). Looking at this place now, you'd never in a million years believe it was once the town's asylum!

Information

The **North-West Regional Tourist Office** (Temple St., tel. 071/916-1201, www.ireland-northwest.ie, 9am-6pm weekdays and 10am-6pm weekends June-Sept., 9am-5pm weekdays Oct.-May) is on the south side of town, in the same building as the Hawk's Well Theatre.

SLIGO

THE NORTHWEST

The Battle of the Books

In AD 561, while abbot of Drumcliffe, St. Colmcille (also known as Columba) borrowed an Italian manuscript during a visit to his friend Finian. When Finian discovered that Colmcille had secretly copied his book, he brought his case to the high king, Diarmuid. Finian claimed that the copy belonged to him, and Diarmuid agreed (though some say a prior grievance between Diarmuid and Colmcille influenced the king's decision).

Colmcille refused to accept his verdict, raised an army, and defeated Diarmuid's forces on the slopes of Benbulben (supposedly aided by an angel). The blood of thousands of men on his hands, Colmcille departed Drumcliffe for Iona off the Scottish coast, where he vowed to convert at least as many people to Christianity as had died on the battlefield that day. Why both Finian and Colmcille were canonized after such a devastating squabble is more or less inscrutable.

Getting There

Sligo Town is 210 kilometers northwest of Dublin on the N4 and 138 kilometers north of Galway on the N17. **Bus Éireann** (Lord Edward St., tel. 071/916-9888) has direct services to Sligo from Dublin (#23, 5/day daily), Galway (#53 or #64, 5/day daily), Belfast (#65 or #66, 5/day Mon.-Sat., 2/day Sun.), Donegal and Derry (#64 or #480, 5/day daily), and Westport (#66, 2/day Sat.-Thurs., 3/day Fri.).

There are at least five **Irish Rail** (tel. 071/916-9888) departures per day Monday-Saturday, from Dublin Connolly to Sligo via Boyle, Carrick-on-Shannon, and Mullingar (7/day Fri., 4/day Sun.).

Getting Around

Sligo Town is totally walkable. Board buses to Strandhill (#472), Rosses Point (#473), or Drumcliffe (#64, #474, #480, or #483) at the bus station on Lord Edward Street.

Rent a bicycle from **Gary's Cycles** (Quay St., tel. 071/913-8060, www.garyscycles.com, €15/25 per half day, €25/45 per day for a hybrid/racing bike). Need a ride? Ring **Sligo Taxi** (tel. 086/121-9111).

NORTH OF SLIGO TOWN
Drumcliffe

A picturesque early-19th-century Anglican church and monastic site a quick journey north of Sligo Town, **Drumcliffe** (Droim Chliabh, "Back of the Baskets," 7.5 km north

of Sligo Town on the N15, tel. 071/914-4956, 9am-5pm Mon.-Sat., 1pm-5pm Sun., free) was founded by St. Colmcille in the year 575—and of course, it is also the final resting place of Ireland's most beloved poet, chosen because his great-grandfather served as rector here between 1811 and 1846. The epitaph on **Yeats's grave** is taken from the poem "Under Ben Bulben," in which he details the circumstances of the burial he intended for himself, finishing with:

Cast a cold eye
On life, on death.
Horseman, pass by!

These last three lines are inscribed on his headstone, which draws thousands of visitors every year. Now, it must be noted that Yeats died on the French Riviera in 1939, and local records indicate his remains were moved to an ossuary in 1946. When he was finally "repatriated" to Ireland in 1948, his friends declared that most of what traveled in the shiny new coffin wasn't actually Yeats. French documents uncovered in 2015 confirm the truth behind this suspicion. Be that as it may, Drumcliffe will always be the place to pay your respects to the great Irish poet. Yeats's wife, Georgie Hyde-Lee, is buried nearby.

For most, Yeats entirely eclipses the historical importance of Colmcille's monastery. All that remains is an exquisite 11th-century high cross (see if you can discern Adam and Eve, Cain and Abel, the Crucifixion, and other scenes) and a **round tower** across the road, reduced to a 16-meter stump after a lightning storm in 1396. Legend states that what's left of the tower will crumble on the wisest person to stand beside it; by all means, hop the wall and see if you're as sagacious as you think.

There's a **visitors center** (tel. 071/914-4956, 9am-5pm Mon.-Sat., 1pm-5pm Sun., €2.50); a ticket will allow you a 15-minute audiovisual on Yeats and Colmcille as well as admission to the church. Frankly, though, the AV is dumbed-down, and the church's interior is mostly unremarkable. There's also a gift shop and tearoom across the lane (always crowded, but worth elbowing your way to a table for some surprisingly good desserts and snacky things).

You would expect **Davis's Restaurant at The Yeats Tavern** (Drumcliffe Bridge, tel. 071/916-3117, www.yeatstavernrestaurant.com, €13-24) to be something of a tourist trap, but it's not. It's a cozy spot, popular with locals and visitors alike, and the menu is surprisingly eclectic. You'll find it on your left just after you've passed Drumcliffe churchyard on the way out of Sligo.

Drumcliffe is a five-minute drive north out of Sligo Town on the N15. **Bus Éireann** (tel. 071/916-0066) offers service from the station on Lord Edward Street (#64, 6/day Mon.-Thurs. and Sat., 7/day Fri., 3/day Sun.) en route to Derry, but be sure to request a stop in Drumcliffe.

Rosses Point

A small but happenin' resort town on Drumcliffe Bay (especially on sunny weekend afternoons), **Rosses Point** (An Ros) boasts a gorgeous Blue Flag strand and bountiful sea fishing; contact **Ewing's** (tel. 086/891-3618, www.sligoboatcharters.com) for a charter. The grassy slopes above the strand are a good spot for a picnic lunch; you have a vantage of Coney Island, namesake of the Brooklyn amusement mecca, and beyond it Sligo's sprawl glittering across the water.

If you have a car, you might want to stay at **Serenity** (Doonierin, Kintogher, signposted off the R291 just east of Rosses Point, tel. 071/914-3351, www.serenitysligo.com, Mar.-Oct., €35-40 pp sharing) even if you plan to spend much of your time in Sligo proper; it's a lovely B&B in a restful setting, a far better value than the B&Bs in town for its sea views, excellent breakfasts, handmade quilts on the beds, and very helpful and knowledgable proprietors.

Your best bet for dinner is the pub fare at cozy, nautical-themed **Harry's** (Main St., tel. 071/917-7173, www.harrysrossespoint.com, food served 5:30pm-9:30pm Mon.-Tues., from 5pm Wed.-Fri., 12:30pm-9:30pm Sat.-Sun., €12-22).

Rosses Point is only 9.5 kilometers northwest of Sligo Town on the R291, accessible by a local **Bus Éireann** route (#473, 7/day weekdays, 5/day Sat.) departing the Lord Edward Street bus station.

Lissadell

The new owners of the stern, Greek Revival **Lissadell** (7 km north of Sligo, signposted off the N15, tel. 071/916-3150, www.lissadellhouse.com, gardens 10:30am-4pm daily June-Sept., house 10:30am-6pm daily mid-Mar.-Sept., garden and house €12), home to the Gore-Booth family from 1834 to 2003, have set about restoring the old gardens to their former glory. After an ongoing dispute with Sligo County Council (during which time the family closed their home to the public), they have apparently settled matters to everyone's satisfaction, and Lissadell is open for visitors once more.

This was the childhood home of Easter rebel Constance Markievicz (the wife of a Ukrainian count) and her beloved sister, the poet Eva Gore-Booth. The sisters devoted their lives to charity work in the slums of Dublin and Manchester, and Constance was the first woman elected to the British Parliament (though she refused to take her seat, being vehemently anti-treaty). Yeats spent a fair bit of time at Lissadell in the sisters' company, and the Yeats Study and his usual guest room are preserved much as he left them (though, in truth, he only visited four times). No student of Irish history should pass up an opportunity to tour the house and demesne. It's a snap to get here from Sligo Town by car; the house is clearly signposted from the N15, though the busy road makes cycling a less than ideal transport method.

Mullaghmore

A tiny fishing village beautifully situated over Donegal Bay, **Mullaghmore** (An Mullach Mór, "The Great Summit") is an angler's heaven on earth (or sea, to be more accurate)—and there's a lovely sheltered strand to boot. Half a dozen charter boat operators, including **Peter Power** (tel. 087/257-6268, www.bayangling.freeservers.com) and **Rodney Lomax** (tel. 071/916-6124, tlomax@eircom.net), can also take you to Inishmurray if the weather's right. On your way here you'll spot 19th-century **Classiebawn Castle** on a cliff to the west, like something straight out of a fairy tale; the castle's original owner, the third Viscount Palmerston, was twice elected English prime minister. You'll pass another fine strand at **Streedagh**, where a Spanish Armada shipwreck in 1588 left 1,100 lifeless sailors on the sand. While away a happy hour hunting for fossils among the rocks.

Once you've arrived at the **Beach Hotel** (on the harbor, tel. 071/916-6103, www.beach-hotelmullaghmore.com, pub food served noon-9pm daily, restaurant 6pm-9pm daily and 12:30pm-3:15pm Sun., €45-65 pp, s €70-90, 15% surcharge on bank holiday weekends), you won't find much reason to leave, what with the ample leisure facilities (gym, pool, sauna, Jacuzzi), seafood pub and restaurant, and self-catering apartments—heck, they even host the occasional Murder Mystery weekend. And of course, you can't beat the view from many of the bedrooms.

If you're spending the night, eat at **Eithna's by the Sea** (on the harbor, tel. 071/916-6407, www.eithnasrestaurant.com, 6:30pm-9:30pm daily Easter-Sept., varying hours in low season, €18-38), which does a smattering of satisfying meat and veggie dishes using organic produce where possible. Unless you've ordered the deluxe seafood platter, try to save some room for a scrummy dessert.

Mullaghmore is 28 kilometers north of Sligo Town off the N15, clearly signposted on the left from the village of Cliffoney (3 km). There's no public transport to Mullaghmore, though Cliffoney is a request stop on the **Bus**

Streedagh Beach, a pristine strand with a sad history

Éireann (tel. 071/916-0066) route from Sligo to Derry (#64, 6/day Mon.-Thurs. and Sat., 7/day Fri., 3/day Sun.).

Inishmurray

Yet another obscure Irish saint, Molaise, founded a monastery on the flat, low-lying island of **Inishmurray** (Inis Muirígh or Inismuireadhaigh), 22 meters above sea level and six kilometers off the Sligo coast, around AD 520. Several ruins lie within a cashel, or ring fort: *clocháin* (beehive huts), several outdoor altars, and three small churches, which were partially "restored" at the end of the 19th century. There was also a separate church and burial ground for the island's nuns. This place is steeped in superstitions and spooky rituals, one of which is the "cursing stones": If you wanted to lay a curse, you would perform the Stations of the Cross in reverse order, turning over the stones beside each devotional station as you went along. Another story said the Leac na Teine inside the Teach na Teine (the "Stone of the Fire" in the "House of the Fire") was said to ignite a brick of turf laid upon it, should every other fire on Inishmurray have been extinguished.

As far as local historians can make out, the monastic community persevered here continuously into the 20th century, making a living selling fish, seaweed, and poteen on the mainland (the last item being, of course, illegal, though due to the remote location law enforcement could never actually catch those mischievous monks distilling it). The last monks, a community of 100, finally left the island in 1948.

Unfortunately, passage to Inishmurray is dependent on the mood of the morning tides. Compounding foul-weather concerns is the fact that boat operators don't find a group of less than six worth their while. On a nice day in high season, though, you might be able to join up with another small group. Ring **Rodney Lomax** (tel. 071/916-6124) or **Keith Clarke** (tel. 087/254-0190, www.inishmurray-islandtrips.com), both of whom operate out of Mullaghmore. Return passage will run you €15-20.

Creevykeel Court Cairn

It won't inspire awe on the scale of Knocknarea or the great passage tomb at Carrowmore, but the **Creevykeel Court Cairn** (30 km north of Sligo on the N15, clearly signposted just east of Cliffoney, always accessible, free) is still the most remarkable memorial of its type. Dating to the third millennium BC, Creevykeel consists of an open oval-shaped central court, with a pair of passage graves and a primary burial chamber at opposite ends.

In 1935 the site was excavated by a team of Harvard archaeologists, who brought to light a collection of decorated and undecorated Neolithic pottery, arrowheads and axes, and four cremation burials (all now in the National Museum of Archaeology and History). The cairn was "restored" after the excavations, which might account for why it's still so *neat*-looking.

This site is worth a stop if you happen to be traveling north to Donegal—but if you're sticking to Sligo Town, a visit to Carrowmore is enough to satisfy most people's interest in megalithic monuments.

EAST OF SLIGO TOWN
Lough Gill

William Butler Yeats's most famous poem, "The Lake Isle of Innisfree" ("I will arise and go now, and go to Innisfree . . ."), was inspired by the ruins of a tiny monastic settlement on **Innisfree Island** (Inis Fraoigh, "Grouse Island") on Lough Gill, which is supposedly hiding a lake monster of its own. You'll find the best vantage of the island at **Dooney Rock,** a small but tranquil nature reserve seven kilometers west of Sligo on the R286 (Yeats wrote a poem about this place, too: "The Fiddler of Dooney"). There are several short wooded walks to enjoy. To get to the lake, keep cycling or driving the R286 past the Dooney Rock car park, and the lakeshore turnoff is another three kilometers down the road.

It's touristy, all right, but an hour-long lake cruise on the *Rose of Innisfree* (Lough Gill, Kilmore, Fivemilebourne, 11 km west of Sligo on the R286/Dromahair road, tel. 071/916-4266, www.roseofinnisfree.com, €15) is the closest you can get to the fabled island. Cruises depart from Parke's Castle in County Leitrim (11am, 12:30pm, 1:30pm, 3:30pm, and 4:30pm daily Easter-Oct.; ring for a shuttle bus from Sligo).

Glencar Lough

Nestled in the Dartry Mountains 11 kilometers northeast of Sligo, Glencar Lough straddles the Sligo-Leitrim border. Along with opportunities for a leisurely walk by the lake or down the backcountry lanes nearby, a pretty (but not terribly remarkable) **waterfall** draws plenty of visitors (especially families with small children) on sunny weekend afternoons. Take the N16 north out of Sligo and you'll see Glencar Lough clearly signposted on your left. There's a car park and small visitors center across the road from the waterfall.

SOUTHWEST AND WEST OF SLIGO TOWN
Carrowmore Megalithic Cemetery

Carrowmore Megalithic Cemetery (Ceathrú Mór, "Great Quarter," 5 km southwest of town, signposted off Strandhill Rd. on the western end of Sligo, tel. 071/916-1534, 10am-6pm mid-Apr.-Oct., €4) is Ireland's largest, with more than 60 tombs—dolmens, cairns, and stone circles—scattered in the fields on either side of the road, within a diameter of only a kilometer or so. This is also one of the oldest funerary complexes in Ireland; archaeologists date the oldest tombs at Carrowmore to 700 years before Newgrange, somewhere around 4370 BC. The primary monument is a huge cairn/passage tomb in the field beyond the small visitors center, which has been excavated and refitted with wire screens to keep the stones in place. If you're visiting in the off-season, it's still possible to jump the fence

and pop inside the passage tomb. Frankly, though, if you only have time for one megalithic monument, get thee to Knocknarea instead.

★ Knocknarea

A 45-minute hike up **Knocknarea** (Cnoc na Rí, "Sacred Hill," 6.5 km southwest of town off the R292, always accessible, free), at an elevation of 329 meters, brings you to an enormous cairn known as Queen Maeve's Tomb. Maeve, of course, was the legendary ruler of Connaught, a notorious troublemaker and Cuchulainn's perennial nemesis. The cairn is 55 meters wide and 10 meters high, and most likely dates to the beginning of the third millennium BC. It has never been excavated, despite widespread speculation that a passage tomb on par with Newgrange lies beneath those 40,000 tons of stone. William Bulfin, who cycled all over the country at the turn of the last century, wrote of Knocknarea that "there is an epic suggestiveness which you cannot miss if you climb the mountain. You cannot keep your hold upon the present while you are up there." These words still ring true despite the modern structures dotting the valleys below.

The climb is easy at first, but the path gets steep the last 5-10 minutes; the panoramic pastoral and sea views are well worth the exertion, however. Many visitors climb the cairn once they've reached the summit, but seeing as this is a Neolithic monument it's in rather poor taste to do so. At any rate, don't leave Sligo without having climbed up to Medbh's Grave. To get there, take the Strandhill road out of the center of town and turn left at the signposts for Knocknarea and Carrowmore. This makes for a nice afternoon of cycling if the weather's fine.

Strandhill

It may be the locals' beach of choice, but the resort town of **Strandhill** (8 km west of Sligo on the R292) has a vaguely run-down feel. There are prettier (and less crowded) beaches at Streedagh and Mullaghmore farther north, though Strandhill does have the best **surfing**. For lessons, rentals, or whatever else you need, try **Perfect Day Surf Shop & School** (on the promenade, tel. 071/912-8488, www.perfectdaysurfing.com). Strandhill also has its own **golf club** (tel. 071/916-8188, www.strandhillgc.com).

The best reason to visit Strandhill is the **Voya Seaweed Baths** (on the promenade, tel. 071/916-8686, www.voyaseaweedbaths.com, 10am-9:30pm Mon.-Fri. and 10am-8:30pm Sat.-Sun. May-Oct., 11am-9pm Mon.-Fri. and 10am-6:30pm Sat.-Sun. Nov.-Apr., 50-minute steam and bath €28, two bathers €55). After 45 minutes in a hot tub full of seaweed plucked from the shore that very morning, you'll feel like a brand-new person. The center also does Swedish and aromatherapy massage.

There's not much in the way of accommodations here, but you might try the smallish, friendly, family-run **Ocean Wave Lodge** (Strandhill Rd., tel. 071/916-8115, www.oceanwavelodge.com, €35-45 pp, dorm beds €18-20). The lodge's 13 rooms are airy and spacious, with pleasingly no-nonsense decor. For lunch or dinner, try **The Venue** (Top Rd., tel. 071/916-8167, www.venuestrandhill.ie, food served 12:30pm-9:30pm daily, €9-13). Ask for a table with a view of the harbor.

Strandhill is eight kilometers west of Sligo Town on the R292. Provided it's not a Sunday, **Bus Éireann** (tel. 071/916-0066) can get you there from Sligo (#472, 7/day Mon.-Fri., 5/day Sat.). The Strandhill bus departs outside the Spar across from the station on Lord Edward Street.

ENNISCRONE

Enniscrone (Innis Crabhann, also spelled "Inniscrone") is a pleasant seaside town despite the smattering of garish amusement arcades. The primary draw is a lovely five-kilometer sheltered strand known as "The Hollow," a surfers' haven; it runs parallel to the main street and is easily accessible from there (it's just behind the houses).

★ Kilcullen's Seaweed Baths

Surfboards aside, don't leave Enniscrone without taking a soak at **Kilcullen's Seaweed Baths** (Cliff Rd., signposted from Main St., tel. 096/36238, 10am-9pm daily May-Sept., noon-8pm weekdays and 10am-8pm weekends Oct.-Apr., steam and soak €25). The therapeutic properties of seaweed and hot water are well known, especially for those suffering from arthritis. There are several reasons why these baths are even better than those in Strandhill: Established in 1912, Kilcullen's is still family-run, and retains its original porcelain bathtubs and other charming Edwardian features; the staff are genuinely friendly; and best of all, there's no time limit! You can soak as long as you like. When you're ready to get out, you pull the handle on the ancient shower above the bathtub and douse yourself in cold seawater, emerging pink-cheeked and fresh as a newborn baby. Massage therapy is available by appointment (soak and half-hour massage €65).

Activities and Recreation

For lessons or equipment rental, head to either the **Northwest Surf School** (on the beach, tel. 087/959-5556, www.nwsurfschool.com) or the **7th Wave Surf School** (on the beach, tel. 087/971-6389, www.surfsligo.com). The **Enniscrone Golf Club** (Enniscrone, tel. 096/36657, www.enniscronegolf.com) is another draw, especially with Irish weekenders.

Food and Accommodations

Enniscrone's kind of short in the eats department, but you're guaranteed a delicious meal at ★ **The Pilot's Bar** (Main St., tel. 096/36131, food served 5pm-9pm weekdays, 1pm-9pm weekends, €7-12)—it does fabulous gourmet pizzas as well as more traditional fare, steak sandwiches and the like. This watering hole is an appealing amalgam of old and new: There's a load of nautical junk on the walls and strung from the ceilings, yet the indie music on the stereo system is playing off an iPod behind the bar.

The rear bedrooms at **Ceol na Mara** ("Music of the Sea," Main St., tel. 096/36351, www.ceol-na-mara.com, €40 pp, s €50-55) offer expansive ocean views. The rooms are modern-minimalist yet comfortable (with excellent showers), and you're welcome to use the owners' sitting room, where there's often a fire burning in the grate. Mr. and Mrs. O'Regan also offer self-catering holiday homes nearby (€350-700/week, highest rates July-Sept.).

Most surfers stay at the **Atlantic Caravan & Camping Park** (on the beach, tel. 096/36132, www.atlanticcaravanpark.com, Apr.-Oct., tent sites €8 per person).

Information and Services

There's no bank in Enniscrone, but you'll find an ATM at the **Spar supermarket** (Main St., tel. 096/36417, 8am-10pm or later daily).

Enniscrone's **tourist office** (Main St., tel. 096/36746, www.discoverenniscrone. com, noon-8pm Mon.-Sat. July-Sept.) is community-run.

Getting There and Around

Enniscrone is 54 kilometers west of Sligo Town on the R297 (from Sligo, take the N4 south, pick up the N59 at Collooney, and then turn off onto the R297 at Dromore West). **Bus Éireann** (tel. 071/916-0066) has a Sligo-Ballina service that stops in Enniscrone (#66 or #458, 5/day Mon.-Sat., 1/day Sun. at 3:30pm, additional departure at 7:10pm Fri.), though you may have to change buses at Dromore West. The Dublin-Ballina bus (#22, 3/day daily) also stops here.

For a lift, ring **Tuffy Taxis** (tel. 087/251-3107).

★ CARROWKEEL PASSAGE TOMB CEMETERY

Owing in part to the remote location in the Bricklieve Mountains, **Carrowkeel**

Passage Tomb Cemetery (6 km off the N4, 33 km south of Sligo Town, always accessible, free) is one of the creepiest megalithic sites in the country—especially in the rain and fog. This Neolithic necropolis of dolmens and cairns was constructed sometime in the third millennium BC, which means it's not as old as Newgrange or Carrowmore. For dramatic location and spooky atmosphere, though, Carrowkeel beats both those sites, hands down. There are 14 cairns, though the entryways of even the largest tombs are too small for more than a peek inside. There are also about 50 circular stone foundations that indicate a Neolithic settlement, perhaps only inhabited while the tombs were being constructed. Even if you find all these archaeological wonders only of mild interest, it's worth venturing out here for the gorgeous panoramic view of Benbulben, Lough Arrow, and plenty of lush countryside. In foul weather it's easy to lose your orientation, so bring a compass if the sky looks threatening.

To get here, take the N4 south from Sligo Town or north from Boyle in County Roscommon (18 km) and follow the signs for Carrowkeel beginning in the hamlet of Castlebaldwin (coming from Sligo, the turnoff is on your right). After a few kilometers you'll come to a cattle fence; open, pass through, and close, and once you reach a large sign with a map of the area, make an immediate left and it's only a kilometer more (down some really narrow and horribly bumpy unpaved roads). You'll know you've arrived when you spot a couple of rusted sign-holders to your left (which, at time of writing, had no signs at all) beside some space for a few cars to park. Public transportation isn't a viable option.

Donegal

It may not be the easiest county to get to, but Donegal's mist-shrouded mountains and dramatic headlands will reward you for your efforts. The Donegal accent (or accents, as there are supposedly 20) is lilting and melodic, so distinctive that after a couple days up here you'll be able to recognize it anywhere. A third of the county is in the Gaeltacht, the Irish-speaking region, and there are more native speakers of the Donegal (or Ulster) dialect than there are Connaught (Mayo and Galway) or Munster (Kerry and Cork). The natives have earned a reputation for genuine friendliness no matter which tongue they're using.

SOUTHERN DONEGAL
Donegal Town
Donegal is far more pleasant than most other county towns, and there are enough sights to keep you here for an afternoon. With so much otherworldly scenery awaiting you farther north and west, though, why linger much longer? Pad your wallet at the ATM, have a pint at the Scotsman, get a good night's sleep, and get an early start.

The center of Donegal Town is marked by "the diamond" (really a triangle), where you'll find nearly all the shops, banks, pubs, and eateries. The Quay runs south from the diamond, leading to the pier, tourist office, and car park (€0.60/hour); Main Street runs east from the diamond; and Tyrconnell Street runs north, passing Donegal Castle before crossing the River Eske.

SIGHTS
Built in 1505 by the first "Red Hugh" O'Donnell, Dúchas-run **Donegal Castle** (Castle St., just off the diamond, tel. 074/972-2405, 10am-6pm daily mid-Mar.-Oct., 9:30am-4:30pm Fri.-Sun. in winter, €4) fell into English hands after the Flight of the Earls in 1607. (His descendant, also known as Red Hugh, lost the O'Donnell ancestral home after

the English won the Battle of Kinsale in 1601.) The castle's new owner, Captain Basil Brooke, was also made governor of Donegal, and he added an English manor-style banquet hall to the original tower house. There isn't a whole lot to see, although the historical exhibit on the tower's top floor is very informative. If you have any interest in Irish history, especially the Flight of the Earls, then take the tour; otherwise just snap a photo from the front gate. In past winters the castle has been open Friday-Sunday, but these hours are subject to change; ask at the tourist office if the gate is closed.

Past the waterbus pier (by the tourist office) are the scant remains of Franciscan **Donegal Abbey,** also built by the first Red Hugh and his wife, Nuala, in 1474. The abbey is pleasantly situated on the mouth of Donegal Bay, but only a few abbey walls are standing, thanks to Rory O'Donnell, who mistakenly dropped a cannonball here during his war with the English (Rory was one of the earls who departed Ireland for good after the disastrous Battle of Kinsale).

The **Railway Heritage Centre** (the Old Station House, Tyrconnell St., tel. 074/972-2655, www.donegalrailway.com, 10am-5pm Mon.-Fri., €3.50) presents the history of the county's two narrow-gauge railroads, the County Donegal Railway and the Londonderry & Lough Swilly Railway, comprising 225 miles of track in total. Featuring restored carriages and an informative presentation, this little museum is worthwhile for anyone with even a mild interest in transportation history.

ACTIVITIES AND RECREATION
The 117-kilometer **Bluestack Way** begins in Donegal, heading north past **Lough Eske** ("Lake of the Fish") and west along the Bluestack foothills to Ardara. You could take a shorter walk (or cycle) along a path encircling the lake before returning to town. You'll

Donegal

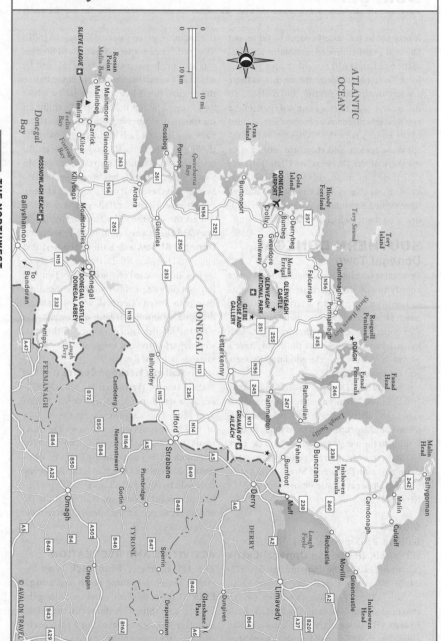

ATLANTIC OCEAN

0
10 km
0
10 mi

SLIEVE LEAGUE ✚

Rossan Point
Malin Bay
Malinmore
Malinbeg ▲
Teelin
Carrick
Kilcar
Killybegs
Glencolmcille
Donegal Bay
Teelin Bay
Fintragh Bay

Ballyshannon
ROSSNOWLAGH BEACH ✚
To Bundoran ↗

263
N56
262
Ardara
261
Rossbeg
Portnoo
Glenties
250
253
252
N56
Burtonport
Gola Island
DONEGAL AIRPORT ✈
Crolly
Bunbeg
Derrybeg
Gweedore
Dunlewey
Mount Errigal ★
GLENVEAGH CASTLE
GLENVEAGH NATIONAL PARK
GLEBE HOUSE AND GALLERY ✚

Gweebarra Bay

Bloody Foreland
Tory Sound
Tory Island

257
Falcarragh
Dunfanaghy
Portnablagh
N56
245
Sheep Haven Bay
Rosguill Peninsula
★ DOAGH
Fanad Peninsula
Fanad Head
246
Rathmullan
247
Rathmelton
238
Buncrana
Inishowen Peninsula
240
Carndonagh
Culdaff
Malin Head
Malin
242
Ballygorman
Inishowen Head
Greencastle
Moville
Redcastle

251
255
Letterkenny
N56
245
N13
GRIANAN OF AILEACH ✚ ★

DONEGAL
N15
N15
Ballybofey
Castlederg
B72
Newtonstewart
B50
B84
B50
B84
B164
N15
N14
Lifford
Strabane
A5
B49
Plumbridge
Gortin
B48
B47
Sperrin
TYRONE
A505
B46
B4
Creggan
B46
Draperstown
B162
A29
B43

DONEGAL CASTLE/ DONEGAL ABBEY ★
Donegal
232
N15
Pettigo
A47
FERMANAGH
Lough Derg

Fahan
Burnfoot
Muff
Derry
DERRY
A2
Lough Foyle
238
240
Limavady
A6
Dungiven
Glenshane Pass
B40
B64
A37
A2
B201

© AVALON TRAVEL

pass through some utterly charming pastoral scenery along the way. Fishing permits are available from **Doherty's** (Main St., tel. 074/972-1119, 9am-6pm Thurs.-Tues.).

In fine weather you can take an informative boat trip across Donegal Bay on the **waterbus** (at the pier by the tourist office, tel. 074/972-3666, www.donegalbaywaterbus.com, 5/day daily in summer, 1/day the rest of the year, €20). The 70-minute tour takes in a seal colony, oyster farm, various castle and monastic ruins, and other points of historical import.

The 18-hole, 73-par course at the **Donegal Golf Club** (Murvagh, Laghey, 10 km south of town on the N15, tel. 073/34054, www.donegalgolfclub.ie) is beautifully situated on the Murvagh Peninsula with a backdrop of the Bluestack Mountains.

FOOD

The cozy **Blueberry Tea Room** (Castle St., tel. 074/972-2933, 9am-7pm Mon.-Sat., under €10) is easily the best eatery in town, serving delicious sandwiches, quiches, cakes, and pies. No wonder it's packed with locals at any time of day. Hostellers and picnickers might stop by **Simple Simon's** (The Diamond, tel. 074/972-2687), a small whole-foods store and

café serving up quiche, tortillas, salads, and plenty of fruit and snacks.

Another excellent lunch option is **Aroma** (Ballyshannon Rd., tel. 074/972-3222, 9:30am-5:30pm Tues.-Sat., daily in summer, under €12), an unassuming café/bakery at the Donegal Craft Village renowned for its melt-in-your-mouth asparagus risotto.

Directly opposite Donegal Castle, the **Olde Castle Bar** (Tyrconnell St., tel. 074/972-1262, www.oldecastlebar.com, food served noon-9pm daily, €15-30) has a fishy reputation, and that's a good thing: The seafood platter is legendary (and might take you all night to finish). There are several options for vegetarians. This is far and away your best dining option in D-town.

If sophisticated modern Irish fare using fresh local produce is what you're after, try **Ard na Breatha** (Drumrooske Middle, a 20-minute walk or 3-minute drive from town, tel. 074/972-2288, www.ardnabreatha.com, 6:30pm-9:30pm Fri.-Sun. for nonresidents, nightly for guests, 5-course dinner €38, à la carte also available), where reservations are essential for nonguests. You might want to stay in the adjoining guesthouse, one of Donegal Town's top lodgings.

Donegal Castle passed into English hands after the Flight of the Earls.

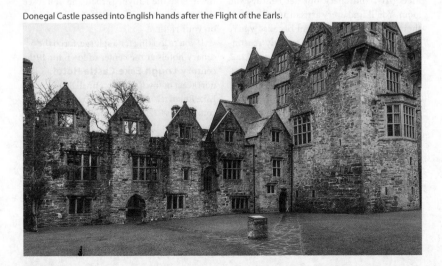

ENTERTAINMENT AND EVENTS

Donegal pubs are the good old-fashioned kind. Most folks, visitors and locals alike, pass the evening at **The Scotsman** (Bridge St., no phone), which has live music nightly year-round. Visiting musicians are encouraged to bring their instruments. You'll also find trad sessions on the weekends at the **Schooner Inn** (Upper Main St., tel. 074/972-1671).

The last weekend in June brings the **Donegal Town Summer Festival** (contact the tourist office for info, tel. 074/972-1148), with street entertainment and more formal traditional music and dance performances featuring musicians from as far afield as Roscommon and Galway. Scarce funding has prevented the festival from running every year, but if you're here in late June or early July keep your eyes peeled for announcements.

SHOPPING

Souvenir hunters shouldn't miss the **Donegal Craft Village** (Ballyshannon Rd., 1.5 km west of town, tel. 074/972-2225, 9am-6pm Mon.-Sat., 11am-6pm Sun.) for its selection of jewelry, tweed, paintings, glassware—even sculptures made of bog wood! Clare O'Presco's handmade tweed scarves, handbags, and bean-bag frogs make particularly nice gifts, and check out her century-old loom. You'll find every artisan at work inside their individual shops, and because you're buying direct the prices are truly reasonable. A **café and bakery** (tel. 074/972-3222, 9:30am-5:30pm Mon.-Sat.) does terrific vegetarian lunches.

Check out **Four Masters** (the Diamond, tel. 074/972-1526) for Irish-interest books and postcards.

ACCOMMODATIONS

The IHH **Donegal Town Independent Hostel** (Killybegs Rd., Doonan, tel. 074/972-2805, www.donegaltownhostel.com, dorms €17, doubles €19-21 pp) gets top marks for friendly reception, clean facilities, comfy beds and common room, and an all-around great vibe. It's one kilometer west of town, but the

walk will only take you 10 minutes, and the distance makes for a quiet night.

A two-minute walk from the diamond, the **Railway Lodge** (Milltown, tel. 074/972-3656, www.railwaylodge.com, €35-40 pp) is in front of the Railway Heritage Centre, although a quiet night's sleep is as good as a promise. You can admire the epic teapot collection in the dining room, and if you ask for porridge it might come topped with fresh blueberries. The owner, Sheila, is so genuinely friendly that you'll feel as if you're spending the weekend at your auntie's. To get here from the center of town, take the castle road, passing the post office on your left.

One of many reasons to stay at **Ard na Breatha** (Drumrooske Middle, a 20-minute walk or 3-minute drive from town, tel. 074/972-2288, www.ardnabreatha.com, closed mid-Jan.-mid-Feb., €35-50 pp, s €50-65) is the excellent bar and restaurant, which is open only to guests during the week (by arrangement). Each of the six rooms in this small and very atmospheric guesthouse features pine furniture, big comfy wrought-iron beds, and Bluestack views. Breakfast is a delight, with a buffet of fruit, cheeses, and homemade breads and smoked salmon with your scrambled eggs. To get here from town, take the Killybegs road and you'll see the restaurant signposted 200 meters down on your right.

If you're looking for a splurge, forgo the ordinary hotels at the center of town for 19th-century **Lough Eske Castle Hotel** (6 km northeast of town via Tyrconnell St. to Lough Eske Road, tel. 074/972-5100, www.solishotels.com, rooms €220-270, dinner €18-32). Built in the 1860s on the site of a 15th-century castle, this five-star hotel and spa offers beautiful views of Lough Eske from many of the rooms.

INFORMATION AND SERVICES

The staff at Donegal's **tourist office** (The Quay, just south of the diamond, tel. 074/972-1148, www.irelandnorthwest.ie, www.donegal.ie, or www.donegaltown.ie, 9am-6pm Mon.-Sat. and noon-4pm Sun. July-Aug.,

9am-5pm Mon.-Sat. Sept.-June) are exceptionally helpful.

ATMs and bureaux de change are available at the **AIB** (tel. 074/972-1016), **Ulster Bank** (tel. 074/972-1064), and the **Bank of Ireland** (tel. 074/972-1079), all on the diamond. **Begley's Pharmacy** (tel. 074/972-1232) is also on the diamond.

GETTING THERE AND AROUND
Donegal Town is 65 kilometers north of Sligo on the N15, 203 kilometers north of Galway on the N15/N17, and 73 kilometers southwest of Derry City on the N15/A5. **Bus Éireann** service (tel. 074/972-1101, www.buseireann.ie, #30 from Dublin via Enniskillen, 7/day Mon.-Sat., 4/day Sun.; #64 from Derry or Galway via Sligo, 5/day Mon.-Sat., 3/day Sun.) in County Donegal is fairly spotty, but private bus companies are picking up the slack. **Feda O'Donnell** (tel. 074/954-8114 or 091/761-656, www.busfeda.ie, buses depart Galway at 9am and 4pm Mon.-Sat., plus 1:30pm and 5:30pm Fri., 3pm and 8pm Sun., return €25) can get you here from Galway City via Sligo.

Hire a cycle from the **Bike Shop** (Waterloo Pl., tel. 074/972-2515, €10/60 per day/week). To get to Waterloo Place, take Bridge Street past the castle, cross the bridge, and turn right.

For a taxi, ring **Quinn's** (tel. 087/262-0670 or 074/913-2000).

★ Rossnowlagh Beach
Rightfully known as "The Heavenly Cove" in Irish, the utterly pristine beach at **Rossnowlagh** (Ros Neamhlach, "ross-NOW-lah") extends for nearly five kilometers. Surfwise, it's a fine alternative to cheesy Bundoran farther south on Donegal Bay. The village also has the dubious distinction of hosting the only Orange Order parade in the republic (on the weekend before July 12, the anniversary of the Battle of the Boyne). There's not much going on otherwise; just make it your business to chill out (literally, if you try to go for a dip; wearing a wet suit would be smart even if you're not riding any waves).

For lunch, try the **Smuggler's Creek Inn** (tel. 071/985-2366, food served 12:30pm-8:30pm daily, closed Mon.-Tues. Oct.-Easter, €14-24), which offers hefty seafood platters and terrace seating overlooking the beach.

The area's best lodging is the four-star, family-run **Sand House Hotel** (on the beach, tel. 071/985-1777, www.sandhouse.ie, €75-100 pp), with individually designed rooms (some with four-poster beds, many with sea views), a rooftop garden, and a spa offering a full range of exotic newfangled treatments (balneotherapy, anyone?).

Rossnowlagh is 18 kilometers south of Donegal Town off the N15, and there is no public transportation.

Bundoran
An overdeveloped resort town just over the Leitrim-Donegal border, Bundoran holds little appeal unless you're a surfer. Rows upon rows of identical holiday homes conjure unpleasant thoughts of an Irish seaside Stepford. That said, wave-riders can contact **Surfworld** (Main St., tel. 071/984-1223, www.surfworld.ie) for equipment rental, or the **Donegal Adventure Centre & Surf School** (Bay View Ave., Dinglei Cush, tel. 071/984-2418, www.donegaladventurecentre.net) if in need of lessons. The center also hosts sea kayaking, canoeing, and snorkeling excursions as well as a long list of non-water sports. All others, keep on driving north.

THE GLEN HEAD PENINSULA
Killybegs
With Ireland's deepest port, **Killybegs** (Na Cealla Beaga, "The Little Churches") has a huge fleet of fishing boats and a fishmeal processing plant on the outskirts of town. Visitors tend to plug their noses at the fishy stink, but the smell isn't nearly as strong as reputed. There isn't much to see in Killybegs (outside the seafood festival in mid-August, which brings fireworks and clowns on stilts), but it's a pleasant enough town that makes a nice stopover if you're driving west from Donegal. And don't miss the gorgeous sandy

strand at **Fintragh Bay** (signposted on the R263 3 km west of town).

Take your tea at one of the harborside hotels—the **Bay View** (Main St., tel. 074/973-1950, www.bayviewhotel.info, €60-70 pp) or the **Tara** (on the harbor, tel. 074/974-1700, www.tarahotel.ie, bar food served 3pm-9pm daily, €13-30, rooms €90-130)—and watch the fishing boats bobbing on the pier and the seabirds wheeling overhead. These are also your best bets for accommodations if you decide to spend the night; the Tara has a sauna, Jacuzzi, and steam room, and ironically, the executive suites at the Bayview are far homelier than the standard rooms. The **Harbour Bar** (on the harbor, tel. 074/973-1049) is a bit of a dive, but the trad's the best in town; **Hughie's** (22 Main St., tel. 074/973-1095, www.hughiesbar.com) has live trad on Tuesday and an open mic on Wednesday.

Don't forget to hit one of the ATMs before you go: **AIB, Ulster Bank,** and the **Bank of Ireland** are all on Main Street.

Killybegs is 27 kilometers west of Donegal Town off the N56. Now affiliated with Bus Éireann, **McGeehan Coaches** (tel. 074/954-6150, www.mcgeehancoaches.com) offers regular service between Dublin, Donegal Town, Killybegs, and Glencolmcille (#490, 2-4/day daily).

Kilcar

A sleepy village between Killybegs and Glencolmcille, **Kilcar** (Cill Charthaigh, "Church of St. Cartha") makes a good base if you're taking a scenic boat trip from nearby Teelin Pier. In addition to a small tweed factory that welcomes visitors, **Studio Donegal** (west end of Main St., tel. 074/973-8194), there are two highly recommended accommodations outside the village: a hostel and a hotel, both atmospheric in their own way.

The IHH ★ **Derrylahan Hostel** (3 km past the village, signposted from the west end of Main St. and thereafter, tel. 074/973-8079, www.derrylahanhostel.ie, dorms €16-18, d €20-25, camping €8 pp) is among the county's best. Shaun McCloskey will greet

you with tea and biscuits—he's the sweetest hostel owner you'll ever meet. Derrylahan is a working farm, and fresh eggs are available for purchase. There's a warm, well-stocked kitchen, cozy common rooms, and en suite rooms in the adjacent building suitable for families. If you don't have wheels, ring Shaun and he'll gladly pick you up. Or if taking the bus, ask the driver to drop you off at "The Rock, Kilcar," which means you'll only have to walk half a kilometer to get there. A 20-minute walk downhill from the hostel leads to the wonderfully sheltered, utterly pristine **Kilcar Strand** (also known as **Portahowley**).

Just over five kilometers east of Kilcar is the **Blue Haven Hotel** (Killybegs Rd., Largymore, tel. 074/973-8090, www.blue-haven.ie, €50-60 pp, food served 12:30pm-9:30pm Mon.-Sat., 3pm-9pm Sun., €11-24), modern yet not at all institutional. The open, airy "dome" lounge is a great spot for an aperitif, and you'll hear mainly Irish spoken at the neighboring tables. The food is just adequate, but at least the prices are reasonable, and the service is cordial and unpretentious. Next door, the elegant **Inishduff House** (tel. 074/973-8542, www.inishduffhouse.com, closed Jan., €40 pp sharing) offers a warm traditional welcome along with the amazing sea views you simply can't find at the few B&Bs in town. You can order a packed picnic basket for lunch.

Kilcar is 12 kilometers west of Killybegs on the R263; make a withdrawal there before you get here, though there's a bureau de change at the newsagent on Main Street if you need it. **Bus Éireann** (#420, 2-4/day Mon.-Sat., 1-2 Sun.) can get you here from Donegal Town.

Teelin

Boat excursions depart from the pier at **Teelin** (Teileann) west of Kilcar. Book one of twelve seats on the *Nuala Star* with **Sliabh Liag Boat Trips** (tel. 074/973-9365 or 087/628-4688, www.sliabhleagueboattrips.com, 90-minute trip €20-35). You'll see birds and dolphins along with the breathtaking Slieve League cliffs. Full- or half-day fishing charters

Irish Phrases

You won't hear a whole lot of Irish spoken outside the Gaeltachtaí, but it's worth picking up a few phrases even if you aren't planning to venture into the farthest reaches of Donegal, Dingle, or Galway. There is now a "standard" dialect using a mix of the three dialects—Connaught (Galway and Mayo), Munster (Kerry, Cork, and Waterford), and Ulster (Donegal)—but Donegal tallies the most native speakers, so here's a quick primer using that dialect. (After all, who speaks textbook Irish outside the classroom? You should be understood wherever you go, and if someone feigns confusion just inform them you're trying out some Donegal Irish.)

- **Welcome** — *Fáilte romhat* (FALL-cheh ROE-it)
- **Hello** — *Dia duit* (GEE-a ditch; literally, "God to you")
- **Hello (to more than one)** — *Dia daoibh* (GEE-a deev)
- **Hello (response)** — *Dia is Muire duit* (GEE-a iss MAU-rya ditch; literally, "God and Mary to you")
- **Goodbye** — *Slán, slán go foill,* or *slán abhaile* (slawn, slawn go foll, slawn a-WALL-eh; literally, "safe," "safe yet," or "safe home")
- **Thank you** — *Go raibh maith agat* (go row MY AH-gut; literally, "may good be at you")
- **Thank you (to more than one)** — *Go raibh maith agaibh* (go row MY AH-give)
- **Please** — *Le do thoil* (leh doe HULL)
- **Excuse me** — *Gabh mo leithscéal* (go mo LESH-cull; literally, "take my apology")
- **We would like to go to . . .** — *Bá mhaith linn dul go dtí . . .* (bah why linn JUL go JEE)
- **I would like a pint** — *Bá mhaith liom pionta* (bah why lum PYUN-tah)
- **Cheers!** — *Sláinte!* (SLAWN-cheh)

are available as well. Those who wish to walk Slieve League can arrange a drop-off in Malinbeg after taking the cruise. To get to the Teelin Pier from Killybegs or Kilcar, take the R263 to Carrick, turn left just before the Óstán Sliabh Liag (it's signposted), and proceed five kilometers to the pier. On the way, you'll pass the **Slieve League Cultural Centre** (tel. 074/973-9077 or 087/770-6334, www.sliabhleaguecliffs.ie, 10am-7pm daily in summer), which dispenses tourist information and organizes hill-walking and archaeology tours. It has a craft shop and a tearoom with homebaked goods.

Glencolmcille

Dotted with Neolithic and early Christian tomb markers, lovely **Glencolmcille** (Gleann Cholm Cille, "Glen of Columba's Church"), with its rolling moorland punctuated by the occasional glade, is within the Donegal Gaeltacht. This is a parish on the western end of the Glen Head Peninsula (also known as the Slieve League Peninsula) comprising five villages; Cashel, the easternmost, has most of the pubs and shops (not that there are many of either!). Sights and accommodations are spread out along the R263 west to the hamlets of Malinmore and Malinbeg.

Glencolmcille is connected to the tweed center of Ardara via the wild and moorgrass-strewn **Glengesh Pass** between the Glengesh and Mulmosog Mountains. The view from the summit, 275 meters above sea level, is as exhilarating in fine weather as it is desolate in the rain.

SIGHTS

An Cláchan, the **Glencolmcille Folk Village** (on the R263 1.5 km west of Cashel, tel. 074/973-0017, www.glenfolkvillage. com, 10am-6pm Mon.-Sat., noon-6pm Sun. Easter-Sept., €4.50) features three cottages furnished to look like authentic 18th-, 19th-, and early-20th-century homes along with a barn and schoolhouse, the idea being that you can see firsthand how your ancestors lived. "Rustic" doesn't quite capture the scene, especially regarding the oldest cottage! The museum was opened in 1967 by Father James McDyer, who opened a cooperative here in the 1950s in an effort to curb emigration. It's the biggest tourist draw in the area, no less worth seeing for its popularity with coach tours. A craft shop, tearoom, and bakery are also on the premises, and there are traditional music sessions in the evenings in high season.

ACTIVITIES AND RECREATION

Part of the Gaeltacht Way, **Slí Cholmcille** (St. Columba's Way) links Glencolmcille with Ardara, 70 kilometers to the north. A far less strenuous alternative is **Trabane Strand** in Malinbeg, a long strand tucked beneath a cliff and accessible by a vertiginous concrete staircase; there's another sandy beach just across the road from the Glencolmcille Folk Village.

Formerly known as the Malinmore Adventure Centre, the refurbished **Áras Ghleann Cholm Cille** (on the R263 in Malinmore, tel. 074/973-0077, www.arasgcc. com) offers the gamut of water-sporting activities as well as accommodation.

FOOD AND ENTERTAINMENT

Dining options are paltry indeed. Your best option is on the road west of Cashel, at **An Chistin** ("The Kitchen," tel. 074/973-0213, noon-9pm daily, €7-12), a delightful spot where Irish language students at Oideas Gael come for a sandwich or snack.

Three pubs stand along Cashel's main street—the **Glen Head Tavern** (tel. 074/973-0008), **Roarty's** (tel. 074/973-0273, www. roartys.com), and **Biddy's** (at the Cashel crossroads, tel. 074/973-0016). Of these, Biddy's has the best *craic*—live trad most summer nights, two open fires, and cheeky barstaff to match the plaques on the walls ("dirty old men need love too").

Glencolmcille is home to one of Ireland's most outstanding Irish language schools, **Oideas Gael** (on the R263, tel. 074/973-0248, www.oideas-gael.com), which offers weekend and weeklong language immersion, music, and art courses April-August.

SHOPPING

If tweed and knitwear are what you're after, look for the family-owned **Glencolmcille Woolen Mill Shop** (tel. 074/973-0070, www. rossanknitwear.ie), which is clearly signposted on the local road to Malinmore. It may be a popular coach bus stop, but the tweeds and sweaters made on the premises are well worth a browse.

ACCOMMODATIONS

As you'll find elsewhere in Donegal, hostels are a popular option even for those not on a budget. The local hotel has closed, and B&Bs are hard to come by.

The **Dooey Hostel** (Cashel, signposted off the R263 at the Glenhead Tavern, 1.5 km up a bumpy road, tel. 074/973-0130, dooeyhostel@ gleanncholmcille.ie, dorms €15, camping €10 pp) is one of Ireland's most distinctive hostels. It's built into the mountainside, so when you open the front door you'll find a sloping rocky wall covered in ivy on your left and paper lanterns overhead (a vaguely tropical effect, were it not for the temperature). Delightful "Mad Mary" O'Donnell serves tea, biscuits, and a generous dose of wry pessimism on your arrival. Each eight-bed dorm has its own kitchen and bathroom, and there are six kitchens in all. The beds aren't terribly comfy, however, and the hostel is nonsmoking in name only. If you need creature comforts (like real mattresses and en suite showers) and don't mind the relative lack of character, stay at the purpose-built **Malinbeg Hostel** (Malinbeg, 9 km west of Cashel at the end of the R263, www.malinbeghostel.com, tel. 074/973-0006, dorms €15, private rooms €14-19 pp), which offers family and private rooms as well as dorms. There's a small grocery directly across the street. Both hostels have amazing sea views.

INFORMATION AND SERVICES

Be sure to withdraw money in Killybegs, as there is no ATM in this remote locale. The Cashel post office does change money, however. The best source of tourist info is the **Glencolmcille Folk Village** three kilometers west of Cashel.

GETTING THERE AND AROUND

The village of Cashel in Glencolmcille parish is 26 kilometers west of Killybegs and 53 kilometers west of Donegal on the R263. Affiliated with Bus Éireann, **McGeehan Coaches** (tel. 074/954-6150, www.mcgeehancoaches.com) offers regular service between Dublin, Donegal Town, Killybegs, and Glencolmcille (#490, 2-4/day daily).

★ Slieve League

One of Donegal's most exhilarating experiences is the eight-kilometer trek along the **Slieve League** (Sliabh Liag) cliffs—at 300-600 meters, these are the highest sea cliffs in Europe. The cliffs start at **Bunglás** (6 km west of Teelin), and the hiking track will take you up One Man's Pass to the summit of Sliabh Liag before winding down at **Trabane Strand** (An Trá Bán) near Malinbeg. South of Bunglás is a much easier option, the "Slieve League view walk," affording you prime photo ops from the south (rather than directly above the cliffs, as on the hike).

Coming from Killybegs, take a left at the **Slieve League Lodge** (tel. 074/973-9973, www.slieveleaguelodge.com; they welcome tourist inquiries) onto the Teelin road. Pass through Teelin village and a fork in the road will appear: If you want to do the easy scenic walk, make a left for Bunglás, and you'll come to a gate fastened with rope; open the gate, drive through, close the gate again, leave your

car in the car park on the left, and proceed for 1.5 kilometers along the winding path.

But if you're up for the hike, take the right at that fork in the road after Teelin and drive for another 2.5 kilometers until the road ends. This is where you begin the four- to five-hour hike up to One Man's Pass and Trabane Strand. Be extremely careful when walking the often-muddy track, as gale-force winds have been known to blow hikers over the edge. Be sure to follow the ridge to avoid slipping in the mud.

Driving yourself to Bunglás presents its own logistical challenge, of course, since you'll have to find a ride back to your vehicle afterward. Contact Joe or Aidan at **Sliabh Liag Tours** (Teelin, tel. 087/286-0471 or 087/671-1944, www.sliabhliagtours.ie), who can either drop you off and meet you afterward, or take you along the scenic route south of Bunglás if you're not up for hiking. But if you are, check out the tips and resources on the **Sliabh Liag Hillwalkers** club website (www.sliabhliagwalkers.com) before you go.

Ardara

A pleasant town with a long handweaving tradition, **Ardara** (ar-DRAH, Ard an Rátha, "Height of the Circular Fort") straddles the trickly River Owentocker at the mouth of Loughros Bay. Other than shopping for tweeds and admiring the **Eas A' Ranca waterfall** (8 km west of town), there isn't a lot to occupy you in the town itself—but it's a good place to spend the night before heading up to Gweedore. Farther afield, the **Kilclooney dolmen** (6.1 km north of Ardara, 400 m east off the R261) reportedly dates from 3500 BC and probably has the country's second-largest capstone (after Browne's Hill in Carlow).

ACTIVITIES AND RECREATION

Ardara is on the **Slí Cholmcille** portion of the Gaeltacht Way, which links the town with Glencolmcille (a distance of 70 kilometers).

Bicycle nine kilometers west of town to **Loughros Head** (on a local road, signposted at the western edge of town). For pony treks along the beaches of Loughros Bay, contact **Castleview Equestrian** (Kilcashel, Ardara, 4 km outside town, tel. 087/275-1334), which also provides B&B accommodations. Follow the sign for Loughros Point from the western end of town, proceed for two kilometers, and you'll see the Castleview turnoff signposted on your left.

FOOD AND ENTERTAINMENT

Your dining options are slim. **Charlie's West Side Café** (Main St., tel. 074/954-1656, 9:30am-10pm daily, under €12) is a relatively classy "chipper" known for its fresh fish. This café also does sandwiches, lasagna, and such-like. It gets quite packed with locals in the evenings.

The best pub in town is **Nancy's** (Front St., tel. 074/954-1187, www.nancysardara.com, food served noon-9pm daily, under €10), which attracts an eccentric older crowd. It feels a bit like having a pint in your grandmother's living room, especially with the collection of porcelain mugs and milk saucers hanging above the tiny bar. There's basic pub grub (and, humorously, only one menu to go around).

Nancy's often has live music, but the town's best venue is **The Corner House** (The Diamond, tel. 074/954-1736). Ardara's *other* best pub has live trad nightly in summer and weekends in the winter. Visiting musicians are welcome to join in alongside the owner, Peter Oliver, who plays a slew of instruments (though only one at a time).

Sadly, most of the other pubs in town have been renovated out of their traditional charm.

SHOPPING

Tweed-stocked gift shops line the main drag, the largest of which is **Kennedy's** (Front St., tel. 074/954-1106). Another big shop on the Donegal end of town, **Tríona Design** (tel. 074/954-1422, www.trionadesign.com), which specializes in classy tweed jackets and trousers, also has a café. Farther along the

Donegal road is the flagship store of **John Molloy** (tel. 074/954-1133, www.johnmolloy.com), uncrowned king of tweed. Along with locally made jumpers, jackets, and other wooly goods, you can also purchase tweed by the yard.

Purists will want to patronize the handweavers, however. **Eddie Doherty** (Front St., tel. 074/954-1304, www.handwoventweed.com) does comfy throws, ponchos, and shearling-lined slippers; call in to Doherty's pub next door if there's no one in the shop.

ACCOMMODATIONS

Ardara has an excellent guesthouse, ★ **Drumbarron B&B** (The Diamond, tel. 074/954-1200, jfeeneyardara@eircom.net , €40 pp). Mrs. Feeney will greet you with tea, freshly made scones, and blackberry jam. The decor is stylishly eclectic; you'll find a cheerful fire, a selection of classic books, and comfy leather armchairs in the sitting room, and the beds have down comforters *and* electric heating pads. Breakfast is lovingly prepared and cheerfully served.

Set on a hill overlooking the lush highland countryside, the Georgian **Woodhill House** (about 1 km outside Ardara, tel. 074/954-1112, www.woodhillhouse.com, Jan.-Oct., restaurant Mar.-Oct., €48-75 pp) was once the home of the Nesbits, Ireland's last commercial whalers. This outstanding guesthouse features a French-inspired restaurant using local produce and fish from Killybegs, a small, cozy bar, and a delightful garden through an old stone archway. Nancy and John Yates are genuinely friendly—the ideal hosts. To get here, go straight through the diamond (rather than following Main Street as it curves left toward the bridge), and you'll see Woodhill signposted at the fork in the road (take a right). If you're driving up from Donegal, you can also get here off the N56; it's signposted about a kilometer outside town. (Also consider Woodhill as an alternative to the Nesbitt Arms Hotel in town, which is mediocre at best.)

INFORMATION AND SERVICES

Whether or not you're interested in the history of the local tweed industry, the **Ardara Heritage Centre** (Main St., tel. 074/954-1704, 10am-6pm Mon.-Sat. and 2pm-6pm Sun. Easter-Sept., free) is a good place to ask questions. **Tríona Design** (tel. 074/954-1422, www.irishhouse.com) on the west end of town offers visitor information as well.

Hit the ATM at the **Ulster Bank** on the diamond. The **Ardara Pharmacy** (tel. 074/954-1120) is on Main Street, just before the bridge.

GETTING THERE AND AROUND

Ardara is 37 kilometers northwest of Donegal Town and 16 kilometers north of Killybegs on the N56. Getting here by public transport is tricky: **Bus Éireann** (tel. 074/912-1309) route #492 links Donegal Town with Ardara, leaving at 9:30am and arriving in Killybegs at 10:15am, with a layover until noon (Mon.-Fri., runs end June to end Aug.); there's another bus at 4:05pm that gets to Killybegs at 4:50pm (Mon.-Fri. all year), and the connection departs 10 minutes later. The return times are also infrequent. **Feda O'Donnell** (tel. 091/761-656 or 074/954-8144, www.busfeda. ie, return €25) offers a Friday-only service from Galway City at 4pm (during the school

year only) and 5:30pm, departing Ardara at 3:30pm Sunday and 8:50am Monday.

Don Byrne (the west end of Main St., tel. 074/954-1658, www.donbyrnebikes.com, €17/80 per day/week), a Raleigh agent, will rent you a bike. Ring **Gerard McHugh** (tel. 087/648-8628, gmchughtravel@gmail.com) for a cab; he's also available for tours of Slieve League.

NORTHWESTERN DONEGAL
★ Glenveagh National Park

Like Killarney National Park in County Kerry, the centerpiece of **Glenveagh National Park** (Gleann Bheatha, "Glen of the Birches") is a Victorian manor house, the fanciful-looking Glenveagh Castle. Covering 160 square kilometers, the park is best known for its proliferation of red deer and rhododendrons, both of which were introduced by Adelia Adair, mistress of the castle. Early summer is the best time of year to visit the park, when the rhododendrons are in full bloom. Other park wildlife includes badgers, hares, stoats, foxes, and the golden eagle, reintroduced in 2000 after a 100-year absence caused by over-hunting.

On the park's western side is Mount

Dramatic windswept vistas abound at Glenveagh National Park.

Errigal, the county's highest peak. The park also encompasses Lakes Dunlewey, Beagh, and Gartan, and the romantic-sounding Poisoned Glen, whose name is the result of a simple misspelling (the Irish name was An Gleann Neamhe, "The Heavenly Glen," which an English cartographer transcribed as An Gleann Neimhe—you can guess what that means).

The national park **visitors center** (entrance off the R251 10 km east of Dunlewey, tel. 074/913-7090, 10am-6pm Feb.-Nov., free) offers a 20-minute audiovisual covering the usual botany and fauna, as well as the stories behind the castle's colorful succession of owners.

Eight kilometers south of the visitors center is the **Glebe House and Gallery** (on Lough Gartan, off the 251, tel. 074/913-7071, www. glebegallery.ie, 11am-6:30pm daily Easter week and July-Aug., Sat.-Thurs. June and Sept.-mid-Oct., €4), which features works by Picasso and Jack B. Yeats—though access is by guided tour only.

There are five signposted walks in Glenveagh National Park, the shortest being 5 kilometers, the longest 22 kilometers. Rule 1: Always wear your bug spray. Pick up a can before you get here, because the midges will bite you something fearsome if you don't.

GLENVEAGH CASTLE

Dúchas-run **Glenveagh Castle** (tel. 074/913-7090, 10am-6:30pm daily Feb.-Nov., €5, plus optional €1.50 one-way shuttle bus fare), built of granite by John Adair in 1870, is nestled between the Derryveagh and Glendowan Mountains on the southern shore of Lough Beagh. The beauty of Adair's estate belies a tragic history: He was a cruel landlord who in April 1861 ruthlessly evicted 244 of his tenants—simply because their presence was spoiling his view!

Professor Arthur Kingsley Porter, an art historian from Harvard University, purchased the castle in 1929 and lived there with his wife until his mysterious disappearance on Inishbofin (an island off the coast of Donegal; not to be confused with the Inishbofin of County Galway) four years later. An American guest of the Porters, Henry McIlhenny, purchased it from Mrs. Porter in 1938, redecorated the mansion, and restored the gardens with great care and attention. Both Porter and McIlhenny entertained a parade of writers, artists, academics, and aristocrats at Glenveagh; as Brian de Breffny writes of this place, "Few are not enchanted by the blaze of rhododendron in June, by the statue-garden, the rose-garden, the mysterious moss-garden on the mountainside and the shimmering lake, and by the atmosphere of the house and the beauty of the furnishings."

If you aren't that interested in examining the china, hunting trophies, and fancy furniture of country manor houses, then you should skip the tour and just enjoy the grounds. Admission is free to the visitors center, and there's a restaurant open from mid-April through September as well as a very charming (if at peak times chaotic) tearoom open daily in high season and weekends in winter.

MOUNT ERRIGAL

Almost perfectly conical, **Mount Errigal** (An tEargail) is visually striking for its cap of white quartzite. At 752 meters, Errigal sounds more formidable than it really is; the reasonably fit can scale it on the five-kilometer "tourist route" in two hours or less. The 3.5-kilometer alternative walk along the scree-covered northwestern ridge is more difficult and is a popular training route for hardcore climbers with loftier ambitions (pun intended). The popular route approaches from the south, beginning at a ruined gateway on the R251 by a bridge just west of Dunlewey village.

Stop in at the national park visitors center or the Dunlewey Lakeside Centre for more detailed information before attempting either route. For either hike, be sure to pick up OS map 1.

DUNLEWEY

You could barely call it a village, but **Dunlewey** (Dún Lúiche, "Fort of Lú") attracts plenty of backpackers in summer for its location under Donegal's highest peak. The brand-new eco-conscious **Errigal Hostel** (on the R251, tel. 074/953-1180, errigalhostel@gmail.com, Mar.-Oct., dorm beds €17-19) is situated right at the foot of the mountain. Along with a cozy sitting room/library and self-service laundry, there's full breakfast (€5.50, includes veg option), packed or eat-in lunches (€5.50/6), and dinner (€10), which is handy seeing as there's no place else to eat! You'll find an ATM as well as groceries at the neighboring petrol station.

Unfortunately, public transportation is so limited in this part of the county that shoestring travelers often end up hitching to get to Dunlewey. There are much livelier places from which to base yourself—such as Bunbeg or Dunfanaghy—but those who aren't all that into the pub culture will find Dunlewey's tranquility a welcome change.

B&Bs are rare along this stretch, but one to recommend is **Glen Heights** (tel. 074/956-0844 or 087/218-8632, www.glenheightsbb.com, €35-40 pp sharing), a lovely dormer with a breakfast conservatory and front patio overlooking Lough Dunlewey. It's signposted from the R251 two kilometers east of the village; make a right at the Poisoned Glen turnoff and continue for about one kilometer. You'll see another sign for the B&B on your left, up a steep driveway.

Mostly of interest to families is **Ionad Cois Locha,** the Dunlewey Lakeside Centre (turn-off at Lakeside Backpackers, tel. 074/953-1699, www.dunleweycentre.com, 10:30am-6pm Mon.-Sat. and 11am-6pm Sun. mid-Mar.-Oct., €10), in the restored home of local hand-weaver Manus Ferry, who died in 1975. There are weaving demonstrations and an audiovisual as well as a boat trip on Lake Dunlewey, narrated with area history and folklore. It's worth stopping by for the cozy café with open turf fire.

Dunlewey is 11 kilometers east of Bunbeg on the R251 and 40 kilometers west of Letterkenny. There is no public transport.

Gweedore

Tucked between the Atlantic and the Derryveagh Mountain range in northwestern Donegal, the parish of Gweedore ("ghee DOH-wer," with a hard "g"; Gaoth Dobhair, "Inlet of the Water") is a visual feast of boggy hills, glens, lakes, and shimmering sea beyond an undulating coastline. You'll also find Ireland's largest community of native Irish speakers.

In Gweedore you'll hear some of the best traditional music sessions on the island; the region has produced many outstanding musicians and groups, among them Clannad on the "first wave" of traditionally influenced Irish "supergroups" in the 1970s, Altan singer Mairéad Ní Mhaonaigh, and Enya. Writing of Altan for *Hot Press*, writer Bill Graham called Gweedore a "slippery and elastic concept and state of mind," but this is often the case when an outsider confuses "village" and "parish." There may be a point labeled Gweedore on your road map, but the name actually applies to the whole region.

It isn't quite as remote as you may have heard, though—not anymore. Ongoing development (cute little holiday homes especially) has scattered the villages of **Bunbeg** (Bun Beag, "Little Root") and **Derrybeg** (Doirí Beaga, "Little Oaks") for several kilometers along the R257. Named for the crimson-hued sunset over the Atlantic, the **Bloody Foreland** (Cnoc Fola) at the northwest tip of Gweedore is arguably the singlemost breathtaking vista in the county—just keep driving north on the R257 from Derrybeg.

Since Gweedore is so spread out, getting around can be a pain without a rental car, but it can be done. If you need a taxi in the area, try **Popeye's Cabs** (tel. 087/248-3888 or 074/953-2633) or **Patrick McFadden** (tel. 074/953-1187). You'll find most of the action in and around the village of Bunbeg; the ATM and bureau de change are there, too, at the **AIB** on Main Street (the R257, tel. 074/953-1077).

Long-Distance Walks in County Donegal

A 111-kilometer stretch of the 900-kilometer **Ulster Way** is located in County Donegal. Beginning in tiny Pettigo on the border, this stretch hugs Lough Derg through the Bluestack and Derryveagh Mountains and into Falcarragh. If basing yourself in Gweedore, you might want to walk part of this route, which forks off the Poison Glen Horseshoe Trail inside Glenveagh National Park.

Another option is the 117-kilometer **Bluestack Way,** which begins just east of Donegal Town, winding around Lough Eske before meandering through the Bluestack Mountains northwest to Ardara. From there, you can join the 70-kilometer **Slí Cholmcille** (St. Colmcille's Way), which loops around Glencolmcille on the Glen Head Peninsula, passing through Carrick, Kilcar, and the Glengesh Pass. This is one of a series of circular walks in Donegal known as the **Bealach na Gaeltachta,** with 290 kilometers of walking trails in all.

Far less traveled is the eerie **Tullaghobegley Walk** ("tull-o-BEG-lee") from Gweedore to Falcarragh, a route used for carrying corpses to the nearest consecrated ground dating back to the 13th century. The five- to six-hour, 11-kilometer walk begins at **Loch na Cuinge,** or Lough Nacung, just east of the village of Gweedore. The route takes you over a mountain called **Taobh an Leithid** (430 meters), with superb panoramic views despite a crop of windmills; local hikers pause for rest at the summit, where you'll find seven cairns. It's tradition to add a rock to the cairns as you pass. Tullaghobegley is not waymarked, so Ordnance Survey Discovery Series map #1 is even more essential; **Údarás na Gaeltachta** in Derrybeg (Páirc Ghnó Ghaoth Dobhair, tel. 074/956-0100, www.udaras.ie) has maps on offer as well. Do not attempt to walk alone, as the weather's inconstancy can pose navigational dilemmas no matter how trusty your compass.

For more information on all walking routes, stop first at the Donegal Town tourist office. The hosts of your B&B can also be a great source of information.

There's no tourist office, but the locals here are some of the friendliest, most eager-to-help folks on the planet.

Patrick Gallagher (tel. 074/953-1107 or 087/233-0888, www.gallagherscoaches.com, ring for fares) provides a one-a-day bus service (two on Friday during the school year) from Belfast to Gweedore (at the Bunbeg crossroads) via Derry, Letterkenny, and Dunfanaghy. The bus leaves Jury's Hotel in Belfast (at 5:30pm Mon.-Sat. and 9:15pm Sun., arriving in Bunbeg at 8:45pm and 12:30am, respectively).

BUNBEG

Six kilometers west of the village of Gweedore is Bunbeg, still laid-back and delightful despite ongoing development. The quaint, tiny Bunbeg Harbour is signposted on the southern end of the village, and from here you can board ferries to Gola or Tory Islands via **Donegal Coastal Cruises** (tel. 074/953-1320, www.toryislandferry.com, daily service Apr.-Oct., weekdays only Nov.-Mar., return fare €20).

One of the best B&Bs in the area is ★ **Teach Champbell** (Bunbeg village, signposted on the left on the R257 a few houses past the AIB, tel. 074/953-1545, www.teac-campbell.com, €35 pp, s €38), a cheerful, deceptively spacious home clad in ivy. The Campbells are lovely people, and you'll feel like you're staying with an old family friend. The back bedrooms have views of Gweebarra Bay. This is a great place to practice your *Gaeilge bhriste* (broken Irish). Another great accommodation, **Bunbeg House** (signposted off the R257, tel. 074/953-1305, www.bunbeg-house.com, €35-40 pp, s €40-45), has a quaint location right on the Bunbeg pier, two kilometers south of the village center—though perhaps the best reason to stay here is the tiny pub and restaurant downstairs.

Gweedore's best hotel is the Óstán Radharc na Mara, the **Sea View Hotel** (on the R257 in the village center, tel.

074/953-1159, www.seaviewhotelgweedore.
com, €55-70 pp sharing). Rooms are comfortable but no-frills (unless you count the trouser press); it's the surprisingly good restaurant (with an open turf fire) and the pub, **Hughie Tim's,** that make the Sea View special. Hughie Tim's is one of the locals' favorite watering holes. The only caveat is the nightclub noise on the weekends; if you aren't planning to dance the night away (no cover for hotel guests), be sure to request a room on the far side of the hotel. The breakfast is outstanding.

A five-minute walk south on the R575 brings you to **Teach Hudí Beag** (tel. 074/953-1016), an unselfconsciously traditional pub offering Gweedore's biggest (up to a dozen musicians!) and best trad session on Monday nights. Whatever you do, don't miss this one.

CROLLY
Tourists and locals alike flock to Leo's Tavern, **Tábhairne Leo** (Meenalick, Crolly, on the R259, signposted from the N56 south of Bunbeg, turnoff right after Paidi Og's pub in Crolly, tel. 074/954-8143, food served 5pm-8:30pm Mon.-Fri. and 1pm-8:30pm weekends, €12-24), because Leo is the father of Enya, that eerily ageless goddess of New Age. This isn't one of those crusty old man's pubs where you can kick back with a pint and a feeling of relative anonymity; it's quite modern on the inside, with too-bright lighting and loud-mouthed American college students often taking up half the tables. That said, the bar food is decent, and there's live music most nights. Plus, you never know which famous Irish songbird you might spot.

FALCARRAGH
The real reason to mention workaday **Falcarragh** (An Fál Carrach, "The Rocky Fence"), 22 kilometers northeast of Bunbeg on the R258 and N56—which is not actually in Gweedore, but just outside it—is the historic **Tullaghobegley Walk,** which starts near the village of Gweedore and ends here. For a lift back to Bunbeg, ring **Joe's Taxis** (Main

St., tel. 074/916-5017) or **Manus McGee** (tel. 087/244-6198).

From Falcarragh, if driving, you can take **Muckish Drive** south through the Derryveagh Mountains, eventually hitting the R251, the northern border of the national park, between Dunlewey and the park entrance. You'll pass plenty of rock- and heather-strewn hills on melancholy Muckish Drive, but you won't see anyone for miles. There are no houses or any other kind of development along this stretch.

GETTING THERE AND AROUND
To cut down on travel time, consider flying directly from Dublin into Aerfort Dhún na nGall, the **Donegal Airport** (Carrickfinn, Kincasslagh, 14 km south of Bunbeg on the R266, signposted turnoff at Crolly on the N56, tel. 074/954-8284, www.donegalairport.ie). **Aer Lingus** (tel. 1890/800-600, www.aerlingus.ie) offers two daily flights to/from Dublin (40 minutes), and there's a flight from Glasgow Prestwick on Sunday, Wednesday, and Friday. You can rent a car with **Avis** (tel. 074/954-8469, www.avis.ie), though you might not be able to get one with automatic transmission.

Dunfanaghy
A delightfully understated resort town of Presbyterian origins, **Dunfanaghy** ("done-FAN-a-hee," Dún Fionnachaidh, "Fort of the Fair-Haired Tribe") is a popular vacation spot for Northern families—yet it's never too crowded, even in peak season. The range of accommodations and variety of exhilarating walks nearby (out to Horn Head, or the wonderfully secluded Tramore Strand), plus its proximity (23 kilometers) to Glenveagh National Park, make Dunfanaghy a fine place to base yourself for a few days.

SIGHTS
If you're feeling even an ounce of self-pity for whatever reason, a visit to **The Workhouse Museum** (just outside town on the N56/Falcarragh Rd., tel. 074/913-6540, www.

dunfanaghyworkhouse.ie, 10am-5pm Mon.-Sat., noon-5pm Sun. mid-Mar.-Sept., €4.50) is a sure-fire way to snap out of it. The exhibit, using mannequins inside life-size dioramas, tells the life story of "Wee Hannah" Herritty, a local woman who spent years wasting away in the 19th-century workhouse on this site. You walk from room to room and listen to "Hannah" speak matter-of-factly of the various horrors she endured in this very building, and the ground-floor rooms give more straightforward information about the workhouse using old photographs and a brief audiovisual. The "wee Hannah" bit might sound like a weird combination of the macabre and the cheesy, but it's a real eye-opener for those who know little about this horrible aspect of Irish history (which is nearly all of us). Fortunately, Hannah eventually found a way out of here and lived to the ripe old age of 90.

The museum has a pleasant tearoom and a gift shop, and the staff are a good source for tourist info.

ACTIVITIES AND RECREATION

Whatever you do, don't leave Dunfanaghy without walking or driving out to **Horn Head** (clearly signposted from the Falcarragh end of town). It's an exhilarating hour-long walk up a few steep, quiet residential lanes out to a heather-covered headland with dazzling clifftop (just under 200 meters high) views of the sea and Tramore Strand to the west.

If there's time, make a detour to the pristine **Tramore Strand** on your way back to town. Turn left immediately after crossing the Horn Head Bridge (or before, if you're coming back from the headland), where you'll find three stone steps down to a small wooden gate. Pastures lie beyond it (as well as a football pitch), but you'll see a path worn through the short grass. It'll take roughly half an hour to get from bridge to strand.

Another Blue Flag strand, **Marble Hill Beach,** lies three kilometers east of Dunfanaghy in the village of Portnablagh.

Fancy a canter along the strand? **Dunfanaghy Stables** (Arnold's Hotel, Main St., tel. 074/913-6208, www.dunfanaghystables.com) can accommodate. The **Dunfanaghy Golf Club** (just east of town off the N59, tel. 074/913-6335, www.dunfanaghygolfclub.com) has one of the most scenic courses you'll ever play.

FOOD

Don't leave town without stopping at **Muck 'n Muffins** (The Square, tel. 074/913-6780, 9:30am-6pm Mon.-Sat. and 10am-6pm Sun. Mar.-Nov., 9:30am-5pm Mon.-Sat. Dec.-Feb., under €7) for a cappuccino. There's a pottery and gift shop on the ground floor and a delightful, friendly café upstairs. You can have a basic-but-tasty lunch (and fabulous desserts) overlooking the garden center next door, teeming with herbs and flowers, and Sheephaven Bay beyond. On Friday night in high season (Saturday too, if the town is jumpin') and holiday weekends in winter, the café transforms into a wine bar serving up antipasto platters and plenty of atmosphere.

For pub grub, **Danny Collins** (Main St., tel. 074/913-6205, food served noon-8pm daily, under €12) is pretty much the only option in town. The menu at **Arnold's Hotel** (Main St., tel. 074/913-6208, food served noon-9pm daily, €8-20) is far tastier and more creative than your average hotel fare.

But the area's finest restaurant is **The Mill** (signposted on the Falcarragh Rd./N56 just outside town, tel. 074/913-6985, www.themillrestaurant.com, 7pm-9pm Wed.-Sun. May-Sept., plus Tues. July-Aug., Fri.-Sun. in low season, set dinner €38, reservations required). You're guaranteed an otherworldly gourmet meal from chef and owner Derek Alcorn, be it lamb, lobster, or slow-roasted duck.

ENTERTAINMENT

Not that there's a whole lot of competition for the title, but the best pub in town is **Danny Collins** (Main St., tel. 074/913-6205), with live trad most nights in summer. Because of its jukebox and television above the bar, **McColgan's** (Main St., tel. 074/910-0947) tends to attract a younger crowd for live blues and rock music several nights a week in high season.

SHOPPING
McAuliffe's (Main St., tel. 074/913-6135) stocks the gamut of souvenirs, from Aran sweaters to locally made greeting cards and Sex-on-the-Beach-scented incense. On a more prosaic note, Ordnance Survey maps are also for sale.

But if it's pottery you're looking for, skip the assembly-line mugs and plates at McAuliffe's for the goods at **Muck'n Muffins** (The Square, tel. 074/913-6780, www.muckn-muffins.com). You can watch the girls at their wheels in the open workshop area. For quality antiques as well as oil and watercolor paintings, visit **The Gallery** (just outside town on the N56/Falcarragh Rd., tel. 074/913-6224, www.thegallerydunfanaghy.com).

ACCOMMODATIONS
Another of Donegal's best hostels is ★ **Corcreggan Mill** (3 km southwest of Dunfanaghy on the N56, tel. 074/913-6409, www.corcreggan.com, dorms €20, private rooms €30-40 pp). Army man Brendan Rohan spent years lovingly fixing up the place, converting a 120-year-old railway carriage into a row of five private rooms using other recycled materials. The kitchen and dining facilities are excellent, and the sitting room with its open fire, comfy armchairs, and spare guitar is second to none. Those not driving should note the hostel's distance from town—it's a 40-minute walk by day along the busy road, but at night you'll need to ring a taxi. And for those who don't fancy spending the night in a sometimes-drafty railway car, Corcreggan Mill also offers en suite B&B accommodations in another restored building on the premises.

On the Falcarragh end of Dunfanaghy's Main Street is a good B&B, **The Willows** (tel. 074/913-6446, www.thewillowsdunfanaghy. com, €40 pp). Electric heating pads, small refrigerators to keep the milk for your tea (no plastic-cup creamers here!), and the open turf fire in the sitting room are all great reasons to stay here. Besides having a fine gourmet restaurant, **The Mill** (signposted on the Falcarragh Rd., tel. 074/913-6985, www.themillrestaurant.com, €55-70 pp) is also the one of the classiest places to stay in Dunfanaghy. The great thing about **Arnold's Hotel** (Main St., tel. 074/913-6208, Apr.-Nov., €70-110 pp), besides the above-average restaurant fare, is that you can arrange bird-watching, horseback riding, or painting excursions.

INFORMATION AND SERVICES
Dunfanaghy has no tourist office, so your best source of info is the **heritage center** (just north of town on the N56, tel. 074/913-6540) at the Workhouse Museum just outside town. The ladies behind the desk are very helpful.

The **AIB** next to Arnold's Hotel has a bureau de change but no ATM.

GETTING THERE AND AROUND
Dunfanaghy is on the N56, 36 kilometers northwest of Letterkenny. **Feda O'Donnell** (tel. 091/761-656 or 074/954-8144, www. busfeda.ie, 4.5-hour trip with a pit stop in Sligo, return €25) serves Dunfanaghy from Galway, departing the Catholic cathedral of St. Nicholas (9am and 4pm Mon.-Sat., with additional Fri. buses at 1:30pm and 5:30pm, Sun. departures at 3pm and 8pm). The bus stops at the square in Dunfanaghy.

Patrick Gallagher (tel. 074/953-1107 or 087/233-0888, www.gallagherscoaches.com, ring for fares) provides a one-a-day bus service (two on Friday during the school year) from Belfast to Gweedore, passing through Dunfanaghy en route. The bus leaves Jury's Hotel in Belfast (5:30pm Mon.-Sat. and 9:15pm Sun., arriving in Dunfanaghy at 8:05pm and 11:50pm, respectively).

Hire a bicycle from Tommy at **Dunfanaghy Bike Hire** (signposted from the N56 just east of town, tel. 086/405-4343, €10/day).

NORTHEASTERN DONEGAL

Letterkenny

Letterkenny (Leitir Ceanainn) is not worth lingering in, but you'll surely pass through Donegal's largest town at some point. Make a withdrawal at one of the ATMs on Main Street before heading north into Inishowen.

If you're making a stop, a good choice for lunch is **The Quiet Moment** (95 Lower Main St., tel. 074/912-7401, www.quietmoment.ie, 8:30am-6pm Mon.-Sat., open Sun. during festival times, under €10), an atmospheric tearoom with a specialty of humongous sandwiches.

If Donegal is the last leg of your trip, you can take a **Bus Éireann** (tel. 074/912-1309, 3-4/day Mon.-Sat., 2/day Sun.) express route from Letterkenny back to Dublin Airport. The bus station is at the Port Road roundabout east of Main Street.

★ Grianán of Aileách

A superbly situated Iron Age ring fort 29 kilometers east of Letterkenny, **Grianán of Aileách** (Grianán Ailigh, "The Solarium of Aileách" or "Fortress of the Sun," signposted off the N13 and a further 2 km uphill, always open, free) served as the royal seat of the northern O'Neills from the 5th century, though the site certainly held pre-Celtic significance. In 1101 the fort was sacked by the king of Munster, Muirchertach O'Brien, as retribution for the destruction of his own seat in Clare. Legend has it that he ordered each of his men to pull a stone from the fort and carry it away. The structure was improperly restored by an amateur archaeologist in the 1870s, and no drawings of the original structure remain. The fort has three walls; the innermost is four meters thick and contains chambers of unknown function. The enclosure, 23.5 meters in diameter, will bring to mind a classical amphitheater. What really sends this ruin into the breathtaking category is the panoramic view over five counties as well as Loughs Foyle and Swilly; it's well worth seeking out. Though there are "official" opening hours posted at the gate, it's possible to view the site at any time.

History buffs should stop by the **visitors center** (Burt, on the N13 near the site turn-off, tel. 074/936-8512, www.griananailigh.ie, 10am-6pm daily June-Aug., noon-6pm daily Sept.-May, €5) before visiting the site. The admission price includes a shuttle bus up to the site.

Grianán of Aileách calls to mind a classical amphitheater.

Those without wheels are best off doing the Grianán as a day trip out of Derry City. You can take the **Bus Éireann** (tel. 074/912-1160) Derry-Letterkenny route (#64, 6/day Mon.-Sat., 3/day Sun., 7 return buses/day Mon.-Sat., 3/day Sun.) and ask to be dropped off at the visitors center; then it's another couple kilometers uphill by foot.

The Inishowen Peninsula

Ask a well-traveled Irishman what his favorite part of Donegal is, and he may very well answer Inishowen. Tourism seems like even less of a priority here, and though there may be a shortage of accommodations and other amenities, you'll be too intoxicated by the view to care. The road up the western side of the peninsula, the R238, is sparsely populated and very dramatic; narrow roads wind through pristine hills and mountains (Slieve Snaght is Inishowen's highest at 615 meters) swathed in heather and evergreens. Follow signs for the "Inis Eoghain 100," a 100-mile scenic drive around the peninsula.

Be sure to withdraw funds before leaving Letterkenny.

MALIN AND MALIN HEAD

There's not much going on in **Malin** (Málainn), 14 kilometers south of Malin Head on the R242, but you should definitely stock up on gas and groceries at the village shop before going any farther.

Ireland's most northerly point, Malin Head is marred a bit by a couple of ugly concrete WWII lookout posts (as well as an older tower dating from the Napoleonic period). A steep rocky path from the car park leads down to a blowhole with the hyperbolic name of **Hell's Hole.** The eight-kilometer Malin Head loop starts at the end of the R242, just north of the hostels, and it's perfect for walking or cycling. If you take the loop clockwise, you'll see the turnoff for the **Wee House of Malin,** a hermit's cave turned Marian shrine (it's more a niche than a cave, so the hermit thing is probably just a legend). Nearby are the ruins of a church used during Penal times. *Star Wars*

fans will be interested to note that scenes from *Episode VIII* were filmed here in 2016.

There's a good hostel on the peninsula, the **Sandrock Holiday Hostel** (Malin Head, signposted off the R242, tel. 077/937-0289, www.sandrockhostel.com, dorms €14), overlooking a small slipway on Trawbreaga Bay a bit farther up the road. If you've been looking out for a place to hide from the world to relax and reflect, here's the perfect spot for it.

CULDAFF

With its sandy beach and excellent pub-cum-guesthouse, quiet **Culdaff** (Cúil Dabhcha, "Back of the Sandhills") makes a good base for exploring the peninsula. No visit to Inishowen is complete without at least one night at ★ **McGrory's** (town center, tel. 077/937-9104, www.mcgrorys.ie, €55-60 pp, s €70-75, food served 12:30pm-8:30pm daily, restaurant €15-24, bar €10-20), an all-in-one complex that admirably manages to feel completely untouristy—perhaps because it's so beloved by locals. McGrory's is best known as Ireland's most northerly concert venue (having hosted Altan, Sharon Shannon, Damien Dempsey, Ron Sexsmith, and Peter Green from Fleetwood Mac), but it also has a guesthouse and a wonderfully cozy pub with friendly waitstaff and sophisticated (not to mention thoroughly delicious) bar food. There's traditional music on Tuesday and Friday nights all year starting at 10pm, and it's worth timing your visit to catch one of these sessions. And of course, there's something going on in Mac's Backroom Bar several nights a week all year long, every night in high season.

Culdaff is 6.5 kilometers east of Malin on the R238, and there is no public transport. Should you need a taxi, ring **Carn Cabs** (tel. 077/937-4580).

DOAGH

Opened in 1997 and added to continually since then, the **Doagh Famine Village** (Doagh, on the R238, tel. 074/937-8078 or 086/846-4749, www.doaghvisitorscenter.com, 10am-5:30pm daily Easter-Oct., €6) is more than a Great Famine museum. This interpretive center offers cottages and other buildings featuring scenes from everyday rural life in the 19th century, from a wake scene in one cottage to a "sod house" used as a refuge for unwed mothers. There's also a "Mass rock," where Catholics would have gathered to meet their priest for Mass during Penal times (this particular Mass rock has been labeled "interdenominational," which doesn't make much sense—but such is the legacy of political correctness). The center makes an admirable effort to connect the 19th-century

tragedy in Ireland with the ongoing problem of starvation worldwide. "If you can walk up to your fridge and find food in it," the center says, "if you have clothes on your back, a roof over your head and a bed to sleep on, then you are richer than 75 percent of the world's population today." They're aiming to provide much more than a history lesson here—and they succeed. The admission price includes a guided tour and a cup of tea afterward.

Doagh is 21 kilometers west of Culdaff on the R238 and is on the Lough Swilly bus route (tel. 074/912-2863 for timetable).

Northern Ireland

Belfast........................ 394

Antrim......................... 404

Derry.......................... 417

Down 426

Armagh 435

Fermanagh 437

Look for ★ to find recommended sights, activities, dining, and lodging.

Highlights

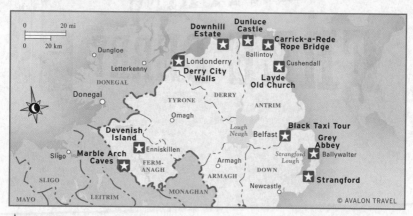

★ **Black Taxi Tour:** Providing an extended glimpse of working-class, sectarian Belfast and a running commentary on the city's political history, this two-hour excursion is a real eye-opener (page 398).

★ **Layde Old Church:** Overlooking the North Channel, this centuries-old graveyard and ivy-clad church ruin is an ideal spot for some quiet reflection (page 408).

★ **Carrick-a-Rede Rope Bridge:** Not for the faint-hearted, this 65-foot suspension bridge sways 80 feet above a sea gorge (page 414).

★ **Dunluce Castle:** Famous for a tragedy in 1639 in which the castle kitchen dropped into the sea, this dramatic stronghold was built precipitously on a basalt cliff, its stability compromised by the caves beneath (page 415).

★ **Derry City Walls:** Built in the 17th century, these are Ireland's only intact city walls, with views of both the old city and the Bogside neighborhood to the west, which features often-poignant peace murals (page 417).

★ **Downhill Estate:** The gutted ruin of Bishop Hervey's 18th-century manor is extremely eerie, and the neo-Grecian Mussenden Temple (which housed the bishop's library) is a lovely sight, perched on a cliff overlooking a pristine strand (page 425).

★ **Grey Abbey:** Founded by the Welsh princess Affreca in thanksgiving for her safe passage to Ireland despite a stormy sea, Grey Abbey is County Down's most important (and spookiest) monastic ruin (page 430).

★ **Strangford:** Possibly the loveliest spot in all of County Down, this seaside hamlet offers short walks through picturesque woodland and nice eateries lining a charming main square (page 433).

★ **Marble Arch Caves:** Full of interesting, whimsically named formations and a network of subterranean rivers, these caves are some of the island's finest (page 440).

★ **Devenish Island:** Take the ferry to this secluded Augustinian monastery on Lough Erne, which features a complete round tower—admire its original conical roof and decorated cornice, then step inside and climb it (page 442).

It may be tempting to regard Northern Ireland as an extension of the Republic, but this region of the United Kingdom has a very distinct atmosphere and character—reserved, even a bit guarded given the long, sad history of the Troubles.

To the first-time visitor, the culture in "the North" can seem like a jarring mix of wistful nationalism (particularly if you find yourself having a pint in a staunchly republican pub in Derry's Bogside neighborhood) and aggressive displays of support for the British crown (the annual Orange parades and bonfires being the most obvious example). Focus on the natural beauty, however, and you'll be creating memories to savor in years to come.

Counties Antrim (Aontroim, "Solitary Farm") and Derry (Doire, "Oak Grove") have most of Northern Ireland's biggest tourist attractions, including Giant's Causeway, the Carrick-a-Rede rope bridge, the Downhill Estate, the early 17th-century Derry City walls, and the Nine Glens—along with the Gobbins, a historic and newly reopened guided cliff path. Antrim in particular is renowned for its coast and glens; its beauty has often been likened to that of County Kerry, and it is by far the most visited of Northern Ireland's six counties.

The political history of these counties is as infamous as their landscapes are pretty. During the Troubles (the summer of 1969 through the 1994 ceasefire), their capital cities were hotbeds of guerrilla fighting between republican and loyalist paramilitary groups. Up North, in Belfast in particular, looking like a tourist has been a good thing. That's not to say early-21st-century Belfast still deserves its reputation for sectarian violence; the shadow of the Troubles still looms in the city's working-class neighborhoods (chiefly in the form of supposedly temporary "peace walls" erected during the Troubles to separate Catholic and Protestant neighborhoods), but unless you take a Black Taxi tour you won't notice much of it. Belfast is a truly cosmopolitan city, boasting some of the island's best pubs and eateries, and its crowded festival roster offers something for everyone at any time of year. Derry City has also geared itself for tourism in recent years, and ironically

Previous: the iconic "Free Derry" mural in Derry City's Bogside neighborhood; Dunluce Castle. **Above:** the Carrick-a-Rede Rope Bridge.

Northern Ireland

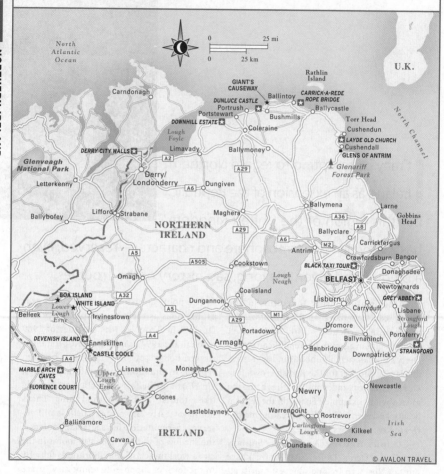

it's those reminders of the city's bloody history that are most attractive to visitors—the Bogside murals in particular, most of which are visible from the southwestern portion of the city walls.

The lesser-traveled counties are worth exploring too, from the Mourne Mountains and classy antiques shops of County Down (An Dún, "The Fort"), to the holy islands of Fermanagh ("fur-MAN-ahh," Fir-Monach, "The Men of Monach"), the cathedrals and apple orchards of Armagh ("ar-MAH," Ard

Mhacha, "Macha's Height"), to the lonely Sperrin Mountains of County Tyrone (Tír Eoghain, "Land of Eoghan"). You could very easily while away your entire vacation up North, without spending a single euro!

HISTORY

Saint Patrick left his mark on Counties Down and Armagh in a big way, founding his very first church in the hamlet of Saul, just east of Downpatrick, in 432; the building was a converted stable donated by a local chieftain, one of the saint's first converts. About 13 years later Patrick made Armagh his base, largely because of the pagan significance of the nearby fort of Emain Macha. (The city calls itself Ireland's "spiritual capital" not just for this, but because it's the seat of both Armagh archbishops—Anglican and Catholic—who also serve as primates of the whole of Ireland.) It's said that Patrick returned to Saul in his "retirement" after three-plus decades of successful pagan conversions.

With the exception of Derry City itself (having a 75 percent Catholic population), Counties Antrim and Derry are known as Protestant (or loyalist) strongholds, with origins in the widespread Plantation of Ulster, or recolonization, starting in the early 17th century. These lands were confiscated from the native Irish after the Flight of the Earls in 1607. Though loyal British soldiers and other subjects were given estates all over the island, more English settled in Antrim and "Londonderry" by virtue of simple geographical proximity. This is why the partition of Ireland in 1921 would reserve for Britain the six counties closest to it.

In the 19th century both Derry and Belfast had flourishing linen industries (and it's said Northern Irish factories provided uniforms for both sides on the American Civil War); the cities were also common points of departure for many emigrants to America and Australia. The *Titanic* was built in the shipyards of Belfast, and you can spend an afternoon at a fancy new museum, Titanic Belfast, on the site.

Nearly three centuries separate the two most vivid chapters in the history of Derry City, and both feature the number 14. During the 105-day Jacobite siege, which began on December 7, 1688, 14 "apprentice boys" had the presence of mind to swipe the keys to lock the Ferryquay Gate against the invaders. The siege killed 7,000 residents and decimated everything within the city walls (apart from St. Columb's Cathedral), but the loyalists managed to hold on to what was known as the "Maiden City" from then on.

And on January 30, 1972, "Bloody Sunday," 14 Catholic demonstrators, among the 20,000 protesting the then-commonplace practice of internment without trial, were massacred by British troops. Bloody Sunday was one day in a long series of clashes between republican and loyalist groups, an epoch rife with terrorist bombings, assassinations, police brutality, and street-fighting known as the Troubles. Memories of devastating IRA bombings in more recent history (1987 and 1998) have marked the collective psyche of both Enniskillen and Omagh, the principal towns of Fermanagh and Tyrone.

In a lesser-known and far happier chapter in Northern Irish history, Amelia Earhart landed near Culmore in Derry (at the Donegal border) on May 21, 1932, thus completing her first solo transatlantic flight.

PLANNING YOUR TIME

The Glens and Causeway Coast can be done in a rigorous one-day arc from Belfast to Derry or vice versa, but it makes far more sense to stop over in Ballycastle, Bushmills, or Ballintoy if you want to experience everything on the route. (Two days will suffice, even if you plan to linger at the Giant's Causeway, but plan on three for a leisurely pace.) Derry warrants a full day's sightseeing, Belfast probably two.

Since you'll be passing through Down on a trip from Dublin to Belfast, it makes sense to pause for a day or two en route. Get to Belfast first if using public transport, because virtually all Ulsterbus routes come out of the capital (and traveling in between towns in Down may even require returning to Belfast). As for the counties less traveled—Armagh, Fermanagh, and Tyrone—you might consider stopping off for an afternoon en route to your primary destinations. The holy islands of Fermanagh's Lough Erne are an easy detour from Sligo Town by car, for instance, or on the way up to Donegal. You could base yourself in Enniskillen and spend a couple days visiting the Marble Arch Caves, Devenish Island, Castle Coole, and Florence Court.

Because of their historical (or legendary) associations with St. Patrick, many towns in Armagh and Down (Downpatrick especially) drag out his feast day into a weeklong carnival. Depending on your capacity for alcohol and crowds, you may want to either avoid these places in March—or arrange your entire trip around St. Patrick's Day!

Belfast

Welcome to the new **Belfast** (Beál Feirste, "Mouth of the Sandbank"), the capital of Northern Ireland, a former industrial town with a population on the rise at 334,000. Whether you want chic or traditional, the city's vibrant pubs and gourmet restaurants alone are worth lingering for a week, and you'll have to go out of your way to observe any reminders of the Troubles.

It's important to note that the friction and segregation are exclusive to the city's working-class communities in west and north Belfast, the same locations of most of the street warfare. Catholics and Protestants, then and now, live side by side in more affluent neighborhoods. The working-class neighborhoods are back to back, along the parallel thoroughfares of **Falls Road** (Catholic) and **Shankill Road** (Protestant), and the barricades between them, meant to be temporary, date to the summer of 1969—the start of the Troubles.

Violence since the 1994 ceasefire has been in the form of isolated flare-ups between the paramilitary groups on both sides (the IRA and the UVF, Ulster Volunteer Force); today, though the tension is sometimes subtly but unnervingly palpable—in, say, the woodpiles in empty car parks, collected by young Protestant boys in anticipation of the marching season celebrations, which mark William of Orange's victory over the Catholic James II at the Battle of the Boyne—Belfast is a perfectly safe city, every bit as cosmopolitan and fast-paced as Dublin.

Belfast is situated on the River Lagan at the mouth of an eponymous Lough, which is a bay rather than a lake. The city center is marked by **Donegall Square,** which encloses the imposing Edwardian **Belfast City Hall;** north of here, along Royal Avenue, you'll find the prime shopping district, as well as the **Cathedral Quarter** around St. Anne's (Anglican), which has emerged (through copious redevelopment funding) as Belfast's "Left Bank." Great Victoria Street, home to the infamous Hotel Europa (bombed 40 times in all) is the start of the **Golden Mile,** a thoroughfare with an exaggerated moniker lined with some of Belfast's best pubs and eateries; the street changes names to Bradbury Place, Shaftesbury Square, and Botanic Avenue, where you'll find **Queen's University** and the lovely **Botanic Gardens.** On Donegall Quay, in the northeastern section, is the **Lagan Lookout,** a weir-cum-pedestrian bridge that's another product of multimillion-pound urban renewal. Sightseeing boats depart here.

SIGHTS

Belfast offers enough attractions to keep you busy for two full days. If this is a fly-by-night visit, at least take the Black Taxi tour for a crash introduction to the city's sectarian politics. You'll learn more in two hours than you might in a semester-long university course.

City Center

If you've got time, take a guided 45-minute tour of the magnificent **Belfast City Hall** (Donegall Sq., tel. 028/9027-0456, tours 11am, 2pm, and 3pm weekdays and 2pm and 3pm Sat. Feb.-Dec., free), with its 173-foot copper dome, built between 1898 and 1906. Admire the classical Renaissance architectural details during your introduction to Belfast civic history. Even if you don't have time for a tour, pop in to admire the lobby and see what's posted in the "What's On" room near the entrance.

Across the street is the **Linen Hall Library** (17 Donegall Sq. N., entrance on Fountain St., tel. 028/9032-1707, www.linenhall.com, 9:30am-5:30pm weekdays, 9:30am-4pm Sun.), the city's oldest, which has a substantial collection of art, political posters, and photographs on the Troubles and the sectarian conflict in general. Linen Hall makes a point of advertising itself as a neutral space in which to ponder the collection. Get a free visitor's pass on your way in.

The great thing about the cavernous, Anglican **St. Anne's Cathedral** (Donegall St., tel. 028/9032-8332, www.belfastcathedral.org, free, £2 donation appreciated) is the warm reception you receive at the door. Volunteers jump to answer any questions you might have—and the answers might turn into a minitour. This Hiberno-Romanesque edifice was built at the turn of the 20th century and features gorgeous gold ceiling mosaics in its Chapel of the Holy Spirit and Baptistery on either side of the entrance. On Sunday at 11am and 3:30pm (excluding July and Aug.) you can hear the Cathedral Choir sing.

The purpose of the 143-foot **Albert Memorial Clock** on Queens Square, built in 1865, is pretty self-explanatory. It stands four feet off center, so locals like to call it Belfast's own Leaning Tower.

The Golden Mile

The late-19th-century **Grand Opera House** (Great Victoria St., tel. 028/9024-0411, www.goh.co.uk) has more than opera on the calendar: Stop in anytime for a drink at the bar and take a look at what's on in the exhibition space.

The exhibits at the **Ulster Museum** (tel. 028/9038-3000, www.ulstermuseum.org.uk, 10am-5pm weekdays, 1pm-5pm Sat., 2pm-5pm Sun., free) run the gamut from contemporary art to Egyptian mummies to interactive natural science exhibits for the kiddos. Just next door are the city's splendid **Botanic Gardens** (entrances at Stranmillis

Rd. and Botanic Ave., daily until dusk, free). The restored **Palm House** (tel. 028/9032-4902, 10am-noon and 1pm-5pm weekdays, 1pm-5pm weekends, shorter hours in winter, free) dates to 1852, and the **Tropical Ravine** features a fishpond with mutant waterlilies (and enough steam to unwrinkle your button-down shirt). These delightful gardens, perfect for a long stroll or jog, are basically the backyard of **Queen's University.** The original college, the ornate English-Gothic **Lanyon Building,** is named for its architect, Charles Lanyon, and was opened in 1849. The Lanyon Building houses the **Naughton Gallery** (tel. 028/9097-3580, www.naughtongallery.org, 11am-4pm Mon.-Sat., free), which showcases local and international artists in an exciting variety of media.

West and North Belfast

It's older (1860s) than St. Anne's, and with its neo-Gothic twin spires it's just as grand, but the interior of **St. Peter's Cathedral** (St. Peter's Sq., off Falls Rd., tel. 028/9032-7573, www.stpeterscathedralbelfast.com) isn't of much interest for non-Catholics. The cathedral is a 15-minute walk west of the city center in the Falls Road neighborhood.

Brian de Breffny offers a few colorful words to describe the 19th-century **Belfast Castle** (off Antrim Rd./A6, 3.5 mi/5.6 km north of the city, tel. 028/9077-6925, www.belfastcastle.co.uk, reception 9am-10pm Mon.-Sat. and 9am-6pm Sun., private rooms 9am-1pm daily by arrangement, free), overlooking Belfast Lough, and the attitudes that shaped its design: "Intellectual and aesthetic values were subordinated to a romantic nostalgia, producing a showy mixture of gables and turrets with strangely contrived proportions . . . massive six-story tower, crow-stepped gables, conical turrets and restless skyline . . . the porch is an uneasy combination of Doric columns and bogus-looking strapwork; two gaunt bow-windows sit spuriously on curved courses of corbelling heavily carved with foliage and flowers." Unsurprising given this description, the refurbished sandstone castle is now one

Belfast

AVENUE GUESTHOUSE
EGLANTINE AVE
CAMERA GUESTHOUSE
WELLINGTON PARK
WELLESLEY AVE
PEARL COURT GUESTHOUSE
MALONE RD

To Raw Food Rebellion, and Dublin

ULSTERVILLE AVE
DUNLUCE AVE
JUBILEE RD
LISBURN RD
COLLEGE GARDENS
ELMWOOD AVE
FITZWILLIAM ST

DONEGALL RD
BLYTHE ST
CITY WAY
SANDY ROW
WELLWOOD ST
GREAT VICTORIA ST
HOLIDAY INN

BOOKFINDERS CAFE
CLAREMONT ST
UNIVERSITY RD

BELFAST INTERNATIONAL YOUTH HOSTEL
SPERANZA
BRADBURY PL
BENEDICT'S
LAVERY'S
DUBLIN RD

STRANMILLS RD
ULSTER MUSEUM
To Lyric Theatre
LANDSEER ST

QUEENS UNIVERSITY
UNIVERSITY SQUARE
MT CHARLES
LOWER CRESCENT
OTHER PLACE

MAGGIE MAY'S
BOTANIC REST
DONEGALL PASS
MARYVILLE ST
BANMORE ST
ORMEAU AVE

MOLLY'S YARD
UNIVERSITY ST

Botanic Garden

UNIVERSITY AVE
RUGBY AVE
FITROY AVE
MCCLURE ST
ORMEAU RD
CROMAC PL

AGINCOURT AVE
STRANMILLS EMBANKMENT
ANNADALE EMBANKMENT
ELGIN ST
DELHI ST
ORMEAU RD
A24

RUTLAND ST
FARNHAM ST
HATFIELD ST
SHAFTESBURY AVE
COOKE ST
BALFOUR AVE
ORMEAU EMBANKMENT

River Lagan

Ormeau Park

To Lurgan

0   200 yds
0   200 m

© AVALON TRAVEL

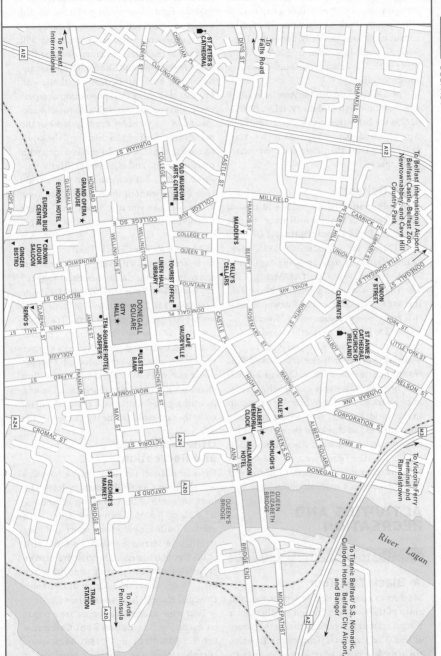

of the city's most popular wedding venues, though you can visit as part of a trip to Cave Hill Country Park. Downstairs, **The Cellar** restaurant (11am-5pm daily, 5pm-9pm Tues.-Sun., 3-course lunch/dinner £20/25), brimming with Victorian atmosphere, is a fine choice for lunch.

The **Belfast Zoo** (off the Antrim road/A6 4 mi/6.4 km north of the city, tel. 028/9077-6277, www.belfastzoo.co.uk, 10am-5pm daily Apr.-Sept. and 10am-2:30pm daily Oct.-Mar., £12) houses more than 160 exotic and endangered species.

East Belfast

No doubt many history buffs and fans of James Cameron's movie will travel to this city especially for **Titanic Belfast** (1 Olympic Way, Queens Rd., tel. 028/9076-6386, www.titanicbelfast.com, 9am-6pm Apr.-Sept., until 7pm June-Aug., 10am-5pm Oct.-Mar., £17.50). The *Titanic* was constructed at a shipyard on this site in 1910-1911, but be forewarned that this fancy new museum offers "interactive" overload to justify the extortionate admission price (not to mention what you'll pay to park and eat). Next door is the dry-docked **S.S. Nomadic** (Hamilton Dock, Queens Rd., tel. 028/9076-6386, www.nomadicbelfast.com, same hours, £7), the last White Star steamship in the world. You may want to skip the fancy museum and just check out the restored 1911 mini ocean liner instead (though it's much smaller than the *Titanic* was). A combo ticket (a "White Star Premium Pass") will run you £25 and includes a souvenir photo.

ACTIVITIES AND RECREATION

TOP EXPERIENCE

★ Black Taxi Tour

Most folks come to Belfast without a solid grasp of the Northern Ireland conflict, but a Black Taxi tour will remedy that in two hours or less. The black taxi dates to the Troubles era in the late 1960s, when renegades on both sides would hijack buses to use as barricades in street fights. Law-abiding citizens needed a safer and more reliable means of transport.

An experienced and articulate driver will take you to the murals and memorial gardens in the **Falls Road** and **Shankill Road** neighborhoods, home to Belfast's Catholic and Protestant working class populations, respectively, and provide you with a thorough background of the Troubles. Frankly, some of the murals are downright frightening—the loyalist ones tend to feature ski-masked men with machine guns, and not even skillfully rendered at that—but you can't say you've truly seen Belfast without them. At the end your driver will take you to a "peace wall" where tourists have been scribbling pacifist messages for years.

There isn't one "Black Taxi" company; there are several with very similar names, and more than one claims to be the "original." Try **Black Taxi Tours** (tel. 028/9064-2264 or 078/1003-3831, freephone tel. 0800/052-3914, www.belfasttours.com) or **Taxi Trax** (tel. 028/9031-5777, www.taxitrax.com). The tour lasts 1.5-2 hours and generally costs £10 per person (for a 3- to 6-person tour; 1-2 people might run you £30 total). If you're traveling alone, ask at your lodging to see if you can join in with a group. Or just ask one of the drivers at the taxi rank outside the Europa Hotel.

Other Activities and Recreation

For a bit of fresh air, there's no better place to frolic than **Cave Hill Country Park** (3.1 mi/5 km north of the city center off the A6, tel. 028/9077-6925, dawn-dusk daily), with marked trails ranging from short and easy strolls to a strenuous walk up Cave Hill (1,182 feet/360 meters). The **visitors center** at Belfast Castle can provide you with a free map. To get there, take Metro bus #1 from Donegall Place (at least 4/hour, fare £2).

Boat trips on the River Lagan are a popular excursion. The **Lagan Boat Company** (tel. 028/9033-0844 or 077/1891-0423, www.laganboatcompany.com, 2-3 trips daily,

75-minute trip £10) departs Donegall Quay beside the Lagan Lookout. A *Titanic*-themed tour takes place three times a day on weekends May-September.

Golfers are well served with the 300-acre, 27-hole **Malone Golf Club** (240 Upper Malone Rd., Dunmurry, 5 mi/8 km south of the city off the M1, tel. 028/9061-2758, www.malonegolfclub.co.uk), a championship course, and the **Royal Belfast Golf Club** (Station Rd., Craigavad, 7 mi/11 km north of the city on the A2/Bangor road, tel. 028/9042-8165, www.royalbelfast.com), established in 1881.

Here on a Sunday afternoon? Catch a **hurling** or **Gaelic football** match at **Casement Park** (Andersontown, West Belfast, tel. 028/9038-3815, www.gaa.ie).

FOOD

Belfast offers loads of upscale restaurants and gastro-pubs, many of which will give you a free glass of wine or a discount on your food bill if you're headed to the Ulster Orchestra or Grand Opera House after your meal.

Cafés

The university neighborhood is your best bet if you're just looking for a cup of coffee and a place to chill. Beloved student haunts include the musty secondhand **Bookfinders Café** (47 University Rd., tel. 028/9032-8269, 10am-5:30pm Mon.-Sat., under £7); **Maggie May's** (50 Botanic Ave., tel. 028/9032-2662, 8am-10:30pm Mon.-Sat., 10am-10:30pm Sun., under £7), famous for its wall murals and huge fried breakfasts; and the **Other Place** (79 Botanic Ave., tel. 028/9020-7200, 10am-8pm daily, until 9pm Thurs.-Fri., 10pm Sat.-Sun., £6-7) for burgers, lasagna, and other hearty grub. Service can be spotty, but the £5 lunch special is tough to beat.

Hankering for a *good* cup of (Fair Trade) coffee? In the Cathedral Quarter, **Clements** (131-133 Royal Ave., tel. 028/9024-6016, 8am-5pm weekdays, 10am-5pm Sat., £3-5), with the likes of Portishead coming through the speakers, can boast cheerful, efficient staff (this may

look like a British Starbucks, but there's table service) and an array of tasty gourmet sandwiches and desserts. There are more branches throughout the city (including at 4 Donegall Sq. W. and 66-68 Botanic Ave.).

Vegans will want to head straight for **Raw Food Rebellion** (336 Lisburn Rd., tel. 077/3006-7704, 8am-6pm daily, under £7) for filling lunches and hip-hop-themed juices and smoothies (e.g., "I got 99 problems and my health ain't one"!) The service is friendly and the coffee is really good, and if you don't feel like eating too healthy you can always save room for a vegan chocolate peanut butter cup.

Restaurants

The perfect place for afternoon tea and pastries, **Café Vaudeville** (25-39 Arthur St., tel. 028/9043-9160, www.cafevaudeville.com, food served noon-3pm Mon.-Thurs. and Sat., noon-5pm Fri., and 5pm-8pm Mon.-Sat., lunches £7-9, dinners £8-12) boasts a truly stunning art nouveau interior with a champagne bar on the mezzanine level. The dessert and cocktail menus are as fantastic as the atmosphere.

Popular with Queen's students for its delicious, good-value gourmet pizzas and pastas, spacious ★ **Speranza** (16-19 Shaftesbury Sq., tel. 028/9023-0213, www.thinkitalian.co.uk, 5pm-11:30pm Mon.-Sat., 3pm-10pm Sun., £6-16) has a relaxed ambience featuring great pop/rock tunes on the stereo that you may not have heard in a while, and decidedly non-Italian decor.

Seafood is a specialty at **Ginger Bistro** (7-8 Hope St., tel. 028/9024-4421, www.gingerbistro.com, noon-3pm and 5pm-10pm Tues.-Sat., 5pm-9pm Mon., lunch £5-17, dinner £15-23), which also gets good marks for helpful service and appealingly quirky decor. Vegetarians will find a wealth of options, and though many of them are au gratin or otherwise loaded with dairy, Ginger is still one of Belfast's best dinner options for vegans. Those on a gluten-free diet have a choice of meals as well. Book ahead.

Reservations are essential at ★ **Molly's**

Yard (1 College Green Mews, Botanic Ave., tel. 028/9032-2600, www.mollysyard.co.uk, noon-9:30pm Mon.-Sat., £13-23), long considered the best eatery in the city. The romantic ambience is perfect for a special night out. The "5-10-5" menu—a three-course meal for £20—is available all day weekdays and until 4:30pm on Saturday. The menu here is modern Irish, though they offer a much better choice of veg options than the average fancy restaurant on this island. And with sparkling cocktails and sublime desserts, it doesn't matter if the service here is ever-so-slightly harried.

Don't feel like eating in a swanky restaurant? Belfast has plenty of top-notch gastropubs too. Try gay-friendly **Union Street** (8-14 Union St., tel. 028/9031-6060, www.unionstreetpub.com, food served noon-3:30pm Mon.-Thurs. and 5pm-9pm Thurs., noon-9pm Fri.-Sat., 1pm-5pm Sun., lunch £6-7, dinner £8-11) in a 19th-century converted shoe factory, where you can get 10 percent off your food bill when you show your Grand Opera House tickets. **Josper's** (Donegall Sq. at Linenhall St., food served noon-10pm daily, £9-26), downstairs at the Ten Square Hotel, offers up huge portions of chicken, salmon, duck, steak, and fresh salads, as well as a terrific homemade veggie burger. **McHugh's** (29-31 Queen's St., tel. 028/9050-9990, www.mchughsbar.com, food served 5pm-10pm Mon.-Sat., 5pm-9pm Sun., lunch £6-8, dinner £8-12) is a city mainstay and one of Belfast's oldest pubs (there was a brothel upstairs in days gone by). Save room for the banana and amaretto cheesecake.

ENTERTAINMENT AND EVENTS
Entertainment

Quaint period watering holes abound in Belfast, and the best way to sample them all is on the **Bailey's Historical Pub Tour** (tel. 028/9268-3665, www.belfastpubtours.com, £7, includes free Bailey's shot). The tour commences from the upstairs dining room at the king of them all, the **Crown Liquor Saloon** (46 Great Victoria St., tel. 028/9027-9901, www.crownbar.com), on Thursday at 7pm and Saturday at 4pm. Book ahead at the tourist office. It's not the old-school über-British groghouse it once was, but **Lavery's Gin Palace** (12-16 Bradbury Pl., tel. 028/9087-1106) has been run by the same family for more than 100 years. There's live music nightly—reggae, rock, and blues—in two of the Lavery's four bars.

You'll find Belfast's best traditional music sessions at **Madden's** (74 Berry St., tel. 028/9024-4114) on Monday, Friday, and Saturday nights; a minute's walk away is the crustier **Kelly's Cellars** (30 Bank St., tel. 028/9024-6058, www.kellyscellars.com), established in 1720, with sessions on Saturday afternoons. There's also a Thursday-night session at **McHugh's** (29-31 Queen's St., tel. 028/9050-9990, www.mchughsbar.com) and live bands in the basement bar on Friday and Saturday.

Belfast's club scene can't compare to Dublin's, but you might try **Ollie's** (Waring St., tel. 028/9023-4888, www.olliesbelfast.com, 9pm-late, cover £5-10) at the Merchant Hotel, which attracts a slightly older (mid- to late 20s) crowd. Drinks are pricey.

The **Ulster Orchestra** (Elmwood Hall at Queen's, 89 University Rd., tel. 028/9066-8798, www.ulster-orchestra.org.co.uk, £8-24) hosts Europe's most distinguished conductors and guest performers. Several concerts are held at Waterfront Hall (2 Lanyon Pl., tel. 028/9033-4455).

It's not all *Figaro* at the **Grand Opera House** (2-4 Great Victoria St., tel. 028/9024-1919, www.goh.co.uk, £5-30). There are plenty of American-style musicals and cheesy children's pantomimes along with traditional opera and ballet. For something more experimental, check out the bill at the **Old Museum Arts Centre** (7 College Sq. N., tel. 028/9023-3332, £6-10). There's always something out of the ordinary going on, be it an interactive play, indie vocalists reinterpreting work from other genres, or off-beat visual art exhibitions. The **Metropolitan Arts Centre** (10 Exchange St., tel. 028/9023-5053, www.themaclive.

LGBTQ Belfast

Northern Ireland's capital isn't quite as gay-friendly as Dublin is, but you'll find several fun night-spots in the Cathedral Quarter. From drag shows to disco night, **Boombox** (1 Union St., tel. 028/9033-2130, www.boomboxbelfast.com, 10pm-3am, cover £5-8) promises a fun time any night of the week, and no trip to the Belfast is complete without a night at **The Kremlin** (96 Donegall St., tel. 028/9031-6061, www.kremlin-belfast.com, 9pm-2am Tues., 9pm-3am Thurs.-Sun., cover £3-10), the biggest (not to mention kitschiest) gay nightclub in Northern Ireland. The theme is all things Soviet, as you'd expect from the name—all but the music, which is mostly techno.

Or if you're just looking for a pint and a chat, try **The Nest** (22-28 Skipper St., tel. 028/9024-5558), the city's oldest gay bar. Also in the Cathedral Quarter, **Union Street** (8-14 Union St., tel. 028/9031-6060) is a gay-friendly gastro-pub definitely worth checking out.

And on a practical note, the city's primary resource center is **Rainbow Project N.I.** (33 Church St., tel. 028/9031-9030, www.rainbow-project.org, 10am-4pm Mon.-Fri.).

com, £7-25) offers an eclectic mix of children's plays, comedy, indie and trad concerts, and adult-only musical theater along with a gallery space.

Northern Ireland's only full-time professional theater, the **Lyric Theatre** (55 Ridgeway St., tel. 028/9038-1081, www.lyric-theatre.co.uk, £10-20) stages both specially commissioned and classic works from an international list of playwrights. The brand-new building is three times the size of the original 1960s theatre, where Liam Neeson got his start in the 1970s.

Festivals and Events

Unfortunately, the revelry during the annual **St. Patrick's Carnival** has resulted in sectarian brawls in the past, prompting the city council's decision (pending appeal) not to fund the event in the future. The week after Paddy's Day brings the **Belfast Film Festival** (tel. 028/9032-5913, www.belfastfilmfestival. org).

The **Belfast Marathon** (tel. 028/9032-0202, www.belfastcitymarathon.com) takes place in early May—the race begins from Belfast City Hall at 9am. You don't have to settle for watching, though; there's a recreational run-walk as well.

Between May and September, **Summer in the City** (www.belfastcity.gov.uk/events) offers an eclectic calendar of

entertainments: classical concerts, guided tours, and art exhibitions. You'll find more art, street theater, and concerts on offer through the **Cathedral Quarter Arts Festival** (tel. 028/9023-2403, www.cqaf. com) in late April and early May, and the **Féile an Phobail** (tel. 028/9031-3440, www. feilebelfast.com) in August. In late October and early November, the **Belfast Festival at Queen's** (tel. 028/9097-1034, www.bel-fastfestival.com) also offers concerts, plays, and art exhibitions at venues all over the city. The **Halloween Carnival** is a five-day event featuring ghost tours and fireworks along with a parade on the 31st.

SHOPPING

The island's oldest continually open marketplace is the delightful 230-stall **St. George's Market** (May St. and Oxford St., tel. 028/9043-5704), always open Friday and Saturday, and sometimes other days for special craft fairs, art exhibitions, and concerts. Along with 23 seafood stalls (it's also the largest fishmarket), you'll find plenty more ready-to-eat nibbles and the occasional stall of gifty things.

Fine yet affordable artwork can be tricky to find, especially in the city. Take a look around the **Belfast Print Workshop and Gallery** (Cotton Ct., 30-42 Waring St., tel. 028/9023-1323, www.belfastprintworkshop.org.uk), which features the work of local artists—be it silkscreen, lithograph, etching, or woodcut.

For Irish-language books (for all levels) and locally made T-shirts, glassware, pottery, and jewelry, stop by the **An Ceathrú Póilí Book & Craft Shop** (216 Falls Rd., tel. 028/9032-2811, www.an4poili.com), part of a larger Irish cultural center, **Cultúrlann Mc Adam Ó Fiaich** (www.culturlann.ie).

ACCOMMODATIONS
Hostels
Belfast has plenty of borderline-sketchy hostels, many of which advertise the cheapest beds in town—a classic case of getting what you pay for. Alas, even the respectable places don't fall into the "excellent" category. The HINI **Belfast International Youth Hostel** (22-32 Donegall Rd., just off Shaftesbury Sq., tel. 028/9032-4733, www.hini.org.uk, dorms £14-15) comes the closest—clean dorms and above-par facilities all around—but it's huge and can be rather noisy. A good budget option—for friends traveling together, anyway—is **Farset International** (466 Springfield Rd., tel. 028/9089-9833, www.farsetinternational.co.uk, £24 pp). Located beside a wildfowl reserve, Farset offers 38 spotless en suite twin rooms with television and hostess tray, and a continental breakfast in the rather antiseptic restaurant is included in the room price. (There's also a self-catering kitchen.)

Bed-and-Breakfasts
For B&B, try a tidy brick townhouse just south of the university—it's a pleasant tree-lined neighborhood with ample on-street parking if you need it and lots of good eateries, and you're only a couple minutes' walk from the Botanic Gardens. One of the best is the **Avenue Guesthouse** (23 Eglantine Ave., tel. 028/9066-5904, www.avenueguesthouse.com, £35-40 pp, s £50-55), which has a lovely little garden out back. It's family owned, unlike many of the guesthouses in this neighborhood, so you can expect a more friendly reception and home baking at the breakfast table. **Botanic Rest** (7-13 Cromwell Rd., tel.

028/9032-4820, www.botanicrest.com, £30 pp) is larger and more anonymous, which isn't a bad thing. The rooms are spotless, the beds comfortable, and the showers hot and powerful, though the staff are phoning it in when it comes to breakfast.

Other B&B options are the **Pearl Court Guesthouse** (11 Malone Rd., tel. 028/9066-6145, www.pearlcourt.com, £30-35 pp, s £40, ask about weekend discounts), which has self-catering apartments available for larger groups in addition to regular guest rooms (not all of which are en suite); and the **Camera Guesthouse** (44 Wellington Park, tel. 028/9066-0026, www.cameraguesthouse.co.uk, £30-35 pp, s £35-40, ask about weekend discounts) in the same quiet, shady tree-lined neighborhood.

Hotels
City hotel room rates generally do not include breakfast. It may be an impersonal chain, but the **Holiday Inn** (40 Hope St., tel. 028/9024-2494, www.hibelfastcitycentre.co.uk, rooms £75) offers laundry service, free parking, a central-but-not-too-central location, and weekend discounts.

The three-star **Benedict's** (7-21 Bradbury Pl., Shaftesbury Sq., tel. 028/9059-1999, www.benedictshotel.co.uk, standard/executive £50 pp, s £85) boasts a great location on the Golden Mile, luxurious bedroom fittings, and an atmospheric neo-Gothic bar and restaurant, converted from an old church, where you can often catch a rock concert at the weekend. This is definitely a hotel for those wanting to sample the Belfast nightlife.

The four-star, beyond-swanky **Ten Square** (10 Donegall Sq. S., tel. 028/9024-1001, www.tensquare.co.uk, rooms £165-210, suites £250), located in a former bank building, offers all the trimmings: fancy toiletries and bathrobes, lush linen sheets on king-size beds, in-room safes, and wet-bars. There's top-notch pub grub downstairs at Josper's. Two things to note: Breakfast is included in the rate, and the weekend rate is higher than midweek.

Another four-star establishment is the

Italianate **Malmaison Hotel** (34-38 Victoria St., tel. 028/9022-0200, www.malmaison.com, midweek/weekend room rate £99/135), with über-chic, individually designed rooms featuring plasma television and DVD. Check out the website for a sweet meal/room/Ulster Orchestra package; a three-course dinner at the Brasserie restaurant, concert ticket, and B&B will run you £120 per person. One caveat: There's no parking.

The four-star **Europa Hotel** (Great Victoria St., tel. 028/9027-1066, www.hastingshotels.com/europa-belfast, rooms £90-250, suites £400, breakfast not included) has the unfortunate distinction of being the most bombed hotel on the planet. Those days are long gone, thankfully, and this business-class hotel is even more a Belfast institution than it ever was. Another Hastings company establishment is the five-star **Culloden Estate** (Bangor Rd., 5 mi/8 km east of the city, tel. 028/9042-1066, www.hastingshotels.com, rooms £160-300, suites £350-700, s £160-190), with a motto of "built for a bishop, fit for a king." The location overlooking Belfast Lough is truly superb, as are the facilities: a deluxe spa and fitness suite with pool, steam room, Jacuzzi, sauna, and gym, as well as comfortable rooms (more homey than chic) appointed with fruit baskets and bathrobes.

INFORMATION

The city's large but efficient **tourist office** (47 Donegall Pl., tel. 028/9024-6609, www.belfastvisitor.com or www.gotobelfast.com) also provides a left luggage service (£5/bag, not overnight though) and bureau de change. Hours vary seasonally (9am-7pm weekdays, 9am-5:15pm Sat., 10am-4pm Sun. June-Sept., 9am-5:30pm Mon.-Sat. Oct.-May).

The **Queen's Visitors' Centre** (Lanyon Building, Queen's University, University Rd., tel. 028/9097-5252, www.qub.ac.uk/vcentre, 10am-4pm weekdays and Sat. May-Sept.) also dispenses tourist info, in addition to a full calendar of art exhibitions.

For information on the republic (including accommodation bookings), stop by **Fáilte**

Ireland (53 Castle St., tel. 028/9032-7888, 9am-5pm weekdays all year, 9am-12:30pm Sat. July-Aug.).

SERVICES

You'll have no trouble finding an ATM. Banks in Belfast include **Ulster Bank** (11-16 Donegall Sq. E.) and **Bank of Ireland** (1 Donegall Sq. S.). **Thomas Cooke** (11 Donegall Pl., tel. 028/9088-3900), the Belfast **tourist office,** and the main **post office** on Castle Place all have bureaux de change.

The **U.S. Embassy** (Danesfort House, 233 Stranmillis Rd., tel. 028/9038-6100, www.usembassy.org.uk, 8:30am-5pm weekdays) is a 15- to 45-minute bus ride from the city center (#8a, frequent departures from Donegall Sq. E. and across the street from the Europa Hotel on Great Victoria St., get off at the Richmond Park stop on Stranmillis Rd.).

Need a pharmacy? You won't have trouble finding one along Belfast's main drags, but head to **Boots** (35-47 Donegall Pl., tel. 028/9024-2332) on a Sunday or if you need a better selection. For medical advice, ring **Health Information Service** (tel. 0800/665-544). Belfast's most centrally located hospital is the **City Hospital** (tel. 028/9032-9241) on Lisburn Road.

GETTING THERE

Belfast is 104 miles (167 km) north of Dublin on the M1 motorway and 72 miles (116 km) southeast of Derry City on the A6. **Ulsterbus** pulls into the **Europa Bus Centre** (adjacent to Europa Hotel, entrance on Glengall St. off Great Victoria St., tel. 028/9066-6630).

If you happen to be coming from Derry City, **Northern Ireland Railways** (www.translink.co.uk) will get you to **Belfast Central Station** (E. Bridge St., tel. 028/9066-6630, 9/day Mon.-Sat., 3/day Sun., single £12) in 2.25 hours.

From the republic, take **Irish Rail** (tel. 01/836-6222, www.irishrail.ie, 8/day Mon.-Sat., 5/day Sun., €15-24 one way) or **Bus Éireann** (#1, tel. 01/836-6111, www.buseireann.ie, €19 one way).

From New York (Newark, change required in Manchester from JFK), Orlando, and Toronto you can fly direct to **Belfast International Airport** (18 mi/29 km west of Belfast on the A57, tel. 028/9448-4848, www.belfastairport.com); nonstop flights are also available to Paris, Amsterdam, Geneva, Prague, Berlin, Rome, and many smaller European destinations. To get to the city center, take the **AirBus** (#300) to the Europa Bus Centre off Great Victoria Street (3/hour, single ticket £7.50). Otherwise, the official airport-to-city-center taxi fare is £31.

There are direct flights from Cork (on Aer Arann), London Stansted, Edinburgh, Glasgow, and other U.K. cities into the **Belfast City Airport** (4 mi/6.4 km east of the city on the A2, tel. 029/9093-9093, www.belfastcityairport.com). Most U.K. flights are on **FlyBE** (tel. 087/1700-0123, www.flybe.com); you can also fly **BMI** (tel. 087/0607-0555, www.flybmi.com) into London Heathrow. **AirLink** (#600) can get you to the Europa Bus Centre (3/hour, £2.50 one way). A taxi will run you £10.

The **Airporter** (tel. 028/7126-9996, www. airporter.co.uk) is the easiest way to travel between Belfast's airports, and there's also service available from Derry City (single/return £20/30).

GETTING AROUND

Provided you plan your sightseeing with efficiency, Belfast is walkable from end to end, though you will want to take a Black Taxi to visit the murals in the Falls and Shankill neighborhoods. You can take **Ulsterbus** (tel. 028/9066-6630, www.ulsterbus.co.uk) route #8 from Donegall Square East south to the Queen's University/Botanic Gardens area, where most of the city's B&Bs are located.

Your easiest option for cycle rental is **Belfast Bikes** (48 Duncrue St., tel. 034/3357-1551, www.belfastbikes.co.uk, 6am-midnight daily, 3-day membership fee £5 plus £3.50 for the first four hours), with 33 docking stations across the city center.

Ring **fonaCAB** (tel. 028/9033-3333) from a landline and a nifty automated system sends a taxi to the address you're calling from; or try **Value Cabs** (tel. 028/9080-9080).

Antrim

CARRICKFERGUS

A rather bland commuter suburb 20 minutes north of Belfast, on the north shore of Belfast Lough, **Carrickfergus** (Carraig Fhearghais, "Rock of Fergus") is known for the island's most complete medieval castle. **Carrickfergus Castle** (Marine Hwy., tel. 028/9335-1273, 10am-6pm Mon.-Sat. and 2pm-6pm Sun. Apr.-May and Sept., 10am-6pm Mon.-Sat. and noon-6pm Sun. June-Aug., 10am-4pm Mon.-Sat. and 2pm-4pm Sun. Oct.-Mar., £3) was Ireland's first Norman fortress. Anglo-Norman adventurer John de Courcy began its construction in the 1180s after a successful invasion, and the building continued after de Courcy was vanquished in 1204 by Hugh de Lacy, Earl of Ulster. King John, worried that de Lacy was becoming too powerful, beseiged the yet-to-be-completed Carrickfergus and took it over in 1210. And that was only the beginning of a long and checkered history. One of its darkest episodes occurred when the Scottish Bruces attacked the castle in 1315; the English garrison survived the yearlong siege by eating their Scottish prisoners (who were already dead, at least).

Considering its dramatic setting and fascinating history, you would think Carrickfergus would be a must-see. Kid-friendly exhibits are one thing, but the National Trust has gone over the top here with melodramatic audiovisuals, amateurish wall murals, and half-size fiberglass statues representing soldiers, archers, John de Courcy and his wife, and so forth. You'll even see one of these creepy figures perched on the throne—the *other* throne.

The castle must have been a far more worthwhile excursion in past years, when it housed the city's military museum (it was used as an armory before 1928). Those artifacts have been transferred to the new **Carrickfergus Museum and Civic Centre** (11 Antrim St., tel. 028/9335-8049, www.carrickfergus.org, 9am-5pm weekdays, 10am-5pm Sat., free), however—and here you'll also find the town's **tourist office** (tel. 028/9335-8000, 10am-6pm Mon.-Sat. and 1pm-6pm Sun. Apr.-Sept., 10am-5pm Mon.-Sat. and 1pm-5pm Sun. Oct.-Mar.). As it is, the castle is of primary interest to middle-schoolers and military history buffs.

Food and Accommodations

If you're spending the night in Carrick (as the locals know it), the best guesthouse in town is **The Keep** (93 Irish Quarter S., tel. 028/9336-7007 or 079/8120-2169, www.thekeepguesthousecarrickfergus.co.uk, £25 pp, s £40), a three-minute walk from the castle on the Belfast end of the main drag. The en suite rooms are capacious and much more stylish than at your average B&B, and Heather and Raymond are very kind and accommodating hosts. Note that many of Carrick's long-established B&Bs have closed or been converted to halfway houses in recent years, so The Keep or the authentically old-fashioned, unpretentious (it's a two-star) **Dobbin's Inn Hotel** (6-8 High St., tel. 028/9335-1905, www.dobbinshotel.co.uk, £40 pp) is your best option, especially if you're a paranormal enthusiast; the presence of Elizabeth Dobbin, murdered by her husband after he caught her having an affair with a soldier stationed at the castle, is well documented.

You can take your chances with the hotel food, but a better choice for lunch or dinner is **Ownie's** (16-18 Joymount, on the same street as the public library, catercorner to the castle, tel. 028/9335-1850, www.owniesbarbistro.co.uk, food served noon-2:30pm and 5pm-8:30pm Mon.-Thurs., noon-3pm and 5pm-9pm Fri.-Sat., 12:30pm-8pm Sun., lunch £6-8, dinner £7-15), a cozy, dimly lighted pub and restaurant with a beer garden and very friendly and accommodating staff. There's a separate vegetarian menu.

Getting There

Carrickfergus is 10 miles (16 km) northeast of Belfast on the A2. Get here via **Ulsterbus** (#163 or #263, tel. 028/9066-6630, www.ulsterbus.co.uk, 2-3/hour, 45-60-minute trip, departs Bridge St. in Belfast, single/return £2.60/4.70) or **N.I. Railways** (tel. 028/9066-6630, www.ulsterbus.co.uk, 2-4 Larne-bound trains/hour, 43-minute trip, single/day return £4.30/6.70) from Belfast's central station.

THE GOBBINS

The dramatic cliff path called **The Gobbins** (Middle Rd., Islandmagee, tel. 028/9337-2318, www.thegobbinscliffpath.com, tours hourly 10am-3pm daily, £8.50) features natural rock tunnels and brand-new bridges with breathtaking ocean views. From the Irish word "gobán," meaning headland, the Gobbins was originally designed by an Irish railway engineer, Berkeley Deane Wise, and opened in 1902; the idea was to drum up holiday railway business, so back in the day an elderly railway employee would give you free entry through "Wise's Eye," a gated hole in the rock-face, if you showed him your rail ticket; if you came on foot, you'd be charged a sixpence admission fee.

The railway company's financial troubles in the 1930s led to the path's closure before World War II, and an attempt to reopen it in the 1950s ended with a major landfall. The path lay in ruin for decades, until finally the local borough council built 15 new bridges (to the tune of £7.5 million) and reopened the cliff path to the public in 2015. Storms in late 2015 and early 2016 necessitated another closure, but at the time of writing local management was planning to reopen the Gobbins for the summer 2016 season. Unlike other walking routes, this one is by guided tour only, and

Antrim and Derry

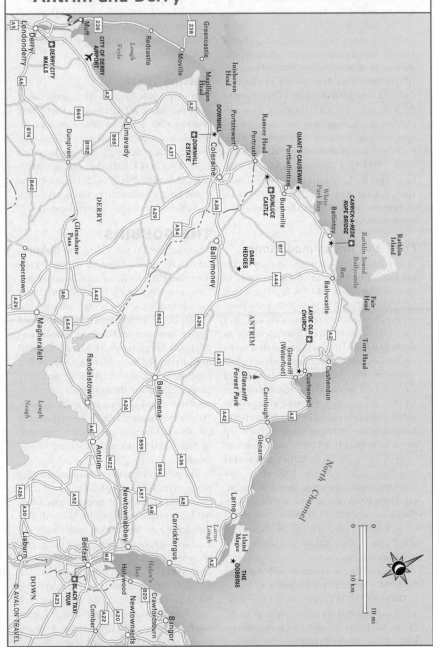

A5
Londonderry
Derry
Muff 238
238
Greencastle
Redcastle
CITY OF DERRY AIRPORT
DERRY CITY WALLS
Moville
Inishowen Head
Lough Foyle
Magilligan Head
A2
A6
B69
B74
Limavady
B68
Dungiven
B192
B40
DERRY
Glenshane Pass
Draperstown
Magherafelt
Randalstown
A29
A6
A42
A54
A29
A54
Coleraine
DOWNHILL
DOWNHILL ESTATE
A37
Portstewart
Portrush
Ramore Head
Portballintrae
GIANT'S CAUSEWAY
Bushmills
DUNLUCE CASTLE
A26
A29
Ballymoney
DARK HEDGES
B62
Ballymena
A26
B17
Ballintoy
CARRICK-A-REDE ROPE BRIDGE
White Park Bay
A44
A2
Rathlin Sound
Ballycastle
Rathlin Island
Ballycastle Bay
Fair Head
Torr Head
ANTRIM
LAYDE OLD CHURCH
Glenariff (Waterfoot)
Glenariff Forest Park
Cushendall
Cushendun
A43
A44
Carnlough
A42
A6
A26
Antrim
M22
Randalstown
A52
A6
B59
B94
A36
A57
A8
Glenarm
A2
Lough Neagh
A30
A26
Lisburn
Belfast
BLACK TAXI TOUR
A23
Newtownabbey
Carrickfergus
M2
Newtownards
Comber
A20
A22
Holywood
Helen's Bay
Crawfordsburn
B20
Bangor
Larne
Larne Lough
Island Magee
THE GOBBINS
North Channel
DOWN

0   10 km
0   10 mi

© AVALON TRAVEL

Ulster Walks

With approximately 560 miles (900 kilometers) of trails, the **Ulster Way** is the island's longest walking route, winding through all six Northern counties as well as central Donegal. Trekking all of it would take about five weeks, though most travelers walk the coastal stretch between the Giant's Causeway and the Glens of Antrim (from Portrush to Ballycastle, or vice versa) known as the **Causeway Coast Way;** there are plenty of accommodations along this route, but be sure to book well advance even in shoulder season. The Ulster Way begins in the suburbs of northern Belfast, by far the least attractive part of the route, before you come to the most popular segment in northern Antrim.

The tourist board is now marketing the longer coastal itinerary between Belfast and Derry as the **Causeway Coastal Route** (www.causewaycoastalroute.com), which is 120 miles (190 kilometers) in total but offers numerous diversions—to the Glens of Antrim or the Dark Hedges for instance. Check out the website for map and suggested itineraries. An alternative for day-trippers is the 2.5-hour guided cliff walk at **The Gobbins.**

While the coastal routes may be the primary draw of the Ulster Way, there are other sections you won't have to share with nearly so many fellow travelers: consider as alternatives the **Central Sperrins Way,** in the mountains of Tyrone and southern Derry, and the **Mourne Trail,** in the mountains of County Down.

As with all signposted walking routes, there are detailed guides with maps available at the local tourist office and bookstore. Websites like the **Ramblers Association** (www.ramblers.org.uk) and **WalkingWorld** (www.walkingworld.com) are helpful planning resources.

since groups are limited to 10, prebooking by Internet or phone is mandatory. The walk lasts about 2.5 hours; your guide can tell you all about the local geology and wildlife, and the admission fee includes transportation to and from the site via shuttle bus.

The **Gobbins Visitor Centre** is in Islandmagee, 9 miles (14 km) north of Carrickfergus via the A2 to the B90. If you're not driving, take **N.I. Railways** (tel. 028/9066-6630, www.translink.co.uk, £6.40/9.90 single/day return from Belfast) to Ballycarry on the Belfast-Larne route. Trains depart hourly Monday-Saturday and every two hours on Sunday. From the Ballycarry train station it's a one-mile walk to the visitors center, although the road isn't the safest for pedestrians; worst case, you can ring **Ballycarry Cabs** (tel. 028/9303-8131) for a lift.

THE GLENS OF ANTRIM

The Northern Ireland Tourist Board may wax poetical on the beauteous Nine Glens of Antrim, but frankly the base towns from which one might explore them—Glenarm, Waterfoot, and Carnlough—are strangely run-down, not particularly friendly, and noticeably lacking in tourist amenities (especially the first two). Cushendall and Cushendun at the northern edge of the Glens are by far the most pleasant, and even they can be sleepy-in-a-bad-way. Furthermore, most of these nine glens are home to a few fortunate locals and aren't tourist attractions as such, the exception being Glenariff Forest Park. Having said all this, the coastal drive north from Belfast on the A2, with the glens on your left, is downright lovely. Take this ride as part of your Causeway Coast tour, and allow two days to do it right.

Glenariff

One of the few glens you can actually traipse through, **Glenariff Forest Park** (signposted on the A43, 8 mi/13 km south of Cushendall on the B14, tel. 028/2175-8232, 10am-dusk all year, cars £4.50) also happens to be the prettiest of them all (Gleann Airimh means "Fertile Glen"). The whole park is remarkably quiet and peaceful. There are plenty of walking trails (from 30 minutes to three hours' duration), but the gem of the park is the substantial **Ess-na-Larach waterfall** ("The Mare's Fall"). Eyeing it from the bridge will give you the distinct feeling you've entered an enchanted forest. Maybe you have.

Cushendall

The glens' largest town, **Cushendall** ("The Foot of the River Dall") is pleasant enough, though it doesn't come near Cushendun's charm. Everything you need—grub and Northern Bank ATM, at least—is within spitting distance of the distinctive sandstone **Turnley's Tower** on Main Street, built in 1817 by the local landlord for double duty, as both curfew lookout and prison for "troublesome citizens." You will probably just want to stop for a meal, as the nightlife is nothing to write home about.

A café without much atmosphere to speak of, **Arthur's** (1 Shore St., tel. 028/2177-1627, 9am-4pm Wed.-Mon., 9am-2pm Tues., under £6) will nevertheless get the job done whether you're after breakfast, lunch, or tea. For dinner, **Harry's** (10-12 Mill St., tel. 028/2177-2022, www.harryscushendall.com, food served noon-9:30pm daily, £7-19), a gastropub serving hearty seafood and local meats (along with a couple veg meals), is pretty much your only option.

If you do want to spend the night, try **Riverside** (14 Mill St., tel. 028/2177-1655, www.theriversidebandb.com, £33 pp, s £40), a small sliver of tranquility right next door to Harry's, or the cheerful **Glendale** (46 Coast Rd., tel. 028/2177-1495 or 078/2105-2597, www.glendale-bandb-cushendall.co.uk, £30-40 pp), which boasts comfortable beds and excellent breakfasts.

If you're driving north to Cushendun, try following the signs for the Glendun Scenic Route instead of continuing up the A2. It may take you 12 or so miles (19 km) out of the way (leaving you back to the A2 about 3.5 mi/5.6 km farther up), but the vistas are worth the extra gas: Glendun is the boggiest of the nine,

with moorlands cloaking the mountain peaks and hazel copses dotting the lower slopes—it all feels dazzlingly remote, despite the sawmill! This is a great option for a long cycle if you're basing yourself in Cushendun (though you've got to bring your own bike).

Cushendall is 48 miles (78 km) north of Belfast on the A2. **Ulsterbus** (tel. 028/9066-6630, #252 or #150/162, 8/day Mon.-Sat., 3/day Sun., £9 one way) has a couple of services to Cushendun and Cushendall from Belfast, but a change in Ballymena is usually required. The journey takes 2-2.5 hours.

★ Layde Old Church

Signposted from Cushendall is the absolutely lovely **Layde Old Church** (0.6 mi/1 km outside town), overlooking the North Channel, an island popularly known as "Paddy's Milestone," and the Scottish coast beyond. Owing much to a babbling brook rushing toward that phenomenal ocean view, these are undoubtedly the most romantic monastic ruins in the north. Once you've admired the McDonnell family monuments, including an exquisite 19th-century high cross—it may not be "authentic," but its lack of age means you can clearly discern the carvings—follow the unpaved path to the right of the ruins for a short coastal walk.

Cushendun

Rather unusually, most of seaside **Cushendun** ("The Foot of the River Dun") is owned by the National Trust—which is why those cute Cornish cottages in the village center, built in the 1920s, are still in pristine condition. Locals still grumble about the row of blank-faced flats built on the far side of the small harbor, and they're the first thing you see when driving into town on the Torr Road, but other than the new apartments and the Mace convenience store on Main Street, Cushendun feels blissfully untouched by modernity. Adding a touch of melancholy to the postcard-prettiness are the two old hotels on the harbor beside the flats, both of them long since closed and inching toward dereliction.

But when the sun rises over the water (a sight well worth dragging yourself out of bed for), you can almost imagine you're here in Cushendun circa 1928. There may not be much to do besides hanging out on the sandy white strand, but does it really matter?

The village pub, **Mary McBride's** (2 Main St., tel. 028/2176-1511), supposedly has the smallest bar on the island (though the pub itself has several rooms, as well as an upstairs restaurant). It's a pleasant enough spot for a pint (despite the TVs tuned to the latest sporting event), but the overpriced food is best avoided. You're far better off heading to Harry's in Cushendall for dinner.

Thankfully, an excellent lunch spot is just across the street: **Theresa's Tearoom** (1 Main St., tel. 028/2176-1506, 11am-7pm Mon.-Sat. and 11am-8pm Sun. Easter-Sept., 11am-6pm weekends Oct.-Mar., £4-9) does heavenly homemade desserts as well as soups, quiches, and salads. Save room for the lemon meringue, served straight out of the oven.

Cushendun has one of the best B&Bs in Northern Ireland. Delightful nonagenarian Catherine Scally ran ★ **The Villa Farmhouse** (185 Torr Rd., tel. 028/2176-1252, www.thevillafarmhouse.com, £30 pp, s £35) for almost five decades (having moved into this atmospheric turn-of-last-century farmhouse all the way back in 1934). Mrs. Scally is no longer with us, but her daughter Maggie is an equally warm and accommodating host. Drop-ins (cyclists, usually) as well as those staying in the self-catering cottage can have a full breakfast (with fresh fruit) for £5. Packed lunches are available too. The bedrooms feature gorgeous antique furniture and real quilts on the beds, and the front rooms have expansive sea views. There are only six rooms and repeat business is considerable, so advance booking is essential from May onward. Coming from points south, turn left at the crossroads on the southern edge of town, and the Villa Farmhouse is one mile (1.6 km) down the road on the left. If you're driving the scenic route south from Ballycastle, you'll spot the

farmhouse clearly signposted on the right-hand side.

Another option, this one just a bit more out of the ordinary, is **Mullarts** (114 Tromra Rd., on the Cushendall road 1.5 mi/2.5 km south of the village, tel. 028/2176-1221, www.mullartsapartments.co.uk, d £175/weekend), three well-appointed self-catering apartments converted out of a whitewashed church built in 1849. Private gardens, patio, an outdoor play area for the kids, and barbecue facilities complete a perfect picture—in fine weather, anyway. Two doubles and one six-person apartment are all available for weekend, mid-week, or weeklong rentals.

Cushendun is 53 miles (85 km) north of Belfast off the A2. **Ulsterbus** (tel. 028/9066-6630, #252 or #150/162, 8/day Mon.-Sat., 3/day Sun., single fare £9) can get you to Cushendun from Belfast.

THE CAUSEWAY COAST

County Antrim's biggest attraction is its north coast, from pleasant seaside Ballycastle with its haunted priory ruins to gorgeous Whitepark Bay and the vertiginous Carrick-a-Rede rope bridge, to Bushmills and its infamous distillery, to the natural wonder of Giant's Causeway. You could drive it in either direction; most visitors start in Belfast, drive north past the Glens and begin in Ballycastle, and wind up in Derry City after a two- or three-day tour. There is also something to be said for driving it west-east, however, since that way you'll have an uninhibited view of the coast from the road.

Got time—and a sturdy pair of kicks? Go for the 10-mile (16 km) **Causeway Coast Way** between Ballintoy and the Giant's Causeway, which will take you about five hours. Without a doubt, this is the best way to experience the Causeway Coast, studded with funky rock formations and breathtaking vistas all around. Stop by the Causeway tourist office for more information before you head off, and plan to spend the night in Ballintoy.

The **Ulsterbus** (tel. 028/9066-6630, www.ulsterbus.co.uk) Portrush-Ballycastle route

The Dark Hedges and *Game of Thrones*

The intertwined beech trees of the Dark Hedges are more than a century past their natural lifespan.

Better known as the Kingsroad on the popular HBO series *Game of Thrones,* the **Dark Hedges,** a tunnel formed of gnarled old beech trees, are shiveringly picturesque. The owner of nearby **Gracehill House** planted more than 150 of them in the late 18th century to create a pretty avenue, though today only 90 or so beeches remain. The Dark Hedges have their own ghost, an unidentified "gray lady" who vanishes as she passes the last tree on the avenue.

Driving from Belfast to the Dark Hedges en route to the Causeway Coast is fairly straightforward: from the A44, once you reach "the Drones" near Armoy, turn left and follow signs for the Gracehill Golf Club. The lane is always accessible because it's actually a public road (Bregagh Road), so you may find yourself driving down it before you even realize you're there. For more on the history of the Dark Hedges and Gracehill House before you go, visit the **Causeway Coast & Glens Heritage Trust** website (www.ccght.org/darkhedges). Gracehill's nearest neighbor is **The Hedges Hotel** (139b Ballinlea Rd., Stranocum, Ballymoney, tel. 028/2075-2222, www. thehedgeshotel.com), which is an option for lunch or tea. You might just want to make a quick pit stop en route to the coast, though, since the place has a bit of a strange vibe.

Hardcore fans of the TV show will definitely want to reserve seats on a daylong **Game of Thrones Tour** (21 Botanic Ave., Suite 180, Belfast, 028/9568-0023, www.gameofthronestours. com), which are usually led by former extras. You have a choice of three itineraries, two Belfast-based (Iron Islands and Stormlands, departing at 8am daily, or Winterfell, departing 9am daily; both tours £40 pp) and one Dublin-based (Winterfell locations, departing 8am daily, €55). Cosplay is encouraged!

(#172) serves Bushmills, Giant's Causeway, and Ballintoy, and you can request other stops along the way (5/day Mon.-Sat., 3/day Sun.).

For visitor information before you go, check out the slick-yet-informative **Causeway Coast and Glens tourism website** (www. causewaycoastandglens.com).

Torr Head

The 11-mile (18-km) scenic route from Ballycastle to Cushendun, **Torr Road,** takes you through some of the most blissfully unspoiled bucolic countryside in Northern Ireland, made even more stunning by panoramic sea views. This winding road is so narrow in places that the dotted line down the center seems a quintessential example of Irish humor. At Torr Head, signposted a short distance off the main road, you'll spot a coast guard building abandoned in the 1920s (to reach it, you can hike up a rocky path from the small car park) and an ice house (used for packing fish) left to ruin around the same time. The hill holds a couple of passage tombs as well, though there isn't much to see. This is Ireland's closest point to Scotland, which is 12 miles (19 km) away.

The downside of such an unspoiled area is, of course, that there are no accommodations to be found until the route's end.

Ballycastle

At the eastern end of the Causeway Coast, **Ballycastle** (Baile an Chaistil) has a lovely Blue Flag beach and a wonderfully friendly vibe. The castle for which the town is named, built by the first Earl of Antrim in the 16th century, is long gone. The town is best known for its annual **Ould Lammas Fair** over the last weekend in August, which features plenty of market stalls and street entertainment, as well as two local delicacies: **dulse,** a dried seaweed, and **yellow man,** hard toffee made from a top-secret recipe. Not here for the fair? You can usually pick up both quirky snacks at **The Fruit Shop** (The Diamond, tel. 028/2076-3348, closed Sun.). Walk up Quay Road away from the harbor and after a few minutes you'll see the tiny shop on your left.

Founded in 1485 by Rory McQuillan (of the same family who built Dunluce Castle), the buildings of the Franciscan **Bonamargy Friary** were built of handsome red sandstone, dark basalt, and granite. On the eastern end of town, these ruins (always accessible) contain the family tomb of the McDonnell clan. But the friary graveyard's most famous inhabitant is Rory's descendant, Julia McQuillan, the "Black Nun" who is said to haunt the grounds . . . missing her head. Centuries-old headstones mossed over and tipped askew, inscriptions long since worn away: The scene is romantic despite the friary's location

beside the 18-hole **Ballycastle Golf Club** (Cushendall Rd., tel. 028/2076-2536, www. ballycastlegolfclub.com). Actually, the golf course surrounds the ruins and graveyard on all sides! To get to the ruins, make a left onto the road just after the big, white, modern golf clubhouse (Cushendall Rd.), and the abbey is signposted on the right, a couple minutes' walk.

Lookin' for live music? Look no further than the locals' favorite watering hole, established in 1766: the **House of McDonnell** (71 Castle St., west of the diamond, tel. 028/2076-2975). Fridays are trad and Saturdays are folk.

FOOD AND ACCOMMODATIONS

Ballycastle doesn't have much in the way of dining options. The food's basic, but **The Bay Café** (26 Bayview Rd.., on the water, tel. 075/9561-8999, 8am-5pm daily, under £7) is a nice spot to sit with a cup of tea and watch the boats bobbing in the harbor. For a proper meal, try out the pub menu at **O'Connor's** (5-7 Ann St., tel. 028/2076-2123, www.oconnorsbar.ie, food served 11:30am-9pm daily, £8-16), which is, of course, all about the local seafood. If you're here on a Thursday evening, you've lucked out: There'll be a traditional music session starting around 9pm.

The family-run, IHH **Castle Hostel** (38 Quay Rd., tel. 028/2076-2845, dorm beds £17) is a good choice for budget travelers. It's clean (if a bit threadbare), with two kitchens and a fire in the common room. The staff are friendly and helpful, the place small enough to attract solo travelers instead of noisy school groups. With colorful, comfortable rooms and a ground-floor tearoom serving lunch and coffee, **An Caisleán** (Quay Rd., tel. 028/2076-2845, www.ancaislean.co.uk, £25-35 pp) is a fine choice a few doors up. (Glenluce Lodge and Corratavey House are alternate names; it's all the same business.)

Glenmore House (4.5 km west of Ballycastle on the B15, 94 White Park Rd., tel. 028/2076-3584, www.glenmore.biz, £35 pp) features Jacuzzis in two of its seven rooms, a private two-acre fishing lake, an outstanding breakfast menu, and simple-but-hearty fare in the downstairs restaurant. This is a great choice for families and anglers. Camping is also an option.

The modern, three-star **Marine Hotel** (1-3 North St., tel. 028/2076-2222, www.marine-hotelballycastle.com, rooms £90-140) offers harbor views from many of the bedrooms. While there's no leisure center on-site, guests can use the facilities at the Marine Country Club (including large pool, sauna, steam room, Jacuzzi, and gym).

PRACTICALITIES

For more information about the fair, stop by the local **tourist office** (7 Mary St., on the eastern side of town, straight through the roundabout by the harbor, tel. 028/2076-2024, 9:30am-5pm weekdays, until 7pm July-Aug.), located in the Moyle District Council building on the way to the golf club and priory ruins.

Ballycastle is 56 miles (90 km) north of Belfast via the A2, A26, and A44. From the capital, take **Ulsterbus** route #131 (change usually required at Ballymena or Larne, 6/day Mon.-Sat., no Sun. service), or from points west on the Causeway Coast take #172 (5/day Mon.-Sat., 3/day Sun.).

Rathlin Island

Eight miles (13 km) out over Rathlin Sound, legend has it that L-shaped **Rathlin Island** (Reachlainn) was cast into the sea by Fionn mac Cumhaill's mother as a stepping-stone between Ireland and Scotland (she was headed there to pick up some whiskey). In fact, Rathlin—Northern Ireland's only inhabited offshore island—did serve as hideaway for Robert the Bruce at the beginning of the 14th century (before he returned to Britain to whup the English good). There isn't anything in terms of megalithic or monastic ruins here, so most of the out-of-towners heading to Rathlin on the ferry are devoted seal- and bird-watchers (who focus their binoculars at the **Kebble National Nature Reserve** on the island's western end)—or those just looking to get off the beaten track.

Soerneog View Hostel ("Kiln," Ouig, a 10-minute walk from the pier, tel. 028/2076-3954, john_jennifer@btinternet.com, Apr.-Sept., beds £15) sleeps only six people (in three private rooms), which means booking ahead is absolutely essential. While making your reservation, mention if you'd like to rent a bike. There's a shop near the pier where you can stock up for dinner, though it's only open 10am-4pm seasonally.

It may sound posh, but the tariffs at the **Manor House** (Church Quarter, on the northside of the harbor, tel. 028/2076-3964, www.rathlincommunity.org/accommodation, £30-35 pp) don't match the name (perhaps in part because it's owned by the National Trust). This wonderfully atmospheric Georgian (with its own walled garden providing fresh herbs for the tearoom/restaurant) is your best bet for an evening meal, though if you aren't staying here reservations are required. (The inn was closed for renovations in 2015, and in 2016 is seeking a new innkeeper; hopefully they'll have found the right person for the job by the time you're reading this.)

Or for a meal-in-a-glass, stop by the island's lone pub, **McCuaig's** (tel. 028/2076-3974), by the pier. (Fascinating side note: The owner discovered what turned out to be a pre-Celtic burial site—4,000 years old!—while digging out a new driveway in 2006.)

The **Rathlin Island ferry** (tel. 028/2076-9299, www.rathlinballycastleferry.com, 45-minute crossing from the Ballycastle pier, £12 return, £15.50 with bike) operates from Ballycastle (10am, noon, 4:30pm, and 6:30pm) and Rathlin (8:30am, 11am, 3:30pm, and 5:30pm) April-September (2/day daily until Oct. 20). The **Boat House Visitor Centre** (near the pier, tel. 028/2076-3951, 11am-4pm daily May-Aug.) dispenses tourist info and historical tidbits.

Ballintoy

Next stop on the Causeway Coast tour is sleepy **Ballintoy** (Baile an Tuaighe, "Town of the Ax"), with fantastic sea and pastoral vistas but not much else to detain you, save the touristy-but-really-fun Carrick-a-Rede Rope Bridge just east of the village. You might recognize the delightfully atmospheric harbor from the second season of *Game of Thrones*; to get there, drive west through the village and turn right at the signpost. There's a harborside cafe (tel. 028/2076-3632, 11am-6pm daily in high season) with basic lunch options. Farther on is the equally lovely harbor at Whitepark Bay, a favorite spot for landscape painters, and if you continue along a westward footpath you'll come to the hamlet of Portbraddan and Ireland's (supposedly) smallest church, **St. Gobnan's.** It's only 6 by 10 feet—yet there are ruins of an even tinier church, **St. Lasseragh's,** perched on a cliff above.

Backpackers have two options. The IHH **Sheep Island View Hostel** (42a Main St., tel. 028/2076-9391, www.sheepislandview.com, dorms £16) is clean and offers good facilities, but it's a magnet for school groups. The quieter option is **Whitepark Bay** (157 Whitepark Rd., signposted off the A2, 3 mi/4.8 km west of the village, tel. 028/2073-1745, www.hini.org.uk, Mar.-Oct., dorms £17-18, twins £20-21 pp), in a totally idyllic beachside location. It's a two-minute walk from the main road; if you're taking the bus, ask to be dropped off at the turnoff.

For B&B, try the homey, 18th-century **Ballintoy House** (9 Main St., tel. 028/2076-2317 or 077/5180-8120, www.ballintoyhouse-bandb.co.uk, £25 pp), on the eastern end of the village. It's the closest B&B to the rope bridge, and you can walk there in less than 10 minutes.

As you would expect in a place like this, the three-star **Fullerton Arms** (22-24 Main St., tel. 028/2076-9613, www.fullerton-arms.com, food served 12:30pm-9pm daily, £7-18, B&B £35 pp, s £45) is a bit on the stodgy side. Christened after Ballintoy's teetotaling 18th-century landlord, the guesthouse rather ironically features a pub with backyard beer garden, live folk and ballad sessions in summer (Mon. and Thurs. starting at 7pm), pool table, and dartboard. This is your best bet for lunch or dinner in Ballintoy (and the pub and restaurant menus thankfully provide veggie lovers with several options). There's also traditional music at the **Carrick-a-Rede** pub (tel. 028/2076-2241) on Tuesday, Friday, and Sunday nights.

To get to Ballintoy, turn off the A2 in Ballycastle and follow the B15 for about 5.5 miles (8.9 km). You'll pick up the A2 again a couple miles west of the village. **Ulsterbus** (tel. 028/9066-6630, www.ulsterbus.co.uk)

Ballintoy Harbour

route #172 can get you here from Belfast (one or two changes required) or all points along the Causeway Coast route.

★ Carrick-a-Rede Rope Bridge

One of the most exhilarating experiences in the north is a walk across the 65-foot **Carrick-a-Rede Rope Bridge** (signposted off the B15, tel. 028/2073-1582, 10am-5:15pm daily early Mar.-May and Sept.-Oct., 10am-6:15pm daily June-Aug., £6), suspended 80 feet above a dramatic sea gorge and swaying in the blustery winds. *Do look down to drink in the whole effect!* There's nothing on the wee island on the far side (which is called Carrick-a-Rede) but pretty ocean views, but most folks take their time snapping photos and watching the birds. Local fishermen used to reassemble the bridge every spring to catch salmon on the far side of this little island, and today it's one of the National Trust's most popular attractions. Needless to say, those with a fear of heights should avoid this one, and opening is always subject to weather conditions; it's wise to call ahead if the forecast is anything less than perfect.

Giant's Causeway

According to legend, this UNESCO World Heritage Site was a footbridge between Ireland and Scotland, destroyed by the warrior Fionn mac Cumhaill to prevent the giant Finn Gall from following him back to Ireland. Under an undulating series of cliffs are towering walls and a seaward staircase fashioned by nature out of gray basalt, some 37,000 hexagonal columns in all. Frankly, while the causeway is genuinely beautiful and well worth a visit, don't expect anything fantastic to look at and you won't be disappointed. Photographers hired by the Tourist Board have a knack for taking dramatic snapshots with impossible hues. Lovely as this place is, it is not the eighth wonder of the world.

On arrival you can either take the cliff route (part of the 10-mi/16-km Causeway Coast Way) to the right or head down a paved road straight to the sea and rock formations. This is, of course, where all the other tourists go (many of them on a shuttle bus called the "Causeway Coaster"; it's only a five-minute walk from visitors center to causeway, and most of those on the bus aren't handicapped or elderly—for whom the shuttle was no doubt intended). The gorse-lined cliff path is easy and dramatic but far less popular. After a mile or so a rather precipitous wooden staircase will bring you down to the paved shore path, or you could keep walking and turn back later.

Giant's Causeway

Walkers and cyclists get free entry, but the admission charge is £9.50 per person (yes, per person!) to park in the official lot. This includes a guided walk and admission to the exhibition in the brand-new visitors center, but it is still ridiculously high. It seems even the National Trust can't resist price-gouging on occasion. And don't waste your money at the visitors center tearoom; get thee to **The Nook,** a fantastic 19th-century schoolhouse-turned-restaurant just beside the Giant's Causeway entrance.

The **visitors center** (2 mi/3.2 km north of Bushmills on the B146, tel. 028/2073-1855, www.giantscausewaycentre.com) also serves as a tourist information point. Hours vary seasonally (10am-6pm daily July-Aug., 10am-5pm daily Mar.-June and Sept.-Oct., 10am-4:30pm daily Nov.-Feb.).

Backpackers will appreciate **Finn McCool's** (32 Causeway Rd., tel. 028/2073-2011, www.finnmccoolshostel.com, dorm beds £18-20, private rooms £55) for much more than the two-minute walk to the Causeway entrance. This hostel offers a hot breakfast included in the price, DIY barbecue facilities, and a scenic view from every room (though none are en suite). You can rent a bicycle (£12/day), golf clubs, or fishing equipment. Pick up groceries in Bushmills on your way out. Travelers who'd ordinarily stay at a budget B&B might want to reserve one of the double rooms here.

Otherwise, **Ardtrabane House** (66 Causeway Rd., tel. 028/2073-1007, www.ardtrabanehouse.co.uk, £89/70 pp with/without breakfast) is equally convenient: You can walk to the Causeway, thereby saving the £9.50-per-person parking and admission fee, but that convenience is unfortunately reflected in the price. You do get a warm welcome, comfy digs, and a big breakfast (be it pancakes or the full fry).

As you would expect, the **Causeway Hotel** (40 Causeway Rd., tel. 028/2073-1226, www.giants-causeway-hotel.com, B&B £35 pp, s £50, lunch £6-11, dinner £8-15) offers unbeatable views of ocean and causeway. The atmosphere may be downright stodgy and the staff not particularly welcoming, but the location is reason enough to stay here. Even if you're staying at the hotel, though, you should take your lunch, tea, and dinner at ★ **The Nook** (48 Causeway Rd., tel. 028/2073-2993, food served 10:30am-8:30pm daily, lunch £4-7, dinner £8-14), an excellent pub-cum-restaurant in a converted schoolhouse just across the road from the hotel and Giant's Causeway visitors center. The menu offers creative and traditional dishes using only local produce (though no vegan dishes apart from the side salad, alas), and the barstaff are pleasant and attentive. You can eat on the original slanted desks beside an open fire (but be careful your dishes don't slide off); the back room, brightened with white Christmas lights, has glass-fronted cupboards filled with vintage toys. You can get a cup of gourmet coffee here, too, sipping it as you muse over whatever memories are brought to mind by the 1980s and '90s pop tunes playing on the stereo.

★ Dunluce Castle

If there were an award for a castle ruin with the most dramatic situation, **Dunluce Castle** (87 Dunluce Rd., signposted off the A2 5 mi/8 km west of Giant's Causeway and 3 mi/4.8 km east of Portrush, tel. 028/2073-1938, 10am-5:30pm daily Apr.-Sept., 10am-4:30pm daily Oct.-Mar., £5) would surely win the distinction. The castle perches precipitously on a cliff over a cave (called Mermaid's Cave, reachable by a steep path down from the castle), and the basalt rock beneath is slowly crumbling away: In 1639 part of the castle tumbled into the sea during a reception, taking most of the servants along with it. Though nothing so tragic has transpired in the intervening centuries, it's only a matter of time before the rest of the castle is lost to the waves.

The earliest extant structures (towers and walls) date from the mid-13th century, though archaeological excavations indicate the land was inhabited as early as the 9th century. Dunluce was home to the McQuillans, the ruling family of north Antrim in the 16th century, and was later owned by Scottish rogue Sorley Boy McDonnell (whose brother married a McQuillan), who added a highly incongruous sandstone loggia (some of which remains).

Even if you haven't budgeted the time for an extended visit, do take a few minutes to admire the view from the grassy hill down from the car park. The Ulsterbus Causeway route makes frequent stops at Dunluce (5/day between Coleraine and the Giant's Causeway Hotel). You could easily walk or bike here from Bushmills (though due caution is required on the busy A2), or walk via the Causeway Coast Way.

Bushmills

If you aren't a whiskey-drinker, then chances are you'll find Bushmills a dull little town. That said, you can certainly base yourself here when visiting Giant's Causeway, which is only a few miles down the road.

The **Old Bushmills Distillery** (Distillery Rd., signposted on the B66, www.bushmills. com, tel. 028/2073-1521, 9:30am-5:30pm Mon.-Sat. and noon-5:30pm Sun. Apr.-Oct., 10:30am-3:30pm weekdays and 1:30pm-3:30pm weekends Nov.-Mar., £7.50) is, of course, the prime attraction. It's been licensed to distill since 1608 (making this the oldest licensed distillery on the planet), and on the tour you'll learn everything you ever wanted to know about the making of *uisce beatha*. Naturally, a shot or two is included in the price of admission.

The new, purpose-built **Mill Rest Hostel** (49 Main St., tel. 028/2073-1222, www.hini. org.uk, dorms £18-20) is popular with tour groups, but it's the place to stay if you're on a shoestring. For B&B, try bright and homey **Portcaman House** (11 Priestland Rd., tel. 028/2073-2286, www.giantscausewayho-tel.co.uk, £35-40 pp). The Priestland Road turnoff is opposite the railway entrance on Dunluce Road.

The **Bushmills Inn** (9 Dunluce Rd., tel. 028/2073-3000, www.bushmillsinn.com, rooms £160-320, food served noon-6pm and 7pm-9:30pm Mon.-Sat., noon-9pm Sun., lunch £10-14, dinner £11-24) is a gorgeously authentic 17th-century hotel where you'll still find gas lamps burning in the downstairs sitting rooms. The rooms in the new wing are relatively characterless (and much more expensive), so you may want to request one of the smaller rooms in the original building. These "budget" rooms overlook the main street rather than the river, but they're absolutely charming. Kill the time before your dinner reservation poking through the spooky old hallways in search of secret passages. The restaurant offers a separate vegetarian menu.

Bushmills is 58 miles (93 km) north of Belfast on the A26 (picking up the B66 in Ballymoney), 13 miles (21 km) west of Ballycastle and 39 miles (63 km) northeast of Derry City on the A2. Bushmills is served by the Ulsterbus Causeway route.

The niftiest way to reach Giant's Causeway from Bushmills (only a 2-mi/3.2-km trip) is via a narrow-gauge **steam locomotive** (Ballaghmore Rd., signposted from the A2, tel. 028/2073-2844, www.freewebs.com/gi-antscausewayrailway, departures on the half hour 11:30am-5:30pm daily June-Sept., single or return ticket £5).

Derry

DERRY CITY/ LONDONDERRY

Vibrant Derry, known to British loyalists as Londonderry, is the island's fourth-largest city. During the war between the Protestant William of Orange and the deposed Catholic James II, Derry got the moniker "Maiden City" because the inhabitants of its walled city were able to withstand a siege that lasted more than a year. To this day, you'll still see the words "never give up—never surrender!" painted on brick walls in unionist sections of town—which leads you to wonder which century these people think they're living in.

A note on the Derry/Londonderry dilemma: Londonderry is the city's legal name, but Derry is the *original* name, preferred by a majority of its inhabitants (the city is roughly 75 percent Catholic and 25 percent Protestant), so henceforth in this chapter "the Maiden City" is referred to as Derry. (Besides, even if you're not a hardcore republican, you've got to admit that "Londonderry" stinks of imperialism.)

There's enough to keep you here for two full days—if nothing else, take a leisurely walk along the early-17th-century city walls, the only ones intact in all Ireland—but don't bank on spending more than three nights here. By your third morning, as in Belfast, all that lingering sectarianism is no longer a sad-yet-fascinating novelty.

On opposite sides of the River Foyle are the **old city walls,** dating to the early 17th century, and the traditionally Protestant **Waterside** section (though in fact the Catholic/Protestant population is nearly 50/50). West of the old city is the **Bogside,** the traditionally Catholic working-class neighborhood that saw so much violence and bloodshed in the late 1960s and early '70s, but which is now completely rebuilt. Waterside and Bogside are connected via the double-deck Craigavon Bridge.

★ Derry City Walls

Constructed between 1614 and 1619, these are the only intact city walls in all Ireland, though the four original gates were rebuilt in the 18th and 19th centuries along with three new entrances. No visit to Derry is complete without making the circuit around the walls to observe the city within and without; it may sound perilous, but these walls are sturdy enough at 30 feet thick and up to 26 feet high. The circumference is about a mile and a quarter (nine furlongs, to be precise), and staircases are located at many points along the inner walls. It'll take you half an hour to make a complete circuit, but you'll want to walk it more than once. They're always open and admission is free. You can view many of the peace murals from the southwestern section of the city wall, including *The Death of Innocence,* but take the time to exit the old city and view them from the street.

Guildhall

Step inside the neo-Gothic **Guildhall** (Guildhall Sq., tel. 028/7137-7335, www.derry-city.gov.uk, 9am-5pm weekdays, free), which houses the Derry City Council headquarters as well as the greatest number of stained-glass windows of any building on the island. The Guildhall was built in 1887, destroyed by fire on Easter Sunday 1908, and rebuilt and reopened in 1912. Its clock face is the largest in Ireland, and at 13 feet and one-quarter inch, its pendulum is one-quarter inch longer than Big Ben's. In the foyer is a larger-than-life (six-foot 10-inch) statue of Queen Victoria at her dowdiest. Fashioned out of Sicilian marble, the statue weighs in at a staggering 2.5 tons—and the pedestal is another three! You can take your time wandering through the building looking at all the windows—though the Main Hall, with its California redwood ceiling

Derry City

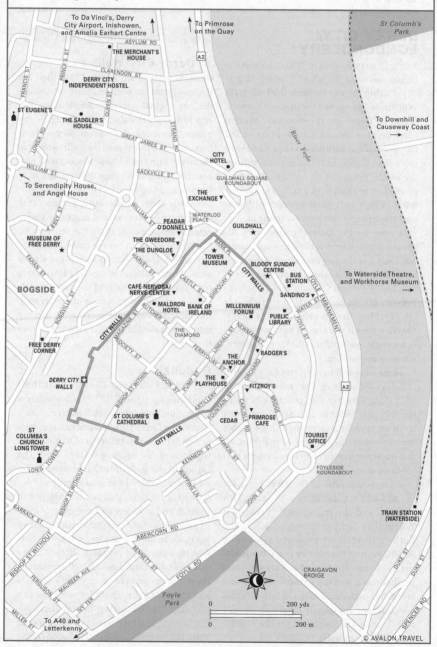

To Da Vinci's, Derry City Airport, Inishowen, and Amelia Earhart Centre

To Primrose on the Quay

St Columb's Park

ASYLUM RD

THE MERCHANT'S HOUSE

CLARENDON ST

DERRY CITY INDEPENDENT HOSTEL

FRANCIS ST

PRINCE'S ST

QUEEN ST

A2

ST EUGENE'S

THE SADDLER'S HOUSE

GREAT JAMES ST

STRAND RD

River Foyle

To Downhill and Causeway Coast

LOWER RD

WILLIAM ST

SACKVILLE ST

CITY HOTEL

To Serendipity House, and Angel House

GUILDHALL SQUARE ROUNDABOUT

WILLIAM ST

THE EXCHANGE ▼

ABBEY ST

WATERLOO PLACE

PEADAR O'DONNELL'S

GUILDHALL ★

MUSEUM OF FREE DERRY ★

THE GWEEDORE ▼

THE DUNGLOE ▼

BANK PL

HARVEY ST

TOWER MUSEUM ★

CITY WALLS

BLOODY SUNDAY CENTRE ★

BUS STATION

FOYLE EMBANKMENT

FAHAN ST

BOGSIDE

CASTLE ST

SHIPQUAY ST

SANDINO'S ▼

To Waterside Theatre, and Workhorse Museum

ROSSVILLE ST

CAFÉ NERVOSA/ NERVE CENTER ▼

MALDRON HOTEL

BANK OF IRELAND

MILLENNIUM FORUM

PUBLIC LIBRARY

WATER ST

FOYLE ST

MAGAZINE ST

BUTCHER ST

THE DIAMOND

NEWMARKET ST

CITY WALLS

SOCIETY ST

FERRYQUAY ST

LINENHALL ST

BADGER'S ▼

FREE DERRY CORNER

BISHOP ST WITHIN

LONDON ST

PUMP ST

THE ANCHOR ▼

ORCHARD ST

DERRY CITY WALLS ✚

THE PLAYHOUSE ■

FITZROY'S ▼

A2

ARTILLERY ST

FOUNTAIN ST

CARLISLE RD

BRIDGE ST

ST COLUMBA'S CHURCH/ LONG TOWER ✚

ST COLUMB'S CATHEDRAL ✝

CITY WALLS

CEDAR ▼

PRIMROSE CAFE ▼

TOURIST OFFICE ●

LONG TOWER ST

KENNEDY ST

HAWKIN ST

FOYLESIDE ROUNDABOUT

BARRACK ST

BISHOP ST WITHOUT

WAPPING LN

JOHN ST

TRAIN STATION (WATERSIDE) ■

ABERCORN RD

BENNETT ST

DUKE ST

DUKE ST

BISHOP ST WITHOUT

FERGUSON ST

MAUREEN AVE

FOYLE RD

CRAIGAVON BRDGE

SPENCER RD

MILLER ST

IVY TER

Foyle Park

To A40 and Letterkenny

0   200 yds
0   200 m

© AVALON TRAVEL

suggested donation £2) date to 1633, and the whole place is a monument to the loyalist triumph against the Jacobites during the siege of 1688-1689—for the relics inside (including a cast-iron cannonball weighing 280 pounds) as well as the fact that the cathedral was the only building still standing afterward. The chancel has a stained-glass window depicting the Ascension along with a series of mosaics of the four Evangelists along with Patrick and Columba. Some of the dust-laden flags above your head are more than two centuries old. To the rear of the church is the chapter house, containing aforesaid historical artifacts, along with the choristers' vestry, featuring a triad of windows glorifying the Williamites' victory. Note that if you take the guided city tour through the tourist office, your admission to the cathedral is covered under the same ticket—and you'll get more out of your visit.

The Bishop's Gate stairs lead up to the Derry City walls.

panels and grand pipe organ, is particularly atmospheric. The organ was built in 1914 and was restored by the same firm 68 years later, after the 1972 IRA bombing.

Tower Museum

The **Tower Museum** (Union Hall Pl., tel. 028/7137-2411, www.derrycity.gov.uk/museums, 10am-5pm Tues.-Sat., plus bank holiday Mon. in summer, £4) has two permanent exhibitions, one a thorough history of the city and the other with various treasures dredged up from a Spanish Armada ship that sank in Kinnegoe Bay, Donegal, in 1588. The shipwreck was discovered by members of the Derry Sub-Aqua Club in 1971 and subsequently excavated by a team of underwater archaeologists.

St. Columb's Cathedral

The oldest parts of **St. Columb's Cathedral** (London St., tel. 028/7126-7313, www.stcolumbscathedral.org, 9am-5pm Mon.-Sat., 9am-1pm and 2pm-4pm in low season,

The Bogside

Head to the Bogside, Derry's traditionally Catholic blue-collar neighborhood, for better views of the **peace murals** as well as the **Bloody Sunday Memorial,** all along Rossville Street and its side roads. These dozen (at time of writing) murals are the work of only three local artists (William Kelly, Tom Kelly, and Kevin Hasson), along with a rainbow-hued 2004 addition that features the work of Derry schoolchildren from both sides. The murals depict Bernadette Devlin, a republican activist elected a mid-Ulster MP at the age of 21; Bobby Sands, shown longhaired and bearded, during the last phase of his fatal hunger strike; and a kaleidoscope of smiling faces, the 14 demonstrators massacred by British troops on Bloody Sunday.

Another mural shows the figure of 14-year-old Annette McGavigan, who was murdered in 1971 by a sniper perched on the city wall; she was carrying a towel on her way to the pool, which the soldier suspected hid a bomb. The oldest mural declares "You are now entering Free Derry" at the intersection of Rossville and Fahan Streets; it was painted in 1969 after the "Battle of the Bogside" of August 12-14,

The Derry City Coat of Arms

You might be wondering what the deal is with that smiling yellow skeleton on Derry City's coat of arms. William de Burgo, the "Brown Earl" of Ulster and ruler of the city of Derry, was having a castle, called Greencastle, built on the east coast of the Inishowen Peninsula in County Donegal. William bricked his cousin Walter de Burgo, an Anglo-Norman knight, into a dungeon in said castle in 1332, where Walter starved to death. Why do this, you ask? William suspected Walter of having an affair with his wife. So that yellow skeleton represents the murdered Walter de Burgo—though no one's sure what he had reason to grin about . . .

when republicans managed to cut their neighborhood off from all British police and paramilitary activity (a period that lasted nearly a year). This wall is all that remains of the old Bogside; all the flats and townhouses you see now are new construction, and the rest of the murals date from 1994 onward. You might be surprised to see how quiet and workaday the Bogside is; it's a perfectly safe place nowadays. You can view all the murals on **The Bogside Artists** website (www.bogsideartists.com).

Developed by the Bloody Sunday Trust, the **Museum of Free Derry** (55-61 Glenfada Park, off Rossville St., tel. 028/7136-0880, www.museumoffreederry.org, 9:30am-4:30pm Mon.-Thurs., 9:30am-3pm Fri., 1pm-4pm Sat.-Sun., £3) chronicles the Catholic struggle for civil rights, including background on individual Bogside neighborhoods and emphasizing the personal experiences of local residents.

Construction of the Catholic cathedral, the neo-Gothic **St. Eugene's** (Great James St., tel. 028/7126-2894), was begun after the Great Famine and dedicated in 1873. There isn't nearly as much here in terms of history as at St. Columb's, but many will find this church's soaring ceiling and quiet austerity reason for a slight detour.

While in Bogside, check out the wonderfully ornate Catholic **St. Columba's Church, Long Tower** (Long Tower St., off Barrack St., tel. 028/7126-7284), which features several excellent reproductions of masterpieces by Raphael, Leonardo, and others (a full-size *Last Supper* is painted above the altar). The church

opened in 1786 (partly through the generosity of Derry's left-leaning Protestant bishop, the infamous Frederick Augustus Hervey), though construction continued for many decades afterward.

Other Sights

Featuring exhibits peopled with the usual creepy mannequins in period dress, the **Workhouse Museum** (23 Glendermott Rd., Waterside, 0.9 mile north of the Craigavon Bridge, tel. 028/7131-8328, www.derrycity.gov.uk/museums, 10am-4:30pm Mon.-Thurs. and Sat., free) is housed in the same building as the Waterside public library. This workhouse was opened in 1840 and only closed in 1948, at which time it was converted into a hospital; the hospital closed in 1991, and the building reopened as a museum in 1997. Along with material on the Great Famine and 19th-century poverty in general, there are rotating historical exhibitions that don't necessarily have much to do with the workhouse itself.

A guide at the **Amelia Earhart Centre** (Ballyarnett Country Park, 3 miles north of the city on the A2, tel. 028/7135-4040, www.derrycity.gov.uk/museums, 9am-4pm Mon.-Thurs., 9am-1pm Fri., ring for an appointment, free) will take you to the very spot where the famous American aviator made her unexpected landing on May 21, 1932.

Activities and Recreation
TOURS
Politically correct, nonsectarian city tours (including a circuit of the city walls) start at

Hang-Gliding in Ulster

Northern Ireland offers opportunities to sightsee from above, as it were. In County Derry, the **Ulster Gliding Club** (tel. 077/0980-8276 for bookings, www.ulsterglidingclub.org, lessons given 9:30am-6pm Sat.-Sun., trial lesson £35), based in Bellarena, 22 miles (36 km) east of Derry City, offers instruction for beginners as well as gliders of all experience levels. Same goes for **First Flight Paragliding** (Newtownabbey, tel. 028/9083-2648, www. firstflightparagliding.co.uk, one-day taster course £120), which is affiliated with the **Ulster Hang-gliding and Paragliding Club** (tel. 028/3834-1544, www.uhpc.co.uk), based in Craigavon in County Armagh, 14 miles (22 km) northeast of Armagh City and 28 miles (45 km) southwest of Belfast. Flying sites include mountains in the Sperrins in County Tyrone and the Mournes in County Down.

the **tourist office** (44 Foyle St., tel. 028/7126-7284)—they're a bit more expensive than other tours but last nearly two hours (tours depart 2:30pm Mon.-Fri. Sept.-June, 11:15am and 3:15pm Mon.-Fri. July-Aug., £5).

Alternatively, ring Martin McCrossan at **Derry City Tours** (11 Carlisle Rd., tel. 028/7127-1996 or 077/1293-7997, www.derrycitytours.com, hour-long tour £4), which depart the office on Carlisle Road at 10am, noon, 2pm, and 4pm year-round. The price includes a cup of tea.

OTHER ACTIVITIES AND RECREATION

Derry is the starting point of the 21-mile (34 km) **Foyle Valley Cycle Route,** which dips into Donegal briefly before delivering you to the Strabane tourist office in County Tyrone. The route is mostly off-road, making it a good choice for a peaceful, if strenuous, day's activity. Ask at the Derry tourist office for more information and a free map.

Foyle International Golf Centre (12 Alder Rd., tel. 028/7135-2222, www.foylegolfcentre.co.uk) has two courses (one 18-hole championship course and a 9-hole par-3 course) as well as a floodlit driving range. The **City of Derry Golf Club** (49 Victoria Rd., Prehen, 3 mi/4.8 km west of Derry City, tel. 028/7134-6369, www.cityofderrygolfclub. com) also offers two courses.

They're over the border in County Donegal, but the **Lenamore Stables** (Muff, tel. 074/938-4022) are only two miles (3.2 km) outside the city.

Food

Derry may not compete with Belfast when it comes to eating out, but you can have yourself a scrummy meal if you know where to go.

The coffee shop at the Nerve Centre, **Café Nervosa** (7-8 Magazine St., tel. 028/7126-0562, 9:30am-5pm Mon.-Sat., £3-5), facing the west wall, is a good place to chill out with a cup of coffee and surf the net for no extra charge. The lunches are simple but hearty, with several vegetarian and gluten-free choices. With an in-house baker and butcher and two locations, **Primrose Café** (15 Carlisle Rd., tel. 028/7126-4622, 8am-5pm Mon.-Sat., 11am-4pm Sun., £7-10) and **Primrose on the Quay** (2 Atlantic Quay, same phone) are the very best spots in town for either a sourdough sandwich or the full fry, though the new waterside eatery has a fancier ambience.

The portions are on the dainty side, but **Badger's** (16-18 Orchard St., tel. 028/7136-0763, food served noon-7pm Mon.-Thurs., noon-9:30pm Fri.-Sat., noon-4pm Sun., £5-11) does the best pub grub in town—the relatively creative menu features tasty Indian-inspired vegetarian dishes. The warm wood paneling, stained glass, whimsical wall murals, and second-floor nonsmoking section (with its own bar) make Badger's a comfy spot for lunch.

Two swanky but laid-back spots for lunch or dinner are **The Exchange** (Exchange

House, Queen's Quay, tel. 028/7127-3990, www.exchangerestaurant.com, noon-10pm Mon.-Sat., 5:30pm-9pm Sun., £8-15), a wine bar/restaurant, and **Fitzroy's** (3 Carlisle Rd. and 2-4 Bridge St., tel. 028/7126-6211, www.fitzroysrestaurant.com, 9:30am-10pm Wed.-Sun., 9:30am-7pm Mon.-Tues., lunch £5-10, dinner £8-12, £13 3-course dinner Wed.-Thurs. after 7pm). These are a couple of Derry's best eateries, offering imaginative dishes with fresh ingredients—no overpriced, microwaved appetizers here!

Owned by a very friendly Irish-Lebanese couple, ★ **Cedar** (32 Carlisle Rd., tel. 028/7137-3868, http://cedarlebanese.webs. com, 5:30pm-9:30pm Wed.-Sat., £5-15) has something for everyone, from vegan moussaka to marinated lamb skewers. Be sure to order the *patata harra,* crispy thin-sliced potatoes drizzled in hot sauce. Later on in the evening the chef will likely emerge from the kitchen to chat with you, not just to make sure you're enjoying your meal but because he's genuinely interested in how your vacation is shaping up. The food is good, but it's the kind reception that makes Cedar such a memorable eatery.

Entertainment and Events
ENTERTAINMENT

No trip to Derry would be complete without a pint (or five) at one of the pubs along Waterloo Street, especially **Peadar O'Donnell's** (59-63 Waterloo St., tel. 028/7126-7295, peadars@ti-scali.co.uk), named for the Donegal-born IRA rebel-turned-novelist. Peadar's has the best trad in town, with different fiddlers, strummers, and singers on every evening at 11pm onward—not to mention the quaintly unsettling decor, mounted boar and ram heads and taxidermied birds of prey. The squeamish should avoid looking above the bar, where you'll find dried pork (including a pig's head decked out in sunglasses) strung from the ceiling. Fortunately, Peadar's attracts mostly locals despite its reputation for great trad. The other two pubs of note along this street are **The Gweedore,** which has a couple of long-haired

strummers singing bluesy rock every night, and is attached to Peadar's by a door at the rear of the pub; and **The Dungloe** (41-43 Waterloo St., tel. 028/7126-7716), which offers trad on Thursday, rock on Friday and Saturday, and karaoke on Sunday. **The Anchor** (38 Ferryquay St., tel. 028/7136-8601, www.anchorbar.co.uk), still family-run, is another excellent spot for live blues most nights of the week.

If you're looking for a trendier spot, the hands-down favorite of 20-something locals is **Sandino's** (1 Water St., tel. 028/7130-9297, www.sandinoscafebar.com)—named after the Nicaraguan guerrilla (makes sense, considering the occasional political events held here). There's always something going on Thursday-Sunday, be it live rock or trad, DJs, or film screenings.

Besides classical, folk, and pop concerts, dramatic offerings at the **Millennium Forum** (Newmarket St., tel. 028/7126-4455, www.millenniumforum.co.uk, £8-20) run the gamut from Shakespeare and Brontë adaptations to classic American musicals. The **Waterside Theatre** (The Ebrington Centre, Glendermott Rd., tel. 028/7131-4000, www. watersidetheatre.com, £5-11) hosts both local and international dance and theater companies, with a few tribute bands and children's plays thrown in for variety's sake. **The Playhouse** (5-7 Artillery St., tel. 028/7126-8027, www.derryplayhouse.co.uk, £7-15) does comedy, jazz and pop concerts, and contemporary (sometimes political) drama.

Catch an indie flick or pop/rock concert at the **Nerve Centre** (7-8 Magazine St., tel. 028/7126-0562, www.nerve-centre.org.uk, screenings £2, concerts £10-15), which also hosts the Foyle Film Festival every November. Part of a Bogside community regeneration project, the **Gasyard Centre** (128 Lecky Rd., Brandywell, tel. 028/7126-2812, www. gasyardcentrederry.com) sometimes hosts concerts in its multipurpose auditorium.

FESTIVALS AND EVENTS

Derry offers a music fest to suit every taste. In mid- to late April, the **Feis Doire**

Cholmcille is the largest festival of Irish traditional music in Derry or Donegal. For more information, contact the **Millennium Forum** (Newmarket St., tel. 028/7126-4455, www.millenniumforum.co.uk), which hosts most of the events. Alternatively, the annual **City of Derry Jazz and Big Band Festival** (tel. 028/7137-6545, www.cityofderryjazz-festival.com) is usually the last weekend in April. And for something you can dance to, there's the **Celtronic Festival** (tel. 078/1491-8452, www.celtronicfestival.com) in late June and early July.

August brings competing cultural events (music, readings, exhibitions, and suchlike) in the form of the Bogside **Gasyard Wall Féile** (tel. 028/7126-2812, www.gasyardcen-trederry.com) and the **Maiden City Festival** (tel. 028/7134-9250) for "Prods."

Autumn brings more entertainments. The culmination of the city's weeklong **Halloween Carnival** (tel. 028/7137-6545, www.derrycity.gov.uk) is fireworks on the night itself. The **Seagate Foyle Film Festival** (tel. 028/7126-7432, www.foylefilm-festival.org), the largest in Northern Ireland, generally takes place in mid-November and features both Irish and international flicks.

Shopping

Derry has two large shopping centers, the **Richmond** (tel. 028/7126-0525, www.rich-mondcentre.co.uk) on the diamond within the old city walls, and the **Foyleside** (tel. 028/7137-7575, www.foyleside.co.uk) just without on Orchard Street. For a quieter, quainter shopping excursion, pop inside the **Derry Craft Village** (entrances on Shipquay St. and Magazine St.); a couple of small shops sell local crystal and jewelry beside a few cheap-and-cheesy souvenir stores. Even if you're not interested in either, it's nice to walk through this lovely little courtyard with its charming architecture and brightly painted doors. There's a sec-ondhand bookstore here worth an extended browse: **Foyle Books** (12A Magazine St., tel. 028/7137-2530).

Accommodations

B&B accommodations are comparatively difficult to come by; you have more hotel choices. Luckily for backpackers, the **Derry City Independent Hostel** (Prince's St., tel. 028/7128-0542, www.derry-hostel.co.uk, dorms £14-15) is pleasantly bohemian and cozy, and prices include continental break-fast. The "fifth night free" policy and nightly barbecues April-September contribute to the phenomenon known around here as the "Derry vortex"—once here, you'll find it dif-ficult to leave.

★ **The Saddler's House** (36 Great James St., tel. 028/7126-9691 or 028/7126-4223, www.thesaddlershouse.com, £30-35 pp, s £40-55) is universally recognized as the best B&B in the city, and deservedly so. Dr. and Mrs. Pyne live in another townhouse around the corner, **The Merchant's House** (16 Queen St., £33-40 pp, s £40-55), which has more rooms with shared bath. Both Georgians have been restored to perfection—grandfa-ther clocks, Hogarth prints, and decorative plasterwork. The breakfasts are outstanding and the resident canine is delightful. Book ahead, especially in high season, and call in to Saddler's when checking in.

If Saddler's and Merchant's are booked up, there's another set of sister B&Bs on the Bogside: **Serendipity House** (26 Marlborough St., tel. 028/7126-4229, www.serendipityrooms.co.uk, £28-30 pp) and **Angel House** (43 Marlborough St., same details). Rooms are small but have lots of character, and there's a generous continental breakfast buffet along with the usual cooked options.

It's surprising that the four-star **Maldron Hotel** (Butcher St., tel. 028/7137-1000, www.maldronhotelderry.com, £40-55 pp, s £60-80), the first built within the old city walls, has such a modern design and impersonal ambi-ence. That said, the location (at Magazine St. and Butcher St., just beside the western wall) is second to none—it's certainly reason enough to stay here. Check out the website for spe-cial deals.

Also boasting four stars is the Great Southern **City Hotel** (Queen's Quay, tel. 028/7136-5800, www.cityhotelderry.com, rooms £90-150), which offers views of the Guildhall and the River Foyle and a deluxe leisure center (full-size pool, steam room, Jacuzzi, and gym).

It may not have the location, but the three-star **Da Vinci's** (15 Culmore Rd., 1 mi/1.6 km north of the city, tel. 028/7127-9111, www.davincishotel.com, rooms £60-140) more than compensates with comfortable business-class rooms and 21 cushy self-catering apartments. While there aren't leisure facilities at the hotel, it offers discounted rates at the Templemore Sports Complex a mile away. You'll find above-average fare in the hotel restaurant and a lot of locals (always a good sign) in all of Da Vinci's three bars.

Information and Services

Tourist office (44 Foyle St., tel. 028/7126-7284, www.derryvisitor.com) hours vary seasonally (9am-5pm weekdays all year, plus 10am-5pm Sat. mid-Mar.-June and Oct.; 9am-7pm weekdays, 10am-6pm Sat., and 10am-5pm Sun. July-Sept.). The *Derry Journal* (www.derryjournal.com) is a good source for news and events in the Maiden City.

Derry's banks (all with ATMs and bureaux de change) are clustered around Guildhall Square and Waterloo Place, including **Ulster Bank** and **Bank of Ireland.** Your best bet for a pharmacy is **Boots** (tel. 028/7126-0432) in the Foyleside Shopping Centre.

Getting There

Derry City is 72 miles (116 km) northwest of Belfast on the A6. Get here from the capital city via **Ulsterbus** (Foyle Street Depot, tel. 029/7126-2261, #212, 32/day Mon.-Fri., 19/day Sat., 11/day Sun., travel time 1 hour 50 minutes, £12 one way). **Northern Ireland Railways** pulls into Waterside Station (tel. 028/7134-2228, www.translink.co.uk) across the Craigavon Bridge and offers service to/from Belfast (9/day Mon.-Sat., 3/day Sun., £12 one way). At 2 hours and 10 minutes, the train actually takes longer than the bus!

Derry City Airport (Airport Rd., Eglinton, 7 mi/11 km northeast of Derry, tel. 028/7181-0784, www.cityofderryairport.com) offers direct flights from Dublin, Glasgow, and Manchester on British Airways, and Liverpool, London Stansted, and Nottingham on RyanAir. The **AIRporter** shuttle runs six times daily between the airport and the Quayside Shopping Centre.

the eerie ruins of the 18th-century Downhill Estate

For bus transport from the republic, Letterkenny-based **John McGinley** (tel. 074/913-5201, www.johnmcginley.com) operates a coach service linking Dublin (city and airport) with Derry before continuing on to Donegal. **Bus Éireann** can get you here from Donegal Town and Letterkenny (#64, 8/day daily).

Getting Around

Derry is small enough that you can walk everywhere you want to go. If you're just spending the afternoon, park your car at the multilevel Foyleside garage across the car park beside the tourist office (£0.80/hour).

For bicycle rental, try **Claudy Cycles** (556 Barnailt Rd., tel. 028/7133-8128, www.claudy-cycles.co.uk, £12/50 per day/week).

For a cab, ring **The Taxi Co.** (3A Lower Clarendon St., tel. 028/7126-2626) or **Foyle Taxis** (10a Market St., tel. 028/7127-9999 or 028/7126-3905), both of which offer 24-hour service.

★ DOWNHILL ESTATE

Blink once and you might miss the loveliest spot in County Derry: Downhill is a tiny place, only on the map for the 18th-century clifftop estate of Bishop Hervey, now a huge and extremely eerie ruin. Beneath that cliff is a pristine beach popular with surfers.

The grand estate of the infamous Bishop of Derry and fourth Earl of Bristol, Frederick Augustus Hervey, has lain in ruin since World War II. More entrepreneur and playboy than holy man, he invented and grew wealthy on Hervey's Bristol Cream (ask for it instead of Bailey's while you're in the North) and built

this rambling mansion in 1774. These ruins are among the very creepiest in all Ireland, especially if visited on a sunless day. Much of the original 395-acre **Downhill Estate** (Hezlett Farm, 107 Sea Rd., Castlerock, signposted from the A2, tel. 028/7084-8728, www.ntni.org.uk, dawn-dusk all year, car £3.80) now makes up **Downhill Forest** (10am-dusk daily, free), which slopes eastward to the little ho-hum resort town of Castlerock. Perched on a cliff over the north coast, a short walk from the mansion ruin, is the delightful **Mussenden Temple** (11am-6pm weekends Mar.-May and Sept.-Oct., daily Easter week and June, 11am-7pm daily July-Aug.), which housed Hervey's library, mistress, or both, depending on whom you ask. This place is a favorite haunt of wedding parties, and a midsummer concert is performed on the lawn.

Just off the beach, the IHH, family-friendly ★ **Downhill Beach House** (Glenhassan Hall, 12 Mussenden Rd., tel. 028/7084-9077, www.downhillbeachhouse.com, Easter-Oct., £19-23 pp) is an absolute gem. A large restored Victorian nestled between cliff, stream, and sea, this place is the perfect get-away-from-it-all spot, especially if you're the outdoorsy type; not only can you rent wet suits and bodyboards here, but nearby Downhill Forest is ideal for a long walk or jog. The owners are a lovely young couple, William and McCall, who take pride in making ongoing improvements to an already fabulous hostel.

Downhill is 29 miles (47 km) east of Derry City on the A2. The **Ulsterbus** (tel. 028/9066-6630, www.ulsterbus.co.uk, 5/day Mon.-Sat., 2/day Sun.) Goldline Express route #234 between Derry and Coleraine can get you here.

Down

Of the six counties in Northern Ireland, Down has the most to offer. Antrim may have the famous coastline, pretty glens, and capital city, but Down's smaller towns and villages are generally more upbeat and better maintained—and the mountain and coastal scenery is nearly as pretty.

BANGOR

A quintessential Victorian seaside resort, **Bangor** ("BANG-grr," Beannchor) began as a 6th-century monastery associated with St. Columbanus. Today it's a Belfast commuter suburb—and the third-largest town in Northern Ireland—with a bustling marina and a few good pubs and eateries. Base yourself here when visiting the capital city for lower-priced accommodations and prettier surrounds, or spend a couple days exploring the Ards Peninsula, south of here.

Sights

Now the headquarters of the North Down Borough Council, mid-19th-century **Bangor Castle** (Town Hall, Castle Park Ave., tel. 028/9127-0371, free to grounds) isn't generally open to the public, though you can ring for an appointment if you'd like to see inside.

Aside from a 15th-century bell tower, what's left of **Bangor Abbey** dates from the mid-19th century. You'll have to find someone in the adjacent Church of Ireland (tel. 028/9145-1087) to let you inside.

There's an eclectic range of exhibits at the **North Down Heritage Centre** (Castle Park Ave., tel. 028/9127-1200, 10:30am-4:30pm Tues.-Sat., 2pm-4:30pm Sun. all year, and until 5:30pm Tues.-Sun. July-Aug., free), one of which traces the abbey's history.

The **Ulster Folk and Transport Museum** (Cultra, A2 Belfast-Bangor road near Holywood, tel. 028/9042-8428, www.uftm.org.uk, train rides Sat. 2pm-5pm, £9 to either folk or transport, combo ticket £11) is

a complex of reconstructed shopfronts with costumed craftspeople and other "villagers." Hours vary seasonally (10am-5pm Mon.-Fri., 10am-6pm Sat., 11am-6pm Sun. Mar.-June, 10am-6pm Mon.-Sat. and 11am-6pm Sun. July-Sept., 10am-4pm Mon.-Fri., 10am-5pm Sat., 11am-5pm Sun. Oct.-Feb.).

Activities and Recreation

The beautifully manicured **Ward Park** (Hamilton Rd., tel. 028/9145-8773 for bowling and putting greens, tel. 028/9145-7177 for tennis, sporting facilities open daily Easter-Sept.) is one of the loveliest town parks anywhere in the country, with a brook cutting through it. You can play tennis or go bowling or putting for a nominal fee.

The **Bangor Marina** (tel. 028/9145-3297) is one of the biggest in Ireland. **John Erskine** (tel. 028/9146-9458 or 078/0157-1830) and the **Blue Aquarius** (tel. 077/7960-0607, www.bangorboat.com) both offer fishing, birdwatching, and general sightseeing trips.

Gransha Equestrian Centre (10 Kerrs Rd., Six Road Ends, 3.7 mi/6 km southeast of Bangor off the A21, tel. 028/9181-3313, www.granshaequestrian.com) has an indoor arena as well as 40 acres of cross-country trails. Or tee off at the 18-hole, 71-par **Bangor Golf Club** (Broadway, 1 mi/1.6 km east of town on the Donaghdee road/B21, tel. 028/9127-0922).

Food and Entertainment

Order yourself a cappuccino and a decadent dessert at **Red Berry** (2-4 Main St. at Queen's Parade, tel. 028/9147-3373, www.redberrycoffee.co.uk, 9am-10pm Mon.-Sat. 10:30am-6pm Sun., £4-8), a sleek and pleasant coffee shop with large windows facing the marina. There are plenty of lunch specials too—burgers, pizzas, and the like.

You'll find decent pub grub at **Jenny Watt's** (41 High St., tel. 028/9127-0401, www.jennywattsbar.com, food served noon-7pm

Down and Armagh

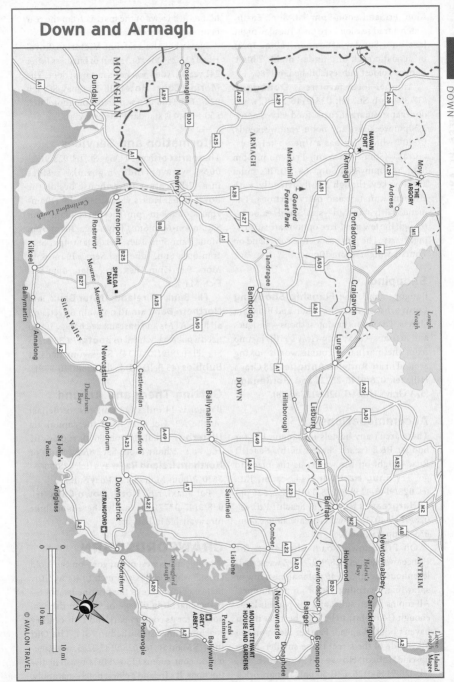

MONAGHAN

Dundalk

Crossmaglen

ARMAGH

NAVAN FORT

Armagh

Moy

THE ARGORY

Ardress

Portadown

Craigavon

Lurgan

Lough Neagh

ANTRIM

A1

A29

A25

A29

A28

B30

A25

A28

Markethill

Gosford Forest Park

A51

A29

M1

A4

Newry

Carlingford Lough

Warrenpoint

Rostrevor

Kilkeel

Ballymartin

Annalong

Mourne Mountains

SPELGA DAM

Silent Valley

B8

B25

B27

A25

A27

A1

Tandragee

Bambridge

A50

A26

A50

A1

Hillsborough

Lisburn

A26

A30

M1

A52

Belfast

M2

A8

Newtownabbey

Carrickfergus

Larne Lough

Island Magee

A2

Newcastle

Castlewellan

Dundrum Bay

Dundrum

Seaforde

St. John's Point

Ardglass

Ballynahinch

A49

A24

A7

A23

A49

DOWN

Saintfield

Comber

A22

Lisburn

A22

A20

Crawfordsburn

Holywood

Helen's Bay

Bangor

Groomsport

Donaghadee

A2

Downpatrick

STRANGFORD

A25

A22

A2

Portaferry

Strangford Lough

Portavogie

A20

MOUNT STEWART HOUSE AND GARDENS

GREY ABBEY

Ards Peninsula

Ballywalter

Newtownards

0   0

10 km   10 mi

© AVALON TRAVEL

Mon.-Fri. and noon-9pm Sat.-Sun., £6-10). Catch a trad session here on a Tuesday night, jazz on a Sunday afternoon (11am-3pm), or acoustic rock on Sunday night. This is Bangor's oldest pub, established in 1780.

Another local favorite is **Donegan's** (37-39 High St., tel. 028/9146-3928, www.donegansrestaurant.co.uk, food served noon-2:30pm weekdays and noon-9pm weekends, £7-10), which also has a fine upstairs restaurant (5pm-9pm Mon.-Fri., noon-9pm Sat., 12:30pm-8pm Sun., £8-18). It's quiet and low-key, though family-friendly, with efficient waitstaff and hefty portions. The menu's fairly standard—steaks and seafood—though the few meat-free options are surprisingly tasty. The pub hosts a live rock band on Thursday nights from 10pm.

Shopping

Bangor's mall, the **Flagship Shopping Centre,** has entrances on Main and Bingham Streets. The town's quaintest shops—antiques and artisans—are along Gray's Hill, just up from the marina. A couple worth poking around in are **Annville Antiques** (28 Gray's Hill, tel. 028/9145-2522) and **Goldenage** (57A Gray's Hill, tel. 028/9127-0938).

Accommodations

There aren't any hostels in Bangor, but for budget B&B (read: shared bath), Seacliff Road—right on the water—is the place to go. Try **Snug Harbour** (144 Seacliff Rd., tel. 028/9145-4238 or 078/3533-8252, £25 pp) or **Hargreaves House** (78 Seacliff Rd., tel. 028/9146-4071, www.hargreaveshouse.com, £33-40 pp, s £45-60).

On Princetown Road, **Shelleven** (61 Princetown Rd., tel. 028/9127-1777, www.shellevenhouse.com, £40-45 pp) is along a row of sprawling, charming Victorian townhomes. All rooms are en suite, and the place is large enough (14 rooms) to be your best bet if you haven't booked ahead. Farther along on the other side of the street is the smaller, more upscale **Hebron House** (68 Princetown Rd., tel. 028/9146-3126, £40-50 pp), a smart brick

home with views of the marina from the rear bedrooms and breakfast room.

Now that the seafront Victorian Royal Hotel (22-28 Quay St.) is out of business (after 241 years!), your best bet is just next door: The **Marine Court Hotel** (18-20 Quay St., tel. 028/9145-1100, www.marinecourthotel.net, £50-80 pp) is standard business class.

Information and Services

The **tourist office** (34 Quay St., tel. 028/9127-0069, www.northdown.gov.uk) resides in a 17th-century tower house beside the Royal Hotel. Hours vary seasonally (10am-7pm Mon., 9am-7pm Tues.-Fri., 10am-4pm Sat., noon-6pm Sun. July-Aug., 10am-5pm Mon., 9am-5pm Tues.-Fri., 10am-4pm Sat., 1pm-5pm Sun. June and Sept., 10am-5pm Mon., 9am-5pm Tues.-Fri., 10am-4pm Sat. Oct.-May).

The **Bank of Ireland, Ulster Bank,** and **Northern Bank** are all on Main Street, and all have ATMs and bureaux de change. If you need a pharmacy, head to **Boots** (79/83 Main St., tel. 028/9127-1134). Suds your duds at **Bubbles** (43 Belfast Rd., tel. 028/9146-9991).

Getting There and Around

Bangor is 14 miles (22 km) east of Belfast on the A2. Get here from the capital via **Ulsterbus** (tel. 028/9066-6630) routes #B1 and #B2 (2/hour Mon.-Sat., 8/day Sun.) or **Northern Ireland Railways** (tel. 028/9066-6630, 2/hour Mon.-Sat., 13/day Sun.).

For a taxi, ring **North Down Cabs** (tel. 028/9147-0777). Strangely, there is no bike hire available in Bangor.

CRAWFORDSBURN

A couple miles west of Bangor—on the "gold coast," which refers as much to its wealthy Belfast commuters as the pristine beaches—is the charming village of Crawfordsburn, notable for its country park and 17th-century coaching inn. Established in 1614, **The Old Inn** (15 Main St., tel. 028/9185-3255, www.theoldinn.com, rooms £136-290) is awash in distinctions. It's Ireland's oldest hotel—naturally,

Grace Neill's pub in Donaghdee

Mourne Mountains aside, the area east of **Strangford Lough** (from the Norse Strangfjörthr, "Strong Ford") is the loveliest part of County Down. A narrows connects the lake to the sea between the tips of the Ards (An Aird) and Lecale (Leth-Chathail, "Cathal's Half") Peninsulas. There's a frequent ferry connection between the two towns on opposite sides of the narrows (Portaferry and Strangford, respectively), so you can bypass the lough's less interesting western shore once you've explored the bucolic, low-lying Ards. The east coast is punctuated by caravan parks, and though there are a few pretty beaches, swimming in the Irish Sea is not recommended due to industrial pollution.

Newtownards

Gateway town to the Ards Peninsula, you'll find **Newtownards'** (Baile Nua na hArda) distasteful abbreviation—"N'ards"—on road signs all over northeast Down; the town itself isn't much more appealing. If you're passing through, you might want to stop at the **tourist office** and craft shop (31 Regent St., tel. 028/9182-6846, www.kingdomsofdown. com, 9:15am-5pm Mon.-Fri. and 9:30am-5pm Sat.) if you have any questions about the peninsula, since the Portaferry office is only seasonal. From the A20/Belfast road, take the town center exit at the roundabout and turn right onto Church Street, which becomes Regent Street.

Scuba divers have another reason to stop in N'ards: **DV Diving** (138 Mountstewart Rd., tel. 028/9146-4671, www.dvdiving.co.uk), which caters to all experience levels (and provides accommodations).

Donaghdee

Claiming to be the oldest pub in Ireland, ★ **Grace Neill's** (33 High St., tel. 028/9188-4595, food served noon-2:30pm and 6pm-9:30pm daily, £7-14) sure looks the part, from the gnome-sized entryway and low, rough wood ceiling to the cobwebby lace curtains and the dirt ground into the flagstone floor.

it's also one of the most haunted. C. S. Lewis, a frequent guest, proclaimed it heaven on earth. And despite somewhat touch-and-go service, the restaurant (food served 7am-9:30pm Mon.-Fri., 8am-9:30pm Sat.-Sun., bar meals £5-14, dinner £14-27) is the best in County Down. Victorian high tea is served 10am-noon daily and 3pm-5pm Monday-Saturday (£18, £22-26 with champagne).

But first work up an appetite at the **Crawfordsburn Country Park** (Bridge Rd. S., Helen's Bay, 2 mi/3.2 km west of Bangor on the B20, tel. 028/9185-3621, 9am-8pm daily Apr.-Sept., 9am-4:45pm Oct.-Mar., visitors center 9am-5pm daily, free), with its two-mile (3.2-km) strand and wooded nature trails, one of which leads over an old railway viaduct to a waterfall near the Old Inn.

Crawfordsburn is just under two miles (3.2 km) west of Bangor on the B20, but you can get here on the Belfast-Bangor train via **Northern Ireland Railways** (tel. 028/9066-6630, 2-3/hour). Get off at the Helen's Bay stop.

Over the centuries, famous visitors have included Daniel Defoe, Franz Liszt, John Keats, and Peter the Great. During slow periods, you've got to ring the brass bell at the bar (stamped 1824) to obtain the bartender's attention. And with all the yellowed photographs on the walls and antique liquor bottles arranged in the glass cases, it might sound like Grace Neill's is a self-conscious tourist attraction, but it's not at all—and the staff are friendly as can be. Food is served in both the modern bistro and "library bar" adjoining.

Otherwise, the little seaside town of Donaghdee doesn't have much going on (and the beach isn't the greatest), but it's only a six-mile (9.6 km) drive east of Bangor, and Ulsterbus serves the town on its Belfast-Millisle route (#7 from Belfast, #3 from Bangor, 2-3/hour daily).

Mount Stewart House and Gardens

One of Ireland's most glorious manor houses overlooks Strangford Lough from the western side of the Ards. Now in care of the National Trust, the 18th-century **Mount Stewart House and Gardens** (on the A20 5 mi/8 km south of Newtownards, tel. 028/4278-8387, www.nationaltrust.org.uk, £8, garden tour additional £4) was the home of the marquess of Londonderry. The gardens are open year-round, but the house is not (house noon-6pm daily July-Aug.; noon-6pm Wed.-Mon. Sept.; 1pm-6pm Mon. and Wed.-Fri. and noon-6pm Sat.-Sun. May-June; noon-6pm weekends and holidays mid-Mar.-Apr. and Oct., gardens 10am-8pm daily May-Sept., 10am-6pm Apr. and Oct., 10am-4pm Nov.-Mar.). Inside you'll find a world-class collection of paintings and sculpture; outside is an equally stunning 78-acre formal garden dating to the 1920s, the highlight of which is the Dodo Terrace, featuring topiaries of mythical and long-extinct animals. A classical Greek folly set on a hill, the Temple of the Winds was built in 1780 and affords an excellent view of Strangford Lough.

Mount Stewart is a 15-minute drive south of N'ards, and the Belfast-Portaferry Ulsterbus routes #9A and #10 pass the gate six times a day Monday-Saturday, three times on Sunday.

★ Grey Abbey

There are two great reasons to pause in **Greyabbey,** a small town just south of Mount Stewart on the western Ards road: a charming stone courtyard lined with antiques stores, and the magnificent ruins of the 12th-century **Grey Abbey** (An Mhainistir Liath, Church Rd., tel. 028/9054-6552, visitors center 10am-7pm Tues.-Sat. and 2pm-7pm Sun. Apr.-Sept., 10am-4pm Mon.-Sat. and 2pm-4pm Sun. Oct.-Mar., free). This Cistercian priory was founded in 1193 with the largesse of the Welsh princess Affreca, wife of Anglo-Norman adventurer John de Courcy, in thanksgiving for her safe passage from the Isle of Man. This is Ireland's first fully Gothic-style edifice—without a single rounded arch to be found—and there are a couple of interesting tomb effigies, a knight and a lady, incorrectly identified as Affreca (since the tomb style is late 13th century). Adding an element of spookiness even in fine weather is the largely 18th-century graveyard out front, with its otherwise dignified headstones tipped askew. This cemetery is more crowded than a U2 concert.

The abbey grounds are lush and immaculately maintained, an ideal spot for a picnic lunch. If the sun's not shining, you can always enjoy a soup or sandwich at the splendidly old-fashioned tearoom at **Hoops** (Main St., tel. 028/4278-8541, 9am-5pm Tues.-Sat., daily July-Aug., tearoom open at 10am, £3-6), a complex of more than a dozen antiques shops lining a cobblestoned courtyard.

Otherwise, the town of Greyabbey is a rather dull little place, with a proliferation of ugly pebble-dashed rowhouses. Plan on a visit of no more than a couple hours, as this is a quiet residential area with scarce accommodation.

Greyabbey is 14 miles (23 km) south of Bangor and is served on **Ulsterbus** route #9A or #10 (6/day Mon.-Sat., 3/day Sun.) between Belfast and Portaferry.

Grey Abbey is County Down's most important monastic ruin.

Portaferry

At the Ards' southern tip, quiet **Portaferry** (Port an Pheire, "Ferry Landing-Place") is still the most happening spot on the peninsula. With its seal sanctuary and displays of aquatic life from Strangford Lough and the Irish Sea, the **Exploris Aquarium** (Castle St., tel. 028/4272-8062, www.exploris.org. uk, 10am-6pm Mon.-Fri., 11am-6pm Sat., noon-6pm Sun. Apr.-Aug., until 5pm Sept.-Feb., adult/family £7.50/24) makes a fine family excursion. Or go for a beach trek with the **Cherry Tree Riding Centre** (5 Newcastle Rd., tel. 028/4272-9639).

Portaferry's **tourist office** (Castle St., tel. 028/4272-9882, 10am-5pm Mon.-Sat., 2pm-6pm Sun. Easter-Sept.) adjoins the ruin of a 16th-century tower house.

Portaferry is 23 miles (37 km) south of Bangor on the A2 (east side of the Ards) or A20 (lough-side). **Ulsterbus** (tel. 028/9066-6630, #9A or #10, 6/day Mon.-Sat., 3/day Sun.) can get you here from Belfast via N'ards and Greyabbey.

Zip across the narrows to Strangford on the **Strangford Lough Ferry** (tel. 028/4488-1637, departs every half hour 7:30am-10:30pm Mon.-Fri., 8am-11pm Sat., 9:30am-10:30pm Sun., single/day return £5.80/10 car and driver, £1/2 pedestrian or passenger).

WEST OF STRANGFORD LOUGH
Lisbane and Around

It's on the main A22 road between Bangor and Downpatrick, yet the hamlet of **Lisbane** (Lisbaun, "White Fort") is surprisingly quiet and pastoral. There are a few things of moderate interest in the area, including the scant remains of the 7th-century **Nendrum Abbey** (Mahee Island, 4.5 mi/7.2 km southeast of Lisbane, tel. 028/9754-2547, abbey ruins always accessible, visitors center 9am-6pm Tues.-Sat. and 1pm-6pm Sun. Apr.-Sept., 10am-4pm Sat. and 2pm-4pm Sun. Oct.-Mar., free) and a nearby wildlife refuge, **Castle Espie** (Ballydrain Rd., tel. 028/9187-4146, www.wwt.org.uk, 10:30am-5pm Mon.-Fri., 11am-5:30pm Sat.-Sun. Mar.-Oct., 11am-4pm Mon.-Fri., 11am-4:30pm Sat.-Sun. Nov.-Feb., £7.50). Only the foundations remain of Nendrum's small churches and beehive huts (along with the diagonally shaped stump of a 12th-century round tower), but the interpretive displays and audiovisual at the adjacent visitors center will help you imagine what this monastery must have been like a thousand years ago. Family-friendly Castle Espie is home to a flock of light-bellied Brent geese during the winter; the staff name each goose and keep close tabs on how each is doing. There's also an interpretive center, though the views of Strangford Lough alone are reason enough to come. To get to Nendrum, turn onto Quarry Road opposite the Maxol Station in Lisbane, proceed 1.5 miles (2.4 km), and you'll see Nendrum signposted at a crossroads. After another three miles (4.8 km) you'll come to a small bridge with a castle ruin beyond it; cross this and you'll see the abbey car park on your right. The wildlife refuge is signposted on the A22 between Comber and Lisbane.

Even if you're just passing through Lisbane, stop for a snack at **The Old Post Office** (191 Killinchy Rd., the A22, tel. 028/9754-3335, www.oldpostofficelisbane.co.uk, 9:30am-5pm Mon.-Sat., £5-8), which includes a gallery, upscale gift shop, and cozy tearooms with loft seating and open fires.

But you really should consider spending the night here. One of the very best B&Bs on the island (if not *the* best) is ★ **Anna's House** (35 Lisbarnett Rd., 0.3 mi/0.5 km off the A22, signposted, tel. 028/9754-1566, www.annashouse.com, £45-55 pp). Consider Anna's a destination in itself. This tranquil farmhouse overlooks a small lough and has a fantastic two-acre garden dotted with whimsical clay busts and other neat sculptures by the owners' son. All the food is organic, down to the instant coffee on your hostess tray, and the breakfast menu is truly without equal. Each of the three double rooms is furnished with gorgeous antiques, a load of good books, pressed linen sheets, a minifridge for your milk, and a fully stocked medicine cabinet. As you would expect from such thoughtful gestures, the Johnsons are wonderfully kind and fascinating people with a genuine *mi casa e su casa* attitude; Anna periodically sleeps in her guest beds to ensure they're still comfortable. Plan to stay at least two nights—and even then you'll be reluctant to leave.

The best restaurant in the area is **Lisbarnett House** (on the A21, tel. 028/9754-1589, www.lisbarnetthouse.com, 6pm-9pm daily, 2-course early-bird special £13 6pm-7pm daily and 6pm-9pm Mon., £10-19). The modern Irish here is fresh and delicious, if a bit unadventurous; though the staff are nice, the dining room is a bit on the stuffy side. There's live trad in the adjoining bar on Saturday nights.

For more atmosphere, drive a little farther to **Daft Eddy's** (Sketrick Island, Killinchy, tel. 028/9754-1615, food served noon-9pm daily, £9-16), a well-established bar-restaurant with a quirky nautical theme (check out the overturned rowboat above your head decked out in Christmas lights, and the busty figurehead on the wall by the bar). The food is good (the token veggie dish is creative, if a bit dainty, but the steaks and seafood are hearty enough), the staff are cordial, but it's the lake views from the dining room and deck that make for a memorable meal. To get here from Lisbane, pass southward through the village and after 2.5 miles (4 km) or so, make a left onto Beechvale Road (you'll see a signpost for Sketrick Castle). After another 2.5 miles you'll come to a narrow causeway with the ruins of Sketrick Castle on the far side; cross it to get to the restaurant straight ahead, up a small hill.

Lisbane is 14 miles (23 km) south of Belfast off the A20, and unfortunately Ulsterbus doesn't serve this stretch of the A22.

Saintfield

A ho-hum town midway between Belfast and Downpatrick, **Saintfield** is worth a stop for its row of wonderful little antiques shops. A little over a mile south of town is the 52-acre **Rowallane Garden** (signposted off the N7, tel. 028/9751-0131, www.ntni.org.uk, 11am-6pm Mon.-Fri., 2pm-6pm Sat.-Sun. Apr.-Oct., 11am-5pm Mon.-Fri. Nov.-Mar., £5.30), with its walled gardens and pretty fields of Himalayan poppies. The best time to visit is early spring, when the azaleas and rhododrons are in bright bloom.

As for the antiques shops, they're all on Saintfield's main street. **Christine Deane** (90 Main St., tel. 028/9751-1334 or 078/0197-9496) has an exquisite collection of Victorian and Edwardian jewelry. **Agar** (92 Main St., tel. 028/9751-1214) has some incredibly neat finds in the way of 19th-century furniture—if you're willing to pay to ship it home! Note that most of these shops close on Sunday and Monday.

Once they're done making the rounds, local antiques-shoppers take lunch at ★ **The March Hare** (Fairview, at the end of Main St., tel. 028/9751-9248, 10am-4pm Wed.-Fri., 10am-4pm Sat., lunches £4-7), a tiny, unself-consciously old-fashioned tearoom with

NORTHERN IRELAND
DOWN

thoroughly delicious homemade soups, sandwiches, quiches, and pies, and very friendly staff. The March Hare is so popular you may not get a table right away, but the food is definitely worth the wait.

Saintfield is just over 15 miles (25 km) south of Belfast on the A24 and is served on the **Ulsterbus** (tel. 028/9066-6630, #15, 2-4/hour daily) Belfast-Downpatrick route.

DOWNPATRICK

County Down's principal town may boast strong historical ties with the island's patron saint, but frankly **Downpatrick** (Dún Phádraig, "Patrick's Fort") is a dismal place.

The Anglican **Down Cathedral** (The Mall, tel. 028/4461-4922, 10am-4:30pm Mon.-Sat. and 2pm-5pm Sun., free) stands on the likely burial place of St. Patrick and so has been a place of pilgrimage for nearly a millennium and a half. Its current incarnation dates from the turn of the 19th century, and the cathedral features a splendid pipe organ. A 10-minute visit should suffice.

Stop by the **St. Patrick Centre** (53a Market St., tel. 028/4461-2233, 9:30am-7pm Mon.-Sat. and 10am-6pm Sun. June-Aug., 9:30am-5:30pm Mon.-Sat. and 1pm-5:30pm Sun. Apr.-May and Sept., 10am-5pm Mon.-Sat. Oct.-Mar.) for tourist info, but don't waste time in the cheesy exhibition center.

Downpatrick is 20 miles (32 km) south of Belfast on the A7 and is served by **Ulsterbus** (tel. 028/4461-2384, #15/A, hourly buses Mon.-Sat., 5/day Sun.).

THE LECALE PENINSULA
★ Strangford

The absolutely lovely harbor village of **Strangford** makes an ideal base for exploring the Lecale Peninsula. From here you can also hop the ferry, with or without your car, across the lough to Portaferry.

The village's romantic atmosphere is defined by the sight of a fleet of colorful fishing boats, a small but perfectly manicured green, and the 16th-century **Strangford Castle,** a well-preserved ivy-clad tower

house overlooking the harbor. Inside there isn't much to see but the bric-a-brac of ongoing neglect, but if you're really curious, the key is available from the caretaker at 39 Castle Street.

Head up Castle Street and hang a left at a shady stone staircase for the **Strangford Bay Path,** a Secret Gardenesque walk with woods on one side and the narrows on the other; the tide has heaved clumps of seaweed onto the grass. Eventually you'll come to the 18th-century, half-Gothic, half-neoclassical **Castle Ward Estate** (Park Rd., tel. 028/4488-1204, house 1pm-6pm Fri.-Wed. June, 1pm-6pm daily July-Aug., 1pm-6pm Sat.-Sun. mid-Mar.-May and Sept., grounds 10am-8pm daily May-Sept., 10am-4pm daily Oct.-Apr., house and grounds £7.30), which includes the Strangford Lough Wildlife Centre and a couple of older tower houses you spotted across the narrows from the bay path. Scenes from *Game of Thrones* were filmed here.

The old-fashioned facade of **The Lobster Pot** (9-11 The Square, tel. 028/4488-1288, www.thelobsterpotrestaurant.co.uk, 11:30am-9pm Mon.-Sat., 12:30pm-8pm Sun., £14-26) belies a spiffy interior complete with aquarium (the fish aren't to eat), portholes in the ceiling, and the likes of Dean Martin on the stereo. The name is misleading too, for there are plenty of alternatives to the seafood dishes, and the chef is surprisingly vegetarian-friendly. The adjoining pub has live trad most nights in the summer.

Your other, equally delicious lunch or dinner option is a pub-cum-restaurant called **The Cuan** (The Square, tel. 028/4488-1222, www.thecuan.com, food served noon-8pm daily in low season and until 9pm Sun.-Thurs. and 9:30pm Fri.-Sat. June-Aug., £12-20, B&B £43-48 pp, s £58-65), which also has nine smallish-but-comfortable (and super-clean) bedrooms on offer upstairs and a quaint little fish-and-chipper next door. Another accommodation option is **Strangford Cottage** (17 Castle St., tel. 028/4488-1208, www.strangfordcottage.com, Apr.-Sept., rooms £115-130, s £65), an ivy-clad Georgian with three en-suite bedrooms and an award-winning breakfast.

Strangford is nine miles (14 km) northeast of Downpatrick on the A25. Get here from Belfast by **Ulsterbus** (#16E, at least 20/day).

The **Strangford Lough Ferry** provides a shortcut across the narrows to Portaferry on the Ards Peninsula (tel. 028/4488-1637, departs every half hour 7:30am-10:30pm Mon.-Fri., 8am-11pm Sat., 9:30am-10:30pm Sun., single/day return £5.80/10 car and driver, £1/2 pedestrian or passenger).

NEWCASTLE

Newcastle (An Caisleán Nua), County Down's other seaside resort, isn't as classy as Bangor. The main street, lined with the usual cheap-'n'-greasy amusement arcades and takeaways, seems darn near endless. If traveling by bus, you'll disembark on Railway Street; make a right onto Downs Road (where you can turn off for the beach), and you'll eventually hit Main Street, which becomes the Central Promenade; keep going and you'll be traveling south on the Mourne coastal road.

Planning to explore the Mournes? Pick up an OS map and guidebooks at the **tourist office** (10-14 Central Promenade, tel. 028/4372-2222, 9:30am-7pm Mon.-Sat. and 1pm-7pm Sun. July-Aug., 10am-5pm Mon.-Sat. and 2pm-6pm Sun. Sept.-June). There are a couple of banks with ATMs and bureaux de change on Main Street.

Newcastle is 30 miles (48 km) south of Belfast on the A24 and is served by **Ulsterbus** (#18 and #20, 13/day Mon.-Fri., 9/day Sat., 6/day Sun.) from Belfast.

SILENT VALLEY

The granite-topped **Mourne Mountains** are the most spectacular scenery in County Down, no doubt about it. You'll drive past pretty gorse-dotted hills and unsettling sectarian road paint to the Silent Valley Reservoir (tel. 084/5744-0088, 10am-6:30pm daily May-Sept., 10am-4pm Oct.-Apr., visitors center 10am-4pm Apr.-Oct., car/pedestrian £4.50/1.60), the source of Belfast's

drinking water since the Spelga Dam was built to span the Kilkeel River. As it should be, this is a beautiful, pristine park where you can walk right up to the reservoir and listen to the water lapping gently at the huge stone basin as you survey the surrounding peaks, each of them crossed by the 22-mile drystone **Mourne Wall.** Eight feet high and three feet thick, the wall was constructed between 1904 and 1922 to enclose the valley (and to provide much-needed work for hundreds of local men, though most of them had to travel miles on foot to get here, and they weren't paid by the hour). As for how the Silent Valley got its name, it's said the noise of the rock-blasting frightened all the birds away—and they never returned. There are easy walking trails throughout; bring a picnic lunch.

Ulsterbus provides service in summer (#405, 7/day) to the Silent Valley, Atticall, and Tollymore; otherwise you'll need a car to reach the reservoir. If you're not here in high season, there are several ways to experience the mountains sans wheels, mostly by way of Newcastle. Take a walk through the foothills via the entrance at Tollymore Forest Park, or climb the 2,795-foot (852-meter) **Slieve Donard** via a route that begins three miles (4.8 km) south of town on the A2 (at a small car park carved into the hill) and winds through six miles (9.6 km) of County Down's most breathtaking scenery. Seeing as it's Northern Ireland's highest peak, Slieve Donard is a difficult four-hour climb—so take all the usual equipment and precautions. Take the Newcastle-Kilkeel **Ulsterbus** route (#37, 14/day Mon.-Fri., 11/day Sat., 6/day Sun.) from Newcastle to reach the starting point.

And if you don't have time for any of this, at least take the A2 coastal road south from Newcastle to Warrenpoint, wedged between gorse-strewn mountains and glittering sea.

You have several options if you'd like to experience the Mournes with a little help. For a guided walk or cycle, contact **Outdoor Ireland North** (14 Shimavale, tel. 028/4372-4372 or 079/7340-8056, www.

outdoorirelandnorth.co.uk). **Tollymore Mountain Centre** (Bryansford, tel. 028/4372-2158, www.tollymore.com) offers one-day mountaineering, rock-climbing, and canoeing courses. Nothing but rain? No worries: There's an indoor climbing wall.

You could base yourself on the Mourne coast in Rostrevor; alternatively, there are a few accommodation options in the mountains, mostly in and around the village of Atticall. Located between the Silent Valley and Spelga Dam, the 28-bed, purpose-built, eco-friendly **Cnocafeola Centre** (Bog Rd., Atticall, 9 mi/14 km east of Rostrevor, 1.8 mi/2.9 km west of the Silent Valley entrance, tel. 028/4176-5859 or 028/4179-2952, www. mournehostel.com, dorms £20, twin/private rooms £45) has two self-catering kitchens as well as a (bring your own bottle) restaurant serving three meals a day (advance booking essential). All rooms are en suite.

For more information, contact the **Mourne Heritage Trust** (87 Central Promenade, tel. 028/4372-4059, www.mournelive.com) in Newcastle.

ROSTREVOR

Rostrevor (Caisleán Ruairi, "Rory's Castle") is easily the most attractive town along the Mourne coastal road, with gorgeous views south over Carlingford Lough (just don't look west to the smokestacks of Warrenpoint). Spend the night here before heading up into the Mournes, and if time allows, go for a walk through the "fairy glen" in the hilltop

Kilbroney Forest Park (Shore Rd., the A2, tel. 028/4173-8134, 9am-10pm daily June-Aug., 9am-5pm daily Sept.-May, free). Early July is a good time to be here, when some of the best traditional musicians in the north gather for the **Fiddler's Green Festival** (tel. 028/4173-9819, www.fiddlersgreenfestival. com).

It's a bit surprising there aren't many accommodations here—just a few nice but no-frills B&Bs. You'll get a warm welcome at the cheerfully furnished and super-clean **Fir Trees** (16 Killowen Old Rd., signposted off the A2 1.8 mi/2.9 km east of town, tel. 028/4173-8602 or 077/1169-4089, www.stay-inthemournes.com, £40 pp). There are three rooms, all en suite, and the twin room has a view of Carlingford Lough and Mountain; the breakfasts are fairly basic.

For dinner, look no further than **The Kilbroney** (31 Church St., tel. 028/4173-8390, food served noon-9pm daily, £7-12), which does fantastic bar meals—it's just burgers and paninis during the day, but the dinner fare is more sophisticated (including a mean mushroom risotto for vegetarians). Save room for the sticky toffee pudding, and ask if there'll be live music later in the evening.

Rostrevor is 22 miles (35 km) southwest of Newcastle on the A2 coastal road. **Ulsterbus** can get you here from Belfast (#238 then #39, 16/day Mon.-Sat., 3/day Sun.), though a change is required at Newry. If coming from Newcastle, you'll have to change at either Newry or Kilkeel (#37).

Armagh

Known for its city cathedrals and apple orchards, mostly rural Armagh is the home of the only cider brewed in Northern Ireland, **Carson's** (www.armaghcider.com). A leisurely drive through northern Armagh's 4,000 acres of orchards in May is one of the highlights of a trip to Northern Ireland. You might even come upon a game of road

bowling, a centuries-old sport that's still popular here and in parts of County Cork.

If you've passed a day too long in Dublin or Belfast, you'll find Armagh City refreshingly laid-back. The city park, **The Mall,** is on the eastern side of town, and most of what you'll need is one block west on English Street, including the **tourist office** (40 English St., tel. 028/3752-1800, www.visitarmagh.com, 9am-5pm Mon.-Sat. all year, 1pm-5:30pm Sun. July-Aug. and 2pm-5pm Sun. Sept.-June).

SIGHTS

The foundation of **St. Patrick's Church of Ireland Cathedral** (Cathedral Close, up the hill from Market Square, tel. 028/3752-3142, www.stpatricks-cathedral.org, 10am-5pm daily Apr.-Oct., 10am-4pm daily Nov.-Mar., free) dates to the 13th century, though the present edifice dates to the 1830s. Legend states that Patrick founded his first church on this small hill in the year 445. Brian Boru is supposedly buried here, too. Between June and August there are guided tours at 11:30am and 2:30pm daily (except Sunday). And when you see the soaring twin spires of the hilltop neo-Gothic **St. Patrick's Catholic Cathedral** (Cathedral Rd., tel. 028/3752-2802, www.armagharchdiocese.org, free), you'll fully understand why Armagh is the "Cathedral City." Between the brilliant stained glass windows, gold mosaics, and flatscreen monitors anchored to the columns, the interior is visually overwhelming—but well worth a visit. A 90-minute **walking tour** (tel. 077/4015-1442, www.armaghguidedtours.com, booking essential, £4) focusing on Armagh's history and architecture departs the tourist office on Saturday at 11am and 2pm and Sunday at 2pm June-September.

FOOD AND ACCOMMODATIONS

If you'd like to spend the night in Armagh City, try **7 Houses** (3 Upper English St., tel. 028/3751-1213, www.sevenhouses.co.uk, rooms £75-95), with an adjoining **pizza restaurant** (6pm-8:30pm Thurs.-Sun., £8-11). But don't miss Northern Ireland's only Australian eatery, ★ **Uluru** (16-18 Market St., tel. 028/3751-8051, uluru_bistro@hotmail.co.uk, noon-3pm and 6pm-9:30pm Tues.-Sat., £8-15). Yes, the menu features the requisite kangaroo steak, but the service is impeccable, the gourmet coffees sublime, and the dessert menu all but brings one to tears. And as for entertainment, the Saturday session at **Turner's** (the Charlemont Arms, English St., tel. 028/3752-2028) starts at 10pm; on Tuesday you'll find trad at the cozy **Hughes' Northern Bar** (100 Railway St., tel. 028/3752-7315), which attracts a fun, youngish crowd, and it has a live band on Saturday.

AROUND ARMAGH CITY

For a walking, cycling, golfing, or angling holiday, contact **Lurgaboy Adventure** (12 Gosford Rd., tel. 079/2114-3010, www.lurgaboylodge.com), which will hook you up with the equipment, a guide (if necessary), and a quaint self-catering cottage with all the mod cons. Or just come for an afternoon of archery or tree-climbing. The adventure center is right beside **Gosford Castle and Forest Park** (7 Gosford Demesne, Markethill, tel. 028/3755-1277, www.forestserviceni.gov.uk, 8am-dusk all year, car/pedestrian £4/1), with an arboretum, walled garden, nature walks, and picnicking facilities. The sadly neglected house itself, an early 19th-century "Normal Revival" manor, is closed to the public. Gosford and Lurgaboy Adventure are six miles (9.6 km) southeast of Armagh on the A28.

The most important archaeological site in Northern Ireland is **Navan Fort,** or Emain Macha ("The Twins of Macha," 2 mi/3.2 km west of Armagh off the B115, tel. 028/3752-1801, www.navancentre.com, visitors center 10am-5pm Mon.-Sat. and noon-5pm Sun. June-Aug., visitors center £5, site free). As Ulster's pre-Christian capital (from 700 BC), the fort is comparable to the Hill of Tara in County Meath, and its legends include all the heavy-hitters of Irish folklore; also like Tara, what the site lacks in dramatic ruins it more than makes up for in a rich and spooky sense of history. It takes less than an hour to walk here from the city, or you can take **Ulsterbus** (#73, 7/day Mon.-Fri., 3/day Sat.) to the village of Navan from the bus depot just north of the Mall.

GETTING THERE

Armagh is 37 miles (60 km) southwest of Belfast on the A3 and 81 miles (130 km) northwest of Dublin on the M1, picking up the A29 in Dundalk. There is ample free parking on the east side of the Mall. **Ulsterbus** (tel. 028/3752-2266, route #551, 20/day Mon.-Fri., 15/day Sat., 8/day Sun.) can get you here from Belfast; the depot is on Lonsdale Road, on the Mall West.

Fermanagh

Fermanagh is very much a lake county, as the Upper and Lower Loughs Erne (though "Lough Erne" generally refers to the larger lower lake) are central to its geography, commerce, and tourism. The nationalist writer William Bulfin cycled around the lakes near the turn of the 20th century, and he offered nought but praise. "You seldom hear of Fermanagh as being a picturesque district," he wrote, "and yet you could linger in it for weeks without tiring of it." *Weeks* may be a slight exaggeration, but it's certainly true that Lough Erne's beauty is underrated. Adding to its romance is a smattering of still-grand manor houses, equally forlorn castle ruins, and vast, lush forest parks.

ENNISKILLEN

Fermanagh's capital is the pleasant market town of **Enniskillen** (Inis Ceithleann), a natural base for exploring the islands of Lough Erne. The nightlife's not half bad either, and there are a few outstanding restaurants (all on Belmore Street, incidentally). The town's Irish name means "Ceithleann's Island," the name of an old Irish warrior (not "Cathleen").

Enniskillen is situated at the southern end of Lower Lough Erne, on an island at the mouth of a river with the same name, which eventually empties into the Upper Lough. Though it's easy to traverse by foot, the town is a maze of one-way streets; the main thoroughfare (changing names from Ann to Darling to Church to High to Downhall to East Bridge Street) moves east on Ann and Darling but west from Church Street. If driving, use the free parking lot by the Erneside bus station and explore the town on foot. Forthill Park is on the eastern end of town, off the Dublin roundabout at the end of Belmore Street.

Sights

Overlooking Lough Erne, the earliest parts of **Enniskillen Castle** (Castle Barracks, tel. 028/6632-5000, www.enniskillencastle. co.uk, 10am-5pm Tues.-Fri. and 2pm-5pm Sat.-Mon. July-Aug., closed Sun. May-June and Sept., 2pm-5pm Mon. and 10am-5pm Tues.-Fri. Oct.-Apr., £2.50) date to the 15th century. The castle's most distinctive feature is a Scottish-style watergate of twin corbelled pepperpot bartizans—in other words, this section looks like it belongs in a fairy tale. The old keep houses a (crammed and creepy) military museum (the Regimental Museum of the Royal Inniskilling Fusiliers, to be precise), the arcaded barracks an exhibition on the monastic history of the Lough Erne islands, and the Fermanagh County Museum is also on the grounds, with small exhibits on Belleek and lace-making as well as the area's natural history. A major renovation was underway at time of writing, with only part of the usual exhibition open to visitors. All in all, the castle is a fine rainy day activity, but in nice weather just admire the watergate—a misnomer, for it isn't actually a gateway—from a picnic bench in the park outside.

For a panoramic view of town and lake, climb the 108 steps of **Cole Monument** (Forthill Park, on the east end of town, tel. 028/6632-5050, 1:30pm-3pm daily Apr.-Sept., free), erected in memory of the son of the first Earl of Enniskillen.

Enniskillen

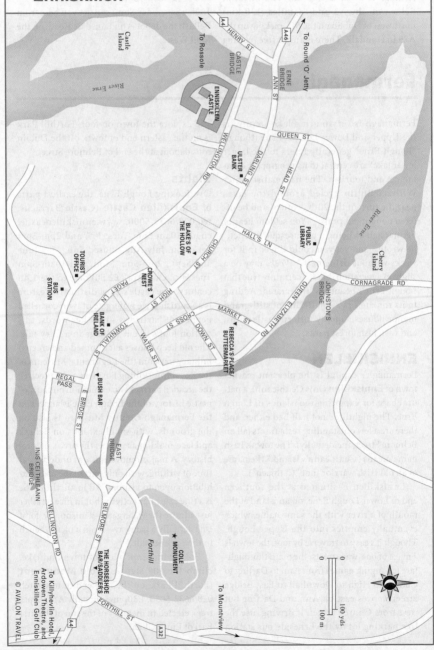

Castle Island

River Erne

To Rossole

To Round 'O' Jetty

HENRY ST

A4

A46

CASTLE BRIDGE

ERNE BRIDGE

ANN ST

ENNISKILLEN CASTLE

QUEEN ST

WELLINGTON RD

DARLING ST

HEAD ST

ULSTER BANK

PUBLIC LIBRARY

HALL'S LN

Cherry Island

River Erne

BLAKE'S OF THE HOLLOW

CHURCH ST

TOURIST OFFICE

CROWE'S NEST

PAGET LN

HIGH ST

MARKET ST

QUEEN ELIZABETH RD

CORNAGRADE RD

JOHNSTON'S BRIDGE

BUS STATION

BANK OF IRELAND

TOWNHALL ST

WATER ST

CROSS ST

DOWN ST

REBECCA'S PLACE/ BUTTERMARKET

REGAL PASS

BRIDGE ST

BUSH BAR

EAST BRIDGE

INIS CEI THLEANN BRIDGE

BELMORE ST

WELLINGTON RD

Forthill

COLE MONUMENT

To Mountview

THE HORSESHOE BAR/SADDLERS

FORTHILL ST

To Killyhevlin Hotel, Ardowen Theatre, and Enniskillen Golf Club

A4

A32

© AVALON TRAVEL

0   100 yds
0   100 m

Activities and Recreation

Go for a waterbus cruise on Lough Erne with **Erne Tours** (Round 'O' Jetty, Brook Park, on the A46 just west of town, tel. 028/6632-2882, departures at 10:30am, 2:15pm, and 4:15pm daily July-Aug., 2:30pm Tues., Sat.-Sun. Sept., 2:30pm Sun. May-June, £10). The trip lasts just under two hours, and the highlight is a (however brief) stop at Devenish Island.

Anglers should head to **Home, Field & Stream** (18 Church St., tel. 028/6632-2114, www.hfs-online.com) for permits and tackle.

Opened in 1896, the 18-hole, par-71 **Enniskillen Golf Club** (1.5 mi/2.4 km southeast of town off the A4, tel. 028/6632-5250, www.enniskillengolfclub.com) is beside the Castle Coole estate.

The kid- and beginner-friendly **Forest Stables** (100 Cooneen Rd., Fivemiletown, 18 mi/26 km east of Enniskillen off the A4, tel. 028/8952-1991) is on the Fermanagh-Tyrone border.

Or go canoeing or windsurfing on Upper Lough Macnean at the **Corralea Activity Centre** (162 Lattone Rd., 14 mi/23 km west of town, tel. 028/6638-6123, www.activityireland.com). There are self-catering cottages available as well. To get here, take the A4 west out of town to Belcoo and make a right onto the B52; the center is three miles (4.8 km) down on the left.

Food and Entertainment

If you're shopping at the Buttermarket, the natural choice for lunch is cafeteria-style **Rebecca's Place** (tel. 028/6632-4499, www.rebeccasrestaurant.net, 7am-7:30pm daily, until 8:30pm Fri.-Sat., under £8), but at peak lunchtime hours it's mobbed with young families.

The Horseshoe Bar (66 Belmore St., tel. 028/6632-6223, www.horseshoeandsaddlers.com, food served 4pm-11pm daily, until 10pm Sun., £9-15) does terrific meat-and-potatoes pub grub. Save room for the amazing sticky toffee pudding. The food in the upstairs restaurant, **Saddler's** (5:30pm-11pm Mon.-Sat., noon-10pm Sun., £12-22), is only slightly more sophisticated, but a fair bit pricier.

It's recently been modernized out of its old-fashioned charm, but on the upside, the **Bush Bar** (26 Townhall St., tel. 028/6632-5210, www.thebushbar.com, food served noon-9pm daily, £8-16) still does burgers, seafood, and stirfries, and there's now a gourmet deli attached.

The amiable barstaff at **Blake's of the Hollow** (Church St., tel. 028/6632-2143, www.blakesofthehollow.com) pour the best Guinness in the north; they also make the best Bailey's coffee. This gorgeous old pub retains much of its original Victorian detail—mahogany wall paneling and high ceilings, ornate pillar lamps sprouting out of the bar, and real snugs in the back. Or stop by the **Crowe's Nest** (12 High St., tel. 028/6632-5252, www.crowesnest.pub) for the trad session on a Monday night (summer only). The Crowe's Nest has a nice beer garden out back, super-traditional pub grub, and live blues or rock every other night of the week.

Locals seem quite proud of Enniskillen's modern, lakeside theater, **Ardhowen** (Dublin Rd., 1.2 mi/2 km outside town, tel. 028/6632-5440, www.ardhowentheatre.com, £7-15), which offers a diverse lineup of dance, concerts (jazz, pop, and the occasional tribute), and both classic and experimental dramatic productions. The town's annual amateur drama competition takes place here in early March.

Shopping

Got any room left in your suitcase? **Cloughcor House Antiques** (tel. 028/6632-4805) sells a lot of neat stuff (bookends, clocks, wooden decoys, picture frames, and suchlike) that just *looks* antique, along with the real thing. And no self-respecting shopper should miss the **Buttermarket** (Down St., tel. 028/6632-4499, closed Sun.), a quaint complex of small shops and galleries. The most extensive of these is the **Boston Quay Craft Shop** (tel. 028/6632-3837), selling lovely handmade greeting cards, French soaps, jewelry, candles, stationery, children's accessories, and fun housewares. Most of the stock is imported, however.

Accommodations

A short walk from the town centre, **Rossole** (85 Sligo Rd., tel. 028/6632-3462 or 078/1245-2526, www.rossoleguesthouse.com, £30 pp), is an imposing Georgian-style stone home with Lough Erne literally in the backyard (you can even borrow a boat from the owner).

The modern **Killyhevlin Hotel** (0.9 mi/1.5 km south of town on the A4, tel. 028/6632-3481, www.killyhevlin.com, £60-70 pp, s £90-100) has a spa and leisure center as well as lake views from many of the rooms, but the walls are thin and the food is mediocre.

Information

Enniskillen's very helpful **tourist office** (Wellington Rd., tel. 028/6632-3110, www.fermanaghlakelands.com, 9am-7pm Mon.-Fri., 10am-6pm Sat., 11am-5pm Sun. July-Aug.; 9am-5:30pm Mon.-Fri., 10am-6pm Sat., 11am-5pm Sun. Easter-June and Sept., 9am-5:30pm Mon.-Fri. Oct.-Easter) also sells fishing licenses.

Services

You'll find ATMs and bureaux de change at **Ulster Bank** (16 Darling St.) and the **Bank of Ireland** (7 Townhall St.). Suds your duds at **The Wash Tub** (12 E. Bridge St., tel. 028/6632-5230) and get your Rx at **Belcoo Pharmacy** (15 Main St., tel. 028/6638-6931).

Getting There and Around

Enniskillen is 42 miles (67 km) east of Sligo on the N16 and 50 miles (81 km) west of Armagh on the A4/A28. **Ulsterbus** (tel. 028/9066-6630) can get you here from Belfast (#261, 8/day Mon.-Sat., 2/day Sun.) or Derry (#296, 1/day Mon.-Fri.). **Bus Éireann** (tel. 01/836-6111) serves Enniskillen on its Dublin-Donegal route (#30, 4-5/day), and there's service from Sligo (#66, 5/day Mon.-Sat., 2/day Sun.) as well.

Ring **County Cabs** (tel. 028/6632-8888) for a taxi.

SOUTH OF ENNISKILLEN

Castle Coole

One of Northern Ireland's grandest manors is the neoclassical **Castle Coole** (4 mi/6.4 km southeast of town on the A4, tel. 028/6632-2690, www.ntni.org.uk, grounds 10am-8pm Apr.-Sept., until 4pm Oct.-Mar., house noon-6pm weekends mid-Mar.-May and Sept., Fri.-Wed. June, daily July-Aug., £4.50), the seat of the earls of Belmore. The saloon, bedchambers, and state rooms have been painstakingly restored by the National Trust to their Regency-era resplendence, with all the original furniture for which it was specially designed in the 1790s. It's said that the building costs so far exceeded estimates that the interior was decorated with restraint, yet the plasterwork and other period details are surely sumptuous enough—this is because the second earl was even more extravagant than his father had been. The most amusing part of a visit to the house is King George IV's bedroom, prepared for his visit in 1821 but never used. George was too busy with his mistress, Lady Conyngham of Slane Castle in County Meath.

Castle Coole is only four miles (6.4 km) from Enniskillen, a walk of 30-40 minutes south on the Dublin road. Even if you aren't all that interested in the manor itself, take a long walk around the tranquil 1,500-acre demesne (10am-8pm May-Sept., until 4pm Oct.-Apr., £3).

★ Marble Arch Caves

In 1895 a French lawyer and speleologist named Edouard Martel ventured into a hitherto-unexplored cave in the Cuilcagh ("KWILL-kuh") Mountains, which locals swore was haunted. He found the **Marble Arch Caves** (Florencecourt, 11 mi/18 km southwest of town off the A32, tel. 028/6634-8855, www.marblearchcavesgeopark.com, 10am-5pm July-Aug., 10am-4:30pm mid-Mar.-June and Sept., £9.50), one of Ireland's few subterranean sights as spectacular as hyped. After a 15-minute boat trip, during which you'll see the junction of the three

Excursion to County Tyrone

Between the heavy pall still hanging over Omagh after the horrific 1998 bombing and a proliferation of super-unionist Plantation towns, you might wonder how a trip through County Tyrone could be worthwhile. First, the **Ulster-American Folk Park** is one of the island's best museums (2 Mellon Rd., Castletown, 5 mi/8 km north of Omagh on the A5, tel. 028/8224-3292, www.folkpark.com, 10:30am-6pm Mon.-Sat. and 11am-6:30pm Sun. Apr.-Sept., 10:30am-5pm Mon.-Fri. Oct.-Mar., £4.50). The indoor museum spans the length of American history, focusing, of course, on the contributions of the Scots-Irish. Outside, the folk park is divided into Old and New World villages, with a reconstructed port and emigrant ship ingeniously linking the two. The idea of a lady wearing a bonnet working at a spinning wheel sounds pretty hokey, but the "costumed interpreters" explain and demonstrate the traditional crafts in a clear, undramatic way. One of the highlights of the Old World park is the original cottage where Thomas Mellon, the Pittsburgh financier, was born in 1813. In the New World section you can tour a replica of the clapboard house his father built in Pennsylvania in 1822 (four years after emigrating), complete with rickety stairs and lumpy beds made with hand-sewn quilts.

Tyrone's second draw is the **Sperrin Mountains,** which can be beautiful in fine weather, rolling moorland all sprinkled with yellow gorse; in the more remote parts there's not a house, human, even sheep for miles on end. The Northern Ireland Tourist Board promotes the Sperrins as perfect for long-distance walking or cycling, and though some travelers will want to seize on this opportunity to veer well off the tourist circuit, there's virtually no place to stay in the mountains; you can either camp or try a self-catering accommodation on the southern fringes. One option is **An Creagan Visitor Centre** (Creggan, on the A505 12 mi/19 km northeast of Omagh, tel. 028/8076-1112, www.an-creagan.com, 11am-6:30pm daily Apr.-Sept., 11am-4:30pm Mon.-Fri. Oct.-Mar., 1-bedroom cottage £120-180 per weekend, £220-280 per week), which offers an exhibition (free) on the flora, fauna, and archaeology of the Sperrins. Bike rental is available (£7/10 per half-day/day), and there's also a pub-cum-restaurant serving lunch, tea, and dinner. There are regular weekend trad sessions.

The **Ulsterbus Sperrin Rambler** service (#403, 2/day) connects Omagh with Gortin and Cranagh, where you'll find another resource: the **Sperrin Heritage Centre** (274 Glenelly Rd., Cranagh, on the B47 23 mi/37 km north of Omagh, tel. 028/8164-8142, 11:30am-5:30pm Mon.-Fri., 11:30am-6pm Sat., 2pm-6pm Sun. Apr.-Sept., £2.50). The center is just south of the Sperrins' highest peak, Mount Sawel (2,230 feet, 680 meters). Outside of the Rambler bus, those not walking or cycling will need a car to explore these mountains.

smaller rivers that empty into the Cladagh, there's a one-hour walking tour jam-packed with geological tidbits. The guides have a clever name for every funny-looking formation. A specially designed cement walkway that parts the subterranean lake is known, appropriately enough, as "the Moses walk." Foam on the ceiling indicates how high the water was earlier in the day—even the Moses walk can flood.

While you're waiting for your tour to commence, check out the excellent 20-minute audiovisual on the geology, botany, and history of the area. The caves and the surrounding **Marlbank National Nature Reserve** have been designated a European Geopark, and the blanket bog on the Cuilcagh Mountains supports a great deal of flora and fauna.

Be smart and ring ahead to reserve a place on a tour in the summer. To get here from Enniskillen, take the Sligo-bound A4, and after three miles (4.8 km) make a left onto the southbound A32. The caves are clearly signposted from there, and you'll pass Florence Court on the way. From Sligo, take the eastbound N16 and look for the Marble Arch signpost in Blacklion.

Florence Court

In the shadow of Benaughlin Mountain—from

the Irish for "Peak of the Horse" because its limestone scree once resembled a horse's profile—**Florence Court** (7.5 mi/12 km southwest of town via the A4 and A32, tel. 028/6634-8249, grounds 10am-8pm Apr.-Sept., until 4pm Oct.-Mar., house noon-6pm weekends mid-Mar.-May, 1pm-6pm Mon. and Wed.-Fri., noon-6pm Sat.-Sun. June, noon-6pm daily July-Aug., Sat.-Sun. Sept., £6) offers a serene walled garden and wooded walking trails through the adjoining forest park. There are three circular trails, 2-7 miles (3-11 km) long; the shortest takes you past the Florence Court Yew, the tree from which all Irish yews the world over originated. The house itself is a Palladian manor, built in the 1740s by Sir John Cole and extended by his son William, the first Earl of Enniskillen, 30 years later. What's even more remarkable about the original 18th-century furniture and rococo plasterwork is that the place could be so well restored after the fire that broke out in 1955.

the pre-Christian Janus Stone of Boa Island

THE HOLY ISLANDS OF LOUGH ERNE
★ Devenish Island

Devenish (Daimh Inis, "Ox Island") has the spectacular ruins of 6th-century Augustinian St. Molaise's Monastery. An astonishingly well-preserved 12th-century round tower, 30 meters high, sports a decorated cornice and its original conical roof. Best of all, you can climb it!

There are many legends surrounding this island, one of which concerns the building of 12th-century **St. Mary's Abbey** nearby; it's said that St. Molaise (who founded the monastery in the late 500s, mind you) listened to the birds singing, communing with the Holy Spirit. When he finally shook himself from his sacred reverie, half a millennium had passed, and his grand abbey stood all around him. The monastic community here flourished for another half a millennium, but despite its remote location it could not escape Henry VIII's decree of the late 1530s—that all the Irish monasteries be dissolved.

The Devenish ferry service was out of operation at time of writing, but you can still get there through **Erne Tours** (tel. 028/6632-2882, www.ernetours.com, operates May-Sept., departs 2:15pm, 4 sailings daily in July-Aug., return fare £10). Departure is from Round 'O' Jetty at Brook Park, Enniskillen, on the A46 a ten-minute walk west of town.

Boa Island

On the northern end of Lower Lough Erne is the largest of Lower Lough Erne's 97 islands, **Boa Island** (from Badh, an Irish war goddess, pronounced "boh"), linked to the mainland by a bridge on either side and spanned by the A47. Boa is noteworthy for its two-faced Celtic idol (also known as the "Janus Stone"). Some 2,000 years old, the Janus Stone is located in the Caldragh cemetery, signposted off the A47. As if its freaky faces weren't enough to give you gooseflesh, just check out the hollow at the top of the stone; archaeologists believe it may have been used to hold sacrificial blood.

White Island

The spookiest of Lough Erne's "holy islands" is **White Island.** Walk through the plain Romanesque doorway of a 12th-century church, and you will find a row of six statues, pagan in aspect, attached to the interior wall. These are flanked by two pieces from a much later date: a mildly grotesque face on the right and a *sheila-na-gig* on the left. Though they were carved in a Celtic style, the six central stones were fashioned by the same hand sometime between the 7th and 10th centuries. Amazingly enough, they were used as ordinary stones during the building of the church, and were only discovered in the 19th century and arranged here for display.

White Island is accessible via a **ferry** (tel. 028/6862-1892, www.castlearchdaleboathire.com, departures on the hour 11am-6pm daily July-Aug., 11am-1pm weekends Apr.-June, return fare £4) from the pier at the **Castle Archdale Country Park** (Lisnarrick, 10 mi/16 km northeast of Enniskillen on the B82, tel. 028/6862-1892, 9am-dusk daily,

free). The ferry allows you a sojourn of about 40 minutes.

BELLEEK

Renowned for its porcelain factory, **Belleek** (Béal Leice, "Flagstone Ford") is a pleasant one-street town on the western end of Lower Lough Erne. Shop to your heart's content at **Belleek Pottery** (on the A46, tel. 028/6865-9300, www.belleek.ie, 9am-6pm Mon.-Fri., 10am-6pm Sat., 2pm-6pm Sun. Apr.-Sept.; opens at 11am Sun. July-Aug.; 9am-5:30pm Mon.-Fri., 10am-5:30pm Sat., 2pm-6pm Sun. in Oct.; 9am-5:30pm Mon.-Fri. Nov.-Mar.). Tours take place every half hour (9:30am-12:15pm and 2:15pm-4:15pm Mon.-Fri., £4).

Belleek is 24 miles (39 km) northwest of Enniskillen on the A46 and 18 miles (30 km) south of Donegal on the N3 (picking up the N15 in Ballyshannon). Ulsterbus service from Enniskillen is quite inconvenient, but fortunately **Bus Éireann** (#30, 7/day Mon.-Sat., 5/day Sun.) passes through Enniskillen and Belleek on the Dublin-Donegal route.

Background

The Landscape 445

History 447

Government and Economy 456

People and Culture 458

The Landscape

GEOGRAPHY

Ireland is 84,079 square kilometers (32,477 square miles); as a size comparison, you might fit the island within the state of New York. The island lies between the Atlantic Ocean to the west and the Irish Sea to the east, which separates Ireland from Great Britain. The island's longest waterway is the River Shannon, stretching 259 kilometers from Lough Allen in County Leitrim south through Lough Derg (bordered by Clare, Tipperary, and Galway); then it empties into the 113-kilometer Shannon estuary, which forms the southern shore of County Clare. The largest lake is the 388-square-kilometer Lough Neagh in Northern Ireland, bordered by five of its six counties. Ireland's mountain ranges form a ring around the flat Midlands region, which features large swaths of bogland and many small lakes farther north, especially in County Cavan. Battered by the Atlantic, Ireland's west coast is far more rugged, characterized by peninsulas, islands, and headlands. The Irish coastline is estimated to be 5,800 kilometers long.

CLIMATE

The North Atlantic Drift, a warm ocean current in the north Atlantic, contributes to Ireland's temperate climate; its temperatures are among the least extreme in Europe, and it rarely snows and even more rarely freezes. Yes, it rains two days out of three, and as Heinrich Böll once wrote, "The rain here is absolute, magnificent, and frightening." But the mild winters and wet summers allow for a green landscape all year long.

May and June are the sunniest months, with an average of six hours of sunlight per day; July and August are the warmest (average temp 14-16°C/57-60°F), though the temperature sometimes climbs into the 20s C/lower 80s F. December and January are the rainiest (70-75 millimeters monthly rainfall), January and February the coldest (4-7°C/39-44°F). August-November is also a very wet time of year (66-70 millimeters), and July and August bring the highest risk of thunderstorms, especially in the west (which is the rainiest region overall). The southeast is Ireland's sunniest region, with Wexford boasting the title of "Ireland's Sunniest County."

ENVIRONMENTAL ISSUES

Ireland has its share of pollution, much of it the product of industry and irresponsible agricultural practices. There is also an acute nationwide litter problem. Those rolling green hills are deceptively pristine, and it's precisely this traditional image of Ireland that is preventing or delaying much-needed reforms. Though a majority of Irish rivers and lakes offer good water quality, the Irish Sea is highly polluted (and there is some evidence that regular bathing in it is a cause of cancer). Plus, several tests have confirmed fecal contamination in the groundwater, but one example of the consequences of improper agricultural practice. Ireland is also well behind much of Europe when it comes to recycling, though the government finally initiated county-run recycling programs in 2005. There are glass receptacles in every strip mall parking lot and home collection for plastic and paper, but because the counties charge for this service, many citizens are not as diligent as they should be. For more information, visit the **Friends of the Irish Environment** (www.

Previous: the graveyard and high crosses at Clonmacnoise; a sun-dappled bed of clover in County Leitrim.

friendsoftheirishenvironment.org) or **An Taisce** (www.antaisce.org) on the web.

PLANTS AND ANIMALS

Ireland has comparatively few plant and animal species because of its geological "youth": The island was created at the end of the last ice age.

Vegetation

Bogs—blanket and raised—feature prominently on the Irish landscape (12,000 square kilometers in all). They were formed when Neolithic farmers first cleared forests for farming: The treeless soil gradually became more acidic, forming heather and rushes; these plants decayed and formed a layer of organic matter on which new growth could begin. Logs of turf—essentially bricks of peat sliced from the bog and laid out to dry—have been a source of fuel since the 17th century. Ireland was heavily forested before the Stone Age, and after the Norman invasion the English exploited many remaining Irish forests for timber for shipbuilding.

Fewer than 1,000 plant species are unique to Ireland. The Burren in County Clare is the most popular region for botanists, as there are both alpine and Mediterranean species growing alongside native species; the mild climate allows such nonnative varieties to flourish.

Mammals

There are only 31 extant mammal species in Ireland, most of which have been introduced by humans over the last 8,000 years. Native species include the red fox, hedgehog, stoat, and badger. Several species, though not endangered, are found mostly in the country's national parks and nature reserves: the pine marten, red deer, and Irish hare. It's speculated that Neolithic settlers first brought cattle and sheep to Ireland sometime around 6500 BC. Rabbits were introduced by the Normans in the 12th century, and the two rat species and common mouse traveled here by boat as well.

Sealife

With all its lakes, rivers, tributaries, and coastlines, Ireland is an angler's paradise, and seafood is an integral part of the Irish diet. Salmon, pike, and brown trout are the primary freshwater species; marine species include bass, cod, haddock, hake, and turbot. Whales and dolphins frequent Irish waters, the common dolphin being the most frequently sighted species. Bottlenose dolphins are often very friendly, following boats for miles and lingering in harbors for long periods of time (a dolphin named Fungie in Dingle is the most famous example). There are dolphin-watching trips available in West Cork and Loop Head in County Clare.

Birds

Most of the island's 400 recorded bird species are migratory, and there are more than 60 bird sanctuaries. Many offshore islands are popular with bird-watchers, including Scattery Island in Clare, Rathlin Island in Antrim (one of few remaining homes of the endangered corncrake), the Saltee Islands in Wexford, and Small Skellig off the Iveragh Peninsula in County Kerry. For more information, contact the **Irish Wildbird Conservancy** (www.birdwatchireland.ie).

Reptiles and Amphibians

Ireland has very few reptiles. It's true that there are no snakes in Ireland, though St. Patrick probably had nothing to do with it! The island features only three amphibious species—the natterjack toad, smooth newt, and the common frog—and just one reptile, the common lizard. For everything else, you'll have to visit the zoo in Dublin or Belfast.

History

PREHISTORY

We know relatively little about pre-Christian Ireland, and what we do is extrapolated from archaeology, mythology, oral tradition, and Roman records. The first human hunter-gatherers arrived between 10,000 to 8000 BC as the ice age ended and the oceans rose to separate Ireland from Britain and Europe. They arrived in small boats, though some may have crossed a narrowing isthmus. Agriculture was introduced from the continent around 4000 BC. Neolithic culture flourished, relics of which still punctuate the Irish landscape: large standing stones, dolmens, burial mounds, and stone circles, some cosmically aligned. The most impressive Neolithic passage tomb is **Newgrange** in County Meath, which predates the Great Pyramid in Egypt and features the famous tri-spiral motifs associated with Irish crafts to this day. Bronze Age artisans produced intricate gold work of a high quality renowned throughout Europe.

THE CELTS

Iron Age society in Ireland was dominated by druids, who functioned as spiritual leaders, doctors, poets, lawmakers, and teachers. The distinct rival kingdoms that began to emerge in Ireland at this time are survived today, more or less, in the traditional counties and provinces of Ireland. It is popularly believed that around this time Ireland underwent a large-scale invasion by the Celts, a creative if warlike race that originated in central Europe. It is more likely, however, that Celtic influences and culture were gradually adopted by the native Irish. Either way, from about 300 BC a strong Celtic society dominated Ireland over the following millennium, and their art and spiritualism are still considered an integral part of Irish culture. The Irish Celts followed an elaborate and surprisingly progressive civil legal system known as the Brehon Laws, though they were not above raiding the British coast and taking slaves.

While Ireland was never formally part of the Roman Empire, the island was influenced by, and engaged in trade with, the Romans. Frequent references to Hibernia, Ireland's Latin name, are found in Roman records, but it remains unclear what kind of relationship existed between Ireland and the vast empire.

EARLY CHRISTIAN IRELAND AND THE GOLDEN AGE

During the 5th century Irish pirates frequently raided the British coast, even forming colonies in Scotland, Wales, and England. Slaves were often taken, among them the adolescent who would become St. Patrick. Though he is popularly credited with single-handedly converting the Irish to Christianity, in fact there were other missionaries sent to Ireland long before and long after Patrick. And while he has had a lasting influence on Irish spirituality, Patrick cannot be solely credited with creating the particular variant of Christianity that embraced Irish traditions and laws (apart from those laws that directly contradicted Christian doctrine, of course). These influential clerics encouraged Ireland to unite its various rival kingdoms under a single authority, a high king.

Irish monasteries soon earned an excellent reputation as centers of Latin learning, and attracted scholars, scribes, and theologians from all over Europe. As scholarship and craftsmanship thrived in these monasteries, and as Christian values discouraged interkingdom warring, Ireland entered its Golden Age. The island's existing artisan traditions saw further advancement, and indeed the finest European artworks of the era were produced in Ireland's monasteries. Several impressive examples survive to this day, such as the delicately detailed **Ardagh Chalice,** on display in the National

Museum of Archaeology and History, and the **Book of Kells,** an illuminated bible housed in Trinity College.

While the rest of Europe was ravaged by the Dark Ages, Latin learning (and Western civilization itself) was preserved in Irish monasteries like Glendalough in County Wicklow and Clonmacnoise in County Offaly. As Europe gradually stabilized, the "island of saints and scholars" sent missionaries back to mainland Europe, where they founded a great many monasteries.

THE VIKINGS

Such enormous wealth attracted barbarian attention, and in the 9th century Vikings from Norway arrived in their imposing longships, raiding the coasts and striking vulnerable towns and monasteries along the Shannon, Suir, and other strategic waterways.

The round tower, a style of refuge almost unique to Ireland, symbolizes this era. Eventually, some Vikings settled in Ireland, appreciating the milder winters. They founded towns along the coasts from which to attack the inland native strongholds, but successive generations embraced Irish culture and adopted Christianity, effectively becoming Hiberno-Norse. In the first decade of the 11th century, **Brian Boru** became high king. The title was mostly honorary for his predecessors, but Boru assumed actual authority over the island; he demanded tributes from the smaller kingdoms, which he used to rebuild churches and monasteries destroyed by the Vikings.

Brian Boru rallied the remaining Irish kingdoms in a bid to break Norse power over Ireland. His combined forces fought the climactic daylong **Battle of Clontarf** outside Viking Dublin in 1014, and Boru is traditionally credited with driving the Vikings "back into the sea." In reality, however, it was more a civil war between the Irish. (The "Viking" army was in the service of the king of Leinster and was composed mainly of Irish and Hiberno-Norse soldiers.) The elderly Boru did not survive the battle, and by this time the Viking and native cultures had already amalgamated. The Vikings had founded many of the seaports that would become Ireland's main towns and cities, including Dublin, Galway, and Cork. They also introduced the use of currency.

THE NORMANS

The second wave of invaders were to have an even more profound impact on Ireland's destiny. The Normans had previously settled in northern France, and in 1066 they conquered England. A century later Dermot MacMorrough, the exiled king of Leinster, petitioned England's Henry II to help him regain his kingdom. The Earl of Pembroke, Richard de Clare (popularly known as Strongbow) agreed to lead an invasion force in return for the hand of MacMorrough's daughter. By 1169 MacMorrough—often singled out as the greatest traitor in Irish history, which is no mean achievement—had retaken Leinster, and upon his death his Norman son-in-law ruled it.

Henry II felt threatened by this rival Norman kingdom growing across the channel and secured a papal bull in order to land a fleet in Ireland. Soon after Henry II arrived in Waterford in 1171, the Normans, with their superior weapons, armor and tactics, conquered the entire east coast and divided the taken land into earldoms as rewards for their knights. They built many distinctive towerlike castles all around the country.

By the 13th century, however, the Normans had retreated to the territory surrounding Dublin, known as **The Pale,** due to several factors. In 1315 Edward Bruce of Scotland invaded England; a long and bloody war ensued throughout the British Isles, in which the Gaelic lords sided against the English. Also, the Black Death hit the more densely populated Norman towns harder than their scattered Irish counterparts. Disconnected from a troubled England, the settled Normans began to consider themselves natives, and became "more Irish than the Irish themselves." Toward the end of the 16th century, England had lost virtually all its control over Ireland "beyond the Pale."

THE REFORMATION AND PROTESTANT ASCENDANCY

For Ireland, the Reformation spelled enduring catastrophe. Henry VIII of England cut all ties with the Catholic Church following his divorce from Catherine of Aragon; while the majority of England, Scotland, and Wales converted to Protestantism relatively painlessly, the more independent Ireland retained its deep-rooted Catholicism. Henry increasingly feared an Ireland-based invasion of either French or Spanish Catholic forces. So the king sought to undermine the most powerful dynasty in Ireland, the Fitzgeralds, who were the earls of Kildare. In 1543 Dublin was stormed by Silken Thomas, son of the reigning earl. This rebellion was quashed, Thomas and his men executed, and the Fitzgeralds' lands confiscated. Henry next turned his sights on the Catholic Church and pillaged several monasteries and churches, eventually "dissolving" them entirely (which is why virtually all of Ireland's pre-Reformation churches are Anglican). In 1541 Henry forced the Irish Parliament to declare him king of Ireland.

The Ulster province was the last outpost of Irish Catholic power, where Hugh O'Neill, Earl of Tyrone, initiated a rebellion. This erupted into the **Nine Years' War,** which raged through the reigns of Elizabeth I and her successor, James I. In 1601 the earls marched south and gathered a large army to meet the English in the **Battle of Kinsale.** The Irish were aided by a Spanish fleet, which besieged Kinsale seaside. Due mainly to misguided tactics, O'Neill and the earls were defeated, though some survived and fled to Europe, a turning point known as the **Flight of the Earls.**

For the first time in the centuries since the Norman invasion, England had resoundingly conquered Ireland. Elizabeth I implemented the **Plantation of Ireland,** where huge amounts of land confiscated from the earls were given to Protestant settlers in a bid to assimilate the Irish. Unlike previous settlers, these Protestants did not integrate with the angry and powerless Catholic majority. The native Irish were further oppressed by the **Penal Laws,** which outlawed all faiths except Protestantism. The majority of Catholics continued to practice their religion in secret.

OLIVER CROMWELL AND THE PENAL LAWS

The disenfranchised Irish supported Charles I, a Catholic, during the English Civil War against the Protestant Parliamentarians. Charles was defeated, and Oliver Cromwell, leader of the Parliamentarians, decided to restore English control of Ireland. There are few historical figures on whom history is more divided than Cromwell. The English thought him a hero of democracy, but his actions in Ireland have rightfully branded him a monster. Cromwell's forces landed in Drogheda in 1649 and cut a swath of destruction upward through the country. Cromwell's brutal campaign left more than a third of Ireland's population either dead or in exile. Approximately 20,000 square kilometers were seized from Irish Catholics and divided amongst Cromwell's supporters. Many of the dispossessed Irish relocated to the wilder, less fertile west. Cromwell's own infamous words were "to hell or to Connaught."

In 1689 Ireland hosted a second conflict between English monarchists and Parliamentarians. James II, also Catholic, arrived in Ireland and was recognized as king by the Irish Parliament. Preparations were made to restore property and status to Catholics. They laid siege to the city of Derry, which caused mass starvation within the city walls. The siege ended when James II was defeated at the Battle of the Boyne by the forces of William of Orange. William was actually James's Protestant son-in-law, invited to the throne by the English Parliament after James's departure.

The Penal Laws were reapplied, though harsher this time: They prevented Catholics from owning land and essentially outlawed all traces of Irish culture.

THE BIRTH OF NATIONALISM

Most of the 18th century was relatively peaceful in Ireland, though unrest escalated as the economic situation worsened. This combined with two very cold winters caused the first **famine** of 1740-1741, which caused the deaths of 400,000 people. Also fueling unrest were the American and French Revolutions, which inspired liberal thinking—even in the "planted" Protestant population, who were beginning to consider Ireland their home. The **United Irishmen** (under the leadership of **Theobald Wolfe Tone,** a high-minded Dublin Protestant) initially sought reform through nonviolent means, but as the French Revolution became increasingly gruesome, the society took on a more militaristic approach. In retaliation the Protestants formed the Orange Society, named in honor of William of Orange.

Tone accompanied the French in a failed attempt to land a fleet in Bantry Bay. The English government began a full-scale nationwide hunt for the United Irishmen, which caused widespread panic among Catholics. In 1798 a rebellion erupted in the traditionally peaceful county of Wexford, led by Father John Murphy. The rebellion was bloodily suppressed after a run of minor victories. Later in 1798 Tone and a second French fleet were defeated at sea. He was captured and committed suicide in prison.

THE ACT OF UNION AND CATHOLIC EMANCIPATION

The Irish Parliament was composed of an increasingly anxious Protestant gentry, and in 1800 the ruling body dissolved itself and joined the House of Commons. This consolidated government, the United Kingdom of Great Britain and Ireland, was an attempt to secure British authority.

Meanwhile, **Daniel O'Connell,** a young Catholic lawyer from County Kerry (though Catholics were denied education, wealthier families would send their sons to study in Europe), fought a successful campaign for the repeal of the Penal Laws. The British Parliament conceded **Catholic Emancipation** in 1826 after O'Connell won a parliamentary seat for County Clare. Though Catholics were not allowed to become members of Parliament, the government feared mass protests and permitted O'Connell to sit in Westminster.

O'Connell, hailed then and now as the "Great Liberator," went on to campaign for more reforms for Catholics, most notably an attempt to repeal the Act of Union. Though O'Connell had the popularity to rally "monster meetings" that drew as many as half a million Catholics, he eventually lost influence over the nationalist movement as it grew impatient with nonviolent methods.

FAMINE AND EMIGRATION

In 1845 a blight caused the failure of potato crops all over the island. This, coupled with exploitative and selfish economic structures, led to Ireland's worst tragedy, the **Great Famine** (1845-1849). The island's population dropped from eight to five million because of mass starvation and emigration. Though there was more than enough food in the country, most of it was exported to Britain and overseas. As historian Roy Foster explains it, "Traditionally, the Famine was seen as at worst a deliberate English policy of genocide, at best willful neglect on the part of the British government."

Under the Poor Laws landlords were responsible for the welfare of their tenants, yet many landlords exercised a less expensive option: paying for their tenants' passage to America. The conditions of the overcrowded and poorly managed ships were atrocious, and many emigrants did not survive the journey on these "coffin ships." The British government eventually granted some aid, but it was far from adequate, and emigration continued.

Tracing Your Roots

Looking for the names and old address of your great-great-grandparents from County Tipperary? Though each county has its own archive, it's more sensible to start at the **General Register Office** (Joyce House, Lombard St., Research Room, 2nd fl., tel. 01/635-4000, 9:30am-4:30pm Mon.-Fri.) in Dublin, where you can look up your ancestor's birth, marriage, or death certificate (all of which should list the addresses of the parties involved) no matter which county he or she came from; the records here start at 1864. The fees are nominal, though they can start to add up if you need to broaden your search: €2-4 per request (you can request up to five annual record books at a time), and €4 for a photocopy. Though the archive is always a hive of activity, the staff is willing to answer quick questions and offer search tips.

You can also check the census records and various databases at the **National Archives** (Bishop St., tel. 01/407-2300, www.nationalarchives.ie, 10am-5pm Mon.-Fri.). Another good starting point, particularly if you need help planning your search, is the **National Library Genealogy Advisory Service** (Kildare St., tel. 01/603-0200, www.nli.ie, 9:30am-5pm Mon.-Wed. and 9:30am-4:45pm Thurs.-Fri., plus 9:30am-12:45pm Sat. Mar.-Oct.). This office has a few databases on offer but is worth a visit mainly for the knowledgeable staff, who will provide you with thorough advice. No appointment is necessary.

The General Register Office in Dublin has birth, marriage, and death records for the Northern Ireland counties as well, but there is additional information available at the **Public Record Office of Northern Ireland** (66 Balmoral Ave., tel. 028/9025-5905, www.proni.gov.uk, 9am-4:45pm Mon.-Wed. and Fri., 10am-8:45pm Thurs.).

If you don't have the time to conduct extensive genealogical research, consider hiring a professional. Ask at the National Library office for a list of private researchers; most are based in Dublin.

At the turn of the 20th century the population was down to four million.

During this time the Irish language fell out of popular use; famine and emigration more heavily impacted Irish-speaking areas. Also, the recently introduced National School system taught only through English by order of the British government. Many Catholics—weary of poverty and observing the economic prosperity of English-speaking America and Britain—began to see Irish as a dying language. Irish was still spoken in the country's more rural and remote reaches, however. The regions in which Irish is still spoken as the primary language—Dingle, Connemara, Gweedore, Ring, and others—are known as the Gaeltachtaí.

PARNELL AND HOME RULE

In the wake of the Great Famine, Ireland's resentment of the British government grew, and several minor rebellions were staged by organizations such as the Fenians and the **Irish Republican Brotherhood** (IRB, a secret society that was to play a considerable role in the struggle for independence). Impoverished Catholic tenants were granted more rights—like the option to purchase the land they rented—by consecutive British governments under pressure from the Land League, headed by the IRB's Michael Davitt and Protestant landowner **Charles Stewart Parnell,** who organized boycotts of landlords who didn't comply with the league's conditions.

Parnell's firm belief in Irish sovereignty led him to found the Home Rule League, and in 1875 he was elected to the British Parliament—where he caused a lot of trouble. Though Parnell was an overwhelmingly popular and charismatic leader (he was referred to as the uncrowned king of Ireland, and he even convinced Prime Minister William Gladstone to back Home Rule twice), he fell from grace in 1890 when his affair with Kitty O'Shea, the wife of a fellow MP, became publicly known. The scandal greatly affected his health and he died the following year.

The wealthy Protestant population of eastern Ulster vehemently opposed the concept of Home Rule; as a heavily industrialized (rather than agrarian) society, they were spared the worst effects of the famine. Though Gladstone's second Home Rule Bill in 1892 had been defeated, they sensed the tides turning; in 1912 Sir Edward Carson founded the **Ulster Volunteer Force** (UVF, a vigilante offshoot of the Unionist Party). The UVF staged massive paramilitary rallies, threatening civil war in the face of Home Rule. In response to the UVF, Eoin O'Neill established the **Irish Volunteers** to defend Home Rule. But when World War I broke out in 1914, the threat of civil war was suspended.

THE EASTER RISING

In 1916 a small splinter group of Irish Volunteers, along with James Connolly's Irish Citizen Army (established in 1913 to protect peacefully demonstrating workers against the British police), staged an armed rebellion. The nationalists marched into Dublin on Easter Monday and took several landmark locations in the city, making the General Post Office their headquarters. From the steps of the GPO the poet Patrick Pearse read aloud the **Proclamation of the Irish Republic,** declaring his group of insurrectionists the provisional government of a new republic, the Volunteers its legitimate uniformed army. Initially most Dubliners condemned the rising, as a week of intense fighting between the rebels and the British Army (who responded with superior firepower and heavy artillery) had effectively wrecked the city. When the rebels finally surrendered to the British, they had to be protected from the mobs of angry Dubliners they had intended to liberate.

The British exacerbated the situation when they executed 15 of the rebels (14 at Dublin's Kilmainham Jail, including Patrick Pearse and James Connolly, and one in London) and sentenced a further 76 to death. (Due to the

mounting pressure of public sympathy for the rebels, the remaining death sentences were commuted to penal servitude.) This effectively made martyrs of the rebels, creating the very blood sacrifice the rising had intended and sparking a new wave of nationalism. Among the prisoners was Eamon de Valera, who was spared from execution by his American citizenship. He and his lieutenant, Michael Collins, a young civil servant from West Cork, were eventually released from prison on amnesty.

De Valera and other republicans formed a political party, **Sinn Féin** (meaning "We Ourselves"), and won the majority of the Irish seats in the 1918 general election. Rather than take their positions in Westminster, they declared Ireland independent and reformed the Volunteers into the Irish Republican Army (IRA), simultaneously declaring war on British troops on Irish soil.

THE WAR OF INDEPENDENCE

This entrenched war commenced with the murders of two Royal Irish Constabulary (RIC) men, on the same day the Dáil (the new independent Irish Parliament) convened: January 21, 1919. The British government tried to regain order by deploying a combined force to Ireland to assist the RIC: regular infantry, Army Auxiliaries, and an RIC reserve force, better known as the **Black and Tans.** This was a vicious and undisciplined paramilitary group comprising mainly ex-soldiers and prisoners, whose unchecked deeds further cemented the general population's embrace of republicanism. The Black and Tans retaliated with excessive force, burning and sacking several towns, including the Cork city center. Unable to engage the better-armed British forces directly with a front line, the IRA pioneered guerrilla and urban warfare, creating "flying columns" to ambush their enemy. This campaign was masterminded by Michael Collins, who in prison with other volunteers had effectively run a military training camp. Collins headed a delegation to London to negotiate, and in December 1921 both sides signed the **Anglo-Irish Treaty.** While granting Ireland considerable autonomy, the treaty allowed for the partition of the six counties that had a Protestant majority. This would create two new nations, each with Home Rule, though Northern Ireland would choose to remain part of the United Kingdom.

THE FREE STATE AND THE CIVIL WAR

The Dáil ratified the treaty in January 1922, forming the **Irish Free State,** and a general election that summer showed support for pro-treaty politicians. De Valera and his followers refused to accept the terms of the treaty, however, and stormed out of the Dáil. Soon afterward the Irish Free State erupted into a treacherous civil war. Arthur Griffith, who had helped negotiate the treaty, became president of the Free State.

Now commander-in-chief of the Free State Army (formerly the IRA), General Collins was forced to hunt down his former comrades and friends. This is an often unspoken chapter in Ireland's history, as uncompromising idealism turned the country against itself—it divided communities and even families down the middle—and atrocities were committed on both sides. Griffith died of anxiety and General Collins was shot dead in an ambush near his home parish in West Cork.

The anti-treaty forces laid down their arms in 1923, but the civil war had cast a long shadow over the young nation. De Valera eventually recognized the government and formed a rival political party in 1927, Fianna Fáil. They won several seats in the election of that year, and entered the Dáil without taking the oath of allegiance to the British crown that had been a controversial condition of the treaty. (The Free State was still a member of the British Commonwealth.)

The Free State faced many difficulties in its early years. There was a global economic depression in the wake of the Wall Street crash of 1929, and several European states were turning to fascism to sustain themselves. Fianna Fáil came into power in 1932—and since it was a peaceful changeover, the Free State achieved a long-awaited sense of stability.

Though emigration, poverty, and unemployment levels were high, Ireland remained a democracy during the uncertain decade. De Valera's Ireland clung to several insular policies in an attempt at self-sufficiency. He oversaw the large-scale cultivation of the bogs for peat as well as the construction of the ambitious Ardnacrusha Hydroelectric Power Station (or "Shannon Scheme"); at the time it was the largest project of its kind ever attempted. De Valera also refused to pay land rates to Britain, contravening yet another condition of the treaty.

The Catholic Church was as influential as de Valera; it directed the Free State away from the liberal and inclusive ideals of the Proclamation of the Irish Republic and toward an oppressively conservative Catholic climate. The church ensured the banning of contraception, divorce, and other so-called immoralities that affronted its dogma; at its bidding the Irish government censored and even banned a great many books and films. The church also controlled the country's schools and hospitals. Many Protestants left the Free State feeling intimidated in an overwhelmingly Catholic environment. Indeed, during the 1920s, a great many Protestant "big houses"—seen as symbols of the Anglo-Irish Ascendancy—were burned to the ground.

In 1937 a new constitution was drawn up that affirmed Irish neutrality and spared it from the ravages of World War II. Many Irish fought in the war against fascism, however, and in truth the Free State was "neutral in favor of Britain." Idiosyncratically, World War II was known as "The Emergency" in Ireland, and heavy rationing was put in place.

THE IRISH REPUBLIC

After 16 years of political dominance, Fianna Fáil lost to Fine Gael, the successors to the original Free State government; Fine Gael quickly declared Ireland a republic and withdrew from the Commonwealth. Sean

Lamass became Taoiseach (prime minister) in 1959, and he implemented sweeping new policies (such as free secondary education) to strengthen Ireland's economic prospects, competitiveness, and infrastructure—and to curb emigration. Successful and popular besides, Lamass was credited with laying the groundwork for Ireland's later economic vitality. Ireland also sought membership in the European Economic Community, but was not admitted until 1973 along with the United Kingdom. Membership initially proved beneficial, but toward the end of the 1970s a harsh downturn slowed the economy considerably. The 1980s were bleak indeed, characterized by high unemployment.

THE TROUBLES

Northern Ireland's first premier, James Craig, proclaimed it "a Protestant state for a Protestant people" in response to the overwhelmingly Catholic Free State south of the border. In the North, a policy of discrimination denied power, employment, and even decent housing to the Catholic minority. A corrupt electoral system and flagrant gerrymandering denied Catholics representation even in Derry, where they were in the majority by 10 percent.

A peaceful civil-rights movement emerged, following the example of Daniel O'Connell, Gandhi, and Martin Luther King Jr. But the Royal Ulster Constabulary and other militant unionists used violence to disperse a peaceful rights march in 1968, sparking counterviolence among the utterly disenfranchised Catholic population. Another march was attacked by a unionist mob in January of the following year, and the situation was only exacerbated by the police, who swept through the Catholic Bogside neighborhood of Derry City.

That August British troops were deployed to Northern Ireland to restore order. While the troops initially were welcomed by both sides, the Catholics soon realized the soldiers were an oppressive occupying force, an instrument of the Protestant majority. The

situation came to a head with the events of January 30, 1972, **Bloody Sunday,** when 14 civilians were massacred by British troops during a civil-rights march. Many were shot in the back.

The IRA—not the original Irish Republican Army, but the ideological descendants of those who had rejected the Anglo-Irish Treaty—saw an exponential jump in recruitment and membership, as many Catholics believed these nationalist paramilitaries to be their lone, true defense force. In this poisonous atmosphere of sectarian hate and paranoia, the worst decade of the Troubles began.

DIRECT RULE AND THE NORTHERN QUESTION

The Troubles—a characteristically Irish euphemism—increased the size and power of various paramilitary groups on both sides, with various contrasting agendas. The IRA split into the Official IRA (OIRA) and the Provisional IRA (PIRA). In 1974 the more extreme Irish National Liberation Army was formed. On the unionist side, the UVF was joined by groups such as the Ulster Defense Association (UDA), the Ulster Freedom Fighters (UFF), and the Red Hand Commandos.

The Northern Irish Parliament was dissolved in 1972, and a new power-sharing system was almost put into place. A widespread strike by Protestant workers derailed the process, though, and for the next 27 years, Northern Ireland was under Direct Rule by the British Parliament. The paramilitary campaigns of both sides now featured bombings, which often resulted in civilian casualties.

The violence also spread beyond the borders of Northern Ireland, with the PIRA (also known as "the provos") setting off several bombs in London from 1973, and the UVF perpetrating bombings in Dublin and Monaghan on St. Patrick's Day 1974. Groups on both sides regularly committed sectarian murders. All such terrorist acts were condemned from both communities and from the British and Irish governments, but the cycle of violence and retribution was well under-way. The Troubles reached a climax in 1981, when republican inmates in the infamous "H-blocks"—including 27-year-old elected MP Bobby Sands—went on a hunger strike in a plea to be recognized as political prisoners. Sands and nine others fasted to death, and to this day they are hailed as martyrs to the nationalist cause. The hunger strikers are often commemorated by Sinn Féin: originally de Valera's political party, now socialist in bent, and oft-accused of being the political wing of the Provisional IRA.

The presence of the British Army reserve and the (predominantly Protestant) Royal Ulster Constabulary (RUC), Northern Ireland's police force beginning in 1922, seemed to discourage ongoing violence—yet IRA splinter groups were preparing for a full-scale "long war," going as far as to procure large arms shipments from Libya. Even the majority of Catholics, who totally condemned the IRA and their methods, were unwilling to trust the British soldiers who'd treated them so horribly in the past. Catholics also suspected collusion between the armed forces and unionist paramilitaries, and in recent years much evidence has come to light to confirm this.

In 1986 the British and Irish governments signed the **Anglo-Irish Agreement,** by which they would work together to bring peace to the North. The 1990s brought economic prosperity to both sides of the border—which, combined with the waning authority of the Catholic Church, helped depolarize attitudes in the North. The Northern Ireland demographics were also moderating, with Catholics now making up 40 percent of the population.

Significant advances in the peace process of the early 1990s included the Downing Street Declaration, which formally declared that Britain had no self-serving strategic or economic interest in Northern Ireland. In August 1994, Gerry Adams, leader of Sinn Féin, announced that the IRA was on a ceasefire. Two months later loyalist groups also announced

a ceasefire. Actual peace talks never began, though, as demands from both sides were not met. The IRA refused to surrender its weapons unless British troops were withdrawn from Northern Ireland and its political prisoners were freed, all of which were demands the British government considered too high. The bombing of London's Canary Wharf in February 1996 brought an end to the first ceasefire.

A second IRA ceasefire was secured in 1997, and on April 10, 1998, negotiations resulted in the Good Friday Agreement. For the first time since the implementation of Direct Rule, a system of power-sharing was brought to the North, with both nationalists and unionists receiving legislative control in several areas of government.

The Good Friday Agreement was overshadowed by riots during unionist marches through nationalist neighborhoods, a rising internal unionist murder rate, and the worst bombing since the start of the Troubles: On August 15, the Real IRA (founded by former members of the PIRA who refused to accept the terms of the Good Friday Agreement) detonated a car bomb in Omagh, County Tyrone. Twenty-nine people were killed, both Catholic and Protestant. The Real IRA's actions were condemned by all governments and parties, including Sinn Féin.

Peace talks have progressed slowly in recent years; many contentious aspects of the Good Friday Agreement have yet to be resolved, such as paramilitary decommissioning and British military withdrawal. Also, since 2002 the power-sharing agreement has been suspended as a result of distrust between nationalist and unionist politicians. Another contributing factor is the recent rise in popularity of the more extreme nationalist (Sinn Féin) and unionist (Ian Paisley's Democratic Unionist Party) political parties over their more moderate counterparts.

The most recent and promising development came in July 2005, when the Provisional IRA announced that its armed campaign had come to an end. In September an international weapons inspector from Canada, John de Chastelain, oversaw the destruction of the PIRA's arsenal.

More than 3,000 soldiers and civilians have lost their lives over the course of the Troubles.

RECENT DEVELOPMENTS IN THE REPUBLIC OF IRELAND

The 1980s were a period of high unemployment and emigration, though policies and reforms were introduced that built on the infrastructures of the 1960s. Such policies finally paid off in the economic boom of the 1990s known as the "Celtic Tiger." The phrase, coined in 1994, refers to Ireland's remarkable period of economic growth between the early 1990s and 2001, which transformed the republic into one of Europe's wealthiest nations. This success has been attributed to a variety of factors, including financial support from the European Union, conservative government spending, and low corporate tax rates (which encouraged many international businesses to open Irish branches). The wealth is not evenly distributed throughout the population, however; the east coast, particularly Dublin, has benefited the most. A global downturn in 2001 was followed by a rebounding Irish economy in 2004, but economists were spot on in their assertion that this second boom could not sustain itself as well as the original "Celtic Tiger." Sure enough, Ireland found itself in a financial crisis when the global recession hit at the end of 2008, and the recovery has been slow.

Birth control, illegalized in 1936, was made legally available again in 1992, and homosexuality was decriminalized the following year; divorce was legalized in 1996. Since these milestones of the mid-1990s Ireland has grown increasingly tolerant. The stigma associated with childbirth out of wedlock, for example, is pretty much a thing of the past in all but the most conservative circles. In keeping with these cultural shifts, Mass attendance has more than halved since 1995. Ireland's young (and young-in-spirit) liberals celebrated the positive outcome of the gay marriage referendum at the end of 2015.

Government and Economy

GOVERNMENT
The Irish Republic

Adopted in 1937 by referendum (thus replacing the Constitution of the Irish Free State in place since 1922), the Constitution of Ireland guarantees a democratic republic for its citizens. There is a bicameral legislature (or parliament) known as the Oireachtas ("o-ROCK-tas"), which comprises a lower house, the Dáil Éireann ("doll AY-rinn"), and a Senate-like house known as the Seanad Éireann ("SHAN-add AY-rinn," informally known as "the Senate"); both houses meet at Leinster House in Dublin. Unlike in the U.S. Congress, however, the Dáil exercises significantly more power than the Seanad. A member of the Oireachtas is known as a Teachta Dala ("TCHOCK-tuh DOLL-uh," abbreviated TD).

There are two primary political parties in the Irish system, the Fianna Fáil ("Soldiers of Destiny") and the Fine Gael ("Family of the Irish"). The former group was founded by Eamon de Valera in 1926 as a radical anti-treaty party, whereas the Fine Gael are the ideological descendants of the pro-treaty forces, founded in 1933 at the merging of three smaller parties. Fine Gael is traditionally considered moderate to conservative, while Fianna Fáil is moderate to liberal, though in reality the party lines are almost indistinguishable even to many native Irish. At time of writing the Fianna Fáil were the opposition party, holding 44 of the Dáil's 158 seats (Fine Gael holds 50).

Sinn Féin ("We Ourselves") is now the largest minority party in the republic, with

23 seats in the Dáil; traditionally considered the political arm of the Irish Republican Army and often associated with Marxism, this party is an even bigger player in Northern Ireland, where it is supported by most Catholic voters. Gerry Adams is the leader of the Sinn Féin party, whose ultimate goal is a united Ireland.

Other minority parties include Labour (founded by Easter rebel James Connolly in 1912), Anti-Austerity Alliance/People Before Profit, the new Independents 4 Change party, the Social Democrats, and the Green Party (founded in 1981 as the "Ecology Party of Ireland").

The Irish prime minister is known as the Taoiseach ("TEE-shock"), meaning "chieftain," and the Tánaiste ("taw-NESH-tah") is the deputy prime minister. The Taoiseach is the leader of his or her party, appointed by the president from among the members of the Dáil for a five-year term—or until the Taoiseach "loses the confidence" of the Dáil, at which time he or she may be compelled to resign (though this has never occurred). An Taoiseach—the formal title—nominates the Irish cabinet (as well as 11 members of the Seanad), and all cabinet members must also be members of the Oireachtas. At time of writing, Ireland's Taoiseach was Enda Kenny of the Fine Gael party; he took office in March 2011 and was reelected in 2016.

The Irish president (Uachtarán na hÉireann in Irish) is essentially a ceremonial figure, elected for a maximum of two seven-year terms. The poet Michael D. Higgins was elected ninth president of Ireland in 2011. Eamon de Valera was the first Taoiseach (and third president) of the Irish Republic, in office 1937-1948 (and president 1959-1973); Douglas Hyde was the first president, in office 1938-1945.

Northern Politics

Northern Ireland is governed by the British Parliament. The North's loyalist parties include the Ulster Unionist Party and the Democratic Unionist Party (DUP), the latter of which is now the largest in the province. Sinn Féin is Northern Ireland's primary republican and nationalist political party, the second being the Social Democratic and Labour Party (SDLP). The SDLP distinguished itself during the Troubles as antiterrorism, while Sinn Féin supported IRA violence as a means of achieving a unified Ireland. Other minority parties include the Green Party and People Before Profit Alliance on the left and the Traditional Unionist Voice (a DUP splinter group) on the right.

ECONOMY

Ireland's economic boom of the 1990s and early 2000s is a thing of memory now—the ghost of the Celtic Tiger is still licking its wounds after the global recession and €85 billion bailout from the European Union and International Monetary Fund. Agriculture has been Ireland's traditional lifeline, though in the last few decades tourism has become the number one industry—the island was welcoming well over seven million visitors a year in the early to mid-2000s. While tourism dropped off sharply in 2009, the figures are steadily climbing again.

Much of Ireland's white-collar workforce is engaged in the IT and investment sectors—international companies having been enticed here with tax incentives back in the boom times—and for a while many long-emigrated sisters and brothers were returning home to work. Ireland is no longer one of the richest nations in Europe, although it is slowly and steadily recovering.

People and Culture

DEMOGRAPHY

Since the recession, Ireland's population is no longer increasing by leaps and bounds. The current population of the republic is 4.7 million (by 2016 estimate), and approximately 1.8 million live in the six Northern counties (with 579,000 in the greater Belfast area). Though Dublin proper has roughly half a million inhabitants, almost 1.3 million Irish live in the greater metropolitan area, meaning that nearly 40 percent of the republic's population lives in the city and suburbs of the capital. The urban/rural population ratio is roughly 3:2, a reversal of the population distribution in the 1920s. Also, there are approximately 29,573 "Travellers," the politically correct term for the island's itinerant populations; each region has slightly different customs and dialect.

The **Central Statistics Office** (www.census.ie) has more interesting stats: Seeing as agriculture is such a historically integral part of the Irish economy, it's worth noting that approximately 6 percent of Irish farmers (who own their own farms) are under the age of 35. Divorce was legalized (by referendum) only in 1996, and today one in ten Irish marriages ends in divorce (the lowest divorce rate in the E.U.). The current life expectancy is 80.9 years: 79 for men and 83.5 for women.

IMMIGRATION

The influx of immigrants and refugees (from eastern Europe and Nigeria, mostly) since the advent of the "Celtic Tiger" economic boom is a remarkable irony: The Irish were so used to emigrating that they couldn't comprehend it when the foreigners started moving in! The percentage of Ireland's residents born elsewhere is roughly 20 percent, and a majority of those residents are eastern European; most successful visa applicants in recent years have been Indian, Russian, and Chinese. There is also a substantial population of African (mainly Nigerian) political refugees, whose

children, when they speak, sound every bit as Irish as the Irish themselves.

RELIGION

The population of the republic is 84 percent Catholic and a little less than 3 percent Protestant. The Northern Ireland population is roughly 48 percent Protestant and 45 percent Catholic, and that split continues to even out as strict Catholics keep on having larger families (the Catholic Church still forbids the use of contraception). Of course, these percentages vary by location; some areas (like Derry City and south Armagh) are predominantly Catholic and republican, and other areas (Plantation towns, mostly) are overwhelmingly Protestant and unionist. Of the North's Protestant population, most are Anglican (or Church of Ireland); the remainder are Methodist, Presbyterian, and many smaller, often evangelical sects. (You'll notice fire-and-brimstone-type notices and biblical quotations posted along the roadways when traveling in the North.) As you'd expect, the percentage of Irish citizens who identify themselves as non-Christian or atheist is extremely small; 0.03 percent are Jewish, 1.07 percent Muslim, and almost 6 percent report no religious beliefs (a further 1.6 percent are "unspecified").

In recent decades Ireland has veered away from its traditionally conservative climate and attitudes, partly due to growing disillusionment with the Catholic Church. Divorce, homosexuality, and most recently gay marriage were legalized through several referenda, birth control was made legally available again (though the Catholic Church still does not sanction its use), and allowances for abortion have been made in extreme circumstances. Church attendance has plummeted in recent decades, from more than 90 percent in the mid-1970s to 60 percent in the mid-1990s to roughly 40 percent in 2010 (and

Irish Expressions

You will probably notice that the Irish have a unique way of responding to a question; for example, if you ask "Did you go to the match today?" they'll say "I did" rather than "yes." This is because there are no real words in the Irish language for "yes" and "no." Instead, Irish-speakers reply with the same verb that was used to ask the question.

You may also notice that the Irish often drop their apostrophes—Murphy's Pub may read "Murphys Pub" above the doorway. Perhaps this also stems from the absence of apostrophes in the Irish language.

The first floor of a building is known as the "ground floor" in Ireland, and what Americans call a second floor is their first. Also, the Irish "ring" instead of "call" someone on their "mobile" rather than "cell phone." To "call on" people is to visit them in person.

Like the Brits, the Irish call french fries "chips" and potato chips "crisps." Soccer is "football" (which is not the same as Gaelic football), and fans are enthusiastic about "sport" rather than "sports."

"Your man" just means the particular person the speaker is referring to, not your boyfriend or husband.

The word *craic* (pronounced "crack") is fairly ubiquitous, and it has no direct translation—"fun" isn't quite adequate. "Fun with music and flowing pints" is more accurate. In any case, you'll brand yourself a tourist if you snicker when somebody uses it.

Here are a few more expressions you may need to know:

- "half-four"—4:30 (i.e., the time of day)

- "Monday week"—a week from Monday

- "fair play to you"—good job, nice going

only 14 percent in Dublin). As in the United States and several other European nations, child abuse scandals are a huge reason why so many disillusioned Irish Catholics are no longer going to church on Sunday.

LANGUAGE

Irish (or Gaelic, as foreigners often call it) is the Republic of Ireland's first official language (though English is far more widely spoken, the Constitution recognizes it secondarily). Irish (Gaeilge in Irish) is an Indo-European language brought to the island by the Celts and related to the native tongues of Scotland, Wales, and the Isle of Man. The Gaelic language most similar to Irish is Scottish Gaelic; it is possible for a Donegal Irish speaker to hold an (albeit halting) conversation with a Scottish Gaelic speaker. Note that it is more precise to refer to the Irish language as "Irish" rather than "Gaelic," as "Gaelic" is more often used to refer to Scottish Gaelic.

Many people are working assiduously to avoid the death of the Irish language, and their hopes are looking up. The problem is that in the post-independence republic, students were "force-fed" Irish and punished if they did not speak it as well as they did English (a remarkable reversal from the age of the Penal Laws!), and as a result many middle-aged Irish retain a marked distaste for the language of their forebears. Outside the Gaeltachtaí, regions where Irish is the primary language, you'll hear it spoken fairly infrequently; another problem with sustaining the native tongue is that the Ulster (Donegal), Connaught (Mayo and Galway), and Munster (Cork and Kerry) dialects are different enough to incite confusion even among native speakers; there have been proponents of a standardized dialect, but unsurprisingly this movement has not progressed. Today there are approximately 70,000 native Irish speakers on the island, and though 40 percent of all those in the republic claim fluency in the language, most admit they use it pretty infrequently.

For more information on the Gaeltachtaí, check out the **Údarás na Gaeltachta** website (www.udaras.ie).

THE ARTS
Handicrafts

Ireland's traditional cottage industries include lace, linen, tweed, and knitting.

Kenmare in County Kerry was a center for the **lace-making** craft in the 19th century and today offers a historical lace exhibition in the heritage center. Virtually all the lace you find in stores now is machine-made, however.

The making of Irish **linen** goes back to the 11th century, when flax was first farmed here; from monastic annals we know that the fabric was worn by the upper classes. From the 17th through the 19th centuries, linen was an exclusively Northern industry, funded by the British government to encourage English and Scottish settlement; women and children toiled in the flax-spinning mills that lined Falls Road in Belfast, a staunchly Catholic neighborhood. Belfast's last linen factories closed in the early 1960s, though it's still possible to buy Irish-made linen products at upscale gift shops.

Donegal is the island's center for **tweed** production, and you can see century-old looms still in use in Ardara, Donegal Town, and elsewhere. Due to financial cutbacks, some of the county's tweed production is now completed abroad; look for the "made in" label when shopping for tweed (again, Donegal and Ardara are two of the best places to shop).

Knitwear is another quintessentially Irish craft. Women on the Aran Islands in County Galway still knit their intricately cabled sweaters by hand, as they have for centuries. The vast majority of the "Aran sweaters" you'll find in Irish gift shops are machine-knit, but it's well worth spending a great deal more on a hand-knit jumper, if you can afford it.

Ireland—County Waterford in particular—is also renowned for its **crystal.** Many counties besides Waterford have their own crystal factories, including Kilkenny, Cavan, and Tipperary, and there are smaller workshops all over the country (many of them run by former Waterford master craftspeople). Waterford may be the most famous, but the crystal produced elsewhere can be every bit as beautiful (and is sometimes less expensive).

Though **pottery** is also a very popular souvenir, most Irish potters import their clay from England. A few do use a local variety of red daub earthenware clay, though, and some glazes used by Irish potters are produced using local materials as well.

Music and Dance

You may already be well acquainted with the music of U2, Van Morrison, the Cranberries, The Pogues, Enya, Damien Rice, and other popular Irish artists and groups, as well as the Riverdance phenomenon that began with the Eurovision performance in 1995 and all the other step-dance shows it's inspired since then. But you may not be as aware of the traditional music of Ireland.

The Irish traditional music session will always feature a fiddle, or two, or three, along with a bodhrán ("boh-RAWN"), a goatskin drum pounded with a two-ended wooden beater. Though they're not indigenous instruments—but to be accurate, very few quintessentially Irish instruments are—banjos, guitars, and bouzoukis are also common on the trad scene. The tin whistle is somewhat less popular despite its low startup (you can get a good whistle for €10) and portability. Accordions (and concertinas for the ladies) are becoming somewhat less common as well. It takes decades of practice to master the uilleann ("ILL-in") pipes, which is part of why uilleann pipers are few and far between these days. Harps are generally reserved for classical concerts and kitschy medieval banquets.

Regarding the music itself, most of the tunes you'll hear are jigs (6/8 time) and reels (4/4 time), with the occasional air—a song without time—thrown in for good measure (no pun intended). *Seán nós* is a traditional unaccompanied singing style, in Irish. Irish

Best Souvenirs

Even if you're on a shoestring budget, you'll want to find something quintessentially Irish by which to remember this trip.

Serious **tweed** lovers must make Donegal the centerpiece of their itinerary. Visit the workshops or showrooms of **John Molloy** (tel. 074/954-1133, www.johnmolloy.com) and **Eddie Doherty** (Front St., tel. 074/954-1304, www.handwoventweed.com) in Ardara and **Clare O'Presco** (Donegal Craft Village, Ballyshannon Rd., 1.5 km west of town, tel. 074/972-2225) in Donegal Town. **Studio Donegal** (west end of Main St., tel. 074/973-8194) in Kilcar is the place to go for Irish tweed yarns for knitting and weaving.

For the signature **Aran sweater,** you'll ideally visit the speed-knitting ladies at the **Kilmurvey Craft Village** (by the entrance to Dún Aengus, tel. 099/61233) on Inis Mór, but if you can't get to the source, definitely stop by **Ó'Máille's** (16 High St., tel. 091/562-696, www.omaille.com) in Galway City.

If you're hoping to pick up some Waterford **crystal,** note that much of it is no longer produced in Ireland; instead, visit the crystal studio showrooms at **Criostal na Rinne** (signposted off the R674, tel. 058/46174, www.criostal.com) on the Ring Peninsula southwest of Waterford or **Kinsale Crystal** (Market St., tel. 021/477-4493, www.kinsalecrystal.ie) in Kinsale, County Cork. **Tipperary** (www.tipperarycrystal.com), **Cavan** (www.cavancrystaldesign.com), and **Kilkenny** (www.kilkennycrystal.com) have their own crystal studios as well.

Irish **pottery** varies greatly in style; for something unique, skip the assembly-line "cottage" businesses and pay a visit to **Yvonne McEnnis** (The Pottery Shop, Church St., tel. 065/683-7020) in Corofin, County Clare, or **Louis Mulcahy** (4 km west of Ballyferriter on the R559, tel. 066/915-6229, www.louismulcahy.com) on the Dingle Peninsula in Clogher, County Kerry.

And for Celtic and Celtic-inspired **jewelry,** you might try **Kinsale Silver** (Pearse St., tel. 021/477-4359, www.kinsalesilver.ie) in Kinsale or one of Dingle Town's well-established jewelry designers: **Brian de Staic** (Green St., tel. 066/915-1298, www.briandestaic.com) or **Niamh Utsch** (Green St., tel. 066/915-2217, www.nugoldsmith.com).

musicians have a strangely organic approach to their repertoires; often one in a group will begin to play and his or her fellow musicians will know which song it is, despite not having a name for it. Even if they don't know the song they will probably still be able to play along.

Traditional Irish dance consists of **step dancing,** in which dancers perform intricate tap dancing with stiff unmoving arms, and **set dancing,** a group dance resembling a quadrille. An evening of traditional music and dancing is called a **ceilidh,** though most of the ones you'll see as a tourist can have a somewhat over-the-top theatricality to them.

Literature

The Irish are consummate storytellers; just walk into a pub, sit beside a local, and wait for him or her to strike up a conversation. This longstanding reputation began with the bards of pre-Christian and medieval Ireland; they were some of the most revered members of society, patronized by petty chieftains and high kings. Until early Christian times Ireland's storytelling tradition was solely oral, but the first monks, learned in Latin as well as Irish, put nib to vellum and recorded many of the island's greatest epics, one of the more famous examples being the *Táin Bó Cúailnge* ("The Cattle Raid of Cooley").

Ireland's most famous writers have tended to be of the Anglo-Irish Ascendancy (not surprising, seeing as the vast majority of the dispossessed Irish were too busy trying to survive to produce much in the way of poetry and prose). Anglo-Irish writers of the 18th and 19th centuries still read today include Jonathan Swift (Dean of St. Patrick's Cathedral in Dublin, satirist, and author of the beloved *Gulliver's Travels*) and Maria

An Architectural Glossary

From the Bronze Age to the opulent faux castles of the Victorian era, here's a rundown of the most common architectural terms. Architecture buffs should also check out **Archeire** (www.irish-architecture.com), an opinionated guide to Irish architecture from Norman castles to O'Donnell & Tuomey.

antae: a pilaster forming the end of a projecting lateral wall, as in some Greek temples, and constituting one boundary of the portico

bailey: a castle's outer wall

beehive hut: a small circular stone building shaped like a beehive

caher: a circular area enclosed by stone walls

cairn: a prehistoric grave covered by a mound of stones

cashel: a stone-walled circular fort

chancel: the eastern end of a church, where the altar is located

cheveaux de frise: a defensive field of sharp stone spikes around a fort, placed to impede the cavalry of an attacking army

clochán: a dry-stone beehive hut usually used for monks' solitary cells in the early Christian period

corbel: a triangular bracket, usually made of stone or brick, that projects from the face of a wall and is usually used to support a cornice or arch

cornice: a horizontal molded projection that crowns a building or wall

crannóg: an artificial island (piled up with rocks and debris) connected by a wooden bridge to the shore, usually containing a thatched house and barn surrounded by a palisade and created for ease of defense

cromlech: a tomb with two upright stones covered by a capstone, synonymous with dolmens; literally a "bent flagstone"

curtain wall: an exterior wall or a section of that wall between two gates or towers

dairtheach: in a monastery, a small room reserved for private prayer

demesne: the land surrounding a castle or manor house, often including gardens

dolmen: a prehistoric tomb made of two vertical stones topped by a capstone, giving the structure the vague appearance of a toadstool

fulacht fiadh: a Bronze Age hearth consisting of an earthen trough filled with water, into which fire-warmed stones would be placed, boiling whatever meats were submerged in the water; it is possible that such troughs were used for laundry, cloth-dyeing, and leather-making as well

gallery grave: a burial chamber shaped like a tunnel

Georgian: a relatively austere architectural style used from the 1710s to the 1830s, named for Britain's four King Georges and characterized by symmetry and proportion with a restrained use

Edgeworth, who produced fictions like *Castle Rackrent* to support her family estate in Longford. The 19th-century Anglo-Irish Gothic writers—Bram Stoker, Joseph Sheridan Le Fanu *(In a Glass Darkly)*, and Charles Maturin *(Melmoth the Wanderer)*—have been given short shrift in the realm of Irish literary criticism; it should be noted that Le Fanu's vampire novella *Carmilla* actually predates Stoker's enormously popular and influential *Dracula*. Maturin, an Anglican minister, was the great-uncle of Oscar Wilde,

one of the country's greatest playwrights; Wilde would use the pseudonym "Sebastian Melmoth" when in exile in Paris.

Engineered by William Butler Yeats and his patron, Lady Augusta Gregory, the Irish Literary Revival of the early 20th century introduced more of the country's brightest luminaries, including John Millington Synge, George Bernard Shaw, and Sean O'Casey *(The Plough and the Stars)*. Today, James Joyce's doorstoppers, *Ulysses* and *Finnegan's Wake*, often eclipse the work of other fine writers of

of classical Greek and Roman elements; examples abound in Irish domestic architecture, especially in Dublin and Limerick

Gothic: an architectural style characterized by pointed arches, used in Irish castles and churches between the 12th and 16th centuries

keep: a castle's main tower, also called a donjon

machicolation: a projecting gallery at the top of a castle wall, supported by corbeled arches and having floor openings through which stones and boiling liquids were dropped on attackers

motte: an early Norman fortification with a raised, flattened mound topped with a keep; many motte-and-bailey structures were erected in the early 1200s

neoclassical: a movement beginning in the mid-18th century, inspired by ancient Greek and Roman architecture and a reaction against rococo and other ornate styles; examples include the Four Courts in Dublin

Palladian: the early 18th-century English revival of the style of 16th-century Italian architect Andrea Palladio, characterized by an adherence to mathematical proportions as well as architectural features like loggias and porticos; the foremost example of Irish Palladian architecture is Castletown in County Kildare

passage grave: a Celtic tomb reached by a passageway and buried beneath an earth and stone mound

ráth: a circular fort surrounded by a wooden wall and earthen banks

reredos: a decorative (usually wood-carved) partition in front of a church altar

ring fort: a circular stone structure with an embankment on all sides, built between the Bronze Age and medieval times

Romanesque: an architectural style characterized by rounded arches and vaulting, popular in Ireland in the 1100s; the style known as **Hiberno-Romanesque** incorporates Celtic motifs in its stone carvings as well as antae and high-pitched corbelled gables

round tower: a tall circular tower built in Irish monasteries between the 9th and 11th centuries, used for a lookout and refuge from Viking invaders (which is why the tower entrance was virtually always at least one story off the ground)

sheila-na-gig: a female effigy, similar to a prehistoric fertility figure in its exaggerated reproductive anatomy, carved in stone on the exterior of churches and castles (literally "Sheila of the teats")

souterrain: an underground chamber or passageway, usually used in ring and hill forts to provide storage for food or an escape route in an emergency

standing stone: a vertically placed stone set in the ground, dating across several time periods; their general purpose is unknown, though some were certainly used as grave markers

voussoir: one of the wedge-shaped stones forming the curve of an arch or vaulted ceiling

the early to mid-20th century on American college syllabi: Flann O'Brien, Sean O'Faolain, Patrick Kavanagh, Kate O'Brien, Elizabeth Bowen, and many others. Ironically, many of Ireland's greatest talents—Wilde, Yeats, Joyce, Samuel Beckett—spent most of their time abroad.

Playwright and author Brendan Behan (*The Borstal Boy*) was, like Wilde, a colorful figure renowned for his witty, self-revealing epigrams ("I only take a drink on two occasions: when I'm thirsty and when I'm not")—and prolific despite an early death in 1964, at age 41. The country's most important contemporary playwrights include Tom Murphy (*The Gigli Concert*) and Brian Friel (*Dancing at Lughnasa*).

Seamus Heaney is Ireland's most famous contemporary poet, having translated *Beowulf* into English and produced an oeuvre worthy of the 1995 Nobel Prize in Literature. Other poets, like Nuala Ní Dhomnaill, write exclusively in Irish (their volumes have English translations by other Irish writers), and still other poets have gone back and forth between Irish and English, like Michael Hartnett and Mícheál Ó Siadhail.

Television and Cinema

Until the founding of the Irish Film Board in 1981, British and American companies produced most of the movies made in Ireland. Though John Ford's *The Quiet Man*, filmed in Galway and Mayo in the summer of 1951, was seen as a Technicolor marvel at the time, the movie is thin on plot and rife with stereotypes and absurd brogues. Fortunately, Irish filmmakers have more than made up for such early American-made blunders with classics like *In the Name of the Father, The Field,* and *My Left Foot* (all directed by Jim Sheridan), as well as *Michael Collins* and *The Crying Game* (by Neil Jordan). Many American movies are filmed here each year too (most recently the latest *Star Wars* installments), and though Irish actors get plenty of work in Hollywood, they tend to remember their roots. Liam Neeson, a native of County Antrim, is the primary patron of the Lyric Theatre in Belfast, the theater in which he learned his craft back in the 1970s.

Architecture

Quaint thatched-roof whitewashed cottages aside, Ireland's most characteristic architecture belongs to the distant past: the Iron Age ring forts perched dramatically atop rocky promontories; the round towers and simple one-room churches of the early Christian monasteries; the solid medieval tower houses of the Gaelic chieftains and Norman conquerors. Because domestic architecture was often of the wattle-and-daub variety, the remnants of the island's prehistoric buildings are found mostly within necropolises, the Brú na Bóinne site in County Meath being the most famous example. Archaeologists have also uncovered the stone foundations of Neolithic farmhouses. Using such remains, some interpretive museums have been able to construct replicas of *crannógs*—artificial islands built up with rocks and topped by a round thatched house—and other ancient dwellings.

Though beehive huts, *clocháin,* are emblematic of the early Christian monastic period—used as the monks' cells, for sleep or solitary prayer—these corbelled structures were first erected in the Neolithic period. Round towers—which functioned as a defense against Viking raiders (not for the monks' lives so much as their treasures, jeweled reliquaries and illuminated manuscripts and suchlike) as well as a geographical touchstone for pilgrims—are unique not only to the Christian monastic period, but to Ireland as well. You won't find any round towers except on this island.

Though the Vikings established their port cities at Dublin, Waterford, Wexford, and elsewhere in the 9th and 10th centuries, their extant architecture is limited to chunks of city walls. The Normans left Ireland with a tremendous architectural heritage, mostly in the form of the fortified castles for which the country is perhaps best known. The Normans also brought the Gothic, which became the most pervasive style of ecclesiastical architecture in the centuries to follow—through the 19th century (and well into the 20th) Roman Catholic churches went up in the neo-Gothic style, sometimes with Hiberno-Romanesque flourishes.

The early 12th century heralded the popularity of the Romanesque style in Irish churches, the most famous example being the tiny, spooky Cormac's Chapel at the Rock of Cashel. Irish stonemasons created an amalgam of Romanesque and Celtic motifs to create a distinctive "Hiberno-Romanesque" style; you'll find excellent examples of this fusion at the Nuns' Church at Clonmacnoise and Clonfert Cathedral in eastern Galway.

Opulent country houses built by English landlords run the gamut from neoclassical and Palladian styles (Castle Coole in Fermanagh and Castletown in Kildare being respective examples) to the neo-Gothic manors of Glenveagh Castle in Donegal and Kylemore Castle (now Abbey) in Connemara, to Victorian mansions like Muckross House in Killarney National Park (not to mention countless renovated boutique hotels and B&Bs). Ireland has a strong Georgian architectural heritage, and not just in cities like Dublin and Limerick. Many smaller market towns were planned by the local landlord, so the extant architecture lining those tidy tree-lined squares echoes the prevailing aesthetics of the time.

Dublin's grandest architecture is also in the neoclassical style; take for example the president's home in Phoenix Park (Áras an Uachtaráin), designed by Francis Johnston, and the Customs House and the Four Courts by James Gandon. Some architects, like William Chambers (who designed the Casino Marino for the Earl of Charlemont), never even set foot on Irish soil. Though such structures as neoclassical Dublin City Hall and the Palladian Leinster House are examples of imperialist style and construction, they are nonetheless some of Ireland's finest architecture of the last 300 years.

SPORTS

Though you'll find plenty of fans of the British football teams, most Irish love to watch Gaelic football and hurling (camogie is the ladies' version of hurling). Formed in 1884 to promote these uniquely Irish pastimes, the **Gaelic Athletic Association** (www.gaa.ie) is headquartered at Croke Park in Dublin. For want of a better comparison, hurling looks like a cross between field hockey, baseball, and lacrosse, with a broad-ended stick used to balance the ball briefly before hitting it; players can also handle the ball. Gaelic football looks more like soccer than anything else. Horse and greyhound racing are popular with bettors.

Essentials

Transportation 467

Travel Tips 474

Food and Accommodations 471

Information and Services 477

Transportation

GETTING THERE
Air

Airfares naturally vary greatly between seasons; when booking ahead for a summer holiday (round-trip, flying from the United States), expect to spend at least US$800; last-minute fares could cost you well over US$1,000. Fares in shoulder season are in the neighborhood of US$600-800. The sooner you purchase your ticket, the better the deal; the only exception is in mid-January through February, when Aer Lingus and other carriers offer very good last-minute fares (around US$500). Fares skyrocket again in the week leading up to St. Patrick's Day.

All ballpark figures noted above factor in taxes and fees.

FROM THE UNITED STATES AND CANADA

Aer Lingus (tel. 800/474-7424, www.aerlingus.com) and **United** (tel. 800/864-8331, www.united.com) offer the best service and options when flying from the United States. Both offer direct flights from New York (JFK or Newark), Boston, Denver, San Francisco, Los Angeles, and many other cities. **Delta** (tel. 800/241-4141, www.delta.com) also offers direct flights.

Transatlantic flights are available to the island's three major airports: Dublin (tel. 01/814-1111, www.dublinairport.com), Shannon (tel. 061/712-000, www.shannonairport.com), and Belfast International (tel. 028/9448-4848, www.belfastairport.com), but not the smaller regional airports.

Air Canada (tel. 888/247-2262, www.aircanada.com) offers direct flights from Toronto to Shannon. **Delta** (tel. 800/221-1212, www.delta.com) and **Aer Lingus** (tel. 800/474-7424, www.aerlingus.com) are other options.

FROM THE UNITED KINGDOM AND CONTINENTAL EUROPE

Despite the inconvenience of flying out of secondary airports, low-cost air carriers are the way to go when flying from the United Kingdom and mainland Europe. **RyanAir** (www.ryanair.com) is far and away the most popular option when flying to both the republic and the North, with **EasyJet** (www.easyjet.com) a close second. You can get a direct flight from Europe to several city and regional airports—Knock, Derry City, Belfast City, and Cork—and there is also more limited service available to Galway, Waterford, Donegal (near Gweedore), and Sligo. Aer Lingus offers frequent flights to Dublin from Heathrow, Gatwick, and London City, as well as Paris, Madrid, Milan, Rome, Naples, Frankfurt, Brussels, Amsterdam, Vienna, Budapest, Prague, Warsaw, Munich, and many more locations.

Sea

International ferry services are available, mostly from the United Kingdom, as well as Roscoff and Cherbourg in France. Booking online can save you as much as 10 percent, but note that not all ferries accept pedestrian passengers. **Irish Ferries** (tel. 01/638-3333, www.irishferries.com) sails from Dublin to Holyhead. **Steam Packet** (tel. 1800/805-055, www.steam-packet.com) sails to Dublin from the Isle of Man. Ferry service is available to Dún Laoghaire, 13 kilometers south of Dublin, via **Stena Line** (tel. 01/204-7777 or 01/204-7799, www.stenaline.ie) from Holyhead in Wales.

Previous: Temple Bar in Dublin; the Old Library at Trinity College Dublin.

Get to Rosslare Harbour from Fishguard in Wales via **Stena Line** (tel. 053/931-3997, www.stenaline.ie), or from Pembroke or France (Cherbourg or Roscoff, the latter Apr.-Sept. only) via **Irish Ferries** (tel. 053/913-3158, www.irishferries.com).

GETTING AROUND
Air

To cut down on time in the car or bus, try flying from Dublin to one of the regional or city airports, usually on **Aer Arann** (www.aerarann.ie): Waterford (10 km south of the city, www.flywaterford.com), Cork (6 km south, tel. 021/431-3131, www.corkairport.com), Shannon (85 km south of Galway City, tel. 061/712-000, www.shannonairport.ie), Sligo (Strandhill, 8 km west of Sligo Town, www.sligoairport.com), Donegal (Carrickfinn, 84 km northwest of Donegal Town, www.donegalairport.ie), Kerry (Farranfore, 16 km south of Tralee, www.kerryairport.com), or Knock (roughly equidistant between Sligo and Galway, both about 72 km away, www.knockairport.com). All airports host car-rental agencies.

Bus

The republic's national bus service, **Bus Éireann** (tel. 01/830-2222, www.buseireann.ie), has an extensive network of national and cross-border routes, as well as local service in the larger towns and cities. An **Open Road** ticket allows unlimited bus travel within the republic during a certain period, three days out of six for €60 with each additional day costing €16.50.

Bus Éireann doesn't run everywhere, though, and several regional companies (sometimes family run) fill in the gaps. Others are commuter buses (also useful for tourists) that are often more comfortable and slightly less expensive than the national bus service. Bus Éireann covers much more of the country and is usually less expensive, but the railroad offers more speed and comfort. One independent company providing very useful Dublin-Galway, Dublin-Cork, and Connemara

services is **Citylink** (tel. 091/564-164, www.citylink.ie). **GoBus** (tel. 091/564-600, www.gobus.ie) offers reliable service to Dublin and Cork. When you book online you'll save at least a euro each way.

Northern Ireland is served by **Ulsterbus** (tel. 028/9066-6630, www.ulsterbus.co.uk), which offers special sightseeing services on the Causeway Coast and the Sperrin Mountains, as well as a summer service through the Mourne Mountains. A steal at £9, the **Sunday Rambler** ticket will get you unlimited travel on all Ulsterbus services within Northern Ireland on Sunday. A Belfast-Dublin ticket can run you as little as £8 if you purchase online.

Train

The Irish national train network is Iarnród Éireann, a.k.a. **Irish Rail** (tel. 01/836-3333, www.irishrail.ie), which serves most of the larger towns and cities. For the most part, the railway map looks like a starfish, with all lines leading from Dublin—meaning that if you want to travel from, say, Sligo to Galway, a change is required. Return fares are always a better value, day return fares especially, though prices rise at the weekend. If you're planning on a lot of train travel, purchase an **Irish Explorer Ticket,** a combination bus-and-train ticket that allows you five days of travel out of 15 (€160) within the republic. There's also a **Trekker pass** (€110) for unlimited train travel over a four-day period. Train passes are not available for purchase online; you can purchase them at any bus station ticket counter, though to be frank these tourist passes are not nearly as good a value as they used to be; tally up the ticket prices for your itinerary (using the website fare finder) and you may very well realize you won't be saving anything. For international train passes, visit **Eurail** online (www.eurail.com).

The **DART,** or Dublin Area Rapid Transit (www.dart.ie) is popular with commuters, and is very useful for visitors staying in Dublin who wish to see more of Counties Dublin and Wicklow. **Luas** (www.luas.ie) is a light-rail service within the city designed to cut down on gridlock.

North of the border, the train operator is **Northern Ireland Railways** (tel. 028/9089-9411, www.translink.co.uk), which provides service from Derry to Belfast, Belfast to Bangor, and Belfast to Drogheda and Dublin.

Car

Driving on the left is a downright scary proposition, and the idiosyncrasies of the Irish roads can leave even the best drivers anxious and stressed out. If you plan to stick to larger towns and cities, you're best off using public transportation. But the Irish bus and rail networks do not serve many remote locations, and many wonderful attractions are difficult, even impossible, to reach without a car (Clonmacnoise is one example). Weigh the stress involved in driving on Irish roads against the benefit of going anywhere you like, anytime you like, and make a decision from there.

TRAFFIC REGULATIONS AND TIPS

First off, you'll be driving on the left (and don't make any wisecracks about "driving on the wrong side" at the Europcar desk!). In keeping with this, the right lane is the "fast" lane. The dread of every foreign driver is the roundabout, a common substitute for an intersection; traffic proceeds in a clockwise direction, and you enter the circle only when there are no vehicles oncoming from your right. The larger roundabouts also have traffic lights. When approaching the roundabout, stay in the left lane if you intend to take the first exit, the right lane for subsequent exits; you'll know which exit you want by reading the big green sign posted before the roundabout.

Parking is generally free in smaller places, though the larger towns and cities operate a "pay-and-display" policy. You buy a ticket from a blue kiosk to leave on your dashboard, €0.60-3/hour depending on the size of the town (not all accept credit cards, so be sure to carry several euros in change). Still other parking lots are "disc-operated," meaning

you'll have to duck into the nearest newsagent to purchase a disc for about the same price. In some towns it's worth seeking out free parking spaces a bit farther from the center; in other situations you'll just have to fork it over. Spend a few minutes when you first arrive in a new place just getting your bearings and scoping out free parking opportunities. Some lots charge €3-3.50 for the whole day. After 6:30pm, though, you won't have to feed the car park kiosk.

In the republic, distances and speed limits are given in kilometers, with the exception of some very old signs still in need of replacement in more remote locales (you'll have no difficulty recognizing them). Northern Ireland is still on the Imperial system, so in the Northern Ireland destination chapters all distances are listed in both miles and kilometers. Always trust your map over the road signs; they're sometimes pointed in the wrong direction (through age and weather, not necessarily mischief). Though this book lists roads by official number ("N" indicating a national road, "R" a regional road, "L" a local road) for ease of navigation, the Irish don't always use them when giving directions—they tend to say "the Dublin road" instead of "the N3." Ireland has been hard at work building new motorways (noted by an "M") in recent years, so small-town bottlenecks aren't as ubiquitous or inevitable as they used to be. There are tolls (€2-7) along these motorways, so carry extra change (otherwise you have to park on the side of the highway and visit the office to use your credit card), although if you're driving the M50 you can pay your toll online using **eFlow** (www.eflow.ie).

It is polite to acknowledge the other drivers you pass on narrow backcountry roads, especially if they pull to the side to let you pass first. Raise a finger or two off the steering wheel in a sort of benediction.

SAFETY

This may be a generalization, but there's a great deal of truth in it: Irish drivers are reckless. They are impatient, they drive too fast, and they take ridiculous risks. Also, the speed limits off the national roads and motorways are too high: 100 kph (62 mph) on a narrow, winding road where even a good driver would apply the brake liberally. Ireland's roads claim lives every weekend of the year, and until the government wises up, lowers the speed limits on regional roads, and then puts the guards on the streets to enforce them, these tragedies will continue to occur. Sadly, alcohol is often involved in such incidents. Avoid becoming a statistic by following all the usual commonsensible rules: Designate a sober driver who won't drink even a single beer, wear your seatbelts, and use the high beams on country roads (dim them if you see a car ahead, though). Drive only as fast as you feel comfortable; Irish drivers have no qualms about passing you, anyway!

CAR RENTALS

To rent an automobile, you must be over 23 years old and have been licensed for at least two years. There are numerous rental companies, most of which are international (and have desks at most airports): **Europcar** (www.europcar.ie), **Avis** (www.avis.ie), **Budget** (www.budget.ie), **Hertz** (www.hertz.ie), and **Enterprise** (www.enterprise.ie). GPS rental is universally available.

Theft insurance is an option, but because car theft is practically nonexistent in Ireland you'd do well to opt out and save yourself a few euros a day.

PACKAGE DEALS

You can find airfare-car rental combined rates on Expedia, Orbitz, and other websites. Otherwise, instead of booking directly through Avis, Europcar, or whichever, go through **AutoEurope** (tel. 01/659-0500, www.autoeurope.com). Clerks at the rental agencies admit that booking through AutoEurope will get you a better rate.

MAPS AND DIRECTIONS

Ordnance Survey (OS, www.osi.ie) publishes detailed scale maps of the national parks, cities, and the larger towns, which indicate one-way streets. Pick up a road atlas—the Collins or Ordnance Survey brands are recommended (about €9)—before leaving the airport, as the map the rental agency gives you isn't detailed enough.

Bike

Bicycle hire will usually run you €15-20 per day (or £10-15 in North Ireland, and as much as €25 in Dublin). Weekly rental is a better value, roughly €50-60 per week. In addition, you're often required to leave a deposit and/or a form of ID. Some cycle shops provide one-way service for an additional fee; check out **Raleigh Rent-a-Bike** (www.raleigh.ie) for participating dealers. Serious cyclists will want to bring their own, of course; your bike will be factored into your baggage allowance. Irish buses usually allow bikes in the cargo hold, though you'll probably have to pay a surcharge. Especially with private companies, ring ahead to ensure you'll be able to bring your cycle along.

Tours

Keep in mind that most tours follow the well-trod tourist tracks—the Cliffs of Moher, Killarney, Adare in County Limerick, Blarney Castle, and the usual spots in Dublin. They are certainly convenient, but they generally provide only a very narrow tourist's view of Ireland. One of the most popular choices (popular with retirees) is **CIE** (www.cietours.com), offering coach tour packages in Ireland and elsewhere in Europe. In contrast, Con Moriarty at **Hidden Ireland Tours** (tel. 087/221-4002, www.hiddenirelandtours.com) offers active, often themed holidays. For the backpacking set, there's the **Paddywagon** (www.paddywagontours.com), a hop-on, hop-off bus tour, and **Shamrockers** (tel. 01/672-7651, www.shamrockeradventures.com).

Food and Accommodations

FOOD AND DRINK

Traditional Irish dishes like colcannon (mashed potatoes, butter, and cabbage or kale), boxty (potato pancakes), and lamb stew are fast disappearing off the pub menus, though black pudding, a sausage made from dried pigs' blood, is still served at B&Bs. When traditional meals do make an appearance, they're usually given the gourmet treatment in chic Continental restaurants, where your plate of bangers and mash (sausages and mashed potatoes) might come served with a sprig of some unidentifiable herb. This gourmet trend, encouraged by the Celtic Tiger, has resulted in hundreds of top-notch restaurants and "gastro-pubs" serving French- and Asian-inspired cuisine; the food is dubbed "Modern Irish" if it emphasizes local, often organic produce, meats (Kerry lamb, for instance), and seafood. Many native Irish chefs were trained on the Continent and have returned home to open their own eateries, and still other chef/owners are foreigners who recognize a growing market. Many pubs still serve defrosted fish-and-chips and gristly lamb stew, but they are becoming increasingly few and far between even in smaller villages. As ever, potatoes and brown bread are staples of the Irish diet.

Beverages

The Gaelic words for whiskey are *uisce beatha,* or "water of life"—which just goes to show you how much the Irish love to drink it. **Jameson** is the most popular brand, with **Bushmills** preferred by the Brits up North. Interestingly, it's said that you can tell the distillery's political affiliation by the shape of the bottle: square bottles are loyalist and round bottles (like Jameson's) are republican.

Of course, **Guinness** is far and away the most popular brand of Irish stout (also referred to as "porter" back in the day); **Beamish** and **Murphy's** are Cork brands,

not readily available elsewhere in the country. Kilkenny-based **Smithwick's** is a popular ale (though it's now owned by Guinness). Imported beers are becoming increasingly commonplace in Irish pubs; favored brands include Stella Artois and Carlsberg. There are various cider brands available, though most of them are U.K. imports; Irish-brewed **Bulmer's** is the top brand (it's the same as Magner's in the United States).

Don't tip at the pub; unlike those back home, Irish bartenders make a regular wage. They'll actually be insulted if you try. Want to savor the music, but not the drink—or seriously short on cash? Try ordering a "blackcurrant," which is just a dollop of blackcurrant syrup in a pint glass of water. The bartender will charge you less than a euro for it, and it tastes like noncarbonated fruit soda.

The Irish do not use ice in their cold drinks, and if you ask for an "iced tea" they'll look at you like you're missing a few marbles (then inform you that "iced tea" is an oxymoron). Indeed, the Irish are fairly particular about their tea; few drink anything besides Barry's brand, and most people have at least one cup with pretty much every meal. Ireland's tea dependence originated in Britain; during the Industrial Revolution, English factory bosses recognized it as the ideal drink for their workers—inexpensive, caffeinated, and nonalcoholic. Low tea prices and comfort against the wet weather made it the natural choice in Irish homes as well. Despite declining tea sales, Barry's is still Ireland's most popular beverage. Indeed, this island has the world's highest per-capita tea consumption (four cups per day and seven pounds a year, to be exact).

And though coffee drinking is on the rise, java-lovers beware: many Irish B&Bs serve instant. In a nation of tea drinkers, very few people have ever seen (or heard of) a coffee grinder. Also, don't order a cocktail unless it's a posh sort of pub. Bartenders will often charge by the shot, meaning a Sex on the Beach could end up costing you €17.

Dining

Many bars offer a "pub grub" menu, featuring hearty traditional meat-and-potato meals at some places and more elegant, Continental-type fare at "gastro-pubs." Pub grub is less expensive than dinner at a regular restaurant, though most pub kitchens close by 9:30pm. The more upscale Irish restaurants generally offer a good-value two- or three-course early-bird menu.

Vegetarianism and Special Diets

Vegetarians, don't believe anyone who says you can't eat well in Ireland. Even halfway decent restaurants have at least one meat-free option, at worst an unimaginative pasta dish; gourmet eateries tend to offer only one choice, though it's generally as good as any other dish on the menu. And in the off chance you find yourself in a rural watering hole—miles from the nearest proper restaurant, with nothing on the pub grub menu but meat and fish— just ask the staff what they can whip up for you; they'll be happy to help you out. Vegans will likely have a tricky time of it outside the larger towns, however, since vegetarian dishes are usually quite heavy on the eggs and dairy. Worst-case scenario, you'll be served boring stirfries and "curries" consisting mostly of rice. (The concept of plant-based protein is not quite understood here yet, alas.) Consider planning your itinerary around the country's best vegan-friendly eateries (a trip to Cork City is a must), and/or using self-catering accommodations in rural areas so you can cook for yourself. For tips and resources, check out the **Vegetarian Society of Ireland** (www.vegetarian.ie), the **Vegan Society of Ireland** (www.vegan.ie), and **Happy Cow** (www.happycow.net/europe/ireland) as you're planning your holiday.

Irish chefs (even in rural areas) are well informed when it comes to gluten allergies, and many menus mark their gluten-free options.

ACCOMMODATIONS
Hostels

Ireland has a rightful reputation for some of the best hostels in Europe. There are the inevitable stinkers, but the various hostelling organizations—**An Óige** (www.anoige.ie), the republic's youth hostel organization; **Independent Holiday Hostels in Ireland** (IHH, www.hostels-ireland.com); **Independent Hostel Owners of Ireland** (IHI, www.independenthostelsireland.com); and **Hostelling International of Northern Ireland** (HINI, tel. 028/9031-5435, www.hini.org.uk)—generally ensure that hostels operating under their banners offer cleanliness and hospitality. Some hostels also have an adjacent campground, where you pay less for a site than you would for a bed but have access to the kitchens, showers, and sitting rooms. Many hostels arrange outdoor activities and other events; some include a light breakfast in the room price, and the very best hostels offer additional meals at dinner. Cramped bunk beds and communal showers can seem like negligible inconveniences when you consider how many new friends you can make while hostelling. Though most hostellers are under 30, generally travelers of all ages are welcomed. In recent years, some hostels have closed their doors to tourists to become immigrant or refugee housing (which is more profitable for the owner).

Also keep in mind that some hostels might start off with good management in the beginning, thus securing the IHH or IHI stamp of approval, only to decline after the business changes hands or for other reasons. A personal recommendation from a fellow traveler is ideal, but if that's not possible and you have your doubts about a particular establishment, ask for a brief tour of the hostel (including the dorm room you'd be staying in along with the shower room) before you check in. Also, most hostels don't issue dorm room keys, so be very careful with your valuables. Checkout is generally 10am.

Bed-and-Breakfasts

B&Bs, which are run out of a family home,

are the most popular form of accommodation, and can be found in every nook and corner all over the country. Though B&B proprietors are among the friendliest, most knowledgeable, and helpful Irish people (after all, their livelihood depends upon it), there are several caveats: There's less privacy than in a hotel, and you may be forced to adjust to the owner's schedule, particularly regarding breakfast times. Also note that prices are per person, often with an unfortunate "supplement" for singles. Nevertheless, B&Bs are nearly always a better value than the hotels and much more comfortable than hostelling.

Also note that proprietors pay for those AA "diamond" ratings; if a B&B doesn't have one, it just means the owners didn't want to pay the AA inspector's fee. In the republic, the shamrock logo indicates the B&B has been approved by the tourist board, though many nonapproved B&Bs are excellent, too. By law, all Northern Ireland B&Bs must be approved by the N.I. Tourist Board.

In theory, B&Bs serve a full Irish breakfast, but most owners skip the time-consuming items like mushrooms, blood sausage, and fresh fried potatoes. (Tinned baked beans may not sound very appetizing now, but you'll grow to like them.) Vegetarians need only ask; proprietors are happy to skip the bacon, and most offer cereal, yogurt, and/or fruit salad. Most places have a set breakfast time of one or two hours between 6:30am and 10am; your host will inform you of these hours. A few B&Bs serve evening meals, mostly in rural areas where there are few restaurants.

Many B&Bs do not accept credit cards, since the fees eat up a percentage of their profits, and those that do sometimes impose a small service charge (2-3 percent). It is customary to pay on the morning of your departure, though, so there's no need to search for the nearest ATM before you check in. Checkout time is generally 11am.

Over the past few years **AirBnB** (www.airbnb.com) has become a very popular alternative—sometimes even traditional B&Bs have listings there. Even if you're going mostly with AirBnB accommodations, you might want to spend at least one or two nights in an old-fashioned B&B to soak up the atmosphere.

Hotels

The more established Irish hotels can be quite grand, old-fashioned, and lovely, but compared to B&Bs they're generally not a great value for the money. Prices range from €40 in remote locales to well over €200 or €300 in converted castles or manor houses, though the higher price bracket is often per room rather than per person. Some hotels have moved away from an inclusive full breakfast, so ask before making a reservation. Checkout time is generally at noon.

Self-Catering Accommodations

If you plan to "stay put" in one place for a week or more, taking day trips rather than moving from town to town, a self-catering cottage or apartment may be a good choice. Some self-catering digs are brand-new apartments or holiday homes; others are quaint thatched-roof cottages. Purpose-built "holiday homes" in highly touristed areas are often excessively priced, though, so look for individuals who rent out a few small properties as a way of making extra cash. Helpful websites with properties nationwide include **Trident Holiday Homes** (www.selfcatering-ireland.com) and **Dream Ireland** (www.dreamireland.com). Another site, **Rent an Irish Cottage** (www.rentacottage.ie), offers rentals in the western counties from Mayo to Cork (excluding Galway). Some proprietors will charge you for the heat and electricity used over the week, so ask about this beforehand.

Travel Tips

VISAS AND OFFICIALDOM
Passports and Visas

Unless you are a citizen of the European Union, you'll need a passport to enter the country (and even if you are, it's smart to carry it anyway). At the customs desk at Shannon or Dublin, North American visitors' passports are stamped with a tourist visa, which allows them a stay of three months. If you plan to remain in the Republic of Ireland for longer than three months, contact the Irish police, the **Garda Síochána** (tel. 01/666-9100, www.garda.ie), to register for a student or work visa. If you ask at the customs desk, they'll provide you with the address of the *garda* station at your destination. Both the Garda National Immigration Bureau (GNIB) and the Irish Naturalisation and Immigration Service are at 13/14 Burgh Quay in the Dublin city center.

Border Crossings

Though there are still a few security checkpoints along the 360-kilometer border between Northern Ireland and the republic, only the most suspicious-looking travelers will be stopped; you as a tourist and a civilian will most likely cross the border without even realizing you've done so. If you intend to remain in Northern Ireland for longer than six months, contact the **U.K. Home Office** (www.gov.uk/browse/visas-immigration) for information on obtaining a visa or work permit.

Customs

When leaving Ireland, E.U. citizens have no limit to the monetary value of goods purchased while in Ireland, so long as the items purchased are not for commercial use. Citizens of the United States, however, are subject to U.S. Customs restrictions: You're allowed only $400 worth of goods tax free (that's $400 per person), and there's a 10 percent tax imposed thereafter. It's possible to mail up to an additional $200 worth of goods home without paying the duty, but your purchases in the duty-free shops in Irish airports count toward that $400 monthly total (that is, you're not paying tax in Ireland, but you may still be required to do so on those same goods upon return to the United States). There are also limits imposed upon cigarettes (200 maximum) and alcohol (one liter maximum). In addition, U.S. citizens should note that bringing fresh food or plants home is not permitted. For more information, visit the U.S. Customs website (www.customs.gov).

CONDUCT AND CUSTOMS

While the atmosphere in most pubs may seem informal enough, and plenty of people lapse into the use of excessive expletives when they've had too much to drink, you should always try to keep your language as clean as possible. The Irish make allowances for those silly drunkards, but they won't consider you very mannerly if you use the same language their inebriated friend does. It's also smart to avoid talking politics, unless you're sure your views won't clash with those of your companions—for example, you can agree wholeheartedly with a bunch of sentimental republicans when they drink to a unified Ireland, whereas you would absolutely avoid talking politics in a pub in Northern Ireland named the "Queen's" or "King's" anything.

During music sessions in the pub, it is polite to pause in conversation to clap for the musicians when a song ends. And if a new friend is kind enough to buy you a pint, it goes without saying that the next round is on you!

Visitors should never make assumptions about the sexual mores of their new friends—suggestive advertising, frank talk on TV and in social situations, and other purported signs of a sexually liberated culture can belie deep-rooted conservative values.

SIGHTSEEING PASSES AND DISCOUNTS

If you plan to do much sightseeing, the **Dúchas Heritage Card** (www.heritageireland.com) is a must-have. For €25 (€10 for students!), you can get into any of the Office of Public Works' 70-plus sites for a full year. Seeing as Newgrange-Knowth combo admission costs €11 now (and many other sites are €4-7 apiece), you'll recoup that money in just a few visits. Obviously, students should pick up the card even if they're planning to use it only a few times. Purchase the card at the reception desk of any site.

In North Ireland, the **National Trust Touring Pass** (www.nationaltrust.org.uk), valid for seven days (£26), gets you "free" admission to more than 300 manors, gardens, and suchlike throughout the British Isles. Another option (island-wide) is the **Heritage Island Explorer Touring Guide** (www.heritageisland.com); buy the €8 info brochure and show it at more than 90 sites for a 2-for-1 or percentage discount. Most discounts are the former, though, so it makes more sense to buy this one if you're traveling in pairs.

ACCESS FOR TRAVELERS WITH DISABILITIES

Guesthouses, museums, and so forth are gradually becoming more accessible for visitors with disabilities. Bord Fáilte publishes an annual accommodations guide, available at any tourist office, that specifies which hotels and B&Bs offer special access. In the North, the booklet to ask for is *Accessible Accommodation in Northern Ireland*. The Dúchas website (www.heritageireland.ie) details which heritage sites are wheelchair-accessible.

Renting a car is probably the way to go, as navigating the public transportation systems can be difficult at best. Irish buses are not wheelchair-accessible, though the trains are possible to ride with some assistance. Iarnród

Éireann's official policy provides for this, but you must call ahead (tel. 01/836-3333).

For information or assistance, contact **Enable Ireland** (tel. 01/872-7155, www.enableireland.ie), a nonprofit organization in the republic, or **Disability Action** (Portside Business Park, 189 Airport Rd. W., Belfast, tel. 028/9029-7880, www.disabilityaction.org) in Northern Ireland. If you are in need of a wheelchair, contact **The Irish Wheelchair Association** (24 Blackheath Dr., Dublin, tel. 01/833-8241, www.iwa.ie).

TRAVELING WITH CHILDREN

Ireland is the ideal choice for a family vacation. To simplify matters, consider making day trips from a single base town (you will find most B&Bs very accommodating) or renting a self-catering holiday cottage (the cooking is up to you, but then you don't have to conform to the serving times of restaurants and B&Bs). You might find the major cities too hectic if small children are involved—think about forgoing Dublin for a more relaxing holiday by lake, river, or sea, punctuated by day trips to heritage museums and medieval ruins. Virtually all sightseeing attractions offer a family admission rate, as do some modes of public transportation (with one or two adults and up to three children under the age of 16). Otherwise, B&Bs and hotels generally offer cots at no extra charge, as well as a children's discount of 20-50 percent.

By law, those under the age of 18 are not allowed in the pubs after 10pm in summer and 9pm in winter. This cutoff time might be earlier depending on the establishment (look for a sign above the bar).

WOMEN TRAVELING ALONE

Ireland is one of the safest places on earth for the single female traveler. The psychological intricacies of the stereotypical Irishman aside, the men of this island are almost always genuinely friendly and eager to help you in any way they can.

Since you will need your sweaters even in July and August, the question of how revealing one can dress when out pubbing and clubbing is pretty much moot. While the occasional eccentric Englishwoman can be found sunbathing in the nude at some of the less touristy beaches, this kind of activity is not recommended. Nor is hitchhiking—though if you must, hitching in Ireland is safer than anywhere else. That said, caution and common sense are your greatest assets. Some parts of Belfast and Dublin simply aren't safe for lone women pedestrians after dark, and incidents can occur even in quiet suburban neighborhoods.

If you will be hostelling during your trip, note that many Irish hostels now offer predominantly mixed-gender dormitories. If you would prefer a girls-only dorm room, be sure to mention that when you check in.

GAY AND LESBIAN TRAVELERS

Ireland has grown increasingly tolerant and open minded regarding homosexuality, as evidenced by the happy outcome of the same-sex marriage referendum in 2015. The local church is mum on the matter, and, thankfully, bigotry is limited to isolated incidents.

The largest cities—Dublin, Belfast, Cork, and Galway—are the best places for socializing, though the smaller cities are slowly beginning to establish pubs and networking groups as well. Excellent resources include **Outhouse** (tel. 01/873-4932, www.outhouse.ie), **Gaire** (www.gaire.com), and **The Outmost** (www.theoutmost.com). **QueerID** (www.queerid.com) is Dublin-centric, and Cork City's best resource is **Gay Cork** (www.gaycork.com). For information on the summer Gay Pride Parade in Dublin (and plenty more), check out **Dublin Pride** (www.dublinpride.org). A parade is also held annually in Belfast, although its participants have met with more hostility than their Dublin counterparts.

There are several switchboards in Dublin and Belfast, and though you can call from anywhere in Ireland the opening hours are quite restricted: **Gay Switchboard Dublin** (tel. 01/872-1055, www.gayswitchboard.ie, 8pm-10pm daily, except for 3:30pm-6pm Sat.); **Lesbian Line Dublin** (tel. 01/872-9911, www.dublinlesbianline.ie, 7pm-9pm Thurs.); and **Lesbian Line Belfast** (tel. 028/9023-8668, www.lesbianlinebelfast.co.uk, 7:30pm-10pm Thurs.).

STD cases are on the rise, especially in Dublin—take all necessary precautions. **The Gay Men's Health Project** (tel. 01/660-2189, www.gmhs.ie), which operates a clinic in the Baggot Street Hospital in Dublin, can offer more information, as can the sites listed above.

SENIOR TRAVELERS

Visitors over the age of 60 are entitled to discounts at museums and other sights as well as on most forms of public transit (including Bus Éireann and Irish Rail). The bus or train may be the best way to go, as car-rental companies will not rent automobiles to drivers over the age of 75 (and usually impose a surcharge for drivers ages 70 to 74).

BUSINESS HOURS

Irish banks are generally open 9am or 10am to 4pm or 5pm Monday to Friday; post offices keep the same hours, closing 1pm-2pm for lunch. Many smaller businesses close during this hour, too, so keep this in mind when running errands. Bookstores, boutiques, and many other shops close at 6pm, and most stores still close on Sunday, especially in the smaller towns and villages.

LAUNDRY

Irish launderettes are mostly full service, and will run you €8-12 per load. Some offer a same-day tourist service. Many accommodations offer laundry service for an additional fee (often less than that of a launderette), so ask at your B&B before looking for a cleaners in town.

TOILETS

Most sizable Irish towns offer public toilets. Those not coin-operated are very basic (not to mention grotty), so always carry a bottle of hand sanitizer. Most establishments reserve their restrooms for customers only, though this rule is often bypassed in pubs by the truly desperate traveler.

The Irish words for "men" and "women" often appear on restroom doors: the men's room is labeled *fir* and the women's is *mna*. The Irish for "toilets" is *leithreas*.

Information and Services

HEALTH AND SAFETY

In the event of an emergency, dial 999 on your cell phone or nearest pay phone, which will connect you with the local police (or *gardaí*) and ambulance.

There is a choice of pharmacies even in the smaller Irish towns, though not all are open on Sunday; general hours of operation are 9am-6pm, and many places are open until 8pm or 9pm at least a few days a week. Your accommodation can direct you to the nearest seven-day pharmacy, if you end up needing medication over the weekend. Condoms are now available at any pharmacy.

Ireland is a very safe country—the vast majority of violent crimes are drug-related, and fortunately this is a world tourists seldom come into contact with. Your biggest safety concern regards your rental car, as there are a staggering number of motor accidents on a daily basis: 1,000 people are injured per month, with an average monthly death toll of 30. Drive conservatively no matter how many speed demons pass you on those narrow roads.

It goes without saying that you should never drink to excess—no matter if your B&B is a five-minute walk up the road, and regardless of how many free pints you're handed. If at all possible, avoid driving late at night even if you're the designated driver; many other motorists won't be so conscientious. And while it seldom happens that blackout drugs are slipped into nightclub drinks when a girl's back is turned, you should still keep your drink with you at all times.

MONEY

Currency

The Irish punt is long gone—the euro has been the official currency since February 2002. Check on the exchange rate before you leave using Google or the **Universal Currency Converter** (www.xe.com/ucc); at time of writing the U.S. dollar was a bit stronger against the euro (compared to before the economic downturn), €1 equaling $1.13. As part of the United Kingdom, Northern Ireland uses British sterling; the exchange rate at time of writing was £1 to $1.43. Many shops and accommodations along the border will accept either currency.

Using your credit or ATM card gets you the best exchange rate, but if you need to change money, visit a bureau de change at a bank. (Bureaux de change at tourist offices, hotels, and commercial agencies offer a poorer rate of exchange, plus commission.)

Taxes

You are entitled to a VAT (value added tax) refund on all goods purchased in the republic upon departure, so long as you aren't an E.U. citizen—saving you 17.36 percent off the original price. Whenever you make a purchase at a gift shop, just ask for a voucher. (Note that it's the VAT on goods, not services, that is refundable.) Fill all your forms in before you get to the airport, then visit the Global Refund Desk, which is located between the security and immigration checkpoints. You'll receive a refund in cash or by credit card, though a credit refund can take as long as two months to process.

Tipping

As bartenders are paid a regular wage in Ireland, there is no need to tip them.

At restaurants, your credit card slip will include a gratuity line. Tip only if your service has been better than average (and if you aren't being served by the owner of the establishment), and do not feel compelled to leave 15 or 20 percent even for excellent service. (Remember that unlike American servers, your waiter is making at least minimum wage.) Also, if a restaurant has imposed a service charge (10-15 percent) and you weren't satisfied with the service, don't hesitate to request the charge be removed from your bill.

Though it isn't necessary to tip Irish taxi drivers, you might want to add a euro or two if he or she has been especially helpful. If you have luggage, there's an automatic surcharge of approximately three euros, which is fair considering the driver will almost always load and unload your bags, and may even carry them to the door for you unasked.

COMMUNICATIONS AND MEDIA

Telephone

Phone numbers in the republic can be five, six, or seven digits. The North has a single area code and eight-digit numbers. (When ringing Northern Ireland, use the area code 028 when dialing from within the U.K. or internationally, but 048 when dialing from the republic.) The area codes 083, 085, 086, 087, or 089 indicate the number belongs to a cell phone (Three, Meteor, Vodafone, or Tesco Mobile).

When calling Ireland from the United States, note that the Republic of Ireland's country code is 353 and Northern Ireland is 44, and you must omit the zero from the area code when dialing. For example, to reach Galway City (area code 091) from the United States, you would dial 011-353-91-555-555; to reach a location in Northern Ireland, you would dial 011-44-28-5555-5555.

If you are planning to stay for longer than a few weeks and need to use a phone regularly for reservations, taxis, and so forth, it might

pay you to get your home cell phone "unlocked" (for a fee of €10) and then spend €10-20 for a new simcard and pay-as-you-go plan. Having said all this, since wireless Internet access is now widely available, you can get by using Skype whenever you're online.

Internet Access

Wireless Internet access is now widely available (and virtually always free of charge) in pubs, restaurants, and accommodations on both sides of the border, rendering the Internet "cafés" of the 1990s and early 2000s more or less obsolete. There's usually a password to log in, so ask a staff member if it isn't posted.

Media

The Irish get their television and radio news from **RTÉ**, Radio Telefís Éireann. **TG4**, pronounced "tee gee CAH-her," is the Irish-language television network, though it does run some English-language programs (and includes subtitles for most of the rest).

The Irish Times (www.ireland.com) is the republic's primary newspaper, available at newsagents nationwide. The *Belfast Telegraph* (www.belfasttelegraph.co.uk) is Northern Ireland's national newspaper.

MAPS AND TOURIST INFORMATION

The tourist board in the Republic of Ireland is **Fáilte Ireland** (www.failteireland.ie). In the North, it's the **Northern Ireland Tourist Board** (www.discovernorthernireland.com). Though these agencies provide information to visitors (tourist office clerks in the North tend to be particularly knowledgeable), they pretty much exist to arrange accommodations (for a small fee, of course), sell books and maps, and provide other profit-based services. Indeed, a tourist office always doubles as a gift shop. Tourist office opening hours vary from season to season; some are closed in winter, and many close for lunch (1pm-2pm).

Ordnance Survey maps (www.osi.ie) are available at tourist offices and bookstores.

The OS Discovery Series consists of 89 maps covering the country; at 1:50,000, they detail practically every stone in the road. If you are doing any walking, cycling, or in-depth sightseeing, be sure to pick up the appropriate map (they run about €9). Unfortunately, bookstores and tourist offices generally stock only maps covering the immediate area, though it is possible to order online.

WEIGHTS, MEASURES, AND TIME

Ireland is officially on the metric system, but in reality, measurements of weight and distance are inconsistent. Meat and produce are weighed and priced in kilograms, but Guinness will be poured in pints until the last day of the world. If you hear something like "I lost three stone on this new diet," know that one stone is roughly 14 pounds.

In the republic, all speed limit signs are given in kilometers. In Northern Ireland, the Imperial system is still the norm—all distances are listed in miles.

Before you leave home, pick up a three flat-pin adapter from an electronics store so you can use your laptop and other electrical gadgets. Ireland's standard voltage is 220 volts at 50 hertz (Northern Ireland's is 230/240 at 50 hertz), and you will need to purchase a voltage converter if any of your appliances are not compliant (though most likely you'll be fine with just an adapter). If you have any doubts, contact the manufacturer of the device in question before departure.

Ireland is on Greenwich mean time (GMT) and uses daylight saving time (GMT plus one hour in summer), though the country goes to daylight saving time two weeks ahead of the United States. Ireland is five hours ahead of America's east coast and eight hours ahead of the west coast, apart from those two weeks (when it is six and nine hours ahead).

Ireland is one hour behind Spain, France, and Italy, and nine and ten hours behind Australia (nine in Brisbane, ten in Sydney and Melbourne). To check the time difference between Ireland and other locations, you might try the helpful website **The World Clock** (www.timeanddate.com/worldclock).

Resources

Glossary

This compilation includes slang and common cultural and historical references in both Irish and English.

afters: dessert

Anglo-Irish: a land-owning Protestant family of English descent, or any descendants thereof

Anglo-Irish Treaty: the 1921 agreement that divided Ireland into British-controlled Northern Ireland and the independent republic in the south; the cause of the Irish Civil War (1922-1923)

ard rí **(ard REE):** high king

bank holiday: an official three-day weekend when banks close and everyone's off work on the Monday; expect crowds at pubs, restaurants, and hostels

banoffee pie: a dessert made from toffee and bananas that originated in England and is now quite popular on Irish menus

banshee: a female spirit whose shrieking and wailing augurs an impending death

bap: a lunch roll, like a seedless hamburger bun

bawn: a yard enclosed by a fortified house

big house: a term used (usually disparagingly) to refer to the home of the local landlord, who would be a member of the Protestant ascendancy

Black and Tans: a brutal and undisciplined British paramilitary force in 1920 and 1921, sent to Ireland to suppress all rebels (especially the IRA)

black pudding: sausage made from dried pigs' blood

Blue Flag: an "eco-label" awarded by an independent group, the Foundation for Environmental Education, that indicates the beach in question is very clean and safe

bodhrán (boh-RAWN): a hand-held goatskin drum used in traditional Irish music

bog: wet terrain with thick spongy layers of moss and other vegetable matter; also slang for toilet

bridle way: path for walkers, cyclists, and horseback riders

camogie: the women's version of hurling

caravan: a trailer or mobile home

céad míle fáilte **(kayd MEE-leh FAWL-cheh):** traditional greeting, meaning "a hundred thousand welcomes"

ceilidh (KAY-lee): a session of traditional dance and music

champ: mashed potatoes and onions

chemist: pharmacist

chipper: a fish-and-chips shop

cider: alcoholic apple cider

clearway: a road without a shoulder

coach: long-distance charter bus, usually for large tourist groups

concession: discounted admission

Connaught: one of the four ancient Irish provinces, encompassing Counties Galway, Mayo, Sligo, Roscommon, and Leitrim

control zone: the area of a town center where cars must not be left unattended

craic **(crack):** a fun time, good music and conversation; sometimes used in greeting, as in "What's the *craic*?"

culchie **(CULL-chee):** an urbanite's derogatory term for a person from the country; a "country bumpkin"

curragh: a rowboat covered with tarred canvas, traditionally used for fishing

Dáil (doll): the lower house of the Irish Parliament

DART: Dublin Area Rapid Transit, the commuter train line running from Howth through Dublin south to Bray in County Wicklow

diamond: town square

drink: alcohol (often called "the drink")

drisheen: pudding made from pigs' blood, a traditional Irish breakfast food

dual carriageway: a divided four-lane highway

Dubs: short for Dubliners

DUP: the Democratic Unionist Party, a hardline unionist (and exclusively Protestant) political group formed by Ian Paisley in the early 1970s

drumlin: a gentle hill formed long ago by retreating glaciers

Éire (air): the Irish name for the Republic of Ireland

eolas **(OH-lahs):** information

feis **(fesh):** a gathering

feis ceoil **(fesh kyohl):** a festival of music

Fenians: a nickname for members of the Irish Republican Brotherhood (IRB), a militant nationalist group founded in 1858; predecessors of the IRA

Fianna (FEE-uh-nuh): a group of mythical warriors whose exploits feature in many Irish legends

Fianna Fáil (FEE-uh-nuh FALL): a centrist political party formed by those nationalists who did not want to accept the compromise of continued British rule in the North

Fine Gael (FEE-nuh GALE): a centrist political party formed by those nationalists who were willing to accept continued British rule in the North to be able to form an independent republic

fir **(fihr):** men; used on toilet doors (singular *fear*)

freephone number: toll-free telephone number

GAA: abbreviation for the Gaelic Athletic Association, the organization founded in 1884 to promote the native pastimes of hurling, Gaelic football, and other sports

Gaeltacht (GALE-tahckt or GWALE-tahckt): a region where Irish is the primary language spoken (plural Gaeltachtaí)

gangway: aisle

gansey: sweater

garda, gardaí (GAR-da, gar-DEE): the Irish police, the full name being An Garda Síochána, "Guardian of the Peace"

H-blocks: literally refers to the H-shaped layout of British prisons, though the term is generally used in regard to the IRA members who as H-block inmates conducted a widespread hunger strike in 1981 in hopes of being reclassified as political prisoners

Hibernia: the Roman name for Ireland; literally "Land of Winter," so misnamed because the Romans thought they had discovered Iceland

homely: cozy, homey, homelike (never means "ugly"!)

hooker: a traditional Galway sailing ship, from the Irish *húicéir*

hurling: a traditional Irish sport, one of the fastest games in the world; a cross between hockey, lacrosse, and soccer

IHH: Independent Holiday Hostels of Ireland; a hostel's membership in this organization is indicative of high standards in safety, cleanliness, and hospitality

interval: intermission

IRA: the Irish Republican Army, the largest republican paramilitary group, founded in 1919 with the aim of a reunited Ireland, achieved by force if necessary

jacks: toilet

jars: alcoholic drinks

jumper: sweater

kerb: just another spelling of "curb"

kipper: smoked herring

knickers: ladies' underwear

leabharlann **(LORE-lahn):** library

Leinster: one of the four ancient Irish provinces, encompassing the southeastern section of the country from Louth down to Kilkenny and Wexford

loo: toilet

lough (lock): a lake or narrow sea inlet

loyalist: one (usually a Protestant) who supports Northern Ireland's continued existence as part of Great Britain; another word for unionist

Luas: the light-rail system through suburban and downtown Dublin

marching season: the time of year between Easter and mid-June when the Northern Irish calendar is filled with loyalist marches in celebration of the victory of William of Orange at the Battle of the Boyne in 1690

minced meat: hamburger

mná **(m'NAH):** women; used on toilet door (singular *bean*)

mobile (MOH-bile): cell phone

MP: member of Parliament (British)

Munster: one of the four ancient Irish provinces, encompassing Counties Clare, Limerick, Kerry, Cork, Tipperary, and Waterford

musha **(MUSH-ah):** indeed (archaic)

naomh **(nave):** saint

nationalism: the belief that Ireland should be reunited; its proponents are called nationalists

off-license: liquor store

ogham (OH-um): Ireland's earliest form of writing (dating from the 5th to the early 7th century), consisting of an alphabetic system of lines for consonants and notches for vowels, usually carved in stone

Oireachtas: the bicameral Parliament of the Irish Republic, consisting of the Dáil (lower house) and the Seanad Éireann (upper house, or Senate)

OPW: Office of Public Works, the republic's governmental agency for town planning as well as conservation and restoration efforts

Orange Order: the largest Protestant group in Northern Ireland, established in 1795

OS: Ordnance Survey, Britain's national mapping agency; Ordnance Survey Ireland (OSi) issues detailed region maps for all Ireland

Partition of Ireland: the division of Ireland into Northern Ireland and the Irish Republic in 1921

pasty (rhymes with "nasty"): a meat pie with a crust

pay-and-display parking: the paid hourly parking system in most Irish towns, whereby motorists are required to purchase a ticket from a blue kiosk to display on their "windscreens"

peat: partially carbonized vegetable matter, found in bogs, that has traditionally been dried and used for fuel; now also comes in briquette form for household use

Penal Laws: laws passed in the 18th century that forbid all Catholics from gathering for Mass, owning land, holding public office, and so forth; officially known as "Laws in Ireland for the Suppression of Popery"

petrol: gas (as in fuel)

Plantation: the settlement of English immigrants on lands confiscated from Irish Catholic farmers in the 17th century

plaster: a Band-Aid

poteen (po-CHEEN): illegal whiskey, potent enough to kill in large quantities, that was usually brewed by dispossessed Irish farmers to make extra money; from the Irish *poitín*

Prod: a Northern Irish Protestant

quay (key): a street along a river or harbor

queue (cue): a line (at the bank, the supermarket, etc.)

quid: slang for pounds (now euros), though it isn't used as often since the conversion

rashers: bacon

republicanism: the militant belief in a reunited Ireland

return ticket: a round-trip fare

roundabout: traffic circle

Rover pass: a euro-saving Bus Éireann bus pass good for 3 days' travel out of 8 consecutive days, 8 days out of 15, and so on

RTE: Ireland's broadcast network, the acronym for Radio Telefís Éireann

rubber: eraser

scrummy: short for scrumptious

SDLP: Social Democratic and Labour Party, the largest nationalist political party in the Northern Ireland assembly

sean nós **(shawn NOHSS):** a style of traditional song with three primary characteristics: the songs are unaccompanied, performed solo, and always sung in the Irish language; literally, "in the old way"

seisún: a traditional music session

single ticket: a one-way fare

síbín **(shuh-BEAN):** an illicit tavern or speakeasy; "shebeen" in English

Sinn Féin: a republican political party whose longstanding goal is a reunited Ireland; it is usually considered the political arm of the IRA despite its assertion that the two organizations are unaffiliated

slagging (off): making fun of someone

slí (shlee): literally "way," a hiking trail

slieve: a mountain, from the Irish *sliabh*

smalls: underwear

snug: a booth tucked away in a pub, meant for a bit of privacy

strand: beach

subway: an underground passageway for pedestrians

Taoiseach (TEE-shock): prime minister of the Republic of Ireland; literally, a chieftain

takeaway: takeout food

taking the piss: making fun of someone

Tánaiste (TAHN-ish-tcheh or TAHN-iss-teh): deputy prime minister of the Irish Republic

Teachta Dala (TCHOCK-tuh DOLL-uh): a member of the Irish Parliament, abbreviated TD

teach, tí, tigh (tchock, tchee): house (often used as in a public house, i.e., pub)

teampall (TCHYEM-pull): church

tinker: a now politically incorrect (and even offensive) term for an Irish person who lives a nomadic lifestyle, traveling in caravans and traditionally making a living as a smith; also (inaccurately) called gypsies

top up: to fill up a drink, or to add credit to your mobile phone account

torc: a neck or wrist ornament made of a band of twisted bronze or other metal, a type of jewelry introduced by the ancient Celts; most Irish examples date from the late Bronze Age and early Iron Age

Tory: the term for a conservative politician in Britain comes from the Irish *toiride,* meaning "pursuer," a word that originally referred to a highwayman

trad: short for traditional music

Traveller: the politically correct word for one of a group of nomadic Irishpeople who travel in caravans and speak a separate language (called Shelta) in addition to English; there are approximately 25,000 Travellers in Ireland today

Tricolour: the green, white, and orange Irish flag symbolizing peace between the (green) Catholic Irish and the (orange) Protestant Irish

turf: another word for peat

turlough (TUR-lock): a small lake that disappears in dry weather

uilleann pipes (ILL-inn): the Irish bagpipes, which are inflated by a bellows and have a range of two octaves

uisce (ISH-keh): water

uisce beatha (ISH-keh BAH-hah): whiskey; literally, "water of life"

Ulster: one of the four ancient Irish provinces, encompassing the six counties of Northern Ireland (Antrim, Armagh, Derry, Down, Fermanagh, and Tyrone) along with three counties in the republic (Cavan, Monaghan, and Donegal); sometimes used to refer to Northern Ireland (especially by the British government)

UVF: Ulster Volunteer Force, a unionist paramilitary group established in 1966

unionist: one (usually a Protestant) who supports Northern Ireland's continued existence as part of Great Britain; synonym for loyalist

victualler: butcher

Wellingtons: knee-high rubber boots, also known as wellies

PLACE-NAMES

Here are Irish words that form place-names in English.

ard: high

baile (BAL-ee or BALL-yuh): village, town

beag (beg): small

bothár (BOH-hir): road

caislean (CASH-lin): castle

carraig (KAR-rig): rock

cath (kah): battle

cill (kill): church

dún (doon): fort

gort: field

lough (lock): lake

mór (more): big

slí (shlee): path, way

teach (tchock): house

Suggested Reading

HISTORY

Duffy, Sean. *The Concise History of Ireland.* Dublin: Gill & MacMillan, 2005. Just what it says on the tin, from a specialist in medieval history.

Harbison, Peter. *Guide to National and Historic Monuments of Ireland,* 3rd ed. Dublin: Gill & Macmillan, 1998. This guide will prove invaluable if you plan to visit archaeological sites.

LITERATURE

Here is an assortment of the contemporary and the classic. Ask at a local bookshop for more recommendations.

Banville, John. *The Sea.* New York: Knopf, 2005. The prolific Banville is one of today's best Irish literary novelists. *The Sea* won the 2005 Booker Prize.

Behan, Brendan. *The Complete Plays: The Hostage, the Quare Fellow, Richard's Cork Leg, Moving Out, A Garden Party, The Big House.* New York: Grove/Atlantic, 1978. Considering all the time he spent in jail (and in the pubs), hard-drinking IRA member Behan was able to write a load of plays and fiction in his 41 years; this volume is a must-have for theatergoers.

Delaney, Frank. *Ireland.* New York: Harper, 2008. Delaney's a master at telling stories within the story.

Enright, Anne. *The Green Road.* New York: Norton, 2016. Enright is one of Ireland's foremost fiction writers, having won the Booker Prize for her novel *The Gathering* in 2007.

Frawley, Oona. *Flight.* Dublin: Tramp Press, 2014. This beautifully written novel portrays the various hardships of Ireland's immigrant population in a very compassionate way.

Joyce, James. *Dubliners.* Many consider Joyce the greatest Irish writer of all time and others find his work pretentious. If *Ulysses* isn't your cup of tea, try this collection of short stories. The final tale, *The Dead,* was inspired by the childhood love of his wife, Nora Barnacle, and the 1987 film version was director John Huston's last.

Keane, Molly. *Good Behaviour.* London: Virago Press, 2001. This ironically titled novel, set in the 1920s, offers up black comedy at the expense of the Irish Ascendancy.

Kinsella, Thomas. *The Tain: From the Irish Epic Táin Bó Cuailnge.* Oxford: Oxford University Press, 1969. The definitive translation of the 8th-century Irish epic featuring the hero Cúchulainn and his nemesis, Medb, the scheming queen of Connaught.

Le Fanu, Sheridan. *In a Glass Darkly* (Oxford World's Classics). Oxford: Oxford University Press, 1999. Dubbed "The Invisible Prince" by his Dublin neighbors, Le Fanu funneled his obsession with the occult into an awesome collection of horror stories, including the vampire tale "Carmilla," for which he is best known.

McCormack, Mike. *Notes from a Coma.* London: Jonathan Cape, 2005. A fine novel, described (albeit simplistically) as a cross between *1984* and *The X-Files,* from one of a younger generation of Irish prose writers.

McGahern, John. *By the Lake.* New York: Knopf, 2003. It may not have much of a plot, but in this gorgeously atmospheric novel (titled *That They May Face the Rising Sun* in

Ireland and Britain) it's hardly a flaw. The much-revered McGahern, who passed away in 2006, is known for darker works than this (such as *The Dark,* which was banned in 1965).

Ní Dhomhnaill, Nuala. *Selected Poems: Rogha Dánta.* Dublin: New Island, 2000. Many of Ireland's finest poets are writing exclusively in Irish, and Ní Dhomhnaill is perhaps the most beloved among them. (Original Irish on the left page and the English translation on the right.)

O'Brien, Kate. *The Land of Spices.* London: Virago Modern Classics, 1988. Banned in Ireland in 1941 for its fleeting and euphemistic mention of a homosexual tryst, this is one of the best Irish novels of the 20th century.

Ó Cadhain, Máirtín. *Cré na Cille (Graveyard Clay),* trans. Liam Mac Con Iomaire and Tim Robinson. New Haven: Yale University Press, 2016. Set in a Connemara graveyard, this 1949 novel follows the grudges and rivalries of the ghosts who linger there.

O'Casey, Sean. *Three Dublin Plays: The Shadow of a Gunman, Juno and the Paycock, and the Plough and the Stars.* New York: Faber and Faber, 2000. These three early plays, generally considered O'Casey's best work, provide a window into inner-city life that only a man born there could have achieved.

Synge, John Millington. *The Aran Islands.* New York: Penguin, 1992. Synge's travel writing isn't as well known as his dramatic works, but this volume is a must-read for Aran enthusiasts and armchair travelers alike.

Synge, John Millington. *Playboy of the Western World and Other Plays.* Oxford: Oxford University Press, 1998. This edition features all of Synge's published plays.

Wilde, Oscar. *The Best of Oscar Wilde: Selected Plays and Writings.* New York: Penguin, 2004. This collection includes *An Ideal Husband* along with four more well-known plays and several pieces of Wilde's literary criticism.

Wilde, Oscar. *The Picture of Dorian Gray.* New York: Random House, 1998. This edition features an introduction by Pulitzer Prize winner Jeffrey Eugenides.

Yeats, William Butler. *Selected Poems and Four Plays,* 4th ed. New York: Scribner, 1996. If you buy only one compilation of Yeats's work, this is a solid choice.

ART HISTORY
Bowe, Nicola Gordon. *The Life and Work of Harry Clarke.* Dublin: Irish Academic Press, 1989. An illuminating study of Clarke, Ireland's greatest stained-glass artist, by a professor at the National College of Art and Design in Dublin.

THE IRISH LANGUAGE
Ó Siadhail, Mícheál. *Learning Irish: An Introductory Self-Tutor,* 3rd ed. New Haven: Yale University Press, 1995. This is one of the best introductory Irish textbooks; it uses Connaught Irish rather than the standard dialect.

FOOD AND DRINK
Arnold, Hugo, and Georgia Glynn. *A Year at Avoca: Cooking for Ireland.* Dublin: Gloss Publications, 2010. Modern Irish cuisine from the country's favorite gourmet chain restaurant.

Cotter, Denis. *For the Love of Food.* New York: Collins, 2011. A fabulous cookbook from the owner/chef of Cork City's famous vegetarian restaurant, Café Paradiso.

NATURE AND WALKING GUIDES

Booth, Frank. *The Independent Walker's Guide to Ireland*. New York: Interlink, 1999. This guide features 35 day hikes nationwide, all 3-15 kilometers long.

Lynham, Joss, ed. *Best Irish Walks*, 3rd ed. Dublin: Gill & Macmillan, 2001. This volume offers 75 hiking routes that are generally longer and more challenging than those in the Booth guide.

LIVING IN IRELAND

McDonald, Christina. *Living Abroad in Ireland*. Berkeley, CA: Avalon Travel, 2012. Whether you intend to stay six months or a lifetime, this book provides all the resources you need to put down roots.

Internet Resources

ENTERTAINMENT

www.culturenorthernireland.org
News and reviews of theater, books, music, fine arts, and sporting events in Northern Ireland.

www.entertainment.ie
Entertainment Ireland has the lowdown on clubs, theaters, festivals, concerts, films, etc.

www.todayfm.com
One of the republic's most listened-to radio stations plays mostly "top 40" interspersed with lots of entertaining chitchat.

SIGHTSEEING AND TOURIST INFORMATION

www.discovernorthernireland.com
The official site from the Northern Ireland Tourist Board.

www.ecotourismireland.ie
A new organization dedicated to promoting environmentally friendly tourism, primarily through walking and cycling holidays.

www.heritageireland.ie
Dúchas, Ireland's Office of Public Works, offers photos, background, and information on national parks and monuments on its official site.

www.lovindublin.com
A popular Dublin-centric blog offering reviews of new and trendy restaurants along with entertainment listings.

www.megalithomania.com
An informative and opinionated gazetteer on the country's megalithic and early Christian remains, including fine color photos.

www.failteireland.ie
The official site of Bord Fáilte in the Republic of Ireland.

ACTIVITIES AND RECREATION

www.irelandwalkhikebike.com
This is your site if you're looking for a guided walking or cycling tour. All tour operators are Tourist Board-approved.

www.irishtrails.ie
The Irish Sports Council provides maps, trail descriptions, and other resources for long-distance walkers.

www.isasurf.ie
The official site of the Irish Surfing Association covers both sides of the border.

www.mountaineering.ie
Virtual home of the Mountaineering Council of Ireland.

www.mountainviews.ie
Before you go, view pictures and tips of individual mountains posted by seasoned hill-walkers.

www.npws.ie
For all you bird-watchers and walkers, the National Parks & Wildlife Service website lists nature reserves and conservation sites in the republic.

TRANSPORTATION
www.aaroadwatch.ie
The Automotive Association website includes a route planner, invaluable for mapping out your road trip.

www.transportforireland.ie/taxi/taxi-fare-estimator
Check out this site if you're not renting a car. It very helpfully provides a list of the maximum fares (by location) that a taxi driver can legally charge you.

NEWS AND PUBLICATIONS
www.bbc.co.uk
The BBC, many Northerners' primary news source.

www.breakingnews.ie
Just as it says, this slightly sensationalist news source lists Irish news first.

www.ireland.com
The *Irish Times,* the best source for nationwide news online and in print.

www.rte.ie
The official site of Radio Telefís Éireann, the republic's radio and television service.

Index

A

Abbey Island: 222
Abbey of the Holy Cross: 228
Abbey Theatre: 35, 66
accessibility: 475
accommodations: 472-473; Belfast 402-403; Dublin 69-72; Galway 298-299; see also specific place
Achill Island: 350-353; map 351
Achill Seaweed Baths: 351
activities: see recreation
Act of Union: 35
Adare: 283
Adare Heritage Centre: 283
Adrigole: 195-196
Adrigole Arts Centre: 195-196
agriculture: 457
Ahakista: 192
Ahenny: 152-153
Aideen's Grave: 77
Aillwee Caves: 271
air travel: 73, 467, 468; see also specific place
Albert Memorial Clock: 395
Allihies: 31, 197, 198
Allihies Language & Arts Centre: 198
Altazamuth Stone: 225
Amelia Earhart Centre: 420
amphibians: 446
An Cláchan: 376
An Creagan Visitor Centre: 441
Anglo-Irish Agreement: 455
Anglo-Irish Treaty: 453
animals: 446
Annascaul: 215-216
Annascaul Pottery: 216
Anna's House: 23, 432
An Trá: 310
Antrim: 404-415; map 406
Aran Heritage Centre: 301
Aran Islands: 12, 16, 300-311
Aran sweaters: 305, 460, 461
Áras an Uachtaráin: 51-53
Áras Ghleann Cholm Cille: 376
archaeology: 29-30, 81, 84, 85-88, 211, 276, 337
Archaeology Centre: 276
architecture: 462-463, 464-465
Ardagh Chalice: 447-448
Ardara: 22, 377-379
Ardfert: 242
Ardfert Cathedral: 242

Ardhowen: 439
Ardmore: 21, 159-160
Ards Peninsula: 429-431
area: 445
Armagh: 435-437; map 427
Arthurstown: 136-137
arts/culture: 460-465; see also specific place
Ashtown Castle: 51
Athlone: 328-331
Atlantic Sea Kayaking: 28, 185
Aughnanure Castle: 322
Augustinian Friary: 283
Avoca: 114-115
Avoca Handweavers: 68, 114-115

B

Ballina (Clare): 255
Ballina (Mayo): 356
Ballinskelligs: 223
Ballinskelligs Priory: 223
Ballintoy: 24, 412-414
ballooning: 57
Ballsbridge: 71
Ballycarbery Castle: 228
Ballycastle (Antrim): 24, 411-412
Ballycastle (Mayo): 30, 355-356
Ballydavid: 214-215
Ballydonegan Strand: 31, 197, 198
Ballyferriter: 213-214
Ballyhack: 137
Ballyhack Castle: 137
Ballykissangel: 114
Ballyrisode Strand: 189
Ballyshannon Folk Festival: 294
Ballyvaughan: 268-271
Baltimore: 31, 186-188
Baltimore Beacon: 187
Bangor: 426-428
Bangor Abbey: 426
Bangor Castle: 426
Bangor Erris: 353-354
Bangor Trail: 348, 354
banks/banking: 477; see also specific place
Bantry: 190-192
Bantry House and Gardens: 166, 190-191
Barley Cove: 31, 188, 189
Barnacle, Nora: 289
Barna Wood: 292
bars: see entertainment

Basilica of St. Vincent de Paul: 170
Battle of Clontarf: 448
Battle of Kinsale: 449
Battle of the Boyne: 89-90
Battle of Vinegar Hill: 125
Baurtregaum: 215
Bealach na Gaeltachta: 382
Bealaclugga: 268
Beamish: 471
Beamish and Crawford Brewery: 171
Beara Peninsula: 15, 20-21, 31, 193-198, 240
Beara Way: 28, 193
Beaulieu House and Gardens: 99
Bective Abbey: 88-89
Bective Mill: 88-89
bed-and-breakfasts: 472-473; see also
    accommodations
Beenkeragh: 234
Behan, Brendan: 463
Belfast: 17, 23, 393-404; map 396-397
Belfast Castle: 395-398
Belfast City Airport: 404
Belfast City Hall: 23, 394-395
Belfast Festival at Queen's: 401
Belfast Film Festival: 401
Belfast International Airport: 404
Belfast Marathon: 401
Belfast Zoo: 398
Belleek: 443
Belleek Pottery: 443
Bellharbour: 268
Bells of Shandon: 169
Belmullet: 354
Benbulben: 357
Bennettsbridge: 145
beverages: 471-472
Bewley's: 66-67
bicycling: 19, 28, 470; Aran Islands 304, 306;
    Burren Cycleway 269-270; Connemara 314;
    Derry 421; Dublin 75; Great Western Greenway
    343; Táin Trail 92-93, 104
birds/bird-watching: 132-133, 347, 446
Bishop Lucey Park: 167
Bishop's Palace: 277
Black Abbey: 139-141
Black and Tans: 452
Black Fort: see Dún Dúbhchathair
Blackfriars Abbey: 153
Black Head: 267
black pudding: 471
Blacksod Point: 354
Blackstairs Mountains: 28
Black Taxi Tour: 13, 17, 23, 390, 398
Blackwater Way: 156
Blarney: 176
Blasket Centre: 213

Blasket Islands: 213
Blennerville Windmill: 241
Bloody Foreland: 17, 24, 381
Bloody Sunday: 454
Blue Raincoat: 360
Bluestack Way: 369-371, 382
Boa Island: 442
boat tours: Belfast 398-399; Connemara 321; Cork
    179; Dublin 55-56; Enniskillen 439; Louth 104
bodhráns: 313
Bog of Allen: 117
bogs: 446
Bogside: 417, 419-420
Bogside peace murals: 13, 17, 24, 390, 419-420
Bog Week: 318
Bolin Island: 282
Bolton Library: 150
Bonamargy Friary: 411
Book of Kells: 11, 14, 34, 41, 448
books/bookstores: 362, 461-464, 484-486; see
    also shopping
border crossings: 474
Boru, Brian: 247, 448
Botanic Gardens (Belfast): 23, 394, 395
boxty: 471
Boyne Valley: 85-91
Boyne Viaduct: 98
Brandon, Mt.: 215
Bray: 116-117
Bray Head Loop: 225
Brehon Laws: 447
Brigit's Garden: 322
Brittas Bay: 117
Browne's Doorway: 289
Browne's Hill Dolmen: 128
Brú Ború Cultural Centre: 150
Brú na Bóinne: 10, 14, 29, 56, 81, 82, 85-88
Brú na Bóinne Visitor Centre: 85
Bull Ring: 129
Bulmer's: 471
Bunbeg: 381, 382-383
Bundoran: 373
Bunglás: 377
Bunratty: 252-254
Bunratty Castle: 16, 26, 253-254
Burren: 16, 28, 30, 268-276; map 269
Burrenbeo: 268
Burren Centre: 273
Burren College of Art: 268
Burren Cycleway: 269-270
Burren Exposure: 268
Burren Nature Sanctuary: 323
Burren Perfumery and Floral Centre: 272
Burren Way: 244, 269-270
Burrishoole Abbey: 349
bus travel: 468; see also specific place

Bushmills: 416, 471
business hours: 476
Butter Gate: 97

C

Caher: 234
Cahercommaun Hill Fort: 272
Caherconnell Stone Fort: 272
Caherconree: 215
Caherdaniel: 221-223
Cahergall ring fort: 31, 228
Cahermacnaughten: 272
Cahersiveen: 31, 227-230
Cahersiveen Festival of Music & the Arts: 229
Cahir: 151-152
Cahir Castle: 26, 124, 151
Cairde Sligo Arts Festival: 361
Caislean Uí Bhriain: 309
Camaderry Mountain: 111
Canadian Embassy: 72
canoeing: 28, 292, 439
Cantwell Fada: 145
Cape Clear Island: 186-188
Carlingford: 103-105
Carlingford Friary: 103
Carlingford Maritime Festival: 105
Carlow Town: 128
Carlsberg Kilkenny Rhythm and Roots Weekend: 143
Carraig ná Finnise: 309
Carramore: 343
Cararoe: 313
Carrick-a-Rede Rope Bridge: 17, 24, 390, 414
Carrickfergus: 404-405
Carrickfergus Castle: 26, 404-405
Carrickfergus Museum and Civic Centre: 405
Carrick-on-Suir: 152-153
Carrigaholt: 260
Carron: 272
Carrowkeel Passage Tomb Cemetery: 29, 334, 368
Carrowmore: 17, 29
Carrowmore Megalithic Cemetery: 366
Carrownisky: 343
Carson's: 435
car travel: 469-470; see also specific place
Casement Park: 399
Cashel: 21, 148-151
Casino Marino: 53-54
Castle Archdale Country Park: 443
Castle Coole: 440
Castle Espie: 431-432
Castlegregory: 215
Castletown: 118
Castletownbere: 196-197
Castletownshend: 186
Castle Ward Estate: 433
Cathaoir Synge: 307

Cathedral of Saints Peter and Paul (Glendalough): 110
Cathedral of Saints Peter and Paul (Trim): 95
Cathedral Quarter: 394
Cathedral Quarter Arts Festival: 401
Catholic Church: 453, 458-459
Catholic Emancipation: 450
Cat Laughs Comedy Festival: 143
Cattle Raid of Cooley: 93, 461
Causeway Coast: 17, 24, 409-416
Causeway Coastal Route: 407
Causeway Coast Way: 407, 409
Cave Hill Country Park: 23, 398
caving: 264, 440-441
Céide Fields: 30, 355
ceilidh: 461
Celbridge: 118
cell phones: 478
Celtic Tiger: 456
Celtronic Festival: 423
Celts: 447
Central Sperrins Way: 407
Charles Fort: 178-179
Chester Beatty Library: 34, 43-44
Chez Hans: 21, 150
children, traveling with: 475
Christchurch: 44-46, 70
Christ Church Cathedral (Dublin): 14, 25, 34, 44
Christ Church Cathedral (Waterford): 153-156
Church of the Ascension: 182
Church of the Assumption: 129
Church of the Holy Trinity: 235
Church of the Immaculate Conception (Clonakilty): 183
Church of the Immaculate Conception (Wexford): 129
Church of the Little Ark: 261
Church of the Nativity of Our Lady: 182
Cill Cean Fhionnaigh: 308
Cill Ghobnait: 309
City of Derry Jazz and Big Band Festival: 423
civil war: 453
Claddagh Arts Centre: 292
Clare: 16, 243-268; map 246
Clare Heritage Centre: 274
Clare Island: 347
Clare Island Abbey: 347
Clare Museum: 248
Clarke, Harry: 47, 57, 129, 169, 170, 182, 186, 204-205, 235, 256, 258, 308, 319, 338, 348, 349, 485
Classiebawn Castle: 364
Clew Bay Archaeological Trail: 337
Clifden: 314-316
Clifden Hill: 274
Cliffs of Moher: 9, 16, 20, 197, 244, 262-264
climate: 18, 445

climbing: 28, 234-235, 346-347, 435
clocháin (beehive huts): 464
Clochan na Carraige: 303
Clogher: 213
Clonakilty: 183-185
Clonfert Cathedral: 326
Clonmacnoise: 16, 27, 286, 327-328; map 330
clubs: *see* entertainment
Cniotáil Inis Meáin: 22, 309
Cnoc Raithni: 309-310
Cobh: 177-178
Cobh, The Queenstown Story: 177
coffee: 471
Cois na hAbhna: 250
colcannon: 471
Cole Monument: 437
Collins Barracks: 48
Collins, Michael: 167, 183, 452-453
Columba: 362
comedy venues: 67
Comhaltas Ceoltóiri Éireann: 66
Cong: 337-339
Cong Abbey: 338
Connemara: 16, 28, 197, 311-323; map 312
Connemara Loop: 316
Connemara National Park: 22, 286, 311, 318-319
Connemara Way: 321
Connolly, James: 452
Conor Pass: 215
Coole Park: 325-326
Corcomroe Abbey: 268-269
Cork: 15-16, 162-198; map 164-165
Cork Arts Theatre: 173
Cork City: 21, 167-176; map 168
Cork City Gaol: 169
Cork Film Festival: 174
Cork International Airport: 176
Cork International Choral Festival: 174
Cork Jazz Festival: 174
Cork Midsummer Festival: 174
Cork Opera House: 174
Cork Pride: 173
Corkscrew Hill: 270
Cormac's Chapel: 21, 148
Corofin: 25, 273-274
Corofin Traditional Music Festival: 275
Corrán Tuathail: 230, 234
Craggaunowen Project: 252
craic: 63, 459
Crane, The: 22, 296
Crawford Municipal Art Gallery: 169, 170
Crawfordsburn: 428-429
Crawfordsburn Country Park: 429
Creevykeel Court Cairn: 17, 29, 365
crime: 477
Croaghaun: 351

Croagh Patrick: 17, 22, 27, 334, 346-347
Croke Park: 47, 57
Crolly: 383
Cromwell, Oliver: 449-450
Crookhaven: 188
Cros na Scraeptra: 328
Cruinniú na mBad: 324
cruises: *see* boat tours
crystal: 156, 157, 181, 460, 461
Cúirt International Festival of Literature: 297
cuisine: *see* food
Culdaff: 24, 387
Curracloe Beach: 124, 129, 132-133
Curraun: 347
currency: 477
Cushendell: 408
Cushendun: 408-409
customs, cultural: 474-475
customs regulations: 474
Cycle Ireland: 28
Cycle Route: 190
cycling: *see* bicycling

D

dance: 460-461; *see also* entertainment
Dark Hedges: 410
de Clare, Richard: 448
demographics: 458
Department of Foreign Affairs: 72
Derreen Gardens: 240
Derry: 17, 417-425; map 406
Derrybeg: 381
Derry City: 24, 393, 417-425; map 418
Derry City Airport: 423
Derry City walls: 13, 17, 24, 390, 417
Derrynane House: 222
Derrynane National Historic Park: 222
Desmond Castle: 178, 283
de Valera, Eamon: 35, 452-453
Devenish Island: 390, 442
Dingle Peninsula: 11, 16, 20, 197, 204-216; map 206-207
Dingle Town: 20, 204-212; 208
Dingle Way: 210
Direct Rule: 454
disabilities, tips for travelers with: 475
discounts: 475
Discover Ireland: 28
Díseart Institute of Education and Celtic Culture: 200, 204-205
diving: 28, 135, 187, 189, 196, 205, 215, 225, 260, 264, 351, 429
Doagh: 387-388
Doagh Famine Village: 387-388
Dog's Bay: 313
Dollymount: 56

dolphins: 205, 258, 260, 446
Dominican Friary: 150
Donabate: 56
Donaghdee: 429-430
Donaghmore: 92
Donegal: 23-24, 333-336, 369-388; maps 335, 370
Donegal Abbey: 369
Donegal Airport: 22, 383
Donegal Castle: 22, 369
Donegal Craft Village: 22, 372, 461
Donegall Square: 394
Donegal Town: 369-373
Donegal Town Summer Festival: 371
Dooega: 350
Doolin: 16, 30, 263-267, 300-301
Doolin Folk Festival: 294
Doolough Valley: 334, 339-342
Doonagore Castle: 264
Dooney Rock: 358
Douglas Hyde Gallery of Modern Art: 41
Down: 426-435; map 427
Down Cathedral: 433
Downhill: 24
Downhill Estate: 26, 390, 425
Downhill Forest: 425
Downpatrick: 433
Downpatrick Head: 356
Dowth: 29, 87
driving: 469-470; see also specific place
Drogheda: 97-101; map 98
Drogheda Arts Festival: 100
Droichead Arts Centre: 100
Drombeg Stone Circle: 185
Dromore Wood: 274
druids: 447
Druid Stone Circle: 219
Drumcliffe: 362-363
Dublin: 14, 20, 25, 26, 29, 32-76;
    accommodations 69-72; activities/
    recreation 55-57; entertainment/events 63-
    67; food 57-63; history 35-39; information/
    services 72-73; maps 36-37, 49, 52, 58-59,
    77; shopping 68-69; sights 34, 39-54;
    transportation 73-76
Dublin Castle: 26, 43
Dublin City Hall: 43
Dublin City Marathon: 67
Dublin City Soul Festival: 67
Dublin Dance Festival: 67
Dublin Gay Theatre Festival: 65
Dublin International Airport: 73
Dublin LGBTQ Pride Festival: 65
Dublin Pass: 40
Dublin Theatre Festival: 67
Dublin Writers Museum: 46
Dugort: 350

dulse: 411
Dún Aengus: 23, 30, 286, 301, 302
Dunbeg Fort: 213
Dun Briste: 356
Duncannon: 136
Duncannon Fort: 136
Dún Chonchúir: 306, 307
Dún Dúbhchathair: 23, 30, 286, 301, 302
Dún Eochla: 30, 303
Dún Eoghanachta: 302-303
Dunfanaghy: 383-385
Dún Fearbhaí: 307
Dún Fhormna: 309
Dunguaire Castle: 16, 26, 323
Dún Laoghaire: 79
Dunlewey: 381
Dunluce Castle: 17, 24, 26, 390, 415-416
Dunmore: 144-145
Dunmore Cave: 144-145
Dunmore East: 15, 124, 158-159
Dunquin: 213
Dursey Island: 31, 197, 198
Dwyer McAllister Cottage: 114
Dysert O'Dea: 25, 244, 275-276
Dzogchen Beara: 197-198

E

Earhart, Amelia: 420
Eas A'Ranca waterfall: 377
East Clare Way: 256
Easter Rising: 35, 50, 51, 452
East Munster Way: 156
economy: 457
Edgeworth, Maria: 461-462
electricity: 479
Elly Bay: 354
embassies: 72
emergencies: 73, 477
English Market: 174
Ennis: 25, 248-251; map 249
Enniscorthy: 125-128
Enniscorthy Castle: 126
Enniscrone: 28, 30, 367-368
Ennis Friary: 25, 248
Enniskerry: 106-109
Enniskillen: 437-440; map 438
Enniskillen Castle: 437
Ennis Trad Festival: 294
Ennistymon: 262
entertainment: Belfast 400-401; Dublin 63-67;
    Galway 294, 296-297; see also specific place
environmental issues: 445-446
Errigal, Mt.: 28, 380
Errisbeg: 313
Ess-na-Larach waterfall: 408
events: see festivals/events

Everyman Palace Theatre: 173
Exploris Aquarium: 431
Eyeries: 196

F

Falcarragh: 383
falconry: 338
Falls Road: 398
Fanore: 267
fauna: 446
Féile an Phobail: 401
Feis Doire Cholmcille: 422-423
Fermanagh: 437-443
ferries: 467-468; see also specific place
Festival of Baroque Music: 361
festivals/events: 294; Belfast 401; Dublin 67;
    Galway 294, 297; see also specific festival;
    specific place
Fiddler's Green Festival: 435
films: 464
Fintragh Bay: 374
fish/fishing: 189, 224, 225, 228, 235, 256, 314, 426,
    439, 446
Fisherstreet: 264
Flaggy Shore: 270
Fleadh Cheoil na hEireann: 294
Fleadh na gCuach: 324
Fleadh Nua: 250
Flight of the Earls: 449
flora: 446
Florence Court: 441-442
food: 471-472, 485, Belfast 399-400, Dublin 57-62,
    Galway 293-295; see also specific place
football: 465
Fort of King Laoghaire: 89
Forty Foot Pool: 79
Fota Arboretum and Gardens: 176-177
Fota House: 177
Fota Island: 176-177
Fota Wildlife Park: 177
Four Courts: 47-48
Foyle Valley Cycle Route: 421
Franciscan Friary (Adare): 283
Franciscan Friary (Killarney): 25, 235
Frank McCourt Museum: 279-280
Free State: see Irish Free State
French Church: 153
Friel, Brian: 463
Fringe Festival: 67
Fungie: 205
Fusiliers' Arch: 43

G

GAA Museum: 47
Gaelic: see language

Gaelic football: 47, 57, 171, 399, 465
Gaeltachtaí: 459-460
Gaiety Theatre: 66
Gallarus Castle: 214
Gallarus Oratory: 16, 20, 214
Galway: 16, 22-23, 284-331; map 287
Galway Arts Festival: 297
Galway City: 11, 16, 25, 30, 288-299; map 290-291
Galway City Museum: 289-292
Galway Film Fleadh: 297
Galway International Oyster Festival: 297
Galway Jazz Festival: 297
Galway Races: 297
Game of Thrones sites: 56, 410
Gap of Dunloe: 31, 234
Garden of Remembrance: 46-47
Garnish Island: 16, 21, 31, 193-194
Garter Lane Arts Centre: 157
Gasyard Centre: 422
Gasyard Wall Féile: 423
Gate Theatre: 66
gay/lesbian travelers, tips for: 65, 173, 296, 401,
    476
Gay Pride Parade: 65
Gaze: 65
Genealogical Centre: 274
genealogy: 451
General Post Office: 46
General Register Office: 451
geography: 445
Giant's Causeway: 17, 24, 414-415
Giant's Grave: 283
Glandore: 185-186
Glasnevin: 53
Glasnevin Cemetery: 53
Glebe House and Gallery: 380
Glenariff: 407-408
Glenariff Forest Park: 407-408
Glenbeigh: 230
Glencar: 230
Glencar Lough: 366
Glencolmcille: 17, 375-377
Glencolmcille Folk Village: 376
Glendalough: 10, 21, 25, 56, 82, 110-111
Glengarriff: 15, 21, 31, 193-195
Glengarriff Bamboo Park: 31, 194
Glengarriff Woods Nature Reserve: 166, 194
Glengesh Pass: 375
Glen Head Peninsula: 373-379
Gleninchaquin Park: 219
Glenmalure: 82, 110, 113-114
Glenmore Lake: 240
Glen of Imaal: 114
Glens of Antrim: 24, 407-409
Glenveagh Castle: 24, 380
Glenveagh National Park: 24, 334, 379-381

Glór Irish Music Centre: 250
glossary: 480-483
Gobbins, The: 24, 405-407
Golden Mile: 394, 395
golf: Antrim 411; Belfast 399; Clare 261; Connemara 314; Cork 179, 183, 189, 194; Derry 421; Donegal 371, 384; Down 426; Fermanagh 439; Galway 292; Kerry 219, 235; Kilkenny 142; Limerick 280; Louth 99, 104; Mayo 343; Meath 95; Sligo 358-359, 367; Waterford 158; Wexford 130
Good Friday Agreement: 455
Gort na gCapall: 303
Gosford Castle and Forest Park: 436
Gougane Barra: 15
Gougane Barra Forest Park: 192
government: 456-457
Government Buildings: 41
Gracehill House: 410
Grace Neill's: 429-430
Grafton Street: 57-60, 68
Grand Canal: 118
Grand Opera House: 24, 395, 400
Grange Stone Circle: 282-283
gratuities: 478
Great Famine: 345, 387-388, 450
Great Western Greenway: 28, 343, 348, 349
Green Holes of Doolin: 264
Gregory, Augusta: 325-326, 462
Grey Abbey: 17, 390, 430
Greyabbey: 430
Greystones: 117
Grianán of Aileách: 24, 334, 386-387
Griffith, Arthur: 453
Guildhall: 417-419
Guinness: 48-50, 471
Guinness Storehouse: 48-50
Gurteen Bay: 313
Gus O'Connor's Pub: 244, 265
Gweedore: 17, 22, 24, 381-383

H

Hag's Head Walk: 263
Half Moon Theatre: 174
Hall of the Vicars Choral: 148
Halloween Carnival: 401, 423
handicrafts: 114-115, 143, 305, 460, 461; see also shopping
hang-gliding: 28, 126, 421
Hawk's Well Theatre: 260
health: 477
Healy Pass: 21, 240
Heaney, Seamus: 463-464
Helix, The: 67
Hell's Hole: 387
Henry II: 448

Henry VIII: 449
Heritage Card: 39-40
Highlanes Gallery: 98
hiking: 28, 348, 382, 407, 486; Aran Islands 304; Bangor Trail 348, 354; Bealach na Gaeltachta 382; Beara Way 193; Blackwater Way 156; Bluestack Way 369-371, 382; Burren Way 244, 269-270; Causeway Coastal Route 407; Causeway Coast Way 407, 409; Central Sperrins Way 407; Connemara National Park 318; Connemara Way 321; Dingle Way 210; East Clare Way 256; Easter Munster Way 156; Glendalough 111; Great Western Greenway 343, 348, 349; Inis Oírr Way 310; Kerry Way 230; Lough Derg Way 256, 280; Mourne Trail 407; Mt. Errigal 380; Royal Canal Way 118; Sheep's Head Way 190, 193; Slí Cholmcille 376, 377, 382; Slievemore 351; South Leinster Way 126, 146; Táin Way 104, 105; Tullaghobegley Walk 382, 383; Ulster Way 382, 407; Western Way 348; Wicklow Way 106, 109, 110, 111, 112, 113
Hill of Allen: 117-118
Hill of Slane: 92, 93
Hill of Tara: 82, 84, 89
history: 29-30, 34-39, 81, 84, 121, 125, 163-167, 201-204, 245-247, 285-288, 333-336, 392-393, 447-456, 484
hitchhiking: 476
Hollow, The: 51
Holy Cross Church: 219
Holy Island: 257
Holy Trinity: 156
Holy Trinity Heritage Centre: 104
Home Rule: 451-452
Honan Chapel: 15, 21, 166, 169, 170
Hook Head Lighthouse: 14, 124, 135-136
Hook Head Peninsula: 135-137
Hore Abbey: 150
Horn Head: 384
horse riding: Clare 256, 261; Connemara 314; Cork 183, 189; Derry 421; Donegal 378, 384; Down 426, 431; Fermanagh 439; Kerry 205, 222, 235; Kilkenny 142; Louth 106; Mayo 338, 343; Meath 95; Sligo 359; Wexford 132, 134
hospitals: 73; see also specific place
hostels: 472; see also accommodations
hotels: 473; see also accommodations
Howth: 76-78
Howth Castle: 76-77
Hugh Lane Municipal Gallery of Modern Art: 34, 47, 66, 170
Hungry Hill: 195
Hunt Museum: 16, 244, 279, 281
hurling: 47, 57, 171, 399, 465

I

Ilnacullen: 31, 193-194
immigration: 458
Inch: 216
Inchagoill Island: 338
Inchydoney Strand: 183
independence: 452-453
information: 477-479; see also specific place
Inisfallen Island: 231
Inishbofin: 316-317
Inishkea Islands: 355
Inishmurray: 365
Inishowen Peninsula: 24, 387-388
Inishturk: 347-348
Inis Meáin: 22, 306-309
Inis Mór: 23, 28, 30, 300, 301-306
Inis Oírr: 309-311
Inis Oírr Heritage House: 309
Inis Oírr Way: 310
Inistioge: 146
Innisfree Island: 365
International Literature Festival Dublin: 67
Internet access: 478
Ionad Árann: 23, 301
Irish Agricultural Museum and Famine Exhibition: 133
Irish Citizen Army: 452
Irish Film Centre: 67
Irish Free State: 453
Irish Hang Gliding and Paragliding Association: 28, 126
Irish language: see language
Irish Literary Revival: 35
Irish Museum of Modern Art: 50
Irish Parachute Club: 126
Irish Republic: 453-454, 456-457
Irish Republican Army (IRA): 452, 454-455
Irish Republican Brotherhood (IRB): 451
Irish Steel Guitar Festival: 100
Irish Trails: 28, 193
Irish Underwater Council: 28
Irish Volunteers: 452
Iron Age: 447
itineraries, suggested: 20-31, 38
Iveragh Peninsula: 16, 217-239; map 240

J

James Fort: 179
James II: 449
James Joyce Tower & Museum: 79
Jameson: 38, 178, 471
Jameson Heritage Centre: 178
jaunting cars: 234
Jazz on the Terrace: 66
Jerpoint Abbey: 15, 21, 25, 124, 146
Joe Watty's: 23, 305

John F. Kennedy Arboretum: 137
Johnstown Castle: 133
Joyce, James: 462-463

K

kayaking: 28, 31, 130, 185, 187, 189, 196
Kebble National Nature Reserve: 412
Keem Bay: 350
Kells: 147
Kells Priory: 25, 147
Kenmare: 20, 31, 217-221
Kerry: 16, 199-242; map 202-203
Kerry Bog Village: 230
Kerry Cliffs: 223-224
Kerry County Museum: 241
Kerry Way: 28, 230
Kilbaha: 260-261
Kilbroney Forest Park: 435
Kilcar: 22, 374
Kilcar Strand: 374
Kilclooney dolmen: 377
Kilcullen's Seaweed Baths: 334, 367
Kildare: 117-119; map 107
Kildavnet Castle: 350
Kilfane: 145
Kilfane Church: 25
Kilfane Glen & Waterfall: 145
Kilfenora: 272-273
Kilkee: 260
Kilkenny: 138-147; map 139
Kilkenny Arts Festival: 143
Kilkenny Castle: 14, 21, 26, 124, 138-139, 141-142
Kilkenny City: 21, 25, 138-144; map 140
Kilkieran: 152-153
Killaloe: 255-257
Killaloe Cathedral: 255
Killarney National Park: 10, 20, 25, 200, 231-234; map 232
Killarney Town: 20, 25, 31, 235-239; map 236
Killary Adventure Company: 28
Killary Harbour: 16, 286, 320-322
Killiney: 56
Killybegs: 373-374
Kilmacduagh: 16, 25-27, 286, 324-325
Kilmainham Jail: 50, 51
Kilmalkedar Church: 214
Kilmore Quay: 134-135
Kilmurvey: 304
Kilmurvey Craft Village: 23, 305, 461
Kilnaboy: 276
Kilree: 147
Kilree Church: 25, 147
Kilruddery House & Gardens: 116
Kilrush: 258-259
Kilrush Woods: 258
King John's Castle (Carlingford): 103

King John's Castle (Limerick): 26, 276, 277-278
Kinsale: 15, 21, 178-182
Kinsale Arts Festival: 180
Kinsale Gourmet Festival: 180
Kinsale Jazz Festival: 180
Kinvara: 16, 323-324
Knappogue Castle: 26, 252
Knightstown: 225
knitwear: 305, 460
Knock: 356-357
Knock Airport: 357
Knockmore: 347
Knocknarea: 17, 334, 358, 366
Knockreer House and Gardens: 231
Knowth: 29, 87
Kylemore Abbey: 16, 319
Kyteler, Alice: 141

L

lace-making: 460
Lacken Strand: 356
Ladies' View: 233
Lady Bantry's Lookout: 31, 194
Lady's Leap: 110
Lagan Lookout: 394
Lahinch: 261
language: 375, 459-460, 462-463, 480-483, 485
Lansdowne Stadium: 57
Lanyon Building: 395
Laragh: 110, 112
launderettes: 476
Lauragh: 240
Layde Old Church: 390, 408
Leaba Diarmuda agus Ghráinne: 303, 307
Leacanabuaile: 228
Leap Castle: 329
Leap travel card: 56, 74
Ledwidge Museum: 92
Leenane: 286, 320-322
Le Fanu, Joseph Sheridan: 462
Leinster House: 41
Lemaneagh Castle: 273
Letterfrack: 22, 317-318
Letterkenny: 386
LGBT travelers, tips for: 65, 173, 296, 401, 476
Lia Fáil: 89
Light Opera Festival: 157
Limerick: 16, 243-247, 276-283; map 246
Limerick City: 276-283; map 278
Limerick City Gallery of Art: 279
Limerick Museum: 277
Limerick Treaty Stone: 277-279
linen: 460
Linen Hall Library: 395
Lisannor: 261-262
Lisbane: 23, 431-432

Lisdoonvarna: 267
Lismore: 160-161
Lismore Castle: 160-161
Lissadell: 363-364
literature: 461-464, 484-485
litter: 445
Loch a'Dúin Valley: 211
Loch na Cuinge: 382
Londonderry: see Derry City
Loop Head: 261
Loop Head Peninsula: 260-261
Lord Brandon's Cottage: 233
Lot's Wife: 187
Lough Caragh: 230
Loughcrew Cairns: 14, 29, 82, 90-91
Loughcrew Equinox Festival: 90
Loughcrew Historic Gardens: 90
Loughcrew House: 90
Lough Derg Way: 256, 280
Lough Erne: 442
Lough Eske: 369
Lough Gill: 365-366
Lough Gur: 244, 276, 280, 282-283
Lough Gur Interpretive Centre: 282
Lough Leane: 231
Lough Neagh: 445
Loughros Head: 377-378
Lough Sheelin: 91-92
Louth: 97-106; map 86
Lower Lake: 25
luggage lockers: 73
Lugnaquilla: 113
Lynch Memorial Window: 289
Lynch's Castle: 289
Lyric Theatre: 401

M

Macalla Farm: 347
Macgillicuddy's Reeks: 28, 200, 234-235
MacMorrough, Dermot: 448
Magdalene Tower: 97
Maharees Islands: 215
Malahide: 26, 78-79
Malahide Castle & Gardens: 78
Malin: 387
Malin Head: 387
Mall, The: 435
mammals: 446
Mannin Bay: 313
Mansion House: 42
maps: 470, 478-479
Marble Arch Caves: 390, 440-441
Marble Hill Beach: 384
Market Arcade: 68
Marlbank National Nature Reserve: 441
Matt Molloy's: 22, 343

Maturin, Charles: 462
Maumturks: 311
Maynooth: 118-119
Maynooth Castle: 118
Mayo: 333-357; maps 335, 340-341
McCourt, Frank: 279-280
McGrory's: 24, 387
measurements: 479
Meath: 85-97; map 86
medical care: 73, 477; *see also specific place*
Meetinghouse Square: 44
Meeting of the Waters: 114, 233
Mellifont Abbey: 14, 25, 101-102
Merchant's Quay Shopping Centre: 174
Mermaid Arts Centre: 116
metric system: 479
Metropolitan Arts Centre: 400
Middle Lake: 231
Midleton: 178
Millennium Forum: 422, 423
Millmount Museum: 97-98
Miltown Malbay: 261
Mint, The: 103
Mizen Head Peninsula: 15, 31, 188-190
Mizen Vision: 31, 166, 188
Model Gallery: 22, 358, 360, 361
Moll's Gap: 234
Monasterboice: 14, 25, 82, 102-103
money: 477
Monroe's: 22, 296
Mothar: 263
Mount Brandon: 215
Mount Errigal: 28, 380
Mountshannon: 257
Mount Stewart House and Gardens: 17, 3430
Mourne Mountains: 17, 23, 434
Mourne Trail: 407
Mourne Wall: 434
Muckross: 231-233
Muckross Abbey: 25, 231-233
Muckross House and Gardens: 31, 233
Muckross Lake: 231
Muckross Traditional Farms: 31, 233
Muiredach's Cross: 102
Mullaghmore (Clare): 274
Mullaghmore (Sligo): 358, 364-365
Mullaghroe Beach: 354
Mullet Peninsula: 354
Mulranny: 349
Murphy, Tom: 463
Murphy's: 471
Murrisk: 27, 345-346
Murrisk Abbey: 345
Museum of Free Derry: 420
music: 13, 261, 265, 294, 460-461; *see also*
    entertainment

Mussenden Temple: 17, 24, 425
Mweelrea Mountains: 342

N
Narcissus Marsh Library: 45
Na Seacht dTeampaill: 301, 302
National Aquatic Center: 56
National Archives: 451
National Botanic Gardens: 53
National Concert Hall: 66
National Craft Gallery: 143
National Famine Monument: 345
National Gallery of Ireland: 14, 34, 41-42
National Library: 42, 451
National Museum of Archaeology and History:
    14, 29, 34, 42
National Museum of Decorative Arts and History:
    48
National Museum of Natural History: 42
National Opera House: 131
National Sealife: 116
National 1798 Centre: 126
National Shrine of Our Lady of Knock: 356
Naughton Gallery: 395
Neachtain's: 23, 296
Neeson, Liam: 464
Nendrum Abbey: 431
Nerve Centre: 422
Nevan Fort: 436
Newcastle: 434
Newgrange: 14, 29, 85-87, 447
New Music Festival: 361
Newport: 348
newspapers: 478, 487
Newtown Abbey: 95
Newtown Castle: 268, 271
Newtownards: 429
Nicholas Mosse Pottery: 145
nightlife: *see* entertainment
Nine Years' War: 449
Nora Barnacle House: 289
Normans: 448-449
North Cross: 103
North Down Heritage Centre: 426
Northern Ireland: 17, 23-24, 389-443, 454, 457;
    map 392
North Kerry: 241-242
North Mayo Sculpture Trail: 353
Northside: 46-47, 62, 71
NUI Maynooth: 118
Nuns' Church: 27, 328

O
O'Brien's Castle: 263
O'Casey, Sean: 462

O'Connell Memorial Church: 228
O'Connell Monument: 46
O'Connell, Daniel: 35, 222, 450
ogham stones: 211
O'Kelly, Michael: 87
Old Barracks Heritage Centre: 227-228
Old Bushmills Distillery: 416
Old Inn: 428-429
Old Jameson Distillery: 38, 48
Old Library: 11, 34, 41
Old Museum Arts Centre: 400
O'Neill, Hugh: 449
opera: 131, 174
Ormond Castle: 124, 152
Oughterard: 322-323
Ould Lammas Fair: 411
Our Lady of Mount Carmel: 25, 45
Oyster Festival: 105

P
packing tips: 18-19
Pairc Uí Chaoimh: 171
Pale, The: 448
Palm House: 395
paragliding: 421
parking: 469
Parnell, Charles Stewart: 451-452
Parnell Monument: 46
Parnell Square: 46-47
passes, discount: 39-40, 475
passports: 18, 474
Pearse Museum: 54
Pearse, Patrick: 50, 51, 54, 313
Pearse's Cottage: 313
Penal Laws: 449-550
People's Garden: 51
pharmacies: 73, 477; see also specific place
Phoenix Park: 50-53, 56; map 52
Phoenix Park Visitor Centre: 51
planning tips: 18-31, 38, 39, 84, 125, 167, 204, 247, 288, 336
Plantation of Ireland: 449
plants: 446
Playhouse, The: 422
political parties: 456-457
Pollatomish: 354-355
Poll na bPéist: 303
Poll na Seantoine: 356
pollution: 445
population: 458
Portaferry: 431
Portmagee: 25, 224
Portrane: 56
pottery: 160, 216, 443, 460, 461; see also shopping
Poulanass Waterfall: 111
Poulnabrone: 16, 30, 271-272

Powerscourt House and Gardens: 14, 21, 82, 106-108
Powerscourt Townhouse: 67, 68
prehistory: 29-30, 447
Proclamation of the Irish Republic: 452
Project Arts Centre: 67
Prospect Cemetery: 53
Public Record Office of Northern Ireland: 451
pubs: 471-472, 474; see also entertainment

QR
Quad Attack Adventure Centre: 126
Queen's University: 394, 395
Quiet Man, The: 337-338
Quiet Man Heritage Cottage: 338
Quin: 251-252
Quin Abbey: 25, 251-252
radio: 478
rail travel: see train travel
Railway Heritage Centre: 369
Ramsgrange: 137
Rathfarnham Castle: 54
Rathlin Island: 412
Ráth of the Synods: 89
Ravensdale: 105-106
Ravensdale Forest Park: 106
Recess: 322
recreation: 28, 486-487; Belfast 398-399; Dublin 55-57; Galway 292; see also specific place
recycling: 445-446
Reformation: 449
Reginald's Tower: 153
religion: 25-27, 458-459
rental cars: 75, 470; see also driving; specific place
Renvyle: 319-320
reptiles: 446
restaurants: 471-472; see also food
restrooms: 477
Riasc Monastic Settlement: 20, 214
Ring of Kerry: 11, 16, 20, 28, 31, 197, 200, 217-223
Roadford: 264
Rockfleet Castle: 349
Rock of Cashel: 10, 15, 21, 26, 124, 148-150
Rossaveal: 300, 313
Ross Castle (Kerry): 31, 231
Ross Castle (Meath): 26, 91
Rosses Point: 358, 363
Rosslare: 133-134
Rosslare Harbour: 134
Rosslare Strand: 129-130, 133-134
Rossnowlagh Beach: 334, 373
Rostrevor: 435
Rothe House: 141
Roundstone: 313-314
Roundstone Musical Instruments: 313
Roundwood: 112-113

Rowallane Garden: 432
Royal Canal: 118
Royal Canal Way: 118
Royal Hospital Kilmainham: 50
Royal Irish Academy: 42
Royal Irish Constabulary: 452

S

safety: 469-470, 477
sailboarding: 158
sailing: 104, 187, 188, 195, 314
Saintfield: 432-433
Saint's Road: 214
Salthill: 292
Scattery Island: 259-260
Schull: 31, 188-189
Schull Planetarium: 31, 188-189
Schull Regatta: 188
Scoil Acla: 352
Scuba Dive West: 28, 319-320
Seagate Foyle Film Festival: 423
sealife: 446
seán nós singing: 460-461
Sea Week: 318
Seipeal Eoin agus Naomh Mhuire gan Smal: 308
Selskar Abbey: 129
senior travelers, tips for: 476
services: 477-479; see also specific place
set dancing: 461
Shanahill East: 216
Shankill Road: 398
Shannon Airport: 254-255
Shannonbridge: 328
Shannon, River: 445
Shaw, George Bernard: 462
Sheep's Gate: 95
Sheep's Head Peninsula: 15, 190-192, 197
Sheep's Head Way: 190, 193
Sherkin Island: 186-187
shopping: Belfast 401-402; Dublin 68-69; Galway 295, 297-298; Kilkenny 143-144; Waterford 157; see also specific place
Shop Street: 288-289
Silent Valley: 434-435
silverworking: 181
Sinn Féin: 452, 457
Skellig Experience: 225
Skellig Islands: 200, 226-227
Skellig Michael: 16, 25, 226-227
Skellig Ring: 200, 223-225
Skibbereen: 186
Skibbereen Heritage Centre: 186
skydiving: 126, 359
Slane: 92-94
Slane Abbey: 92
Slane Castle: 92

Slea Head Drive: 11, 20, 200, 205, 212-215
Slí Cholmcille: 376, 377, 382
Slieve Donard: 434
Slieve League: 17, 28, 334, 377
Slieve League Cultural Centre: 375
Slievemore: 351
Slievemore Deserted Village: 350
Sligo: 22, 333-336, 357-368; maps 335, 340-341
Sligo Abbey: 358
Sligo Art Gallery: 358
Sligo International Choral Festival: 361
Sligo Jazz Project: 361
Sligo Museum: 358
Sligo Town: 29, 357-362; map 359
Small Skellig: 226
Smithwick Brewery: 141, 471
snakes: 446
South Great Georges Street: 60-61, 68
South Leinster Way: 126, 146
Spanish Arch: 289
Sperrin Heritage Centre: 441
Sperrin Mountains: 441
Spinc Mountain: 111
Spirit of Voice: 297
sports: 28, 465; see also specific sport
S.S. Nomadic: 398
St. Aidan's Cathedral: 126
Staigue Fort: 221
stained glass: 170
stand-up paddleboarding: 359
St. Anne's Cathedral: 395
St. Anne's Church: 15, 21, 166, 169
Statutes of Kilkenny: 125
St. Audoen's Church: 45-46
St. Barrahane's Church: 186
St. Canice's Cathedral: 14, 139
St. Colman's Cathedral: 177
St. Colmcille: 362
St. Columb's Cathedral: 419
St. Columba's Church, Long Tower: 420
St. Declan's Monastery: 15, 21, 124, 159-160
St. Declan's Well: 159
St. Enda's National Historic Park: 54
step dancing: 461
St. Eugene's: 420
St. Fachnan's: 273
St. Fin Barre's Cathedral: 169-171
St. Finbarr's Oratory: 192
St. Finghin's Church: 252
St. Finian: 362
St. Flannan's Oratory: 255
St. Francis' Abbey: 141
St. George's Market: 401
St. Gobnan's: 413
St. Iberius: 129
St. John's Cathedral: 279

St. Kevin's Bed: 110
St. Kevin's Church: 110-111
St. Laurence's Gate: 97
St. Mary's Abbey (Dublin): 46
St. Mary's Abbey (Fermanagh): 442
St. Mary's Cathedral (Killarney): 25, 235
St. Mary's Cathedral (Limerick): 244, 276, 279
St. Mary's Church (Cong): 338
St. Mary's Church (Dingle): 205
St. Mary's Church (Kilkenny): 146
St. Mary's Pro-Cathedral: 46
St. Michan's Church: 25, 34, 48
St. Molua's Oratory: 255-256
St. Nicholas' Collegiate Church: 289
St. Nicholas' Roman Catholic Cathedral: 289
Stoker, Bram: 462
Stoneyford: 145
St. Patrick: 84, 392-393, 447
St. Patrick Centre: 433
St. Patrick's Carnival: 401
St. Patrick's Cathedral: 25, 45
St. Patrick's Church: 170, 348
St. Patrick's Church of Ireland Cathedral: 436
St. Patrick's Festival: 67
St. Patrick's Rock: 21
St. Peter's Cathedral: 395
St. Peter's Church of Ireland: 99
St. Peter's Roman Catholic Church: 98-99
Strandhill: 358, 359, 366-367
Strangford: 23, 390, 433-434
Strangford Bay Path: 433
Strangford Castle: 433
Strangford Lough: 429
Strawberry Fair: 125
Streedagh: 358, 364
Strongbow: 448
St. Senan's: 258
St. Stephen's Green: 14, 34, 42-43, 56, 70-71
St. Stephen's Green Shopping Centre: 68
Studio Donegal: 374
Summer in the City: 401
surfing: 28, 189, 215, 216, 261, 343, 367, 373
Swift, Jonathan: 461
Swiss Cottage: 151
Synge, John Millington: 307, 462

T

Taaffe's Castle: 103
Táin Bó Cúailnge: 93, 461
Táin Trail: 92-93
Táin Way: 104, 105
Talbot Castle: 95
Taobh an Leithid: 382
Tavern, The: 27, 345
taxes: 477
taxis: 76; *see also specific place*

tea: 471
Teach an Phiarsaigh: 313
Teach Ceoil: 344
Teach Hudí Beag: 22, 383
Teach Synge: 22, 307
Teampall an Cheathrair Áileann: 303
Teampall Bheanáin: 303
Teampall Chaoimháin: 309
Teampall Chiaráin: 303
Teampall na Seacht Mac Rí: 307
Teelin: 374-375
telephone services: 478
television: 464, 478
Temple Bar: 44, 60, 69-70
Temple Bar Food Market: 44
Temple Ciarán: 328
Temple Connor: 328
Temple Finghin: 328
Temple na Griffin: 242
Templenahoe: 242
Temple na Skellig: 110
Tetrapod Trackway: 225
theater: 66-67; *see also* entertainment; *specific place*
Theatre Royal: 157
Tholsel: 103, 138
Thomastown: 145
Thoor Ballylee: 16, 326
Tigh Coili: 22, 296
Tigh Fitz: 23, 305
Ti Joe Mac's: 23, 304
time zone: 479
Timoleague: 182-183
Timoleague Abbey: 182
Tintern Abbey: 124, 135
Tipperary: 148-153; map 149
tipping: 478
Tir Sáile: 353
Titanic Belfast: 398
Tivoli Theatre: 67
Tobar Chinndeirge: 307
Tobar Éinne: 309
toilets, public: 477
Tone, Theobold Wolfe: 450
Torc Waterfall: 233
Torr Head: 410-411
tourism: 457
tourist information: 478-479, 486; Belfast 403; Dublin 72; *see also specific place*
tourist visas: 18, 474
tours: 470; Aran Islands 303; Derry 420-421; Dublin 55-56; Galway City 292; Meath 85; *see also specific place*
Tower Museum: 419
Trabane Strand: 376, 377
Trácht: 323

Tradfest: 67
traffic regulations: 469
train travel: 468-469; see also specific place
Tralee: 241-242
Trá Leirtreach: 308
Trá Mhóir: 313
Tramore Strand: 384
Tranaun: 347
transportation: 19, 467-470, 487; see also specific place
Trawmore Strand: 350
trekking: see hiking; specific trail
Trim: 94-97
Trim Castle: 26, 82, 94-95
Trinitarian Friary Church: 283
Trinity College: 14, 40-41
Trinity Tree: 205
Triskel Arts Centre: 173-174
Tropical Ravine: 395
Troubles, The: 454-455
Tullaghobegley Walk: 382, 383
Tullycross: 319
Turnley's Tower: 408
tweed: 460, 461
Twelve Bens: 311
Tyrone: 441

U

Uamhain Ghríora: 308
Ulster-American Folk Park: 441
Ulster Folk and Transport Museum: 426
Ulster Museum: 395
Ulster Orchestra: 24, 400
Ulster Volunteer Force (UVF): 452
Ulster Way: 382, 407
Union Hall: 185-186
United Irishmen: 450
United States Embassy: 72, 403
University College Cork: 169
University Concert Hall: 281
University of Limerick Activity Centre: 255, 256
Upper Diamond Hill: 318
Upper Lake: 25, 233

V

Valentia Heritage Centre: 225
Valentia Island: 225-226
Valentia Island Sea Sports: 28, 225
Vandeleur Walled Garden: 258
VAT (value add tax): 477
vegetarian/vegan food: 472
Ventry: 212
Vikings: 448

Vinegar Hill: 126
visas: 18, 474
Voya Seaweed Baths: 367

WXYZ

walking, long-distance: see hiking; specific trail
Ward Park: 426
Waterford: 153-161; map 154
Waterford City: 153-158; map 155
Waterford Crystal Visitor Centre: 156
Waterford Treasures: 156
Waterford Walls: 153
Watergate Theatre: 143
water pollution: 445
Waterside: 417
Waterside Theatre: 422
weather: 18, 445
websites: 486
Wee House of Malin: 387
Wellington Monument: 51
West Cork Arts Centre: 186
West Cork Model Railway Village: 183
West Cross: 102-103
Western Way: 348
Westgate Heritage Centre: 129
Westport: 22, 342-345; map 342
Westport Arts Festival: 344
Westport House & Country Park: 342-343
Wexford: 125-137; map 127
Wexford Arts Centre: 131
Wexford County Museum: 126
Wexford Opera Festival: 131
Wexford Town: 128-132; map 130
Wexford Wildfowl Reserve: 132-133
wheelchair accessibility: 475
whiskey: 48, 178, 416, 471
White Island: 443
White Strand: 228
Wicklow: 106-117; map 107
Wicklow Mountains National Park: 14, 21, 25, 110
Wicklow Town: 116
Wicklow Way: 28, 82, 106, 109, 110, 111, 112, 113
Wild Atlantic Way: 197, 336
Wilde, Oscar: 462
Willie Clancy Summer School: 261, 294
windsurfing: 134, 314, 439
Wolfsonian Foundation: 170
women travelers, tips for: 475-476
Woodstock Gardens: 146
Workhouse Museum (Derry City): 420
Workhouse Museum (Dunfanaghy): 383-384
Yeats, William Butler: 325-326, 357, 362-363, 365
yellow man: 411

List of Maps

Front Map
Ireland: 2–3

Discover Ireland
chapter divisions map: 15

Dublin
Dublin: 36–37
Greater Dublin: 49
Phoenix Park: 52
Dublin Food and Accommodations: 58–59
Vicinity of Dublin City: 77

Around Dublin
Around Dublin: 83
Meath and Louth: 86
Drogheda: 98
Wicklow and Kildare: 107

The Southeast
The Southeast: 122–123
Wexford: 127
Wexford Town: 130
Kilkenny: 139
Kilkenny City: 140
Tipperary: 149
Waterford: 154
Waterford City: 155

Cork
Cork: 164–165
Cork City: 168

Kerry
Kerry: 202–203
The Dingle Peninsula: 206–207
Dingle Town: 208
The Iveragh Peninsula: 218
Killarney National Park: 232
Killarney Town: 236

Clare and Limerick
Clare and Limerick: 246
Ennis: 249
The Burren: 269
Limerick City: 278

Galway
Galway: 287
Galway City: 290–291
Connemara: 312
Detour to Clonmacnoise: 330

The Northwest
The Northwest: 335
Mayo and Sligo: 340–341
Westport: 342
Achill Island: 351
Sligo Town: 359
Donegal: 370

Northern Ireland
Northern Ireland: 392
Belfast: 396–397
Antrim and Derry: 406
Derry City: 418
Down and Armagh: 427
Enniskillen: 438

Photo Credits

All photos © Camille DeAngelis except page 10 © Patryk Kosmider | Dreamstime.com; page 11 (top) © Pajda83 | Dreamstime.com, (bottom) © VanderWolfImages | Dreamstime.com; page 20 © Rafalstachura | Dreamstime.com; page 24 © Diro | Dreamstime.com; page 27 © Andrews71 | Dreamstime.com; page 29 © National Monuments Service/Dept. of Arts, Heritage and the Gaeltacht; page 102 © Bjoernalberts | Dreamstime.com; page 212 © Adamlaws | Dreamstime.com; page 226 © Jiriko | Dreamstime.com; page 251 © Patryk Kosmider | Dreamstime.com; page 277 © Sean O'Dwyer | Dreamstime.com; page 331 © Igabriela | Dreamstime.com; page 350 © Mkallstrom | Dreamstime.com; page 466 (top) © Spanishjohnny72 | Dreamstime.com, (bottom) © Trondur | Dreamstime.com

Acknowledgments

No one deserves greater thanks than my good friend Diarmuid O'Brien, who stepped in to write the history section when I realized I needed help making my deadline. He did a fantastic job, and I'm tremendously grateful for all his hard work in research and writing.

An adventure, in Ireland or elsewhere, is only as great as the people with whom you share it, and those kind and generous souls you encounter by providence. So I'll mention my traveling companions over the years—Kate DeAngelis, Aravinda Seshadri, Leah Smith, and Kelly Brown. I got to see and enjoy more of Ireland every time we slung on our backpacks.

Naturally, my time at the National University of Ireland, Galway better equipped me to tackle this guide, and I owe thanks to all the friends I made there: Ailbhe Slevin and Christian O'Reilly, Seanan McDonnell (and his wonderful family—Bán, J. P., Fergal, and everyone), Megan Buckley, Patrick Curley (and Tara, and Breda!), Lindsay and Trev Ward, Sinéad Ní Ghuidhir, Áine McHugh, Meg Ginnetty, Liam Kuhn, Deirdre Sullivan, and Diarmuid O'Brien (again!). Thanks also to the dear friends I've made more recently: Shelley Troupe and James Mullaney, Emily Goldstein and Vince Murphy, Brendan O'Brien (and Margaret and Joe), and Damien Cahill. Whether you showed me around your hometown, tipped me off to your favorite pubs, put me up, drove me around, came out to dinner, or made me laugh: thanks a lot.

Way back in high school, Pamela Fisk encouraged my budding interest in Irish history. Thanks are also due to my professors in the Irish Studies program at New York University, Padraig Ó Cearúill and Mick Moloney especially, as well as my teachers at NUI Galway—Adrian Frazier, Joe Woods, and Sinéad Mooney—and Mike McCormack in particular.

Jennifer Flores ("Ní Bhlathanna"), I am so lucky to have met you in Irish class at NYU. Our idyllic afternoon on the Causeway coast along with Natalie Mason and Genevieve Handy is always going to be one of my favorite memories of Ireland. Genevieve, thanks so much for your company. Hanging out with you and Dave Wright in Dublin was another highlight.

Tom Sullivan, thank you for cheerfully changing my flat tire and feeding me delicious meals you pulled out of your hat. Kevin O'Cuinn, thanks for your company in Westport and elsewhere. You both made bumming around in Leenane one of the most memorable parts of my original road trip. I am also grateful to Andrzej Syski for his company in Doolin and the Burren, John Renway Strohmeyer for allowing me to drag him all over Derry City, and to the lovely Susen from Germany for lending me her camera batteries in Ballycastle. Thanks to Brendan Stafford at Tintern Abbey, Michelle at Trim Castle, and all the other excellent tour guides who didn't think I was weird for taking notes. Many thanks also to Yvonne McEnnis of The Pottery Shop in Corofin for her help with getting my bearings in the area. As for the revision trip, I'm most grateful to Lucy and Ultan at Gort Na Nain, my new favorite Irish B&B (outside Kinsale, County Cork). You guys treated me like a friend from the second I pulled into your driveway. I'm so happy I found you. Thanks also to Tony Roche in the Department of Arts, Heritage and the Gaeltacht at the National Monuments Service for his kind and efficient assistance.

I am indebted to the works of David Monagan, Anthony Bailey, Heinrich Böll, Pat Boran, Brian de Breffny, William Bulfin, Roy Foster, Mike McCormack, Frank McDonald, H. V. Morton, Kate O'Brien, Patrick Pearse, George Bernard Shaw, Paul Theroux, David A. Wilson, and W. B. Yeats. I quoted these authors to add a little flavor to my write-ups, and I like to think the book is a much more entertaining read for all their wise observations.

As for the team at Avalon, thanks go to Elizabeth Hollis Hansen and Grace Fujimoto for giving me the opportunity to revise *Moon Ireland*; to my editor, Kathryn Ettinger; to Darren

Alessi for his work on the photography; to Kat Bennett for the cartography; and to everyone else who put so much time, energy, and enthusiasm into this guidebook. (Plus a retroactive shout-out to Kristen Couse and Tom Haslow, my editor and co-author on *Hanging Out in Ireland*, which we researched all the way back in 2000.) I'm also extremely grateful to my agent, Kate Garrick, who holds my hand whenever I need it, and to Debka Colson and all my colleagues at the Writers' Room of Boston, who cheered me on as I raced to finish work on the second edition.

A hundred thousand thank-yous to the Murphy family: Gene, Betty, Sharon, Yvonne, and Justin. They have overwhelmed me with their friendship, kindness, and generosity time and again, and I count myself incredibly privileged to be related to them. (Plus, Yve and Sharon gave me loads of great tips for dining and drinking in Dublin, and the book is so much better for them.) I am so very grateful to Dick Wahner (may he rest in peace) for putting me in touch with our Irish family.

Lastly but mostly, thank you to my sister Kate, my parents, my grandparents, and the rest of my family for their encouragement and support. My father deserves special thanks for fortifying me every summer morning in 2006 with big breakfasts and half a dozen cups of gourmet java. Otherwise, with the deadline for the first edition looming, I might've forgotten to eat altogether.

Also Available

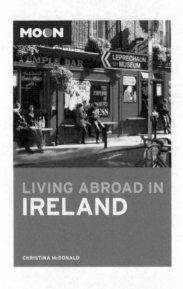

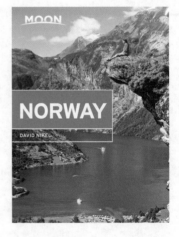

MAP SYMBOLS

▬▬▬	Expressway	○	City/Town	✈	Airport	⚓	Golf Course
═══	Primary Road	◉	State Capital	✈	Airfield	🅿	Parking Area
──	Secondary Road	⊛	National Capital	▲	Mountain	▲	Archaeological Site
─ ─ ─	Unpaved Road	★	Point of Interest	✛	Unique Natural Feature	⛪	Church
───	Feature Trail	•	Accommodation				Gas Station
- - - -	Other Trail	▼	Restaurant/Bar	🐚	Waterfall	◎	Glacier
··········	Ferry	■	Other Location	▲	Park		Mangrove
═══	Pedestrian Walkway			▣	Trailhead		Reef
▭▭▭	Stairs	⋀	Campground	⛷	Skiing Area		Swamp

CONVERSION TABLES

$$°C = (°F - 32) / 1.8$$
$$°F = (°C × 1.8) + 32$$

1 inch = 2.54 centimeters (cm)
1 foot = 0.304 meters (m)
1 yard = 0.914 meters
1 mile = 1.6093 kilometers (km)
1 km = 0.6214 miles
1 fathom = 1.8288 m
1 chain = 20.1168 m
1 furlong = 201.168 m
1 acre = 0.4047 hectares
1 sq km = 100 hectares
1 sq mile = 2.59 square km
1 ounce = 28.35 grams
1 pound = 0.4536 kilograms
1 short ton = 0.90718 metric ton
1 short ton = 2,000 pounds
1 long ton = 1.016 metric tons
1 long ton = 2,240 pounds
1 metric ton = 1,000 kilograms
1 quart = 0.94635 liters
1 US gallon = 3.7854 liters
1 Imperial gallon = 4.5459 liters
1 nautical mile = 1.852 km

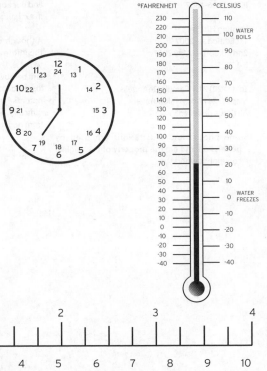

MOON IRELAND

Avalon Travel
An imprint of Perseus Books
A Hachette Book Group company
1700 Fourth Street
Berkeley, CA 94710, USA
www.moon.com

Editor and Series Manager: Kathryn Ettinger
Copy Editor: Deana Shields
Graphics Coordinator: Darren Alessi
Production Coordinator: Darren Alessi
Cover Design: Faceout Studios, Charles Brock
Interior Design: Domini Dragoone
Moon Logo: Tim McGrath
Map Editor: Kat Bennett
Cartographers: Brian Shotwell, Karin Dahl, Kat Smith
Indexer: Deana Shields

ISBN-13: 978-1-63121-419-6
ISSN: 1936-1807

Printing History
1st Edition — 2007
2nd Edition — May 2017
5 4 3 2 1

Front cover photo: Ross Castle near Killarney in County Kerry © nagelestock.com / Alamy Stock Photo
Back cover photo: Connemara in County Galway © Tonybrindley | Dreamstime.com

Printed in China by RR Donnelley